REGENERATION THROUGH VIOLENCE

REGENERATION THROUGH VIOLENCE

The Mythology of the American Frontier, 1600-1860

By RICHARD SLOTKIN

Wesleyan University Press, MIDDLETOWN, CONNECTICUT

Library of Congress Cataloging in Publication Data

Slotkin, Richard, 1942–
    Regeneration through violence.

    Bibliography: p.
      1. American literature—History and criticism.
    2. National characteristics, American. 3. Mythology in litera-
ture. I. Title.
PS88.S5   810'.9   72–3725
ISBN 0–8195–4055–2

The cover illustration reproduces a line-cut depicting Daniel Boone rescuing his daughter from Indians from *The First White Man of the West,* or *The Life and Exploits of Col. Dan'l. Boone, the First Settler of Kentucky* by Timothy Flint (Cincinnati, 1851).

Paperback ISBN 0–8195–6034–0

Manufactured in the United States of America

First paperback edition, 1974

TO IRIS

Contents

Acknowledgments

I am greatly indebted for the aid, advice, criticism, and encouragement given me by Professors John L. Thomas and Albert D. Van Nostrand of Brown University and by Mr. Thomas Adams of the John Carter Brown Library. This book has also benefited from the many comments, corrections, and suggestions offered by Professor Joel Porte of Harvard University and Professors George Creeger and Joseph Reed of Wesleyan University. I want also to thank Alan Levensohn of Cambridge for his many helpful suggestions and Puffin D'Oench of Middletown for her assistance with the index and to express my gratitude to Brown University and Wesleyan University for financial support of my research. And I thank my wife, for all of the above.

REGENERATION THROUGH VIOLENCE

There was, thank God, a great voluptuary born to the American Settlements against the niggardliness of the damming puritanical tradition; one who by the single logic of his passion, which he rested on the savage life about him, destroyed at its spring that spiritually withering plague. For this he has remained since buried in a miscolored legend and left for rotten. Far from dead, however, but full of a rich regenerative violence he remains, when his history will be carefully reported, for us who have come after to call upon him.

William Carlos Williams, *In the American Grain*

But you have there the myth of the essential white America. All the other stuff, the love, the democracy, the floundering into lust, is a sort of by-play. The essential American soul is hard, isolate, stoic, and a killer. It has never yet melted.

D. H. Lawrence, *Studies in Classic American Literature*

CHAPTER 1

Myth and Literature
in a New World

THE mythology of a nation is the intelligible mask of that enigma called the "national character." Through myths the psychology and world view of our cultural ancestors are transmitted to modern descendants, in such a way and with such power that our perception of contemporary reality and our ability to function in the world are directly, often tragically affected.

American attitudes toward the idea of a national mythology have been peculiarly ambivalent. There is a strong antimythological stream in our culture, deriving from the utopian ideals of certain of the original colonists and of the revolutionary generation, which asserts that this New World is to be liberated from the dead hand of the past and become the scene of a new departure in human affairs. Nonetheless, we have continually felt the need for the sense of coherence and direction in history that myths give to those who believe in them. The poets of the early years of the republic — taught, as part of their classical education, that national mythologies are embodied in literature and begin with national epics in the manner of Homer — attempted to fabricate an "American epic" that would mark the beginning of a national mythology, providing a context for all works to come after. Their concept of myth was essentially artificial and typically American: they believed, in effect, that a mythology could be put together on the ground, like the governments of frontier communities or the national Constitution, either by specialists or by the spontaneous awakening of the popular genius. Like the Constitution, such myth-epics would reflect the most progressive ideas of American man, emphasizing the rule of reason in nature and in human affairs, casting aside all inherited traditions, superstitions, and spurious values of the past. The freedom and power of man were to be asserted against the ideas of necessity, of historical determinism, of the inheritance of guilt and original sin. From Barlow's *Columbiad* and Dwight's *Greenfield Hill* in the late eighteenth century, through Whitman's "Song of Myself" and Melville's *Moby-Dick* in the nineteenth, to Hart Crane's *The Bridge* and Williams's *Paterson* or the "great American novel" in the twentieth, American writers have attempted the Homeric task of providing, through epic poetry or epic fiction, a starting point for a new, uniquely American mythology.[1] Even scholarly critics who address themselves to the problem of the "myth of America" have a marked tendency to engage in the manufacture of the myth they pretend to analyze in an attempt to reshape the character of their people or to justify some preconceived or inherited notion of American uniqueness. Such critics are themselves a part of this national phenomenon of myth-consciousness, this continual preoccupation with the necessity of defining or creating a national identity, a character for us to live in the world.

Works like the *Columbiad* and *The Bridge*, whatever their artistic merit, failed (at least in their authors' lifetimes) to achieve that quasi-religious power throughout the whole of a culture that is the characteristic attribute of true myth. The premises of such works do not take into account the facts that myth-making is a primary attribute of the human mind and that the process of mythogenesis in a culture is one of continuous activity rather than dramatic stops and starts. True myths are generated on a sub-literary level by the historical experience of a people and thus constitute part of that inner reality which the work of the artist draws on, illuminates, and explains. In American mythogenesis the founding fathers were not those eighteenth-century gentlemen who composed a nation at Philadelphia. Rather, they were those who (to paraphrase Faulkner's *Absalom, Absalom!*) tore violently a nation from the implacable and opulent wilderness — the rogues, adventurers, and land-boomers; the Indian fighters, traders, missionaries, explorers, and hunters who killed and were killed until they had mastered the wilderness; the settlers who came after, suffering hardship and Indian warfare for the sake of a sacred mission or a simple desire for land; and the Indians themselves, both as they were and as they appeared to the settlers, for whom they were the special demonic personification of the American wilderness. Their concerns, their hopes, their terrors, their violence, and their justifications of themselves, as expressed in literature, are the foundation stones of the mythology that informs our history.

The failure of writers and critics to recognize and deal with the real mythological heritage of their time and people has consequences that go beyond the success or failure of their literary works. A people unaware of its myths is likely to continue living by them, though the world around that people may change and demand changes in their psychology, their world view, their ethics, and their institutions. The antimythologists of the American Age of Reason believed in the imminence of a rational republic of yeomen farmers and enlightened leaders, living amicably in the light of natural law and the Constitution. They were thereby left unprepared when the Jeffersonian republic was overcome by the Jacksonian Democracy of the western man-on-the-make, the speculator, and the wildcat banker; when racist irrationalism and a falsely conceived economics prolonged and intensified slavery in the teeth of American democratic idealism; and when men like Davy Crockett became national heroes by defining national aspiration in terms of so many bears destroyed, so much land preempted, so many trees hacked down, so many Indians and Mexicans dead in the dust.

The voluminous reports of presidential commissions on violence, racism, and civil disorder have recently begun to say to us what artists like Melville and Faulkner had earlier prophesied: that myths reach out of the past to cripple, incapacitate, or strike down the living. It is by now a commonplace that our adherence to the "myth of the frontier" — the conception of America as a wide-open land of unlimited opportunity for the strong, ambitious, self-reliant individual to thrust his way to the top — has blinded us to the consequences of the industrial and urban revolutions and to the need for social reform and a new concept of individual and communal welfare. Nor is it by a far-fetched association that the murderous violence that has characterized recent political life has been linked by poets and news commentators alike to the "frontier psychology" of our recent past and our long heritage. The first colonists saw in America an opportunity to regenerate their fortunes, their spirits, and the power of their church and nation; but the means to that regeneration ultimately became the means of violence, and the myth of regeneration through violence became the structuring metaphor of the American experience. How that myth evolved and gained credence and power is the subject of this study.

Three critical problems lie in the path of any study of the so-called myth of America. The first is the question of the Americanness of its origin. Myths are human creations, and the people who composed the vast majority of the American population before 1800 were European by ancestry, by language, and by religious and literary heritage. The only non-European native cultures were those of the Indians. Like the colonists, the Indians had mythologies based on their experience in the world — in the Indians' case, the American wilderness. Did those same conditions, operating on European immigrants, impose on or induce in the colonial mind a similarly "American" mythology? We know that the colonists adapted their ways of living, farming, hunting, and fighting in order to survive in the Indians' world. Did they also (to some degree) acquire an Indian-like vision of the New World, an Indian-American mythology? Since the Indian is, from our point of view, the only one who can claim to be indigenously American, it seems important to question whether our national experience has "Americanized" or "Indianized" us, or whether we are simply an idiosyncratic offshoot of English civilization.

The second critical problem arises from the fact that this artificially created American nation — the self-baptized "American people" — first saw light in the age of the printing press. Mythologies arise spontaneously in the preliterary epochs of a people's history and consequently are "artless" in their portrayal of the world and the gods, appealing to the emotions rather than the intelligence. American myths — tales of heroes in particular — frequently turn out to be the work of literary hacks or of promoters seeking to sell American real estate by mythologizing the landscape. One of the problems with which this study has to deal is the question of the relationship between myth and literature. Is the dominance of printed literature inconsistent with the initiation and development of myth, and is the post-Gutenberg period also necessarily postmythological?

The third problem is that which lies at the source of every study of myth in history and literature: the problem of defining myth and of distinguishing between archetypal myth, folk legends, and artistic mythopoesis. Such a definition must be made before we can understand what has been involved in the process of myth-making in America, what the stages of that process have been, and how our mythology acquires and exercises its power in human thoughts and affairs.

Mythogenesis

A mythology is a complex of narratives that dramatizes the world vision and historical sense of a people or culture, reducing centuries of experience into a constellation of compelling metaphors.[2] The narrative action of the myth-tale recapitulates that people's experience in their land, rehearses their visions of that experience in its relation to their gods and the cosmos, and reduces both experience and vision to a paradigm. Reference to that myth or to things associated with it — as in religious ritual — evokes in the people the sense of life inherent in the myth and all but compels belief in the vision of reality and divinity implicit in it. The believer's response to his myth is essentially nonrational and religious: he recognizes in the myth his own features and experience, the life and appearance of his ancestors, and the faces of the gods who rule his universe, and he feels that the myth has put him in intimate contact with the ultimate powers which shape all of life. Thus myth can be seen as an intellectual or artistic construct that bridges the gap between the world of the mind and the world of affairs,[3] between dream and reality, between impulse or desire and action. It draws on the content of individual and collective memory, structures it, and develops from it imperatives for belief and action.

The ultimate source of myth is the human mind itself, for man is essentially a myth-making animal. He naturally seeks to understand his world in order to control it, and his first act in compassing this end is an act of the mind or imagination. On the basis of limited, finite experience, he creates a hypothetical vision of a universal, infinite order and imposes that hypothesis on his perception of the phenomena of nature and his own behavior. He tests his vision by acting in accordance with the principles of behavior that seem to be demanded by reality as he envisions it. Insofar as that behavior is consistent with the universal order, it will seem to prosper him and acquire the name of virtue.[4] Aside from its function as a guide to behavior, his vision is regarded as a source of power, since it tells him how to propitiate and control the forces that order the world.[5] Thus myth-visions, which are generated by the mind, ultimately affect both man's perception of reality and his actions. Myth describes a process, credible to its audience, by which knowledge is transformed into power; it provides a scenario or prescription for action, defining and limiting the possibilities for human response to the universe.

In order to understand the process of myth-making in America and to establish criteria by which we can discover and define both the nature of the "American myth" and the manner and time of its emergence, we must begin by examining the state of mind that transforms experience, perception, and narration into the materials of a myth. Philip Wheelwright calls this state of mind the "mythopoeic mode of consciousness" and finds it present in the psychology of both the myth-making artist and the artist's people — his audience.[6] The mythopoeic mode of consciousness comprehends the world through a process of thought- and perception-association, a process of reasoning-by-metaphor in which direct statement and logical analysis are replaced by figurative or poetic statement: the sudden, nonlogical perception and expression of "an objective relation between parts of reality, or between objective and subjective realities." [7] The nature of the mythopoeic perception, in both maker and audience, is mystical and religious, drawing heavily on the unconscious and the deepest levels of the psyche, defining relationships between human and divine things, between temporalities and ultimates.

> There is a strong tendency of the different experiential elements to blend and fuse in a non-logical way. And not only that, but the self-hood of the observer tends to blend with them; that is to say he becomes a full participant and not a mere observer. Finally, there is a blending, or partial blending, of worshipper and sacred objects and ceremonial acts with certain transcendent Presences.[8]

Myth-making, by this definition, is simultaneously a psychological and a social activity. The myth is articulated by individual artists and has its effect on the mind of each individual participant, but its function is to reconcile and unite these individualities to a collective identity. A myth that ceases to evoke this religious response, this sense of total identification and collective participation, ceases to *function* as a myth; [9] a tale that, through the course of several generations — or even several retellings within one generation — acquires this kind of evocative power has evolved into myth.

The mythopoeic mode of consciousness is dependent on — but distinct from — the myth-artifact, which is the actual tale or some sacred image or object connected with the myth-narrative. The artifact symbolically embodies the mythopoeic perception and makes it concrete and communicable.[10] The legends and stories we commonly call myths are simply the artifacts of the myth, and they retain their mythic powers only so long as they can continue to evoke in the minds of succeeding generations a vision analogous in its compelling power to that of the original mythopoeic perception. The myth-artist, priest, or fabulist uses the artifacts of myth to evoke the "sense" of the myth and its complex of affirmations in the audience. He may use these artifacts in two ways — either deliberately, in an effort to make propaganda for his cause, or unconsciously, under the compelling association of perceived event and inherited mythology.

As artifacts, myths appear to be built of three basic structural elements: a protagonist or hero, with whom the human audience is presumed to identify in some way; a universe in which the hero may act, which is presumably a reflection of the audience's conception of the world and the gods; and a narrative, in which the interaction of hero and universe is described. Hero and universe may be readily abstracted as "images," which may in turn be evocative enough to become equated in our minds with the whole of the myth itself. The narrative as a whole is more difficult to abstract, since its action defines (explicitly and implicitly) the relationship of hero to universe and of man to God — and so establishes the laws of cause and effect, of natural process, and of morality. It is the narrative which gives the images life by giving them a mode of interaction.

Images of the hero and the universe are devices that enable us to identify with (and thus enter) the world of the myth, and these may change fairly rapidly to accommodate new perceptions or requirements of the myth-makers and their audience. This is certainly the case with American mythology, in which (as Henry Nash Smith shows in *Virgin Land*) the image of the wilderness east of the Mississippi changes from "desert" to "Garden" in a century and a half, while that of the Great Plains exhibits a similar change in less than half that time — from its purchase in 1803 to the realization of its economic potential before the Civil War. However, while the images may readily exhibit changes in response to the play of social and psychological forces, the narrative or narratives which relate them to each other have or acquire a certain fixity of form. Their structure and character may be more clearly articulated through the passage of time and the operation of historical forces on the mind of the audience, but their essential nature remains substantially the same. Only truly radical alterations of the images of hero and universe effect significant changes at the narrative structural level of the myth, for such changes (by definition) reflect a fundamental alteration of the culture's conception of the relationship of man to the universe, a revolution in world view, cosmology, historical and moral theory, and self-concept. Hence such changes may be seen as marking the point at which a new epoch of cultural history or perhaps even a new culture can be said to begin.

Stories that exhibit this kind of power persistently in many cultures over long periods of time are termed *universal archetypes*. Those which exhibit similar persistence within a single culture (and which are variants of universal archetypes) are what I term *cultural archetypes* and *cultural myths*. (The former term refers to an abstraction or "narrative of narratives" derived from and expressing the common structural form of a constellation of related myth-narratives.) This study is an attempt to define at least one of the cultural archetypes which emerged from the historical experience of the American colonial frontier to function as myth in our culture.

The distinction between mythopoeic consciousness and myth-artifact is helpful in dealing with the problem of the relationship between the archetypal and the tribal or culture-bound qualities of myth. The so-called myth critics have been justly criticized for attempting to reduce all literary narrative to paradigmatic archetypes, obscuring all authorial and cultural differences and all distinctions of literary artistry and aesthetic response

— in effect, reducing all the varieties of myth and literature to a single psychological or anthropological datum.[11] The study of archetypes is based upon an analysis of the underlying structure of myth-narratives or -artifacts; the term is most frequently used to describe those paradigmatic structures that seem to be common to all mythologies, of whatever place or cultural epoch. Since myth begins as a mythopoeic mode of consciousness — a state of mind and a mode of perception — it is reasonable to assume that myths are archetypal or universal to the extent that certain conditions of life and psychological states or concerns are universal among men. All men are born and must die, feel the need for love and begetting children, dream of immortality and an amenable universe, suffer the pangs of guilt and frustration, experience the wastage of time and the waning of their powers. All men share certain perceptions of the relationships between the universals in their human condition, such as the mirroring of seasonal patterns in human life, the echoing of vegetable death and rebirth in the perpetual deaths of fathers and successions of sons. Myth-narratives that embody and explain these conditions and perceptions — the death and resurrection of the nature-god; the sacred marriage of the divine king and the earth goddess, or spirit of place; the hero's quest in the kingdom of death for the boon of life — are common to all cultures, of whatever technological level or place, differing in particular details but not in their structural patterns.

Archetypal myths combine and correlate individual experience and psychology with collective history and with the processes of cosmic evolution. This drawing together of experiential and historical or cosmogonic threads can be seen in the myth of the heroic quest, which is perhaps the most important archetype underlying American cultural mythology. The quest involves the departure of the hero from his common-day world to seek the power of the gods in the underworld, the eternal kingdom of death and dreams from which all men emerge; his motive is provided by the threat of some natural or human calamity which will overtake his people unless the power of the gods can be borrowed or the gods themselves reconciled with the people.[12] The quest is also an initiation into a higher level of existence and power, echoing the movement of the boy from childhood into manhood: the departure from the world of parental nurture and law into the world of maturity and independent responsibility, in which the forces of the cosmos operate without parental amelioration. For the initiate, the achievement of maturity depends on his ability both to understand and take upon himself the power and knowledge of his parents (quest for the source) and to differentiate himself from them (the triumphant return on completion of the quest). The most significant rituals of the tribe center about the rites of initiation, since these must provide a continuing supply of competent men to sustain the society. Therefore it is not surprising that myths of heroic quest and initiation are among the first coherent myth-narratives formulated by a culture, the bases of national epic poetry (the *Odyssey*, the *Aeneid, Gilgamesh, Beowulf,* the Arthurian epics).

Archetypal myths derive from and mirror archetypal states of mind. In *Thresholds of Initiation,* J. L. Henderson (developing a Jungian thesis) characterizes the basic psychological tension as a conflict between "Moira" and "Themis" — between the unconscious and the conscious, the dream or impulse and the rational idea, the inchoate desire and the knowledge of responsibility, the gratification-world presided over by the mother and the world of laws and reasons ruled by the father. The process of maturation, of initiation into adulthood, requires the reconciliation of these two elements, these two modes of relating to life; and since, as infants, we are absorbed in the maternal world of Moira, the initiation requires us to move toward the paternal figure (Themis) for a confrontation and some form of reconciliation. This tension and the psychological processes it evokes are echoed (according to Jung) in the processes by which myths evolve. Moira was a prehistoric earth-goddess, predating the Olympian deities of Greece, a goddess ruling both personal destiny and the allotment of "moieties" of land, a maternal spirit of place. She represents the mythopoeic pole of the myth-making process, existing at "the undifferentiated matrix of the archetypal world of prehistory," her nature established by the impulses, dreams, and inchoate desires that characterize the human unconscious. About her gathers "the fresh and timeless phenomenon of a ritual dance, drama, or painting which serves the function of providing religious, aesthetic, social, and philosophical experience all at once." [13] Just as individuals, in the course of normal maturation, leave the womblike maternal world of childhood for the world of men, of activity, of the disappointment of dreams and the difficulties of achievement, cultures presumably move from the maternal, Moira vision of their character and destiny toward the Themis vision. This vision centers on the paternal principal in deity, Olympian Zeus rather than pre-Olympian Moira, and on the activity and responsibility of social life as opposed to passivity and absorption in the mother. Themis represents "the final socio-religious, artistic, or philosophic cultural form of any given community, varying in its character from nomadic hunting cultures and the herdsmen to settled agricultural groups and larger organizations of hieratic city-states." [14] Henderson also notes that as this transition takes place, "the archetypal content [of myth] is spread out and becomes much thinner than it was at its primordial source. Finally Moira and Themis are separated and may be in conflict with each other." [15]

This "conflict" between Moira and Themis — between the unconscious and conscious, the mythopoeic and the artificial, the archetypal and traditional elements in myth — is not one which is capable of resolution through the victory of one or the other. Perhaps "conflict" does not describe their relationship so well as "tension," since elements of both persist in all mythologies, as in most human psychologies. Although Moira ceases to dominate the gods, she or her avatars retain a subordinate position under Zeus and periodically assert their primordial power against paternal authority. Bacchus or Zagreus — or the drunken "Indian Joes" of American literature — are their children, embodiments of the childish and primitive impulses of the unconscious: hunger for food, power, pleasure, dissolution of the self in passionate love, and cruelty. These qualities make the children of Moira a perpetual source of disorder, inciters of female or youthful violence against paternal agents of order like the king of Thebes and the artist Orpheus. As Henderson says, this mythic tension reflects the individual human need to reconcile mother and father, the male and female sexual principles, the unconscious and conscious realms of the mind.[16]

The stages of development in the evolution of myth-artifacts mirror the psychological alternation between movements away from the mythopoeic source (Moira) and attempts to return and reacquire the power of original mythopoeic perceptions. Philip Wheelwright identifies three stages in the development of myth: "primary," "romantic," and "consummatory." [17] The primary stage is that in which the "mythopoeic mode of consciousness" predominates both in the activity of the myth-maker and in the perceptions of his audience. Through repetition of the formulas or repeated use of the artifacts of this primary myth, however, a convention of form is established and identified with the content of the primary myth. In this romantic stage, the attainment of an original experience of mythopoeic insight into the nature of reality becomes less important than fulfilling the social obligations established for the myth and for the priests who keep and ritualize it. Fulfillment of the literary and social requirements that custom has established for "artists" likewise becomes of primary importance for the tribe's official or semiofficial artificers of myth-stories. Thus in this phase the metaphoric surface of the myth may be overelaborated in such a way as to obscure or even twist its original meaning or content, to repress and even deny the faiths and values that were inherent in the original mythopoeic experience. In highly sophisticated cultures, such as that of modern Europe and the West, artists and thinkers become aware of this corruption of the modes of belief and expression and attempt to overcome it, either by reachieving the mythopoeic, spontaneous element in artistic perception and creation or by critically separating the "gold" of archetypal myth from the "dross" of particular traditions. This consummatory stage is marked by a conscious attempt to "recapture the lost innocence of the mythopoeic attitude by transcending the narrative, logical and linguistic forms which romantic mythologizing accepts and utilizes." [18] In this stage of myth-making the artist acts as prophet rather than as priest or ministrant to his people, shaking minds and hearts with new visions rather than providing customary balm for normal social and personal anxieties. The novelists and poets who attack the conventions of thought, feeling, and expression by transforming and revolutionizing literary and linguistic forms — the Romantics in their day, for instance, and the post-Joycean novelists in ours — belong to this phase of mythic endeavor, as do the Protestant revivalists who prophesy against conventionalized, normalized, formalized religious experience in the name of a spontaneous mythopoeic experience of faith in God.

In the attempt to recover the world of primary myth and universal archetypes, the consummatory myth-maker must draw upon the vocabulary of myth-images and -structures that is his cultural heritage. Hence his approach to the reenvisioning of the universal archetype necessarily involves the reenvisioning of the cultural archetypes that lie behind the variegated surface of his culture's myth-media. Moreover, the consummatory myth-maker brings to his efforts a critical awareness which sets him apart from his forebears. First, he is aware of and capable of articulating the need for myth *as myth* — that is, as a construction of symbols and values, derived from real and imaginary experience and ordered by the imagination according to the deepest needs of the psyche. In addition, he has the benefit of historical knowledge and can look back over a span of time in which myths have developed and decayed, have shaped and been shaped by human and national history. Given this double awareness, the consummatory myth-maker has a degree of critical distance from his material and his works which does not exist for the mystic of the primary myth or the conventional imitator of romantic myth. This creates barriers to the acceptance of the vision of the consummatory myth-maker as a social myth, since it is the function of myth to provide a formula for credence and faith, not an apparatus for critical analysis. Thus a novel like Melville's *Moby-Dick* or Joyce's *Ulysses*, which are attempts at consummatory myth-making, fails to achieve recognition and credence among the people and in the historical time to which it is addressed.

Although primary, romantic, and consummatory stages in the development of myth can be generally discerned, it would be a mistake to assume that any given period or specific work can be classified as belonging exclusively to one of the three.[19] Romantic myth partakes of the original power of the primary myth, despite the fact that it obscures its origins. To the extent that consummatory myth-making succeeds, it becomes identical in quality, power, and function with primary myth; it may in fact be the primary stage of a new myth evolution. At the same time, the symbolic language elaborated in the romantic stage of the myth's development provides the basic vocabulary of the consummatory myth. Like Moira and Themis, these stages or phases coexist in mythologies, providing formal tension as well as a tension in meaning or content. Myth is essentially conservative, depending for its power on its ability to play on conscious and unconscious memory, to invoke and relate all the narratives (historical and personal) that we have inherited, and to reach back to the primal levels of individual and collective psychology.

National Mythology: A Summary View

The universal archetype is essential to myth, since all myth, to be credible, must relate the problems and aspirations of particular cultures to the fundamental conditions of human existence and human psychology. But the viability of myth also depends upon the applicability of its particular terms and metaphors to the peculiar conditions of history and environment that dominate the life of a particular people. This principle of distinction is implied in Joseph Campbell's definition of myth as "traditional metaphor addressed to ultimate questions." [20] The ultimate, archetypal questions of human existence are spoken to by the myth; but the success of the myth in answering these questions for a people depends upon the creation of a distinct cultural tradition in the selection and use of metaphor. It is in their development of traditional metaphors (and the narratives that express them) that the mythologies of particular cultures move from archetypal paradigms to the creation of acculturated, even idiosyncratic myth-metaphors.

In this process of traditionalization it is the artifact of myth — the narrative — that exhibits change and development. Thus it is in this stage that the nature of the artifact, the medium through which the mythic perception is transmitted, becomes of crucial importance. In addition, it is at this stage that the role of the artist, the intelligent manipulator of media and artifacts, becomes important as a means of controlling and directing the development of myth, limiting or augmenting its power to induce the mythopoeic affirmation in its audience. It is at this stage that various cultures move away from the universal vision of the archetype toward some particular interpretation of the archetypal narrative that will reflect their characteristic approach to life. It is at this point that the Christian variant of the myth-narrative of the dead-and-resurrected god diverges from the Norse or the Dionysian, and it is here that the farming culture's version of the sacred marriage varies from that of the hunting or the industrial culture. Hence it is at this point that myth provides a useful tool for the analysis of the particularity of a human culture.

The Europeans who settled the New World possessed at the time of their arrival a mythology derived from the cultural history of their home countries and responsive to the psychological and social needs of their old culture. Their new circumstances forced new perspectives, new self-concepts, and new world concepts on the colonists and made them see their cultural heritage from angles of vision that noncolonists would find peculiar. The internal tension between the Moira and Themis elements in their European mythologies (and the psychological tension that is the source of this myth-duality) found an objective correlative in the racial, religious, and cultural opposition of the American Indians and colonial Christians. This racial-cultural conflict pointed up and intensified the emotional difficulties attendant on the colonists' attempt to adjust to life in the wilderness. The picture was further complicated for them by the political and religious demands made on them by those who remained in Europe, as well as by the colonists' own need to affirm — for themselves and for the home folks — that they had not deserted European civilization for American savagery.

Added together, these conditions ensured that the colonists would be preoccupied with defining, for themselves and for others, the precise nature of their constantly changing relationship to the wilderness. This made for a highly self-conscious literature with a tendency toward polemic and apology, in which the colonist simultaneously argued the firmness and stability of his European character and (paradoxically) the superiority of his new American land and mode of life to all things European. The fact that the colonial experience began in the age of the printing press gave this kind of literature wide currency. The very nature of print made it the perfect medium for this sort of literature, allowing the writer to draw on a vast vocabulary of literary conventions in making his case for America.

This set of circumstances created a pattern of evolution for the American myth that is somewhat different from the pattern suggested by Wheelwright for primitive cultures. The colonists whose writings form the body of the mythology were working in a literary tradition and a medium of communication that had been highly structured and conventionalized through centuries of European practice. The primary sources from the New World, written by early explorer-conquerors, are couched in the imagery of this romantic European mythology and seem at this distance highly artificial and literary. References to images of the Golden Age, as depicted by Greek and Latin poets, abound both in the writings of court and church historians and in the accounts by the explorers themselves. Howard Mumford Jones notes that Columbus's first description of the New World is colored by the traditional imagery of the earthly paradise:

> This island and all others are very fertile to a limitless degree. . . . In it there are many harbours on the coast of the sea, beyond comparison with others which I know in Christendom, and many rivers, good and large, which is marvellous. Its lands are high, and there are in it very many sierras and very lofty mountains, beyond comparison with the island of Teneriffe. All are most beautiful, of a thousand shapes, and all are accessible and filled with trees of a thousand kinds and tall, and they seem to touch the sky. And I am told that they never lose their foliage, as I can understand, for I saw them as green and lovely as they are in Spain in May, and some of them were flowering, some bearing fruit, and some in another stage, according to their nature. And the nightingale was singing, and other birds of a thousand kinds. . . . In it are marvellous pine groves, and there are very large tracts of cultivable lands, and there is honey, and there are birds of many kinds, and fruits in great diversity. In the interior are mines of metal. The people of this island . . . go naked. . . . They never refuse anything which they possess, if it be asked of them; on the contrary they invite anyone to share it, and display so much love as if they would give their hearts. . . . And they do not know any creed, and are not idolators; only they believe that power and good are in the heavens. . . .[21]

As Jones notes, the description is generalized, abstracted, and vague to a fault; and the nightingales are either pure fiction or the error of a perception dominated by conventional imagery, since no such birds exist in the New World. The accounts of the conquest of Mexico written by Cortés, Gómara, and Díaz del Castillo (which are discussed in chapter 2) reflect the strong influence of secular chivalric romances. Díaz's Indians, viewing the ruins of Mexico City, speak "in much the same way that we would say: 'Here stood Troy.' "[22]

The later myth-literature of the Colonial and early national periods was intended as a kind of consummatory myth-making: an attempt by art-ful moderns to recapture the unsophisticated, passionate, believing spirit of the primitive "natural" man. In so doing, these later writers (Cooper, Longfellow, Melville, and others) reached back to the only sources of truly primary American myth — the myths of the Indian aborigines and the per-sonal narratives of the unsophisticated, almost primitive colonials (and their slicker, sensationalistic successors of the popular press) who fabri-cated a mythology out of their real and imagined experiences with the In-dians. The story of the evolution of an American mythology is, in large measure, the story of our too-slow awakening to the significance of the American Indian in the universal scheme of things generally and in our (or his) American world in particular. As Kenneth Rexroth says:

> Our memory of the Indians connects us with the soil and the waters and the nonhuman life about us. They take for us the place of nymphs and satyrs and dryads — the spirits of the places. They are our ecolog-ical link with our biota — the organic environment which we strive to repudiate and destroy. . . . the flooding tide, full of turmoil and whirl-pools, of the unconscious, or the id, or the "dark forces of the blood" — the actual, savage environment that reason and order and humane relationships can penetrate but cannot control.[23]

Thus the evolution of the American myth was a synthetic process of reconciling the romantic-conventional myths of Europe to American expe-rience — a process which, by an almost revolutionary turn, became an analytical attempt to destroy or cut through the conventionalized mythol-ogy to get back to the primary source of blood-knowledge of the wilder-ness, the "Indian" mind, the basic, Moiratic, myth-generating psychology of man. Yet our only sources of primary knowledge about the Indian mind (aside from a few incompetent studies of Indian ritual and legendry by missionaries) were works by those who regularly battled the Indians or by those who stayed with them as war captives or adopted tribesmen. These were the people who lived near or among the Indians, learning their modes of thought and behavior so well that they could successfully fight them or even integrate themselves into Indian society. Even at the source of the American myth there lies the fatal opposition, the hostility between two worlds, two races, two realms of thought and feeling.

"The land was ours before we were the land's," said Robert Frost. The process by which we came to feel an emotional title to the land was charged with a passionate and aspiring violence, and "the deed of gift was many deeds of war." Because of the nature of myth and the myth-making process, it is a significant comment on our characteristic attitudes toward

ourselves, our culture, our racial subgroupings, and our land that tales of
strife between native Americans and interlopers, between dark races and
light, became the basis of our mythology and that the Indian fighter and
hunter emerged as the first of our national heroes. In order to understand
the complex and many-leveled influence of our history on our mythology,
and of mythology on our culture, we must understand the nature of the peculiar forces that shaped mythology in America.

Generally speaking, the basic factors in the physical and psychological
situation of the colonists were the wildness of the land, its blending of un-
mitigated harshness and tremendous potential fertility; the absence of
strong European cultures on the borders; and the eternal presence of the
native people of the woods, dark of skin and seemingly dark of mind, mysterious, bloody, cruel, "devil-worshipping." To these must be added the
sense of exile — the psychological anxieties attendant on the tearing up of
home roots for wide wandering outward in space and, apparently, backward in time. The sense of loss was heightened by the inevitable lapsing of
communication with the homeland, the divergence of colonial from homeland historical experience, and the rise of new generations more acculturated or acclimated to the wilderness, less like the remembered grandparents in the fixed image of Europe. Exploration of new lands was one
necessity imposed on them; fighting Indians, enduring captivity among
them, and attempting to convert or enslave them were others. All emigrants shared the anxious sense that they had been, willingly or unwillingly, exiled from their true homes in the motherlands of Europe; all faced
the problem of justifying their emigration to more stable folk at home, of
trying to sell them either actual land or the idea of a colony. All felt impelled to maintain traditions of religious order and social custom in the
face of the psychological terrors of the wilderness. Later, the sons of these
emigrants strove to justify their title to the land they took for their own.

Around each of these problems a body of literature with distinct formal conventions gathered: narratives of discovery, narratives of Indian war
and captivity, sermons, and colonization and anticolonization tracts. These
accounts purport to be first- or second-hand reports of day-to-day events
and topography in the new world. The authors usually had ulterior motives
in publishing them — a desire to explain or justify, through imaginative reconstruction of events, a course of action they had taken or their right to
possess the land; or simply an attempt to persuade potential European settlers of the beauties and wealth of the strange new world. In any case,
their appeal to the reader was carried by the metaphors that, implicitly or
explicitly, informed their accounts. At the outset these metaphors were

drawn from a purely European context, either the literature of the classical age and medieval and Renaissance romances, or the religious and political thought of the Reformation. Gradually these metaphors, constantly adjusted to suit American conditions, began to metamorphose, to take on some of the shape and coloration of the colonists' experience of America and her landscape.

As American society evolved through years of historical experience, the differentiated literary forms were gradually drawn together by writers who more or less deliberately sought to create a unified and compelling vision of the total American experience — an American myth. This process of reintegration was logically inevitable. The more a writer or preacher understood of the American environment, the less he could simplify or compartmentalize his approach to analyzing it. One could not discuss exploration, for example, without mentioning the chance of Indian attack and captivity. One could not maintain religious discipline by purely theological argument or pure civic force, if parishioners were willing and capable of seeking their fortune by itinerating on the edges of the wilderness; so sermons merged with accounts of frontier hardship. Any work capable of attaining that unified and compelling vision of the whole American experience would have to contain in its terms — narrative, character, imagery, values — the sum total of all these experiences reduced to a basic and universal archetype of all the colonists' experiences, the one presenting the most vital psychological difficulties, and present its vision in terms appropriate to the historical experience of a wilderness people.

Printed literature has been from the first the most important vehicle of myth in America, which sets it apart from the mythologies of the past. The colonies were founded in an age of printing, in large part by Puritans, who were much inclined toward the writing and printing of books and pamphlets and the creating of elaborate metaphors proving the righteousness of their proceedings. Since Americans turned readily to the printed word for the expression and the resolution of doubts, of problems of faith, of anxiety and aspiration, literature became the primary vehicle for the communication of mythic material, with the briefest of gaps between the inception of an oral legend and its being fixed in the public print. How this occurred is one of the chief issues to be dealt with in this study. For the student of the historical development of America as a culture, the visibility of the several stages in the evolution of "traditional metaphors addressed to ultimate questions" is an invaluable aid. It also presents several difficulties. In order for us to examine myth, we must rely on artifacts which are translations of the mythopoeic perception of reality. A tale handed down in the oral tradition from generation to generation presents, if examined at a late period, a distorted and adulterated image of the original. As a vehicle of myth, literature enjoys the advantage of formal permanence. The process of writing, however, necessitates a certain distortive distancing between the author and his experience — a distortion compounded where the author has the experience only at second hand or where he attempts to recall it after the passage of many years. Furthermore, myth as literature is subject to the movements of the literary marketplace. Authors and publishers interested in book sales might deliberately shape their narratives to suit current fashion; moreover, writers desiring a wide reputation shaped their narratives to English audiences as much as, or more than, to American audiences, introducing extraneous characterizations of their material which have little to do with the American colonists' attempts to understand their situation in their own terms.

On the whole, the development of narrative literature in the first two hundred and fifty years of American history is one of the best guides to the process by which the problems and preoccupations of the colonists became transformed into "visions which compel belief" in a civilization called American. Repetition is the essence of this process. Certain instances of experience consistently recurred in each colony over many generations; translated into literature, these experiences became stories which recurred in the press with rhythmic persistence. At first such repetition was the result of real recurrence of the experiences. The Indian war and captivity narratives, for example, grew out of the fact that many pious and literate New Englanders were continually falling into the hands of the Indians or attempted to explain their actions in battle. Once in literary form, the experience became available as a vehicle for justifying philosophical and moral values which may have been extrinsic to the initial experience but which preoccupied the minds of the reading public. Thus Cotton Mather and others wrote "improvements" of the captivity narratives and used them in jeremiads and revival sermons. Through repeated appearances and recastings in the literary marketplace, a narrative which proved viable as a bestseller or a vehicle for religious or commercial persuasions would be imitated by more or less professional writers (where such existed) or those emulous of literary or ecclesiastical reputation. Thus the experience would be reduced to an imitable formula, a literary convention, a romantic version of the myth. When enough literature had been written employing the convention, it might become a sort of given betweeen writer and audience, a set of tacit assumptions on the nature of human experience, on human and divine motivations, on moral values, and on the nature of reality. At this point the convention has some of the force of myth: the experience it portrays has become an image which automatically compels belief by a culture-wide audience in the view of reality it presents. Thus in tracing the development of the conventions of narrative literature, we are tracing the development — by accretion of symbols characteristic of cultural values — of a distinct world vision and an accompanying mythology emerging from the early experiences of Europeans in the wilderness.

The cultural anxieties and aspirations of the colonists found their most dramatic and symbolic portrayal in the accounts of the Indian wars. The Indian war was a uniquely American experience. Moreover, it pitted the English Puritan colonists against a culture that was antithetical to their own in most significant aspects. They could emphasize their Englishness by setting their civilization against Indian barbarism; they could suggest their own superiority to the home English by exalting their heroism in battle, the peculiar danger of their circumstances, and the holy zeal for English Christian expansion with which they preached to or shot at the savages. It was within this genre of colonial Puritan writing that the first American mythology took shape — a mythology in which the hero was the captive or victim of devilish American savages and in which his (or her) heroic quest was for religious conversion and salvation. As their experience in and love for America grew, however — and as non-Puritans entered the American book-printing trade — the early passion for remaining "non-American" (or non-Indian) became confused with the love the settlers bore the land and their desire to gain intimate knowledge of and emotional title to it. If the first American mythology portrayed the colonist as a captive or a destroyer of Indians, the subsequent acculturated versions of the myth showed him growing closer to the Indian and the wild land.[24] New versions of the hero emerged, characters whose role was that of mediating between civilization and savagery, white and red. The yeoman farmer was one of these types, as were the explorer or surveyor and, later, the naturalist.

But it was the figure of Daniel Boone, the solitary, Indian-like hunter of the deep woods, that became the most significant, most emotionally compelling myth-hero of the early republic. The other myth-figures are reflections or variations of this basic type. In numerous popular narratives devoted to Boone's career, the experience of America that first appears in the captivity and Indian war narratives is reduced to a paradigm. The values, beliefs, and experience of life for which the captives and Indian-killers or -converters had spoken were concentrated in this new figure and in the narratives that define his ways of relating to the cosmos. Moreover, these older values were compounded with the newer, more acclimated view of

America symbolized by the farmer and the naturalist or surveyor. The figure and the myth-narrative that emerged from the early Boone literature became archetypal for the American literature which followed: an American hero is the lover of the spirit of the wilderness, and his acts of love and sacred affirmation are acts of violence against that spirit and her avatars.

In its structure this myth-narrative follows a variation of the initiation into a new life or a higher state of being or manhood that is a myth-theme as old as mankind.[25] The boy's coming of age, the fall, the Christian conversion, and the success myth (the American dream of perpetual self-improvement and -transcendence) are variations of the basic theme. Usually the experience of initiation is portrayed as an individual accomplishment, an experience of life which each man must come to in his turn. In America, however, the experience of initiation into a new life was shared by all members of colonial society simultaneously during a certain, relatively brief period of time. The pivotal position of the Indian war narratives and John Filson's legend of Boone's "baptism by combat" in the development of American mythology and literature is explained by their applicability to the universal problem of the colonial period: the problem of acculturation, of adjusting the mores and world view of one's native culture to the requirements of life in an alien environment. The English colonists had to remake their values, their concepts of law and religion, and their images of their role and place in the universe in order to survive in the wilderness. This necessity was difficult to acknowledge, since the colonists felt it their duty to remain loyal to their English heritage. It was far easier to define their cultural identity by negative means, through attacking or condemning alien elements in their society, by casting out heretics like Roger Williams and John Underhill, whose ideas were strange or whose behavior smacked of an Indian-like lack of orthodox discipline. The Indian wars, in which culture was pitted against culture, afforded a perfect opportunity for this sort of definition by repudiation. In opposing the Indian culture, the Puritan symbolically affirmed his Englishness. Even as social and religious issues grew complex and clouded, as men who had been orthodox in England grew heretical in America, as men grew unsure about whether the true church was presbyterian or congregational, antinomian or orthodox, English or universal or American, there remained a fundamental simplicity in the opposition between Indian and settler.

Writers of the Indian war narratives, a circle which included both actual participants and clerical outsiders like the Mathers, generally composed their accounts as if their audience's belief in certain concepts of morality and theology and the frontier could be taken for granted. Their works were unconscious experiments, designed to test the power of certain ideas of human experience (and in particular the American experience) to produce conviction in an audience. Revival preachers employed Indian war tales as a tool for arousing pious anxiety in their congregations; land speculators used them as advertising ploys; representatives of social, religious, and political factions used them to justify their particular conceptions of the truth. Frontiersmen used them to mock the ways of town-bred tenderfeet; town-bred preachers used them in chastising the restless indiscipline of frontier life.

[margin note: Indian war tales were used for various political purposes.]

Any experiment was successful to the extent that its assumptions about life, America, Indian, God, and the wilderness coincided with those of its particular audience. But during the first centuries of its existence, colonial society was fragmented into hostile cultural enclaves and rival governments, each speaking for separated and isolated fragments of that society. Even after the Revolution, sectional and local differences persisted and to some degree intensified. This heterogeneity, coupled with the constant pressure of European immigration and expansive emigration to the frontier, made for a constant agitation of issues, values, and ideas. In this fluid culture, the success of any given attempt at myth-making was usually brief, until Filson's first study of Daniel Boone appeared in 1784. This figure caught and held the national attention for half a century, despite varying sectional evaluations of the moral and social character of the frontier hero.

Even in the pre-Boone literature, however, throughout all the changes and developments, certain themes and values persistently recurred. These are the core of the American frontier myth — the symbolic formulations of the American experience which carried the world view of the first colonists from generation to generation. This study therefore begins with an investigation of the two cultures that battled for the New World. It is followed by an analysis of the Puritan literature of the Indian wars and of the captivity narrative, which emerged as the Puritan myth of America. Changes in the symbolic roles of Indians, frontiersmen, and Europeans in the eighteenth century are then traced to their culmination in Filson's *Kentucke,* which formulated the myth of the hunter as archetypal American and mediator between civilization and the wilderness. The divergence of American and European treatments of this figure from 1784 to the Jacksonian era, and the divergence of treatment in the literatures of various sections of the United States, are dealt with in the following section. Finally, the emergence of an American literature firmly based on an American mythology is treated through the works of Cooper, Melville, Thoreau, and other writers of the American Renaissance period.

CHAPTER 2

Cannibals and Christians:
European vs. American Indian Culture

> "*Brother;* . . . We are told that your religion was given to your forefathers, and has been handed down from father to son. We also have a religion, which was given to our forefathers. . . . We worship in that way. It teaches us to be thankful for all the favors we have received; to love each other, and to be united. We never quarrel about religion.
>
> "*Brother;* We do not wish to destroy your religion, . . . we only want to enjoy our own. . . . As we are going to part, we will come and take you by the hand, and hope the Great Spirit will protect you. . . ."
>
> As the Indians began to approach the missionary, he rose hastily from his seat and replied, that he could not take them by the hand; that there was no fellowship between the religion of God and the works of the devil.
>
> This being interpreted to the Indians, they smiled, and retired in a peaceable manner.
>
> *Chief Red Jacket and a Missionary*[1]

THE culture and literature we call American was born out of the confrontation between cultures that embodied two distinctly different phases of mythological evolution, two conflicting modes of perception, two antagonistic visions of the nature and destiny of man and the natural wilderness. The European cultures that sought to transplant themselves to these shores possessed a sophisticated, romanticized mythology, in which the land of what was to become the American West figured long before its actual discovery. The Europeans were met by native Indian cultures whose mythology was closer to the primary, Moira stage, whose vision of the American landscape was mythopoeic rather than conventional, whose values and mores (derived from their environment and their mythic vision) were in important respects antagonistic to those of Europe. Yet between European and Indian there was a fundamental bond of sympathy, a mutual recognition of a brotherhood of consciousness (or perhaps of the unconscious). The whites appreciated and envied what they took to be the Indian's ease of life and sexuality, the facility with which he adjusted to the land, the fidelity and simplicity with which he worshiped his wilderness gods, and the gratification of mind and body such worship brought him. The Indian perceived and alternately envied and feared the sophistication of the white man's religion, customs, and technology, which seemed at times a threat and at times the logical development of the principles of his own society and religion. Each culture viewed the other with mixed feelings of attraction and repulsion, sympathy and antipathy.

Human cultures on the North American continent, whether they were of European or Indian origin, have been shaped by the interaction of their migrant peoples with the American landscape, the wilderness. The one constant in the American environment has been the wilderness in its varying forms of forest, plain, mountain, and desert. The French and English settlers of Canada and the eastern seaboard of the United States confronted essentially the same physical environment as the Abnaki (Wabanaki), Iroquois, Algonkian, and Cherokee who preceded them in the land. As the American environment was the same for each of these cultures, one might reasonably expect that in the process of adjusting their lives to the wilderness, each of these cultures would acquire certain elements or qualities distinctly derived from and suited to that environment. Differences between them might be accounted for by considering their differing points of cultural and historical origin. Also, their presence together in the land, resulting in both violent and amicable cultural interaction, would affect the development of each culture, just as the constant of the wilderness would. If we are to understand the mythology and the cultures derived from this complex of interacting factors, we must have some understanding of the nature of the hostile cultures involved (Indian and European), of how they reacted to their environment, and of their vision of both their own role in the cosmos and that of their opposites.

The European Myths: Chaos and Arcadia

Colonists from Europe were the inheritors of a long and elaborate mythoreligious tradition, one in which the primary mythic consciousness had been submerged in a complex of social and literary conventions, hidden behind apparently arbitrary and nonfunctional rules and ornaments. The Indians, having no written literature beyond a few glyphs, were closer to the primary sources of myth and more capable of perceiving the life around them with the mythopeoic eye of the godmaking believer. Where the settlers could see only chaos and wilderness, the Indian's eye and mind could construe an order, a kindred intelligence in all things. The historical conflict between these peoples was intensified — and ultimately trans-figured — by the psychological conflict implicit in European confrontation of the New World wilderness. D. H. Lawrence expresses and partially explains the intensity and significance of the white-Indian conflict in his description of the hostility between "blood"-knowledge and brain-knowledge:

> . . . the blood *hates* being KNOWN by the mind. It feels itself destroyed when it is KNOWN. Hence the profound instinct of privacy.
>
> And on the other hand, the mind and the spiritual consciousness of man simply *hates* the dark potency of blood-acts: hates the genuine dark sensual orgasms, which do, for the time being, actually obliterate the mind and the spiritual consciousness, plunge them in a flood of suffocating darkness.
>
> You can't get away from this.
>
> Blood-consciousness overwhelms, obliterates, and annuls mind-consciousness.
>
> Mind-consciousness extinguishes blood-consciousness, and consumes the blood.
>
> We are all of us conscious in both ways. And the two ways are antagonistic in us.[2]

·   In the Colonial period the Moira-Themis tension between blood and brain, common to all cultures, mythologies, and personalities, made itself felt on two levels. Within the body of European myths about America were two antagonistic pre-Columbian conceptions of the West: the primitive belief in the West as the land of the sea, the sunset, death, darkness, passion, and dreams; and the counterbelief in the West as the Blessed Isles, the land of life's renewal, of rebirth, of reason and a higher reality. Once colonization began, this tension found an objective correlative in the conflict between the cultural values and mythologies of the settlers and those of the Indians. It is this coincidence of the terms of dream dilemma and of the actual culture conflict that is the starting point of the American mythology.

In the myths of Europe, the islands of the West had been fabled before the Age of Discovery as the place of the underworld or afterworld, the mystical kingdom of dreams, of death and dissolution, the maternal womb and tomb of the sea or the night (in which the sun would sink), the world below consciousness, the realm of Moira. Before the outlying islands of a New World defined themselves on Columbus's horizon, the West had been conceived as a group of island gardens set in the wine-dark sea. The Blessed Isles of the Greeks swam somewhere in the West, a land of dead souls dwelling in permanent bliss. But the sunny, templed isle of Atlantis had been whelmed under by that same limitless dark sea. It was to the west of Greece that Odysseus and Aeneas found the door of Hades; and other legends less happy than those of the Hesperides cast a melancholy pall about the imagined landscape of the West — Valhalla of the doomed Norse gods, the *Abendsland*, Land of Nightfall, as it is still called in German. But even in death's dream kingdom there was hope for the renewal of life, for a day of resurrection for the fallen kings of men. Arthur of Britain passed westward over the water into Avalon, but from the west he would return, the once and future king.[3]

In the mythology of Europe, the West and its peoples were strongly associated with the kingdom of death and dreams, the underworld — in psychological terms, the unconscious. In the archetypal mythology of the heroic quest, which informs all accounts of the Age of Discovery, it is the journey to the underworld that is the essential, necessary action. In this dark, hidden realm abide the forces that silently and inscrutably shape the destiny of men, nations, and the physical universe. When overwhelming need — the failure of crops or game, of cultural or personal vigor, of religious faith, of self-knowledge or self-acceptance — drives the hero to seek aid from powers beyond his own or those of his world, his quest takes him out of the world and into the realm of dreams, of death, of secret magic, of the unconscious. There he finds a "boon" — a golden bough or other magic talisman — which he seeks to bring back to his commonday world for the salvation of that world. Before he can do so, however, he must submit himself to the underworld, or (in Conrad's terms) immerse himself in the destructive element; he must be tested by the forces underpinning the world, be initiated into the wisdom of the dead and the ever-living. He risks destruction of self, either personal destruction in death or the mystic-erotic dissolution of the death in love and the death in God. Should he be fortunate enough to escape, he remains a man marked by the gods, alienated psychologically from the commonday reality by his possession of dark and fundamental knowledge.[4]

In its primary form the hero myth reflects the mental journey of the mystic, the man who drowns his consciousness in the inner ocean of his mind or the ocean of the universal god. The hero myth itself, however, presents this quest of consciousness in social and historical terms: it takes place in the "real" world, the world of time and event; and it involves a hero who is the symbolic vessel of the whole culture's collective consciousness and the agent of their will to survive or their aspiration to power. In Europe during the Age of Discovery, however, such myths were better known in their romantic, conventionalized forms than in their primary forms. Centuries of literary and philosophical embellishment had substituted artifice and convention for mythopoeic spontaneity in epic poetry and tragedy. The Romans imitated the forms of the Greek poems and plays that inexplicably moved them, and in their concern with formal imitation they lost the sense of life inherent in the myths. The medieval scholars and troubadors ornamented and elaborated the received tradition, hiding the core of myth under a panoply of social and religious conventions, imposing rigid artistic categories on the received material, rather than illuminating the mythic essentials that transcend artificial distinctions of genre.

A significant example of this romanticization is the medieval and Renaissance treatment of the myths and rituals of sacred marriage, an archetype in which the hero-king achieves sexual union with the goddess of nature in the wilderness, thus ensuring the seasonal renewal of human and vegetable life. Underlying the myth and its attendant rituals is the psychological quest of the *anima*, the feminine principle of passivity, passion, and acceptance within the reasoning, cold, masculine consciousness. Achievement of reconciliation between these halves of the mind means the attainment of psychological identity, self-containment and self-contentment. But rather than plumb the metaphor of the sacred marriage, European Christians elaborated the metaphor, ornamented it, and bowdlerized it of those elements that spoke too intimately and too directly to the deeply sexual, unconscious yearning for psychological unity. The result was the literary convention of courtly love, in which sexual union is perpetually frustrated or else rendered sterile, impotent to produce heirs to hero-kings. The passions are cultivated and exalted through frustration, which becomes a kind of holy exercise; marriage ceases to represent the culmination of union and becomes rather the artificial barrier that keeps the true lover from his true beloved.[5]

This world of elaborately conventionalized thought, feeling, and expression reacted to the discovery of the western world in conventionally appropriate terms. Its response was structured by the romantic mythology it had inherited and by the formulas of literary genres devoted to exploiting that mythology. The New World gradually perceived by the discoverers was vast, unknown, exotic, uncultivated, and peopled by diverse nations of savages, some of whom lived in burrows and grubbed for insects and some of whom were masters of imperial civilizations; but European writers responded to the discovery in the conventional terms of utopian treatise-fiction, arcadian poetry, and the chivalric romance-epic. More's *Utopia*, for example, was set in an imaginary American Indian empire and based in part on reports of the actual accomplishments of Aztec, Inca, and Chibcha Indians. Bacon's *New Atlantis* evoked a more venerable and abstract Platonic image of an imagined western kingdom.[6] Mapmakers, painters, and colonial publicists played on images of the Hesperides, imaging forth the New World as a collection of jewellike islands in the mystic sea, each a *hortus inclusus* or wall-enclosed garden,[7] a kind of natural cloister in which wild nature is, through its own ordained internal workings, orderly, obedient, and chaste. Less medieval in some respects was the arcadian image of the New World, which at least removed the walls from about the garden. But as in the enclosed garden, the arcadian nature was not wild and chaotic but orderly and symmetrical, reflecting the cultivating hand of a reasoning and compassionate God whose mind was not unlike that of a superior man. The arcadian view of the New World was that of an Eden from which the serpent and forbidden trees had been thoughtfully excluded.

The predominating theme in all these works is that of European renewal through discovery and conquest of the New World. For More and Bacon the renewal was a moral and intellectual one: the expansion of knowledge gained through discovery gives man the power to reform and purify his social and religious institutions. The mere fact of discovery was enough to serve their needs; details of Indian life or of American geography were, for them, beside the point. The arcadian view of the New World postulated a different kind of renewal — a renewal of physical and sexual vigor, of the power of the heart and of sentiment, achieved through a return to a more "natural," less civilizedly "corrupt" mode of life.

This idea was also related to the theme of the romance-epic, in which the heroic adventure is seen as a means to renewing the vigor and restoring the power of Christianity and of the hero's nation. Michael Drayton's ode "To the Virginian Voyage" portrays the colonization attempt as a quest for recovery of the Golden Age and sees in it the promise of a renewal of England's national vigor, perhaps even a resurrection of the heroes of English myth and legend. The ode begins with an invidious comparison between those heroes who go a-questing and the "loyt'ring Hinds" who "Lurke here at home, with shame." The object of the English quest is an unspoiled natural world, shaped by divine artifice for the support and complement of human life, an artfully wrought garden, out of the strife of nations and the harshness of the real natural world:

> And cheerefully at Sea
> Successe you still intice,

> To get the Pearle and Gold,
>   And ours to hold,
> VIRGINIA
> Earth's onely Paradise.
>
> Where Nature hath in store
> Fowle, Venison, and Fish,
>   And the fruitfull'st Soyle,
>   Without your Toyle,
> Three Harvests more,
> All greater then your Wish.
>
> . . . the golden Age
> Still Natures lawes doth give,
>   No other Cares that tend,
>   But Them to defend
> From Winters age,
> That long there doth not live.

In this winterless land of perpetual spring, perpetual fructification, a new race of heroes and bards will spring to renew England's glory:

> And in Regions farre
> Such *Heroes* bring yee foorth,
>   As those from whom We came,
>   And plant Our name,
> Under that Starre
> Not knowne unto our North.
>
> And as there Plenty growes
> Of Lawrell every where,
>   APOLLO's Sacred tree,
>   You it may see,
> A Poets Browes
> To crowne, that may sing there.[8]

Such romanticizing of the New World was not restricted to those who stayed behind to write books and plays about a land they never saw. The explorers and conquerors themselves tended to see the landscape of America through lenses colored by their reading of romance-epics and pastoral verse. Romantic myth also created perception-altering expectations for the Elizabethan and Jacobean navigators who founded the first English settlements in the New World. The Indians of Carolina and Virginia were not the material on which to build a fabulous empire; they had no gold, no floating, terraced cities, no subtle crafts, no very elaborate or striking religious rituals. (Spanish chroniclers found it easier to obscure commercial aims and political ambitions behind the facade of the romance, since the reality of Mexico and Peru to some extent supported the extravagant claims of the romancer.) The reality of Virginia finally required a different metaphor, and the values and aspirations of Elizabethan England suggested a number of alternatives: national aggrandizement to counter Spanish imperialism, expansion of the English Protestant faith to contest with Rome for the souls of the American gentiles, and the Renaissance drive for expansion of human knowledge.

The acts of British seamen-adventurers, soldiers, and scholar-navigators were physical testimony to the vitality of these imperatives, and discovery was invested with the sanctifying aura of heroic myth. Hakluyt's great compendium of tracts, *Principall Navigations*, juxtaposed accounts of exploration in Arctic and American waters with tales of sea fights with the Armada and the plate fleet, commercial treaties with the Muscovites, and combats with the savages of Labrador. It created a strange kind of national epic out of a series of fragments written by participants and contemporaries, whose variously motivated works were united only by an underlying nationalism, a robust intellectual curiosity, a Faustian sense of human power, and an excited sense of the limitless variety of God's creation.

It was in the pages of Hakluyt that the English image of the newly discovered lands began to take shape. Navigators skimming its coasts were drawn by the promise that fable assured them was concealed in the wasteland, but at the same time they were repelled by its outward aspect — its disproportionate extremes of climate, the strange shapes of its topography, its unheard-of plants and animals, and its men of an aspect so strange as to seem ogreish. The account of Martin Frobisher's voyages is typical: the word *monstrous* constantly recurs throughout the work and comes to seem the most characteristic adjective applied to the New World: the ship is surrounded by "monstrous" islands of ice, the "huge and monstrous mountains" promise "Earthquakes or thunder." The natives, like their land, are also monstrous, "altogether voyd of humanity," attacking the explorers without warning, slaying themselves rather than surrender to mercy. An old woman captured in one of the battles is taken for a devil, and the sailors "had her buskins plucked off, to see if she were cloven footed, and for her ougly hew and deformity we let her goe." Confessing ignorance of their religion, the chronicler supposes from their appearance and manners that they are "Anthropophagi, or devourers of mans flesh," and thoroughly "loathsome." [9] Yet despite the threatening aspect, faith in the hidden promise endures. The voyagers expect to find a certain sort of land, and they persist in finding evidence to support the expectation that Arcadia is just over the next, seemingly forbidding horizon:

> Here, in place of odoriferous and fragrant smels of sweete gums, & pleasant notes of musicall birdes, which other Countreys in more temperate Zones do yeeld, wee tasted the most boisterous Boreal blasts mixt with snow and haile. . . . Little birds, whiche we judged to have lost the shore, by reason of the thicke fogges which that Countrey is much subject unto, came flying into our ships, which causeth us to suppose, that the Countrey is both more tollerable, and also habitable within, then the outward shore maketh shew or signification.[10]

The Spanish accounts, more obviously than the English, were shaped by the literary style and values of the romance and by the literature of chivalry — the Grail legends, *Jerusalem Delivered*, the Roland epics, and *Amadis de Gaul*.[11] To be sure, in the case of the Spanish the New World lived up to and perhaps surpassed the expectations engendered by literature. One of the best and most representative of their accounts is Bernal Díaz del Castillo's history of the conquest of Mexico, in which he himself was a common soldier. Díaz describes himself as the son of a petty noble and minor official and speaks as an old soldier whose deeds shine in his memory by the reflected glory of the true heroes under whom he served. He promises to tell the tale "quite simply, . . . without twisting events one way or another," [12] and is in the main sincere. Yet the metaphors of wonder, enchantment, and chivalry are so entangled in the remembered experience as to be inseparable from it. The armored Christian knights march against a mighty pagan empire, ruled by a noble and tragic priest-king. They wander over incredible deserts, in the shadows of fantastically splintered barren peaks, some of which burst spontaneously into flame at their approach. Hostile tribes assail them, or affront their eyes with unspeakable rituals of human sacrifice, or, presenting another face, offer them exquisitely wrought presents of jewels, gold, and feathers. At the end of the unslaked and savage desert, so like the wasteland of the Grail legends, they behold Mexico — great, white, castellated cities, heaped with greenery, floating in the midst of vast blue lakes. Within the enclosed luxuriant gardens of these enchanted cities live an exotic people, dressed in a fantastic garb of woven and many-colored feathers, intricately wrought gold, turquoise ornaments, and printed cotton.

Yet these fair islands are rotten at the heart: within each towering white temple are chambers reeking of blood from human sacrifices and human filth. So reality blends with romance, blood myth with art myth, as obscenity is discovered at the heart of an otherwise perfect reproduction of an enchanted kingdom. In the process of purifying the kingdom — and of taking from it its wealth and power for the invigoration of Spain — the enchanted realms themselves are utterly destroyed, exorcised, all but banished from memory, to Díaz's sorrow.[13]

Díaz's chronicle touches the heart of the problem of Europe's confrontation with the New World. Although the conventional myths and metaphors of Europe distorted the conquerors' perception, the strange and troubling reality of the Indian's world did impinge on their consciousness. Chivalric romance provided metaphorical justification for the man-on-the-make in Mexico but did not explain the troubling nature of the conqueror's response to Indian "virtues" and Indian "obscenities." The Aztec blood-myths and the sacrificial rites of Huitzilopochtli were, after all, not unrelated to the Spanish auto-da-fé; and the Spanish liberators planned, from the first, to reimpose slavery on those tribes they freed from the Aztec yoke. Nor did the chivalric romance explain the aftermath of conquest. Instead of remaining in Mexico to labor for king and God and to found a Christian kingdom to rival the Aztec, the conquering soldiers atomized their society and deserted the colors to wander off, singly and in groups, tracing down Indian legends of hidden gold or untapped mines or fountains of youth. The Spanish came to bring order, but as individuals they succumbed to the temptation of freedom, of disorder, that the New World held out to them.[14]

The most striking quality of life in the New World was the relative absence of social restraints on human behavior, the relative ease with which a strong man could, by mastering the law of the wilderness-jungle, impose his personal dream of self-aggrandizement on reality. In Europe all men were under authority; in America all men dreamed they had the power to become authority. To men of the sixteenth and seventeenth centuries, and perhaps to any others as well, this freedom was itself both promising and threatful. While there was much good to be found in freedom from social restraint, from the imposition of restraints by a collective conscience, there were grounds for anxiety in the fact that each man's conscience had, without external aids, to maintain him in a state of virtue and social conformity in the face of unheard-of temptations. Pre-Columbian legends of the West reflect this fear of the dream kingdom, countering the Hesperides image with that of Valhalla's *Götterdämmerung*, Atlantis's demise, the mouth of Hades. In Norse sagas, which recount an attempt to colonize Vinland the Good half a millennium before Columbus, the dark spell of the land atomizes and ruins the colony. Although the settlers find the land fruitful, the natives are brutish *skrelings*, hostile and bloody-minded; and in that far place, assailed by the fears natural to isolated men in a hostile world, the Norsemen turn on one another in murder and fratricide, breaking the order of the colony in fragments, leaving only a dark saga of jealousy and slaughter.[15]

The Norse experience was shared to some extent by the Spanish and by all subsequent settlers in the New World. Like Shakespeare's Prospero, the conqueror in America stepped out of the "real" world into one in which he had the power to will his dreams. But the magic of the place was of a dual nature; it had both an Ariel and a Caliban face. On the one hand, it led to the execution of good designs; on the other, it stimulated a monstrous ambition against authority, an obscene Faustian lust to satisfy nature by violating all bonds of obedience, religion, and morality. But even the Ariel face of the New World was somewhat treacherous, tempting the good-willed dreamer into simple, natural willfullness, a delight in the exercise of forbidden benign powers. While Caliban might ruin and destroy the body, too long intimacy with Ariel might woo man too far in spirit from the commonday world of human responsibility, the European world.[16]

The Indians played a curious role in exciting Faustian lusts in the conquerors. Their wealth and beauty stimulated the Europeans, their power challenged them, their fatal weakness tempted them to prove their strength. It was Indian legends of golden cities and immortality-giving springs that tempted Ponce de León and Coronado to death. The Spanish found, as did the English after them, that the wilderness could isolate them from their civilization, captivate and imprison them, and compel them to learn and live by its laws. The narrative of the Indian captivity of Alvar Nuñez Cabeza de Vaca, a conquistador captured by the Indians on an expedition to Florida, offers a keen insight into this aspect of the New World (and incidentally anticipates by more than a century the most important genre of Puritan writings about the New World). Cabeza de Vaca and his compatriots sail to Florida to seek more golden cities, following nothing more solid than the romantic mythology that has been given new life by Cortés. Romantic myth provides a totally inadequate guide to conquest: they lose their way, deal incompetently with the Indians, smash their ships, and lose their provisions. When their ineptitude leads to final shipwreck and disaster, Cabeza de Vaca is cast away and captured by Indians. He lives among them several years, gradually learning their language and woods skills and adjusting to their ways, although maintaining his allegiance to Spain and the church. As a result of this education, a subtle change comes over his descriptions of the Floridian wilderness. Land that he found barren and waste when he was with the blind and blundering

Spaniards now appears to flower and be abundantly fruitful for the Indians, who know how to see and how to use it. It is the Indian who teaches the Spaniard to see more in the land than gold or its lack and how to make his way with profit and honor in the land.[17]

Such characters, after their return to civilization, remained divided in their attitudes and values between the world they were born into and the world they had just been educated to, between the European world to which they returned and the Indian world they left. Like Cabeza de Vaca refusing to join Coronado's hunt for Eldorado, they could no longer be as blinded by their romantic mythology as they had been; and many would maintain the patterns of thought and behavior acquired in captivity. Such men and their accounts were essential if the colonists were to learn enough about the New World to be able to survive in it and to pursue their search for Cibolas and fountains of youth. Yet such men were a danger, positing within the European camp the alternative, Indian vision of the world.

To those charged with the rule of colonies, the problem was more political than psychological: how to keep the colonists from dispersing to hunt for gold, glory, and the satisfaction of their hearts' Faustian desires. Economic incentives for preserving colonial solidarity went far in maintaining order; so long as it was profitable to stay together, an acknowledged leader might rule his people. Where economic benefit was in any way or degree dubious, military force or the leader's strength of character might still hold the colony subject. But without a shared commitment to a single goal among all members of the colony, the atomistic tendencies might swiftly destroy it. Every colonial leader shared this same problem: the governors of Cuba failed to check Cortés's westward sally into Mexico, Cortés himself was plagued by men deserting to the gold fields, and La Salle was murdered and Hudson abandoned by disaffected followers. Puritan Massachusetts, itself a fugitive from England, considered itself plagued by the tendency of its people to emigrate into the woods, beyond the pale of its godly rule.

A shared sense of mission, embodied in a vision or metaphoric image, was a chief source of cohesion in colonial enterprise, both in the psychological and, consequently, the practical sense. By appealing to a shared view of the meaning of their life in the New World — a kind of myth — leaders could quell or hold in check the atomistic individual wills of their people.[18] This is an appropriate function for myth and for art to play in the universe. Both serve as means of ordering and explaining a chaotic and threatening environment.

The remythologization of the West began with attempts by French and Spanish Jesuits and English Puritans to order the chaos of the New World and its citizens by providing the colonists (and those Indians who would convert) with a sense of shared mission — a belief that their presence in the New World was decreed from above with definite ends in view and that deviation from those ends was equivalent to mortal sin. This sense of mission provided the colonial with a much-needed psychological insulation from the shocks and temptations of wilderness life. It gave him the sense that the present hardships were temporary and therefore of minor significance. By the same token, it served to distract him from the tempting aspects of wilderness life: from indulgence in sensual pleasures, get-rich-quick schemes, or Faustian rebellions for personal power. By concentrating on the *idea* of America, orthodox mythology fostered what was thought to be a salutary neglect of the immediate, savage America. Concentration on the ends of American colonization also distracted attention from some of the less palatable means employed in achieving those ends. It could, in fact, make men quite callous about the method and manner of their approach to the wilderness and the Indians in the conscious rectitude of their missionary purposes.

The Puritan Myth: Pilgrim's Progress[19]

The English Puritans who settled British America exemplified this European approach to the New World. They were drawn largely from the rising Protestant middle classes of the English cities and country towns: merchants, artisans, professional men, landowners, clerics. Their religion portrayed the progress of the soul as a rising up from the degradation of man's condition at birth to ultimate sanctification through divine grace — a kind of spiritual upward mobility. They repudiated the blood myths and blood rituals of the quasi-pagan lower classes, whose sports and revels and theaters seemed more of Dionysos than of Christ, and also the rituals of Anglo-Catholicism, which likewise had the pagan smack of blood about them. The Faustian spirit of the Renaissance both attracted and appalled them. If man could be a semidivine hero, wielding perfect power in the universe, then man was alone with his freedom and power, without the sustaining prop of an external divine authority. Such loneliness was insupportable: what evils might man not do if left totally to his own devices? The Puritan solved the dilemma by imagining a God whose authority was absolute and arbitrary and a human race utterly depraved and dependent; but through the infusion of divine grace, God might purify man, make him a visible saint, perfect and pure in both motive and deed. Such a man might enjoy (under God) the most complete power and freedom without fear, attaining a state of being beyond the grasp even of Faust.

Puritan preconceptions of the nature of the American lands seem at first glance a conventional blend of promises and threats. As William Bradford reported, they thought of the land as "fruitful and fit for habitation," indeed a place where failing fortunes, health, and physical and spiritual vigor might be renewed.[20] On the other hand, the climate was unknown, and disease was to be feared. Above all, they would be

> in continual danger of the savage people, who are cruel, barbarous, and most treacherous, being most furious in their rage and merciless where they overcome; not being content only to take away life, but delight to torment men in the most bloody manner that may be; flaying some alive with the shells of fishes, cutting off the members and joints of others by piecemeal and broiling on the coals, eat the collops of their flesh in their sight whilst they live, with other cruelties horrible to be related.[21]

Of all the anticipated perils, the threat of Indian cannibals evoked the strongest emotion. Bradford generalized about disease and famine but was quite specific in detailing the terror of the Indians. Unlike the Spanish, the Pilgrims did not wish to discover and conquer Indian empires; nor were they interested in discovering an arcadian people in an American garden, living a model of the Golden Age. What they desired above all was a tabula rasa on which they could inscribe their dream: the outline of an idealized Puritan England, a Bible commonwealth, a city on a hill exemplifying the Word of God to all the world. Thus Bradford's first thoughts on the New World emphasized the virtual emptiness of the land and dismissed the few Indians present as having little claim to humanity and less to the land:

> The place they [the Pilgrims] had thoughts on was some of those vast and unpeopled countries of America, which are fruitful and fit for habitation, being devoid of all civil inhabitants, where there are only savage and brutish men which range up and down, little otherwise than the wild beasts of the same.[22]

This land, so ripe for preemption, was not to be taken simply in the name of conquest, nor in the hope of great personal aggrandizement. The Puritans developed an elaborate concept of their mission in the New World, their "errand into the wilderness," in which their emigration was an analogue of the Exodus of Israel from Egypt — a temporary exile for fugitives from an idolatrous land, a period of trial which would make them worthy of entering into a new Promised Land and a New Jerusalem. Just as the wandering in the wilderness purified and converted the community of Israel to valid worship of the one God, the Puritans hoped that their communities and social, religious, and political institutions would be purified through trial in *America deserta*.

Since the "community of Saints" was made up by the gathering together of converted individuals, the Puritan emigrants paid careful attention to the religious experiences of individual members of the transplanted community in order to discern the positive and negative effects of emigration. This concern created a view of the individual experience as community experience in microcosm; and the community's development in the New World was seen primarily, not in the physical terms of the chivalric romance, but in terms of a psychological and spiritual quest, a quest for salvation in the wilderness of the human mind and soul. The physical world of America was but the physical type of this primary wilderness.

The closest literary analogue of the Puritan model of the heroic quest is John Bunyan's *Pilgrim's Progress*, in which an archetypal Christian departs from his family and home, to journey from the City of Destruction to the Heavenly City through a landscape featured with the various qualities and states of the human mind and soul. The justification of the Puritan pilgrim's departure is the biblical injunction: "If any man come to me, and hate not his father, and mother, and wife, and children, and brethren, and sisters, yea, and his own life also, he cannot be my disciple" (Luke 14:26).[23] The quest for salvation — for the Heavenly City — is undertaken by each individual man in the solitude of mind and soul. The hero of the Puritan quest is not the captain of conquering soldiers but a figure fleeing in solitude from sin-begotten humanity. Actual landscapes are less important than the landscape of the mind. *The Pilgrim's Progress* is cast "in the similitude of a dream," and the first paragraph of the book takes us down several levels to the interior of a mind. Bunyan portrays himself as walking "through the wilderness of the world," dreaming a dream in a "Den."[24] In the dream he sees the figure of Christian, who walks through the wilderness of Bunyan's mind, past features of his psychological geography: the Slough of Despond, Vanity Fair, and the like. Christian dwells in the City of Destruction, which will soon be visited by God's wrath, and feeling the burden of his sins he flees. The appeals of his family and friends, ties of love and of blood, the comforts of society — all must be cast aside for this paramount duty.

Like Christian, the Puritans saw their voyage to the New World as a spiritual journey, and the landscape of their New World often seems to owe more to their concept of the spiritual features of the soul than to the actual topography. The Indians were emblems of external temptation to sin or of the human mind's dark impulses to sin. England was often portrayed in terms of the City of Destruction — a place from which the righteous must, at all costs, flee. This metaphor, however, posed a problem for seventeenth-century Englishmen bound by ties of tradition and emotion to England's land and ways, to their homes and families. Where was the Promised Land to be located, in the New World or in England? Were the emigrants like the Israelites, bound from Egypt to a true Promised Land, or like the Babylonian captives, doomed to a painful exile among heathen before they could return to a renewed home country? The emigrants were bound to England by ties of kinship and emotion. How could they abandon it wholly to the prelates and see former neighbors compelled to the damnation of their souls?

The issue of the extent to which the Saints ought to separate from unpurified social and religious institutions had been debated long before the establishment of a separate Puritan nation became a real possibility. Medieval thought had viewed society as an integral unit, an organism in which church and state, man and community were indivisible. The Tudor period and the rise of an English national consciousness had confirmed and even exaggerated this concept of the church-state. Treason and heresy were analogous crimes; excommunication from the church was civil banishment raised to the highest power. The Puritan sects, with notable exceptions, aimed at reform of the existing church and state from within; even the Nonconformists justified their doctrines by warrants in the Bible of the Church of England and perpetually reaffirmed their English national character. To the psychological anxieties attendant on physical separation by emigration to America, there were thus added the burdens of religious and civil accusations of separatism. To the orthodox Anglicans, the Puritan emigrants were making a separation and schism and were therefore heretics. To the Puritans who remained in England, they were men fleeing from the task of rebuilding the church in England. To the crown they were, potentially at least, political separatists seeking to escape from the requirements of civil law and duty.[25]

Thomas Shepard's "Defense of the Answer," an apology for the emigration to New England, provides a good index to the depth and quality of the Puritan anxiety about having broken those ties of blood, custom, fealty, obligation, and religion that bound them to England. Shepard cites numerous incidents to prove that God has had the emigrants in his care and justifies the settlement on the grounds that it will do God's work among the heathen, as well as liberate some English Christians from Anglican tyranny. In justifying emigration he notes the fear and anxiety with which they broke their social bond to England and entered the terror and temptation of the Indian wilderness, echoing Bunyan's pilgrim:

> When we look back and consider what a strange poise of spirit the Lord hath laid upon so many of our hearts, we cannot but wonder at ourselves, that so many, and some so weak and tender, with such cheerfulness and constant resolutions against so many persuasions of friends, discouragements from the ill report of this country, the straits, wants, and trials of God's people in it, yet should leave our accommodations and comforts, should forsake our dearest relations, parents, brethren, sisters, Christian friends and acquaintances, overlook all the dangers and difficulties of the vast seas . . . and all this to go to a wilderness, where we could forecast nothing but care and temptations, only in hopes of enjoying Christ in his ordinances, in the fellowship of his people.[26]

The concept of the errand into the wilderness was developed to still these objections and to quiet the inner voice that called them back to England.

Numerous tracts were written by the preachers and governors of the emigrant colonies justifying their emigration. Most mentioned the benefits accruing to the state from the establishment of trading stations and food-producing regions and from the extension of the national dominion to check Spain. Uppermost in their thoughts was the religious duty of propagating the gospel to the heathen Indians; for the Puritans, the additional duty of propagating the gospel in England was imposed. New England was to be an exemplary community of saints, an experiment in Puritan government that would train leaders and develop institutions suitable to the government of a redeemed England. To some extent, the Puritan attempts to convert the Indians were to be models for the conversion of English heathen, and tracts detailing the method and process of Indian conversion were circulated in England with the view of admonishing the English: See how these heathens embrace the gospel. Why will you not do the same?

This association of European English and Indian Americans — symbolic poles of the American Englishman's world — is a crucial element in the development of American Puritan thought. Both the Indian and the English prelate threatened the Puritan community with destruction; both tempted men to leave godly for ungodly ways more pleasing to the flesh. Dissolution rather than renewal faced the Puritan community if it fell under the spell of either. As time went by, the Puritans became more preoccupied with working out the details of their Bible commonwealth and with keeping the Indians and home English at a safe distance; later, as missionary efforts with the Indians lagged, so did their efforts to redeem their brothers across the sea. Their attitude toward the native American heathens underwent another sort of change. The heathens' presence in the land made it impossible to neglect or entirely ignore them, and years of conflict with the intransigent Indians made it increasingly clear that they would never entirely convert to English Christianity, although it was conceivable that colonists might revert to the wild. Moreover, the Puritans, unlike the Spanish and French, had come to the New World for land rather than for gold or furs; their aim was to fill up the land with a new people, not to start a few stations to trade with the natives.

The pressure of demographic expansion, coupled with the psychological fear of acculturation, moved the Puritans toward a policy of exterminating the Indians or, at best, reducing them to a semicaptive status on strictly and narrowly delimited reservations (called, at that time, praying towns). It is interesting to note the adoption of similar policies by Puritans colonizing in Ulster and on the Celtic border of Scotland, where systematic assaults were made on Celtic tribalism, native bardic myth-historians were forbidden to sing, isolated clans were exterminated, and the rest of the population was ravaged. Cromwell even attempted to establish a "wild Irish" reservation in western Ireland. His brutal conquest of Ireland seems to have been conceived, in part at least, as an English equivalent of the Spanish jihads against the Indians, which Cromwell had read about in a book dedicated to him by the nephew of John Milton; his wholesale slaughter of the Irish and his selling of many into West Indian slavery parallels exactly the policy adopted by the American Puritans in King Philip's War two decades later.[27] That the situation of the New Englanders — whose opponents were racially and religiously more alien to them than the Catholic Irish were to the English Protestants — evoked similar attitudes and policies is not at all surprising, given the character of their ambitions and their religious and cultural convictions.

Aboriginal America: The Big House[28]

In many ways our Puritan ancestors seem to have shown in exaggerated form, almost in caricature, the patterns of thought and behavior, the religious and literary tendencies, and the sociopolitical and psychological preoccupations of all the Europeans who colonized the islands and forests of the primitive New World. The Puritans were perhaps the archetypal colonizers; they were certainly the most extremely antipathetic to the culture and institutions native to the aboriginal population of America.

Indian land tenure, for example, did not envision the absolute individual possession of the land and its fruits. Tribal lands were tribal property, and the right to hunt or plant thereon could be granted or leased to outsiders; the tribe, however, could retain its original rights to hunt the land along with the lessees. The economic philosophy of the Puritans, by contrast, was intensely bound up with the concept of private property, absolutely possessed by its owner, who had full power to use or sell it. Bound up with this concept of property was a social and religious philosophy derived from centuries of struggle between lord and tenant and between merchant and tax collector in the complexly stratified society of England. To the Puritan his right to absolute possession of his property was akin to the right to absolute possession of his own soul and conscience, his right to worship God after his own fashion despite the prevailing official orthodoxy. It was both the badge and the real basis of his improving status in the world and hence symbolic of his value as both Englishman and Christian.

Nor did Indian and Puritan agree in their conceptions of economic value and the significance of value exchanges. The Indian feared that all economic exchanges were potentially productive of evil — either simple ill will or the magical malice of witchcraft, either the poison of resentment or some real poison to blight soul and body. The giving of wampum was "medicine," protecting the giver of wampum and the recipient against "spiritual infection," purging the transaction from latent evil force. The European concept of "intrinsic value" currency (with its concomitant ideas of the methods for economic success) was antithetical to the Indian concept of currency as a mask for "spiritual and supernatural interplay."[29]

> The [Calvinist] Dutch in buying Manhattan for 60 guilders worth of trinkets undoubtedly drove a shrewd bargain with the Delawares. But who has told us that in the eyes of the Delawares the currency was the symbol[,] not the value equivalent[,] of their hereditary rights to the land as well as its products? This ridiculous price was to them a symbol over which they transferred their good-will and spiritual power over forces dormant in the land, clearing away the poison that might have been engendered by the inequality of value in the transfer.[30]

The divergence in Indian and English Puritan economics is symptomatic of more fundamental cultural disparities. For the Puritan, political, social, and religious theory dealt with the ordering of society in terms of the problem of authority. Institutions were thought to possess the power to bind men and societies because of their derivation of intrinsic value from the ultimate authority of the divine Word. Political controversies therefore concerned the reconciliation of conflicts between persons and institutions sanctioned with authority, such as the crown and the parliament, the tax collector and the proprietor. Solutions to political controversies — like those old class or interest conflicts, or even religious disputes — could best be settled by appeal to ultimate authority. With the lapsing of medieval Christianity and feudalism and the rise of the Protestant bourgeoisie, the character of this ultimate authority and the concept of who has the right to appeal to that authority had undergone vast changes. The pope, the king, the Scriptures, and even the individual conscience were variously cited as partial expressions of the ultimate authority which resides with God himself. This divine authority was now conceived of as otherworldly, nonhuman, transcendent, incomprehensible to natural reason or earthly minds. Thus the political-social theory also implied a metaphysical theory, in which there was a dichotomy between the worlds of divinity and humanity, between authority and those who must obey authority. The Puritans, as members of a tendentious and persecuted religious minority and a rising, ambitious, new middle class, were peculiarly sensitive to distinctions between the sanction of authority and the limits of obedience. And it was the Puritans who most clearly enunciated the concept of the utter division between the realms of divinity and humanity and who sought to create new and more authoritative institutions for governing their own realm.

For the Indian the problem of government arose, not from the conflict of older authorities with new powers, but rather from the organic need of essentially free men to band together for survival. Indian population in the vast continent of North America was sparse, permitting the formation of small, discrete tribal cultures, each developing in its own way with peripheral intercourse and conflict with other tribes. However, a certain general similarity of social needs and environmental conditions produced patterns of belief, ritual, and government that were common to most tribes within each of the major geographical divisions of the continent (eastern woodlands, plains, mountains, deserts, coasts) and some that were almost universal among Indians of the whole continent.

The Indian tribes of the woodlands (and later, the plains), with whom the English settlers had their earliest contact, were small cultures composed of clan-communities, generally seminomadic and of slight technological development. Their tribal histories of migration through varying geographic and climatic zones had made their institutions more flexible, more freely adaptable to new circumstances than those of the Europeans. They had had to adapt to the conditions of wilderness life, since the possibility of controlling or remaking their environment was not open to them (as it seemed to be open to the Europeans). They worshiped the world-as-it-is, and their institutions were therefore shaped to the conditions of their life by a process simultaneously pragmatic and theistic.

While the Europeans, in making laws for the governance of life in a new world, had to reconcile human and divine authority (as these had been defined through centuries of political and philosophical debate), the Indians could concern themselves solely with discovering the readiest way to reconcile personal freedom with individual and collective survival. This they achieved, although the delicate equilibrium of their relationship with the environment, as well as their internal polity, could be easily upset and destroyed by the intrusion of a technologically and numerically superior culture into their world. Puritan political and religious institutions tended to be authoritarian, even where the authorities granted broad liberties to the public. Indian government was strict by necessity, but its roots and its methods were nonauthoritarian. There was no hereditary nobility, and chiefs were usually elected spontaneously for particular occasions when specific kinds of leadership were necessary. Councils of tribal elders and priests were largely consultative rather than magisterial bodies.[31] The Indians' love of personal liberty and freedom soon became proverbial among the colonists; and as we shall see, the passion of the Revolutionaries for independence was often traced, by friend and foe alike, to their having imbibed the Indian passion.

On the level of myth and ritual the divergence of the Indian and Puritan, or European, minds becomes more apparent. For the Puritan the figure of God was purely patriarchal, sternly just, logical, and absolutely transcendent and unworldly. He was primarily the fountainhead of authority, continuing to rule his world according to the law of Logos, his Word. The Catholic maternal deity, mother of the Son of God, was likewise an asexual being in her relationship with the Father; and her Son's presence in the world was a temporary one, to be consummated in a bliss beyond the world. The Indian conception of creative divinity was, in contrast, distinctly sexual, combining both paternal and maternal aspects. The earth was a primary, female deity — maternal, sympathetic, loving, passionate, violent, and absolutely bound up in the tangled veins and arteries of the world. She did not administrate or rule the world, nor did she function as an intermediary for men in some unworldly heaven. Rather, she was the world itself. The paternal aspect of divinity, actively fathering life upon the passive earth, was conceived by the Delaware Indians as Kickeron, which is "Life, Light, Action or Energy . . . [or] the abstract conception back of all these." The Indian term for "governor," sometimes applied to the paternal deity in post-Christian times, was a corruption of the older word and was only applicable to a man.[32] Both male and female principles were spoken of as "kindred," rather than transcendent, beings.

The distinction in their attitudes toward the wilderness becomes clearer as we examine Indian and Puritan myths of creation. Puritan theology begins with the Old Testament version of the fall of man. The woman Eve violates the authority of both the paternal deity and her husband, robbing the divine orchard of forbidden fruit. Her husband compounds the error by succumbing to female authority (in terms of another tradition, to Moira) and disobeying his God. Their punishment is to leave the womblike Garden of Eden, in which their wants have all been anticipated and satisfied, and to enter a wilderness in which they will have to till the soil and produce children, both of which entail pain and hardship. In this crime and punishment the human race has its genesis, conceived in and bound forever by original sin; humanity's very presence in the world is the confirmation of its evil beginning.

Indian versions of this myth are diametrically opposed to the Puritan in values, although strikingly similar in basic structure. The Delaware (Lenni-Lenape) version of creation seems typical of that held by many North American tribes. In the beginning the people live under a lake, in darkness, grubbing roots and vegetables for sustenance. Although these are adequate for existence, they conceive their lot to be miserable or, at least, feel an obscure hunger for something better. One day the tribal hero discovers a deer and pursues it as a hunter. The deer leads him to a hole permitting escape from the underworld. He pursues the deer into the forest, kills it, and eats of its meat; in that moment he perceives the goodness and beauty of his Mother the Earth. He returns to his people with the meat. They partake of it, are awakened, and follow the hunter out into the world to populate, enjoy, and worship the maternal spirit of the woods.[33]

Both myths explain the genesis of the human race and its movement into the world. But whereas the Christian myth deplores this as a fall from a gracious satisfyingly womblike condition, the Indian myth rejoices in the discovery and in the movement into the world. The exile of Adam and Eve results from their disobedience to their transcendent Father, but it is the loss of the foetal or infantile relationship to the life source that is their chief misery. For the Indian it is virtue that leads man into the world, and this virtue finds its highest expression in the exercise of masculine powers (as in hunting). The hunter of the deer (like the father-god Kickeron) is capable of engaging the earth goddess as a sexual equal, of exchanging and mingling powers with her to produce a people and populate a wilderness. The Christian mourns the loss of sexual dependency and abases himself before the masculine power of the paternal god, not daring again to assume his prerogatives.

Blood myth and blood ritual are reflections of the human unconscious, the hidden mind of man — perhaps especially of the id, in which is found the innate urge toward sexual fulfillment, that is, toward self-perpetuation and self-immolation. Sexual mores as well as myths are therefore a revealing source of insight into the mind of a particular culture and its techniques for dealing with human nature. The suppression and reorganization of sexual impulses (in marriage customs and the courtly-love mystique) were a central feature of Christianity and of European culture in particular. The Puritans' attitude toward the way in which myths express man's passional nature is a good index to their sexual attitudes. Sexual expression was synonomous with the sin of lust, save where such expression was placed under patriarchal authority in marriage and where the passional element was repressed in favor of more reasoned and social behaviors. For the Indian, on the other hand, sexual freedom for the unmarried was an assumed right, and even married men to some extent remained sexually free. This freedom was deemed essential to the health of both individual and tribe, besides constituting a pleasurable and at times sacred source of personal gratification. The taboo against adultery by married women was essential to the preservation of social order and was somewhat offset by the freedom of both consenting marriage partners to dissolve their marriage at will. These sexual practices, which horrified the Puritans, were not simply the result of a natural overflowing of free animal spirits; they represented an essential element of the Indian's adaptation to his wilderness world. Indian populations were usually marginal, liable to fatal diminution in poor hunting or growing seasons. Sexual freedom for the young revealed the best breeders and enabled the tribe to benefit from even the earliest years of female fertility.[34]

It would seem from these myths and mores that the Indian cultures tended to value the free exercise of the natural impulses and powers of men, while the Christian emphasized the repression of those impulses and the subordination of those powers to authority. This distinction similarly applies to religious rituals and practices in the two cultures. The basis of Indian ritual were the so-called blood myths that are the primitive roots of Christianity as well. Ritual was chiefly employed for the purpose of propitiating the gods or even controlling them by means of sympathetic magic — by ritual imitation of the gods' behavior or by the reenactment of ancient myths in which contact between gods and men was beneficial and immediate.

The Delaware Indian Big House ceremony was a reenactment of the creation and life history of the world and, at the same time, a pattern for the life of the tribe and of individuals within the tribe. It was thus both the source and the seal of tribal identity for the Delawares, or Lenape. The ceremony involved a tribal dance down the white path, symbolizing the transit of life of all men and of all created nature, under the staff-pole of the Great Spirit. The dance consumed twelve days, symbolizing the twelve moons of the year, so that a yearly life-cycle was symbolically experienced. The heart of the ceremony was the preparing, arming, and sending out of hunters, in the name of the tribe, to hunt and kill some sacred animal and return with it to the tribe. The animal was presented to the people in the Big House and eaten by them in a blood ritual — a pattern which strikingly resembles that in the creation myth of the lake, the hunter, and the deer.[35] The rite partook strongly of the nature of ritual cannibalism, in the manner of the Christian Eucharist, for the animal's body was the vehicle of the divine, animating spirit which moves all things that live and urges them perpetually to begin again the ritual dance of life. But unlike the Eucharist, the Indian ritual frankly employed real flesh and blood rather than emblematic wafer and wine.

The Big House or longhouse was a fairly common eastern-Indian model of the universe and may serve to illustrate the different conceptions of the cosmos in Indian and European cultures. The sixteenth-century European universe appeared as a series of concentric spheres, rigidly geometric in shape and bound in fixed order by the law of God. God himself stood outside the spheres of the universe, bound to man on the innermost sphere only by the figurative chain of being, an ordered hierarchy of levels of existence, power, and virtue. The Delaware Big House was, literally, the large dwelling in which the most important tribal ritual is performed. But it was also a model of the larger universe, and on ceremonial occasions it was mystically equated with the totality of that universe, becoming (for that moment) the thing which it represented. The Big House was the nexus that joined "the celestial universe embraced in terms of time and space [and] the tangible realm of the human in the midst of the concrete." [36] The floor of the Big House was the earth, beneath which was the underworld; the four walls were the quarters of the world; the roof was the "visible sky vault . . . atop which resides the Creator in his indefinable supremacy." The center post that supported the Big-House universe was "the staff of the Great Spirit with its foot upon the earth, its pinnacle reaching to the hand of the Supreme Deity." A door on the east side was "the point of sunrise where day begins and at the same time the symbol of the beginning of things," of the life of each man and the life of all created things. The western door was "the point of sunset and symbol of termination." From east to west ran the "White Path, / Symbol of the transit of life" of men and tribes and of the seasonal growth and decay of living things. The earthly path corresponded to the Milky Way, the white path of man in the world of afterdeath, where the "dance" and the white path persist forever.[37]

Within the circle of the Big House, two figures dominated the cosmos, each defining a way of approach to the reality that the tribe craved to know and worship. These were the "hunter" or "warrior" and the "shaman," as Joseph Campbell terms them in *The Masks of God*.[38] The hunter goes forth from the tribal circle to exploit and dominate nature for his own glory and the benefit of the tribe. He comes to appreciate and worship the power of nature and its spirit through his killing and eating of the beasts who carry that spirit in the world. The shaman's way is the way of passiveness and suffering. He gains insight into the world through adventures of the mind and spirit, risking his life and sanity by putting himself at the mercy of the forces that govern man and the universe. Each figure's actions are defined in myth, and each myth implies an ethic — the hunter's code of war and killing, the shaman's morality of self-abnegation, kindness, and peace. In the Indian way of life, and in the mythology, these figures often appeared paired and balanced with each other, since the hunter's courage is as essential to the shaman as the latter's spirit of kinship with nature is to the good hunter. Thus gentle Quetzalcoatl spoke for peace against the man-eating Huitzilopochtli of the Aztecs; the gentle prophet Deganawidah, reforming rather than warring with the cannibal warrior Hayowentha, became the founder of the Iroquois League of Peace before the coming of the white man; and the warrior Tecumseh's charismatic leadership of the Indians in the first decades of the nineteenth century derived from his pairing with his brother, the Prophet. Sometimes the two were united in a single figure, such as the Sioux Crazy Horse.

Both the hunter and the shaman had their counterparts in white mythology. Indians were generally quick to notice the similarity between the laws of shamans like Quetzalcoatl and Deganawidah and the tenets of Christianity (especially those of Quaker Christianity). The spirit of the hunter likewise corresponded to the entrepreneurial spirit of the colonist-adventurers, the traders in furs and hides and land. Although the white man's economy of trade and exploitation of the land's resources was technologically more advanced, it was not so different in practice from the Indian economy of hunting and barter that the tribes could not see a good thing in the trade nexus. The Indian hunter became quite rapidly the accomplice of the white entrepreneur in the destruction of the wilderness and the beings that derived existence from it.

The shaman is a more complex figure, in both white and Indian societies. Among the whites, and to a degree among the Indians as well, the lifeway represented by the shaman came to be thought of as the way of the victim, the sufferer, the captive. In situations of extreme fear and insecurity, such as those which occur when one culture feels itself in danger of being absorbed or destroyed by another, the balance between the shaman and hunter as equal symbols of value is destroyed. The shaman then becomes symbolic of weakness in man, the hunter symbolic of strength. This was the case with the Aztec and the Iroquois, the tribes most like the Europeans in their attitudes toward war, trade, and government. As small warrior populations in a hard land filled with many enemies, they could ill afford to live entirely by the pacific doctrine of Quetzalcoatl or Deganawidah. Although they continued to propitiate these gods and the values they stood for, the ceremonies became reenactments of the Aztecs' and Iroquois' recurring nightmares of captivity, loss of strength, and impotence. The Europeans, who like the Iroquois and Aztecs were conquerors and imperialists, developed (as we shall see) a similar dichotomy in their mythology and culture between the dominating hunter and the helpless captive. The consequences of such a dichotomy are severe: the natures of shaman and hunter become intensified, and the warrior feels driven to prove his strength and power through acts of incredible cruelty, which is exacerbated by his fear of being at one with the totally helpless victim he destroys. This was the development that took place in both the Iroquois and the Anglo-American mythology in the period we are examining.

The concept of the Big House as an emblem of the universe, and the rituals associated with the Big House, enabled the Indian to reconcile man and nature. These relationships were typically those of consanguinity: the high gods, the beasts of the forest, the trees, fire, and water were regarded as blood relations, as kin sharing the Big House among them. The chief deities were "grandfathers" or "elder brothers," depending on their stature. The eagles, air, planets, thunders, and other portentous beings were also grandfathers, as were certain ancient and respected neighboring tribes. The earth was "mother," as was the sea, but herb medicines and life-sustaining corn were "grandmother." Animals and human tribes were "brothers," occasionally "elder," or otherwise "nephews" or "sisters," according to some obscure scheme of relationships.[39] Similar notions are found among other tribes, including the Sioux, who made no distinction between men and animals, dividing creatures only into "two-leggeds" and "four-leggeds." [40]

Ultimately, these differences in theology, in myth and ritual, in politico-economics, and in psychological theory produced entirely different conceptions of the place of man in the natural world and of the divine scheme of the cosmos. To the Indian the wilderness was a god, whether its face at the moment was good or evil; as a god it deserved and received worship for both its good and its evil, its beauty and its cruelty. Similarly, all the gods and the earth itself were referred to as members of one's own immediate family, as close blood relations. For the Puritan the problem of religion was to winnow the wheat from the chaff, the good from the evil, and to preserve the former and extirpate the latter. The evil was of the world, of nature; the good was transcendent and supernatural. Hence it was quite appropriate to destroy the natural wilderness in the name of a higher good — and quite inappropriate for anyone to worship, as the Indians did, the world or the things of the world, such things being evil by nature.

Like the Puritans, the Indians had abstracted from their mode of life a concept of a "way." The Indian way and the Puritan way were, however, antithetical concepts. The Puritan way aimed at the creation of a sanctified civilization, a society ordered on rigid principles of divine authority. Their concept of social form was dictated by their past experience in urban England or in the country farming villages. They prized cultivation: the bringing of wild man, wild passions, and wild nature under the check of order. The Delaware way, by contrast, was called "wilderness life" (te^{e}keneau-'s.uwak.an): "Not only are wild animals pure in contrast with domestic brutes. . . . It will also be noticed that the term is applied to . . . the unadulterated new fire made without manufactured articles like matches or other unclean material." [41] For their initiation rites, boys were sent into the wilderness to dwell in free solitude till their voices — the expression of the breath or soul — had changed to men's voices.[42] The Puritans, by contrast, initiated boys by bringing them in under the yoke, rigorously subjecting them to social discipline, and examining the state of their souls most carefully before initiating them into the congregation.

Both Indians and Puritans were much concerned with the process of initiating newcomers and young children into the responsibilities and powers of their society. Their theories of initiation reflect their theories of human nature and psychology as well as their conceptions of man's place in his society. Initiation into the community was of peculiar interest to the

Puritans, since their community was drawn out from the larger English community by a process of harsh selection. Since they were dissenters from prevailing religious belief, the Puritans' impulse 'to withdraw from the larger community was accelerated by persecution. Perhaps more important than this circumstantial source of Puritan exclusivity and clannishness was Puritan belief itself. Confronting a church in which traditional ecclesiastical authority and scriptural interpretation were discredited, the Puritan could rely only on his own reading of Scripture and his own conscience for light. How could he avoid falling into heretical error, lacking any authoritative voice to whom he might appeal? Only God himself could give the necessary light for a man to truly read either the Bible or his conscience, since without God man's corrupted reason would lead him astray. God could only reach directly to a man through the miracle of grace, as manifested in the conversion experience. In this experience God miraculously gives man a new and truer sight of himself and his sins and, with it, a new heart capable of feeling remorse for those sins. Without this intervention by a transcendent God, man would be incapable of redeeming himself. Nor can man do anything to bring or induce God to perform the miracle, since man's understanding of God is totally incompetent and since God himself has no moral or other obligation to man. The experience of conversion is therefore arbitrarily granted by an omnipotent and inhuman God to those few whom he has elected or chosen to be among the saved.[43]

Entrance into the Puritan community was dependent upon the manifestation of God's grace to a man in a bona fide conversion experience. For both the man and the community, therefore, there was need to establish some means of identifying and evaluating apparent conversion experiences and ratifying them for the community. For the individual this meant a rigorous course of soul-searching and self-examination, hopefully leading to an awakening of the aspirant's sense of his sinfulness, his utter loneliness and alienation from the God on whom he depends. In this dark night of the soul, a light of hope or relief-giving breath of air might suddenly make itself felt, perhaps stimulating a flood of emotional release, a sense of a burden cast off, of hope and rescue, of "sanctification." Was this light an infusion of grace or simply a relapse of the weak soul into complacency? Only more soul-searching, more disciplined introspection, could begin to establish the truth. Once the man himself was convinced, it was necessary for him to face examination by the church elders, who would inquire minutely into the quality and character of his experience, perhaps requiring further meditations and humiliations and further examinations before ultimate acceptance — or rejection.

These initiatory rites hinged on the intellectual analysis, the breaking down and reordering of experience in terms of an elaborate sacred paradigm. The tests were obstacles to entrance into an exclusive circle, the company of the visible saints. Obedience and self-denial, the acceptance of prohibition, were demanded. Once accepted into the community, the convert had joined an aristocracy of sanctity analogous to the aristocracy of wealth and birth that ruled the world of the unconverted. His primary obligations lay within that group, and even within it his first obligation was always to God and his authority. Although the Puritans did not, as a matter of doctrine, believe that sanctification was inherited by the children of the converted, in practice they tended toward the belief that, at the very least, their sons were more prone to conversion than the children of the gentiles. This aristocratic sense of community was further augmented by their concept of property inheritance, which did in fact make attained standing in the community an inheritable quality.

Full acceptance to honor and dignity in English and Puritan society was conditional upon the attainment of either a certain economic or a certain spiritual solvency. This tended to be less true of Indian tribal societies, in which a man's claim on the sympathy and care of his fellows was his right by virtue of his having been born into the tribe. While the English developed elaborate legal and moral concepts for avoiding the responsibility for care of the aged, indigent, or sick, Indian tribes developed ceremonial practices which integrated the charitable provision for such tribesmen with religious and festive occasions.[44]

This same concept of the organic unity of the individual and the tribe shaped the Indian rites of initiating boys into full manhood and citizenship. Where the Puritan's initiation into full citizenship was hedged about with prohibitions and checks on his personal power and desire, Indian ritual emphasized positive preparation for the role that the boy would inevitably have to play as member of the community. Puritan initiation might end with either overt rejection or relegation to social inferiority and disfranchisement. Indian initiation had perforce to end with the boy's full membership in his community. Like the Puritans, the Indians placed much weight on the experience of conversion, or rather of the attainment of full rapport with the culture's gods. As part of the rites of initation, the Indian youth had to undergo a trial by hunger in the wilderness, in isolation, in order that the gods might speak to him in a dream-vision and reveal to him his true character and personal destiny. The tribal response to the initiate's confession of his vision was, however, very different from the Puritan response. Where the Puritan elders analyzed the experience, picking it to pieces in a search for nonauthentic elements, the Indians treated all dreams — whether of men or priests or fledgling boys — as essentially and, to some extent, equally sacred: "Each of us respected his brother's dream." [45] This the Puritans did only during the peaks of their great revivals. Rather than engage in destructive analysis of a dream, the tribe would communally ratify the burden of the dream for the returning initiate by celebrating with him as he recited and acted out the dream before his assembled people. In cases of dreams that seemed of greater import than the usual, the whole tribe might gather under the youth's direction to act out his dream for him, in the hope that the entire community and its young prophet might gain better understanding of the sacred dream and the gods' demands.[46]

These Indian initiatory practices derived from their belief in the multiplicity of deities and the possession by each man and tribe of its special and unique divinity. Just as the Indians worshiped both the good and the evil, the pleasant and the threatening face of nature, as equal reflections of the divine power in the world, so they accorded a kind of equality of respect to other tribal and personal divinities. An English or other Indian captive accepting adoption into an Indian tribe simply exchanged his tribal god for that of his adopted tribe and was brought in under the latter's protection. In much the same way, visitors with the tribe might place themselves temporarily under the protection of the tribe's deity (under the codes of hospitality); or a member of the tribe visiting the English might worship with them as a mark of respect to his hosts and their god. For the English, however, the act of worship was worth only as much as the intrinsic value of the deity worshiped; and since there was but one true god, their own, they regarded the paying of respect to Indian gods as apostasy, and Indian respect to Jehovah as a sign of imminent conversion. Conversion itself, they made clear, would mean for the Indian an utter casting off of the old god and the life pattern of the tribe. To be truly saved the Indian would have to purge himself of his Indianness; he must become totally English in style of life as well as Christian in spirit. (This subject is discussed in some detail in chapter 5.)

The English Puritan and the American Indian represent a polar opposition in cultural values. Certainly, this was the attitude adopted publicly by many Puritan spokesmen. Yet the Indian's way of life was not totally alien to the Puritan. In it he recognized just enough of his own behavior and feelings to be deeply troubled with self-doubt. Indian religious rituals were strange enough to seem repulsive, yet similar enough to the Eucharist to be disturbing. Indian sexual customs were entirely different from the

Puritan, but they dealt with the facts of human sexuality that Christianity likewise recognized and attempted to control. Racially the Indians seemed alien, yet they were undoubtedly (in many instances) a physically and morally attractive people, not fundamentally dissimilar from the colonists in shape and sympathies. And were their religious customs so very different from the remnants of pagan worship that remained in practice in their own English countryside? The strangeness of the Indian was a threat to the outer man and to Puritan society; the Indian's familiarity, his resemblance to the primitive inner man, was a threat to the Puritan's soul, his sense of himself as English, white, and Christian.[47]

This resemblance between whites and Indians became more troublesome as time went by. It was at times an embarrassment to Puritan writers and a source of guilt to Puritan soldiers that under the pressures of battle in the tangled and isolated wilderness, white troops often behaved precisely like their Indian enemies — burning the villages of their enemies; slaughtering not only the warriors but also the wounded, the women, and the children; and selling their captives into slavery. Official historians of the wars, like Hubbard and Mather, had no trouble explaining the massacres as divinely sanctioned extirpation of the "Amalekites"; but narratives by participants like Captain Underhill (1638) and Captain Church (1716) reflect either a strong sense of guilt or outright moral indignation at the troops' behavior.

In point of fact, the Puritan and Indian responses to the life of the wilderness were, at bottom, strikingly similar. For the whites the wilderness was an extremely difficult place to survive in, especially when climatic difficulties were complicated by the presence of savage, warlike tribes. Earlier agriculturists like the Ohio Mound Builders and the Algonkian tribes had been all but exterminated by the hunting Iroquois, even before the arrival of the Europeans[48] — which suggests that where marginal tribal societies were involved, the warlike had a better chance for survival in the American wilderness. Likewise, the arrival of the populous, technologically advanced, disease-bearing Christians made survival infinitely harder for the Indians. Survival in the wilderness, for Indians and Puritans alike, required perpetual vigilance on the borders and the maintenance of strict order and allegiance within the tribe or community. Survival made a strong military posture necessary to resist inroads by hostile outsiders. More significantly, in order for the tribe to grow and expand its power and food-gathering territory, it had to extend its borders and win its peace by military or quasi-military conquest. The Puritan could not afford to think in purely defensive terms. If he wished to protect what he had won from the wilderness's edge, he had to descend into the heart of its darkness, to master its territory and its Indians, to check the ambitions of the French and Indians seeking to expand into its territory. Just as the Mound Builders fell before the militaristic Iroquois and the way of Deganawidah before that of Hayowentha, Puritan missionary spirit gave way to the military spirit. Puritans came to define their relationship to the New World in terms of violence and warfare. Narratives of the Indian wars of New England became the first significant genre of New World writing and formed the literary basis of the first American mythology.

CHAPTER 3

A Home in the Heart of Darkness:
The Origin of the Indian War Narratives (1625–1682)

> The wilderness had found him out early, and had taken on him a terrible vengeance for the fantastic invasion. I think it had whispered to him things about himself which he did not know, things of which he had no conception until he took counsel with this great solitude — and the whisper had proved irresistibly fascinating. . . .
>
> I tried to break the spell — the heavy, mute spell of the wilderness — that seemed to draw him to its pitiless breast by the awakening of forgotten and brutal instincts, by the memory of gratified and monstrous passions. This alone, I was convinced, had driven him out to the edge of the forest, to the bush, toward the gleam of fires, the throb of drums, the drone of weird incantations; this alone had beguiled his unlawful soul beyond the bounds of permitted aspirations.
>
> Joseph Conrad, *The Heart of Darkness*

LOOKING at the culture of the New World in which they had come to live, the Puritans saw a darkened and inverted mirror image of their own culture, their own mind. For every Puritan institution, moral theory and practice, belief and ritual there existed an antithetical Indian counterpart. Such analogies were never lost on the Puritans, who saw in them metaphors of God's will. Clearly the Indian cultures were the devil's city on a hill, emblematic opposites to their own Bible commonwealth. Yet the Indian was not totally alien to the world of the Saints: like the Indians they too had been, before conversion, under the dominion of the devil. Through grace they might be able to capture the devil's city and turn his demons to good men (if not angels).

As the Indians are, so civilized men once were: this notion had a troublesome side as well. Indian blood myth and blood ritual corresponded, in their primitive trappings and dramatic ceremony, to the ancient revels of England and the "paganism" of Catholic ritual and lore. The Puritan's horror of Indian myth and ritual derived from the very marrow of his own religious tradition. Puritanism began in a revulsion against Catholic and Anglican ritual (and against Elizabethan and Jacobean drama) — a revulsion in large measure against the very idea of blood myths and blood ritual. As in the Indian myth and ritual, the worshiper in the Catholic Eucharist ate of bread and wine that were believed to become the actual body and blood of Christ. That such a miraculous transformation could in fact take place daily in the Mass, under the ministrations of individuals as corrupt as the parish clergy, seemed to the Puritans an offense to reason and logic.[1] It smacked too strongly of other pagan rites then practiced among the English peasantry and urban proletariat, from whose ranks the Puritans were bent on escaping — the Dionysian May revels and the attendant worship of the goddess Flora, against whom Increase Mather preached.[2] Puritanism was founded on opposition to blood myth and blood ritual and on repression of those dark, passionate human impulses that such myth and ritual reflect. In England opposition to such paganism was complicated by the Christian aura of the ceremonies and the civilized surface of daily affairs. In America the issues were graphically simplified by the racial character of the pagan antagonists. The Puritan could stand for reason and religion against utter and passionate infidels.

New Canaan vs. New Israel

The consequences of this state of mind were dramatically revealed in the Puritans' attempts to deal with the licentious Thomas Morton of Merrymount. Morton's activities confirmed their darkest nightmare: that the Indian would give strength to the pagan, the Dionysian elements in the English character and weaken or degenerate the power of order, authority, and Christianity. To the Plymouth Separatists — whose adherence to Puritan principles was in some ways more rigorous and extreme than that of the dominant Massachusetts Puritans — Morton was the symbol of everything evil and threatening in both the New World and their own culture.

Morton had come to the country with another planter sometime between 1622 and 1624, escaping from a tedious lawsuit involving his wife and her son by a former marriage, from debt and poverty, and from other disagreeable circumstances of his life. When his patron abandoned New England for Virginia, Morton gaily usurped his prerogatives. The religion-charged life of the Separatists had no charms for him. He avoided their tight little community, refused to subject himself to the rigors of their discipline, and met their remonstrations with raillery and abuse. His spiritual and physical separation from the Separatists was strongly underlined by the intimacy his settlement enjoyed with the Indians. He traded with them, avoiding Plymouth regulations, and consorted and slept with them, violating Plymouth morality. His attempt to reinstitute the May games at his settlement and to bring the Indians into the pagan rout brought Plymouth's wrath to a head. Morton was arrested, tried, and deported to England. Plymouth charged him, with some justice, as a violator of the ban on selling arms and rum to the savages. He replied, with equal justice, that Plymouth had gotten rid of him to eliminate competition in the trade and to satisfy its priggish scruples about "revelling" with Indians. Some time after his return to Europe he published *The New English Canaan, or New Canaan* . . . (Amsterdam, 1637), in which he added to these charges that of religious bigotry: Plymouth had expelled him for being an Anglican, thus making him a religious martyr.[3]

The New English Canaan is one of the most entertaining and at the same time revealing works about the earliest period of colonization. By detailing Morton's Elizabethan vision of the New World, it points up the character and depth of the controversy between the Puritan and the pagan spirit in old England and primitive America. Where the Puritan saw the New World as a desert wilderness, like that through which Bunyan's pilgrim travels, Morton saw it as a new Arcadia, a land rich in the promise of spiritual and erotic fulfillment and renewal.

Morton saw this promise in overtly pagan terms. His title page is a clue to the argument of the entire book: he calls New England "New Canaan," rather than invoking the then conventional image of the "New English Israel." He begins his examination of the country with an account of the primitive land and savage inhabitants, rather than the conventional account of a "desert" being discovered and settled by Europeans. His metaphors are pagan-classical rather than scriptural: New England is portrayed as the geographic exemplification of Aristotle's "golden meane." He is infinitely more attracted to the "Canaanites" than to the self-appointed "Israelites" of New Plymouth. In their primitive character the Indians seem emblems of the innocent childhood of man. At the same time, they evoke primitive memories of an Heroic Age: their language, which is said to resemble Latin and Greek, leads Morton to speculate that they are the remnants of "the scattered Trojans." Thus not only are they lineal descendants of Greek heroes; they also share a common Trojan ancestry with ancient Britain itself, which according to legendary account was established by a

Trojan Brutus. The government of the Indians is described as nothing short of "Platonic." [4]

Notwithstanding the pagan glories of the American Golden Age, Morton feels New Canaan is ripe for Christianity. The native religion is "no worship or religion at all," and a recent plague preceding English settlement has made the natives susceptible to the coming of new gods in the shape of Englishmen. They present no impediments to conversion and limited Anglicization; on the contrary, they are most "tractable" and exhibit "Love towards the English." Their natural affections, their honesty and fidelity, and their innate sense of mercy and justice have in fact made them ripe for the touch of Christianity. In this union of pagan Indian and Christian Englishman, Morton finds the hope of a great renewal of power, fervor, and goodness in the religious and social life of the human race. The great erotic energy, the beauty, and the natural piety and wisdom of the Indian will be enhanced by the intellectual light of Christian civilization to produce a more powerful, virile, fecund race. The sexual mingling of the races is, in Morton's imagery, the germinal moment of this renewed human race, this renewed Christianity.[5]

The Pilgrim settlers are the chief and only obstacle to the consummation of this natural, fruitful union. Where the Indians have been just, honest, generous, wise, respectful of age, and open in sexual love, the Pilgrims have responded with injustice, venality, hypocrisy, folly, malice, and touch-me-not bigotry. They withhold their hearts and their persons from the Indians and the wilderness, seeking only the corruption and destruction of both for their own gain. It is interesting to set Morton's account of Plymouth history beside those of Governor Bradford and other Pilgrims. The latter emphasize the nobility of their efforts to convert the Indians, their strenuous attempts to deal fairly, their frequent rebuffs and betrayals by the Indians, and their partial reconciliation in the Thanksgiving feast. In Morton's account, Indian virtues are played off against Pilgrim defects. There is no Thanksgiving feast; rather, the Plymouth men invite some Indians to a banquet and there murder their guests in order to provoke warfare between whites and Indians. Incidents of Indian justice are played off against accounts of Plymouth perfidy, such as the legal lynching of a corn thief and the shoddy treatment of Morton himself by the court. "By this you may easily perceive the uncivilized people, are more just then the civilized." [6]

It is clear that Morton's conception of the meaning of plantation in America was different in both spirit and letter from that of the Pilgrims, or Puritans. The latter portrayed themselves as an ascetic, self-denying army, mortifying their flesh in the wilderness to bring God to the heathen and light to their trans-Atlantic brethren. When the plenty of the land and their own organization caused their fortunes and their population to increase, they took it as a sign of divine favor, granted them for their adherence to purified English piety and social discipline. Morton, noting the same phenomenon of New England's growing wealth and population, saw in the same facts the presence of another sort of god. If the planters of New England, like their farms, are more prolific than those of old England or Anglican Virginia, it is because of the tremendous erotic energy latent in the climate, soil, and food.[7]

Morton regarded his own colony of Merrymount (also called by him Marry-Mount, Mary-mount, or Mare-mount) as the fountainhead of that erotic energy, to which all the new and old worlds might have recourse. The naming of the plantation reveals Morton's thoughts about the kind of colony the New World demanded, as well as the character of his own vision and wit. "Merrymount" was the name the Pilgrims preferred, as it suggested mere revelry and riot; Morton himself would not have caviled at the ascription, although he might have omitted "mere." "Marry-mount" hit closer to his purpose, since the colony was a marrying-ground for two worlds and two races, in both a literal and a figurative sense. "Marymount" — a mountain sanctified to the Virgin — was a congenial interpretation for Morton when he chose to parade as an Anglican martyr; it also did nicely (considering the rituals of the place) as both a bawdy blasphemy and a subtle allusion to the link between Christianity's Virgin Mother and the pagan goddesses of the Greeks and Indians. "Mare-mount" evoked the image of sodomy, or buggery, a crime that troubled New England not a little (by Bradford's account);[8] but like "Mary-mount," the name was also evocative of primitive legend and ritual, and in the "Revells" of Merrymount such rituals were mimed by men and women dressed as beasts for the occasion. This punning on the name of his colony marks Morton as a man of the English Renaissance, and not of the meanest wit, since the wordplay is both a game in itself and suggestive of deeper significances.

The meaning and the peculiar power of his colony are described in Morton's "history" of his plantation. Unlike the straightforward, straight-faced Pilgrim-Puritan histories, Morton's account is richly embroidered with poetic and dramatic devices and literary allusions. Bawdry and wit are abundant; and Pilgrim "grandees," under fictional names like "Little-worth" and "Captaine Shrimpe," are satirized unmercifully as prigs and hypocrites. Yet beneath the banter, Morton remains true to his major theme: that the Englishman must withhold nothing of himself from the wilderness and the Indian but merge thoroughly with them and refresh himself at the sources of human passion and affection. The results of such immersion in the wilderness as was possible at Merrymount are suggested by Morton's parable of the "barren doe of Virginia" who becomes fertile in Merrymount. "This goodly creature of incontinency" had fallen into a melancholy fit over the death of her child and her desertion by a paramour. The cold lover was English, the woman "a great Squa Sachem," or Indian queen. After bathing her in an outpouring of humorous verse, Morton thinks it fit that what he (euphemistically) terms "the water of the fountaine at Ma-re Mount . . . be applyed unto her for a remedy." This phallic "fountaine" mysteriously cures her, causing her barren Virginia womb to "become teeming here." [9] Passion expressed in openly sexual relationships between whites and Indians here becomes the source of a renewal of the virility and fertility of both races. But this is hardly the renewal of spiritual, unworldly, self-disciplined religion that the Pilgrims sought.

Morton's dream and that of the Pilgrims clashed most directly over the "Revells of New Canaan," in which conflict the Pilgrims won the American field and lost the battle of books in England. Shortly after establishing his colony, Morton attempted to revive the pagan English ritual of the May revels. The Pilgrims had been dead against such reversions to the primitive among the peasants and urban proletariat in England; in New England, where the necessity of overcoming or converting a savage and strange race pressed on their minds, the reappearance of English paganism was doubly disturbing. It suggested that their fears (and the fears of their opponents) about English Christianity's potential degeneration in the wilderness were proving true. May Day was "of distinctly Pagan origin, whether traced back to the druids or the Romans. It represented all that was left of the worship of Flora; and in the last half of the sixteenth century there was a great deal of that worship left." [10] The rite was presided over by characters variously named the Lord (and Lady) of Misrule, the King and Queen of the May, or Robin Hood and Maid Marian.[11] Dances and processions, often centering about the phallic maypole, characterized the celebration, along with the giving of gifts, including presents of clothing, food, and drink. Other things were likewise given and taken. A sixteenth-century source reports that "of fourtie, threescore, or an hundred maides going to the wood [a-Maying] there have scarcely the third part of them returned home againe as they went." [12] Clearly the May rituals began as a kind of fertility rite in which the free expression of sexuality for the purpose of magically restimulating nature's fecundity was the chief glory. Note the association of the ritual with Robin Hood or Robin of the Wood, a traditional English version of the archetypal "King of the Woods" [13] and a figure of increasing importance in the Americanized literature of the colonies. Daniel Boone and Leatherstocking are his lineal descendants. (Morton was, by his own account, an avid hunter.)

The Lord of Misrule was the name by which this figure became part of the conventional celebrations of the English court and ultimately a court officer. Under a new title, Master of the Revells, he supervised the planning of the May games and the presentation of ceremonial plays and masques for the court. His association with court drama was thus extremely close, and the Puritans' antipathy for his primary function was reinforced by their disgust with the London theater and the impiety of the court.[14] The function of the Lord of Misrule, however, extended below the level of convention. In resigning their sway to the mock prince for a day or a week, the rulers of the land and their subjects could vicariously escape from the daily regimen and the discipline of civilization. Under his sway all values became inverted, incontinency and riot being more desirable than chastity and respect for law, and repressed drives or impulses could find acceptable release and expression. To the Puritan, believing simultaneously in the absolute authority of his God in the universe and the precariousness of divine law and order in the wilderness, this function too was pregnant with catastrophe — particularly when the Lord of Misrule was one who had flouted the law out of season as well as in.

"The Revells of Ma-re Mount" is the most delightful chapter in Morton's book, as well as being its hero's catastrophe. Biting sarcasm at Plymouth's expense is joined with enthusiasm for Indian, English, and Greek paganism and for the joys of the flesh. The language is highly figurative and allusive, to such a degree that it is, at times, almost undecipherable. The scene is conceived as a kind of theatrical masque — a form of theater most popular with the official audience Morton hoped to appeal to — in which all characters are disguised by fictitious names and elaborate metaphorical costumes.[15] The pagan rite of the maypole is performed, with Indians and whites mingling freely in the dances and about the ale barrels. They sing songs that flow spontaneously from the rich poetic imagination of their "Host," Thomas Morton. These songs invariably invoke all the libidinous deities of pagan mythology and the human subconscious. The invocation is addressed to Oedipus and other mythic heroes whose sexual proclivities were both peculiar and pronounced. Their community's hymn echoes the cry "Jo [*sic*] to Hymen," the pagan goddess of the wedding feast and of the virgin's marriage bed. Marriages, both literal and figurative, are concluded between whites and Indians, all of whom are reeling with drink and dressed in the heads and hides of forest beasts or in the traditional garb of the Indians.[16]

This proceeding, says Morton, called down the wrath of priggish Plymouth: "Hee that played Proteus (with the helpe of Priapus) put their noses out of joynt as the Proverbe is." The revelers were doffing their English characters with their clothes, metamorphosing into Indians and beasts in the manner of shape-shifting Proteus in order to play Priapus with the Indian girls at the feast. Thus they were the very type of the Puritan nightmare, in which Englishmen merged with the wilderness and lost all self-restraint, all reverence for authority, all sexual and racial integrity. "The great Monster" whom "Captain Shrimpe" (Miles Standish) came to destroy at Ma-re Mount was, at least in Morton's view, the two-backed beast.[17]

Morton's activity seemed, to the Pilgrims, going native with a vengeance. This Lord of Misrule, like the libertarian Indians, challenged the principles of authority on which civilization and its colonial outposts were based. In Bradford's *Of Plymouth Plantation*, Morton appears as a demonic emissary of atheism, lechery, paganism, and democracy. Although he is a lawyer, he is treated by his patron's servant as an equal. When that patron, Captain Wollaston, sends some of his indentured servants to Virginia to be sold, Morton stirs the rest to throw out Wollaston's lieutenant in order to assert their freedom from the law in America. In Bradford's eyes, Morton as the Lord of Misrule is no figure from a comic masque but a proto-Satan ruling a tribe of resurrected satyrs and primitive demons: "They also set up a maypole, drinking and dancing about it many days together, inviting the Indian women for their consorts, dancing and frisking together like so many fairies, or furies rather; and worse practices. As if they had anew revived and celebrated the feasts of the Roman goddess Flora, or the beastly practices of the mad Bacchanalians." [18] If all men behaved as he did, surrendering to the lusts of the flesh, the godly community would dissolve, and laxness of rule such as prevailed in England would become the practice in New England. But whereas England had the machinery of civil law and social custom to maintain the minimum health of the state, the New England colonies had nothing. If they slipped, it would not be into simple disorder but into either oblivion or barbarism.

Morton's offense seemed to the Pilgrims to threaten the physical life of the colony by violating its psychological commitment to maintain an English identity, to resist acculturation to the Indian's world. The emotional commitment involved in marrying an Indian posed the threat of overinvolvement with "the wilderness of this world," an "intang[ling]

. . . intricate . . . labyrinth" inhabited by the creatures of sin, the temptations of the devil. Even in Virginia, where the pervasive Puritan spirit was somewhat diluted, the marriage of John Rolfe to Pocahontas required an elaborate soul-searching and self-justification by the Englishman. Rolfe's letter to the governor on his marriage reveals his fears that his countrymen will think him carried away by lust or driven to barbarism through despairing of his ever coming home to England.[19] A spirit of self-denial and submission to discipline was essential; to enjoy or revel in the pleasures of a New World was psychological treason. In Connecticut, colonists who chose to "departe . . . and joyne or settle with the indians," could receive three years in jail, plus fines and whipping.[20]

The Development of Genres in Colonial Literature

The Puritans' opposition to the primitive elements of human experience was reflected in their choice of artistic media, specifically their marked preference for the printed word. Their objection to Morton's masque-revel and the drama was of a piece with their opposition to blood myth and blood ritual. The Elizabethan drama or the court masque was threatening to them, not only because of its gamesome lewdness and impiety, but because the drama itself was a kind of sophisticated pagan ritual. In it sins and ill humors were exorcized, mythic kings were slain with symbolic ritual and impressive pomp, and Dionysian Falstaffs were allowed to summon the unconverted people to "holy drunkenness." When they came into power in England, the Puritans suppressed the theater; and in New England, where their control was established from the outset, all attempts to institute games, revels, and "harlotry plays" were sternly rebuked. Their preferred medium for art and argument was the book or pamphlet, in which the orthodox censor or author could exercise more firm control of his materials and, presumably, of his audience's emotional reaction and doctrinal interpretation. Their preferred literary fictions were allegorical works, and lest the foolish reader be led astray, they often provided complete keys to interpreting the allegory in marginal notes. The preferred subjects in the literature of New England were theological argument and polemic, in sermon form. In these preferences the Puritans again typified the distinction between the Indian and the European. The Indian's literature was entirely dramatic, as was his religious ritual. His mythology, the history of his tribe, and the personal confessions of his brothers were communicated through dramatic performance and communal reenactment. Theoretical rigorousness was impossible in such a literature, although Indian dramatic ritual could invoke unanimity of emotional reaction and religious sentiment.

As the Puritans' experience in the New World lengthened, the peculiar features and problems of their new environment were assimilated into the vocabulary of symbols that expressed their vision of God and the world. The wild Indians, flitting unseen, omnipresent, and threatening through the dark wilderness, were visible emblems of the dark motions of the human soul, trapped in original sin. In order to survive in the Indians' world, the English settlers would have to adjust their habits and ways of thinking to that world; but this adjustment involved some diminution of their sense of Englishness, a figurative marriage with the Indians that threatened damnation. They might go to the Indians as missionaries bringing light, as warriors to scourge the devils, or as involuntary captives — but never as husbands. The Indians, and perhaps the Negro slaves as well, were seen as peoples most closely associated with the "Spirit of Place" in America, but they became more and more strongly associated with devils, cannibals, and witches.

Along with the development of the Puritans' vocabulary of symbols came a development of narrative forms, expressing the relation between the Puritans and these symbolic forces in literary terms. Accounts of missionary work, of warfare, and of captivity among the Indians constitute the bulk of the narrative literature produced in New England during the seventeenth century. The missionary tracts were most often printed in London or for the British book trade; they were addressed to English audiences, since the Puritans wished to quash criticism of their lagging efforts in this field. Works printed for New England consumption were dominated by the accounts of warfare and captivity, a fact which is highly suggestive of the nature of Puritan-Indian relationships in the period. The narratives themselves were embedded in extended sermons, and the dramatic events were framed by the rigorous formality of Puritan logic and Puritan rhetoric.

Literature to the Puritan was purely functional: its purpose was to instruct, to teach students the rudiments of a skill or to inculcate moral principles through precept and example.[21] The material which framed the sermon-narrative was carefully designed to restrict the reader's freedom of interpretation, to point him unswervingly toward the "correct" interpretation of the drama he was about to read, to enable him to draw the proper lessons from it.[22] Sermon form was a mold into which the writer could pour his thoughts — and the reader his attention — in the assurance that the product would remain true to the Puritan vision of the nature of human experience. The sermon, like all events of the world, begins with the given word of God, in this case a biblical *text*. The entire sermon is simply the exfoliation of that text to express its uttermost meaning; each step in that exfoliation is set forth plainly and with rigorous attention to the terms and machinery of formal logic. All the events recounted in the sermon, all prophecies, and all moral lessons are seen as having been implicit in the original text, just as every event occurring to every individual atom of nature was predetermined in God's first "Fiat." After the text, the next major division of the sermon was the *doctrine*, in which the major premises of the sermon were carefully laid out in a series of enumerated points and were related to the text at hand and other relevant texts. Following the doctrine was the section called *reasons*, in which the doctrine was explained and justified by precept and example. When narratives were embedded in a sermon, they preempted the reasons section, implying that the tale was being offered as justification of a theological point, not to cater to a baser sort of interest in American events. Following the reasons was the section on *uses* or *application*, which instructed the reader on the lessons he ought to have drawn from the account for his moral betterment and behavioral reform. Since the Puritan account of personal experience in the New World was thus narrowly directed toward the goal of personal conversion or redemption, it was inevitable that the experiences of the Puritans with the Indian and the wilderness should be seen as a metaphor of the personal conversion experience.

The sermon-narrative was the first formal vehicle that proved adequate for the transmission of an American mythology, and it was developed during King Philip's War under the pressure of mortal dangers. Sermon-form narratives, replacing the metaphorically shapeless "reports" of the early days, became the Puritan establishment's first line of intellectual defense against the unruliness and atomism of their people, the criticism leveled against them by the home English, and their own uneasiness about their situation vis-à-vis the Indians. The attitudes implicit in the very form of the narratives, and in the interpretations that were worked into the narratives, dominated thinking about the American wilderness from King Philip's War to the third decade of the eighteenth century.

The literary subject that best suited the demand of Puritan society for a vision of its unique experience, and the requirements of society's leaders for an appropriate vehicle of propaganda and doctrine, was the Indian wars. The experience itself was sufficiently unique to make it outstanding as a characteristic of life in the New World; and such wars were sufficiently frequent to warrant their use as a subject for Puritan historians. In such accounts the Puritans could pit their own philosophy, doctrine, culture, and race against their cultural opposites and could illustrate God's favor to their way of life in recounting their triumph and the discomfiture of both the heathen enemy and those of their own people who had been less than rigorous in their faith. Such narratives were at once an answer to the carping criticism of English Puritans and prelates and a means of reinforcing morale in New England.

The Indian wars proved to be the most acceptable metaphor for the American experience. To all of the complexities of that experience, it offered the simplicity of dramatic contrast and direct confrontation of opposites. It became a literary means of dealing with all sorts of social tensions and controversies — between English and American Puritans, between classes and generations within American society, and between political and religious controversialists. Part of the reason for its wide acceptance as a myth-metaphor derives from its recognition that the most significant peculiarity of the American environment was its substitution of racial and cultural divisions for the traditional English divisions of class and religion. The colonial societies during the early years of settlement were more simple and homogeneous than that of England. New England Puritans did not have an Anglican majority to contend with in America, and the "country" party of southern planters had no opposite "city" party of tradesmen within their own borders. Although there were class divisions sharply drawn in all the colonies, and class antagonisms in each, the points of contention between classes — and the nature, numbers, and proportionate strength of the classes — did not correspond to English norms. Distinctions were drawn between "commonality" and "men of note," but "middling" men were more numerous proportionately in New England than in old, and there was no landed aristocracy to check the rise of tradesmen and artisans to the highest social rank. Conversely, the gap between indentured servants or Negro slaves and masters was wider than that between peasant and lord. The English vocabulary of social values and distinctions was thus to a large extent inapplicable to the American situation. The presence of the Indians and, later, of large numbers of Negro slaves made racial difference a more obvious and important source of social distinction than that between farmer and city man or between peasant and gentry.

In societies that are still in the process of achieving a sense of identity, the establishment of a normative, characteristic image of the group's character is a psychological necessity; and the simplest means of defining or expressing the sense of such a norm is by rejecting some other group whose character is deemed to be the opposite. The English country gentleman might be most easily identified by setting him next to an ambitious and thrifty London merchant, the Puritan by setting him alongside the Cavalier. For the Anglo-American the most important distinction was that between himself and the Indian, the native product of the world which the emigrant had adopted as his own and to which he was in the process of adapting. This shift of emphasis from social to racial distinction had serious consequences. At the least, it made reconciliation between white and Indian virtually impossible, since racial opposition presupposed no common ground between the groups. (Cavalier and Puritan, peasant and lord, were at least white, English, and Christian together.) More significantly for American literature, the shift from a social to a racial vocabulary of distinctions transferred the sphere of contention to a deeper psychological plane and brought unconscious fears and desires more overtly into play. It also meant that the social tensions usually dealt with bloodlessly in narrative literature — the distinctions of class and rank and income, the clash of class mores and moralities — would be conceived in the harsh and melodramatic terms of racial warfare, all but negating the possibility of the kind of social satire practiced by Morton and later by the eighteenth-century poets and novelists.

The Pequot War and the Genre of Indian War Narratives

John Underhill's *Newes from America: or, A New and Experimentall Discovery of New England,* and Philip Vincent's *A True Relation of the Late Battell Fought in New-England,* both published in London in 1638, illustrate the applicability of such narratives to a variety of social and political functions and the aptness of the genre for expressing the anxieties of New England. Underhill and Vincent were parties to a political and religious strife between radicals and conservatives in the Massachusetts government, and their narratives of the military conquest of the Pequot Indians were pamphlets in their paper war. The narratives thus used the first major Indian war in New England as a text from which to demonstrate the validity of their divergent religious and social philosophies and their different visions of the New World. Underhill's vision of a Calvinist Garden of Eden was pitted against Vincent's picture of orderly Boston, like an enclosed island awash in a sea of Indian and heretical chaos.

Vincent was opposed to the expansion of the coastal settlements into the deeper wilderness without strong supervision by men of proven orthodoxy and social position. It is also clear that he viewed the limitation of movement to the frontier as a key to the maintenance of moral and social order in the coastal towns themselves and that he viewed the establishment of a stable, limited New England as essential to the fulfillment of their mission — the building of the exemplary city on a hill. Underhill was Vincent's opposite in temperament and theology. He saw in the New World a promise of freedom for personal religious development and expression, with no restraints but those of God and conscience. In his enthusiasm for the land he closely resembles Thomas Morton.

The immediate occasion of the Underhill-Vincent quarrel was, on the surface, a relatively minor question. Vincent's account of a battle unjustly accused Underhill, a leader of troops, of cowardice in the face of the enemy. Underhill denied the charge. Beneath this quarrel the signs of a more fundamental clash can be seen. Underhill was a spokesman for the heresy of antinomianism, as well as for those who wished to live deep in the wilderness. His writings and speeches linked the pietistic urge for moral freedom with the desire for establishing new, independent settlements in the wilderness. He spoke as if the exploration of the wilderness, with a view toward making a permanent settlement separated from England and the English churches, was an endeavor comparable in holiness to the practice of religious discipline. Thus the opposed views of Underhill and Vincent on the nature of the wilderness became caught up with the tension between "Antinomian" and "Conservative" (or non-Separatist) elements in the Puritan movement itself.[23]

Underhill shaped his narrative as he ordered his life — under the impulse of a passionate enthusiasm for religion, for land, and for the exercise of his powers as a soldier and man of action. His passions, religious and otherwise, were apparently the cause of his undoing in New England. As the son of an English mercenary serving with the Dutch, he was bred to arms and was a professional soldier in the Dutch army at the time of his conversion to Puritanism by English exiles. He was a prominent magistrate and soldier after his arrival in Massachusetts in the Great Migration of 1630/1. In 1637 he returned from the Pequot War expecting a hero's welcome for his services. Instead of being honored, he was soon disfranchised and humiliated at the hands of the General Court (on which he had once served as the first Boston deputy), first for signing a petition for the toleration of Anne Hutchinson and the Antinomians and later for adultery. His unsuccessful defense was passionate and intemperate, based on a sense of the scope for personal and religious freedom offered by the wilderness. In the same year he left for England, where he wrote the *Newes from America*. In the book he combined a religious and legal defense of his actions with an advertisement for available lands on the frontiers beyond the immediate grip of the Bay magistrates. He enumerated places like Long Island and the Hudson River, which were controlled by the Dutch, and "*Casko*, with about an hundred Islands neere to *Casko*," on the far frontier of Maine.

Returning to America after the publication of his book, Underhill continued to utilize his intimate knowledge of frontier life for the establishment of an antinomian church-state free of institutional checks. He attempted to found a church colony at Dover, New Hampshire, but his minister and congregation were forced to disperse by the Bay magistrates. Defeated, Underhill returned to recant his earlier denial of the charge of adultery and pray for readmission to the company of Saints. Denied reenfranchisement and again excommunicated, he fled first to the Dutch in New York, then to libertarian Rhode Island, saw service in further Indian wars as a privateersman and magistrate, and eventually married one of the outcast sect of Quakers.[24]

The title page of Underhill's tract is particularly interesting as a key to his point of view. The publishing conventions of the time dictated the use of the title page as both advertisement and brief table of contents. Often the title page was struck off singly and distributed as handbills to stimulate interest in the book. For this reason the author commonly arranged his title to give most prominent display to the aspect of his book which might excite particular approach to the subject at hand. Underhill subtitled his book "A New and Experimentall Discoverie of New England" and enumerated areas of the frontier that were ripe for settlement, although his main subject was the Indian wars. "Experimentall" was a term equivalent at that time to "experiential" and was often used by the Puritans (especially by later revival preachers like Jonathan Edwards) to indicate a profoundly real *sense* of the "power" of religion. Thus Underhill was implying that an experience or discovery of the essential significance of New England was to be gained through a true sight of the Indian wars.

Underhill's work is loosely structured, clearly the work of a man more devoted to exploit and enthusiasm than to literary craft. He moves erratically from battle scenes to paeans to the new lands, and from these to passionate meditations on the goodness and justice of his God. The result is a portrait of the wilderness that, in the course of a few paragraphs, includes a massacre and a rhapsody, a view of the enemy and a view of the land's beauty:

> Before [the Indians] came to attempt [the fort], they put into a certain river, an obscure small river running into the main, where they

encamped, and refreshed themselves, and fitted themselves for their service, and by break of day attempted their enterprise, and slew nine men, women, and children. Having finished their action, they suddenly returned again, bringing with them two maids captives, having put poles in their canoes . . . and upon them hung our English men's and women's shirts and smocks . . . and in way of bravado came along in sight of us as we stood upon Seybrooke fort. . . .

This fort lies upon the river called Conneticot, at the mouth of it, a place of a very good soil, good meadow, divers sorts of good wood, timber, variety of fish of several kinds, fowl in abundance, geese, ducks, brankes, teals, deer, roebuck, squirrels, which are as good as our English rabbits. . . .

The truth is, I want time to set forth the excellence of the whole country; but if you would know the garden of New England, then you must glance your eye upon Hudson's River, ... [There follows a view of each of the places listed on the title page.] [25]

Vincent had no inclination to explore the wilderness in such detail. He saw New England as a stable, established entity requiring maintenance, rather than as a springboard to active voyages of new and perhaps unthinkable discovery. The full title of his work is: *A TRVE RELATION of The late Battell fought in New-England, between the English and the Pequet Salvages. In which were slaine and taken prisoners about 700 of the Salvages, and those which escaped had their heads cut off by the Mohocks: With the present state of things there.* Where Underhill's title page gives the emphasis to "discovery," Vincent's concentrates wholly on hostility — the battle between an established good and an established evil, and the triumph of good.

Vincent builds his narrative carefully on a formal analogy to the conventions of classical drama. After referring briefly to the temperate climate and fertile soil of New England, he declares: "This is the stage. Let us in a word see the actors." Toward the end of his piece he recalls the analogy to drama: "I have done with the tragic scene, whose catastrophe ended in a triumph." [26] Not until the dramatic structure is complete does he allow himself the luxury of expanding on the virtues of the land — unlike Underhill, whose enthusiasm for the land disrupts his narrative.

Nor is Vincent's appeal for further colonization couched in the enthusiasm of Underhill's work. Rather, Vincent insists that emigration be carefully organized, undertaken for sound economic and religious reasons, and directed by sober men of standing and consequence. "The transcribing of all colonies is chargeable, fittest for princes or states to undertake." [27] He says further:

[Colonies] must be well grounded, well followed, and managed with great stocks of money, by men of resolution, that will not be daunted

by ordinary accidents. The Bermudas and Virginia are come to perfection, from . . . base beginnings, and almost by as weak means,
beyond all expectation and reason. But a few private men, by uniting
their stocks and desires, have now raised New England to that height,
never any plantation of Spaniards Dutch, or any other arrived at, in so
small a time. Gain is the loadstone of adventures. . . . But whilste
men are all for their private profit, the public good is neglected. . . .
The New-Englanders, therefore, advanced the public all they could,
and so the private is taken care for.[28]

The fertility of the ground is next mentioned, but more emphasis is given
to the combination of "racial" vigor and social-religious discipline that
created the enclave on the coast:

In a word, they have built fair towns of the land's own materials,
and fair ships too . . . ; they have overcome the cold and hunger, are
dispersed securely in their plantations sixty miles along the coast, and
within the land also, . . . and are assured of their peace by killing the
barbarians, better than our English Virginians were by being killed by
them. . . .

Their present small numbers would be increased by emigration, but more
by "a faculty that God hath given the British . . . , to beget and bring
forth more children than any other nation of the world," and also by the
"propagation of religion" among the heathen.[29]

Both narratives deal with the same events in the same general sequence: the Indian provocations, the attack on "Seybrooke" fort, the deliverance of the "captive maids," the final battle in which the Pequot fort was
destroyed and the tribe massacred, and the near-disastrous retreat of the
English to their boats. Both regard the Indians as the guilty parties in com-
mencing hostilities out of spite and hatred, as well as a fear of the growing
power of the English. Underhill refers to them as the "devil's instruments"
and the "insolent nation" and records that in his dealings with their ambas-
sadors he refused to consider them capable of keeping a pledged word. Indeed, in an access of distrust he was actually guilty of treachery himself:
having rejected an embassy during the preliminary stages of the conflict,
he turned the ambassador loose and "followed suddenly after before the
war was proclaimed," precipitating a battle.[30] No Englishman, not even
Vincent, thought of condemning him for what they must have regarded as
mere expedience.

Yet Underhill is no blind hater of Indians. In narrating the terrible
final battle and massacre, he twice praises the Pequots' courage. During
the initial assault, he says, "most courageously these Pequats behaved
themselves";[31] and when the infighting grew too deadly for the English

and compelled them to burn the Pequots out, they proved themselves again:

> Many courageous fellows were unwilling to come out, and fought most desperately through the palisadoes, so as they were scorched and burnt with the very flame, and were deprived of their arms — in regard the fire burnt their very bowstrings — and so perished valiantly. Mercy they did deserve for their valor, could we have had opportunity to have bestowed it.[32]

Vincent has no praise for Indian courage, depicting the allies of the English as cowards and giving the Pequots no credit for a strong resistance. The initial assault, which Underhill portrays as hotly opposed with a hail of arrows and bullets, is for Vincent a simple exercise in terrorizing ignorant and cowardly heathen: "The seventy English gave the fort a volley of shot, whereat the salvages within made a hideous and pitiful cry. . . . Pity had hindered further hostile proceedings had not the remembrance of bloodshed, the captive maids, and cruel insolency of those Pequets hardened [the] hearts of the English." After a brief account of two hand-to-hand fights between apparently invulnerable English and doomed Indians, the fire is set, and "in little more than an hour betwixt three and four hundred of them were killed, and of the English only two — one of them by our own muskets. . . . The whole work ended, ere the sun was an hour high, the conquerors retreated. . . ."[33] Underhill gives a different emphasis to the account of casualties by mentioning that twenty English were incapacitated by wounds and indicating that they had been in danger of being destroyed.

As a nonparticipant, Vincent was not compelled to see Indian courage and English savagery at first hand. In any case, he was more interested in asserting the superiority of New England arms and institutions than in giving an accurate view of the Indians; he naturally wished to make the confrontation seem like an inevitable and reasonably easy conquest. Thus he omitted the fact that the cowardice of the supporting troops left the battered English army to be decimated by hunger and untreated wounds in a disastrous retreat.

The case of the "captive maids," which Vincent treats cursorily as a reason for English hostility to the Indians, receives an interesting and lengthy treatment in Underhill's account. Although one of them "told us that they did solicit her to uncleanness," Underhill reports, the Indians did not harm them but "showed them their forts and curious wigwams and houses, and encouraged them to be merry." The girls, whose condition he compares with that of "captive Israel," were "much taken up with the consideration of God's just displeasure to them, that had lived under so prudent means of grace as they did, and had been so ungrateful toward God, and slighted the means. . . ." [34] Thus their captivity became the occasion for a meditation on their own sins and for an awakening in the older girl of a sense of God's justice and mercy, which her redemption "experimentally" confirmed.

Underhill makes much of this direct confrontation between the pietism of an English victim and the terror imposed on it by the alien world. It becomes the occasion for a digression justifying the disorders of opinion and social organization that attended the plantation of New England:

> Sure I am, that sanctified afflictions, crosses, or any outward troubles appear so profitable, that God's dear saints are forced to cry out, Thy loving kindness is better than life, than all the lively pleasure and profits of the world. . . . Better in a prison . . . Better in a fiery furnace, . . . Better in a lion's den, in the midst of all the roaring lions and with Christ, than in a downy bed with wife and children without Christ. . . . The greater the captivities be of his servants, the contentions amongst his churches, the clearer God's presence is. . . . [35]

Like the apologist for emigration, John White, and the later writers of captivity narratives, Underhill portrays the wilderness as a place of trial rather than of physical ease by drawing an implicit analogy between the wilderness and the lion's den or fiery furnace. But he is careful to insist that the presence of great trials is the sign of the presence of God and of the concentration of God's concern for their salvation. In one sense, this is an articulation of the Calvinist "sense of God," which is most acute in times of grave trial; in another, it is a dangerous flirtation with the idea of a fortunate fall. This latter interpretation Underhill seeks to dismiss:

> But now, my dear and respected friends and fellow soldiers in the Lord, are not you apt to say, If this be the fruit of afflictions; I would I had some of those, that I might enjoy these sweet breathings of Christ in my soul, as those that are in afflictions. But beware of those thoughts, . . . for it is against the course of Scripture to wish for evil, that good might come of it. [36]

Thus Underhill lets his reader anticipate both eating a cake and having it. He first offers the possibility of greater intimacy with God through suffering, hinting that even evil in America is charged with the goodness of God, then warns the reader that it is his sacred duty to anticipate only the good and profit (to soul as well as body) of living in the Bible commonwealth.

Vincent takes the negative view of New England's contentiousness and proneness to controversy: "No man is wise enough to shun all evils that may happen; but patience and painfulness overcame all." The use of the past tense indicates that Vincent viewed the colony as the emblem of a stable, finished work of God and man, but Underhill is all anticipation: "You that intend to go to New England, fear not a little trouble. . . . Proceed with courage. . . . More good than hurt will come out of it." [37]

There is, however, one common thread which binds the two narratives together. This is their shared anxiety for the effect of the frontier on the mind and racial character of the English. The Puritans' sexual anxieties, reflected in their feeling that the Indians were lewd and sexually "unclean," was one aspect of this overall anxiety. Indian sexual mores were held to have arisen from the necessities of life in a godless wilderness. To the Puritan mind, the absolute sexual freedom of the unmarried Indians was a sign of corrupt lechery, and they took little cognizance of the rigor of Indian taboos against marital infidelity. This sexual freedom was associated in the Puritan mind with the factiousness and lack of racial or national solidarity that divided the Indians into petty warring kingdoms. The Puritans' own outbreaks of controversy and disorder seemed to signify that the power of the wilderness, which had created a Babel among the savages, might be capable of doing the same to the English.

In addition to the Indians' attitude toward women, their animallike savagery in combat was a sign to the Puritans of their degeneration. The massacre of the Pequot women and children by Underhill's troops in a moment of hysterical rage therefore required a good deal of explaining and justification:

> Many were burnt in the fort, both men, women, and children. Others forced out, . . . which our soldiers received and entertained with the sword. Down fell men, women, and children. . . . Great and doleful was the bloudy sight to the view of young soldiers that never had been in war, to see so many souls lie gasping on the ground, so thick, in some places, that you could hardly pass along. . . . Sometimes the Scripture declareth women and children must perish with their parents. Sometimes the case alters; but we will not dispute it now. We had sufficient light from the word of God for our proceedings.[38]

Vincent's attitude toward the frontier contains a number of striking associations. He begins by asserting that the Indian nature is barbarous because it is so readily fired to vengeance: "[All] provocation moveth choler; and choler inflamed becometh a phrensy, a fury, especially in barbarous or cruel natures." [39] Clearly, Vincent meant this latter judgment to refer to the Indians; yet in light of it, how are we to take his later assertion that the English hearts were enraged and hardened to pitilessness because of the

Indian's provocations? Vincent, perhaps unconsciously, draws from the massacre of the Pequots the implication that under the strain of frontier warfare, Puritans became as choleric and as subject to "phrensy" as Indians — became, in fact, cruel and barbarous like the Indians.

In the opposed viewpoints of the Indian war narratives of Underhill and Vincent, we see the emergence of a characteristic ambivalence of vision. To Underhill the New World offered the possibility of pure and libertarian church government and of personal growth in grace. To Vincent it offered the distinct possibility of moral and spiritual degeneration to a bestial state. In addition, we can see in these narratives the first stage of development of the characteristic image of the New World as it appears in Puritan narratives. The wilderness was seen as a Calvinist universe in microcosm and also as an analogy of the human mind. Both were dark, with hidden possibilities for good and evil. Through the darkness the Indians flitted, like the secret Enemy of Christ or like the evil thoughts that plague the mind on the edge of consciousness. Like the devil, Indians struck where the defenses of good were weakest and, having done their deed, retreated to hiding. Often they carried off good men and pure virgins into hellish captivity and sexual temptation, as an evil thought will carry a good man forever out of the light.

The analogy between Indian warfare and the strife between good and evil for the soul of man was too obvious for the Puritan mind, keen for such images, to miss. Was not the least misstep in moral life, the smallest defeat of virtue, possible signification that the soul had been predestined to damnation? Then (as the "captive maids" discovered) so was the least defeat in an Indian skirmish the beginning of a series of temptations leading toward a possible ordeal in a fiery furnace — in this case a torture stake. The apparent disproportion in the Calvinist concept of punishment for simple venality was echoed by the disproportionate penalties for unwariness in the wilderness. "It is not good to give breadth to a beaten enemy, lest he return armed, if not with greater puissance, yet with greater despite and revenge." [40] Vincent was referring to the Indians, but he might well have meant the devil or the evil thoughts of men. Does not the devil return in power and spite, however often one defeats him? And do not evil thoughts return, however frequently we try to put them by?

At the basis of this Calvinist-Puritan vision of the New World was the perception that the most terrible power on the continent was not in the physical wilderness but, rather, was locked in their own heads and hearts. Having thrust themselves into a new and unformed world, they had the responsibility to create there stability and order. If their own minds faltered or if they failed to hold in consciousness the ideal of order, then order on the continent would in fact cease to exist. If their minds turned to evil, or lost the idea of good, or suffered that idea to be confused by heresy, then the only potential source of good and order in the worldly wilderness would have been lost. Self-restraint had to be maintained by each individual man. When that restraint slipped, as in the frenzy of the Pequot massacre or the captives succumbing to bodily terror, the darkness asserted its power. Given the power of darkness in the wilderness, could Puritan society rely on individual conscience to maintain itself, or did it require strong and authoritarian institutional support?

The works of Underhill and Vincent posit different theories of world order and different methods of achieving the necessary power over human passion and the power of the wilderness. Vincent's narrative aims at restricting his audience's freedom of interpreting the frontier experience. His final exhortation to virtue and good works — echoed in similarly appended sermons and exhortations by writers of Indian war narratives until 1800 — is intended to set all imaginative speculations to rest with an authoritative statement of the uses of the experience. Literarily, his work is as authoritarian as he wished colonial governments to be.

Underhill's work also posits a theory of order, but his concept relies more on a belief in personal self-restraint than on imposed discipline. He paints a picture of a Calvinist utopia growing naturally out of the struggle of saints against the wilderness. Military affairs and the opening of new lands are simply an extension of the Protestant ethic beyond the counting-house. Simple farmers and patriarchs could discover, in Underhill's version of the war, a calling (in the Puritan sense) to military or pioneer life; and in the presumably rational and virtuous order of the Bible commonwealth, such men were to rise easily and naturally to posts of command. This was the subtle key to his plan for bringing order and vision to the development of the wilderness. His outward-looking viewpoint would, like Vincent's conservatism, find its echoes in later narratives, but not until the orthodox had fully had their day.

The King Philip's War Narratives

Historical events ratified the dominant position of Indian war literature in American literary life. Indian wars increased in number and intensity from 1638 onward, ultimately drawing all the colonies into battle with both the Indians and European powers. The Indian wars became the distinctive event of American history, the unique national experience.

The first stage of this escalating spiral of conflicts was King Philip's War (1675–78), in which the New England colonies were driven nearly to the brink of destruction by a loose confederation of formerly friendly tribes led by Metacom of the Wampanoags — or King Philip, as the English in friendship had named him. It was in many ways an archetype of all the wars which followed. It was, moreover, the occasion for a great outpouring of Indian war literature, which crystallized the orthodox Puritan view of the war and gave the genre many of its most lasting characteristics. One of the most important background factors was that in this crisis New England possessed its own presses and therefore could speak directly to a native audience and its concerns, without shaping the argument to an English audience. Still, many of the narratives were addressed to England, for the Puritans hoped, even during the Restoration, to convert England to their own more godly ways.

King Philip's War was extraordinary from an historical standpoint: it was the last of the wars fought by New England without the aid or intervention of outside powers. After 1678 colonial wars were tied to the world wars between France and England, and the New World enemy was the papist French as well as the pagan Indians. Even in 1674 relations with England were changing. The Restoration government, freed of the danger of civil war, was attempting to organize and assert some control over New England for the first time in a serious fashion. The appointment of Andros as governor in New York, with a commission to control the New England colonies, was a sign of the change in policy. Andros went so far as to attempt an annexation of Connecticut territory while that colony reeled under the pressure of the war.

Strife between the colonies of New England was also great. Rhode Island and Massachusetts were pressing complaints against each other, the one inveighing against "tyranny" while the other cried "heresy." Massachusetts men like Increase Mather took occasion to cast doubt on Connecticut's contribution to the cause, dwelling on the number of victories lost through Connecticut's tardiness in sending troops to the field and concluding that that colony was due for "a future tryall" for having passed "unscathed" through the war.[41]

Part of this intercolonial rivalry was based on the growing religious dissidence in New England. The semiindependent church government set up by Stoddard on the Massachusetts frontier was one sign of this. Another can be found in two of the tracts published by Rhode Island men, blaming Massachusetts for the war. John Easton, then deputy governor of Rhode Island, blamed the intolerance of Massachusetts as displayed toward a squaw sachem (woman chief) as the event which wrecked his own attempts to compose the quarrel without war. In *A Relacion of the Indian Warre*, published as a report in 1675, he wrote:

> . . . we knew what [the Indians'] Cumplaints wold be, and in our Colony had removed sum of them in sending for Indian rulers in what . . . Crime Conserned indians lives, which they very lovingly accepted. . . . thay had a great fear to have ani of ther indians should be Caled or forsed to be Christian indians.[42]

In his negotiations Easton offered the Indians equal treatment of laws, the freedom of their own lands, and protection from the violence of rebellious tribes or other colonial governments. The Bay and Plymouth magistrates, however, would not be bound by Easton's agreements, nor would they abandon the idea of converting the Indians to Christianity — for although work in that line had lagged, some souls had been harvested among the Indians. Nor could the Bay seem to acquire the knack of dealing with the Indians, as their treatment of the squaw sachem showed. Easton charges:

> I Can sufitiantly prove . . . that shee had practised much [that] the quarrell might be desided without war, but sum of our English allso in fury against all Indians wold not consent she shold be reserved to our Iesland.[43]

In 1675 Edward Wharton, an exiled Massachusetts Quaker, published in London a more explicit attack on Massachusetts, so virulent that it was suppressed by the Quakers in whose defense it had been written. Wharton's pamphlet, *New-England's Present Sufferings, Under Their Cruel Neighbouring Indians*, scourged Massachusetts as that colony had scourged the Quakers. His tone became unacceptable when he went so far as to imply that the rebellious Indians were the agents of God, visiting punishment on a people who had rejected the light:

> The *Indians*, I hear, insult . . . the English Warriers that God is against them . . . ; and that the English shall (for their Unrighteousness) fall into their hands. Our rulers, Officers and Counsellors are like as men in a maze, not knowing what to do; but the priests spur them on, telling them the *Indians* are ordained for destruction; bidding them go . . . to Warr, and they will Fast and Pray at home in the mean time; yet their General with some other Officers, complained and say, They see not God go along with them.[44]

Wharton and Easton, although representative of groups dwelling on the margins of New England society, were not unique in viewing the war as the consequence of English bad faith in dealing with Indians and political opponents. The so-called King Philip's War tracts, a series of folios and quartos published between 1676 and 1678, are filled with a sense of the burden of New England's sin and the justice of the divine chastening. Indeed, the circumstances of the war fell out in such a way that it would have been difficult not to read into the events a design to test New England. Rhode Island's commitment to religious liberty and majority rule was severely tested when a majority government of Quakers refused to prepare sufficiently for war until it was too late. The result was the decimation of the mainland settlements and the destruction of Providence. Massachusetts's test was more subtly searching. The larger colony did not come so close to destruction by the Indians, but the war revealed profound defects in certain canons of the New England way. The solidarity of Puritan society (including the relationship between the first and second generations of American Puritans) and the ideal of conversion of the Indians were revealed as weak or impotent in the face of mounting internal and external disorder.

The New Englanders published, in both Boston and London, a series of narratives that formed a running record of the war's course. These narratives, which comprise the bulk of the King Philip's War tracts, can be divided into three basic types: (1) those written by men of the outlying colonies or of minority views, like Easton and Wharton, whose narratives were propaganda against the Bay; (2) those written in the form of newsletters by Massachusetts spokesmen to friends in London, structured only by the course of events and by the religious and political preoccupations of their authors; and (3) those which attempted to build the presentation of an historical record around a religious and social thesis.

The newsletters, despite their dispatchlike nature, offer a number of insights into the nature of Massachusetts's "testing." Nathaniel Saltonstall's *The Present State of New-England with Respect to the Indian War*, published in London in 1675, indicates that the war exposed virulent class antagonisms, hatred of the Indians, and hatred as well of those engaged in the holy work of converting the Indians. He gives an account of the trial of a group of Praying Indians who had been jailed with a group of "hostiles" taken in a skirmish. "These Men were at several times tried for their Lives" and were defended before the General Court by the Reverend John Eliot and Captain Guggins, the minister and judicial magistrate appointed to the local bands. Saltonstall indicates that Eliot was heard with respect for his age and wisdom but that Guggins somehow overbore the court with "Impertinences and multitudinous Speeches"; Guggins's "taking the Indians Part so much hath made him a Byword both among Men and Boys," and one of the judges felt he "ought . . . to be confined among his Indians." [45]

Apparently no guilt could be attributed to the Indians, although Saltonstall does not explicitly admit this. Rather, he says that the Indians were confined and "let loose by Night" — a measure which was taken apparently because no Indian, Praying or otherwise, would have been safe in Boston. Events justified the precaution, if such it was. The escape "so Exasperated the Commonality"

> . . . that about the 10th of September, at nine o'clock at Night, there gathered about forty Men (some of Note) and came to the House of Captain James Oliver, . . . to desire him to be their Leader, and they should joyn together and go break open the Prison, and take one Indian out thence and Hang him: Captain Oliver hearing their Request, took his Cane and cudgelled them stoutly. . . .[46]

Law and order in Boston was apparently weaker than the passions engendered by an Indian war. Nor could reverence for one's religious and social superiors stay these aroused passions, for "the Commonality were so enraged against Mr. Elliot, and Captain Guggins especially, that Captain Guggins said on the Bench, that he was afraid to go along the Streets." Not even the hanging of the Indian, accomplished soon after, could stay "the Peoples Rage." A company of Roxbury militia unanimously deposed their appointed captain in favor of the militant Captain Oliver, Guggins's chief opponent on the court.[47]

There is a peculiar emphasis given in all these accounts to the "rage of the Commonality" and the opposition of "men of note" — a sign that the war was converting the social convention of class consciousness into an explosive force. In these narratives it is usually the "sober men," the "men of note," who defend order in society; they are ranged with those who defend the Praying Indians against the popular rage for their destruction.* A *Farther Brief and True Narration of the Late Wars Risen in New-England* (London, 1676) repeats the idea that "our Commonality would have all Indians . . . declared Enemies" and identifies the ground of the Indians' defense by the "sober" men as a great concern for the difference between true guilt and true innocence.[48] Such discrimination was the essence of the Puritan way in religion and could not be sacrificed to passion by those men charged with keeping that way intact. Moreover, the conversion of the Indians had been a primary mission of the Puritans in coming to America. To declare all Indians renegade would have been to deny even the limited headway they had made in that mission.

---

* In Bacon's Rebellion, which occured in Virginia at this time, the same indiscriminate rage against all Indians led to similar atrocities and to even greater rebellions against government authority by the "Commonality."

The conduct of the war, marked by lynchings and "much Intestine Heart-Burnings and Complainings (not to say Mutinies)" [49] — and by massacres like those of the Pequot Fort in 1637 — gave a new edge to the moral and social anxieties of New England; and the narratives formulated these anxieties and made them into the basis for an orthodox myth of the frontier. In the newsletters these anxieties break into the narrative account as recitations of "special Providences." In the early stages of the war these "Providences" are almost exclusively "Judgments" against the sinfulness of New England; only later do accounts of providential redemptions begin to leaven the lump. Thus Saltonstall interrupts his narrative to mention the amounts taken in collection at Increase Mather's church in Boston on the day of the great defeat of Boston troops by the Indians, "which Thing was taken especial Notice of, by all those who desire to see the Hand of God in such sad Providences, which did occasion another Fast to be kept by Mr. Mathers Church . . . Wednesday following." [50]

Increase Mather saw the war as a judgment on New England's "backsliding." In 1676 he published *A Brief History of the Warr with the Indians in New-England*, to which he appended "An Exhortation" (which was also published separately). He followed this in 1677 with *A Relation of the Troubles which have hapned in New-England, by Reason of the Indians There*, to which he appended "An Historical Discorse concerning the Prevalency of Prayer." (His works were published in both Boston and London.) Mather's accounts of the varieties of backsliding can serve as an index to the explosive tensions in Puritan society stirred by the war. He condemns first the "formality" of the religion of the second generation of Puritans and (in a typical Puritan paradox) the lack of formal religion among those moving to the frontier, then the failure to convert the Indians, and finally the "Commonality's" lack of order and respect.

Mather's works were attempts to restore the idea of order to men's minds and the sense of God's power to their hearts. He wanted to reassert the power of "experimental" religion to overcome the compulsions of the frontier. He therefore imposed on his account of the war a sermonlike structure, which was intended to convert the narrative into a means for producing religious conviction in the reader. Normally he adhered to the four-part structure characteristic of Puritan sermons:

Text: Biblical texts appear on the title pages of his narratives (and of those which copied his structure). Typically, texts are chosen to give a dual injunction: to remember and retell the deeds of the fathers and to extirpate the enemy in holy war. A typical formula is Mather's adaptation of Exodus 17 : 17: "And the Lord said unto Moses, write this for a Memoriall in a

Book, and rehearse it in the ears of Joshua; for I will utterly put out the remembrance of Amalek from Under Heaven."

Doctrine: Mather's doctrine in the *Brief History* is representative. It is given in one paragraph, which crystallizes the anxieties of his people:

> That the Heathen People amongst whom we live, and whose Land the Lord God of our Fathers hath given to us for a rightfull Possession, have . . . been planning mischievous devices against that part of the English Israel which is seated in these goings down of the sun, no Man that is an Inhabitant of any considerable standing, can be ignorant.[51]

Here Mather formulates the concept of New England as the new Israel, the new abiding place of a newly chosen race, and attempts to answer the moral questions posed by the hostility of the natives after so many years' acquaintance with English justice and piety. He also appeals to the more "considerable" classes as the bulwark of reason and good sense. He continues:

> Nor were our sins ripe for so dreadfull a judgment, untill *the Body of the first Generation* was removed, and another Generation risen up which hath not so pursued, as ought to have been, the blessed design of their Fathers, in following the Lord into the Wilderness, whilst it was a land not sown.[52]

Reasons: The narrative itself corresponds to the reasons section. In the *Brief History* it is a circumstantial demonstration of the truth of Mather's doctrine — that the second generation of Puritans is rife with infidelity and that the war is a judgment on their sins. A typical example is his account of the death of Wakely, a pious resident of Casco:

> This old Wakely was esteemed a godly Man. He would sometimes say with tears, that he believed God was angry with him, because although he came into *New England* for the Gospel's sake, yet he left another place in this country, where there was a Church of Christ, which he once was in Communion with, and had lived many years in a Plantation where was no *Church* nor *Instituted Worship.*[53]

Wakely's anxieties were the counterpart of the earlier anxieties felt by the nonseparating Puritans when they left the English churches for New England. Mather, as will be seen, agreed that there were grounds for anxiety in moving beyond the edge of settlement so far as Casco Bay.

Uses: The "Exhortation" which follows the narrative corresponds to the application or uses section. It formulates the lesson of the sermon and makes explicit practical means of reversing the course of infidelity.

The crisis in Mather's narrative, and of the war, came with the great

Fort Fight or Swamp Fight of 1675. In this battle an English expedition under Josiah Winthrop wiped out a concentration of Narragansett Indians, perpetrated a massacre, and were decimated by winter and lack of food in their retreat. The victory was won when the troops broke into the Indian fort and burned to death all the women, children, and wounded men in the wigwams. Mather offers no justification for this but mentions that among the prisoners was "a wretched English man that apostatized to the Heathen, and fought with them against his own Country-men." [54] Here was the perfect emblem of the backsliding peculiar to America — a spiritual likeness to the Indians. "God seemed to withdraw" at this point, and Mather recalls the prophecy of Jesus that he would remove "*Candlesticks* out of their places, because of *Contentions*, and loss of first Love. Surely when those places are destroyed where Churches have been planted, Candlesticks are removed out of their places." [55] Malignant distempers afflicted the people, and omens appeared in the sky.

Yet as the judgment of God brought destruction, so the grace of God brought triumph. For no apparent reason, a squaw sachem of the Sekonit Indians came in to surrender; and a party of whites and Indians under Capt. Benjamin Church began taking Indians and converting them into soldiers for the English (if not into Christians). Then "a small party of souldiers whose hearts God had touched," [56] captured Philip's wife and son. Within a few days Philip was betrayed by one of his own men, and an Indian in Church's company killed him.

Why did not God ordain that a white man should kill Philip? "To prevent us from being lifted up, without success, and that we might not become secure," is Mather's answer.[57] For if the war were to become grounds for the redemption of New England, emphasis had to be placed on the war's having been a wrathful judgment. And the sins which called down that judgment, which still flourished, had to be isolated and cut down.

This task Mather assigns to the "Earnest Exhortation," which follows the narrative itself. Here he focuses on the war as "a lesson lest we be laid waste":

> And shall it be said of thee? O *New-England* shall it be said of thee, the Lord hath poured on thee the fury of his Anger, . . . yet thou laydst it not to Heart. A Sword, a Sword is sharpened, and also fourbished . . . to make a sore slaughter, *should we then make mirth*.[58]

The essence of the current evils, which included wining, wenching, foreign fashions, and periwigs, is crystallized in the present generation's "taking up a form of godliness without the power of it." The reasons for this backsliding are discerned in the nature of wilderness life. On the one hand, the saints' fear of the physical terrors of the wilderness has distracted them from true religion and decent behavior by leading them to neglect the spiritual terrors of a fervently worshiped Jehovah in order to obtain ease of mind about their relation to the wilderness:

> Getting bread with the perill of their Lives, because of the Sword of the Wilderness, when they can scarce look out of doors, but they are in danger of being seized upon by ravening Wolves, . . . the sword of the Enemy and fear is on every side.[59]

At the same time (and somewhat paradoxically), Mather finds that the promise of the wilderness has drawn the settlers into an idolatrous worship of *"Land! Land!"*:

> [Whereas] the first Planters here that they might keep themselves together were satisfied with one Acre for each person, as his propriety, and after that with twenty Acres for a Family, how have Men since coveted after the earth, that many hundreds, nay thousands of Acres, have been engrossed by one man, and they that profess themselves Christians have forsaken Churches, and Ordinances, and all for land and elbow-room.[60]

More than a century and a half later, Daniel Boone was to acquire a bad name in New England for his putative advocacy of the identical principle of "elbow-room."

As Jehovah's agent, Mather seeks to shake his audience out of its spiritual complacency by reminding it that the present misery of New England is but a metaphor of the trial to come. In the sufferings of the Indians' victims can be read the torments reserved for the damned at the Last Judgment; and even the defeats inflicted on the Indians by the English ought to offer no comfort, since this too is but an example of the fate of those who fall unconverted into the hand of God. The Indian himself is an image of what the Puritan who succumbs to the threat or the promise of the wilderness may become. Although Mather condemns the persecution of the Praying Indians by vengeful Englishmen, he sees the Indian as a symbol of that spiritual, cultural, and racial degradation to which the spiritual thralls of the wilderness are brought:

> How many that although they are Christians in name, are no better then *Heathens* in heart, and in Conversation? How many families that life like *profane Indians* without any *Family Prayers*, . . . [or] Publick Invocation of the Name of God, . . . [or] Instituted Worship (whereby Christians are distinguished from heathens).[61]

Mather's *Brief History* — and the *Relation* which followed it — established not only a formal structure for the Indian war narrative but also a point of view toward the frontier that characterized the literature of the Indian wars until well into the eighteenth century. Thomas Wheeler's exciting account of the siege and defense of Brookfield and the town's rescue by Boston troops follows the structural pattern established by Mather. The full title is: *A Thankfull Remembrance of Gods Mercy to Several Persons at Quabaug or Brookfield: Partly in a Collection of Providences about Them, and Gracious Appearances for Them; and Partly in a Sermon Preached by Mr. Edward Bulkley, Pastor of the Church of Christ at Concord, upon a Day of Thanksgiving, Kept by Divers for Their Wonderfull Deliverance There*. Wheeler was the military commander at Brookfield, and he gives a firsthand account of the course of events as they occurred. The citation of special providences serves to direct the reader toward the lesson to be learned. The narrative itself occupies ten pages, while Bulkley's sermon occupies thirty in a lengthy discourse against the "wantonness of spirit" that brought the calamity. His text is adapted from Psalms 116 : 12: "What shall I render unto the Lord for all his Benefits towards me." He answers in the manner of the covenant theology: "God hath give you your desires, and Answered your prayers, therefore do you Answer his Expectation. . . . This will open Gods heart and hand to give more." [62]

The leaders of Puritan church and society, following Mather's example, used the Indian war narrative as a means of securing the psychological defenses of their society. Beyond the rim of settlement, the Englishman was the victim of forces beyond his understanding; within the fold, he could be a hero, conquering the forces of sin within the body politic or in his own mind. Defense of present gains and a psychological turning inward for fields of conquest and development are the major themes of the King Philip's War tracts.

For example, Samuel Nowell delivered an artillery election sermon in 1678, which he subsequently published, entitled *Abraham in Arms; or The first Religious GENERAL with his Army Engaging in A WAR For which he had wisely prepared and by which not only an eminent VICTORY was obtained, but A Blessing gained also*. His audience was the body of newly elected militia officers, and the burden of his address was that New England must concentrate as much on military preparedness as on moral fortification against the power of the wilderness. Training in arms is seen to be no less essential to the colony's safety than training in the catechism: "Our Military Strength is, under God, the appointed means, or in the ordinary way of Providence, is the proper and only means. . . . It is a strange piece of dotage befallen this crazy-headed Age, that men should not use the Sword." [63] Nowell, an active combatant in the Swamp Fight, may have been criticizing the moralistic preoccupation of noncombatants Mather and Hubbard, who devoted more attention to public prayer and fasting than to the efficiency of the military organization. Yet his concessions to the practical exigencies of wilderness warfare were minimal, for he could point to only two justifications for pursuing Indians into the woods: the rescue of captives, and the defense of the coastal enclaves. The most notable successes of the colonies were those obtained by men who, like Benjamin Church, ventured boldly into the woods to fight the Indian on his own terms, far from the refuges of the coast. It must also be said that if Nowell saw military training as no less essential than prayer, he saw it as no more essential than spiritual activity.

This philosophy of self-defense carried with it an implicit view of the wilderness as a place in which the Puritan settler might undergo a martyrdom or lose his soul to the devil. William Hubbard's *Narrative of the Troubles with the Indians*, published in Boston and London "By Authority" of the Massachusetts General Court, presents the official version of this point of view. He begins by disclaiming the name "History" for his account, because the "matter" of his book consists more of "Massacres, barbarous inhumane Outrages, than Acts of Hostility, or valiant Atchievements" such as characterize a "war." Like Mather, Hubbard refers to the Indians as "Wolves" or "lions," scarcely human beings. Indeed, he carries the logic of the image a step further than Mather by insisting that the Indian wars resemble the extirpation of vermin more than civilized warfare. The New Englanders are the martyrs or victims of the New World, suffering "Passions" at the hands of their enemies.[64] The Indians are motivated by "the Instigation of Satan, that either envied at the Prosperity of the Church of God here seated; or else fearing lest the Power of the Lord Jesus, that had overthrown his Kingdom in other Parts of the World should do the Like here. . . ." [65] The implication is that "here," the New World, has in fact been part of the devil's kingdom and, in its natural wild state, remains Satan's.

Benjamin Tompson's two proto-epic poems on King Philip's War, *New-Englands Crisis* and *New-Englands Tears*, both published in Boston in 1676 and in London in 1677, evolved symbolic readings of the colonial sense of "victimization" by a wrathful God and a wicked devil. The poems are actually a sequence of loosely related verses centering on particular events and can be read together as a single unit or group of poems. The series begins with a "Prologue" and is followed by "New England Crisis," an account of the origins and early stages of the war. The rest of the cycle is a succession of accounts of particular disasters: "Marlburies Fate," "Providences Fate," "Upon the setting of that Occidental Star John Winthrop, Esq., Governour of Conneticott Colony," and the like.

Tompson's "Prologue" begins with an arcadian view of old New England, in which all men were pious, poor, plain, and brotherly in affection and in the sharing of "substance":

> The times wherein old *Pompion* was a Saint,
> When men far'd hardly yet without complaint
> On vilest *Cates;* the dainty *Indian Maize*
> Was eat on *Clamp-shells* out of wooden Trayes
> Under thatcht *Hutts* without the cry of *Rent,*
> And the best *Sawce* to every Dish, *Content.*
>
> . . . .
>
> And men as well as birds had chirping Notes,
>
> . . . .
>
> These golden times (too fortunate to hold)
> Were quickly fin'd away for love of gold.

Then, in the reign of the first Puritans,

> . . . *puritanick* capes, . . .
> Was comlier wear our wiser Fathers thought
> Than the cast fashions from old *Europe* brought.[66]

Tompson's grievance, like Mather's, is against both Europe (which ignored the New England message) and homegrown dissenters, second-generation backsliders, and controversialists in religion and politics. Such men Tompson associates with the Indians, those barbarians who need "no grounds but lust to make a Christian bleed." Philip and his "peers" are seen as rebels against the wisdom of old Massassoit, Philip's grandfather and the Puritans' first friend. Philip, a "greazy *Lout,*" declares to his men: "[Our] Fathers were not half so wise / As we our selves who see with younger eyes." The Puritan fear of the temptation posed by the "laxness" of Indian sexual mores gives Tompson license to have Philip say, "Wee'l have their silken wives, take they our Squaws."[67]

The forces of disorder, greed, cruelty, lust, class conflict, and filial ingratitude destroy Tompson's arcadia. Interestingly, it is Tompson's Indians who embody these forces. They are even accused of destroying the trees of the wilderness to make a fortress, thus victimizing the woods along with the colonists. The Indians embody all evil in this poem. They are "monsters shap'd and fac'd like men" and function as a scapegoat for Puritan self-doubts and feelings of guilt. Appropriately, they are sacrificed in a fire during the Great Swamp Fight:

> The flames like lightening in their narrow streets
> Dart in the face of everyone it meets,
> Here might be heard an hideous indian cry
> Of wounded ones who in the Wigwams fry
>
> . . . .
>
> Had we been *Canibals* here might we feast
> On brave *Westphalian* gammons ready drest.[68]

This passage sounds a bloody and ambiguous note in the poem. Frying Indians like German hams might be taken simply as a rather horrid conceit; but it is highly suggestive that the savage slaughter of the foe brought to Tompson's mind the possibility of the white settlers feasting on the dead. In the nightmarish atmosphere of a battle deep in the wilderness, in a night made terrifying by the flames and shots and screams of the dying, all kinds of unspeakable acts might be contemplated or committed. Such "temptations" were matters of course in the Indian wars and might be counted on as a source of continuing moral misery to the soldier returned from massacre to congregation.

Cannibalism had traditionally been associated with the Indians of America since the discovery of the New World by the men of the Renaissance.[69] The practice was not restricted to certain tribes of cannibals but was practiced as a ritual by almost all tribes. The Tarrantine Indians of New England would (by one Puritan account) tie captives to a tree and gnaw their flesh piecemeal from the bones.[70] Saltonstall's account in *The Present State of New-England* of the execution of an Indian contains a description of one such ritual and clarifies the motivation for Indian cannibalism: "[The] Executioners (for there were many) flung one End [of the rope] over the Post, and so hoised him up like a Dog, three or four Times, he being half alive and half dead; then came in an Indian, a Friend of his, and with his Knife made a Hole in his Breast to his Heart, and sucked out his Heart-Blood." The whites "asked his Reason therefore" and received the following reply: "Me stronger than I was before, me be so strong as me and he too, he be ver strong Man fore he die." [71] Eating a bit of one's slain enemy (the word "Friend" is a bit of sarcasm here) was to primitive men a ritual means of taking on the strength of that enemy. For the same reason they would cut a piece of a just-killed bear or wolf and eat it raw, believing that they were thus taking on the bear's strength or the wolf's cunning.

Tompson's cannibalistic image of the Indians as fried "gammons" may well be an unconscious symbol for the profound ambivalence with which the Puritans approached the New World. In one sense they did wish to cannibalize the Indian — to take into themselves the Indian's strength or prowess, his ability to live within the environmental laws of the wilderness. They wished to make the Indian and the wilderness their victim, the subject of their will and their vision, and they could impose that will only by gaining the ability to meet the Indian on the terms imposed by the Indian's world. Fascinated by their opportunity for creating a world, the Puritans were also repelled by the nature of the means necessary to their conquest. In order to create a world of divine law pure and simple, they had to subject themselves in part to the law of the devil. In order to convert the Indian, they had themselves to become more like the Indian. But when eventually the obstacles were overcome and they could establish their vision as law without external hindrance, how could they be sure that their immersion in the corrupting element, their figurative cannibalization on the Indian, their partaking of a savage Eucharist, had not permanently corrupted their vision? The only hope lay in a force external to both colonist and wilderness, the Calvinist God of arbitrary grace and redemption. By dramatizing themselves as victims rather than heroes — as passive recipients of God's grace and the devil's malice — the Puritans could view their relationship to the wilderness in more comfortable terms.

Tompson's "Epilogue" formulates the vision of the American experience as it had developed under the dual pressures of the war's events and Calvinist pietism. He sees the present chiefly as an ordeal which makes a future redemption possible:

> Let this dear Lord the sad conclusion be
> Of poor New Englands dismal tragedy.
> . . . .
>
> But in its funeral ashes write thy Name
> So fair all nations may expound the same:
> Out of her ashes let a Phoenix rise
> That may outshine the first and be more wise.[72]

New England is symbolically destroyed in the poem, so that it may be the blank on which God will inscribe the emblem of his will. A significant transfer has taken place: an image originally attached to the New World as a whole — that of the tabula rasa, the void waiting to be filled by the substance of Christian order — is now narrowly applied to the civilized enclave that had been established there. Tompson's prayer is that God should make New England the passive recipient of his will, where the first settlers had hoped to impose their will on the wilderness.

The Puritans' crisis of confidence in their prospects for communal success was partly the result of a series of historical defeats and partly the logical development of the Puritan conception of man's incapacity for virtuous heroism. After the initial successes of their colonies and the triumph of Puritanism under Cromwell in England, the taste of victory began to sour. Cromwellian parliaments and administrators were as troublesome to New England's religious theory and polity as royal officials had been; and with the Restoration even the illusion of Puritan victory went glimmering. Within their own society, internal divisions, controversies, and heresies marred the peace and orthodoxy of the Bible commonwealth; and the savages all but prevailed against them on the borders.

Yet even without these setbacks, the Puritans' confidence in their mission might have been undermined by their antipathy for the Faustian and the heroic in themselves. The lack of human heroes in the King Philip's War tracts is remarkable. Jehovah is the only hero; of the earthly protagonists, very few individuals and no heroes stand out. Special providences to individuals like "old Wakely" are mentioned, but the nature of the incidents makes it clear that God, not man, is the heroic agent. The true earthly protagonists are not men but communities, the colonial governments on the one side, the Indian confederation on the other. Not that heroes were lacking in the war. As we shall see, there was at least one preeminent figure, Captain Church; but references to his exploits are scanty, and his own account would not see print until 1716. John Mason, hero of the Pequot War, refused to publish his account of his exploits, deeming them too immodest and likely to detract from the glory ascribed to God in those events. The only genuine hero to publish during the period was Captain Underhill, a man clearly out of step with the Massachusetts way and one proscribed and exiled by the Puritan community.

The King Philip's War tracts established the characteristic genre conventions for narratives of the Indian wars. God, never man, is the hero, and the community is the central human subject. The narrative itself functions as part of a sermon-polemic, exemplifying a biblical text and reflecting the divine will revealed therein. The narratives are designed to be compelling demonstrations of the Puritan world view — the conception of natural man as a depraved creature, Indian-like, requiring rigid chastisement by God and government. However, the necessity of recounting colonial victories in these narratives made them inappropriate as dramatizations of God's displeasure with New England backsliding, with the tendency of Puritans to drift off into the Indian's world and way of life. They did not inspire virtuous self-recriminations because they allowed the colonists the luxury of putting the whole burden of evil on the Indian's back.

To meet this need, another genre assumed increasing importance. Whereas early emigration pamphlets and Indian war tracts portrayed English colonization metaphorically as Exodus — the journey of Israel from a fallen Egypt to the Promised Land — the captivity narratives portrayed it as a figurative Babylonian captivity, an exile from a lost, conquered, and debased promised land of England.

CHAPTER 4

Israel in Babylon:
The Archetype of the Captivity Narratives (1682–1700)

> Son of man, thou dwellest in the midst of a rebellious house, which have eyes to see, and see not; they have ears to hear, and hear not: for they *are* a rebellious house.
>
> Therefore, thou son of man, prepare thee stuff for removing, and remove by day in their sight; and thou shalt remove from thy place to another place in their sight: it may be they will consider, though they *be* a rebellious house.
>
> Then shalt thou bring forth thy stuff by day in their sight, as stuff for removing: and thou shalt go forth at even in their sight, as they that go forth into captivity.
>
> Ezekiel 12 : 2–4.

ALMOST from the moment of its literary genesis, the New England Indian captivity narrative functioned as a myth, reducing the Puritan state of mind and world view, along with the events of colonization and settlement, into archetypal drama. In it a single individual, usually a woman, stands passively under the strokes of evil, awaiting rescue by the grace of God. The sufferer represents the whole, chastened body of Puritan society; and the temporary bondage of the captive to the Indian is dual paradigm — of the bondage of the soul to the flesh and to the temptations arising from original sin, and of the self-exile of the English Israel from England. In the Indian's devilish clutches, the captive had to meet and reject the temptation of Indian marriage and/or the Indian's "cannibal" Eucharist. To partake of the Indian's love or of his equivalent of bread and wine was to debase, to un-English the very soul. The captive's ultimate redemption by the grace of Christ and the efforts of the Puritan magistrates is likened to the regeneration of the soul in conversion. The ordeal is at once threatful of pain and evil and promising of ultimate salvation. Through the captive's proxy, the promise of a similar salvation could be offered to the faithful among the reading public, while the captive's torments remained to harrow the hearts of those not yet awakened to their fallen nature. This is the pattern suggested by Underhill in his account of the captive maids, whose condition he likens to that of "captive Israel" and whose adventure is presented as a parable of the colonists' collective salvation-through-affliction.[1]

The first captivity narratives were genuine, first-person accounts of actual ordeals, and for that reason it is possible to view the genre as a natural, spontaneous product of the New World experience. However, Puritan ministers and men of letters were quick to realize the polemical and theological potential in the tales and began to exercise direct control over the composition of the narratives, shaping them for their own ends. Under their hands, the genre became very flexible, serving (often simultaneously) as literary entertainment, material for revival sermons, vehicle for political diatribes, and "experimental" evidence in philosophical and theological works. The great and continuing popularity of these narratives, the uses to which they were put, and the nature of the symbolism employed in them are evidence that the captivity narratives constitute the first coherent myth-literature developed in America for American audiences. The nature and extent of the captivity narratives' popularity is attested by the fact that they completely dominate the list of frontier narratives published in America between 1680 and 1716,° replacing narratives of soldierly exploits in the sermon-narrative literature.[2] It almost seems as if the only experience of intimacy with the Indians that New England readers would accept was the experience of the captive (and possibly that of the missionary). Even after 1720 the tales of captivity continued to be popular, although they shared the market with other types of narrative; and the first tentative American efforts at short fiction and the "first American novel" (Brown's *Edgar Huntly*) were very much in the vein of the captivity narratives.

Mary Rowlandson's *The Soveraignty & Goodness of God . . . a Narrative of the Captivity and Restauration* was the first and by far the most widely distributed book devoted to a single captivity. It was printed first in Boston in 1682 and as *The True History of the Captivity* went through two other editions (in Cambridge and London) that same year. These separate

---

° Land-promotion brochures and legal documents also appeared in profusion throughout the period but did not have the imaginative charge of the narrative literature.

editions were not only testimony to the book's extraordinary popularity; they also insured its wide distribution in England and in the colonies. (Colonial printing of Indian war literature during this period was largely restricted to the Boston area presses and the London presses. It was from the latter that books were distributed to England and the southerly colonies, while Boston served eastern New England.) Mrs. Rowlandson's work continued to be popular for a century and a half. It was reissued in Boston in 1720, 1770 (two editions), 1771, and 1773; in New London in 1773; and frequently thereafter in various colonies and states well into the nineteenth century. Another popular early narrative was John Williams's *The Redeemed Captive,* an account of his captivity among the French Indians in Canada. It was published in Boston in 1706 by Cotton Mather himself, in an edition that was hastily and badly printed to meet the immediate demand for it: it sold one thousand copies in a week. Its popularity also was long-lived; it was reissued in Boston in 1707, 1720, 1758, 1774, and 1776 and in New London in 1773. Of the four narrative works which attained the status of best seller between 1680 and 1720, three were captivity narratives; the fourth was *Pilgrim's Progress.* Not until the nineteenth century did a novel gain similar popularity.[3]

But popularity alone is not the best sign by which to recognize the presence of a myth. More relevant is testimony to the power of the captivity narratives to express the community's sense of the meaning of its experience, to rationalize its actions, and to move its people to new actions. The captivities were presented in sermon-narrative form, each beginning with a biblical text and prefaced by a doctrine section in which the moral principles demonstrated in the narrative were defined and offered to the reader as a lesson and a warning to reform his life. Mrs. Rowlandson's narrative, for example, was offered "to her dear Children and Relations" for the purpose of reminding them of their religious duties. Cotton Mather used the narrative of Hannah Dustin's escape from captivity as the core of a series of revival sermons in 1694, attempting to envoke in the backslidden younger generation the religious consciousness of the Puritan fathers by recounting this myth of the Puritan experience. Even the writings that emerged from the witch hysteria of 1692 derived images and narrative patterns from the captivities. Revival preachers persisted in using captivities in their sermons well beyond the Great Awakening of the 1740s. Perhaps the most extraordinary of these was that preached in 1741 by Solomon Williams, a relation of captive John Williams, on the occasion of John Williams's daughter's return after thirty-eight years of captivity.

By the late 1740s the captivities had become so much a part of the

New England way of thinking that they provided a symbolic vocabulary to which preachers would refer almost automatically in any attempt at stirring a revival of religious sentiments. Even Jonathan Edwards's "Sinners in the Hands of an Angry God," the most perfect of the revival sermons, employs images from the captivities. Divine wrath hovers all about the sinful community, and invisible devils haunt the outskirts like Indians waiting for the chance to assault: "The devils watch them; they are ever by them at their right hand; they stand waiting for them, like greedy hungry lions that see their prey. . . . If God should withdraw his hand, by which they are restrained, they would in one moment fly upon their poor souls. . . . The arrows of death fly unseen at noonday; the sharpest sight cannot discern them." God's wrath is likened to a "bow" with a fiery arrow bent and aimed at the sinner's heart, needing but a movement to fly and (like the cannibal bowman) be "drunk with your blood." Even the torments of hell bear peculiar resemblance to Indian fire-torture.[4] Edwards was able to capture the Puritan sense of spiritual isolation and peril in a series of poetic images; but the power of his prose-poetry was made possible by the fact that his audience was saturated in the imagery and emotion of the captivity narratives.

Several identifiable factors brought about the development of the captivity mythology, shaped its course, and gave it its special character and direction. The prime source of its peculiar concerns and images is the psychological condition of the Puritans, their theory of human psychology, and their therapeutic rituals designed for dealing with states of mind or soul. The accuracy with which the captivities reflected this Puritan psychology gave them their great popularity and made them viable as components in Puritan sermons and other rituals; for this reason, discussion of the captivities must center around an analysis of their psychology. Other factors, however, conspired with psychology to make the captivities the starting point of an American mythology, especially the historical circumstances of the Indian wars and the deliberate intervention of conscious artists (notably Cotton Mather) — representatives of the Puritan ruling classes — in the process of myth-making.

The historical impact of the captivity experience on the New England mind can be suggested by a brief glance at the statistics of captivity and the reports of captives' fates that circulated in New England. Emma Lewis Coleman's *New England Captives Carried to Canada*, published in 1925, lists some 750 individual captivities between 1677 and 1750; and there is little doubt that this represents less than half of the total number of captives. Only those who were carried all the way to Canada and integrated into French-Canadian society are listed, since only these appear in Canadian records. Hundreds of children and women (and some men) who vanished into Indian villages have never been traced, and these were more likely than the Canadian captives to remain in captivity for life or to accept adoption into a tribe. Moreover, the inefficiency of colonial record-keeping, especially before 1700, makes it impossible to identify all those taken from New England villages. Other statistics indicate that two were captured for every name that was recorded. Of the 750 whose names and fates are known, 300 were ransomed and returned to New England after captivities ranging from six months to twenty years. Twenty-one captives were returned to the English after longer stays among the Indians and French. Of the remaining captives, 92 were killed in captivity, and more than 100 disappeared after brief stays in Canada — either dead, or escaped to other colonies, or carried into the deep woods by the Indians. One hundred and fifty captives were converted to Roman Catholicism (13 eventually returned to New England); most of them married, and a substantial number of the women became nuns. No fewer than 60 of the captives became Indians outright; and many of those listed as long-term captives were noted for their retention of Indian habits after their return.

From the viewpoint of New England, then, Indian captivity was almost certain to result in spiritual and physical catastrophe. The captives either vanished forever into the woods, or returned half-Indianized or Romanized, or converted to Catholicism and stayed in Canada, or married some "Canadian half-breed" or "Indian slut," or went totally savage. In any of these cases, the captive was a soul utterly lost to the tents of the English Israel.

Another reason for the success of the captivity as an archetype of the American experience lies in its aptness as an expression of the Puritans' anxieties about their social and spiritual position. They had left England voluntarily, although exhorted to remain; to compensate they had resisted, to the best of their ability, the tendency to acculturate to the Indian way of life fostered by the wilderness. Now the anxiety occasioned by their leaving ancestral England was being borne out by their American-born children: just as they themselves had left the ways of their parents and grandparents, so the children were growing up strangers to their parents' culture. The fathers had sharpened their piety in England on the persecutions by Anglican prelates and the hot-gospeling of an evangelical age; their children suffered no such persecution, and the fervor of their piety was markedly less. It was as if the sin of the first generation against their own English parents were being visited upon them through their own children. Tompson's reference to the times when "old *Pompion* was a Saint," before plain "*puritanick* capes" gave way to profane fashions, plays on this anxiety. John White had thought of the relationship between new and old England as a "marriage," but that relationship had long been allowed to lapse; and the Puritans would make no new marriage with the wilderness people. Thus they were guilty of breaking the familial bond binding father to son and man to society, and they felt alienated in their guilt.

In the captivity narrative, the Indians become the instruments of God for the chastisement of his guilty people — a reversal of the missionary and war narratives' insistence that the whites are God's means for the salvation or destruction of the Indians. All interest in the landscape of the wilderness disappears. Underhill's "garden of New England" is seen only as a waste-land of starvation and hardship. Natural terrain is suggested in horrific abstractions; the landscape of the Puritan mind replaces the real wilderness. In place of Underhill's outward-looking spirit, the captivity narratives speak for an inward turn: Underhill's "garden" was free and open to airs and impulses; the "garden" of the captivity is a small, cultivated plot, protected from the encroaching wilderness by a stiff "hedge" of religious dogma and rigorous government. The younger generation, seeking land beyond the "hedge," are equated with the Indians for the breaches they make in good order and filial piety.

Cotton Mather's *Short History of New-England* formulizes the history of the colony in terms of this tension between the generations. He exaggerates his father's strictures against the idolatry of land and elbowroom and echoes in his anathemas the very phrases that had been hurled at the Puritan fathers by their British elders:

> Observe *Goings out* as well as *Breakings in,* if you would see where the *Hedge* is deficient. . . . Ah! Lord! Is there no way for us to hinder our Sons, from *Going out* at our *Wall,* that they may among, I know not what Cursed *Crues, Offer* themselves a *Burnt Offering* unto the *Devil?* . . . Do our *Old* People, any of them, Go out from the Institutions of God, Swarming into New Settlements, where they and their Untaught Families are like to Perish for Lack of Vision? [5]

The opulent promise of America is itself viewed primarily as a temptation of the devil: one of the promises made by the Indian-like "Black man" during the witch hysteria was that he would take those who signed his book "to a Golden City." [6] Such thinking is indicative of the change in the New England mind. The Puritan was no longer sure of his ability to conquer the wilderness in a righteous manner; instead he felt himself weak enough to be debased by the wilderness to the level of the depraved natural man, the

Indian. The safest way of discovering the wilderness, therefore, was as the unwilling captive of the wilderness's familiar demons. One could then justify the gaining of intimate knowledge of the Indian life as the result of divine agency.

The situation of the captive presented an exaggerated and emotionally heightened illustration of the moral and psychological situation of the community. The New Englanders had left their homes voluntarily, albeit under compulsion of conscience, and come to dwell close to the Indians. Their ties with their families, with civilization itself, had been forsaken for the sake of their God's will. But of all New Englanders, the Indian captives were forced into the closest relationship with the Indians. Even the missionary was not so totally bound to the Indian community: his spiritual ties were with civilization, his activities aimed at creating a facsimile of civilization in the wilderness. For the captive, ties to civilization were violently severed, and there was little or no hope of their being restored. The families they brought out of civilization with them were butchered before their eyes. Under compulsion they might be forced to attend the rites of the savages, even to join them. For their fellows at home this was only a distant temptation, although a present one; for the captives the temptation to accept the Indian way of life was great, since it promised escape from immediate torments. The Puritans feared both a "marriage" of the English and "American" cultures and a symbolic cannibalization of Indians by whites. For the women captives there was the immediate threat of a literal forced marriage to an Indian brave. As for literal cannibalism, all captives had to eat, and who could be sure whether the meat offered were human or animal unless the animal's carcass was seen? God would sustain the Puritan community — did not many pious men and women resist temptation in captivity through God's grace? — but the community was still in gravest peril, for many of the captives "fell."

John Williams's narrative, *The Redeemed Captive*, taught that the ultimate salvation of the soul itself was really at stake in the trial by captivity. One of Williams's daughters, who was very young when captured, could not be won from her captors in time for repatriation with her father. The result was typical of the fate of many captives: she forgot her language and her catechism and became at once a papist and a pagan savage, married to an Indian. Despite the efforts of her father and her family to bring her back, she refused all opportunities to resume her former life. On one occasion she returned to the neighborhood of her birthplace (Deerfield, Massachusetts) dressed as an Indian. Her friends clothed her in the English fashion and sent her to meeting, but "she indignantly threw off her clothes in the afternoon, and resumed the Indian blanket." By her own declaration she preferred the Indian way of life. When offered a tract of land, she declared that she would never move again from Canada to New England because to do so would "endanger her soul." [7] Her visit occurred in 1740–41 at the height of the Great Awakening, and her presence in the congregation had been the occasion for "A Sermon Preached at Mansfield, August 4, 1741, at a Time set apart for Prayer for the Revival of Religion," by Pastor Solomon Williams. It was perhaps Williams's attempt to use her as an example of God's delivering a soul from bondage to the devil that made her afraid of "losing" in New England the "soul" she had developed in thirty-eight years of captivity.[8]

Indian captivity victimization by the wilderness was the hardest and most costly (and therefore the noblest) way of discovering the will of God in respect to one's soul, one's election or damnation. The captivity narratives were ideal for expressing this anxiety and for symbolically resolving it. They were based on an experience which was a unique feature of the community's American experience but which was strongly reminiscent of older myths intrinsic to Christianity: the fall of man, the apocalypse, and divine judgment. The structure of the captivity narratives embodied, in symbolically heightened terms, the experience of personal conversion (as the Puritans conceived it), as well as the pattern of the traumatic experience of emigration that had brought the Puritans to New England in the beginning.

The analogies among the structural formulas of the captivity narratives, the Christian myths, Puritan psychology, and the community's historical experiences make it clear that the captivity narrative was a primary vehicle for the American Puritan's mythology. It reduced a complex of religious beliefs, philosophical concepts, and historical experiences to a single, compelling, symbolic ritual-drama. Transmuted into myth, each of these experiences — emigration, conversion, and captivity — like the myths of the fall and the apocalypse,° begins with man in a happy condition of innocence or complacence. By divine intervention, this happiness is disrupted; man is alienated from his happy state and plunged into a trial and ordeal in which his soul is in peril. Ultimately (assuming the soul is not predestined for hell) the experience results in a figurative rebirth, the attainment of a new soul. All are myths of self-transcendence, of initiation into a new state of being. Fallen man is initiated into the corrupted mortal life that we

---

° Other biblical analogues of the captivity are the Babylonian captivity, Job's sufferings, and the parable of the prodigal son. References to all three abound in Mrs. Rowlandson's and all subsequent captivity narratives and in the jeremiads of the clergy on New England's supposed spiritual decline.

know as our own, but the souls brought to judgment pass through trial into heaven, purged of earthly dross. The convert is said to have overcome original sin, to have been "reborn" as a new and sinless being. Like Israel's Babylonian captivity, the experience of emigration is supposed to have initiated the Puritans into a better way of following the divine ordinances. The captivity narrative partakes of all these meanings and adds another: it constitutes the Puritan's peculiar vision of the only acceptable way of acculturating, of being initiated into the life of the wilderness. This last meaning was the most crucial because it spoke directly to the anxieties that arose from the situation of all European colonists in America. It was this that made the captivity narratives the root of a growing American mythology in which self-transcendence through acculturation and acculturation through acts of violence were the basic themes.

The first and perhaps the best of the captivity narratives was Mary Rowlandson's *The Soveraignty and Goodness of God, Together with the Faithfulness of His Promises Displayed: Being a Narrative of the Captivity and Restauration of Mrs. Mary Rowlandson*, first published in 1682. Mrs. Rowlandson's narrative is, in the sense in which I have defined the term, an archetype — that is, the initiator of a genre of narrative within American culture, the primary model of which all subsequent captivities are diminished copies, or types. This is not the same as the Jungian definition of an archetype as a narrative which is at once a cultural phenomenon and an organic component of the individual mind; nor is it the pancultural ur-narrative, or monomyth, described by Campbell in *Hero with a Thousand Faces* and by Frazer in his discussion of the primitive myths of the divine king. If Jung is right, her narrative is reducible to the common terms of a universally internalized mythology. Certainly the terms of her narrative, its structure and its symbolism, are derived from older European mythologies, which in turn derive from still more primitive biblical and Indo-European myths. She frequently acknowledges her debt by using biblical stories as archetypes and precedents for her own situation. However, it is the purpose of this study, not to trace these myths to some primeval source, whether in a collective unconscious or a primitive Indo-European root-culture, but rather to trace the evolution of particularized myths as they function within the history of a single culture. In this limited context, Mrs. Rowlandson's narrative functions as an archetype, creating a paradigm of personal and collective history that can be discerned as an informing structure throughout Puritan and (with modifications) in later American narrative literature. It was the captivity narrative that provided the effective means of assimilating the colonial inheritance of primitive and European-

Christian mythology to the circumstances of American life, of making the universal mythology applicable to a special cultural situation.

The internal coherence of the captivity-based mythology as a representation of personal and collective history, its breadth and depth of influence in New England thought and literature, and its long-term maintenance of its evocative power can be suggested by comparing Mrs. Rowlandson's narrative with other key documents of the Puritan canon. Bunyan's allegory of the soul's quest and pilgrimage in *Pilgrim's Progress* and the emigration tracts of Bradford and John White are useful for suggesting the relevance of the captivity to the Puritans' vision of their life pattern, their quest, and their historical emigration from England. Michael Wigglesworth's *Day of Doom* (1662), the classic Puritan vision of the apocalypse and judgment, also offers suggestive parallels with the captivity myth. And Jonathan Edwards's "Sinners in the Hands of an Angry God" (1749) — the archetypal revival sermon by the most subtle student of the psychology of personal conversion — suggests the relevance of the captivity to the psychology of conversion. Analogies between the captivity and Edwards's sermon are especially interesting because of his "sensationalist" rhetoric: the sermon is designed to impose a series of sense perceptions on the hearer, which will bypass or overwhelm the defenses of his corrupted reason and operate directly on his "affections," thus carrying him into the emotional crisis of religious conversion. This is precisely the way in which myth-tales (such as Mrs. Rowlandson's) operate on their audiences; and the success of Edwards's sermons is testimony to the evocative power of the captivity-myth imagery.

Mrs. Rowlandson's captivity begins typically, with the heroine-victim in a state of relatively complacent ease. She is only vaguely troubled by her easy situation, vaguely wondering why God goes not "try" her in some way. Others of her acquaintance have been so tried, and some have fallen; the Bible promises that all will be tried and should be prepared. Presumably her minister-husband reminds his wife and the community of this each Sunday. But there is only the vaguest suspense or anticipation of threatening evil in the community or in Mrs. Rowlandson's heart. Somehow the victim has forgotten the true meaning of these warnings and portents, believing that the sword will always be kept from the family. She takes peace for granted, but as a good Puritan she longs for some "affliction" of God to be visited upon her, in order that her sinful will might be overborne by a stronger and purer force of holiness than her own. Like Underhill's prospective emigrants, she views the holy afflictions of her fellow Saints in the wilderness and in her complacency thinks (in Underhill's words), "Would I had some of those." In so doing she tempts God, committing the sin of pride, failing to realize what the experience of God's wrath might be, and believing herself capable of sustaining it:

> Before I knew what affliction meant, I was ready sometimes to wish for it. When I lived in prosperity, having the comforts of the world about me, . . . and yet seeing many (whom I preferred before myself) under many trials and afflictions, in sickness, weakness, poverty, losses, crosses, and cares of the world, I should be sometimes jealous lest I should have my portion in this life. . . . Hebrews xii. 6, *For Whom the Lord loveth he chastiseth, and scourgeth every son whom he receiveth.*[9]

Implicit in this point of view is the fear of the double-edged promise of the New World: the opulent rewards, which might make the spirit too secure and unready for the test, and the freedom from artificial restraints, which placed the whole weight of responsibility for the maintenance of virtue in thought and action on the lonely individual. Yet it was for this very reason that the Puritan emigrants had come to América, seeking a hard way to do the Lord's work, not (as their critics charged) fleeing the holy war to live in greater ease. Thomas Shepard, John White, William Bradford, and all the other Puritan emigration tractarians emphasized the arduousness of the task, the ascetic and self-mortifying spirit of the emigrants. Not the "pleasure, profits and honors of the world," but the trials and pains of a land ruled by "death, the king of terror," is their dwelling-place.[10] Like Bunyan's Christian, they must take unto themselves a painful "cross" and love it more than "the treasures of Egypt." [11] Similarly the captivity experience, with its pains and trials, brings a forced end to comforts and pleasures. The cross is thrust upon the Christian — to love it, accept it, and be saved; or to rail against it and perish.

The situation of the Puritan soul, for all its outward security, is thus extremely precarious. His farm is rich, and the landscape is bright and open, but it sits on the brink of the abysmal woods, within whose shadows devilish Indians move. Surrounded by his fellows, he knows that at the ultimate judgment he must stand alone — that even now, when he faces God within his conscience, he is solitary. The world seems secure, but apocalypse lies just below the surface of the mind, of the world. When the moment of judgment or conversion or massacre comes, this latent truth becomes manifest. The sinner beholds his sinfulness; the already damned, the fact of damnation; the backslidden frontiersman, the physical form of his degeneration. Thus Edwards takes as his text the line "Their foot shall slide in due time" and reads it as a prophecy:

[The wicked] . . . were always exposed to *destruction;* As one who walks in slippery places is every moment liable to fall. . . . That the reason why they are not fallen already, and do not fall now, is only that God's appointed time is not come. For it is said, that when that due time . . . comes, *their foot shall slide.* Then they shall be left to fall, as they are inclined by their own weight . . . as he that stands on such slippery declining ground, on the edge of a pit, he cannot stand alone, when he is let go he immediately falls and is lost.[12]

The good, beloved land on which they walk and the very air they breathe are seen as perilous, embodying an implacable hostility toward themselves. The land and creatures they believed they had conquered and tamed are still in the hands of God, ready to turn and visit his judgment upon them:

Were it not for the sovereign pleasure of God, the earth would not bear you for one moment; for you are a burden to it; the creation groans with you; the creature is made subject to the bondage of your corruption, not willingly; the sun does not willingly shine upon you to give you light to serve sin and Satan; the earth does not willingly yield her increase to satisfy your lusts. . . . And the world would spew you out, were it not for the sovereign hand of him who hath subjected it in hope.[13]

The advent of judgment, of conversion, or of captivity breaks into the troubled complacency of the consciousness with sudden violence, catching the soul unprepared. Wigglesworth's poetic vision of the "Day of Doom" employs the same imagery and pattern of events as Mrs. Rowlandson:

Still was the Night, Serene and Bright, when all Men sleeping lay;
Calm was the season, and carnal reason thought so twould last for ay.
Soul, take thine ease, let sorrow cease, much good thou hast in store;
This was their Song, their Cups among, the Evening before.

Edwards's exemplary "natural man" sings the same song, depending "upon himself for his own security," in his stored-up good works, instead of forgetting himself and depending upon the person of Christ. As Wigglesworth shows, such egocentric dreams are disrupted suddenly, without warning, violently:

For at midnight brake forth a Light, which turned the night to day,
And speedily an hideous cry did all the world dismay.
Sinners awake, their hearts do ake, trembling their loynes surprizeth;
Amaz'd with fear, by what they hear, each one of them ariseth.

Straightway appears (they see't with tears) the Son of God most dread;
Who with his Train comes on amain to Judge both Quick and Dead.[14]

Mrs. Rowlandson likewise is caught all unprepared, roused from her bed by the advent of a judgment. The hideous cries of the savages, the sounds of battle, and the sight of several houses burning amaze her with fear: "When we are in prosperity, Oh, the little that we think of such dreadfull sights, and to see our dear Friends, and Relations bleeding out their heart blood upon the ground." Yet these sights are but the outward manifestations of a divine judgment; behind the faces of King Philip and his horde of savages, she discerns "the Son of God most dread": "Oh the dolefull sight that now was to behold at this House! *Come behold the works of the Lord, what dissolations he has made in the Earth* [Psalm 46 : 8]." [15] Like the sinners in Wigglesworth's poem, she is unready for her ordeal:

> I had often before this said, that if the Indians should come, I should chuse rather to be killed by them then taken alive, but when it came to the tryal my mind changed; their glittering weapons so daunted my spirit, that I chose to go along with those (as I may say) ravenous Beasts, then that moment to end my dayes.[16]

The larger patterns of the apocalypse and captivity are also present in the Puritan conception of the individual conversion experience as detailed by Edwards. Judgment for salvation or damnation comes without warning, catching will and consciousness asleep. If we could speak with the damned who have experienced judgment, says Edwards, they would give the following account (which repeats, in its essentials, the pattern of the captivity):

> No, I never intended to come here [to hell]: I had laid out matters otherwise in my mind; I thought I should contrive well for myself: . . . I intended to take effectual care; but it came upon me unexpected; I did not look for it at that time, and in that manner; it came as a thief: Death outwitted me: God's wrath was too quick for me. Oh, my cursed foolishness! I was flattering myself and pleasing myself with vain dreams of what I would do hereafter; and when I was saying, Peace and safety, then suddenly destruction came upon me.[17]

Edwards saw the use or application of his sermon as the "awakening" of "unconverted persons in this congregation" to their actual condition, their real solitude and helpless nakedness in the cold eye of God. This same awakening is achieved for Mary Rowlandson at the advent of the Indians, as it is for Wigglesworth's sinners at the advent of Christ. They are immediately plunged into isolation. Family ties, above all, are violently disrupted; and the essence of their trial is whether they can accept this judgmental disruption as the work of God's grace. Mrs. Rowlandson's elder sister cannot: "Seeing those wofull sights, the Infidels haling Mothers one way, and Children another, and some wallowing in their blood: and her elder Son telling her that her Son William was dead, and my self wounded, she said, And, Lord, let me dy with them; which was no sooner said, but she was struck with a Bullet, and fell down dead over the threshold." [18]

The breaking of family ties continues and is progressively intensified throughout the narrative, leaving Mrs. Rowlandson increasingly isolated. Her wounded baby dies after some days of torment, her son is separated from her, and she herself is carried further into the wilderness. The Indians assure her that they will waylay and kill her husband, who had been in Boston during the attack on Lancaster, if he comes to seek her. She stands alone in her trial, and the first test imposed on her is that she accept her isolation and her family's destruction as God's will.

The trial is identical with that imposed on Bunyan's pilgrim, Christian, who must desert his wife and children to be tried by his God, obeying the biblical injunction: "If any man come to me, and hate not his father, and mother, and wife, and children, and brethren, and sisters, yea, and his own life also, he cannot be my disciple." [19] Thomas Shepard, justifying the Puritan emigration to hostile stay-at-homes, presents the New England adventure in terms of the same injunction:

> When wee looke back and consider what a strange poise of spirit the Lord hath laid upon many of our hearts, wee cannot but wonder at ourselves, that so many, and some so weak and tender, with such cheerfulnesse and constant resolutions against so many perswasions of friends, discouragements from the ill report of this Countrey . . . yet should leave our accomodations and comforts, should foresake our dearest relations, Parents, brethren, Sisters, Christian friends . . . and all this to go to a wildernesse.[20]

Mrs. Rowlandson, echoing the language of both passages, laments the destruction of her family but is able to reconcile it with her vision of God's justice and the ordained condition of man:

> We had Husband and Father, and Children, and Sisters, and Friends, and Relations, and House, and Home, and many comforts of this Life: but now we may say, as Job, *Naked came I out of my Mothers Womb, and naked I shall return: The Lord gave, and the Lord hath taken away, Blessed be the Name of the Lord.*[21]

Mrs. Rowlandson's captivity narrative does more than echo the literature of Puritanism and emigration. By the nature of its theme, setting, and structure, it comments on the "come-outer" tracts of White, Bradford, Winthrop, and Shepard. She dramatizes and brings to the surface the ambivalent feelings of desire (for emigration) and guilt (for "deserting" England) — feelings that undergulf the earlier writings — by casting her emi-

gration as an unwilling captivity to heathens and by conceiving it not as a
crusader's quest but as a sinner's trial and judgment. This vision provides
her with an ethical code to sustain her in her trials. The captivity is an act
of divine providence akin to God's "calling forth" of Abraham, Bunyan's
Christian, and Shepard's Puritans. To question or rail against the breaking
of the family is therefore to question the judgment of Jehovah himself. Yet
it is humanly impossible not to lament the separation, misery, suffering,
and death of loved ones. Mrs. Rowlandson's problem is the same as that of
the "saved" in "The Day of Doom." The souls of men are brought alone
before Christ the Judge, and "their own Consciences / More proof give in
of each Man's sin than thousand Witnesses." The bonds of the family are
dissolved: the saved are forbidden to pity the damned, for "such compassion is out of fashion." [22]

> The tender Mother will own no other of all her numerous brood
> But such as stand at Christ's right hand acquitted through his Blood.
> The pious Father had now much rather his graceless Son should lie
> In Hell with Devils, for all his evils burning eternally.[23]

Mrs. Rowlandson, unlike her sister, accepts the judgment and its consequences: *"my Grace is sufficient for thee."* When her baby dies, she does
not rail; rather, she thanks God for enabling her to bear her loss with the
spirit of Job and concludes: "There I left that Child in the Wilderness, and
must commit it, and myself also in this Wilderness-condition, to him who is
above all." [24]

The fact that the breakup of families is at the center of the trial by
captivity suggests something of the state of the Puritan mind during the
period of captivity narratives. The trauma of emigration centered on the
emotional consequences of their leaving the ancestral English home voluntarily, doing violence to the ties of blood, friendship, and custom. Apolo-
gists like Shepard, Bradford, Winthrop, and White all attempted elaborate
justifications of the act, which serve to underline their justifiable anxieties.
But the captivity narratives invoked the criticism leveled at the first Puritans as admonitions to the American generations, bidding them keep the
old ways and stay behind the "hedge" of settlement. These narratives
imply that unwilling captivity is the only acceptable excuse for going into
the wilderness — that the Puritans themselves were "captives" of the prelates, forced by them to leave a happy English home for a howling wilderness. The departure of the emigrants and Mrs. Rowlandson's acceptance of
the butchery of her family are the American equivalents of Bunyan's
Christian's farewell to his family, his shutting out their cries to return by

putting "his fingers in his ears." [25] The crucial difference between Wigglesworth's division of the family into saved and damned and Mrs. Rowlandson's image of the family's destruction is that Wigglesworth exults in the breaking, identifying gleefully and self-confidently with Christ the Judge, while Mrs. Rowlandson doubts her own sanctity, sympathizes with victims and devils, and acknowledges a sharing of responsibility with the home-destroying Indian.

Once in the wilderness condition, the captive is figuratively in hell. Like the "natural man" in Edwards's sermon, whose piteous and hopeless situation moved his audience to identification and terror, the captive speaks to his reader directly from hell. He is surrounded by men who appear to be devils. He is tempted to share in their sinful orgies. He has an acute sense of his own depravity, his inability to resist temptations and compulsions toward uncleanness. Living beings demonstrate before his eyes his human bondage to sin. Witnessing this picture, whether as actual captive or as imaginative reader, the unconverted man or woman feels the pain of separation from all the good things of God's world and heaven. For the captive, the wilderness is the physical type of metaphysical hell. For the reader, the wilderness is a vivid analogue of the condition of his own inner being — a paradigm of his mind and soul in which his sins, hidden under hopes and rationalizations, are suddenly made manifest.

The throes of the soul's regeneration begin with a sense of separation, a perception of the distance one has fallen from grace. With this comes the perception of sin and sinfulness as a total environment, a world like hell, in which one breathes, gnaws, drinks one's own spiritual filthiness. Thus, for Mrs. Rowlandson and her reader, time is marked not in temporal days but in "Removes," spatial and spiritual movements away from civilized light into Indian darkness. The nadir of her spiritual and physical "progress" in captivity finds her at "twenty removes" from civilization and Christianity. Her choice of the word *removes* and her use of this method of marking the passage of time reinforce the impression of captivity as an all-environing experience, a world in microcosm, complete even to having its own peculiar time-space relationships.

Mrs. Rowlandson swiftly identifies the wilderness of her exile with hell in a vivid portrayal of an Indian bacchanal. Having glutted their appetite for slaughter, the Indians now begin killing and roasting a profusion of domestic beasts:

> Oh the roaring, and singing, and danceing, and yelling of those black creatures in the night, which made the place a lively resemblance of hell. And as miserable was the wast[e] that was there made,

of Horses, Cattle, Sheep, Swine, Calves, Lambs, Roasting Pigs, and
Fowl . . . some roasting, some lying and burning, and some boyling to
feed our merciless enemies.[26]

This gluttony takes on an added significance as the tale of captivity continues, for hunger is the pervasive misery that dominates the lives of captives and Indians alike, driving them to all manner of sins, making Mrs.
Rowlandson eventually their sister in guilt.

At first her restraint is strong in the face of temptation. She is brought
before King Philip himself, who "bade me come in and sit down, and asked
me whether I would smoke." Mrs. Rowlandson here reassures her reader
that this, although "a usual compliment nowadays amongst Saints and Sinners" in Christian Boston, is a temptation the poor Indian captive can still
resist: "For though I had formerly used Tobacco, yet I had left it ever since
I was first taken. It seems to be a Bait, the Devil lays to make men lose
their precious time." [27] But, though she will not partake of the Indian's ceremonial herb, hunger forces her to share the Indian's meat. She roundly
condemns Indians who steal her ration from her. Yet toward the end of her
ordeal she is so far weakened as to be guilty of the same Indian crime toward two captive children:

> I went to another Wigwam, where they were boyling Corn and
> Beans, which was a lovely sight to see, but I could not get a taste
> thereof. Then I went to another Wigwam where there were two of
> the English Children; the Squaw was boyling Horses feet; then she
> cut me off a piece, and gave one of the English Children a piece also.
> Being very hungry I had quickly eaten up mine, but the child could
> not bite it, it was so tough and sinewy, but lay sucking, gnawing,
> chewing and slabbering of it in the mouth and hand, then I took it of
> the Child and eat it myself, and it was savoury to my taste. Then I
> may say as Job, chapter vi. 7. *The things that my soul refused to touch
> are as my sorrowful meat.*[28]

She feels herself metamorphosed into a beast, a wilderness thing. The experience of captivity thus leads her to the perception of her own fallen, debased, even beastlike condition, her absolute dependence on God, her
weakness in the face of sin, and the precarious nature of all human conditions. "I have seen the extreme vanity of this world," she declares.[29] With
this awakening and the arrival of a ransom, the chastened victim is returned to society and restored to her family and the community of Saints.

In the formula that was to become conventional, the return and restoration of the God-wounded sinner marks the conclusion of the captivity.
The captive is not initiated into an entirely new way of life; rather, he is re-

stored to his old life with newly opened eyes. Thus the pain and anxiety of
the captive — particularly his traumatic alienation from family and people
— are partially resolved. And in the symbolic resolution of the captive's
trial, the community's anxieties about emigration and about the conflict
between generations are likewise resolved. Yet the captive, like the regenerate convert, has experienced a thing that his fellows have not, and his return to their presence is therefore not complete; for part of him always
senses, always relives the moment of insight. He has perceived that life is
lived on the brink of an abyss, and this perception stays with him as an
acute and continuing anxiety for the state of his soul and the wrath of
God's judgment on sinful people. Edwards again provides the perfect expression of this sense of isolation and perpetual peril:

> O sinner! Consider the fearful danger you are in: it is a great fur-
> nace of wrath, a wide and bottomless pit, full of the fire of wrath, that
> you are held over in the hand of that God, whose wrath is provoked
> and incensed as much against you, as against many of the damned in
> hell. You hang by a slender thread, with the flames of divine wrath
> flashing about it, and ready every moment to singe it and burn it asun-
> der; and you have no interest in any Mediator, and nothing to lay hold
> of to save yourself, nothing of your own, nothing that you have ever
> done, nothing that you can do, to induce God to spare you one mo-
> ment.[30]

The Puritans believed that the sense of grace, of acceptance by God
the Father, grew directly out of such moments of intense fear, anxiety, and
loneliness. They therefore hoped that the experience of grace, the sensible
apprehension of God by the soul in conversion, would end this feeling of
anxious isolation. Thus the saved man in Wigglesworth's "Day of Doom"
finds a new home in Christ's bosom, and the Puritan fathers hoped to find
in the New World a true "home" for their families and their faith. Hence
arises the movement of the captivity myth through images of exile to images of reconciliation and abiding rest. But Mrs. Rowlandson's experiences
have marked her and left her spiritually alienated from her family. The restoration to the paternal bosom is incomplete. She has seen through the veil
that covers the face of God and cannot lose the sorrowful, necessary
knowledge in the bosom of her restored family and church:

> I can remember a time, when I used to sleep quietly without work-
> ings in my thoughts, whole nights together, but now it is other wayes
> with me. When all are fast about me, and no eye open, but his who
> ever waketh, my thoughts are upon things past, upon the awful dis-
> pensation of the Lord towards us . . . through so many difficulties,
> . . . returning us to safety. . . . I remember in the night season, how

the other day I was in the midst of thousands of enemies, and nothing but death before me: It was then hard work to perswade myself, that ever I should be satisfied with bread again. But now we are fed with the finest of Wheat and, as I may say, with honey out of the rock.[31]

Nor is Mrs. Rowlandson's alienation only emotional. She has acquired a view of the war that is at odds with the orthodox histories. She interrupts her account of her rescue to criticize the policies and behavior of the colonial governments and their neglect of the frontier. Moreover, she has found that the Indians are truly her kindred in spirit: they are as much capable of charity as her own people, and she is as capable of doing evil as they. The text chosen for her narrative, "Out of the eater has come forth meat," thus has an ironic significance. She has partaken of the Indians' world, their bread and wine; she has devoured it as it would have devoured her. She became (for a while) Indian-like in her behavior; she gained insight into the Indian heart and lived intimately with the Indians. This partaking of the "Black Eucharist" was an inevitable part of her experience. Her resistance to adopting the Indians' ways has prevented her captivity from becoming a complete initiation into the American wilderness, as well as an experience of alienation from the security of the past. The Boone myth and other later myths would express the growing consciousness of an American national identity in terms of a partial acceptance of initiation into the Indian's world, but for the Puritan this was impossible. Even the metamorphosis of a white man into an animal later became an acceptable part of the Puritan myth, but not the loss of one's identity as English and Christian.

Mrs. Rowlandson's literary success during her lifetime and her more enduring success as the originator of a major stream in the American mythology were not due to artistic skill. She was a sensitive woman, a careful observer of both external circumstances and conditions of the mind or soul, reasonably well read in Scripture, and capable of writing clear, vigorous, often moving narrative prose. But the power of her narrative to touch and illuminate the deeper structures of Puritan thought, feeling, and tradition is due less to conscious art than to the fact that her experience, training, and state of mind were accurate reflections of the experience and character of her culture as a whole. Her greater degree of natural sensitivity and her experience as a captive made her more capable than her fellows of discovering and revealing the character of her soul, but the soul she revealed mirrored the aspirations and anxieties of Puritan America.

The use of captivity narratives in revival sermons was the most typical form of ritual-therapeutic use of the captivity mythology. A typical example of this ritual use is Cotton Mather's retelling of the captivity of Hannah

Dustin (or Dustan) in *Humiliations follow'd with Deliverances* (1697). The narrative was embedded in a revival sermon, an avowed purpose of which was to stimulate the people to remorseful prayer and self-indictment, to awaken in them the sense of their own baseness and helplessness and their utter dependence on Jehovah. Unlike Mrs. Rowlandson, Mather was a conscious artist, careful in his selection of material and in his presentation of a consistent point of view. Whereas Mrs. Rowlandson was absorbed in her confession and her memory, Mather is detached, highly conscious of his audience and its reactions, and determined to illuminate fully the theological and historical character of the events he portrays.

The subtitle of the work indicates its structure: *A Brief Discourse On the Matter and Method, Of that HUMILIATION which would be an Hopeful Sympton of our Deliverance from Calamity. Accompanied and Accommodated with A NARRATIVE Of a Notable Deliverance lately Received by some English Captives From the Hands of the Cruel Indians and some Improvement of that Narrative.* It begins with a "Lecture" delivered by Mather at Boston on "2 Chron. XII. 7. *They have HUMBLED themselves, I will not destroy them but I will grant them some Deliverance.*" In the lecture he sketches the steps toward that necessary humiliation before God, beginning with a confession revealing our consciousness of sin. There follows a list of the social vices of New England, including drinking, swearing, foreign fashions, and the overzealous persecution of dissenters.

Having sketched the pattern of humiliation in the abstract, he turns to the narrative of Hannah Dustin for the concrete justification of his argument. Mrs. Dustin's narrative briefly and piously sketches her capture, the murder of her children, and her own enslavement. It concludes with an account of how she, with two other captives, awoke in the night, seized axes, and butchered and scalped (for the bounty) their sleeping captors. The three then made their way back to New England. Mather follows this account with an "Improvement" of his own, designed to make clear the precise theological and moral implications of the factual account. "The *Use* which you are to make of [the experience], is, To Humble your selves before the Lord Exceedingly." The redeemed captives should not judge themselves better than those who were not rescued by God, nor should they be considered as great sinners for having been captured themselves. They should rather consider that they have been "under the Hand" of God, have been favored in feeling his power and thus acquiring a knowledge of him. This is God's grace to them, requiring that they in turn "will sincerely render [their] very Selves unto the Lord." Having been slaves to Indians, they must now be "servant" to the Lord. They have been "bought" by "His Blood" from the "Dungeon," from their imprisonment in the real forest and from their bondage in the wilderness of original and personal sin that had held them.[32]

Mather's treatment of Hannah Dustin's account succeeds in the negative aim of eliminating all suggestions of human heroism from the published narrative. However, as the case of Mrs. Rowlandson demonstrates, even the most pious returned captives acquired altered outlooks on the nature of the wilderness and the Indians. Having tasted the "Black Eucharist" of the wilderness and the Indians, they became, to some extent, symbolic amalgams of Indian and white characteristics; and to that extent they resembled the most horrid figure in the Puritan hagiography, the spiritual half-breed. Even Hannah Dustin killed and scalped her former captors in the Indian manner.

Since human experience on the frontier as elsewhere is susceptible of numerous interpretations, accounts of the captivity experience had to be set within a framework that would limit the possible interpretations to those acceptable to the Puritan oligarchy. The addition of prefaces and "improvements" to the narratives by careful ministers was one of the best means for restricting the reader's (and often the writer's) interpretive freedom. Narratives were most often used, as was Mrs. Rowlandson's, as testimony of man's utter dependence on God. Otherwise, captives who escaped from the Indians by strength or cunning might suggest that man could rely on his own strength for salvation.

Many contemporaries of Mrs. Rowlandson shared her intimacy with the Indians, not as captives, but as willing friends and associates. They reached the same conclusions she did about the ineptness and inaptness of the orthodox Puritan Indian policy, and they carried their disagreement far deeper into matters of politics and doctrine. Benjamin Church, for example, actively pursued adventures in the wilderness in association with unregenerate Indians and took an almost unholy relish in dealing with them. His account of his life, in which he is as much a hero as Providence, has a most un-Puritan title, *Entertaining Passages Relating to Philip's War*. But although his adventures were contemporary with Mary Rowlandson's captivity, his book was not published until 1716 and not reissued until 1772.

Before men of Church's stamp could have their day in American letters, New England reaped the full moral, literary, and social consequences of the mythology implicit in the captivity narratives. After 1690 dramatic changes in the character of the Indian wars and the status of the Puritan colonies placed Cotton Mather and men of his stamp at the head of New England's religious and political life. Part of their technique for maintaining the sway of Puritan traditions in New England was their use of a restricted interpretation of the captivity myth as a weapon for restraining the atomism and individualism reflected in the movement of people from the coast into the Indian wilderness. This use of the captivity myth to suppress certain natural tendencies, both within the society as a whole and within individuals, ultimately produced the brief tragedy of the witchcraft hysteria and the enduring tragedy of a permanently distorted image of the American wilderness and the dark, American races.

CHAPTER 5

A Palisade of Language:
Captivity Mythology and the Social Crisis (1688–1693)

> Their courage, had they been gifted with a full knowledge of the New World they had hit upon, could not have stood against the mass of the wilderness. . . . They could not afford to allow their senses to wander any more than they could afford to allow a member of their company to wander from the precinct of the church, even from Boston to Casco Bay, FOR WORLDLY PROFIT. . . . The jargon of God, which they used, was their dialect by which they kept themselves surrounded as with a palisade.
>
> William Carlos Williams, *In The American Grain*

THE character and consequences of the captivity myth can only be understood in the context of the historical origin of the myth. Mrs. Rowlandson's narrative appeared in 1682, but it was not until 1689–92 that a series of dramatic events compelled the Puritans to look to the captivity narrative for their mythological sustenance. In 1688 the beginning of King William's War revealed a drastic change in the character of Indian warfare: the Catholic French of Canada entered the fray on the side of the Indians. In a series of three dramatic raids during 1690, the French and Indians destroyed settlements from Schenectady to the Maine coast and initiated a systematic policy of capturing and converting or ransoming whole townships of Englishmen. Thus the Puritans were faced on the frontier by an alliance of their Manichaean opposites, the pagan Indians and the papist Catholics.

Coincident with the outbreak of this new kind of war (which was to last, in effect, until the Canadian War of 1812–15) came the overthrow of the Catholic King James II in England and his replacement by the Protestant William III. This was accompanied in America by the overthrow of the royal governor Andros in Massachusetts, an act which ratified the alienation of Puritan America from paternal English care that the Puritans had for years so vehemently denied. The first venture of the new government (in which the Mathers played a conspicuous part) was a reprisal assault against Quebec, which failed dismally. Finally, the strain and anxiety of revolutionary times culminated in the witchcraft delusion of 1692–93, in which Cotton Mather and his reworkings of the captivity mythology played a conspicuous part.[1]

Microcosm: The Salmon Falls Captivities

These events were both causes and symptoms of some rather sinister tendencies in the American Puritan mind. The neurotic atmosphere of apocalyptic crisis, the prevalent sense that immanent horror lurked behind the facade of commonday existence, and the consequences of this state of mind can be suggested by an examination of the tragedy of the frontier village of Salmon Falls, an exemplification of New England's nightmare and New England's tragedy. Salmon Falls was one of the villages devastated in the raids of 1690; its people were either massacred or carried into captivity. Some captives remained with the French and Indians, others were ransomed during the abortive Quebec Expedition of 1690. One of the ransomed girls brought back with her the seeds of the virus that was to infect New England with its witchcraft hysteria. As a patient of the spiritual physician Cotton Mather, this girl, Mercy Short, was to become a test case of Puritan psychoanalysis and ritual exorcism, a symbolic example to be employed in justifying the Matherian captivity mythology, and ultimately a Fury who accused and destroyed innocent men and women for being "witches."

Even before its transfiguration in the Indian raid of 1690, Salmon Falls was a microcosm of the Puritan frontier, reflecting in exaggerated form the paradoxes and ambivalences of the Puritan attitude toward the New World. The Anglo-American settlers in the seventeenth century had, as we have seen, two opposed visions of the nature of the wilderness and two contradictory justifications for their having left England to live in that wilderness. Was the western wilderness, in which untrammelled nature held absolute sway, capable of providing a starting place for the renewal and revival of purified Christianity in Europe; or was it to be a place in which Christians would be tempted by devilish seductions to degenerate into base Indians, lecherous, materialistic, demonic? Was nature itself, as revealed in the New World, benevolent and restorative or gross and evil, the reflection of a divine and intelligent light or the shadow of a demonic and irrational darkness? Implicit in the variant views of nature were variant courses of social action. If nature in the New World were benevolent and light, ought the settlers come there to live permanently, or ought they (out of filial duty) stay in America only long enough to acquire light and then return with it to their English home? If the wilderness were wholly darkness, ought they stay and bring it light, or should they flee its precincts as they would the wrath to come?

The debate, difficult enough on an abstract plane, was made even more difficult by the fact that the Puritans found the New World sufficiently pleasant to wish to stay permanently and perhaps to go deeper into the wild continent. This impulse was natural, given their circumstances; but it was psychologically and politically unacceptable to men whose traditional ties of loyalty, memory, emotional affiliation, and blood relationship bound them to their English homes. The result was the anxiety of the emigration trauma, whose symptoms we have already discussed.

Preoccupied with their dilemma of loyalty and conscience, the Puritans were something less than open-minded in their approach to the most articulate phenomena of the wilderness, the Indians. They examined Indians and their folkways for clues as to the character of nature in the New World. As discoveries were made, they projected various means of dealing with their basic problems through the adoption of varying stances toward the Indians. When they felt strong in their spiritual power and pride as Englishmen, they aimed at the conversion of the Indians and the extirpation of their culture. When assurance gave way to self-doubt, they thought of exorcizing the Indians through physical extermination. In both of these moods, their attitude toward the Indians was marked by an inability (or perhaps unwillingness) to perceive the Indians' humanity. When the Puritans began to sense the power of the wilderness working on their minds, hearts, and social institutions, their fears that they might degenerate and become "monstrous" were reflected in a revival of the idea (current in the sixteenth century) that the Indians were nonhuman monsters and had been made so by their exotic, un-European environment. Thus in 1675 some "rude sailors" visiting the neighborhood of Salmon Falls (near the present Berwick, Maine, on the New Hampshire border) took the infant son of the Sokoki chief Squando from his squaw and threw the child in the river to see if Indians knew how to swim from instinct. The child of course drowned, and Squando immediately threw in his lot with King Philip. He later went to Canada, and it was braves of the Sokoki tribe that returned to burn Salmon Falls in 1690.[2]

The sailors' action seems either sadistic or insane, at this distance. However, it reflected a state of mind that was prevalent throughout New England, notably a belief that the Indians enjoyed a special and more-than-human relationship with nature, which gave them a kind of demonic power. New England's survival depended on the discovery of the sources of that power, so that it could either be circumvented or employed by the English against the Indians themselves. The individual Indians, like Squando's son, were not to be appreciated as real, individual beings, but rather as symbolic "masks" of the demonic wilderness. The real interaction was that which took place between the Puritan and the "invisible world" behind the Indian world. What happened to the mediating Indian world in the course of that interaction was of secondary importance.

In 1682 a new chapter in that ghostly dialogue was written at Salmon Falls and reported to Increase Mather, who recorded it for posterity. A spectral figure visited the home of Antonio and Mary Hortado. The disembodied voice asked the Hortados the question that had troubled all New England from the first moment of the decision to emigrate: "the said Mary heard a voice at the door of her Dwelling, saying, What do you here?" Some hours later the invisible stranger struck her a blow in the eye; and in ensuing days pans rang mysteriously, and boulders flew in the windows, about the rooms, and up the chimneys. "Whereupon the said Mary and her Husband going in a Cannoo over the River, they saw like the head of a man new-shorn, and the tail of a white Cat about two or three foot distance from each other, swimming over before the Cannoo, but no body appeared to joyn head and tail together." Such visitations continued until the Hortados were forced to abandon their house as bewitched, although they continued to plant the fields about it. The last visitation was perhaps the most eerie: a woman in Puritan gray garb laughing at Mary Hortado, "but no voice heard."[3]

The Hortados' experience suggests that the atmosphere of the frontier settlement was pervaded by an obscure sense of terror, liable to break out momentarily in aberrant behavior. But this was not always the case. Puritan frontiersmen often were capable of living on terms of ease with the wilderness and with Indian neighbors. Salmon Falls, however, was troubled by the presence of a minister, the Rev. John Emerson, whose spiritual affinities were for the Matherian view of the wilderness. It was he who reported the Hortados' bedevilment to Increase Mather; and less than a decade later, on the eve of the witchcraft hysteria, Emerson (now minister at Gloucester) reported a further visitation to Cotton Mather. This time the devils took the form of Indians who appeared and disappeared at will in the heart of "safe" settled territory.[4] Mather concurred in Emerson's suspicion that these were "Spectres," offering as proof the observation that no reasonable man could believe the Indians capable of roaming at will in a settled area near the Boston garrisons:

> I entirely refer it unto thy judgment (without the least offer of my own) whether Satan did not now Set Ambushments against the Good People of Glocester, with Daemons, in the Shape of Armed Indians and Frenchmen appearing to considerable Numbers of the Inhabitants and mutually Firing upon them, for the best part of a Month together . . .[5]

The premises on which Mather and Emerson based their conclusions were, of course, false. The Indians were capable, without demonic agency, of penetrating almost any part of the colony and on several occasions, in the very suburbs of Boston, assassinated particular individuals who had especially offended them. Ignorance of the Indians' ways produced an irrational fear of them culminating in the belief in their demonic power.

It was into the kingdom of the demons that the people of Salmon Falls were carried when the French and Indian raiders struck in March 1690. The attackers seemed to observers like Cotton Mather the very incarnation of the evil against which the Puritan crusade had set its spears. Pagan Indians and Roman Catholic Frenchmen combined in the assault, and Mather saw them as a physical and spiritual miscegenation of bloods and spirits, monstrous offspring of an unholy marriage between European and Indian: "half Indianized French, and . . . half Frenchified Indians."[6]

The psychological impact of this encaptivation was enormous. The three raiding parties (two of which hit New England) had carried off more captives than all the desultory raiding of the previous decade. Most of the captives were women and children, whose "weakness" left them open to Indian-French blandishments, threats, and corruptions. From the outset it was clear that the dominant theme of the war would be the captivity of New England settlers and that redeeming the captives would be New England's first aim. The very necessity to do so was the sign of New England's total humiliation. The sense of humiliation in turn intensified Puritan self-doubt, particularly when it later became clear that many of the captives preferred to stay in Canada or the Indian villages or, if they returned, preferred Indian modes of living to Puritan ones.

The most serious consequence of the wave of captivities was that it forced the Puritans to reexamine the basic assumptions of their sense of mission, their errand into the wilderness. Their concept of the city on the hill had been based on the principle of resistance to the forces of superstition, paganism, passion, nature, and unreason symbolized by Catholicism and tribalism. To create this city they had been compelled to breach and violate the ties of blood, custom, and affection that bound them to England. The traumatic experience of breaking those bonds made rigid adherence to remembered English ways a psychological necessity, and the criticism heaped on them by English Puritans and royal magistrates made it a political necessity as well. Which would prove the stronger for them — the tie to England and the dream of an orderly, cleanly, symmetrical, Christian city on the hill; or the temptations of the Indian village in the tangled depths of the dark woods, where freedom of impulse and action turned order to anarchy, purity to bestiality, symmetry to monstrosity, and Christianity to paganism?

Their doubts about their power to cleave to the vision of the city on the hill are reflected in the stridency with which they replied to all accusations of their "Americanization" — and in their paradoxical, simultaneous assertions that American Puritanism was purer than English Protestantism. Yet even when they censured fellow Englishmen, like Catholic James II or Governor Andros, they portrayed them in the guise of their native American enemy, the miscegenate Indo-Catholic:

> Libells . . . were carried up and down against the Govern't and those in Authority, — how the Governour had confederated with the freemen [French or bushrangers?], Mohoques and other Indians to destroy the Colony and cut off the People. . . . that the Governour had drawn all the Youth of the Country to the Eastward, on purpose to destroy them [i.e., sent them to Maine to fight Indians]. . . . That the Indian war was but a sham, for hee design'd noe evil to the Indians, but the destruction of the Country. That he admitted the Squaws dayly to him; or else he went out and lodged with them, that noe Soldier durst kill an Indian because the Governour had given positive orders to the Contrary [probably to prevent outbreak of hostilities].[7]

Andros was the representative of the king, who asserted the throne's newly resumed power to act in loco parentis to colonial governments. The rebellion against Andros, coinciding with England's Glorious Revolution, represented the Puritan oligarchy's most emphatic break with the principle of England's paternal power since the original emigration.

God's displeasure, however, was not so easily appeased as the throne's. As if in punishment for this renewed breach of filial obedience,

King William's War broke upon the Puritans' heads. It was to be a war characterized by the taking of captives, for whom the French offered a bounty — a war distinguished by the breaking of family ties, the separation of parents and children. The Puritans quickly discovered in the repeated patterns of these captivities an obscene parody of their own breaching of the social covenant in 1630. Now their women and children were torn from their patriarchal roof and carried into a farther wilderness, this time to dwell in a dark and hellish wigwam, the very antithesis of a city on a hill. Thus the events of 1689–90 seemed to the Puritans like the gradual and progressive concretion of their recurrent nightmare, the unfolding of a patient and thorough retribution for their own departures from sanctity and society, in which the captivity of their wives and heirs was the culminating horror.

The ordeal of the Salmon Falls captives began with the massacre itself and the difficult journey to the Indian villages on the upper reaches of the Kennebec. The French and Indians had trekked for three months over the icebound streams and mountain passes between Lake Champlain and the Maine–New Hampshire border. An equally difficult return journey, encumbered with prisoners, wounded, and the mud of the thawing forest, faced them after the attack. The weak and unfit died; the slow had to be killed lest pursuit or starvation overtake the group. The Indians made a devilish game out of this necessity. A townsman named Robert Rogers, so fat that he had been nicknamed "Robin Pork," attempted to escape. The Indians "stript him, . . . beat him, and prickt him," then fastened him to a tree and piled wood around him. While he waited in terror, they "made themselves a Supper, Singing, Dancing, Roaring, and uttering many Signs of Joy." After supper they formed the other captives in a circle around Rogers and set him ablaze "with much Laughter and Shouting." Children who wept or weakened on the trail were beaten, mutilated, and killed by their captors. When a woman named Mary Plaisted complained of her inability to march quickly because of the infant she carried in her arms, an obliging brave dashed out the child's brains against a tree and, like the sailors who had killed Squando's child, threw the body in the river, and bade her "walk faster than she did before." [8]

Once the captives arrived at the Indian villages and Canadian towns, their captors' attitudes underwent a change. To be sure, some of the Indians persisted in torturing their prisoners, but the propinquity of the French and the lure of bounties effectually checked the spread of excesses. More significantly, there was in most New England Indian tribes a resident French priest — a Jesuit, Sulpician or Recollet father —'who ministered to the tribe and sought through them to gain English converts for the Church. To this end they employed both blandishments and the threat of Indian anger. While greed for ransom and the desire for religious converts ameliorated the captives' lot, other factors exercised a more subtle influence on their condition. At least since the coming of the white man, northeastern Indian tribes had traditionally augmented their numbers by adopting captive children and marrying captive women. Older men, warriors or priests, might in some cases also be adopted into the tribe. The custom of integrating adopted Indians fully into the life of the tribe was perhaps one means of successful tribal adjustment to the disastrous decline of tribal population and health that followed the arrival of the Europeans.

To the young captives, the freedom of impulse, action, and sexual expression that Indian society offered might have been enough, in themselves, to tempt them to remain. When one adds to this temptation the captive's unsureness of rescue or ransom, hence the likelihood of his having to remain forever a slave if he did not achieve adoption as a member of the tribe, one can understand why so many captives succumbed, if only temporarily, to the lure of the wigwam or the church. Orphaned children, whose parents had been killed by the Indians, were adopted by bereft Indian parents° and raised with all the openness of affection and depth of concern they would have given to a child of their own blood or a similarly adopted child of a deceased relation. Widowed wives and marriageable girls were offered the solace of husbands and providers. The boys and men could win complaisant, hardworking wives and, if their skills warranted it, places in the military and religious councils of the tribe.[9]

Still other temptations to Indianization were more subtle than these. Although the Indian village seemed to be the antithesis of the city on the hill, there were in fact (as we have seen) certain fundamental and disturbing affinities between them. Indian ritual and sexual customs in particular were characterized by the overt expression of basic human desires and states of mind that Christianity had long suppressed and concealed beneath an elaborate scrollwork of conventional symbols and complex mores. Puritan reaction to the sexual freedom of the Indian culture, for example, coupled with their racial antipathies, caused them to view the prospect of marrying an Indian or bearing Indian children with horror and revulsion. Yet mingled with the horror and revulsion was the recognition that the In-

---

° Or rather, by the clan or band, since family relationships were established, not on the nuclear model of European cultures, but as diffused kinship over a wide circle.

dian practice was somehow "natural" and that all men, if left to their own devices, would soon succumb to its logic and attractiveness.

Indian religion touched chords of primitive memory and antipathy in the same way. Cannibalism played an important role in Indian ritual. An Indian might eat a piece of a slain enemy to gain a portion of his power; certain animals could become avatars of a god, and these too were killed and eaten as a sacrament. The resemblance of these cannibal rituals to the Eucharist or Lord's Supper was sufficiently obscure to make them seem obscene, yet sufficiently close to make them threatening. The presence of French Catholic priests among the Indians reinforced this terror of Indian cannibalism, rather than allaying it. Although the priests nominally opposed Indian pagan ritual, they were practical enough not to attempt to extirpate paganism among their people but to blend Catholic and Indian rites wherever possible. Certain priests openly condoned and even (for political motives) incited the Indians to acts of cannibalism and torture. In any case, to the Puritan mind the Roman Catholic doctrine of transubstantiation in the Eucharist, in which the wine and bread become the actual blood and body of Christ, had a sufficiently cannibalistic smack to it, which association with pagan cannibals could only emphasize.

Puritan fears that captives might be compelled to or might voluntarily participate in cannibal rituals were not wholly ungrounded. A common Indian torture was to cut off some part of a man's anatomy — an ear, a strip of flesh, a finger — and force the victim to eat it. Beyond this, however, there remained the possibility that even among Indians who practiced no ritual cannibalism, the exigencies of starvation and a long march might compel captives to share man's flesh with the Indians in order to survive. Capt. Peter Schuyler, pursuing the French and Indians who had attacked the Mohawk towns in 1694 in company with some friendly Iroquois, sat down to share some broth with them. The pursuers had been starving for days. Schuyler, about to take a sup of the broth, noticed a hand floating in the mixture and gagged. The Indians, who in this case were not habitual cannibals but had no prejudices against eating human flesh to keep alive, finished the broth and continued the pursuit.[10] It seems likely that the French and Indians and their Salmon Falls captives were reduced to the same exigency, since they were able to carry less with them over the long trail. In any case, incidents of cannibalism among the English in starvation times were not unknown; even in a later era, the Donner party were reduced to cannibalism when winter froze them in while they were attempting to cross the Sierras. But whether viewed as primitive blood-ritual or as dire necessity, cannibalism seemed to the Puritan one of the dark things that the spell of the wilderness might compel Christian men to enact.

The Puritans' terror of both Indian marriage and cannibalism derived from their fear of allowing themselves to adjust to and merge with the environment of the New World, their fear of acceding to the new demands for freedom that the New World stimulated. Marriage symbolized this process of acculturation in terms of a sexual merging of the races. In cannibalism, the image of merging is heightened and intensified, is carried to a spiritual plane through its use in ritual; beginning with the acquiring of special powers by consuming parts of the slain (heart, hand), it culminates in the total absorption of the eater and the eaten in each other, a total sharing of identities. For the Puritan, the traditional revulsion against cannibalism was heightened by the horror implicit in the idea of sexual marriage with the wilderness. As a corollary, Puritan writers show a marked preference for recounting incidents of cannibalism and rape, rather than of voluntary marriage between white captives and Indians or Canadians. The only instances of sexual communion mentioned by Cotton Mather are those in which women are violated by their captors, despite the fact that because of their tribal mores the eastern Indians almost never committed rape. In this, as the court records show, they differed from their white counterparts.

The preference for images of Indian cannibalism and rape reflects a growing Puritan belief that the only acceptable communion between Christian and Indian, civilization and wilderness, was the communion of murder, hunger, and bloodlust. Cannibalism is the hunter's or warrior's expression of the marriage between the human spirit and the spirit of place or of nature, and it appears as such in the American Indian mythology. But the Puritan hunters and warriors (and their spiritual counterparts, the missionaries), because they feared too intimate contact with the wilderness, were unable to accept the mythic logic of their situation. They were bent simply on destroying the wilderness and replacing it with New England. They wished to refuse the cannibal Eucharist that, as in the Indian myth, waited at the end of their sacred hunt; yet their need to survive forced them to cannibalize the spirit and substance of the wilderness and the Indian, against their will and conscience. Later generations, as we shall see, accepted the symbolic cannibalism and marriage of the wilderness Eucharist as part of their mythology. And even contemporaries of Mrs. Rowlandson, like Benjamin Church, were capable of accepting the wilderness Eucharist, although Puritan literary censorship (and the poverty of their own insight) limited their power to express it.

In view of the development of this ambiguous attitude toward cannibalization, it is important to note that in England the powerful symbol of
Indian cannibalism became conventionally associated with all dwellers in
the New World, white and red alike. Swift was perhaps simply exercising
his wit when, in his *Modest Proposal*, he referred to consulting for advice
on cannibalism "a very knowing *American*" with "frequent Experience" in
that art. More striking is the testimony of Admiral Walker, who justified his
failure to carry out an attack on Quebec (in 1711) by conjuring up an imaginary host of horrors from a frozen American landscape. Chief among these
was the fear that the rigor of the climate would compel the English to cannibalism: "I must confess the melancholy contemplation of this (had it happened) strikes me with horror; for how dismal it must have been to have
beheld the seas and earth locked up by adamantine frosts, and swoln with
high mountains of snow, in a barren and uncultivated region; great numbers of men famishing with hunger, and drawing lots who should die first
and feed the rest." [11]

The consequence of this horror of intimacy with the Indians was a
tendency, especially marked among prelates and magistrates, to regard the
frontiersman as a being tainted by too intimate association with the Indians. Indeed, to Increase and Cotton Mather, Puritans who ventured voluntarily beyond the pale of settlement were to be directly equated with the
Indians. Increase Mather's *Brief History* made the point during King Philip's War, as has already been seen. Far from dissipating with the passage of
time, this doctrine became part of the New England and later the American canon. The case of old Wakely, who agonized over having left the
Massachusetts congregations for territory where there was no instituted
worship, became a classic model and was used repeatedly by Cotton
Mather, especially in his magnum opus, the *Magnalia Christi Americana*
(1702). Cotton Mather condemned the settlers at Maine for having grown
"too like the *Indians,* among whom they lived in their *unchristian* way of
living; and instead of erecting churches among themselves, they neither
Christianized the *pagans,* nor, by avoiding the vices which they rather
taught the *Pagans,* did they take a due course to preserve themselves from
losing *Christianity* in *Paganism.*" [12]

This official attitude made social pariahs of a class of men whose skill
and knowledge was essential to the victory of English arms in the New
World, and the evolution of an acculturated American mythology is in part
the story of our gradual acceptance of the frontiersman as a hero rather
than a racial traitor. In this, however, the French were generations ahead
of the English — a fact which helps to explain their success in both mili-

tary and missionary alliances with the Indians. Compare the Puritan attitude toward Indian sacraments — the fear and disgust that found expression in the image of cannibalism — with the French Jesuit Sebastien Râlé's
dialogue with an Indian on the same subject. Râlé at first refused to taste
the Indian's boiled meat, and the Indians perceived his "repugnance."
"Thou must conquer thyself, they replied; *is that a very difficult thing for a
Patriarch who thoroughly understands how to pray? We ourselves overcome much, in order to believe that which we do not see.* Then it was no
longer a time to deliberate; we must indeed conform to their manners and
customs, so as to deserve their confidence and win them to Jesus Christ." [13]
Râlé is willing to exchange sacraments with his parishioners. English missionaries, on the other hand, demanded that the Indian give up all his Indian ways and become thoroughly Anglicized before he could gain acceptance as a church member. Far from accepting and joining in Indian
customs, the English demanded their total extirpation.

The French attitude toward military men of Indian inclinations was
likewise rather liberal, as is evidenced by the case of François Hertel,
leader of the Salmon Falls raid. Hertel had been a captive in the hands of
the English-oriented Iroquois in his youth. Although tortured by the Indians by having one finger cut off and another burned in the bowl of a pipe,
and despite the deep personal piety reflected in his letters to his mother
and confessor in Montreal, Hertel was preparing after a year's captivity to
join an Iroquois war party as an adopted Indian. He was saved for Canada
by the Jesuit father Le Moyne, who came to ransom him. Le Moyne's
preaching against "evil influences" and giving oneself "up to vice and embracing the life of a Savage" were aided miraculously by the lad's wounded
hand's becoming infected. The delay in his departure gave Le Moyne a
chance to bring him around. Hertel's skill and Iroquois inclinations, however, were not frustrated by the French, who gave him scope to exercise
his talents and inclinations at Salmon Falls and other frontier settlements.
Far from bringing obloquy on his head, Hertel's exploits earned him the
Canadian epithet of "l'Héros," and he was ennobled by Louis XIV just before the monarch's death.[14]

The English attitude toward Râlé-type missionaries or preachers who
went too far into the forest and toward frontier fighters like Hertel, who
imitated Indian methods too well, has already been seen at work in the
cases of John Underhill and Thomas Morton. In 1692 the outbreak of the
witchcraft hysteria brought into sharp relief the mindless fears on which
these attitudes were based and allowed them scope to act directly and dramatically on Puritan and frontier society. In this drama the stage was dom-

inated by several figures connected with the tragedy at Salmon Falls: Mercy Short, a teen-aged returned captive who became an accuser of witches; Rev. John Emerson, former minister of Salmon Falls; Rev. George Burroughs and Capt. John Alden, frontiersmen who participated in the negotiations that ransomed captives from the Maine coast; and Cotton Mather, chronicler of the Salmon Falls disaster, spiritual father to Mercy Short, and above all the man whose literary works helped to create and establish the orthodox mythology of Puritan America.

Witchcraft: The "Captivity to Spectres"

In the summer of 1692 Mercy Short, living as a servant with a Boston family and then seventeen years old, went on an errand to the jail in which accused witches were kept. (The hysteria was just then beginning to spread.) She had been captured by the Indians at her home in Salmon Falls when she was fifteen. Her father and mother and three of their children were murdered before her eyes, and she herself was carried to Canada, where she was ransomed by Phipps the following year.[15] Her captivity (if nothing else) might have inclined her to compassion for the accused wretches, but compassion was far from her. She cursed one old woman and was cursed in return. That night she fell into a fit that lasted for weeks, in which she neither ate nor prayed. The fit passed, then came upon her again in the winter. She lay insensible or raving, rising up once to rip a page from the minister's Bible as he read to her. Cotton Mather was called in to minister to her apparently possessed soul and rescue her from the gripe of the devil.

Although it is difficult to diagnose at this distance in time, Mercy Short's ailment seems explicable in terms other than those of demonology. She was suffering a psychotic form of the neurosis which all returned captives experienced. Mrs. Rowlandson speaks of it in her conclusion, when she notes her inability to sleep, her perpetual watchfulness, and her peculiar awareness of the power of God and the wilderness that alienates her from her unawakened kindred. The captivity archetype demanded that the ordeal culminate in both a physical and a psychological rescue from the devil, but for most captives the latter was either incomplete or impossible. Many captives, especially children, simply succumbed to the Indian way of life, which spoiled them for New England once they were ransomed. Many older captives were "infected" with Indian superstitions or "Indian" inclinations toward license and disorderly behavior.[16] Most were simply so stricken by the horror of their ordeal that their minds were permanently impaired and they became prey to strange guilts and torments. Only they knew how close they might have come to succumbing to Indian threats and temptations or to their own primitive fears and longings. They might in fact have participated, even enjoyed, sexual indulgence with Indian men or women, or eaten human flesh in ritual or in fear of starvation. Their fellow citizens could have no conception of the ordeal or their response to it, and thus their experience alienated them from their fellows.

To break through this alienation, this dense accretion of residual horror, became the obsession of many returned captives and the source of violent behavior and a pathological urge to public confession. But the captive's confession, like Mrs. Rowlandson's narrative and Hannah Dustin's, was a two-edged sword. He hoped to ingratiate himself with his society by portraying himself as its symbolic martyr and scapegoat, yet at the same time he wished to express his sense of alienation and to release his hostility and contempt for his society and its smug ignorance of his true plight. These motives underlay Mercy Short's rejection of the accused witch and her later accusations of respectable Puritans. But although it was ignorant of the true basis and depth of the captive's feelings, Puritan society had lived long enough with the threat of captivity and the presence of returned captives to share some of their psychic burden — or at least to recognize in their ravings the symptoms of its own malaise. For this reason, it was especially appropriate that Cotton Mather should be called to Mercy Short's aid. Better than any contemporary, he felt and articulated the captivity psychology that pervaded his society.

Mather had long been preparing for just such a confrontation with the devil. He was then at work on the gathering and systematizing of historical and theological materials that was to culminate in his masterwork, the *Magnalia Christi Americana.* That massive work was to be the history of New England "under the aspect of Eternity"; it would explicate the New England experience in terms of a total world view in which Puritans and Indians would find their true valuation and be placed in the context of the divine drama of history, as it unfolds from Eden to Calvary to Boston to Apocalypse. His confrontation with Mercy Short's devils clarified issues for him and enabled him to draw connections between the several "assaults" on pious New England that he and his father had resisted for years: the assaults of the Indians and of frontier paganism, the assaults of ministerial frauds and heretics, the assaults of the Quakers, the assaults of the royal governor on colonial prerogatives, and the final assault of the witches and the Invisible Kingdom in 1692. Mercy Short helped Mather discover that the common pattern in each of these assaults was precisely that of the captivity narrative: a devilish visitation, an enforced sojourn in evil climes under the rule of man-devils, and an ultimate redemption of body and soul through the interposition of divine grace and the perseverence of the victim in orthodox belief. In the years following his treatment of Mercy Short, Mather's several books on the witchcraft trials, his study of the Indian wars (*Decennium Luctuosum*, 1699), and his *Magnalia* translated the myth-structure inherent in the captivity narrative into a coherent vision of his culture's history.

There can be little doubt that Mather was tending toward this conception of American history even before his meeting with Mercy Short. His anathemas against emigration attest to this tendency, as do his philippics against the Quakers. One of these, reprinted in *Decennium Luctuosum*, is an indication of the direction of his thinking in 1692. He makes it clear that, for him, the Indian wars are one phase of the continuing war between Satan and Christ. In the strategy of that war Indian attacks, the "visitation" of specters, devils, and witches in 1692, and the growth of "heretical" sects on the frontier are related phenomena, are pieces in Satan's grand design of conquest. Thus he concludes his study of the Indian attacks with a diatribe against the Quakers. He equates them with the Indians, partly because of their opposition to English usurpation of Indian lands, but primarily because of their doctrine of human freedom and the inner light — their tenet that Christ is contained within each man and that pure introspection, without inhibition by books and creeds, can yield personal revelation. This tenet Mather equates with the beliefs of the Mohammedan sect of Assassins or "Batenists," "who were the Enthusiasts that followed the Light within, like our Quakers; and on this principle . . . did such Numberless Villainies." [17] Like the Indians, the Quakers have made incursions into frontier settlements, converting the citizens and throwing the churches into confusion:

> If the Indians have chosen to prey upon the Frontiers, and Out-Skirts, of the Province, the Quakers have chosen the very same Frontiers, and Out-Skirts, for their more Spiritual Assaults; and finding little Success elsewhere, they have been Labouring incessantly . . . to Enchant and Poison the Souls of poor people, in the very places, where the Bodies and Estates of the people have presently after been devoured by the Salvages.[18]

The Quakers thus act as a kind of fifth column for the Indians.

Mather's attack on the Quakers' spiritual raiding parties and their friendliness toward the Indians reflects his incomprehension of the basis of Quaker Pennsylvania's success in its dealings with the Indians. The Quakers acted with scrupulous fairness, for the most part, and treated them with respect. The Indians in turn found that the Quakers lived more closely than the Puritans to the letter of the Christianity they preached; and since the Quakers lacked the orthodox creed of the Puritans, they made fewer demands on the Indians' understanding in their attempts to convert them. Further, their doctrine of the inner light and their concept of human relations and community structure echoed patterns in the Indians' own religion. By contrast, Mather's incomprehension of Indian culture and warfare was vast, as is attested by his account of the "spiritual war" conducted against New England by devils in Indian shape:

> The Story of the Prodigious War, made by the Spirits of the Invisible World upon the People of New England, in the year, 1692, . . . [has] made me often think, that this inexplicable War might have some of its Original among the Indians, whose Chief Sagamores are well known unto some of our Captives, to have been horrid Sorcerers, and hellish Conjurors such as conversed with daemons.[19]

At the very time when Mercy Short became possessed, Mather received further dramatic confirmation of his belief in the organic link between heresy, the Indians, and the devil. This was the letter from Rev. John Emerson of Gloucester, former minister at Salmon Falls, reporting the presence of spectral Indians. (Emerson was later to figure as an inquisitor and accuser of witches.) The coincidence of the Indian attacks, the ambushes of Emerson's ghostly Indians, the defeat of Phipps, the tyranny and overthrow of the royal governor, and the persistent spread of witchcraft and possessions evidenced by the case of Mercy Short led Mather to conclude that the crisis was approaching. Now the devil was coming forth, and the battle could be fought in the limited wilderness of a girl's mind and a small room, instead of the dark and limitless wilderness outside.

Mather clearly regarded Mercy Short's case as an archetype of New England's condition, and he presented it as such in *A Brand Pluck'd Out of the Burning* — a narrative of his dealings with the girl that was widely circulated in manuscript. The structural pattern invoked in this account is clearly that of the captivity narrative; but here it is transformed into a ritual exorcism of an Indian-like demon from the body of the white, female "Saint." That Mather regarded his own handling of the case as exemplary is attested by his frequent application of lessons learned from the Short case in exposing other witches.[20]

Mather begins his account by briefly sketching the pattern of Mercy Short's captivity. The pattern contains all those elements we have noted as typifying the captivity narratives, and special emphasis is placed on the destruction of her family:

MERCY SHORT had been taken Captive by our cruel and Bloody Indians in the East, who at the same time horribly Butchered her Father, her Mother, her Brother, her Sister, and others of her Kindred
and then carried her . . . unto Canada: after which our Fleet Returning from Quebeck to Boston brought them with other Prisoners that
were then Redeemed.[21]

The captivity pattern thus invoked is echoed in the account of her early
seizures. After her first "Distinct and Formal Fits of Witchcraft" had apparently remitted, she went to church on a Sabbath in company with her
master and mistress. There the malignant spirits came on her suddenly and
unexpectedly; like the victims of King Philip's War described by Increase
Mather, she was surprised in church on the Lord's day and unexpectedly
plunged into torments. The weight of association and implication in these
first pages of the narrative points the reader directly toward the conclusion
that Mather himself explicitly draws soon after taking up the case: that
Mercy Short is undergoing a second captivity, is being held by "Barbarous
Visitants" in a "Captivity to Spectres." [22]

Mather begins his treatment of the girl by questioning her (as she lies
in a swoon) about the character and appearance of her devils. Her response again suits both Mather's expectations and those of his readers:

There exhibited himself unto her a Divel having the Figure of a
Short and a Black Man; . . . he was a wretch no taller than an ordinary Walking-Staff; hee was not of a Negro, but of a Tawney, or an
Indian colour; he wore an high-crowned Hat, with straight Hair; and
had one Cloven-foot.[23]

He was, in fact, a figure out of the American Puritan nightmare of Thomas
Morton's day: Indian-colored, dressed in a Christian's hat, with a beast's
foot — a kind of Indian-Puritan, man-animal half-breed.

Under the watchful eyes of Cotton Mather, Mercy Short relives the
events of Indian captivity. Sometimes the devils pinch her, bite her, or
slash her skin, as the Indians did to their captives as they fled northward
from Salmon Falls. Like the Indians, the devils force her to fast; like the
pious Jesuits or Abnakis, they forbid her her English prayers, her Bible,
and the speaking of holy names. It becomes increasingly clear that, as in
the case of Mary Rowlandson, her restoration to the communion of the
Saints is incomplete, that part of her remains alienated, the captive of the
demons of the wilderness. Mrs. Rowlandson's alienation took the mild form
of unquiet dreams, an acute sense of the world's vanity, and a mildly critical attitude toward the rulers of church and state. In Mercy Short's case,
each of these tendencies is heightened, intensified, exaggerated to the

point of grotesqueness. Instead of unquiet dreams, she falls into seizures and fits of increasing violence. Instead of acknowledging the world's vanity, she plunges through the physical world directly into the underlying, supernatural abyss. She is not simply critical of the ministry: she rejects all sacred words, accuses her elders and ministers of hypocrisy or infidelity, and blasphemes — all under the "compulsions of the Devil." She herself is not responsible for these things: she refuses to sign the devil's book and so retains her place with the elect. Her vagaries express the devil's malice, not her own. This, at least, is Mather's conclusion.

The wilderness-hell into which she is mentally plunged is itself an inversion of the heavenly Puritan city on the hill, and her experience is an inverted experience of conversion. Although she lies in a well-lighted room in Boston, surrounded by ministers and "persons of quality," she cries out, "Tis a sad Thing to ly starving in the Dark one Day after another, and to see none but Hellish Fiends all the While, and suffer all manner of cruelties from them." [24] Cotton Mather stands by her bedside, offering her counsel and prayer and partaking of sacraments. But her cries are not addressed to him, but to Another in the room, who also offers her sacraments and "redemption" through serving the devil. The kind of sacraments offered by the devil are more explicitly described by one of Mercy's fellow "possessed," Deodat Lawson, in her *Brief and True Narrative of Some Remarkable Passages*. They are clearly of cannibal nature, like the imagined rites of the Indians:

> [The] witches had a Sacrament . . . and . . . they had Red Bread and Red Drink . . . like Mans Flesh, and would have had her eat some: but she would not; but turned away her head and Spit at them, and said, "I will not Eat, I will not Drink, it is Blood. . . . That is not the Bread of Life, that is not the Water of Life; Christ gives the Bread of Life, I will have none of it!" [25]

Mercy exhibits what Mather calls a "Frolick Wit" in her maliciously clever inversions of the conventions of Puritan familial piety and the exaltation of the piety of the older generation. She reverses the traditional positions of the generations, hurling at the heads of her elders the accusation of backsliding that the elders delighted in hurling at the younger generation. It is essential to note, however, that these accusations are indirect, disguised as the ravings of one possessed by a devil.

Her confrontation with the old "witch" in the jail and her loss of father and mother are uppermost in her mind when she embarks on the accusation of the elders. In her delirium, old women visit her and demand that she obey her elders and sign the devil's book:

What that? Must the Younger Women, do yee say, hearken to the Elder? — They must bee another Sort of Elder Women. . . . Pray, do you for once Hearken to mee. — What a dreadful Sight are You! An Old Woman, an Old Servant of the Divel! You, that should instruct such poor, young, Foolish Creatures as I am, to serve the Lord Jesus Christ, come and urge mee to serve the Divel! [26]

Mercy at once demands that the elders fulfill the function they have arrogated to themselves (that of ruling her for her good) and denies that they are able to do so, demanding that they take lessons from or "Hearken" to *her*. Although they have redeemed her body and given her legal title to sustenance in the community, they have not freed her from the burden of guilt she bears — the guilt of having survived her parents' murder, perhaps also the guilt of having succumbed, in mind or body, to the temptations of the Indians. In point of fact, she regards the community as her persecutors, complaining that they gossip about her "fits" and perhaps about her activities while an Indian captive:

'Twas an ordinary thing for the Divel to persecute her with Stories of what this and that Body in the Town spoke against her. The Unjust and Absurd Reflections cast upon her by Rash People in the coffee-houses or elsewhere, Wee discerned that the Divel Reported such Passages unto her in her Fitts, to discourage her.[27]

(It is worth noting that many women captives, Mrs. Rowlandson among them, were subjected to innuendos about their supposed "unchastity" while among the Indians and that such suspicions are present even in the early narrative of John Underhill.)

The failure of the community to save Mercy Short gives her madness a double edge. On the one hand, she yearns for acceptance by the community as the only hope of healing her psychic wounds; on the other hand, she bears a deep hostility toward the community for having failed to understand the truth of her problem. Her ambivalence focuses around her relationships with her dead father (Clement Short), her spiritual father (Cotton Mather), and several father figures drawn from her fantasized captivity experience. The sense of her loss of a father is an acute torment to her, as she reveals in her conversation with her invisible captors:

Well; and what if I am Fatherless? How often have you told mee of That? No, I been't Fatherless. I have God for my Father and I don't Question but Hee'l provide well for me . . . will yett deliver me out of your Cruel Hands.[28]

Just prior to this, the witches had offered to play a father's role toward her by "providing" for her through marriage to a husband. This would have been the Indian method of providing for the orphaned girl captive, although it clearly is not the Puritan way. Her reaction to the devil's proposal is one of exaggerated revulsion, which presumably parallels either her real response to the Indian proposals or the response she would have wanted to give had her flesh not been weak:

> Fine Promises! You'l bestow an Husband upon mee, if I'l bee your Servant. An Husband! What? A Divel! I shall then bee finely fitted with an Husband: No I hope the Blessed Lord Jesus Christ will marry my Soul to Himself yett before Hee has done with mee, as poor a Wretch as I am! [29]

The problems of her sexuality were not so easily exorcised. There is some suspicion that the girl's "vicious courses" after her "salvation" (reported by Calef in his *More Wonders of the Invisible World*) involved sexual promiscuity.

Mather now offers himself as a surrogate father, but she rejects his proposal as well — and rails at Mather into the bargain. Although he has presumably prayed for her "ten times a day" and rarely left her side for long, she accuses him of not having prayed for her "so much as Once!" [30] Whether this accusation was the fruit of psychosis or the exhibition of a malicious wit, it was a keen stroke. Mather had in fact been using her as a symbol, praying for his own purposes rather than hers, expressing more interest in the shape and color of her devils than in her soul. Compassion, never Mather's strong point, played no part in his attempt to win his battle over these particular devils. He entered her dream-wilderness, not as a man who shared its terrors with the sufferer, but as the unsullied agent of righteousness, able to grapple with the devils without being soiled through contact. He came, in effect, as an alien conqueror, representative of a world which totally transcended her jungle and bore no moral or ancestral connection with it. His role was that of a rescuer, a hero redeeming the captive from the invisible, omnipresent, spectral Indians. His assistants struck about them with swords; he himself grappled the devils in mental combat, with the girl's mind as the field. He would give her questions to ask the devils and suggest answers to confute the devils' questions. In such a battle, any device was fair, and any pain caused to the sufferer was worth the expense.

The grim young man and the hysterical girl make a symbolic tableau of the captivity myth: the victim feminine, helpless, and possessed body and soul by the Indian-devils; the rescuer masculine, ruthless, and self-righteous. These two figures embody the only forms of relationship to the

wilderness possible to a Puritan community in the grip of the captivity mythology. Either they succumb to its destructive power, resigned to destruction, or they seek to destroy the wilderness spirit itself, to exorcise it and its
Indian avatars, to wipe the American slate clean.

A comparison of Mather's psychoanalytic technique with that of the
Indians (who were great students of dreams and dream therapy) further illuminates the depth of the struggle between the "American" and "European-Christian" cultures in the New World and the values and practices
that were at stake in the contest. Mather entered the wilderness of the
human mind bent on extirpating its "Indians," exorcising its demons.
These Indian-demons were the impulses of the unconscious — the sexual
impulses, the obscure longings and hatreds that mark parent-child relationships, the proddings of a deep-rooted sense of guilt. The goal of his therapy
was to eliminate these impulses, to cleanse the mind of them utterly, to
purge it and leave it pure. In much the same way he wished to purge the
real wilderness of Indians, to raze it to ashes and build an utterly new
world, uncorrupted by a primitive past, on the blank of the old.

The Indian attitude toward the mind likewise resembled their attitude
toward the wilderness. Just as they worshiped every aspect of creation and
creatureliness, whether it represented what they called good or what they
called evil, so they accepted every revelation of the dreaming mind as a
message from a god within, a world spirit manifested in the individual.
They responded to the dreams of individuals as a community, seeking to
assimilate the dream-message into their own lives and to help the dreamer
accept the message of the dream for himself. "Dreams are not to brood
over, to analyze, and to prompt lonely and independent action," as they
are in the Puritan concept of the conversion experience or in the Matherian inquisition of Mercy Short. Rather,

> the community rallies round the dreamer with gifts and ritual. The
> dreamer is fed; he is danced over; he is rubbed with ashes; he is sung
> to; he is given valuable presents; he is accepted as a member of a
> medicine society. A man whose dream manifests a wish to attack and
> kill is satisfied by being given a coat, a man who dreams of sleeping
> with a woman does not attempt to woo his mistress, he is given an
> available female by the chief's council.[31]

The solution of the dreamer's problem, posed to the community as a "riddle," took precedent over all other social proprieties. "Normally the Iro-
quoian peoples were modest in dress, often rather shy in heterosexual contacts, and although premarital affairs were freely permitted to the young
people and divorce and remarriage were easy for adults, chastity and mari-

tal fidelity were publicly recognized ideals." But on these occasions sexual taboos and restraints were wholly set aside. Indeed, the frequency of overtly sexual dreams gave Indian missionaries "great concern," since such dreams often ended in "therapeutic orgies" or at least in adultery. Frequently repeated dream-wishes led to the creation of formalized "therapies," such as the "Andacwandat feast," which involved "many fornications and adulteries." [32]

Like the Puritans, the Iroquois were fascinated by the terror and the attractiveness of being bound helpless as a captive to terrible antagonists. They too were obsessed by dreams of captivity, of enforced passivity before the malice and power of the wilderness or their enemies. The terrified Indian in such a dream was the obverse of the masterful, all-powerful Indian of the waking world, the world of war and hunting. Similarly, the cowed Puritan of the Sunday jeremiad or the captivity narrative was likely, on the battlefield, to respond to Indian savagery with savagery in kind, to meet massacre with massacre, burning with burning, atrocity with atrocity. The Puritan could never understand the nature of the relationship between these two faces of his character, and he was certainly unable to see this as proof of his human kinship with the Indians. Yet the consequences of this psychological kinship might have been a warning to him.

Like the Puritans, the Indians developed an elaborate community ritual for exorcizing nightmares of captivity. That ritual was a ceremonial reenactment of the nightmare itself. In one such ritual, observed among the Huron in 1642, a man who dreamed that he had been captured was made to suffer ordeals like those put upon captives by the Iroquois. Finally a dog was substituted for the "captive" and killed and eaten (as the Iroquois were said to eat their human captives). A Jesuit named Lalemant observed similar ceremonies among the Iroquois in 1661–62: "One man, in order to satisfy the dictates of his dream, had himself stripped naked by his friends, bound, dragged through the streets with the customary hooting, set upon the scaffold, and the fires lit. 'But he was content with all these preliminaries, and, after passing some hours in singing his death-song, thanked the company, believing that after this imaginary captivity he would never be actually a prisoner.' " [33] Mather's use of literarily imagined captivities was meant to serve a similar function.

Like the Indians in their dream dance, the Puritans entered into and participated in the dream life of Mercy Short and the other "possessed" girls and exalted them to a level equivalent to members of the medicine society, with the task of witchfinding (an honored profession among the Indians). They came to this participation through the persistent invocation (by

Mather and Mercy Short) of the myth of the captivity. It becomes increasingly clear in Mather's narrative that he and his society have internalized the captivity myth, made it a part of their mental vocabulary, and that the girl's ravings strike a chord of recognition in their hearts to which they cannot help but respond. When she cries out that the devils are forcing poison down her throat, Mather and his fellows feel fingers thrusting against the hand they place to block her mouth. When she cries that the devils are rushing about the room, people feel themselves pushed about. Whether through the deliberate malice of her inverted view of the world or through the genuine activity of her psychosis, she makes the healers dance about the room at her whim, crying out that the devils are over here, or down there, and bidding the people strike about them in the air with swords, which they do.

As her fits increase in intensity, the pattern of her Indian captivity becomes more concretely manifested in the pattern of her raving. A crisis arrives on Christmas day. She warns those in the room that the devils would then hold a dance, and her mere words — with the credence lent them by Mather — draw the people into her fantasy, making them direct participants in her agony: "Immediately those that were attending her, most plainly Heard and Felt a Dance, as of Bare-footed People, upon the Floor." Again we are reminded of Mrs. Rowlandson's account of the Indian bacchanal, "the roaring, and singing, and danceing . . . of those black creatures in the night" that made the woods "a lively resemblance of hell." [34]

Soon after this crisis, a long fast and much prayer produce a remission of her fits, and she seems to have been delivered once again from the red devils. Her second captivity seems ended, and Mather chooses an appropriate text to celebrate the fact: "Meat came out of the Eater" — the identical text chosen for Mrs. Rowlandson's account. But as if to underline the precariousness of all redemptions from captivity and the peril of eating the eater's bread and wine, Mercy Short is again assailed by devils which surprise her in church, and the entire sequence of captivity and estrangement begins again. This time there is no ambiguity about the nature of her possession or the place of her captivity: she is in an Indian camp, and French Canadian priests are using the threat of the Indians to force her to take their communion. Mather's treatment of this particular part of the delusion is either very naïve or else the product of his own inventive brain. He professes astonishment that Mercy Short (a former captive in Canada) should have such explicit visions of the Indian camp, although, as he says, she had no knowledge of the confession by a Salem witch that French Canadians and Indians had attended the witch meetings to plot New England's ruin. Here Mather's work with Mercy Short, his polemic histories of the Indian wars, and his theological assaults on Catholic doctrine and writings merge:

> One who was executed at Salem for Witch-craft had confessed That at their Cheef Witch-meetings, there has been present some French canadians, and some Indian Sagamores, to concert the methods of ruining New England. Now tho' Mercy Short had never heard, as far as I have learn't, of any such Confession, . . . shee told us . . . That there were French Canadiens and Indian Sagamores among [her tormenters], diverse of whom shee knew, and particularly Nam'd em.[35]

They offer her their prayer book and claim that they have stolen it from Mather's own library. "It was a Book that indeed came from Canada; a French Book of Idolatrous Devotions, entituled, *Les Saints Devoirs de L'Ame Devote*." And although Mather takes all precautions against further theft, the devils purloin the book again, turning down three of its pages.[36]

Once again Mercy Short is hauled out of the "Horrible Pitt" by God's grace and the zeal of her ministers. To Mather, this final redemption from captivity is an archetypal triumph over all the evil forces that the captivity mythology had attempted to reduce to order. Mercy was first rescued from a physical captivity to the Indians. Her second captivity and rescue put to rout the shades of those Indians and the "Frolick" spirit that questioned the piety and virtue of all elders. Her last captivity again ends with her rescue from Canadians and Sagamores, with the added fillip of a triumph over popish priests and their idolatrous missals. The first redemption was the result of human agency; the latter two are achieved within the mind and soul of the captive by purely spiritual and psychological means.

The precariousness of all redemptions in a world of temptations and the persistent power of inherited sin is underlined by the case of Mercy Short. Her repeated seizures and captivities to specters are graphic demonstrations of the vanity of man's feeling secure in his virtue, and they thus offer superb material for revival sermons attacking Puritan complacency. This was the use Mather hoped to make of the account, the use to which he turned it in his histories.

But Mather's structuring of the narrative of Mercy Short and his later writings in the captivity vein reflect a growing divergence between the orthodox version of the captivity myth and the vision of reality vouchsafed to the captives and the other people of New England with experience on the frontier. It became ever more obvious that colonial incompetence in the wilderness was a result of the refusal to become intimate with the wilderness life practiced by the Indians. Those who lived beyond the "hedge" still felt the power of the promise that had attracted them there and took personal satisfaction in their considerable accomplishments. If they were victims, they often felt they were as much the victims of administrative stupidity as of the wrath of Jehovah and Satan. This was certainly the case after the witch hysteria burned itself out, and a reaction against Mather's handling of it gathered strength. His misunderstanding of Mercy Short, which resulted in his writing the ultimate captivity narrative, is of a piece with his misunderstanding of the nature and meaning of the frontier experiences of his people. He had not succeeded in identifying or rooting out the causes of her psychosis; she soon experienced further afflictions and again began denouncing old women, ministers, and fathers as witches.[37] The pattern of her captivity became the pattern of New England's nightmare.

In all this it is Mather's reactions that are the most surprising. Mercy Short may have been a wretched psychotic or a malicious adolescent wretch, but Mather was neither. Yet each of her revelations evokes an immediate sympathy in Mather and his fellow ministrants. Before her revelations have progressed very far, he concludes that she is in "a Captivity to Spectres," himself invoking the framework of the captivity. It is he who becomes the focus of her fear and guilt for having fallen from the bright circle of Christianity and her family into the hellish pit of captivity, where she may have succumbed to terror or temptation and become disloyal to the memory of her martyred parents. The role is seized upon by Mather, who speaks for the generation of the pious fathers to the generation of the backslidden sons and employs Mercy's narrative to reawaken filial piety. Mercy Short's anxieties about her parents and the consequences of her captivity make her, like the protagonist of the captivity narrative, a symbolic type of all first-generation American Puritans, who broke the social circle of English Christianity to live in an Indian wilderness. When she cries out that she is tormented by her "fatherlessness" and seeks a heavenly father in compensation, their sympathy is immediate and visceral. So close is their sympathy that they share every delusion, hear the obscene dance on the floor, feel the movement of spirits about the room, feel them thrusting poison down her throat.

Mather's recognition of and willingness to invoke the captivity archetype in his account of Mercy Short's possession had its consequences. If nothing else, his words made more apparent the link between Puritan anxieties about their souls and their fears of the Indians. He also gave a certain sanctity to the girl's ravings, a mythological significance that she turned to great account. Having won acceptance from Mather with her first fits, she proceeded to join the accusers, the hysterical, adolescent girls whose words damned innocent men and women to the jail, the gallows, and death by "pressing." The captivity myth allows only two responses to the Indian and to evil, either passive resignation or violent retribution in the name of a transcendent and inhuman justice. From passive suffering, Mercy Short turned to vengeance, and by her side stood Cotton Mather.

His successful exorcism of Mercy Short's demons was one stimulus toward Mather's intensification of the witchcraft prosecutions. He got the utmost propaganda advantage out of the case, augmenting public hysteria by publicizing and playing up her "revelations" and his own sagacity. Another stimulus was provided by a tragedy in his own family, his wife's untimely delivery of a malformed infant shortly after Mercy Short's final remission. That his wife might have fallen victim to the atmosphere of terror he himself helped to create, never occurred to him. He automatically concluded that she had been bewitched by one of the imprisoned old women, who "affrighted [her] with an horrible Spectre" some weeks before her time, "which Fright caused her bowels to turn within her." [38]

Vengeance was not restricted to the elder women of the community. As in the persecution of John Eliot and Captain Guggins during King Philip's War, it fell with particular heaviness on certain representatives of the frontier settlements whose association with the Indians had been rather close. Mather reports in detail the accusation of two such figures, Capt. John Alden and Rev. George Burroughs, both of whom had figured prominently in the negotiations for the return of the captives from the Salmon Falls, Casco, and Pemquid raids of 1689–91. The accusation against Alden recalls that leveled against Thomas Morton; it invoked the traditional image of Indian eroticism as a demonic power, tending to seduce and racially debase white Christians. Alden, a doughty fighter then in his eighties, was accused as follows: "[There] stands Aldin, a bold fellow with his Hat on before the Judges, he sells Powder and Shot to the Indians and French, and lies with Indian Squaes, and has Indian Papooses." [39] He was rebuked for treason, lechery, and disrespect for the court.

George Burroughs, a former Salem minister who had moved to the Maine frontier, was also haled before the jury as a witch. He was accused of performing various prodigies, feats of strength such as frontiersmen are presumed to have delighted in. Although he was "a very Puny man," he had "often done things beyond the strength of a Giant." The specific feat that doomed him was his lifting a seven-foot gun with one hand gripped behind the stock and holding it "like a Pistol, at Arms-end." Witnesses testified that "strong men could not steadily hold it out with both hands." Burroughs replied that "an Indian was there, and held it out at the same time." Cotton Mather, reporting the trial, seizes on the statement with glee as absolutely damning: "None of the other Spectators ever saw any such Indian; but they suppos'd that the Black man (as the Witches call the Devil; and they generally say he resembles an Indian) might give him that Assistence." [40]

Although this type of accusation acquired tremendous currency and power in 1692, it was but a climactic outbreak of tendencies that had always been present in Puritan society. In 1653 a woman was hanged for borrowing "gods" of the Indians, which she worshiped, and for taking the Indian devil-god Hobbamock for a husband. Another confessed to fornication with devils in the shape of forest deer, a third to having let her own child die in order to suckle that of an Indian, a fourth to having converse with a "Warraneage" (Indian for "black cat," an Indian evil spirit).[41] In brief, the Indian (and the forest animals to whom he was likened) was the white frontiersman's familiar spirit, his personal demon, a being who gradually acquired possession of his soul and mind.

The crowning irony of the witchcraft delusion is that the Puritans' hysterical fear of the Indian devils led them to behave precisely like the Indians. The Indians traditionally feared the exercise of black art among them, since a warrior slain by witchcraft would be denied glorification in the afterlife. His blood would not mingle with the earth after battle, but he would be blasted and withered like a diseased plant. Mrs. Mary Jemison, a captive and adopted Indian, wrote in 1824 that she had known brothers to slay one of the fraternity for having killed a number of deer when no other of the expedition could bag one. Like Rev. Burroughs's feats of strength, this was taken as proof of an inhuman power. An ancient chief of the Senecas, who quarreled with the other elders in council, was condemned as a witch because he could not "account for" his long span of life in any specific way. But if the Puritans realized that their fears had led them into behaving like the Indians they rejected, they gave no sign of it.[42] Although Puritan writers frequently mentioned that the Indian religion was a witch-religion, they never equated the Indian casting out of witches with their own. Recognition of the Indian custom was not widespread until the publication of more sympathetic Indian-study treatises in the early nineteenth century (notably that by Heckewelder). Not until 1824 did any historian of the Indians point out the ironic parallels between their exorcisms and those of the Puritans and their common root in a primitive, superstitious fear.[43]

The more experience the Puritans acquired in the New World, the more they had to recognize the power of the Indian to live on viable terms with the wilderness, to succeed where traditional European civilization failed. The longer they stayed in the Indian's world, the more they felt themselves succumbing to the Indian mind, the wilderness mind. There was warrant in the experience of Indian-fighting soldiers for the notion of an Indian familiar in the frontiersman's heart. The experience of Underhill at the Pequot fort was repeated numerous times during King Philip's War. After a long march through the threatening woods and the fury of a desperate battle, white troops would become hysterical with rage and massacre the Indian wounded, women, and children with a fury unmatched even by the Indians themselves. To the returning soldier, this hideous lapse from civilized self-restraint would remain a guilty memory, requiring explanation and justification. Such a transformation was psychologically unacceptable. It was easier to explain the lapse in terms of the spell of the Indian's wilderness, a sudden infection of the Christian soul by an Indian familiar or demon.

As we have seen in the case of Mercy Short, New England's response to this "infection" was an attempt at ritual exorcism in terms suggested by the captivity mythology and the psychological ambience that surrounded it. Exorcistic psychotherapy applied to Mercy Short was intended to rid her — and symbolically New England — of the Indian demon. In fact, however, the ritual and the captivity mythology on which it is based reveal New England's psychological unity with the Indian in responding to the wilderness environment. Once the English arrived in large numbers to preempt the land, the circumstances of the American environment compelled Indian and Puritan alike to join in a constant struggle for survival, to act a heroic role each hour of each active day. Like the Puritan, the Indian felt the need to surrender his will to a stronger will, to place himself beneath a powerful protector, to be captive instead of captor; and this state of mind was reflected in his dreams. For the Iroquois, for example, "the culture of dreams may be regarded as a useful escape valve. . . . In their daily affairs, Iroquois men were brave, active, self-reliant, and autonomous; they cringed to no one and begged for nothing. But no man can balance forever on such a pinnacle of masculinity, where asking and being given are unknown. Iroquois men dreamt; and, without shame, they received from their tribesmen in dream-rituals the fruits of their dreams and their souls were satisfied." [44]

The other side of this duality in Indian psychology is reflected in his treatment of prisoners, his apparent delight in prolonged torture. The warrior, newly escaped from death in battle or on the trail, had to reassert the masculine powers that recent experiences had tested and threatened. He did so by inflicting on his defeated enemy the very torments he had feared for himself, thus exorcising his fears for the moment. This, as we have seen, was also a Puritan response to stress: the massacre of those who threatened massacres, the magical exorcism of those who used black magic.

The Puritan situation differed in some respects from that of the Indian. The Puritan was nominally a subject being — subordinate to and dependent on God, the church, and the magistral authority — and conscious of his subordination. Life in the New World stimulated his repressed dreams of heroism and tempted him to play a titan's part in the conquest of the wilderness, to win and savor the strange rewards of the Indian's world. Those who consented in the repression of this ambition could find support in the public rituals and the public mythology of the captivity. Those who succumbed to the spell of the wilderness and followed the Indian's path could find in the captivity myth and ritual the same solace that the self-reliant Indian found in succumbing to his dreams of passivity and enjoining the tribe to enact his dream wishes for him.

The response of Puritan society, however, went far beyond ceremonial confirmation or reenactment of the dream of captivity. In the hands of the ministers and magistrates, such dreams became a weapon for enforcing a social and psychological regimen in Puritan America. Instead of seeking in the Indian manner to balance the desire for heroic activity with the dream desire for passive submission to authority, the Puritans sought to subordinate the former to the latter. Mather's treatment of Mercy Short and his use of her case to invigorate the witch-hunt is most revealing in this connection. He mustered the forces of nightmare, of the Puritan's captivity- and Indian-haunted dreamworld, for an assault on the active, outgoing, wilderness-seeking component of the Puritan mind and society. Yet he did it all in the name of exorcizing evil dreams and the Indian-like, primitive inclinations of mind and soul that are expressed in dreams.

The consequences of the captivity psychology did not fully appear even in the witchcraft trials. Cotton Mather and other Puritans of his mind employed the years between 1693 and 1740 in creating a vision of history and deity in which the roles of captive, tormenter, and avenger defined the New Englanders' relationships with one another, with the Indians, and with Jehovah. Sermons, histories, antiemigration tracts, and personal narratives all centered around the theme of captivity; between 1682 and 1716 captivities were the only narratives about the frontier published in America. The captivity psychology made only one relationship between white and Indian conceivable — that of captive to captor, helpless good to active evil. Captivity psychology left only two responses open to the Puritans, passive submission or violent retribution. Since submission meant defeat and possibly extermination, New England opted for total war, for the extirpation or imprisonment on reservations of the native population. The third option — seeking an accommodation, a reconciliation, a deeper and more intimate sympathy with the Indians — remained inconceivable until historical changes weakened the foundation of the Puritan mythology of the Mathers.

CHAPTER 6

The Hunting of the Beast:
Initiation or Exorcism?
(1675–1725)

> The boy . . . drew the head [of the slain deer] back and the throat taut and drew Sam Fathers' knife across the throat and Sam stooped and dipped his hands in the hot smoking blood and wiped them back and forth across the boy's face . . . the white boy, marked forever, and the old dark man sired on both sides by savage kings, who had marked him, whose bloody hands had merely formally consecrated him to that which, under the man's tutelage, he had already accepted . . . so that he would continue to live past the boy's seventy years and then eighty years, long after the man himself had entered the earth as chiefs and kings entered it. . . .
>
> William Faulkner, "The Old People"

> All visible objects, man, are but as pasteboard masks. But in each event . . . some unknown but still reasoning thing puts forth the mouldings of its features from behind the unreasoning mask. If a man will strike, strike through the mask! . . . To me, the white whale is . . . outrageous strength, with an inscrutable malice sinewing it. That inscrutable thing is chiefly what I hate; and be the white whale agent, or be the white whale principal, I will wreak that hate upon him.
>
> Herman Melville, *Moby-Dick*

THE mythology based on the captivity narratives embodied the dark side of the Puritan attitude toward the natural world in general and toward the American wilderness in particular. It spoke for the anxieties of the Puritans — their vague sense of guilt for having left England, their sense of isolation, their fears of adjusting to a new and strange environment. It defined their attitudes toward the threatening aspect of the New World and toward the cultural and religious backsliding of the American-born younger generations. There was, however, another tendency in the Puritan mind which looked on the new land with deep and growing affection and dwelt on its promises as much as, or more than, on its threats. These two attitudes of fear and hope coexisted in the minds of most Puritan writers: even Cotton Mather preferred Boston to any city of Europe, and New England to old, as a dwelling-place. The predominance of captivity narratives and antiemigration polemics in the latter part of the seventeenth century was a reflection of specially motivated policy, as well as of one side of the community's sentiments.

Changing Perceptions of the Wilderness

As their experience of the New World increased, the colonists tended to portray the American landscape in more realistic, less nightmarish terms. The wilderness landscape took on more appealing qualities and played a healing or restorative role in relation to the human soul, as well as the punitive role described in the captivities. Changes in the image of the wilderness reflected changes in the colonial concept of the role Europeans should play in America and of their relation to the land and the Indians. The Europeans who colonized the New World had conceived their adventure as an epic quest for some incredibly valuable, incredibly potent elixir or talisman or power which could be found only in the primitive setting of America. The Spaniard, like Díaz del Castillo, conceived this quest and its objects in terms appropriate to the romantic Christian epics of chivalry. The Puritan likewise sought a physical "heavenly city" or garden in the New World; but in the manner of Bunyan's pilgrim, he also saw his quest as one for personal salvation, for the redemption of his soul from the burden of original sin. Extended experience of the New World wrought subtle changes in these concepts of the quest. In Díaz's mind, worship of gold and a romantic, retrospective adoration of the conquered Aztec were substituted for Christian humility. The terms of the New World adventure thus replaced the conventional terms of European romantic mythology. An analogous change occurred in American Puritan literature. Although the Puritans came to America with the ostensible aim of stepping out of "the world" to seek salvation in the internal wilderness of mind and soul, they readily substituted the dark landscape of America for the mental landscape of the sinner in the toils of grace. The image of the city on the hill grew vaguer, while the image of the dark city of the Indians loomed ever more concretely before them.

This natural encroachment of American experience on the European-Christian mythology of the Puritans wrought significant changes in the imagery and the direction of Puritan religious discipline. The heart of Puritan religion was its concept of conversion, in which the man born in sin first discovers the truth of his sinful nature and seeks to purge himself. Entrance into the Puritan community and congregation was dependent on conversion, whether of adults or precocious children, since the Puritans rejected the notion of blood membership in the community of Saints. Each man, they held, inherits the dregs of Adam's original sin with his blood, and his corrupted nature must be purged and renewed before he can be saved. The quest for salvation is thus in large measure a ritual exorcism of the evil that is organically inherent in human nature — a warfare with the blood that prepares the spirit to receive an influx of divine grace and leads the convert to a further inward quest, seeking to discover if, in fact, the signs of God's grace are present within him and he is one of the elect.

The extended collective experience of Puritan communities in the Indian's America made it easy for Puritans to transmute the exorcism of sin from the individual soul in conversion into the exorcism of the Indian and backslidden white from the wilderness. The process of transmutation, however, did not stop at exorcism. (This was what troubled the Mathers.) The introspective quest for positive signs of salvation likewise metamorphosed into a quest in the real wilderness for some contact with divinity, for some image or pattern of the godhead or the good man, or (less romantically) for that aspect of man or nature which is innately worthy of receiving grace. Thus acculturation became an equivalent of conversion. Samuel Sewall, one of the judges at the witch trials and a distinguished Puritan elder, went so far as to declare that the land of New England, by its very *nature*, is suited to bring forth a sturdy race of Christians; in evidence, he cites John Smith's *General History of Virginia*, which declares that the original (Indian) people of the land are "goodly, strong and well-proportioned." Sewall's hope is that the Puritans' heirs will grow in the physical pattern of these Indians, coupling the best traits native to Indian-American soil with the spiritual fruits of European religion. He symbolically equates the Christianizing education of the young with the cultivation of "Indian corn":

> As long as *Plum Island* shall faithfully keep the commanded Post; Notwithstanding all the hectoring Words, and hard Blows of the proud and boisterous Ocean; As long as any Salmon or Sturgeon shall swim in the streams of *Merrimack*, or any Perch, or Pickerel in *Crane-Pond*; . . . As long as Nature shall not grow Old and dote; but shall constantly remember to give the rows of Indian Corn their education by Pairs: So long shall Christians be born there; and being first made

meet, shall from thence be Translated, to be made partakers of the Inheritance of the Saints in Light.[1]

The landscape of the captivity narratives had been described in abstractions of darkness — a wilderness, a dungeon, a hell. The conversion of the soul related in the narratives was violently and painfully accomplished. In Jonathan Edwards's *Personal Narrative*, written some sixty years after the Rowlandson narrative, the landscape is lovingly portrayed and somewhat more specifically featured, and it plays a positive, helpful role in his achievement of conversion. A comparison of Edwards's account of his conversion with that of Thomas Shepard, one of the original planters, reflects the subtle shift in Puritan attitudes from British-born to American-acculturated generations. Shepard's conversion takes place in Cambridge, England, and begins with his hearing a sermon on the text "I will not destroy for ten's sake" (from the dialogue between God and Abraham prior to the destruction of Sodom). He is shaken but returns to his lewd habits, until he awakes one morning after a drunken bout, afflicted with a sense of his brutishness and "beastly carriage."

> When I awakened, I went . . . in shame & confusion . . . out into the feelds, and there spent that sabboth lying hid in the corne feelds, where the Lord who might justly haue cut me off in the mids of my sin; did meet me with much sadnes of hart & troubled my soul for this & other my sins.[2]

Edwards's experience likewise begins with a biblical text, but one filled, not with an overt threat of divine wrath and destruction, but with a promise of grace to the devout worshiper: "Now unto the King eternal, immortal, invisible, the only wise God, be honor and glory for ever and ever, Amen." From this time he begins to have a sense of the "sweetness" of Christ and of an ideal relationship to him, experiencing "sometimes a kind of vision, or fixed ideas and imaginations, of being alone in the mountains, or some solitary wilderness, far from all mankind, sweetly conversing with Christ, and wrapt and swallowed up in God." [3]

Like Shepard, Edwards wanders into the fields lost in introspection. But where in Shepard's narrative the landscape is vague to his inward-looking eye, Edwards's profound introspection is coupled with a detailed perception of the natural beauties that surround him. After his conversion,

> the appearance of every thing was altered; there seemed to be, as it were, a calm, sweet cast, or appearance of divine glory, in almost every thing . . . in the sun, moon, and stars; in the clouds, and blue sky; in the grass, flowers, trees; in the water, and all nature. . . . I often used to sit and view the moon for continuance; and in the day,

spent much time in viewing the clouds and sky, to behold the sweet glory of God in these things; in the mean time, singing forth, with a low voice my contemplations of the Creator and Redeemer.[4]

Even thunder, formerly the fearsome emblem of God's wrath, becomes a source of rejoicing. Edwards watches the play of lightning and rolling thunderheads and sings aloud his joy in God's presence.[5]

The God that his world reveals to Edwards (through the medium of the landscape of the New World) is a God of mercy as well as anger, of infinite love as well as rigorous justice, of infinite promise as well as eternal threat, of maternal joy as well as paternal rigor. The rejoicing of the heart is more precious to him than the intellectual delight of philosophy or even the hard introspection of the search for sin in the soul. Edwards associates the quality of grace with joy, with nature, and (most interestingly) with the "feminine" principle — specifically with his wife-to-be, Sarah Pierrepont, whom he portrays "walking in the fields and groves" in a sweet, mystical revery and who "seems to have someone invisible always conversing with her," as if she were the priestess of some New England "sacred grove." (Edwards's reaction to her conversation with invisible beings in the woods stands in sharp contrast to the reactions of Mather and his associates during the witchcraft hysteria.) Nor was Edwards's experience of the American landscape restricted to the pastoral fields of the coast. He was born in the Connecticut Valley, preached in the frontier community of Northampton, Massachusetts, and represented the Connecticut Valley version of Puritan orthodoxy in controversies in Boston.[6] After his rejection by his congregation, he became a missionary to the Indians at Stockbridge, Massachusetts, where he lived for several years under the threat of imminent attack by French and Indians from Ticonderoga.

Yet even Edwards's attitude is characterized by a fundamental ambivalence toward the natural world and natural man. In "Sinners in the Hands of an Angry God" he several times declares that God's natural world is sweet but that natural man by his will has put the world to corrupt uses and that the world is ready to spew man out. This too is the perception of a frontiersman, whose tenure in the land is of short duration and threatened by a storm of darkness born of the native wilderness. But he is not consistent in his argument that the world is good and man the sole fountain of evil. The evil within man becomes inextricably associated with evil in the composition of the natural environment, just as the Puritan sense of guilt was projected onto the Indians in the captivity narratives.

There is no more striking testimony to the nature of Edwards's ambivalence than the contrasting depictions of the spider in "Sinners in the

Hands of an Angry God" and "Of Insects," a descriptive essay written when he was sixteen. In the latter work the spiders are shown as the most "wonderfull" of insects, the weavers of beautiful webs that figuratively build a bridge between earth and heaven, between the soul of the beholder and the divine source:

> Of these last every One knows the truth of their marching in the air from tree to tree . . . nor Can any One Go out amongst the trees in a Dewey morning towards the latter end of August . . . but that he shall see hundreds of Webbs made Conspicuous by the Dew that is lodged upon them . . . Glistening against the sun and what is still more wonderfull: I know I have several times seen in a very Calm and serene Day . . . standing behind some Opake body that shall Just hide the Disk of the sun and keep of[f] his Dazling rays from my eye . . . multitudes of little shining webbs and Glistening Strings of a Great Length and at such a height as that one would think they were tack'd to the Sky by one end were it not that they were moving and floating, and . . . a Spider floating and sailing in the air with them.[7]

Spiders are seen as a beautiful, intrinsic part of God's plan of nature. Yet in the same work he regards insects as "collections of nauseousness" in the air and describes spiders as "collections of these collections"; their annual flying out to sea is thus a purging or exorcism of the land's ill humors.[8] In "Sinners in the Hands of an Angry God," the spider's symbolic function has been heightened and exaggerated, the naïve wonder at the beauty of natural creatures and processes lost in the image of natural depravity and divine wrath:

> The God that holds you over the pit of hell, much as one holds a spider, or some loathsome insect over the fire, abhors you, and is dreadfully provoked. . . . You hang by a slender thread, with the flames of divine wrath flashing about it, and ready every moment to singe it, and burn it asunder.[9]

Yet in the "Personal Narrative," written less than two years before, nature and divinity are one harmonious expression of the godhead; and even in "Sinners in the Hands of an Angry God," nature occasionally functions as a complement to God's wrathful castigation.

Edwards's ambivalence toward nature and the landscape reflects both the colonists' incomplete acculturation to the wilderness and the Puritan belief that divinity and goodness are inhuman, supernatural, unworldly, and transcendent. There remained, as we shall see, a further stage of acculturation, reflecting a greater sympathy with the natural world and a tendency to invest the Indian wilderness with an immanent, divine spirit.

This movement, covering the years from 1700 to 1790 and culminating in the myth of the hunter Daniel Boone, reflects a shift in attitude favoring the Anglo-Americans' adoption of an Indian-like, mythopoeic view of the landscape.

This Indian view of the relationship between man and nature is illustrated by the primary religious vision of Black Elk, a Sioux holy man, which offers many points of comparison with the conversion experiences of Edwards and Shepard. As a youth, Black Elk was driven into melancholia by the condition of his people — their starvation, their submission to the white men, their desertion of the old tribal ways and heroes. At the age of nine he had a vision in which he was taken into the other world and given the power of a priest-king to bind the nation together and to make it grow healthy and multiply. For years he concealed this vision, growing more and more fearful that he was failing in his duty by not expressing it. Like Edwards, he feared the thunderstorms as a sign of divine wrath and confessed his vision; as in Edwards's experience, fear of thunder then turned to delight in it. However, Edwards's initial vision came to him as a result of reading in the Bible and manifested itself in a discontent with worldly things. The God he sensed was of an unearthly and transcendent sweetness, the dispenser of a severe and immitigable justice. Black Elk's gods were not transcendent but immanent in the living blood of men and beasts and trees. In his vision they appeared in the shapes of Six Grandfathers, divine embodiments of the six sacred directions (earthward, skyward, and the points of the compass). The substance of their message was that he should become the brother and "relative" of all things of the world, especially of men and beasts. Thunder threatened him, calling with a human voice; but after he confessed his vision before the people and became a priest, "the fear that was on me so long was gone, and when thunder clouds appeared I was always glad to see them, for they came as relatives now to visit me. Everything seemed good and beautiful now, and kind." [10]

The powers of divinity, for the Indian, were resident in the trees, animals, people, and tribes about him. The gods were kind in the sense of belonging to the same species and blood. Hence they were capable of domination and use by man, amenable to emulation by man, perhaps even vulnerable to the assaults of man. The gods, nature, and man were of one essence, not of three distinct characters. The Indian religion was that of the hunter, who experiences the transfer of identity between hunter and prey and thus learns his brotherhood with all life. Appropriately enough, two Indian-like hunters, Benjamin Church and Daniel Boone, were the first heroes of the emerging myth of the frontier.

Two opposed images of the Indian developed from the ambivalence of the European colonists. The image of the good savage, which gained its greatest credence in the eighteenth century, presents the archetypal American as a blend of Christian and Indian, European and American, cultivated and wild nature. Opposed to this literary mythology is the older one, based on the exorcistic half of the Puritan quest for salvation. These myths, if logically developed, posit antithetical approaches to the American wilderness and the Indian. The exorcist abhors the Indian for making the forest a dark wilderness instead of a bright city; his opposite number sees in the unique character of wilderness and Indian a unique opportunity to discover the wellsprings of virtue and faith. This latter certainly wishes to substitute himself for the Indian as lord of the kingdom, but he wishes also to learn from the Indian, to be partially initiated into the wisdom by which the Indian has learned to live with and master the wilderness.

The cleavage between these two halves of the Puritan mind becomes most strikingly apparent after 1700, with the emergence of literary spokesmen for the initiatory viewpoint within the Puritan community. Before 1700 most such spokesmen were, like Thomas Morton, foreigners to Puritanism. By 1700 the expansion of the population and frontier boundaries of New England, as well as her increased experience of the American wilderness, brought into existence new social cleavages, reflecting the intellectual cleavage in the Puritan attitude toward man in the wilderness. The most significant of these changes was the maturation of two new generations of American-born children, who had no acquaintance with the persecution and little sense of the dedication and fervor of the preemigration days in England. They did not acquire the piety of their fathers; rather, they complacently accepted their circumstances, with a formalistic bow to religion, or else attempted through excess of enthusiasm to recreate their fathers' world view and so reinvoke that pietistic fervor. Supplementing this cleavage, and complicating it, was the developing breach between town and frontier settlement, between those like the Mathers, who theorized about the desperate evils of the wilderness from the environs of Boston, and those who willingly pursued and enjoyed the wilderness life. If it was natural for the authority-minded Mathers to denounce pioneering as Indian-like degeneracy and to call for the exorcism of the Indian spirit from New England and the church, it was equally natural for the others to speak for the idea of living on Indian terms with the wilderness, of accepting the wilderness as the source of whatever natural divinity or salvation was appropriate to an American people.

The acculturated element in Puritan society surfaced literarily in 1716 with the publication of Benjamin Church's *Entertaining Passages Relating to Philip's War*. The book and its author were the antitheses of Puritan attitudes toward life, the wilderness, and literature. Church's book clearly addressed itself to the profrontier element in Puritan society by satirizing the incompetence of Puritan historians and Puritan soldiers in dealing with Indian warfare. More significantly, it reflected the two most significant cultural and literary trends during this phase of American development: the tentative emergence in the colonies of a felt affinity for the wild Indians, and the concomitant emergence of a greater realism in portraying the wilderness, a willingness to acknowledge more of its promises in proportion to its terrors.

Before 1716 the literature of the Indian wars had been entirely a literature of exorcism. Mather's use of the captivity myth to cast the devils out of Mercy Short was the most obvious use of the captivity motif in ritual exorcism; the use of Indian war materials in revival sermons signified a broader application of the material for purposes of exorcizing the evils inherent in the generation gap, the decline or backsliding of the younger generation, and the anxieties of progressive acculturation. The Indian (like Edwards's spider) functions as a scapegoat in this literature of exorcism. In officially sanctioned narratives relating to King Philip's War, and later in Cotton Mather's more systematic New England mythology, the exorcism of the Indian is likened to the hunting down and slaying of rabid beasts embodying all qualities of evil. In the captivity narratives, bestial Indians are seen as the outward type of the beast that is in every man. The captive, too, hunts a beast in the forest; but, like the sinner in Edwards's "Sinners in the Hands of an Angry God," the captive's salvation (and his reader's) depends on his ability to see that the "hellish principles" are within himself. He must hunt out the inner beast and slay it before he can be redeemed.

Cotton Mather's *Magnalia Christi Americana* (1702) — the most complex and extensive statement of Puritan historical-theological theory — and William Hubbard's officially authorized history of King Philip's War (published 1677–78) both treat the war in terms of the hunt-exorcism metaphor. Unlike the Indian captives and Benjamin Church, neither Mather nor Hubbard was a participant in the hunting of the beast. Their works are attempts to interpret the experiences of others in an orthodox fashion, to discover beneath the surface of the events an archetype that would conform to their conception of life in a Calvinist universe. Mather and Hubbard are essentially typologists, seeking to reduce the events of the hunting of King Philip to conformity with the will of God as manifested in certain biblical texts — texts which have themselves been interpreted in such a fashion as to make them archetypal, universally applicable.

The typological exploration of the Indian wars was also intended to keep a check on any further development of the mythology of the frontier. Cotton Mather's conclusion to his account of King Philip's War in the *Magnalia* is representative of his method. The section begins with an elaborate interpretation of an unimportant text from Exodus, relating in three verses the conquest of the land of Og, king of Bashan. Bashan, by Mather's account, was reputed to be "woody" territory. He then traces various pagan versions of this conquest, in which Bashan and Og are associated with the Python, the oracle of Apollo's temple at Delphos, and the monster Typhon. The conquest of woody Bashan thus becomes a metaphor for the destruction of various monstrous creatures, serpents in particular, and the false prophets of the pagans. This in turn becomes a metaphor for the recent victory over the Indians, in which each detail of the war corresponds to a part of the biblical and classical conquests. The Indians are serpents, "generations of the dragon," and giants. The resemblance between woody New England and woody Bashan is emphasized. King Philip is compared to Og, to the Python, to a "great leviathan sent to [the victors] for a *thanksgiving-feast*." Mather then makes clear the purpose of this method:

> We have by a true and plain history secured the story of our successes against all the *Ogs* in this *woody* country from falling under the disguises of *mythology*. . . . No, it is our Lord Jesus Christ worshipped according to the rules of his blessed gospel, who is the great Phoebus, that *SUN of righteousness*, who hath so saved his churches from the designs of the *generations of the dragon*. . . . [It] is *our own backsliding heart*, which has plunged the whole country into so wonderful a *degeneracy*.[11]

Note that the physical type of New England's degeneracy is a figure from pagan mythology (which Mather paradoxically urges writers to abjure), half man and half beast, a figure analogous to the "spiritual half-breed" who blended Indian and white characteristics.

Mather's strictures against the use of allusions to classical mythology is an integral part of the effort of official Puritan historians to check the imaginative impulses of interpreters of the American experience. Yet even this formal restriction was soon to be violated on a broad scale. Mather himself could not leave the Greeks and Romans alone; later Puritan historians, such as Penhallow, and epic poets, such as the Puritan general Roger Wolcott, deliberately employed classical mythology and history as a source for structuring metaphors in their works. But it was the writing of men like

Benjamin Church, a veteran Indian fighter of heroic stature and irrepressible gusto, that posed a more fundamental threat. Church's account of his own efforts in the hunting of that great leviathan, King Philip, was completely unrestricted by any desire to fit the narrative into one of the orthodox metaphorical molds. Neither did Church turn to the classics for preconceived models. Just as he took his method of fighting from the Indians he fought with, he took the pattern of his book from the pattern of events in his extended hunt of King Philip. In the process he created the prototype of the myth that was to mingle with the Puritan mythology as a characteristic American vision of American experience.

In the course of his hunt for the Indian king, Church became more and more like the Indian. Furthermore, he not only accepted this amalgamation of white and Indian characteristics; he actively and enthusiastically sought it. To some extent, this pattern is a reflection of the circumstances of the act of hunting itself. On an extended hunt for a single beast, the hunter is forced to follow in the animal's footsteps, to eat when he eats, sleep when he sleeps, and move when he moves. This contributes to that mysterious sense of identification between hunter and hunted that so many writers have remarked. The pattern also represents, in dramatic fashion, the process of acculturation that frontiersmen of Church's generation were undergoing.

This myth of the hunter is not a totally new and unprepared-for departure in Puritan literature. It draws strength from its relevance to traditional Indian-war writing. Notably, it shares some of the essential features of the captivity myth: the use of the wilderness as a metaphor for the human unconscious and of the beast as a symbol for the secret, darkened soul within each man. In its essential structure the myth of the hunter follows the pattern of the archetypal quest for the source of divine power. The quest is a searching both of the two worlds (the temporal and the underworld) and of the hero's soul. These two quests lead him to the arms of the earth goddess, who is also his "lost half," his anima, the hidden part of his male consciousness where feeling subordinates intellect: passive, feminine, essential. It is in the union with this other self, this goddess–soul mate, that the hero achieves both personal salvation and the boon of power that will save his people. Edwards himself says almost as much when he portrays his wife-to-be, Sarah Pierrepont, as the living embodiment of that state of grace which he must study and strain to achieve.

In later versions of the hunting myth, particularly those myths relating to Daniel Boone, the anima is the obvious object of the hunter's quest. The beast of the woods is transformed into an object of love, a woman (perhaps the goddess of the place) to whom the hero is wedded in symbolic sexual violence. This, it will be recalled, was the core of American Indian mythology as well. The Puritan version of this quest involves an exorcism rather than a wedding and regards the secret self as conceived in sin and featured with darkness. Still, its parallel metaphorical structure is well defined, and the mythic pattern is systematically clarified by many authors.

Church's narrative stands somewhere between these two fully realized mythologies but is not itself a conscious attempt to create a new myth. The myth-pattern that does emerge from Church's work can therefore be seen as the result of a simple interaction between a frontiersman and his environment — the end product, not of a bardic, myth-making consciousness, but of Church's letting his words and thoughts shape themselves to the events of the hunt.

The Archetype of the Hunter Myth

Church was of the first generation born in America and raised on the frontier. After his birth in 1639, he and his family moved frequently from farm to farm on the fringes of the settlements. Church himself continued to follow this pattern, planting first at Bristol in Plymouth Colony, then at Fall River, then — in his middle thirties — on Little Compton Neck, deep in Indian country. This last remove, which he made just before the outbreak of King Philip's War, and the others which followed it were not simply the behavior of a restless youth prior to a final settling down. They were, on the contrary, the life style of a mature man. The pattern, so typical of frontier life, was anathema to Puritans like the Mathers, who believed that a permanent, settled dwelling place, close to the "Institutions of God," was the first necessity of moral government. Although Church was "constant and devout in family worship, wherein he read and often expounded scriptures to his household," [12] he was proud of having moved beyond the precincts of instituted worship. In his preface he boasts that he was the "first Englishman" to plant at Little Compton, "which was full of Indians." [13] Although he served the confederate colonies of New England as a soldier and a magistrate, he preferred to dwell far from their towns. Eventually granted an official commission as a colonel, he was always happier leading Indian and white irregulars in a guerrilla-style battle than acting as a prestigious commander of regular forces.

Thus Church was a pivotal figure in the transition between two cultures and two generations in the colonies. Born and educated as a Puritan, he valued hard work, prosperity, piety, and public service. He was a prosperous landowner, a sharp trader, a slaveholder, and a magistrate. Yet he was also an itinerant farmer and hunter, delighting in accomplishments that were not comprehended in the Protestant ethic: capturing whole tribes single-handedly with the aid of his wit and a jug of rum, ambushing Indians and beating them at their own war, hunting wily hostile chieftains through swamps in the dead of a New England winter. He treasured equally the praises of a New England governor and an Indian chief.

The dominant theme of Puritan writings on the Indian wars was the dependence of man on the will of God and on the institutions of a moral government, both as interpreted by the orthodox clergy. Church's familiarity with the wilderness and his perception of the clergy's and government's ignorance of the conditions there made him strikingly independent of their authority in his judgment of events, policies, and the state of affairs. At the height of the war with Philip, he decided to move his family (his pregnant wife and their first son) to Rhode Island, then a beleaguered outpost on the edge of the battlefield. He was advised by those in authority to remain instead at Clark's garrison; but he disregarded their advice, accurately assessing the strength of the Rhode Island position and the weakness of Clark's, which was destroyed by Indians shortly after he left.[14]

More striking than the act itself is the frank manner in which he expresses his confidence in his own judgment and his lack of confidence in that of the authorities. The several tracts written during the war by Increase Mather reflected an atmosphere of terror: New England felt threatened by dangerous foes, foreign, domestic, and supernatural. Official histories, written as many as thirty years later, reflect the same viewpoint. But Church's work (written forty years after the war) reflects a confidence based on a thorough acclimatization to the wilderness. The only thing that seems to worry him, as he recalls it, is the incompetence of the Puritan leadership, and this amuses him as much as it disturbs him. His chief aim is not to resign himself to the will of God. His one desire is to obtain an independent command with sufficient forces, after which he is confident he can end the war in a season. And, as the book reveals, he did just that. Even if we discount the historicity of this self-confidence (which must have been augmented in the forty years since the war), the fact that Church would express such self-confidence is in itself significant; and the fact remains that his most unorthodox decisions seem to have been as successful as he could have wished.

Church's book departs from both the form and the values of the other tracts and histories of King Philip's War. The title reflects this difference: *Entertaining Passages, Relating to* PHILIP'S *War . . . with Some Account of the Divine Providence towards Benj. Church, Esqr.* No thesis, religious or otherwise, is suggested in the title; the only purpose suggested for the writing of the book is that of entertaining, rather than reforming, the reader. Divine providence is mentioned, but seems to figure anecdotally in the history, rather than as an organic causative principle. It will not appear in the same way or with the same emphasis as in the sermon-histories and captivity narratives.[15] The title of Mary Rowlandson's captivity, by contrast, details a doctrinal thesis and emphasizes with a deeply pious tone the importance of God and the littleness of man: *The Soveraignty and Goodness of GOD, Together with the Faithfulness of His Promises Displayed; Being a Narrative of the Captivity and Restauration of Mrs. Mary Rowlandson . . . Written by Her own Hand for Her private Use, and now made Publick at the earnest Desire of some Friends, and for the benefit of the Afflicted.*

Mrs. Rowlandson's title concludes with a biblical quotation, reflecting the omnipotence of the Deity: "Deut. 32. 39. See now that I, even I am he, and there is no God with me; I kill and I make alive, I wound and I heal, neither is there any can deliver out of my hand." Church's title page lacks any biblical reference, as does the text of his work — in striking contrast to the captivity narratives and official histories, which are heavily larded with biblical quotations and allusions. So striking is this lack that a grandson of Church felt called upon to write a new preface for the 1772 edition of the book, in which he assures the reader of Church's piety.

The extent of Church's departure from the literary and religious values of seventeenth-century Puritanism can be measured by comparing *Entertaining Passages* with Increase Mather's war tract of 1677. The tract follows the formal conventions typical of works on the Indian wars written before 1716. In aim and structure it is diametrically opposed to Church's book. Church seeks to entertain, Mather to teach and reform. Church's work is structured by the human hero's experiences, Mather's by the formal and logical conventions of the sermon form and the demands of his theory and doctrine. Mather titled his work *A Relation of the Troubles which have hapned in New-England, by Reason of the Indians There,* and subtitled it with an outline of his thesis: *Wherein the frequent conspiracyes of the Indians to cutt off the English and the wonderfull providence of God in disappointing their devices is declared. Together with an historical discourse concerning the prevalency of prayer; shewing that New-Englands late deliverance from the Heathen is an eminent answer to Prayer.* Thus the narrative begins with a thesis and a doctrine, which the events of the war are seen to justify. The lessons learned from the events are immediately applied to the larger questions of theology — in this case, the problem of the efficacy of prayer. The hero of the narrative is God, the causal agent on whose acts victory or calamity depend. The final message is that man must humble himself and "pray, pray, pray, never more need than now." [16]

Church, on the other hand, considers himself (with some justification) as much the hero of the war as providence. In his preface, in which he personally addresses the reader in his most pious tone, the conventions of humility before providence are subtly converted into assertions of human heroism. The praise of God is formal, conventional:

> Altho' many of the Actions that I was concerned in, were very Difficult and Dangerous; yet, myself and those who went with me Voluntarily in the Service, had our Lives . . . wonderfully preserved by the over-ruling Hand of the Almighty from first to last ·. . .

The conclusion of the passage, however, violates the convention:

> . . . which doth aloud bespeak our praises: And to declare his wonderful works is our indispensible duty.[17]

In other words, God's preservation of Church bespeaks Church's glory as much as the Lord's.

Throughout his preface, it is Church himself who is most clearly in focus. Even at the end of the preface, where he invokes Christ's aid in his "spiritual warfare," he offers the reader a whimsical and attractive image of himself and, by a biblical allusion, compares *himself* to the pillars of smoke and fire that protected the Israelites in the Sinai deserts:

> I hope the Reader will pass a favourable Censure upon an Old Souldier, telling of the many Ran-Counters he has had, and yet is come off alive. It is a pleasure to Remember what a great Number of Families in this and the Neighbouring Provinces in *New-England* did during the War, enjoy a great measure of Liberty and Peace by the hazardous *Stations* and *Marches* of those Engaged in Military Exercises, who were a Wall unto them on this side and on that side.[18]

In contrast, Increase Mather systematically refutes the concept of human agency in the victory, giving all credit to the Lord for the victory. The only efficacious human acts he admits are the passive acceptance of divine chastisement and engagement in prayer and fasting: "How often have we prayed that the Lord would take those his Enemies into his own avenging Hand. . . . This Prayer hath been heard; . . . Yea the Indians themselves have testified, that more amongst them have been cut off by the Sword of the Lord . . . then by the Sword of the English." [19]

These differences in form and style are significant of more profound departures in Church's attitude, style of life, and literary production. His attitude toward God and divine providence is distinctly different from that of the Puritan establishment; and his attitude toward the establishment itself, as reflected in his satiric jibes at their behavior during the war and at the official postwar histories written by William Hubbard, is irreverent and sharply critical. These differences are symptomatic of the divergence not only of the generations but also of the frontier and town sections of Puritan society. Church's book, the most popular history of that war, is clearly oriented toward the values of acculturated frontiersmen, who would share his amusement and rage at Bostonian tenderfeet in the woods. More profound are Church's divergent conceptions of the nature of man — of man's capability for heroism, in particular — and his affection for the unredeemed "natural man," the pagan Indians. Out of these concepts, Church's narrative develops a distinctly different myth-interpretation of the Indian wars themselves.

Church is closer to the frontier hero of later literature than to the Puritan victim-hero of the seventeenth and early eighteenth centuries. He is totally at home in the new environment, skilled and competent at overcoming foes and natural obstacles. His adaptation to the wilderness has not cost him his civilization and his self-possession. Because of his understanding of the laws of life in the woods, he can impose an order of his own on events, employing the best of both Puritan and Indian cultures for his own purposes. Moreover, he is conscious of his power and makes no bones about portraying himself as the chief hero of the war. The Puritan townsman, in contrast, believes the wilderness is a chaos because he does not understand the laws of survival in the forest. When war forces the Puritan into the woods, he is lost, both physically and spiritually adrift. Having lost his moral bearings, the Puritan's response to stress is likely to be a disproportionately violent and hysterical savagery, or else an abject cowardice.

In effect, Church is denying the two basic premises of the Puritan view of the war: that God brought about the victory, and that the victory was a vindication of the virtue and social efficiency of the Puritanism of the fathers. Church himself prefers to lead Indians of the unconverted sort into battle and views the Puritan armies with contempt. His work abounds in instances of unconverted Indians fighting bravely with Church against their tribe and kin because of their respect for him and their promise to obey him. Colonial troops are often seen getting out of hand or fleeing like cowards. On one occasion Church has to threaten to shoot the captain of a sloop before the Englishman will come close enough to shore to rescue Church and his men.

In his report of the Great Swamp Fight of 1675, Church's personal bravery and good sense are sharply set against the stupidity and cowardice of the Puritan army. After the Indian fort has been carried in a bloody assault and the last of the Indians driven out (in part by a Church stratagem), the colonial army riots and begins a massacre. The thrice-wounded Church attempts to quell the butchery, but in the nightmare atmosphere of the burning fort this is impossible. When Church calls on General Winslow to control his troops, a wild-eyed captain threatens to shoot him down, and a "gentleman" doctor says that if Church persists, he will see him *bleed to Death like a Dog before he would endeavour to stench his blood.*" [20]

According to Church, the Mathers and Hubbard (who glorified the massacre as the essence of retribution on the Enemy) misunderstood the meaning of victory and defeat in the context of wilderness warfare. By massacring the Indian women and children and burning the fort after the Swamp Fight, the colonial army was denying its own wounded the shelter from the winter night offered by the wigwams. Further, if they had spared the camp, the Indians who fled would have been forced to return and submit, perhaps even to become allies, in order to escape exposure and starvation. Mather might exult that the Indians were justly "Berbikew'd" and Hubbard that they "fried with their Mitchin"; [21] but Church knew that the chief advantage possessed initially by the English was their reputation for showing mercy to prisoners who surrendered. It was on the strength of this that Church did most of his recruiting among the unconverted tribes. Yet the Puritans not only massacred their captives but also lynched friendly Indians and went back on Church's promises of mercy to sell their captives into West Indian slavery.

Church's attitude toward the Indians is his most striking departure from the official Puritan line. His relations with them are characterized by a mixture of shrewd policy and genuine affection. His approach to potential malcontents among his battlefield recruits is to "clap them on the back, and tell them, *Come, come, you look wild and surly, and mutter, but that signifies nothing, these my best souldiers were a little while ago as wild and as surly as you are now; but by that time you have been but one day with me, you'l love me too, and be as brisk as any of them.* And it prov'd so." [22] Increase Mather's version of Church's successes makes no mention of his diplomatic skill, his backslapping, or his power to make the Indians love and depend on him as a war chief. Nor does he treat Church's Indians as loyal soldiers and friends of the captain: "Yea many of those bloudy and deceitful Indians who were taken by Capt. *Church,* would frequently destroy and betray their bloudy and false-hearted Comrades." [23]

Church's indignation at white treatment of the Indians is partly based on his affection for Indian friends and partly on tactical considerations; the Indians' cooperation was a necessary ingredient of victory. It is not based on moral principles or on the traditional errand into the wilderness, as were the objections of Gookin, Eliot, and other proponents of Indian missions. Double-dealing in truces might be immoral, but its immorality is less important than the fact that it made the Indians less willing to come in and submit to the English. Church grows warmly passionate in his plea that surrendering Indians ought not to have been sold to the West Indies — as warm as Cotton Mather in his condemnation of backsliders — but he does not address himself to the moral question involved:

> [He] perswaded them (by a friend *Indian* he had employed) to come in. And had their promises to the *Indians* been kept, and the *Indians* farely treated, 'tis probable that most if not all . . . had soon followed the Example . . . which would have been a good step towards finishing the War. But in spite of all that Capt. *Eels, Church,* or *Earl* could say, argue, plead, or beg, some body else that had more Power in their hands improv'd it; and without any regard to the promises made them on surrendering themselves, they were carry'd away to *Plymouth,* there sold, and transported out of the country; being about Eight-score Persons.[24]

The moral judgments of the Mathers and Hubbard are based on the social tradition and church doctrine derived from England. Obedience, humility, and asceticism are cardinal virtues. Church's moral judgments are based on a code of behavior derived from the necessities of life in the wilderness: coolness and courage in action, open-mindedness on Indian policy, an ability to live with the Indians, and subordination of all considerations to the efficient prosecution of the war. A case in point is Church's attitude toward drink and tobacco. Mrs. Rowlandson, it will be recalled, regarded her resistance to Philip's offer of a pipe of the Indian weed as an important instance of her moral strength, a major victory in her resistance to the terrors and temptations of her captivity, and a lesson to her children. Church, on the other hand, is quite happy to smoke a ceremonial pipe when the needs of Indian diplomacy require it, and (as we will see) he makes a pleasure of his necessity. He condemns the use of tobacco only where its use by white soldiers gives away a planned ambush. Efficiency, not morality, motivates his rebuke: "But Capt. *Fullers* party, being troubled with the Epidemical plague of lust after Tobacco, must needs strike fire and Smoke it; and thereby discovered themselves."[25]

Church's code, derived from experience, is tested in the battles and negotiations recounted in his narrative; the code of the Mathers and Hubbard is likewise affirmed in their accounts of these same events. God's presence in Church's narrative is small; references to providence are few and, when they occur, are brief, formal invocations of God's name. This is in sharp contrast to the extended meditations on providence indulged in by the Puritan historians and such captives as Mrs. Rowlandson. The rather hasty and offhand references to God in Church's account of his first important fight with the Indians at Almy's pea field is typical of him. He *"Bless'd God, and called to his Men not to discharge all their guns at once, lest the Enemy take the advantage . . . and rush upon them with their Hatches."* Again, he *"had confidence that God would yet preserve them . . . [and] bid them be Patient, Courageous, and Prudently sparing of their Ammunition."* Hubbard, in reporting the same event, speculates that Church must have felt "some divine inspiration in his heart"; but Church, writing forty years after Hubbard, does not take up the suggestion.[26]

These attitudes in themselves, as the expressions of a representative of the New England frontiersmen, are significant signs of shifts and divisions in Puritan thinking about the New World. But Church's greatest accomplishment lies in the fact that his attitudes, his values, and his images of men, Indians, and God are woven into a work of literature in which the character and deeds of a central human hero provide both thematic and structural unity and a hero-centered vision of the American experience. Heroic agency replaces divine agency in historical causation; the character and inclinations of Benjamin Church, "Esqr.," are of greater moment than the character and inclinations of a Calvinist Jehovah.

Church is a singularly unpompous hero. High spirits, good humor, and an almost Falstaffian gusto characterize his portrayal of himself. Even when he is underlining his own bravery and sagacity, his manner is humorous. He enhances his own heroism by satirizing the stupidity and poltroonery of the Puritan soldiers, officers, and historians. Nor does he take his heroism with Matherian solemnity: even in moments of high heroism and grave crisis, he is capable of observing his heroic posturings with an eye for the absurd or the farcical. In an early engagement in which boastful Puritan troops have fled from an incompetent Indian ambush, Church portrays himself standing alone on the field to bring off the single wounded man, providing ample evidence that the Indians could barely hit the crowd of them with a volley. Turning to his men, he cries for a rally, but the cowards refuse to move. He then gives a graphic portrait of himself working up into a storming, foot-stamping rage at the troops amid the misdirected but constant fire of the Indians: "Mr. *Church* perswaded, at length stormed and stampt, and told them 'twas a shame to run" — but to no avail. He stalks off the field alone, bringing the wounded man with him.[27]

Since official historians like Hubbard and the Mathers had carefully invested even the smallest incident with overtones of cosmic significance and the aura of miracle, Church's refusal to take his own heroism seriously is significant. He is sure enough of his heroism to poke fun at it. Humor and irony are the signs of his self-possession, his sense of himself and of his place in his environment. It is impossible to imagine one of the Mathers treating their New England Jehovah or his human subagents with the same irreverence which Church applies to himself. Indeed, Cotton Mather had already given Church warrant for a more solemn interpretation of his own significance. Mather found an appropriate symbolic role for Church in his typological "myth of New England" (in the *Magnalia*) by playing on his name, which "might suggest unto the miserable salvages, *what* they must be undone by fighting against." Mather later referred to Church as "our Lebbeus" and compared him to the dragon- and giant-slaying knights of the "silly old romances" in an effort to increase his typological significance in the reader's eyes.[28] Yet Church persisted in defining himself in his own terms.

The Puritan who lost his self-restraint in the terrors of an Indian fight knew that he had been overthrown by the powers of his own inner darkness, allied with the darkness of the woods. Church feared no such overthrow, and his humor is a sign of his enjoyment of himself and his hard life. It is also an indication that by 1716 there was an audience in America for portrayals of the frontier from a frontiersman's point of view, for Americanized visions of a good life beyond the "hedge," beyond the New Zion and the reach of its crusading divines.

Church's satire depends for its force on the existence in his frontier audience's mind of a certain commonsense view of life, based on its experience in the wilderness. Thus Church mocks both Indian and tenderfoot — the one for his superstition, the other for his innocence — and contrasts them with his audience's sense of their own prowess and competence. The frontiersman's mind, with its sense of proportion, is the only controlling force in the wilderness where the "Entertaining Passages" occur. It is not a mind which projects visions but one which tests all previous visions against its commonsense knowledge of reality and, if they fail, mocks and negates them.

This sort of mind could not sustain a concept of a pure hero. Church's ironic views of himself are consistent with his concept of reality and his moral neutrality. He is a hero in the peculiarly American tradition described by F. O. Matthiessen in *American Renaissance*: "All mythical heroes have been exaggerations, but they have been serious ones. America came too late for that. Her demigods were born in laughter; they are consciously preposterous; they are cockalorum demigods." [29] Church could afford to portray himself as such a cockalorum demigod because he had a sense of security within his environment. He had gained this security by adapting to the pressure of facts and events, by developing what Mather anathematized as a "Lack of Vision" (a lack of preconceptions about the wilderness) and an intimacy with wild nature. His derivation of a moral point of view from the facts of his life in the American wilderness is a sign of a developing equilibrium between the colonists' conceptions of their place and role in America and the realities of the wilderness.

Just as the Puritans had defined their identity by the negative means of rejecting and condemning the Indians, so Church enhances his own prowess and that of his Indians and rangers by setting their virtues against the vices of the New England soldiery. The tone, however, is satiric rather than anathematic and thus reinforces the reader's impression of Church's lightheartedness, his lack of bitterness. He is hard on Puritan poltroons in his book and (if his account is to be trusted) gave them short shrift during the war itself. On one expedition the commander of the troops refused, on the grounds of danger, to act on a Church-given opportunity to ambush Philip. "Pray sir," Church replied sarcastically, *"please to lead your company to yonder wind-mill on Rhode-Island, and there they will be out of danger of being killed by the enemy, and we shall have less trouble to supply them with provisions."* [30]

Church's criticism of the Puritan officers springs from a shrewd sense of the psychology of fear under which they operated. He is unsparing in his condemnation of the foolish policies that resulted from this psychology, as his account of the Swamp Fight, with its riot and massacre, reveals. His account of the building of a fort on Mount Hope Neck gives him scope to condemn not only the Puritan officers but also the writers and clerics whose ideas of Indian warfare provided the underpinnings of the foolish design and justified it to the people. The expedition began as an attempt to hunt Philip down, but this proving too difficult, the troops paused and constructed a fort that would "starve" Philip out of the swamp. Philip simply walked the long way around the fort and escaped to an even more advantageous position for raiding the frontiers and intimidating other tribes into alliance. Church declares that he spoke out at the time against the action, strongly and with "contempt": "And to speak the Truth, it must be said, That as they gain'd not that Field, by their Sword, nor their Bow; so 'twas rather their fear than their courage, that oblig'd them to set up the marks of their Conquest." Not content with this, he condemns Cotton Mather and Hubbard by directly contradicting their accounts of the affair, ridiculing those who "pleased themselves" to "fancy a mighty conquest." [31]

Hubbard's account of the affair does portray it as a conquest and accepts the ridiculous strategic concept of besieging a swamp with a single fort. Moreover, he reveals the nature of the "fear" that obliged them to set up so many "marks of their conquest":

> Capt. *Henchman* and the *Plimouth* Forces kept a diligent Eye upon the Enemy, but were not willing to run into the Mire and Dirt after them in a dark Swamp, being taught by late Experience how dangerous it is to fight in such dismal Woods, when their Eyes were muffled with the Leaves, and their Arms pinioned with the thick Boughs of the Trees, as their Feet were continually shackled with the Roots spreading every Way in those boggy Woods. It is ill fighting with a wild Beast in his own Den. They resolved therefore to starve them out of the Swamp. . . . To that End they began to build a Fort, as it were to beleaguer the Enemy.[32]

The recurrent images are those of captivity: "mufflled," "pinioned," "shackled." Church's experience, by contrast, had taught him the opposite lesson. He delighted in fighting the wild beast in the mire and dirt of his own den, with the beast's own methods and the beast's own kin for helpers. It was this that brought him success in hunting down Philip, where all others had failed.

The hunt for the Indian king begins with a diplomatic coup, carried off by Church in characteristic fashion. By his own account, he had long planned an embassy to the Sogkonate Indians, his neighbors at Little Compton; their woman chief or squaw sachem Awashonks is a friend. On a visit across Narragansett Bay he spies some Sogkonates fishing and decides to seize the opportunity to begin negotiations:

> It fell out that as they were in their Voyage . . . some of the Enemy were upon the Rocks a fishing; he bid the *Indians* that managed [his] Canoo to paddle so near to the Rocks as that he might call to those *Indians;* told them, That he had a great mind ever since the War broke out to speak with some of the *Sogkonate Indians* . . . *That he had a mighty conceit that if he could gain a fair Opportunity to discourse them, that he could draw them off from Philip, for he knew they never heartily loved him.*[33]

Despite the disapproval of the authorities, Church arranges to meet Awashonks and appears at the rendezvous alone and unarmed, with a roll of tobacco and a jug of rum. The Indians appear, armed and hostile, but

Church jokes and bullies them into putting down their weapons. To allay Awashonks's fear that the rum is poisoned, Church takes a mouthful from his "callabash" by way of demonstration, then pours the rum on his hand and "supps" it with obvious relish, then "took the Shell and drank to her again and drank a good Swig which indeed was no more than he needed." He then passes round the jug and arranges the terms of peace before the festivities get out of hand.[34]

At the same time that the reader is admiring Church's diplomatic skill and physical courage, he is entertained by the sight of the bold captain growing slightly tipsy on his treaty rum, passing the bottle about with an Indian squaw and her retainers. After a second crisis in the negotiations, when Church almost fails to reach the rendezvous to receive the formal capitulation, the captain's enjoyment of his role and successes prompts a further breach of solemnity. He has left a Mr. Howland some distance from the rendezvous site and determines to play a practical joke on him to kick off the lengthy celebration of the peace at the Indian camp. Awashonks's Indians fall in with the spirit of the jest (apparently Church's sense of humor was as appealing to Indians as to frontiersmen, a fact which may be significant):

> Mr. *Church* being of a Mind to try what Mettal [Howland] was made of, imparted his notion to the *Indians* . . . & gave them directions how to act their parts; when he came pretty near the Place, he and his *English* Men pretendedly fled, firing on their Retreat towards the *Indians* that pursued them, and firing as fast after them. Mr. *Howland* being upon his guard, hearing the Guns, and by & by seeing the motion of both the *English* and *Indians,* concluded his friends were distressed, was soon on the full career on Horse-back to meet them, until he perceiving their laughing mistrusted the Truth.[35]

Hubbard and Increase Mather, in their accounts of the events that gave New England its most effective allies, the Sogkonates, make no mention of Church's hilarious negotiations nor of his practical joking. Hubbard does not mention Church's early intention of beginning negotiations when an opportunity should arise; the first meeting of the Indians and Church and the successful negotiations are (by Hubbard's account) all the result of either fortuitous or providential chance, in which human will does not figure at all.[36] Increase Mather's account does not even mention Church's presence, being more concerned with the prevalence of prayer than the efficacy of rum: *"How often have we prayed that the Lord would take away Spirit and Courage from [the Enemy] and cause those Haters of the Lord to submit. . . . In this Thing also the Lord hath had Respect to our*

Requests . . . e.g. . . . the *Squaw-Sachim* of *Saconit,* with above an hundred Indians submitted themselves to Mercy. . . ." [37]

With the conclusion of the alliance, Church receives the commission and powers he has been seeking and turns to hunt Philip to the ground at last. He looks forward to the hunt with pleasure and engages in it with enthusiasm, reveling in the exercise of his powers of leadership, the affection of his white and Indian troops, his successes in battle, and his ability to recruit soldiers from the enemy. It is his personal delight in the activity of the hunt — and the growth of his spirit, power, and prestige which occurs in the course of the hunt — that gives the latter half of the book its structure. Interestingly, the emotional climax of the book is, not the killing of Philip alone, but the killing coupled with the running down of Annawon (Philip's lieutenant) and the strange primitive ritual that follows. Here Church differs significantly from Hubbard and Cotton Mather, both of whom regard the killing of Philip as the perfect capstone and climax of the war, the very type of retributive justice.

The difference lies in the concept of the experience of the wilderness that structures each of the works. Church, approaching the woods as a willing hunter, embraces the ways of the chief he hunts to the death. Mather and Hubbard view the hunting of Philip as an instance of retributive justice and a kind of exorcism of Puritan anxieties by the slaying of an evil wilderness beast. The facts are simple. Church harried Philip from camp to camp, depriving him first of rest and food, then capturing his wife and heir. In an insane rage, Philip killed one of his own Indians, and the man's brother informed Church of Philip's whereabouts. Thus Philip was brought to bay by his violation of family ties. The immediate instance was that of an Indian family; but in the accounts of Mather and Hubbard, his crimes against white families are figured in the event.

To Church, the capture of Philip's family simply means that his quarry is near and gives him a psychological edge on the despairing Philip. To Hubbard the capture is much more: it makes Philip feel the pain he has inflicted on the families of his white captives, forcing him to experience in his person all their suffering and all their fear. Thus the capture of the queen and prince gives a grand symmetry to Hubbard's portrayal of the war:

> [Philip was] made acquainted with the Sence and experimental Feeling of the captivity of his Children, loss of his Friends, slaughter of his Subjects, bereavement of all Family Relations, and being stript of all outward Comforts, before his own Life should be taken away . . . an Object of Pity, but a Spectacle of Divine Vengeance.[38]

In Philip's death all of the anxieties that were embodied in the captivity mythology are projected onto the Indian king and exorcized in his slaughter. Cotton Mather underlines this by comparing Philip to all manner of mythic beasts — the "dragon," the "Python," the "leviathan" — each representative of some great evil in the souls of men. The moment of Philip's death is therefore a solemn and tragic one, and Mather and Hubbard are careful to give the glory of his killing to God alone. Hubbard, employing the metaphor of the hunt, declares that only by divine license and permission was the hunt consummated successfully:

> *Philip*, like a Salvage and wild Beast, having been hunted by the English Forces through the Woods . . . at last was driven to his own Den, upon *Mount-Hope*, . . . which proved but a Prison to keep him fast, till the Messengers of Death came by Divine Permission to execute Vengeance upon him.[39]

Mather rejoices that the killing itself was done by an Indian, for an Englishman who did the deed might be tempted to take the credit on his human shoulders: "And indeed, if any *Englishman* might have had the honour of *killing* him, he must have had a good measure of *grace* to have repressed the *vanity of mind* whereto he would have had some temptations." [40]

Church's account of the hunting of Philip moves too quickly to have the solemnity of Hubbard's and Mather's accounts, nor is Church inclined to regard Philip's death as the war's real ending. Whatever he might mean in Mather's symbolism, Philip was in reality only one of many warring chiefs. Certainly Church is satisfied with the hunting down of Philip, but his satisfaction is not expressed in terms of a ritual exorcism or retributive justice. He looks on the dead Philip as a "great, doleful, naked, dirty beast" but reveals no special animus or admiration for his qualities as a man or his symbolic significance. He orders Philip beheaded and quartered, and a note of humorous vulgarity enters the proceedings when the Indian delegated to the task boasts that though Philip was strong in life, "he would now chop his Ass for him." [41] After complaining that the government paid too low a bounty for Philip's head (to keep Church from "vanity of mind"?), he returns to hunting the rest of Philip's band, led by Annawon — a subchief who, in Church's eyes, is at least as significant a figure as Philip, if not in fact a greater.

Annawon is Philip's chief advisor and lieutenant, a powerful and fearless man despite his great age. At the ambush of Philip his great, booming voice could be heard crying "Iootash! Iootash!" ("Fight! Fight!") to the

frightened braves, while Philip himself ran for the woods without attempting to rally his men. Annawon is a strong link to the past, a contemporary
not of Philip but of Massasoit, the Indian chief who came to the first
Thanksgiving — and hence a representative on his side of the generation
of the first Winthrop, Bradford, and the elder Mather. His name signifies
both "chief" or "ruler" and "nurse," which suggests the esteem in which
his own people hold him.[42] Church evidently shares the Indian, rather than
the Matherian, scale of values, and the capture of Annawon is therefore
the climax of his book.

The capture of Annawon contains, along with Church's usual mixture
of humor and hairbrained daring, a ritual that is distinctly opposite in form
and content to the ritual exorcism envisioned in Hubbard's and Mather's
narratives. With a handful of Indians, Church approaches the camp of Annawon and more than a hundred armed braves. Crawling and hiding, he
reaches the place at the head of the camp where Annawon and his son are
sleeping next to the stacked arms of the war party. With a bound, Church
knocks the son senseless and seizes Annawon, while his assistants grab the
stacked weapons. The son's cry arouses the camp, and the Indians surround them with arms in hand; but with great coolness, Church turns to
them and threatens them with instant annihilation by his surrounding
"army." Then, to distract the Indians while his men disarm them, he declares, "I am come to sup with you," and accepts a meal of "cow-beaf"
and green corn. He then lies down next to Annawon to sleep for the rest of
the night.[43]

In the darkness Church lies unsleeping, while Annawon crawls into
the bushes. Suspecting treachery, Church rises to follow, but Annawon
suddenly returns.

> The Moon now shining bright, he saw him at a distance coming
> with something in his hands, and coming up to Capt. *Church*, he fell
> upon his knees before him, and offered him what he had bro't, . . .
> *"Great Captain, you have killed Philip, and conquered his Country for
> I believe, that I and my company are the last that War against the
> English, so suppose the War is ended by your means; and therefore
> these things belong unto you."*

Church accepts, with perfect willingness, an Indian's acknowledgment
that he personally (rather than Jehovah) was the "means" to his country's
salvation. A more orthodox man would have made an editorial objection, if
not an immediate protest. But Church's scene continues:

> Then opening his pack, he pull'd out Philips belt, curiously wrought
> with *Wompom*, being Nine inches broad wrought with black and

white *Wompom,* in various figures, and flowers, and pictures of many
birds and beasts. This, when hanged upon Capt. *Churches* shoulders,
reach'd his ancles. And another belt of *Wompom* he presented him
with, wrought after the former manner, which *Philip* was wont to put
upon his head, . . . and another small belt with a Star upon the end of
it, . . . edged with red hair, which Annawon said he got in the Muh-
hogs country.[44]

These were "Philips Royalties, which he was wont to adorn himself with
when he sat in State." Church has thus been symbolically crowned the
new king of the woods and decked in regalia which includes the scalps of
what are probably redheaded whites. Although he does not make this explicitly a symbolic ceremony, he says nothing which would prevent the
reader from assuming that he was aware of and enjoyed the symbolism.
God's name occurs nowhere in the passage.

Only an Indian would have been capable of such a gesture of exchange, and only a man attuned to Indian values could have accepted the
gift in Church's manner. For the Indian, exchanges between men were
fraught with peril for both soul and body, whether these were economic
exchanges, exchanges of words, exchanges of gifts, or exchanges of blows.
In all such transactions they employed wampum or ceremonial objects to
draw off the latent evil, to avert the malice or resentment possible in economic exchange or discussion or gift-giving, and to placate the spirits of
those they have injured or killed. Such exchanges therefore involved complex "spiritual and supernatural interplay," rather than an exchange of objects with "intrinsic value." [45] An anthropologist's description of the significance of the Indians' sale of Manhattan (already quoted) lets us appreciate the nature of the exchange between Church and Annawon from the
Indian's viewpoint:

> [In] the eyes of [the Indians] the currency was the symbol[,] not the
> value equivalent, of the relinquishment of their hereditary rights to
> the land as well as its products. This . . . price was to them a symbol
> over which they transferred their good will and spiritual power over
> forces dormant in the land, clearing away the poison that might have
> been engendered by the inequality of value in the transfer.[46]

Annawon had lost his king, his land, and most of his tribe; he may have
known he was about to lose his life as well. His gesture, after the exchange
of battle, reflected his desire to transfer his people's "power over forces
dormant in the land" to a proven worthy successor and to draw off the
"poison" from the exchange by means of the wampum ceremony.

The night of Annawon's tribute is evidently one of Church's fondest memories, for he dwells on it at great length and is unusually particular in his description of the weather and the scenery, as well as the details of the ornaments. He spends the rest of the night swapping tales of his adventures with Annawon and promises the chief his life. A bond of affection is created between them. But as with those Indians who were sold after their surrender, Annawon falls victim to the anger of the victors, and Church later finds "to his grief" the head of Annawon perched on a pole in Plymouth. The act was "so hateful to Mr. Church, that he opposed it, to the loss of the good will and respects of some that before were his good friends."[47]

Hubbard's account of Church's transactions with Annawon barely mentions the surrender of Philip's royalties and certainly does not attach the importance to them that Church does. Nor does Hubbard portray Church's talk with Annawon as a congenial exchange between old soldiers. The only appropriate speech, from Hubbard's viewpoint, would be a confession of guilt by Annawon in which the acts of God, rather than those of Captain Church, would be acknowledged with trembling:

> The said *Annawan* confesseth also, that he did believe by all those late Occurents, that there was a great God that over-ruled all; and that he had found, that whenever he had done to any of those, whether *Indians* or English, the same was brought upon himself in after-time. . . . But Whatever his Confessions of this Nature were, being forced from him by the Power of Conscience, after he was delivered up to Authority, he was put to death.[48]

Church, of course, mentions nothing of this, although he knows Hubbard's book rather well.

Where the Mathers and Hubbard rejected the Indian as the emblem of the devil and the "hellish principles" inside each man, Church accepted the Indian as a man whose adjustment to his beloved wilderness was perfect and complete. Church's purpose in life was to enjoy the things which gave him pleasure — arduous deeds which would test his strength and sagacity to the fullest, bring all his powers into play, earn him honor among white men for his service and among his enemies for courage and honorable dealings, and secure him self-respect for having fulfilled all his potential and become as great and secure as he wished to be. In order to achieve these things he had found it necessary to learn from the Indians, and he found the necessity enjoyable. He indulged his appetites, where such indulgence did not affect his power to function. Even when he was in his sixties and as fat as Falstaff, he was still able to harry the Indians through the woods of Maine (with the aid of two sergeants to lift him over fallen trees).[49] His account of the hunting of Philip crystallizes this philosophy.

The mythic pattern in the narrative arises quite naturally from the circumstances of Church's time and personality. Even his symbolic identification with the object of his long hunt is explicable from the peculiar psychology of the hunting situation.

Yet the narrative does conform to the archetypal myth of initiation into kingship. The failing king, on whose homeopathic sexual powers the fertility of the tribal woods depends, is slain by his successor, who has undergone ordeals to become worthy of the deed. The dead king's blood refreshes the earth, and his slayer takes his place. Even minor details in the hunting of Philip contribute to the impression that a mythic ritual of some sort has taken place. The hand of the sacrificed king had been maimed in an earlier accident when a white man's pistol, given as a gift, exploded. Thus Philip's weakness, impotence, and decline are figured in the fact that he is a "wounded king," and his particular sort of wound has distinct sexual overtones. Appropriately, Church not only inherits his regalia but by right of capture is the legal possessor of Philip's wife.

In effect, Church accepts the mantle of a wilderness kingship that Philip himself had borne. He becomes Philip's heir and successor. The conclusion of his hunt is, not a ritual exorcism of projected evil, but the achievement of a higher state of being. His experience is an initiation into the kingship of the American wilderness, undertaken willingly. In its structure, Church's tale is strongly related to the captivity myth and to that extent draws on tradition. It begins with his happy residence in the bosom of his family and ends with his restoration after an ordeal in the wilderness. But where the captive is wrested unwillingly from his family, Church leaves voluntarily. Where the captive is a prisoner in a dungeon-wilderness, Church is a hunter and a seeker, who derives new strength from the wilderness. The captive remains alienated after his return, just as he has been alienated during his captivity; he is psychologically in bondage to a vision of life incompatible with that of the "world" as he finds it. Church is also changed by his experience, but he is not simply alienated from his old way of life. Rather, he finds a new home in the wilderness and a role suited to the prowess and wisdom he has gained in his long hunting of the king of the woods.

Church's narrative is archetypal in the same sense that Mrs. Rowlandson's is: it initiates a genre and a vision of individual and collective history that becomes an informing structure of American narrative literature. Like Mrs. Rowlandson's narrative, it draws broadly and deeply on the cultural properties of the immediate society; and like hers, it links the American experience to older myths. However, where her mythic antecedents are biblical, Church's are distinctly primitive, closer in imagery and spirit to the myths of the Indians and of primitive Europe than to the Christian mythology of Puritanism. Mrs. Rowlandson is conscious of her antecedents, having internalized as archetypes of experience the stories written in the Bible. Church refers to no literature, biblical or otherwise. The archetypes that enter into his narrative arise from the imagination of a fairly primitive civilized man as it plays over the content, both conscious and unconscious, of its memory. This evocation of primitive archetypes, and of the states of mind that give them rise, gives to Church's narrative that quality of coherence and of reference to a grand, universal, primeval cosmology that makes mythology out of simple narrative.

Primitive mythological patterns figure strongly in Church's tale, as a glance at Frazer's *Golden Bough* will reveal. The central myth from which Frazer's study of human mythology springs is that of the king of the wood in the sacred grove of Nemi:

> In that grove grew a certain tree round which, at any hour of the day and probably far into the night, a grim figure might be seen to prowl. In his hand he carried a drawn sword, and he kept peering warily about him as if at every instant he expected to be set upon. He was at once a priest and a murderer; and the man for whom he was watching was sooner or later to murder him and hold the priesthood in his stead. . . . The post which was held by this precarious tenure carried with it the title of King of the Wood. . . .[50]

The description certainly suits King Philip, who was indeed the native king of the woods — simultaneously a priest, an overlord, and (from the white viewpoint) a murderer. Certainly he was harried and hunted, in the manner suggested by Frazer, by his successor, Church.

The function of the priest-king was clearly that of a spirit of natural and sexual vigor or fertility. His annual killing and replacement figured the change of seasons and of generations that was essential to the preservation of life. The manner in which his body was disposed of was also crucial. The god Osiris, "the first to teach men the use of corn," had a function analogous to that of the priest of Nemi, and "his mangled remains were scattered up and down the land and buried in different places. Taken all together these legends point to a widespread practice of dismembering the body of a king or magician and burying the pieces in different parts of the country in order to ensure the fertility of the ground and probably also the fecundity of man and beast."[51] The parts of the dismembered body of the slain king-priest-god were either buried, or worn by the slayers, or hung from trees. Philip's severed head and quartered limbs were similarly displayed in several New England towns. His mutilated hand was worn as an ornament by the Indian who had killed him (a gift from Church); and Church himself, as we have seen, adorned himself with Philip's robe and crown.

In mythic terms, this treatment of the "hanged and mutilated god" was intended either to utilize his magic power for the soil (burying) or to preserve or ressurect his power among men by endowing other men with its accouterments. The wearing of parts of the slain king, or the flayed skin of a substitute victim, was "a means of effecting his resurrection, and with it the revival of vegetation in spring." [52] Many Indian tribes had similar rituals, in which an animal representing a king-god would be slain and his skin borne by a man, who would acquire the power and virtue of the divine beast.

There is, however, a sinister implication in the ritual. The priest-king-murderer is not exorcized; he is replaced by a man who in turn becomes priest, king, and murderer. Church replaces King Philip by donning his regalia of beast skins and human scalps; and he gains the kingship by Philip's means, the means of murder and violence. Church admires the Indians, in his way, and his feeling for his last opponent, Annawon, is deeper than simple admiration or respect. Certainly he loves the Indian's world as much as the English towns. Yet his means of relating to Indians and wilderness are the means of violence and murder; he achieves kingship over his preferred world and people by destroying them in battle. Like the hunter-heroes of Indian mythology, who kill and devour the mystic deer that embodies the spirit of their earth mother, his creative act of love, of self- and societal regeneration, is an act of violence.

Church himself remains blissfully ignorant of the mythic implications of his narrative. He is absolutely immune to conscious mythologizing. He makes no "improvements" on the scene with Annawon, allowing the facts to speak for themselves. He does not explicitly claim to be the king of the wild frontier, nor does he go to elaborate lengths to explain the meaning of the pattern of events that structures his narrative, as do Mather and Hubbard and as will the interpreters of the careers of Daniel Boone and Cooper's Leatherstocking. Clearly he does not see the landscape as the nightmare country of the captivities, but he does not offer an alternative; his book is singularly devoid of landscape portrayal. This acceptance of the Indians and unwillingness to force them into a cosmic metaphor is admirable from a certain standpoint: it enables him to avoid the savage bigotry of a Mather. But the hard-headedness of his ethics and his perceptions also prevents him from sensing the tragic overtones in the image of Philip's queen and heir, surrounded by weeping women and retainers, waiting on a Boston dock for the ships to carry them into West Indian slavery. It also makes it impossible for him to offer a theory of historical causation, or of direction and meaning in history, to counter the Matherian vision of history as a concatenation of providence and affliction (although he mocks Mather's conclusions rather effectively). The narrative is in itself an implicit argument for an heroic theory of history, but Church is not interested in achieving the critical distance from his tale that would enable him to generalize broadly.

Typical of his attitudes and his mode of "critical" expression is the irreverent anecdote with which he concludes. After the anger and the ordeal, after the reconciliation-in-violence of Church and Philip and the mystical ceremony of Annawon, Church records the capture of an old Indian named Conscience. "*Conscience,* said the Captain (smiling) then the War is over, for that was what they were searching for, it being much wanting." [53] Thus Church, with a grin, discovers Mather's beloved conscience in the wilderness in the shape of an old, backslidden Indian. The image is both an explicit parody of the concept of the war's purposes put forward by Increase and Cotton Mather and an implicit parody of the mythic ceremony of identity exchange that Church himself has invoked.

Church's narrative is the first literary vaulting of the hedge of rigorous social and intellectual government and an anticipation of the literary developments that were to culminate in the Daniel Boone legends as the myth of the hunter. It draws on existential and psychological sources that the Puritan excluded from his literary production: direct and positive emotional responses to the wilderness and the Indian, and mythopoeic (perhaps primitive or atavistic) states of mind. This turn toward the Indian ultimately liberated the myth-making mind of the colonists and awakened them to at least a partial awareness of their own special psychology.

The seventeenth-century Puritans had, nonetheless, left an indelible mark on American literature and on the psychology and ideology that sustained it. It was they who developed the sermon form for the Indian war narrative and made it a genre where religious and social beliefs could be expressed in the drama of narrative action. This conjunction was necessary to the production of American historical fiction, which was in turn the base upon which a broader imaginative literature could be founded. It is important to note that while the structure of the myth of the hunter used by later American writers will resemble that of Church's narrative, much of their imagery and symbolism will be drawn from the rich typology of the Mathers and the Puritans. Cotton Mather's symbols for Philip — the leviathan, the serpent, the dragon — figure as symbols of the enigmatic power and character of nature in Melville's *Moby-Dick*, Cooper's Leatherstocking tales, and Faulkner's "The Bear" (to name the most notable instances). The reason for this lies partly in the fact that Puritan literature was based on a metaphoric equation of the physical wilderness with the (presumably depraved) soul of mankind. The Puritans viewed the Indians as projections of the evil within themselves, as well as agents of an external malice — a vision whose paradox is fruitful ground for a wide range of imaginative speculation on the nature of reality and of history and on the possible roles and powers men can assume in the world. Moreover, the terms in which this pregnant paradox was couched were established by Puritan writers as the characteristic images of America's unique geographical and historical character.

Church himself is evidence of the imaginative latitude offered by the Puritan paradox to an imagination capable of a certain amount of daring or unorthodoxy. His positive attitude toward his identification with the Indian king is the obverse of the Puritan captive's recognition of his own evil nature in the nature of the Indian. The difference between the two visions is a reflection of the changing attitude toward the character of the aboriginal, archetypal American (the Indian) that was a consequence of colonial acculturation to the wilderness. But the achievement of this acculturated vision by Church and his successors in the hunter-myth vein is simply that of correcting the imbalances of the Matherian vision of pioneer history and character. Myth is conservative, or the imagination which creates it is retentive of past visions. The Mather-Rowlandson myths were not purged from cultural memory but rather were integrated with the Benjamin Church–derived mythology of the hunter in a gradual process. In the crowning expressions of these myths — *Moby-Dick* and the Leatherstocking tales — the antithetical mythologies of Mather-Rowlandson and Church are seen as variant expressions of a single vision, ambivalent and divided against itself but nonetheless characteristic of American culture. Philip of the maimed hand is the lineal father of the leviathan with the maimed fin. Both are at once independent natural beings, demonic expressions of the power and promise (for good or ill?) of wild, untamed nature, and reflections of or counterparts to the hunters who seek them in the wilderness of trees or oceans.

But the most significant contribution of the Puritans was the development and articulation as myths of several basic points of view in regard to the wilderness — the outward-looking, wilderness-loving viewpoint of Underhill and Church; Mrs. Rowlandson's combination of Calvinist sensibility and frontier realism; and the superheated vision of those like the Mathers, who saw the wilderness as a nightmarish dream-kingdom, in which the afflicted soul alternated between a fantastic hope of total transcendence of all human and natural frailties and a fear of the devil's hideous shape and immanent power to cast him utterly into hell. These visions were expressed in four basic narrative formats or mythological structures, each of which is a variation on the great central myth of initiation into a new world and a new life that is at the core of the American experience:

1. *Conversion,* typified by the confessional narratives of Shepard and Edwards, in which the soul interacts directly with God in spiritual exercises, achieving a sense of salvation after affliction of spirit, through the gracious intervention of a transcendent God;

2. *Sacred Marriage,* typified by Morton's union with the "barren doe of Virginia" and perhaps by Edwards's account of Sarah Pierrepont, in which the human protagonist is united with a female who is both the embodiment of the god-spirit immanent in nature and the "other half" of his own individual nature (anima);

3. *Exorcism,* typified by the captivity narratives, in which the same beings, components of psychology, races, or powers conceived of as the anima in the sacred marriage are treated as if they were representations of the id, being sought out and recognized only that they might be repressed or destroyed; and

4. *Regeneration through Violence,* typified by the narrative of Church and the subsequent myth of the hunter, in which the anima-id paradox is embodied (not resolved) in an intimate conflict between male avatars of wilderness and civilization for possession of the white female captive — a figure who embodies the Christian moral and social law that the hunter both defends and tries to avoid and who therefore, like the Indian opponent, is at once the hero's anima and his soul's most feared enemy.

Not all of these patterns received equal weight or attention in Puritan writing, but all were in one sense or another generated by the confrontation of Puritanism with the wilderness and its promises and threats. The variant myths, and the states of mind that gave rise to them, continued to conflict and evolve in the changed climate of the eighteenth century and on into the beginning years of the new nation.

CHAPTER 7

The Search for a Hero and the Problem of the "Natural Man" (1700–1765)

> If we have depicted Americans as being a race of men who have all the faults of children, as a degenerate species of the human race, cowardly, impotent, without physical strength, without vitality, without elevation of mind, we offer nothing in such a portrait that would surprise the imagination by its novelty, for the history of man in his natural state has been more neglected than one might think.
>
> Abbé de Pauw, *Recherches Philosophiques* (1768)

ALTHOUGH the captivity myth remained potent, the publication of Church's *Entertaining Passages* in 1716 marks a turning point in the literary mythology of the Indian wars. Church substituted a realistic acceptance of the conditions of moral and physical life imposed by the wilderness for the Puritan rejection of the wilderness as a chaotic and devilish environment. Further, in the course of imaginatively reconstructing his adventures, he unconsciously employed a myth-archetype which differed considerably from that most often employed by the Puritans. He substituted the ritual of initiation for that of exorcism and the figure of a hunter-hero for that of a god- and devil-bullied victim. Although negative interpretations of the wilderness persisted — and the distrust of emigration and frontiersmen did remain a persistent strain in New England (and later in the United States) — the books which followed Church's tended to treat the landscape of the wilderness with more realism, denying neither its harshness nor its beauty. Their authors aimed more at increasing the colonists' sense of security, of at-homeness in the wilderness, than at compelling them to reject the New World and cling to the remembered old. Between 1716 and

1784, from the appearance of Church's book to that of Filson's *Discovery, Settlement and Present State of Kentucke*, the Puritan vision of the New World underwent a drastic change, shifting its basis from the captivity myth and the Westminster Confession to a more secularized world view, based on rationalistic philosophy and continuing experience on the frontier.

The development of this new, acculturated world view was in large measure the result of the continued expansion of New England into the wilderness. The fact of expansion itself indicates that the people had moved away from the hedged-in Puritan concept of the coastal enclave. The expansion increased the fund of knowledge about the Indians and the land, at the same time that it created an imperative demand for such information. The settlers needed practical advice on how to live with the Indians in the wilderness, what to expect of them and of the land, and how to fight against both. They required a manual of information about the Indians and the wilderness, not a religious tract anathematizing them — a literature shaped by experience rather than biblical exegesis. Against this new realism in the literary approach to the frontier the orthodox preachers of the Revival set their faces. In New England the early stages of the new, evolving myth of the frontier were shaped by the struggle between the revivalists, who drew on the strong tradition of the period of the captivities, and those writers who followed the path opened by Benjamin Church.

New Images of a Frontier Hero

It was symptomatic of the shift (in New England attitudes, at least) that the captivity narratives no longer preempted the literary marketplace, as they had from 1680 to 1716. After 1725, even the revivalistic preachers turned to narratives of battle for their material, employing accounts of victories and defeats as they had employed the captivities: as a scourge to the back of sinful New England. The treatments of Lovewell's defeat of 1725 reveal the division in the New England idea of man's power in the wilderness. Lovewell was the leader of a group of New England rangers who harried the Indian villages in the same manner as the Indians harried the English frontier — burning, killing, taking captives and scalps. On a raid against the Piggwackett Indians, Lovewell's company was ambushed; Lovewell himself was killed, and most of his company were shot down. But in the vicious fire-fight that decimated Lovewell's troop, the Indians suffered such heavy losses that they fled without taking any scalps, leaving their war chief Paugus dead on the field. The power of the tribe was broken for the duration of the war.

The first narrative dealing with Lovewell's defeat was a sermon-narrative by Thomas Symmes, who saw the defeat as a sign of divine wrath and an occasion for self-mortification. The second was in the form of a popular ballad, which celebrated in Church's manner the bloody deeds of Lovewell's men in their last fight. Symmes's work went through two editions under two titles within a year. The first title details his theme: *Lovewell Lamented. Or, a sermon occasion'd by the fall of the brave Capt. John Lovewell and several of his valiant company, in the later heroic action at Piggwacket.* The second title — *Historical Memoirs of the Late Fight at Piggwacket* — perhaps reflects the publisher's sense that his readers' real interests centered on the battle rather than on its improvement. The double publication within the year suggests both the popularity of the account and the authorities' approval of its thesis.

Symmes's Captain Lovewell is but one short remove from the victim-hero of the captivities. Symmes's primary interest is in Lovewell's defeat by the wilderness, and he carefully omits details that might create in his audience more pride in Lovewell's power than humiliation at his fall. The point of departure is not the event itself but a biblical text, David's elegy on Saul and Jonathan. The sermon proper is a kind of literary-critical exfoliation of the elegy as "a very bright example, how to behave upon, and what improvement to make, of the death of useful men." [1] He discusses various "reasons" why it is "decent and becoming," "useful and advantageous," and "pious and Scriptural" to weep for the death of such men. Such lamentations have "uses" as "spur[s] to virtue," that is, to humility. Lovewell's fall is proof that boasting (by New England pamphleteers) of the Lord's favor before a battle is both impious and liable to be upset and that even great skill in war is no shield against defeat. Therefore, in Indian or "spiritual-warfare," "soldiers had need to be truly religious and well-prepared for death. So, then, a well grounded perswasion of a part in Christ, and an interest in the favor of God, is what all that go forth to war, would do wisely . . . to obtain." [2] To put the matter more plainly, they would do well to become converted, through a consciousness of their sin and their dependence on God for grace. The use of the defeat is to make us, as readers, come to conversion through a perception of our sin and dependence: there are "tokens of His displeasure to be seen in this affair."

> Have not our sins as really slain our magnanimous soldiers, as ever, David slew Uriah the Hittite by the sword of the children of Ammon? . . . Should we not endeavor to find out and put away the accursed

thing from the midst of us? And to turn to him that smites us? How many calls have New England had, from the pulpit, and by the press also, from year to year; to remember whence we are fallen and repent and do our first works! . . . But alas, How many hate to be reformed! [3]

Yet New England did not wish to see Lovewell's defeat only as the revivalists desired them to see it. If Lovewell died at Piggwackett, so did Paugus, his opposite number among the Indians. Frontiersmen might mourn the fallen, but they knew that the Indian victory had crippled the Piggwacketts and weakened their power fatally. The "Song of Lovewell's Fight" reveals that a segment of New England took more pride in its ability to fight like the savages than in its supposed spiritual superiority to Indian ways. Verse 16 of the ballad boasts:

Our worthy Captain Lovewell, among them there did die;
They killed Lieutenant Robbins, and wounded good young Frye,
Who was our English chaplain: he many Indians slew,
And some of them he scalped, while bullets round him flew.[4]

The image of the English chaplain scalping his slain enemies is a symbol of the division between the clergy of the towns and the people of the frontier. Frye's fiancée, an Andover girl whose father felt Frye was too poor and ill-educated to be a proper husband, preferred to elegize him as "that young student, Mr. Frye, / Who in his blooming youth did die, . . . / A comely youth and pious too." [5] Yet he carried a scalping knife with his Bible.

The conflict between Symmes and the balladeer is rooted in divergent ideas of the efficacy of human heroism, the value of natural or even primitive human behavior, and the wisdom of trusting personal experience of the wilderness rather than orthodox theory. Later attempts to employ the Indian wars in revival sermons take greater cognizance of this popular demand for a human hero to represent New England's pride and its Americanization. Thomas Prince's edition of John Mason's *A Brief History of the Pequot War*, published in Boston in 1736, characteristically attempts to blend the revivalists' evocation of "humiliation" with a slight bowing to the reading public's need for heroes to worship. Prince's hero, John Mason, is (unlike Lovewell) a man long dead, one of the first generation of Puritans. His heroism is qualified by a strong sense of dependence on God, analagous to that expressed by the captives. Yet Mason *is* a hero; and his narrative remained unpublished from its initial abridgement in Increase Mather's history of King Philip's War (1677) to the end of the period of the captivities. Yet if Mason is not a victim, like the protagonist of the captivity narrative and of Symmes's *Lament*, neither is he a frontier hero on the model of Benjamin Church or the scalp-hunting Chaplain Frye. Mason is, rather, a symbol of a past heroism, a power lost with the faith of the fathers and their intimacy with God. By revivifying this symbol, Prince seeks to awaken in New England a sense of the relative weakness of the present generation. For Prince, like Symmes and the Mathers, is interested in combating the dangerous sense of security, not in finding images that would justify continued emigration to the frontier.

Prince was a prominent clergyman, book collector, and historian, author of *A Chronological History of New England*, which became a classic work in the genre of Puritan theodicy-histories. Typically, that work began with Adam and Eve and set out to trace in outline the whole cycle of history, culminating in the settlement of New England by the new chosen people — a sort of Newer Testament, supplementing the Bible and placing New England's history in context with that of the other Chosen People. The first volume was published in the same year as his edition of Mason's history, but Prince's thirst for recording every detail of God's "activity" made it impossible for him to complete his major work.

In the context of the unfinished theodicy-history, Mason might have figured as the modern type of an Old Testament soldier on the model of Gideon or the young David: a man who manifestly enjoys the favor of God in overcoming the outnumbering host of his enemies, yet who modestly effaces himself before the people and gives all the glory to God alone. Mason had shared with John Underhill the command of the colonial forces who assaulted and destroyed the Pequot fort in 1637. It was he who had led the assault against the palisade and who, at the height of the action, hurled a flaming brand into a wigwam and set the whole village ablaze. Unlike the ambitious Underhill, Mason does not portray the action as an occasion for glorious battle between equally valorous foes. Rather, he shows it as the chastisement of the children of darkness by agents of the Lord, who recognize their own impurity in the eyes of God and so remain humble. Where Underhill reaped censure and exile for his various "enthusiasms" (both religious and economic), Mason earned the praise of the magistrates and social and political advancement.

To Mason's pious and straightforward narration of these events (not including the postwar rewards) Prince adds a series of prefaces and introductions, interpreting the significance of the work in terms appropriate to each of the audiences addressed by them. Prince's edition of Mason adopts the same sermonlike form which characterizes the narratives of Wheeler and Increase Mather. The text is Psalm 44 : 1–3:

> We have heard with our Ears, O God, our Fathers have told us, what Work Thou didst in their Days . . . . : How Thou didst drive out

the Heathen with thy Hand, and plantedst Them: how Thou did
afflict the People and cast them out. For they got not the Land in Possession by their own Sword, neither did their own Arm save them: but
thy right Hand and thine Arm, and the Light of thy Countenance, because Thou hadst a Favour unto them.

Prince's choice of a text recalls Church's criticism of the fort builders who
set up the "marks" of a victory, because of their fear, on land that they had
not won with their arms. But where Church allowed the implication that
his own arm might have won them a field elsewhere, Prince is careful to
emphasize God's power to bring victory, just as Mason himself concluded
that the "use" of the war was to awaken our remembrance of God: "Let us
therefore praise the Lord for his Goodness and his wonderful Works to the
Children of Men!" [6] Mason saw the Puritan soldiers as victims of the
power of the wilderness, or as feeble victors upheld by God's power and
not their own:

[We] repaired to the Place of our Abode: where we were Entertained with great Triumph and Rejoycing and Praising God for his
Goodness to us, in succeeding our weak Endeavours. . . . Thus was
God seen in the Mount, Crushing his proud Enemies and the Enemies
of his People.[7]

Such was Mason's view of the battle in which the English burned and shot
to death most of the tribe in the Pequot fort. In contrast to the new trend
set by Church's self-glorifying account of personal triumphs, Prince's edition of Mason marks a sort of reversion to type in the development of the
genre.

Hampered by a tradition which did not accept the wilderness as an
environment productive of good, writers like Prince took their visions of
the good life from the era of the first settlements, when the orthodox congregations of the civilized coastal enclaves were themselves outposts on
the frontier and when ministerial sway was strong to the edge of the clearings. Their vision of the orderly, symmetrical, and organic unity of man,
God, commonwealth, and natural wilderness — a unity which was supposedly realized in the time of the fathers — became a benchmark against
which the fall of the present generation could be measured and its appalling distance comprehended. Prince's several prefaces, corresponding to
the doctrine section of a sermon, are intended to force the reader to draw
invidious comparisons between the former time and the present. Prince
begins by comparing Mason to the biblical heroes, who conquered "By
Faith" rather than by dependence on their own strength. Yet Prince feels
called upon to justify this biblical comparison, as if his audience might not

accept such comparisons as a matter of course, as did the audiences of
Mather and Hubbard:

> The Judicious Reader that knows the New English History, cannot
> think these Scripture Phrases or religious Turns unsuitable on this Oc-
> casion: For as these Colonies were chiefly, if not entirely Settled by a
> Religious People, and for those Religious Purposes; It is as impossible
> to write an impartial or true History of them, as of the ancient Israel-
> ites, . . . without observing that Religious Spirit.[8]

The last lines in particular suggest the alienation of his readers from the
"Religious Spirit"; they are thought to prefer "true History" and to be put
off by religious "Turns" of phrase or imagery. Yet later in the preface
Prince offers those same readers the Puritan version of the Pequot War victory as the work of God and remarks that the account is a "standing Monu-
ment" both to "the courage of our pious Fathers" and to "the eminent Appearance of Heaven to Save them." [9] There is a clear distinction between
the piety of Prince and that of Benjamin Church: Prince more frequently
pays tribute to the power of providence. Yet when one compares Prince's
statement with Mason's own praise of the Lord, Prince's seems flat and formalistic. This is not to say that Prince did not believe that God's power had
saved New England; it does indicate that the faith of Prince and his readers had to compete seriously with secularism.

Prince includes in his edition several other prefatory statements by
various anonymous hands. One of these, which is significantly addressed
"To the American Reader," epitomizes many of the forces that were at
work in the society and the literature of the early eighteenth century. Its
title is in itself a symptom of the growing sense of national identity which
was the product of a century of living in the new land. It begins with a reference to the burgeoning literature produced by the press and to the
growth of publications unrelated or downright hostile to religious concerns
— particularly political pamphlets: "Although it be too true indeed that
the Press labours under, and the World doth too much abound with pam-
phleting Papers; yet know that this Piece cannot or at least ought not to be
disaccepted by thee; For by the help of this thou mayst look backward and
interpret how God hath been working." This reminder of the reality of our
dependence on God, says Prince, ought to effect a revival of religion by
overcoming our "lethargilike Security"; for though our souls still confront
the same devil, we can see (by comparing our faith to Mason's) that we
have not the saving sense of God our fathers had.[10]

Prince's inclusion of this preface suggests that he concurred, in spirit
at least, with its author's belief in human insignificance before God and the

church. It is interesting, therefore, that Prince chose a personal narrative like Mason's for his vehicle and that he emphasized in his preface the heroic stature of Mason. The conscious creation of culture heroes is not usually associated with the Puritans, who subordinated personal glory to a desire to glorify God. Church's narrative was an exception to this rule of humility, and Church's creation of a heroic vision of himself was accomplished by dramatic implication rather than by avowed intention. Yet Prince offered Mason to his readers as a potential culture hero, an idealized symbol of the vision of the whole people of New England, a mythic emblem of their historical and religious experience. The device was unsuccessful: Mason was not in fact accepted by a large public as the embodiment of the American dream. But Prince's use of a hero-figure as the key to an evocative appeal to the whole of society was in itself a significant development.

Prince's hero fails literarily because his very nature precludes his open assumption of the hero's role. Mason's own words are directed to turning aside any interpretation of his narrative as a metaphor for the total course and meaning of the war. In a statement to the General Court of Connecticut (reprinted by Prince), Mason protests: "You well know how often I have been requested by yourselves to write something in reference to the Subject of the ensuing Treatise, . . . and how backward I have been, as being conscious to my own unfitness; accounting it not so proper, I being a Chief Actor therein myself." [11] It was at his own instigation that his narrative was unprinted (in its entirety) for a full century.

The trend in frontier literature was toward more self-conscious and egotistical models of the American hero. For example, Major Robert Rogers, leader of the guerrilla-type ranger companies of the last French and Indian War, attempted in the 1760s to dramatize himself to the British court and public as the American hero par excellence. In 1765 he published in London his *Journals* in which he claimed that the "several Excursions he made" had provided a key to "the most material Circumstances of every Campaign upon that Continent." But this attempt at hero-creation failed to gain an American audience. Since Rogers's primary purpose was to convince an English audience of his qualifications for the post of governor at Michillimackinac, he published the work in England and apparently sought no American edition of it. Still, he was a product of the New England–New York frontier, and as such his life, his egotism, and his Benjamin Church-like attitude toward Indians and Indian fighting are of value as indications of the direction in which images of the frontier hero and the Indian were developing.

The careers of Mason, Church, and Rogers mark the stages of the developments which took place in Indian war literature and in American culture from the early to the late Colonial period. All three men were renowned Indian fighters, but their successive campaigns show an increasing proficiency in woodcraft and the gradual adoption of Indian modes of dress and combat. Each of the men participated in the massacre of Indian tribes by white troops. Mason justifies the wiping out of the Pequots as a judgment of God upon the heathen. Church condemns one massacre (in the Swamp Fight) which he believes served no purpose; he later perpetrates a small massacre himself, when he orders some French prisoners "knocked in the head" because he has not enough troops to fight the enemy and also guard the prisoners. In both cases he avoids moral justifications, preferring to claim considerations of efficiency as his motives. Rogers's greatest exploit was his epic trek through the wilderness to attack the Indian village of St. Francis. The massacre perpetrated there appears deliberate and cold-blooded, presented as a matter of strategic policy and justified by the cruelty of these Indians in their incessant raids on the settlements. Where Mason's massacre was begun in panic and justified by theology, where Church's was unsystematic and offhand, Rogers's is the product of a thorough comprehension of the nature and necessities that govern successful strategy in an Indian war. Moral considerations play absolutely no part in his account; he recognizes only the pragmatic values imposed by war in the wilderness. Even the harrowing return from St. Francis, in which his men all but starve to death, occasions no pious reflections on providence. The killing of a partridge when his men are at the last extremity is regarded simply as an instance of "good fortune." [12]

The Mason-Church-Rogers development indicates an intellectual movement toward secularization, a tendency to imitate Indian ways of fighting in the wilderness, and a somewhat clearer image of Americans' concept of themselves and their land as embodiments of a new and promising order, derived from the conditions of life in the American wilderness. Mason is careful to set himself off from the Indians as an exponent of an alien, European civilization. Church implies his closeness to the Indians in his account of his recruitment of Indian soldiers and his pride in being able to live chiefly in unsettled parts. Rogers is explicit about his affinity for the wilderness (although careful to draw a line between Indians and himself) and is not even as settled a man as Church. Rogers is no farmer but a ranger and trader in the wilds from his youth:

Between the years 1743 and 1755 my manner of life was such as led me to a general acquaintance with the British and French settlements in North America and especially with the uncultivated wilderness, the mountains, valleys, rivers, lakes, and several passes that lay between and contiguous to the said settlements. Nor did I content myself with the . . . information of hunters but travelled over large tracts of the country myself, which tended not more to gratify my curiosity than to inure me to hardships and, without vanity I may say, to qualify me for the very service I have been employed in.[13]

The development also suggests that American writers (and their readers) were attempting to work out for themselves a clear concept of a representative American — a hero who could be set off against the culture heroes of Europe and express the Americanized Englishman's new sense of himself, his new perception of his place in the wilderness and the world. The frequency with which hero-narratives begin to occur in American writing about the frontier suggests the growing sense of need for such a hero. At the same time, the Indian begins to appear in a more positive light, as a representative of the kind of heroism that natural, uncultivated, American man is capable of. Even though the Indian is consistently portrayed as inferior to whites, his presence remains necessary to the revelation of the heroic stature of the Anglo-American hero. The Indian is his foil, the opponent against whom he exercises and develops his heroic powers as a representative of civilization.

The colonists, then, required an image, a symbolic heroic figure, whose character and experiences would express their own sense of history, of their relationship to the American land, of their growing away from Europe. The need for such an image extended to all the colonies — and indeed to Europe, whose writers sought an image of the American "type" that would express their sense of the colonists' having become un-European in the course of their American experience. The evolution of the new myth of the frontier was not exclusively the result of internal tensions in Puritan New England. In the seventeenth century, however, New England was virtually the only section of the country with a substantial printing and bookselling trade sustained by an American popular audience. Further, its literature was the only one characterized by an intense striving for metaphors and myths that could define a peculiar place for its readers in the cosmos. No other section experienced Indian wars of the same duration and intensity, and no other had the same inclination to make this struggle the basis of a religion-charged mythology.

As communication between the colonies improved and as contacts with England became easier, the parochial literature of New England was cross-fertilized by metaphors and traditions from Europe and from the southern and middle colonies. This process was accelerated by the growth of the printing and bookselling trade and by the establishment of a system of distribution which by 1800 linked all the colonies to the bookselling capitals of New York and Philadelphia. Cadwallader Colden's study of the Indians, published in New York in 1727, and Provost William Smith's *Historical Account of Bouquet's Expedition* (Philadelphia, 1766) were the first important studies of Indian warfare published outside New England. The breakdown of New England's literary isolation, coupled with the native trends resulting from the realist-revivalist split, led to an increase of secularism in its Indian war literature — a tendency to employ classical rather than biblical texts for metaphoric allusion (in defiance of Cotton Mather's strictures against "mythology"), to take a more positive view of the Indian and the natural man, to accept the possibility of human heroism.

This trend was paralleled by a growing consciousness of America's distinctiveness vis-à-vis Europe. Political disagreements with England, revolving around fundamental disagreements in political theory as well as policy, sharpened this sense of American identity throughout the colonies. Finally, the rediscovery of America by the French philosophes, and the consequent opening of a dialogue between French and American intellectuals, helped provide Americans with a philosophic rationale for their new acceptance of the primitive frontier as their home.

European Images of the American Character: Indianization

The definition of an American hero depended upon the answers to two questions: What is characteristically American, and to what extent is man capable of heroic action in Jehovah's and nature's universe? The answers to both questions involved an investigation of the nature of the Indian, for the Indian was not only the characteristic human product of the American land but also, to Europeans and colonists alike, the type of the natural man. Since nature in America had developed unchecked by civilized institutions or arts, whatever man was by nature capable of in the way of virtue and heroism, or evil and degradation, ought to reveal itself in the Indian. The colonists themselves, however, were not Indians but Europeans transplanted to the Indians' world. Hence the American hero would have to bridge the gap or mediate between the European past and the Indian present. While part of his development to heroic stature must be the consequence of evolution through experience in the Indian's world, part of his nature is inherited from Europe.

The Puritans expressed the difference between Indian and English character in terms of the distinction between the "light of nature" and the "light of revelation." Like the Indian, the colonist used the natural reason of fallen man to establish justice and religion in the wilderness; but unlike the Indian, the white man had also inherited a surer guide: the revealed Word of God. Continental rationalists of the later eighteenth century, on the other hand, expressed the difference between the Indian and the European in terms of natural innocence and civilized experience. The Indian, in this view, had just embarked on the course of social evolution that would take him toward civilization and its discontents. The colonist was no longer innocent of history; he had already experienced the "fall" from savage innocence to the guilt and anxiety of civilized life. The savage trusted his natural passions, innocent of the consequences of his individualism and self-indulgence; the colonist had learned to use his intellect and conscience to keep his nature within bounds. But both Puritans and rationalists came to conceive the American experience as a blending of Indian and European characteristics, although there were wide variations in judgment as to whether this had improved or degenerated the colonials.

Although fear of racial degeneration as a result of intermarriage persisted as a significant force in American and European thought, a counter-trend developed in the eighteenth century. This line of thought emphasized the capacity of the savage to become "white" and the natural ability of man to attain both Christian virtue and heroic stature. A new concept of the nature of the Indian and Indian-European relationships was the touchstone of this new development. In the specialized literature devoted to systematic study of Indian mores and racial theory, we can see not only the evolution of this new conception of the Indian but also a divergence between American and European treatments of the frontier. From the outset, Europeans viewed the colonization of the New World as a metaphoric marriage between civilization and savagery. Once this view became conventionalized in English comic drama and satiric poetry, the convention itself became the starting point for all writing on the colonists and the Indians. For the Americans, who had to live with the Indians, continually renewed experience of the Indians had to be the starting point. Moreover, since the colonists were the ones actually faced with acculturation to the Indians' world, the marriage metaphor was unacceptable. The British employed it as a comically pejorative convention in dealing with the rustic foibles of provincial American characters; the colonists resisted it with an emotional intensity amounting at times to hysteria. But even while the New Englanders were resisting all tendencies in their population to behave like the Indians, in European eyes the association of Indian and emigrant was firmly fixed.

As early as 1605, British playwrights were employing this and other stereotypes of America with humorous effect. Ben Jonson, George Chapman, and John Marston collaborated on a comedy called *Eastward Hoe*, in which the Roanoke Virginians are satirized as Indian-cuddlers and More's *Utopia* is ironically invoked in parody of the utopian projects envisioned by the Virginia promoters. The play was performed in both London and Virginia, which apparently could still laugh at itself. In act 3, scene 3, a Virginia recruiter employs the metaphor of an Indian virgin's seduction to describe the achievement of the colony:

> *Seagull:* Come, boyes, Virginia longs till we share the rest of her maidenhead. . . . A whole country of the English is there man, bred of those that were left [at Roanoke's lost colony]; they have married with the Indians, and make them bring forth as beautifull faces as any we have in England; and therefore the Indians are so in love with 'hem that all the treasure they have they lay at their feet.[14]

This association of Indian America with the liberation of sexual impulses became an integral part of the European vision of the American. The less flattering association of Americans with blood ritual and cannibalism likewise persisted.

Ned Ward of Grub Street, pamphleteer, satirist, and author of *The London Spy* (1699), gave a comprehensive view of English stereotypes of America. Ward produced a series of travel satires, one of which takes him (or rather his putative correspondent) to New England. *A Trip to New-England*, printed in London in 1699, roasts the Puritans thoroughly as sharpers and cheats, niggard lovers and husbands of doubtful manhood; their wives are ripened at thirteen and worn into hags by twenty-four but still defy the harsh laws against adultery to "be reveng'd on Matrimony." Part of their ill nature is the result of their religion, says Ward, but much of it is the result of their living too close to and too much like the Indians. Like Mrs. Rowlandson, he condemns the New England love of tobacco and rum, but his tone is far less that of the outraged minister than the disgusted dandy: "The women (like the men) are excessive smokers; and have contracted so many ill habits from the Indians, that 'tis difficult to find a woman cleanly enough for cook to a squeamish lady, or a man neat enough for a valet to Sir Courtly Nice." Like the Indians, they are lazy and work their women to death, while they themselves eat, drink, sleep, and smoke their lives away.[15]

Ward and other English writers of the late seventeenth and early eighteenth centuries shared the anxieties of Puritan writers of Cotton Mather's ilk about emigrant acculturation to the wilderness, but their attitude was a spectator's amused condescension. They did not share the hagridden intensity of an agonist like Mather, for whom this was the fundamental dilemma of culture, politics, and spiritual government. Daniel Defoe's novels *Colonel Jacque* and *Moll Flanders* (both 1722) exemplify the uses to which these conventional images of America might be put. In the former, the highwayman Jacque is transported to the New World for his crimes. There he discovers a land in which a man can redeem himself and rebuild his life — in effect, create a new world for himself. He comes to Virginia under an indenture and leaves a free, prosperous planter. For Moll, on the other hand, Virginia turns out the sort of place that the Puritan nightmare envisioned — a mysterious land in which the darkest dreams of the hidden self are coaxed to the surface and acted out beneath a brightly smiling sun. She meets a planter in Virginia, marries him, and bears him a child; their life is perfectly blissful and prosperous, until she discovers that he is in fact her long-lost brother and that for years she has been lecherously reveling in an incestuous bed. All happiness destroyed, she returns to Europe, where her fortunes are, for the moment, ruined again; but she far prefers this bodily ruin to the corrupted happiness of Virginia. The vision of the New World in *Moll Flanders* is similar to that in Morton's *New English Canaan*, in which the invocation to Oedipus and Hymen promises libidinous pleasures to the revelers, although Defoe's heroine clearly goes unwillingly and unwittingly down Morton's path.

Ebenezer Cooke's *The Sotweed Factor* (London, 1708) carries this image to its humorous extreme, expatiating broadly on its humorous possibilities and employing it as a general anathema on the whole race of Anglo-Americans. The Indian appears as the American Priapus:

> But *Indians* strange did soon appear,
> In hot persuit of wounded Deer;
> No mortal Creature can express
> His wild fantastick Air and Dress;
> His painted Skin in colours dy'd,
> His sable Hair in Satchel ty'd,
> Shew'd Savages not free from Pride:
> His tawny Thighs and Bosom bare,
> Disdain'd a useless Coat to wear,
> Scorn'd Summer's Heat and Winters Air;
> His manly Shoulders such as please,
> Widows and Wives, were bath'd in Grease
> Of Cub and Bear, whose supple Oil,

> Prepar'd his Limbs 'gainst Heat or Toil.
> Thus naked Pict in battel fought,
> Or undisguis'd his Mistress sought;
> And knowing well his Ware was good,
> Refus'd to screen it with a Hood. . . .[16]

Cooke's curse upon the Americans is that they be devoured by "cannibal" slaves imported from Africa — in punishment for their having preyed, canniballike, on traveler Cooke — and that Europe abandon them to turn Indian:

> May they sustain the Fate they well deserve:
> May they turn Salvage, or as *Indians* wild,
> From Trade, Converse, and Happiness exil'd;
> Recreant to Heaven, may they adore the Sun,
> And into Pagan Superstitions run
> For Vengeance ripe ——
> May Wrath Divine then lay these Regions wast
> Where no Man's Faithful, nor a Woman chast! [17]

It is only the acculturated, the true "Americans" that Cooke hates; he exempts "any of the English gentlemen resident there." The Americans are clearly degenerate racially. Their skin has become "as tawny as a Moor"; they are monstrous figures molded "by wanton Nature . . . in Jest," rather than by God in his own image. Cooke's reaction to the white planters is identical with his reaction to the Indian he meets. His first acquaintance with the planters suggests that Maryland is "the Land of Nod; / Planted at first, when Vagrant Cain, / His Brother had unjustly slain" and came to dwell in a wigwam in America, "the first [who] in Furs and Sot-Weed dealt." [18]

Yet for all its bitter vividness of detail, Cooke's portrait of America is clearly not an attempt at critical realism, countering the booster rhetoric of colonial promoters. A second edition of the poem ("Sotweed Redivivus," 1730), published in the colonies after Cooke's emigration there, reveals a general toning-down of the earlier version's bitterness, with the substitution of a mild word of warning to tradesmen and a pleasant (if qualified) tribute: "that Land where Hospitality / Is every Planter's darling Quality." [19] The difference can be accounted for by noting the shift in Cooke's audience from English to American, from an audience prepared for one set of conventional images to one prepared for another.

Changes in American Images of Indian Character

European writers thus tended to describe the acculturation of the colonists in terms of an unholy marriage between the Christian and the savage in the wilderness. To the American Puritans this marriage metaphor was so intensely threatening as to be intolerable. The captivity narratives provided them with one acceptable metaphor, as we have seen; the Indian missionaries provided another. Just as it was acceptable for a man to be captured by Indians if that would chasten and save his Christian soul, so it was acceptable for a missionary to go willingly to the Indians for the purpose of converting them to Christianity. The missionaries conceived of their mission in both cultural-racial and religious terms: they were out not only to convert the savages but to English them. The Praying Indians, whose praises were sung by the great missionaries, John Eliot and Daniel Gookin, were mediating figures of a sort. But their goodness, if they had any, was the result of their having become English, of having left the Indian culture and acculturated to the colonial civilization — thus reversing the process that the colonists so feared.

The seventeenth-century missionaries saw the Indians as embodiments of the spirit of nature in America, the type of fallen natural man. Since they lacked acquaintance with revealed religion, the Indians' degenerate state was a heightened and exaggerated type of the fallen state of the Christianized English. Even their good friend Thomas Shepard said of them (in 1647), "What Nation of people ever so deeply degenerated since *Adams* fall as these Indians?" [20] While there is no doubt that the missionaries sincerely wished to benefit the Indians, their writings reveal a curious lack of interest in them as Indians and as men. The missionaries were chiefly interested in the Indians as converts or as a symbol that could be useful in chastising those whose interest they had most at heart: English and New England Christians.

Henry Whitfield's tract of 1651, *The Light Appearing More and More*, is representative. Addressed to the "Christian Reader," it concludes with a summary view of the Indians' symbolic function in Puritan theology. They are seen to respect authority, to seek Christ's love for its own sake, to pursue virtuous ways industriously, to have a keen sense of sin, and to be constant and attentive at services. The whites, by contrast, waste their Christian gifts, are disrespectful of civil and ecclesiastical authority, and are self-seeking, dissipated in drink, lazy, and complacent in their lack of a sense of sin. They neglect the Sabbath and sleep in meeting. In effect, the Indians have exchanged their Indian ways for English, and the English have become as swinish, lazy, and ignorant of their sin as the Indians. In case the reader has missed the point, Whitfield underlines it:

> For this my heart is sad, fearing that if the Lord do not mightily step in, the next generation will be betrayed to *Ignorance* of the *Truth*

as it is in Jesus, to Delusions and Profanenesse, . . . and that these Indians will rise up against us in judgment against us and our children at the last day. Brethren, the Lord hath no need of us, but if it please him, can carry his Gospel to the other side of the world, and make it there to shine forth in its glory, brightnesse, power and purity, and leave us in an Indian darkness.[21]

The missionaries demanded a complete change in Indian religious, social, and filial customs. Eliot urged them to abandon their "scattered" way of living and gather in communities and congregations on the model of the New England township.[22] The Indian economy of hunting and marginal farming was to become purely agrarian, since the settled life of the industrious farmer was more congenial to the Protestant ethic of hard toil in the vineyards. The taciturn braves, used to expressing religious feelings of pride and military power in communal dances, were bidden to confessional inquisitions in which the state of their souls was rigorously examined by their English ministers. Like their English brethren, they confessed their sense of sin, their loneliness before God's wrath, their sense of their own unworthiness — and, in every case, cited some characteristic form of Indian behavior as the hallmark of their sin. Under Eliot's ministry, for instance, they confessed: "I did greatly love hunting, and hated labor: but now I beleeve that word of God, which saith, Six dayes thou shalt labor: and God doth make my body strong to labor." [23] Since hunting was the calling of men and "labor" that of women in Indian societies, the converted Indian surrendered part of his manhood in accepting Christianity.

The Indian custom of mourning loudly for the dead was condemned as hellish, and the Indians were required to adopt a seemly resignation. Their abiding affection for their children — the tribe's only hope of immortality in a harsh world — was proverbial. Especially strong was the love for a son, a future warrior and vessel of his father's name. To mourn exceedingly for a dead son, however, went against the Puritan creed, as it seemed to question God's righteousness in taking the child away. Thus Eliot has Toteswamp make the following confession (citing a favored biblical text) before the committee designated by the government to examine the Indians on their progress in Christianity:

> Christ saith, He that loveth father, or mother, or wife, or Child, better than me, is not worthy of me. Christ saith, I must correct my Child, if I should refuse to doe that, I should not love Christ. . . . I am greatly grieved about these things, and now God tryeth me whether I love Christ or my Child best.[24]

To the missionaries, such a trial was not grievous. It was necessary to bring the Indian to a consciousness of the true God, unlike his old "pauaus," or medicine men, whose regime gave him "libertie to sinne." [25]

The Indian's pride in himself, his tribe, and his power was the key to his maintenance of barbarous religion. Pride of any sort had to be broken before the sinner could perceive his damnation and begin the process of conversion. Breaking the Indian's pride was therefore the first task, and among the converts it succeeded. One such convert confessed to the examining committee:

> I Confess that before I prayed, I committed all manner of sins, and served many gods: when the English came first, I going to their houses, they spake to me of your God, but when I heard of God, my heart hated it; but when they said the Devil was my God, I was angry, because I was proud. . . . I had greatly sinned against God, and had not beleeved the Word, but was proud: but then I was angry with myself, and loathed myself, and thought God will not forgive me my sins.[26]

After his pride was broken and his soul shrank onto the bosom of an English Christ, the Indian's estrangement from his tribal circle was effected. The love that bound him to his tribe turned into a wish that the tribe would die or vanish and thus resolve the conflicting demands of preacher and *pauau:*

> Before I prayed unto God, the English . . . often said unto me, Pray to God; but I having many friends who loved me, and I loved them, and they cared not for praying to God, and therefore I did not: But I thought in my heart, that if my friends should die, and I live, then I would pray to God; soon after, God so wrought, that they did almost all die. . . .[27]

Thus, while Indian conversions could be compared with New England backsliding to suit the revivalist's purposes, the ultimate significance of the missionary work was its confirmation of the eternal righteousness of English and New England institutions. The Praying Indians were to be made into copies of Englishmen. Eliot is quite open about this aspect of his mission and worked it into the catechism he gave the Indians:

Q: *How many Gods are there?*
A: There is one onely God.
Q: *Have not some Indians many Gods?*
A: They have many Gods.
Q: *How doe you know these Gods are no Gods?*
A: Before the English came we knew not but that they were Gods, but since they came we know they are no Gods.
Q: *What doe you find in the true God, that you find not in false Gods?*

A: I see in the English many things, that God is the true God.

Q: *What good things see you in the English?*

A: I see true love, that our great *Sachems* have not, and that maketh me think that God is the true God.[28]

In the eighteenth century, however, a noticeable change in the missionary tracts can be seen. David Brainerd, intended son-in-law of Jonathan Edwards, was an Indian missionary before and during the period of the Great Awakening. His journal, edited and in part reprinted by Edwards, reflects a new motivation for the missionary's going to the Indians. The older quest for the Englishing of the Indians is subordinated to the missionary's own quest for religious fulfillment. The journey to the Indian village is, for Brainerd, more of an inward than an outward journey. He sees himself as subjecting his unmalleable soul to a term of trial in order to abase his pride, humble himself, and make himself conscious of his sin and of his dependence on God for salvation. To achieve this self-knowledge, he seeks out the Indians — those symbolic types of the natural man's most degraded state — and fairly revels in the debasement he suffers by going to them:

> Saw much of my nothingness most of this day: but felt concerned that I had no more sense of my insufficiency and unworthiness. O it is sweet lying in the dust! . . . and I should have been ashamed to see the most barbarous people on earth, because I was viler, and seemingly more brutishly ignorant than they.[29]

When he preaches, his eyes are still turned inward. He worries intensely about his own state of grace, even as he expresses a vague "hope" that God will show mercy to his Indians. One Sunday he "perceived that the men were in some measure afraid of me" and longs that "some dear Christian knew my distress." Likewise, his achievement of some success among the Indians goes to solace his ego: "My heart rejoiced in my particular work as missionary; rejoiced in my necessity of self-denial in many respects; and still continued to give up myself to God, and implore mercy of him, praying incessantly. . . ."[30]

Brainerd's interest in the Indians and their community is negligible. He scarcely spends a word describing the landscape of the place, the composition of the village, or the faces and characters of his parishioners. Their symbolic character for him is identical with that given them by the Puritans and Europeans: they are savage, benighted, proud, stubborn, degenerated, inclined toward evil. What is different is Brainerd's approach to his experience with them. He is not seeking to make them English so much as to discover and exorcise the Indian in himself.

Brainerd died in 1747, and Edwards published his account of him shortly thereafter. Yet in 1753, only four years after the revivalistic fervor of the Great Awakening, Samuel Hopkins published an account of the Indian missions that — in a sharp departure from the manner and matter of Eliot, Whitfield, and Brainerd — adopted a rational and quite secular rationale for Indian missions. The fact that Hopkins's son became the founder of the neo-Edwardsian movement in New England theology makes the change even more striking. Hopkins's *Historical Memoirs Relating to the Housatunnuck Indians* begins with an account of the Reverend John Serjeant's successes among the Indians in pacifying and increasing piety in the tribe. There are no extended Indian confessions. As in the sermon-form narrative, a section on the uses of Serjeant's missionary work follows the main text, but Hopkins's application is political rather than religious. The Indians ought to be made friends "because they have the Balance of Power in their Hand." His primary plea is not for the conversion of the Indians, whether for their salvation or for the fulfillment of one's own religious duty. Rather, it is for a more pragmatic Indian policy, in which missionary work is accompanied by a change in certain odious trade practices. Self-interest as well as charity must be consulted. Further, he asserts that the Indian holds in his "Hand" the power to save or defeat the colonies. Such a statement would have been unthinkable for an orthodox Puritan of Cotton Mather's generation, for whom all victories were exclusively of God.[31]

To a large extent this change in attitude was the logical result of the colonists' extended experience in the New World. This experience, coupled with the influence of intellectual trends in Europe, worked to alter their vision of both nature and natural man, hence their concept of the Indian and their belief in their own human capacity for heroism.

Cadwallader Colden's study of the Iroquois Five Nations, published in New York in 1727 and in an expanded edition in 1747, offered an image of the Indian shaped by the new scientific thought of both Europe and America, as well as by older traditions. In Colden's view, the Indian is still the natural man, closer to Adam than are the Europeans and representing an early stage of human social, political, and religious evolution. His chief point, however, is that the Indian contains within him the form of modern Christian man, while his institutions offer examples of the earliest and most natural forms of human polity. He compares the Indians with the Romans of the heroic Republican age in their personal characteristics:

> The Five Nations are a poor Barbarous People, under the darkest *Ignorance*, and yet a bright and noble Genius shines thro' these black

> Clouds. None of the greatest Roman Hero's have discovered a greater Love to their Country, or a greater Contempt of Death than these Barbarians have done, when Life and Liberty came in Competition: Indeed, I think our Indians have out-done the Romans. . . .[32]

Moreover, he draws close parallels between their political institutions and those of the American colonies, implying that the colonial governments have, by forming in the Indians' world, taken on the best characteristics of the Indians' proto-Roman republic and combined it with the political wisdom learned since tyrants usurped the first republics of men.

A crucial point in Colden's argument is the antiquity of the Indians' system of government, which supports his contention that "the *Indians* are living Images" of the ancestors of Christendom:[33]

> The Five Nations (as their Name denotes) consist of so many Tribes or Nations joyn'd together by a League or Confederacy, like the United Provinces, without any Superiority of any one over the other. This Union has continued so long that the Christians know not the Original of it.[34]

He accepts the Lockean view that man in the state of nature was free of all political restraints and that he banded with his fellows in a social compact for their mutual protection and benefit. To this end he sacrificed some of his freedom for legal liberty, purchasing security with the acceptance of restraints. Thus the first government was the most natural form of government, since it developed directly from the situation of mankind in a hostile world and answered man's basic needs. Subsequent governmental institutions, acquiring lives of their own, independent of men and situations, usurped more authority than was necessary for the security of the members of the community — a case of art debasing rather than improving nature. Since Locke's theory provided the rationale for that era of revolution and reform in English politics, Colden's presentation of the Five Nations as a justification of both the Lockean thesis and the colonial system of government is highly significant. It points toward a developing national consciousness in the colonies and suggests the political direction which that nationalism was to take.

The Indian community is portrayed as a nearly ideal republic, governed by the ancient, wise, and brave. The power of the chiefs is derived from the people of the community. The chiefs are customarily poorer than their subjects, and they must exhibit a perfect selflessness in their conduct of affairs or be pulled down:

> Each Nation is an absolute Republic by its self, govern'd in all Publick Affairs of War and Peace by the Sachems or Old men, whose Au-

thority and Power is gain'd by and consists wholly in the Opinion the rest of the Nation have of their Wisdom and Integrity. They never execute their Resolutions by Compulsion or Force upon any of their People. Honour and Esteem are their Principal Rewards, as Shame & being Despised are their Punishments.[35]

Colden emphasizes that as this is "the most Ancient and Original Condition of almost every Nation," its institutions are "the Original Form of Government"; the patriarchal, monarchical, and other political formulas have no claim to the title.[36]

The Lockean theory employed by Colden is environmentalist in its conception of the nature of man and society. It assumes that institutions and racial characteristics are derived from the physical environment — in the Indians' and colonists' case, from the wilderness. The Puritans tacitly made the same assumption in seeing the Indian as the human embodiment of the devilish essence of the wilderness. Colden and Locke accept this evaluation of the Indian-wilderness relationship, but they see nature as productive of good rather than evil. The Indian, left to his own devices, had embarked on the road to civilization long before the coming of the Christians. This belief in the essential goodness of nature was not a late importation from England. As we have seen, Samuel Sewall associated the bounty and loveliness of the landscape with a spirit of natural goodness. John Wise, writing in 1717, went even further in asserting that the principles of good and moral government ought to be based on natural law, as exhibited in the environment. Jonathan Edwards attempted to make a philosophic reconciliation between Lockean sensationalism and Calvinist orthodoxy, and his recollection of his own conversion experience emphasized the operation of the frontier landscape on his mind, couching Lockean theory in imagery appropriate to an American experience.

Colden's Indians, like the missionaries' Praying Indians, are a mixed people, combining white and Indian traits. The difference between the two viewpoints is that where the missionary finds it necessary to impose Christian characteristics upon the essential pagan, Colden (like the Rousseauists) sees the Christian contained within the pagan, waiting to blossom in the fullness of time. The French philosophes of the eighteenth century began with assumptions very much like those of Colden and Locke and developed from them an elaborate theory of nature, anthropology, and politics. Since American contacts with the Continent were increasing throughout the century, culminating not only in the Franco-American alliance of 1778 but in a quarter-century of intensive intellectual exchange, the French use of the theory to evolve images of the characteristic American type — the American "hero" — merits investigation. Moreover, the difference between their American myth and the one evolved at the same time by the Americans suggests the nature and direction of America's continuing, gradual growing-away from Europe.

The wars of religion that characterized the seventeenth century had permanently soured many European intellectuals on the Heavenly City of orthodox Protestant and Catholic Christianity. They dreamed instead of a City of Man, founded on a humanistic code of laws derived from human experience in the world, rather than on special or traditional revelation. The growth of scientific knowledge and methodology stimulated this movement by providing clear concepts of the operation of natural processes, scientific truths which could be used to test traditional theology and political thought, challenge their natural defects, and support their natural virtues. Yet the aftereffects of the Christian past could still be discerned beneath the new wrappings. No one was more delighted than an Enlightenment philosopher whose scientific and philosophic researches confirmed his belief in the moral principles whose worth he had been taught from his childhood.

The philosophes began their investigations of human life and morals with an examination of environmental conditions, seeking to derive a new decalogue from nature. Their concepts of nature, however, tended to take on traditional shapes. Two characteristic visions of nature appeared in the literature and painting of the period, the pastoral and the sublime. The latter presented a vision of nature as an all-powerful deity, inspiring in man a sense of terror and exaltation through the exhibition of tremendous powers, dwarfing and dominating the human. Sublime landscapes were commonly composed of violently exaggerated and contorted rock formations or huge, conflicting masses of rock and water, with man a tiny victim under the great mass of nature. The New World, by reputation, was a place in which nature, untutored by the hand of civilized man, had long developed in unchecked freedom. To philosopher-scientists like Buffon, de Pauw, and Raynal, this world of pure or unameliorated nature seemed as appalling as it had to Cotton Mather. Like Mather they saw it as a force of overwhelming power, dominating and controlling man, reducing him to cannibalism, causing even Europeans to degenerate physically and morally, to become (like the Indian) a degenerate form of man.

In one crucial respect, the French writers of the degeneracy school differed from their American counterparts. Where Mather and his cohorts saw the Indian as insatiably lustful, a being of overbearing sexual power, these European writers saw him as sexually weak, cold-blooded, insensitive to pleasure or pain, passionless° — perhaps even defective in his manhood.[37] Both images, however, reflect the same fear: the European's fear of becoming powerless, sexually and in other ways, before the power of nature revealed in the wilderness. The French, at a distance, saw this in terms of sexual degeneration (through the ravages of syphilis) and loss of potency. The Puritans, living beside the wilderness, felt both its potency and its power to excite in them a desire to express their own potency of spirit and of sexuality.

Just as, in the New World, men of Church's kind grew to delight in their powers and those of the wilderness, so in Europe there was an affirmative vision of the New World contrasting with the degeneracy theory. The pastoral vision of nature saw the natural world as a garden cultivated and dominated by the mind of man or by a reasonable God. It was a vision of nature as humanized and gentled, symmetrical, orderly, and peaceful — nature as the farmer shapes it, not the wilderness encountered by an exile or outcast. It was, above all, a vision of nature as the vehicle of civilized European values, that is, a field for the physical realization of humanistic ideals. Like the sublime, the pastoral concept carried an implicit theory of man's relationship to nature. It assumed that the laws of human nature, if left to work without the hindrance of artificial institutions, would inevitably produce a "natural" society in which all of Europe's cultivation and none of its debauchery would flower. Rousseau and the physiocrats who espoused this vision also reexamined the American experience with untrammeled nature. They agreed with Buffon, de Pauw, and Mather that nature had presided over the actions of the natives of America, both red and white; but they concluded that the ultimate consequence of this was the uplifting of men, rather than their degeneration — the realization rather than the destruction of Europe's best nature.

The French conceived of America as a stage on which the drama of man's evolution was being replayed for a civilized audience hopeful of its final outcome: the creation of civilization. The New World was a kind of experimental laboratory in which revolutionary theories of human nature and divinity were being tested and proven. Nor was the result of the experiment of purely scientific or philosophic interest. The philosophes, even the most conservative, were attacking the intellectual foundations of the ancien régime in France and European Christendom. The symbolic figures of

---

° Their philosophical opponents saw in the same behavior (insensibility to pain, coolness, etc.) the exhibition of the classic virtues of the Stoics.

the good savage and the good Quaker, which occupied the center of the American stage (as the French saw it), were part of the myth that led the intellectual elite of France into its infatuation (and later disillusion) with revolution, liberty, and the unchecked expression of the popular will.

The concept of the good savage epitomizes a belief in the essential natural goodness of man. But the good savage, although his thought contains potentially all the best ideals of Christianity, is a tragic, doomed type. He is totally innocent, unaware of the capacity for evil and selfishness that lies within himself and his fellows and of the power of human institutions to acquire an inhuman power of their own. The good Quaker, on the other hand, is a figure who mediates between the natural, naïve goodness of the savage and the cold wisdom of the European. This figure was first detailed by Voltaire in his *Lettres Philosophiques* (1734) in an account of Penn's Quaker colony, which Voltaire saw as a return to a Golden Age, an arcadia.[38] Benjamin Franklin's tours of France in 1767 and 1769 reinforced the good Quaker image, as did the political *Letters* of a "Pennsylvania Farmer," John Dickinson. These two men also served to link the image with the political reforms desired by the physiocrats. It is important to note that they took their symbolic American from the cultivated, pastoral portion of the American landscape and chose to ignore the half-savage frontiersmen and barbarous Indians. The intelligent agrarian, not the libidinous, unrestrained savage, was their type of the ideal American.

The implication of the pastoral concept of nature's amenability to civilized ideals is that the closer one lives to nature, the more human and therefore civilized one will become. But Rousseau's vision came to extend beyond the simple pastoral and into the area governed by the terrible forces of superhuman nature. Here he prefigured Romanticism (as did sublime painting in general) by conceiving that a sense of all the powers of nature, including the savage and the dark, is essential to natural life — that the contemplation of a landscape in which cosmic terrors clash is as uplifting and humanizing to the soul as the contemplation of pastoral harmony. It follows, for Rousseauists, that the good Quaker can exist only in close proximity to the good savage. He must learn from the savage that he has forgotten about his own nature, even while he teaches the savage the hard-learned virtues of Christian restraint.

Americans who investigated the literature of Europe thus found two prime stereotypes of themselves and their Indian neighbors — on the one hand, the good Quaker and good savage image; on the other, the image of degeneracy, whose chief signs were intermarriage and racial amalgamation. Despite the difference between these images, certain basic patterns were identical. The most important of these was the association of the Indian with the forces of the unconscious, the suppressed drives and desires that undergulf the intellect. The proponents of the good savage theory saw this hidden self as inherently good in its motivating principles and were willing to trust its expression when its passion had been curbed a bit by intellect. The proponents of the degeneracy theory regarded the intellect as weak in comparison with the forces of the hidden mind, which they considered the dark side of human nature, the source of its bestiality. (This, as we have seen, corresponds to the Puritan vision of the wilderness and the Indian.) For the proponents of the degeneracy theory, the marriage myth-metaphor — in which a white Christian mingles his blood with the dark savage, submerging conscience and intellect in the passions of the darker self — remained characteristic and presaged the biological and moral decline of the race in America. Those who took the pastoral view of American nature conceived of the exchange as an intellectual marriage of the best of Indian life with the best of Christianity and saw the outcome as a natural movement of all Americans toward a republican-arcadian polity.

Historical Experience and the Evolution of American Heroes

American hero-figures and metaphors for the American experience were not so much derived from postulates about nature as they were from extended experience in the wilderness. The French required mediating figures like the good savage and good Quaker as a philosophical necessity. For the colonists, mediating figures were the sine qua non of their continued health. Despite their intense fear of racial blending, the psychological consequences of hanging between the old world and the new were too much to be borne for very long. Gradually the colonists adopted a more favorable attitude toward the Indians, beginning with a more objective treatment of them and ending (in 1773–1800) in the advocacy of a systematic imitation of the Indian way of life as a means to national independence and identity. This advocacy took the form of theoretical argument for the adoption of Indian tactics and even modes of government, and of literary argument in the appearance of heroes who act as mediators between the two cultures. The mediating figure of the frontier hero was not only a psychological but a social and political necessity. White Americans required such a figure in order to deal successfully with the Indians in battle, trade, and diplomacy and to live successfully in the wilderness. They also required a moral rationale for claiming and conquering Indian lands; otherwise they would simply be exercising, like the Indians, the right of the mighty over the weak. Lacking such a rationale, the Mathers had had to set their faces against expansion into the wilderness. Once it became clear that people would not be deterred from going to the woods, it became necessary (if one was not to cast out *all* the people from the church) to rationalize their going.

Each section of the colonies, however, had had a somewhat different sort of experience with the Indians; each had a distinctly different literary tradition and a different literary tie to Europe. New England's experience had been unique. Her conflict with the Indians and the French was intense and protracted, and the peculiar sense of mission that pervaded New England thought had given the conflict extensive mythic interpretation. Virtually alone among the colonies, New England had a distinctive literary tradition, based on the large number and local sales of books printed in New England for New Englanders. Under the influence of changing attitudes, even orthodox New Englanders were taking a more heroic view of their ancestors, comparing them as much with the heroes of classical epics as with passive Christian martyrs. In view of their warlike past, it was appropriate that the war narrative and the military epic should be preferred forms.

Roger Wolcott, a Puritan general and magistrate, was one of the earliest writers to employ the new attitudes, in his epic poem on the Pequot War, "A Brief Account of the Agency . . . of John Winthrop" (Boston, 1725). Like the revivalist Prince, Wolcott harked back to the distant past of New England in his search for a hero for his epic. The extent of the change in the Puritan mind can be seen in the comparison of Wolcott's epic with Benjamin Tompson's epic on King Philip's War, "New Englands Tears" (1676). Tompson's title reflects the melancholy nature of his subject; his epic is a sequence of accounts of New England's defeat and humiliation, following the structural and imagistic pattern of the captivity narrative. Wolcott's title emphasizes the "agency" of a human hero. Tompson addresses himself to the moral crisis of the moment by reference to contemporary events. Wolcott reaches into the past for symbols and heroes that shed light on a broader spectrum of time and on the broader social concerns of national identity and relations between colonials and home English. Ignoring Cotton Mather's strictures against the use of pagan mythologies and unorthodox interpretations of the American wilderness (like the legend-making of Benjamin Church), Wolcott draws his structuring metaphors from Greek and Roman classics and the conventional European images of the New World.

Wolcott was considered a reasonably orthodox Puritan, a respected member of the upper class, who later made a name as a general during Sir William Pepperrell's Louisbourg expedition in 1744–45. By the time Wolcott wrote his poem, it had become painfully obvious that the Puritan experiment had failed in its effort to convert old England to that form of Christianity. Instead, the English had turned on New England with lectures condemning their politics and religious intolerance. Wolcott, far from protesting this state of affairs, adopted English literary values and conventions, departed from Puritan "plain style," and went so far as to portray John Winthrop, Jr., solemnly agreeing with the merry monarch, Charles II, on basic religious and political principles. Although Wolcott used native subject material (the war, the Indians, the landscape), he dressed his characters in accordance with European literary fashions to render his subject acceptable.

The subject of the poem is Governor Winthrop's embassy of 1662, seeking from Charles a royal charter to protect Connecticut's liberties and form of government. Political questions concerning the definition of the proper roles of colonial and English governments were to come increasingly into the fore as the eighteenth century progressed. Conflicts of interest and policy between England and America were to force Americans to define ever more clearly their own political aims and ideals and to stimulate attempts at defining the American nationality. Yet Puritan Winthrop and Anglo-Catholic Charles meet in Wolcott's poem without any doctrinal rancor or sense of religious division. Both share the same political ideals, and this agreement is all that is necessary for the total reconciliation of Puritanism and the head of the English prelacy.

Agreement between the Puritan and the Anglican in Wolcott's poem extends even to their perception of America, for Winthrop's "justification" of Connecticut takes the form of an Indian war narrative. The narrative Winthrop tells is not, however, the typical Puritan sermon-account. The thesis of the poem is not theological but political, and there is no Puritan humility but rather an inflated sense of epic grandeur. Hubbard refused to give Indian conflicts the name of "war" in his officially authorized *Narrative of the Troubles with the Indians* of 1677, preferring "outrage" or "murder" as appropriate to the subhuman nature of the Indian. Wolcott does not boggle at comparing the Pequot War to the battles before Troy.

Winthrop begins his account to Charles with a description of the American landscape from which all elements of the devilish have been expelled and replaced by pastoral deities of the Golden Age:

> After the *Meadows* thus have took their Place.
> The Champion Plains draw up to fill the space.

Fair in their Prospect, Pleasant, Fruitful, Wide,
Here *Tellus* may be seen in all his Pride . . .
In shady Vales the Fruitful *Vine* o're whelms,
The Weaving Branches of the bending Elms.

Within the Covert of these shady Boughs,
The Loving *Turtle* and his Lovely Spouse
From Bough to Bough in deep Affection move,
And with Chast Joy reciprocate their Love.
. . . .
Zephirus Whispers a Delightful Air.
. . . .
The Muses hence their ample Dews Distill.
. . . .
More than was feigned from the twy topt Hill.
. . . .
Or *Latmos* which *Diana* stops upon,
There to salute her dear *Endimion*.[39]

Just as the wilderness is transformed into Arcadia to suit the fancy of an
English monarch, so the "greazy Lout" Sassacus is transformed into the
head of a "Kingdom" or "Empire":

Of the brave *Pequot* Nation he was Head,
And with such Conduct had their Armies led
That by the Power of his Martial Bands,
He had subjected all the Neighbouring Lands.
. . . .
Great was his Glory, greater still his Pride,
Much by himself and others Magnify'd.[40]

Thus one of the first steps by which Wolcott justifies his native land is a
glorification of the Indian and the landscape. But their beauty depends, in
Wolcott's poem, on their resemblance to a European Arcadia and the roy-
alty of classical antiquity.

The Puritan also is transformed into a Christian Aeneas or Ulysses,
motivated by a drive for personal fame rather than a zeal for virtuous self-
abasement before God. Wolcott has John Mason (the same whose narrative
Prince reprinted as an example of the virtue of the fathers) harangue his
troops in a most un-Puritan manner:

Looking on his Cheerful Soldiery,
True son of Mars, bred up in Brittany;
Each firmly bent to Glorify his Name
By Dying bravely in a Bed of Fame.[41]

The last line here contains a conventional conceit on the word *death*, which compares the *petite mort* of the lover in sexual fulfillment with death on the battlefield and so equates battle with bed. This is hardly an analogy Increase Mather would have drawn. In addition to this blood-wedding metaphor, Wolcott plays with the notion of cannibalizing the Indians by partaking of a wilderness Eucharist. He describes Hooker as having exhorted the troops to attack the Indians — and "they shall be your bread." [42]

The passage continues with Mason's address, in which he cries, "The more the Danger is the more's the Fame," and "Leave the Success to Him whose boundless *Powers* / Will doubtless bless so just a War as ours." [43] Mason himself, as we have seen, refused to publish his account during his own lifetime because it seemed immodest and sinfully proud to claim personal "Fame." Nor would so devout a Puritan have admitted a belief that God would "doubtless" favor him: God's favor is withheld or granted according to His arbitrary will, and it is "complacent" in a man to be sure that God will prosper him in any given endeavor.

Wolcott carries his conceptions through to their logical conclusions. Just as he glorifies Sassacus as a king, he refers to the Pequot wigwam as a "stately Palace." [44] The firing of the fort creates a "dreadfull Emblem of the flames of Hell," [45] but Wolcott is far from asserting that Mason is here the instrument of divine wrath. Instead of dwelling (like Benjamin Tompson) on the "frying" of the heathen, Wolcott attempts to excite the sympathies of the reader by again playing with the love-death conceit. In this instance he makes a rather macabre comparison between the love-burnings of a young Indian couple, the fire of the sexual union, and their incineration in the burning fort. A significant point in this incident is that Wolcott does not burn his Indians and send them to hell. Rather, his consumed lovers ascend from the fort, supported on wings of sentimental pathos: "Then souls united both at once repair, / Unto their place appointed thro' the air." [46] No mention is made of the postbattle massacre of the Pequot women and children by the Indian allies and the Puritan soldiers — the consummation of the opposition of the two races in a moment of shared violence.

The conclusion of the piece, corresponding in its placement and function to the uses section of the sermon-narrative, is a political (rather than a religious) application of the tale. Charles grants Winthrop his charter and recites the ethical maxim that public office is a civil trust requiring action in the public interest. The finale is a lecture in political ethics to the people of Connecticut:

> Then, let the Freemen of your Corporation
> Always be ware of the Insinuation,

Of those which always Brood Complaint and Fear,
. . . .
. . . these [heretics] outdo him in that way of evil
And will for God's sake play the Devil.
And Lastly, Let Your New *English* Multitude,
Remember well a Bond of Gratitude
Will Lye on them and their Posterity
To bear in mind their *Freedom* came by *Thee*.[47]

Wolcott's image of the New World is drawn from the extensive vocabulary of conventional images and symbols that had, since the Renaissance, been the basis of European visions of the New World. The overtones of a pastoral Golden Age, the association of the love-death conceit with the dark people of the wilderness, the chivalric imagery — all belong to this tradition. The seventeenth-century Puritans modified these traditional images to make them conform to the Calvinist conception of the universe and to enforce the vision of an evil, inimical wilderness that their peculiar religious and social order seemed to require. Wolcott, in harking back to the older European tradition, translates the Puritan vision of America's promise and threat back into conventional, secular terms. Puritan anxieties about the traumatic experience of emigration, which earlier generations had dealt with through the intensely religious captivity myth, are peacefully adjusted in Wolcott's poem by means of politics and an agreement among soldiers and gentlemen.

The middle colonies shared something of the Puritan heritage that shaped Wolcott's work. Philadelphia, their cultural capital, was a Quaker town, founded by a radical offshoot of the Puritan movement. Intellectual emigrants from the Puritan rigors of New England, like Benjamin Franklin, reinforced the Puritan aspect of the city. Philadelphia was, however, a cosmopolitan town, tied to Europe by trade, shipping, and politics. Unlike the fugitives who settled New England, Pennsylvania Quakers and other citizens belonged to a proprietary colony, whose rulers generally resided in England. Pennsylvania also differed from New England in its relations with and attitudes toward the Indians. Quaker relations with the Indians had, since the time of Penn, been excellent. Penn and his heirs had enjoyed a deserved reputation for fairness in dealing with the Indians, and the pacifist sympathies of the Quaker settlers made it clear that the Pennsylvanians posed no military threat. Pennsylvania, however, was never unalloyedly Quaker, and Quaker strength declined as emigrants from Europe and the north swelled its population. The strain of Quakerism, however, remained strong, partly through Quaker strength in the Philadelphia schools and printing trade, partly through the political dominance of Quaker proprietors and the Quaker party in the legislature.

John Woolman spoke for the best of the Quaker spirit in his journal, published in 1774. Woolman was a Quaker missionary and itinerant preacher, an early advocate of abolition and a spokesman for reconciliation with the Indians. His approach to an Indian town where he intended to work for conversion was in sharp contrast to the egocentricity and sense of superiority evident in the missionary journals of Brainerd and his Puritan colleagues. Believing that the Indians were men like himself and hence vessels containing the inner light — the knowledge of God and his expression in love — Woolman came to learn as well as teach, to receive as well as give:

> I was led to think on the Nature of the Exercise which hath attended me: Love was the first Motion, and then a Concern arose to spend some Time with the *Indians*, that I might feel and understand their Life, and the Spirit they live in, if haply I might receive some Instruction from them, or they be in any Degree helped forward by my following the Leadings of Truth amongst them: And, as it pleased the Lord to make Way for my going at a Time when the Troubles of War were increasing, and when, by Reason of much wet Weather, Travelling was more difficult . . . I looked upon it as a more favourable Opportunity to Season my Mind, and bring me into a nearer Sympathy with them.[48]

Like the Puritans, Woolman saw in the Indian an image of the natural man: man in his most basic, primitive, prerevelationary form. Unlike the Puritans, he believed that natural man to be the vessel of the inner light and undertook, in this journey to the Indians, a pilgrimage to his own sources. Thus he prepared himself during his journey by projecting himself imaginatively — by attempting to feel with the Indians, to share their sympathies and perceptions, to bring himself into a more profound intimacy with and adjustment to the conditions of their world. The adjustment would, of course, be temporary, since his mission was to redeem the Indians, to develop the seeds of grace that God had planted in their red souls. Nevertheless, the fact that he conceived of the first step in this process of conversion as an adjustment of his Christian mind to the Indians' world marks a striking departure from traditional missionary attitudes.

Woolman spoke for a relatively small and special segment of Pennsylvania society, which combined sincere Quaker piety with enlightened attitudes on politics, social action, and racial and religious tolerance. Non-Quakers from Puritan New England and non-Puritan old England constituted the majority of Pennsylvania's population and predominated in the outlying countryside and frontier. Quaker intolerance and insensitivity exhibited themselves in the political strife that divided these people from the proprietors and their partisans, the Philadelphia Quakers, whose political ascendency, regardless of voting strength, was guaranteed by proprietary rule. For political and economic as well as religious reasons, the Pennsylvania legislature refused to defend the frontiers against Indian raids or to grant the frontier towns permission and means to defend themselves.

The spokesman for non-Quaker Pennsylvania was Benjamin Franklin. This chief exemplar of Philadelphian intellectuality was a transplanted New Englander who had come to Philadelphia in his young manhood. His wide-ranging interests and later diplomatic career made him an intellectual go-between for European and American thinkers. In Franklin the religion-charged world vision of the Puritans was tempered by the cosmopolitan rationality of the great seaport city and mingled with the strains of Quaker tradition, English deism, and Continental philosophy. His use of literary forms was typical of his relationship to Puritan thought. His autobiography, for instance, is in the genre of Puritan confessional narratives; but where Shepard and Edwards focus on the emotional experience of their conversion, Franklin details the rational processes by which he has culled secular lessons from experience and achieved moral and intellectual wisdom.

His treatment of the Indians also bears striking resemblance to Puritan writings, but the anathematic spirit has been tempered by the Quaker Pennsylvanian tradition of a long-standing peace with the Indians. Military strife provides metaphors for the New England writer, but Franklin takes his metaphors from a milder, more gradual form of conquest. Evolutionary development, rather than destruction, will make the American land amenable to the colonists and less so to the Indians.

In 1749, Franklin accompanied the Pennsylvania commissioners to treat with the Indians at Carlisle. After the treaty rum was distributed and the Indians had become drunk, the commissioners went down to see what their revels were like:

> We found they had made a great bonfire in the middle of the square; they were all drunk, men and women, quarrelling and fighting. Their dark-colour'd bodies, half naked, seen only by the gloomy light of the bonfire, running after and beating one another with firebrands, accompanied by their horrid yellings, form'd a scene most resembling our ideas of hell that could well be imagin'd.[49]

Franklin's attitude owes much to the traditional imagery of the captivity narratives and less to the kind of experience and values espoused by such as Benjamin Church. Church described Indian dances with affection and amusement, noting that fat Awashonks led her tribe in dancing "in a foaming Sweat." Mrs. Rowlandson's vision was very much like Franklin's: "Oh the roaring, and singing, and danceing, and yelling of those black creatures in the night . . . made the place a lively resemblance of hell." Like Mather, Franklin concludes that the Indians must be destroyed — but by the natural consequences of their love of rum, not by their sinfulness or transgression against God and his people, nor by the criminal vigilantism of Indian-killers like the Paxton Boys:

> And, indeed, if it be the design of Providence to extirpate these Savages in order to make room for cultivators of the earth, it seems not improbable that rum may be the appointed means. It had already annihilated all the tribes who formerly inhabited the sea-coast.[50]

The conquest of the New World, in Franklin's imagery, is a natural or an economic process, not the result of a willful march into the wilderness. The farmers who cultivate the soil naturally seek empty lands, and the savages' love of rum has emptied their former lands. What could be more righteous than that the zone of cultivation should expand into formerly savage precincts? Thus the farmer, like the Puritan captive, is a mediating figure between the American wilderness and the civilized world. Christianity and civilization are strongest in his mind; he does not seek the Indian in his wilderness. Rather, he waits until the land is free of Indians and open for cultivation. Once the curse is off, there is no harm in his seeking out and farming the land. Just as the Puritan captive is drawn into the wilderness unwillingly, passively obedient to the will of God, Franklin's farmer enters in obedience to the "will" or the force of natural process. The Puritan combination of acceptance of the wilderness and a fearful reserve of full commitment is thus translated by Franklin into terms amenable to the eighteenth century.

William Byrd of Westover, Virginia, spoke for the southern colonies, as Woolman and Franklin did for the middle and Wolcott for New England. Unlike Franklin, however, Byrd's literary roots were in London rather than in the New World. Literature was a pervasive presence in New England, and the Boston presses turned out metaphorical treatments of American history for a wide, literate, New England audience. In the South the level of literacy was lower, the native presses fewer and not concerned with printing literature by Americans, and the literary audience more limited.[51] It was characteristic of the South that Byrd's work should circulate only in manuscript in the upper circle of Virginian society [52] and that when he should consider publication, he should think of London. Most books read and written by southerners were printed abroad, and the southerners' favorite writers were not the homegrown ideologists and frontiersmen who were read in New England and New York.[53] Fiction and poetry for Byrd meant the novels of Defoe, the verse of Pope and Dryden, and the ancient classics. Southern poets writing of the New World dealt with it in terms imitative of the English poets, most frequently adopting the pose of the urbane poet-wit, mocking the rusticity and crudeness of America. Less frequently they adopted the equally inappropriate pose of the pastoral poet, romanticizing the landscape by describing it awry. Beyond these literary imitations, the southerner's writing on the New World was in the form of factual history or description, rather than Puritan-like sallies into cosmic metaphor.

"Southern verse-writers," Kenneth Silverman observes, "rarely idealized the country or, until the mid-eighteenth century, indulged in grand speculations over what it might become. Usually Southern poets either wrote about matters unrelated to the New World, or else they dispraised it. Southern dislike for the country radically distinguishes Southern verse from Northern." [54] This "dislike" was different in quality from the fears and antipathies of the Puritans for the wilderness. The Puritans saw in the wilderness an incalculable potential to produce good or evil, a true City of God or a true City of Satan; they feared and loved both the physical wilderness and the Faustian dreams they projected upon it. The southern antipathy for the wilderness was a kind of snobbery, reflecting a desire to associate their culture with that of London by criticizing the country "provinces" in which they had perforce to dwell. (Thus Ebenezer Cooke could gain the favorable attention of Marylanders by making a few strategic changes in *The Sotweed Factor*, while retaining its general spirit of humorous denigration.) Southerners affected unconcern or humorous annoyance with their surroundings when in a literary mood. When speaking of business and of their real concerns in the wilderness, they spoke in the matter-of-fact tone appropriate to purely economic transactions.

Yet these factual accounts and descriptions of territory acquired, through repetition, as distinct a formulaic structure as the Puritan sermon-narratives. Accounts such as Beverley's *History and Present State of Virginia*, Lawson's account of Carolina, and Hewatt's history of Carolina and Georgia commonly began with a description of the landscape and a sketch of its agricultural prospects. This was followed by a section dealing with the colony's settlement, another on its government, and a final section describing the local animals and the local Indians. Unlike the Puritan accounts, these studies of the Indian dealt in detail with the Indians' character, their religious and social institutions, and their manner of hunting and fighting. The portrayals were low-keyed, reasonably free of the anathematic spirit of the Puritan chroniclers.

Thus when Byrd composed his *Histories of the Dividing Line* (an account of a surveying expedition to the backwoods), he had two different literary traditions to draw on. The first was that of the historical-geographical account, which possessed a distinct form but no ruling metaphor. The second was the English tradition of the southern imitators, which was avowedly literary and dealt extensively with image and metaphor but which offered no appropriate language to deal with Byrd's subject. The account which emerged was an amalgam of the two traditions, in which Byrd stands as a peculiar kind of mediator between civilization and savagery.

The *Histories* are actually two manuscripts, one labeled "Secret History of the Dividing Line." Both were circulated in Virginia, the latter presumably to a circle of intimates. The "Secret History" was probably composed first in 1728 and reflects Byrd's first attempt to order his experiences for literary expression. A salient characteristic of this private version is the novelistic altering of names of personages to reflect humorously on their characters. Byrd himself is referred to as Steddy, the hotheaded Richard Fitz-William is Firebrand, an inquisitive Carolinian is Puzzlecause, and a boring preacher is Dr. Humdrum. Byrd's attitude toward the frontiersmen in the "Secret History" is quite favorable, and the lechery of the gentlemen surveyors is amusingly dealt with. In the more public record of the "History of the Dividing Line," however, he adopts the pejorative image of the frontiersmen that had been conventional in European literature since at least the beginning of the century. Moreover, he parodies the conventions of the historical-geographical description and draws on direct experience of Indian life to exercise his wit on various stereotypes of the Indians. He adopts the conventional metaphor of the settlement of the wilderness as an act of love, a sexual wedding of the civilized man and the Indian. He acknowledges the threat of degeneration in such an act; but far from regarding this with the distaste of the Puritan or the European, he toys with its attractive possibilities.

His *History of the Dividing Line* begins with a wittily irreverent narrative of the discovery and settlement of Virginia. He compares the sudden fashion for American voyages with the fashion for pilgrimaging to the Holy Land, but he mocks this metaphor so dear to the Puritans by terming such voyages "Quixot Adventures" and a "Modish Frenzy." Nor are the American pilgrims saintly by any means; they are, rather, "Adventurers . . . Idle and extravagant." The great failure of the colonists, in Byrd's account, is their failure to convince the Indians of their friendship by the only possible means, that of intermarriage. Such alliances would have been "prudent" and helped to civilize and convert the savages, could the colonists "have brought their Stomachs to embrace [it]." [55] While acknowledging that it would take "stomach" to marry with the savages, Byrd immediately begins to expatiate on the pleasures of such an alliance, as well as its political and religious benefits. An essential part of his argument is the equation of the Indians with the colonists themselves as heathen:

> The Indians are generally tall and well-proportion'd, which may make full Amends for the Darkness of their Complexions. Add to this, that they are healthy & Strong, with Constitutions untainted by Lewdness, and not enfeebled by Luxury. Besides, Morals and all considered, I cant think the Indians were much greater Heathens than the first Adventurers, who, had they been good Christians, would have had the Charity to take this only method of converting the Natives to Christianity. For, after all that can be said, a sprightly Lover is the most prevailing Missionary that can be sent amongst these, or any other Infidels. [56]

The French, despite the idolatrous nature of their religion, have employed this very means to good effect among the Indians. The New England Puritans, who carried the aversion to intermarriage to extremes, are seen as suffering more by the hands of the Indians as a consequence:

> These Saints conceiving the same Aversion to the Copper Complexion of the Natives . . . would, on no Terms, contract Alliances with them, afraid perhaps, like the Jews of Old, lest they might be drawn into Idolatry by those Strange Women.
> Whatever disgusted them I cant say, but this false delicacy creating in the Indians a Jealousy that the English were ill affected towards them, was the Cause that many of them were cutt off, and the rest exposed to various Distresses. [57]

The pragmatic ground for intermarriage is further developed by Byrd: intermarriage would give the English more right and title to the land they were claiming, since it would come as a marriage portion.

Byrd reiterates his belief in marriage between Indian and white at the beginning and at the end of his account of his march into the Indians' country, reiterating the theme of sexual merging or marriage as a metaphor for his experience in the land. Unlike the Europeans of the degeneracy school and the Puritans, Byrd reiterates the belief that intermarriage will improve or whiten the Indians, rather than darken the whites:

Nor wou'd the Shade of the Skin [of the children of Indian-white unions] have been any reproach at this day; for if a Moor may be washt white in 3 Generations, Surely an Indian might have been blancht in two.[58]

Had the English done this at the first Settlement of the Colony, the Infidelity of the Indians had been worn out at this Day, with their Dark Complexions, and the Country had swarm'd with People more than it does with Insects. . . . All Nations of Men have the same Natural Dignity, and we all know that very bright Talents may be lodg'd under a very dark Skin. The principal Difference between one People and another proceeds only from the Different Opportunities of Improvement.[59]

Beneath his banter, there is serious matter in Byrd's argument. His statements provide an accurate hint of the racial theory that was to dominate American thought in the eighteenth and nineteenth centuries and influence the slavery question as well as the Indian problem. His assumption is that the dark races are departures from the ideal model of humanity, their outer differences corresponding to a characteristic barbarism, brutality, stupidity, or "Infidelity." In much the same way, the French assumed that beneath the skin of the good savage lurks the spirit of the good Quaker — that is, beneath the surface of a dark, troubled nature there moves a divine human intelligence, like their own in kind if different in quality. Buffon, de Pauw, and the American proponents of the "degenerate" view of the Indians held a contrary theory: that racial characteristics, once established, are as immutable as the lines that divide the species. The consequence of intermarriage must infallibly be (in this view) the degeneration of the species. In the crucial decades before the Civil War, southern thought shifted emphatically away from the views of Byrd and Rousseau, and even the northern leaders of the antislavery movement were strongly affected by the fear of racial amalgamation. But between 1720 and 1790 the trend in American thought was not only toward acceptance of the Indian as a potential racial brother but toward identification with the Indian as the hallmark of American nationality. In the light of this development, Byrd's use of the marriage metaphor is highly significant. That metaphor — like the hunter myth of Benjamin Church, the Puritan captivity mythology, the traditions of the New England Indian-war narratives, and the agrarian thought of Franklin — was to become part of the Boone legend that would dominate American mythology in the formative years of nationhood.

Byrd's surveying expedition takes him deep into the frontier, moving from the coast westward along the Carolina-Virginia line into the Indians' country. As the surveyors leave the settled land, Bird's narrative becomes increasingly concerned with the problem of amalgamating the Indian and the English ways of life. European stereotypes come to the fore, and the frontiersmen are seen as racially degenerate, sickly, lazy, lustful, and stimulating lust. Yet simultaneously a countertendency operates to convey a sense of the promise inherent in the landscape. This latter tendency is significant; but by far the greater emphasis is placed on a critical, satirical view of the frontiersmen, such as would please an audience raised on the conventional literary treatments of the frontier.

As the surveyors penetrate the land, it becomes progressively more difficult, more ugly, more pestilential. The darkening of the landscape is paralleled by their meetings with a series of erotic figures and temptations, each one more vile than the last. The first of these is a self-styled "Hermit," who is actually a Maroon, or escaped slave, living in the Indian fashion with a "wanton Female." Their home is "a Bower . . . in the Indian fashion"; their food is gathered from the abundance of nature. Byrd's comment refers us to the French conception of the good savage, who differs from these only in his innocence, his inability to know the degradation of his condition: "Thus did these Wretches live in a dirty state of Nature, and were mere Adamites, Innocence only excepted." [60] The next meeting is with another couple who have fallen from civilization into barbarous habits and superstition — a fortune-teller and "a Young Wench he had carry'd off." [61]

Eros's power over the surveying party itself waxes as they move deeper into the wilderness. On several occasions members of the party attempt (with varying success) to ravish women who come their way. Byrd and Shoebrush (the "Secret History" reveals) take a walk in the woods and meet with "a Dark Angel" who "surpriz'd us with her Charms." Byrd is smitten, and Shoebrush is excited to the point of violence:

> Her complexion was a deep Copper, so that her fine Shape & regular Features made her appear like a Statue in Bronze done by a masterly Hand. Shoebrush was smitten at the first glance, and examined all her neat Proportions with a critical Exactness. She struggled just enough to make her Admirer more eager, so that if I had not been there, he wou'd have been in Danger of carrying his Joke a little too far.[62]

In this instance, as in others, Byrd's is the voice of reason and moderation. He jestingly decries extreme aversion for the dark races of the woods, but when placed in close proximity to them, he resists the temptation to respond to their darkness with the darkness of his own lust. Lesser men — a category to which Byrd relegates most frontiersmen — lack his self-restraint and are debased by their life in the wilderness. The women are sallow or sandy in complexion and inclined to lechery; they strongly tempt the surveyors at every turn. The men are lazy and as shiftless as Indians in matters of religion and industry:

> Some, who pique themselves upon more Industry than their Neighbours, will, now and then, . . . cut down a Tree whose Limbs are loaden with the Moss aforemention'd. The trouble wou'd be too great to Climb the Tree in order to gather this Provender, but the shortest way (which in this country is counted the best) is to fell it, just like the Lazy Indians. . . . The Men, for their Parts, just like the Indians, impose all the Work upon the poor Women.[63]

Carolina itself, by virtue of its agricultural potential, is a land of promise that is wasted on the frontier "lubbers." Yet Byrd sees some promise in them too, recalling that imperial Rome began with just such a group of outcasts and fugitives from justice as compose the Carolina settlers.[64]

Since they are in the wilderness, they must hunt the Indians' natural food in the Indian manner. Byrd is aware of Indian and frontier animal myths and begins to subscribe to some of them. One of the hunters kills a bear, an animal sacred to the Indians — and, in fact, worshiped in ancient Europe and Britain — and the company partakes of its flesh. The bear was an old god of fertility and sexual vigor, and Byrd reports that " 'tis too rich for a Single Man, and enclines the Eater of it strongly to the Flesh. Inasmuch that whoever makes a Supper of it, will certainly Dream of a Woman, or the Devil, or both." [65] Such dreams would naturally have been sought by Indian worshipers; and certainly the Puritans' horror of men who ate the meat and bread of the wilderness expressed itself in their nightmares of witch-women, or the devil, or both. But Byrd's reaction to wilderness meat is hardly puritanical. After the killing of a wild turkey, Byrd in a mood of high spirits founds the Order of Ma-ooty, an Indian word meaning "a Turkey's Beard." Half-mockingly, he speaks of it as a "religious" order as well as an order of knighthood; the travelers are given badges, or totems, symbolic of their place in the new order.[66]

Although they neglect their own worship somewhat, Byrd and his fellows spend one Sunday examining an Indian named Bearskin on the particulars of his religion, which they find to contain "the three Great Articles of Natural Religion: The Belief of a God; The Moral Distinction betwixt Good and Evil; and the Expectation of Rewards and Punishments in Another World." Although Byrd finds the Indian notion of heaven "a little

Gross and Sensual," he feels that such beliefs are inevitable "in a People that are contented with Nature as they find Her" and have not the light of revelation.[67] Yet though he thus sets himself apart from the Indians, his sympathies are reflected in his easy adjustment to Indian customs and ideas and his respect for the light of nature.

Byrd's affection for the Virginia landscape, revealed in the lovingly detailed descriptions of it in his diary, does not extend to the landscape of the Carolina Indian country. As the surveyors proceed, they pass through the Dismal Swamp, a veritable Slough of Despond, whose chief source of beauty is also the source of its corrupted, malign air:

> It had one Beauty, however, that delighted the Eye, tho' at the Expense of all the other Senses: the Moisture of the Soil preserves a continual Verdure, and makes every Plant an Evergreen, but at the same time the foul Damps ascend without ceasing, corrupt the Air, and render it unfit for Respiration. Not even a Turkey-Buzzard will venture to fly over it, no more than the Italian Vultures will over the filthy Lake Avernus, or the Birds in the Holy Land over the Salt Sea, where Sodom and Gomorah formerly stood.[68]

As with the land, so with the people. The surveyors invite a "Tallow-faced Wench" to drink with them, "and when they had rais'd her in good Humour, they examined all her hidden Charms, and play'd a great many gay Pranks." The fair exterior soon yields signs of foulness and self-indulgence, and the erotic game becomes a trifle disgusting: "While Firebrand, who had the most Curiosity, was ranging over her sweet Person, he pick't off several Scabs as big as Nipples, the Consequence of eating too much Pork." [69]

After passing through the Dismal Swamp, the surveyors reach an Indian village where, presumably, Byrd can put his theory of Indian relations to the test. It is worth noting that while the "Secret History" recounts a number of erotic passages before the arrival at the Indian village, the more widely circulated text mentions rather few — a fact which gives the events in the Indian camp a special emphasis. The travelers enter the camp, saluted by the cries of the women and the dismal howling of the men, and are treated to a war dance. Unlike Franklin and the New Englanders, Byrd sees no resemblance between the savage dance and the capering of demons in hell. He observes their menacing gestures with the confidence that these are but ceremonies, rather childish ones at that, which pose no threat to his strength.

At this point the women appear, and Byrd describes them carefully, choosing his metaphors to emphasize the erotic potential of the situation:

They were Wrapt in their Red and Blue Match-coats, thrown so Negligently about them, that their Mahogany Skins appear'd in Several Parts, like the Lacedaemonian Damsels of Old. Their Hair was breeded with white and Blue Peak, and hung gracefully in a large Roll upon their Shoulders.

This peak Consists of Small Cylinders cut out of a Conque-Shell . . . Strung like Beads . . . the Blue being of much greater Value than the White, for the same reason that Ethiopian Mistresses in France are dearer than French, because they are more Scarce. . . . Tho' their Complexions be a little Sad-Colour'd, yet their Shapes are very Strait and well proportioned. Their Faces are Seldom handsome, yet they have an Air of Innocence and Bashfulness, that with a little less dirt wou'd not fail to make them desirable. Such charms might have had their full Effect upon Men who had been so long deprived of female conversation, but that the whole Winter's Soil was so crusted on the Skins of those Dark Angels, that it requir'd a very strong Appetite to approach them.[70]

In the end, it is not racial scruples nor even a gentlemanly aversion to uncleanliness that keeps Byrd from the "Copper Colour'd" beauties. Rather, the scarcity of available women prevents the Indians from offering the whites the accustomed hospitality:

We were unluckily so many, that they cou'd not well make us the Complement of Bed-fellows, according to the Indian Rules of Hospitality, tho' a grave Matron whisper'd one of the Commissioners very civilly in the Ear, that if her Daughter had been but one year Older, she should have been at his Devotion.[71]

The "Secret History" reveals that some of the men did dally with the Indian girls and that Byrd himself took the lack of bedfellows "unkindly." [72]

Byrd then discourses on the failure of the English to Christianize the Indians and returns to his earlier theme: that marriage with the Indians, since it is the sole method of keeping them friendly and converting them to Protestant Christianity, ought to be an English policy, instead of the present situation in which cohabitation with squaws is restricted to the character of a passing debauchery for wandering surveyors. At length, after setting up their marks at the extreme border of the colonies, which Byrd likens to Hercules setting up his pillars at the western edge of the ancient world, the surveyors make their way home.

Franklin and Byrd, along with John Mason in Wolcott's poem, were the American alternatives to the European image of the good Quaker, the figure mediating between civilization and the wilderness. Wolcott's Mason was a Puritan rendered heroic by the ambience of a martial epic, complete with metaphorical allusions to the heroes of pagan mythology. Franklin, although he spoke for the farmers of the Quaker Penn's colony, was no good Quaker (although he played that role while traveling in France). Like Wolcott he saw the English presence in the wilderness as a direct confrontation with the Indians. Unlike Voltaire and Rousseau, who were enchanted by a stable tableau of good Quaker juxtaposed with good savage, the practical Franklin saw the situation as dynamic and changing, with the English farmer naturally replacing the Indian by virtue of his moral and economic superiority.

Byrd was also a mediating figure, who portrayed himself as a hero in the wilderness — the man who controls all situations, imposes restraint on whites and Indians, passes judgment on the mores of Indians and frontiersmen, and speaks with the voice of reason. He was, in character, exactly what his stylized, quasi-fictional name in the "Secret History" said he was: Steddy the Chief Surveyor, observant, orderly, and self-possessed. Unlike Franklin and Wolcott, he sought a consummation of sorts in the wilderness; but even he placed strict limitations on the extent to which he would merge with the wilderness. Marriage with the Indian must be undertaken — but for the proper reasons, for John Rolfe's reasons. In this way the Indian could be both Christianized and whitened in the course of two generations. Otherwise, the fate of the Carolina lubbers — sallow-faced, lecherous, indigent, diseased — awaited us all. Racial degradation would redden and darken, instead of blanching, the American skin.

CHAPTER **8**

A Gallery of Types:
The Evolution of Literary Genres
and the Image of the American
(1755–1785)

> What then is the American, this new man? He is either an Euro-
> pean, or the descendant of an European, hence that strange mix-
> ture of blood, which you will find in no other country. . . . *He* is an
> American, who, leaving behind him all his ancient prejudices and
> manners, receives new ones from the new mode of life he has em-
> braced.
>
> Crèvecoeur, *Letters from an American Farmer*

THE sermons, tracts, and narratives that grew out of the last French and
Indian War (1755–64) reveal some of the changes that had taken place in
American thought since the turn of the eighteenth century. The reactions
of New England, Pennsylvanian, and Virginian writers reflect emerging nationalism and, simultaneously, a distinct sectional orientation. The trend
toward human heroes is evident; but still more striking are the emergence
of the Indian as the model for an American heroism and the tendency of
writers to set this American-model hero against the British model. Coincident with this rehabilitation of the Indian is a renewed interest in the wilderness landscape. Before 1716, captivities and Indian-Puritan battles
were depicted against a generalized, nearly featureless background. By
1784, when John Filson published his life of Daniel Boone, landscape description was a major interest, and nature was functioning in literature as a
godlike agent for the regeneration of man. This trend involved the development of new types of literature, with forms and conventions suited to
the new interest in specialized study of the Indian and the landscape.

At the same time there was a revival of interest in the writing and
reading of fiction. Before the mid-eighteenth century, fiction as such was

frowned on as a diversion unworthy of the pious. Handbooks, sermons, captivity narratives, and tracts for children dominate F. L. Mott's list of popular, best-selling books from 1660 to 1740. After this period, novels by Richardson and Defoe became popular, especially in the 1770s. American writers of fiction, however, did not figure as best sellers until the nineteenth century.[1] Some American writers did attempt setting American history in traditional literary forms, such as the drama and the epic poem, in an effort to impress Europe with the signs of cultural strength. But neither the reading public nor the book printers of London and the colonies expected fiction of American authors: it was out of their literary tradition and, in any case, liable to reflect provincialism.

Within the traditional, nonfiction genres—the Indian war narrative, the captivity, the travel narrative—the new interest in fiction produced a gradually increasing tendency to substitute imagination for experience, to offer a fictionalized, sensationalized account as a true narrative. Two results of this increased plumbing of the imagination were the more obvious and explicit use of mythological elements in the narrative literature and the concurrent heightening of the symbolic interpretation of the Indians. (We have seen foreshadowings of this in the narratives of Church, Byrd, and Rowlandson.) In their search for salable literature in quantity, the writers reduced the narrative forms evolved by the Puritans to their basic formulas; as a result, the artful exploitation of archetypal situations became more important than the recounting of actual personal experience. The symbolic vocabulary of the Puritans became conventionalized through habitual employment, and it changed under the pressure of usage to better suit the temper and define the experiences of later American generations.

The French and Indian War and National Self-Image

Like King Philip's War, the last French and Indian War was a watershed in American history. King Philip's War was the last in which New England fought without the aid or the complications of British involvement in the war. The war of 1755–64 was the last in which the colonists fought as agents of the British in a worldwide struggle against European powers. It achieved the aims of the New England crusaders of the late seventeenth century in the destruction of the popish power in Canada. It brought a greater and more efficient British involvement in military affairs in America and exposed a generation of native militia to the military discipline of Britain's professional soldiery. It brought Americans closer to England's national spirit than they had ever been and made them feel more than ever before the pride of belonging to the British Empire, of joining in admiration of British heroes like Amherst and Wolfe. When, after the war, the British Parliament persisted in treating the colonies like half-alien and isolated dependencies of the crown, it flouted this unifying spirit and turned the colonists' new nationalist sentiment against Britain.

Parliament may have aggravated the American sense of alienation from Britain, but it did not cause it. Even the most pro-British accounts of the war indicate that the "imperial spirit" of the Americans was as much an expression of "Americanist" patriotism as it was of fellow feeling toward the British Empire and the home islands. If close contact with the British as comrades in arms led to a sense of comradeship, it also revealed the sharp differences in education, experience, and attitude that separated the colonial from the Briton after a century and a half of American history. Writers expressed the sense that American and British heroism, as found on the great battlefields, were of two different natures and derived from different historical and military traditions. The American style of heroism, because it was derived from experience in the wilderness and close study of the Indians, had proved the more appropriate to American warfare. Those British generals who, like Amherst and Wolfe, could adapt to that style and express admiration of it, became heroes to the Americans. Those who rejected the style out of hand — like the unfortunate Braddock — were regarded, with all due sympathy, as fools. Indeed, only his deathbed conversion to appreciation of the fighting style of the provincial troops, "my noble Blues," entitled Braddock to any great share of American sympathy.

The war also brought into direct contact and alliance the military forces of the various colonies. Hitherto, the colonies had fought their own wars singly or in small combinations. Thus New England and New York bore the brunt of Canadian assaults that, until 1755, left Pennsylvania and the South relatively untouched. Carolinians fought the Yemassee and the Cherokee, as Georgians did the Spanish, with no assistance from Massachusetts or Connecticut. The latter colonies fought King Philip while Virginia was fighting the Susquehannas and Bacon's rebels; but these wars were not organically related, and neither colony sent support to the other. In 1755–64 the war was general, and for the first time most of the colonies were in some way directly assaulted as part of a grand Indian-French conspiracy.

This circumstance revealed a further development in the cultural evolution of the colonies: the growth of what we may, with hindsight, call sectionalism or sectional nationalism. The war afforded opportunities for New England to compare her style of life and warfare with that of Pennsylvania and Virginia and to make the same distinctions between colonial characteristics as were made between American and British. The writers in each group of colonies were reacting to essentially the same phenomena: events such as Braddock's defeat and Wolfe's victory were everywhere recognized as crucial. In the reactions of writers to these events, one can see the emerging characteristics of their sectional cultures — distinct and varying social and political concerns, prejudices, ideas about the wilderness and man's relation to it, and literary traditions. A brief overview of literary responses to a few major events as evinced in a single, well-defined genre — the sermon — may serve to suggest some of the differences in the cultural and literary values and inheritances of the three sections.

The war began with the massacre of Braddock's army by the Indians at Fort Duquesne. The battle was a classic example of the failure of European tactics in the wilderness: Braddock's troops, forced by their officers to form in close order in a clearing, were all but massacred by a smaller number of Indians fighting from concealment. Of all the colonies, Virginia suffered most directly the consequences of this disaster. Her own troops were involved in the massacre, and her frontiers were laid open to Indian raids via the wide — and now undefended — road that Braddock had cut into the woods from the Virginia frontier. In 1756 Samuel Davies published a pair of sermons on the defeat, titled *Virginia's Danger and Remedy*, which differ from the New England model, most significantly by drawing on the marriage metaphor employed by Byrd and his English and Virginian literary ancestors. Byrd had envisioned a direct, organic connection between the land and its inhabitants. In his *Histories*, as the land darkens and grows wilder, Byrd's men grow more lustful and difficult to curb, while the women grow more slatternly and libidinously exciting. The "lubberliness" of the Carolinian frontiersmen is reflected in the land's continuance in natural decay, despite its potentiality for development. Davies's sermon similarly associates the human defeat and the human sin that made defeat inevitable with a purely natural disaster, the extended drought that struck Virginia in 1755–56. It is this use of a symbolism pairing human with natural events that separates the Virginian from the Puritan writer, whose vision pairs human ("visible") events with divine or spiritual ("invisible") events.

Davies's doctrine resembles the earlier Puritan sermons in its insistence that military and natural disaster is the consequence of communal persistence in sin. He makes no attempt, however, to follow the rhetoric of the Puritan sermon. The narrative of Braddock's defeat, undertaken in the first sermon, subtly prepares the reader or listener for the causal linking of the human and the natural disaster. When Braddock falls, Davies exclaims: "How are the mighty fallen, and the Weapons of War perished! Ye Banks of *Monongahela,* upon you let there be no Dew, neither let there be Rain upon you. . . ." [2] The death of the hero-leader, it is suggested, results in the curse of infertility falling on the land for which the hero fought. This view of the sympathetic relationship between man and nature is essentially the same as that in primitive mythology and ritual. Davies does not commit himself on the question of whether the cause of the disaster is human, natural, or divine; rather, he implies that a mythic combination of the three is responsible.

As in Byrd's narrative, the land is associated with women (or goddesses), and the hero enters the wilderness for a marriage or sexual union that, by association, is equated with the reproductive power of nature. With the hero's fall at Fort Duquesne, the union is terminated, and drought is the result: hopes of sexual union and rebirth give way to sexual violence and death. The blood is not passed to a new generation but is squandered on the ground or selfishly drunk by cannibals in a perverse inversion of the marriage metaphor. Thus Davies dwells on the horrid fate of the frontier women, who are "ripp'd up, and left in a Posture too monstrous to be express'd, and even their *Blood drank!*" Instead of the merging of white and Indian to produce a white Indian (as Byrd had envisioned), the reverse is threatened: naked Indians from the wilderness "and some of our own gloomy Domestics" — the dark races in league — threaten white Virginia with possession by the powers of darkness, working both at the borders and from within the community.[3] Davies's sermon suggests the potential within the South for the same kind of hysteria that swept New England during the witchcraft delusion; but it also suggests that the South's attitude toward the wilderness was not as antinatural as that of New England.

New England's reactions were shaped by its more formalized mythology of the Indian wars and its rigid conception of sermon form. In 1755 William Vinal of Newport, Rhode Island, preached *A Sermon on the Accursed Thing that Hinders Success and Victory in War*, in the tradition of Symmes's sermon on Lovewell's defeat and of Cotton Mather's captivity sermon of 1694, *Humiliations follow'd with Deliverances.* He followed the rigid structure of sermon form devotedly, numbering the points of his doctrine, reasons, and uses. His thesis — that sin is the accursed thing that must be cast out before we can redeem the defeat — is what tradition would lead one to expect in such a sermon. The sense and content of Vinal's sermon, however, go somewhat beyond the traditional bounds of Symmes and Mather. The sin he preaches against is chiefly attributed to "notables and Rulers," rather than to the commonality — in contrast to Mather, whose chastisement was directed at commoners moving away from the control of the magistrates. Braddock himself, although deemed brave enough, is said to have erred through pride and English snobbery in refusing to heed the warnings of experienced American Indian-fighters. His tactics were too "regular," and he had no opportunity to "acquaint himself with the Irregular Manner of fighting, . . . the *American* way of fighting." Part of Vinal's conclusion calls for the redemption of a "degenerated" New England and cites her *"Self-Confidence in War,"* her "fall" from her "first Love" of true religion, as the reason for her becoming an Anglo-American monster, a "degenerate Plant of a strange Vine." Yet Vinal is also concerned with politics and military tactics, and he recommends the adoption of the Indian style of fighting (characterized as "American") as most suited to the wilderness. His use of the term "American" instead of the traditional "New-English" or "English" suggests a growing sense of nationality in New England.[4]

Charles Chauncy's *Letter to a Friend*, on Braddock's defeat and the American Sir William Johnson's victory at Lake George, states the case for nationalism and militarism more strongly than Vinal's account. Chauncy was a moving spirit in the ecclesiastical and intellectual affairs of Boston, the archopponent of the Edwardsians and a founder of the liberal Unitarian movement. His letter follows the sermon-narratives in having a particular thesis or doctrine, a narrative of defeat that justifies the doctrine, and a section on the uses or application of the doctrine to future affairs. He even echoes the phraseology of Matherian attacks on Puritan complacency in his suggestion that the chief use of the defeat is its terminating our sense of "security." But Chauncy's doctrine and its application are entirely secular. The good end he has in view is, not the revival of a sense of man's dependence on God, but the improvement of the military establishment along lines suggested by New England's long experience with Indian warfare. Here he draws on New England's unique experience of more than a century of uninterrupted warfare against the French and Indians. He asserts that New England troops are superior to those of the southern and middle colonies, and to English regulars as well, because their "temper and character" have been formed in the hard school of the Indian wars. Their supposed possession of the ark of an English Israel is not mentioned. "English

Sparta" would seem a more appropriate appellation than "English Israel" in Chauncy's work.

Chauncy presents New England's experience as a dramatically heightened and intensified image of the experience of all the colonies in America. The century of Indian warfare is seen as a dramatization or archetype of the national experience. Braddock's defeat on the Ohio suggests the need for a greater assertion of national pride in an American identity, and that identity is to be defined in military terms. But the New England or American soldier-hero, as Chauncy sees him, is essentially Indian in his manner of fighting: "*American irregulars*, in an *American* war, are full as necessary as *British regulars*. . . . If one of the good effects following upon the *Ohio-defeat*, so inglorious to the *British* arms, . . . is not a greater care to distinguish *American* merit, it will not be because it is not . . . fitted to point out the political Wisdom of such a conduct." [5] The victory of William Johnson in that same year is seized upon by Chauncy as proof of his doctrine. (Twenty years later, the tactics lauded by Chauncy triumphed for New England at Concord and Lexington.) Even more to the point is the manual of arms composed later in the war for the American rangers by their New England commander, Major Robert Rogers. Rogers codified the Indian methods of fighting so that these could be taught to troops inexperienced in Indian warfare. He systematized the same tactics that Benjamin Church learned piecemeal from his Indian scouts and applied them so successfully that he became, next to Generals Wolfe and Amherst, perhaps the chief military hero of the war.

The New England writers, in treating the Braddock defeat, reflect the nature of the New England literary tradition in their employment of sermon form, their use of their experience in Indian warfare as the characterizing feature of their communal personality, and their envisioning of their community as a peculiar, isolated nationality caught between the hostile worlds of Indians and Englishmen. The reaction of the middle colonies to the war was also characteristic. In Pennsylvania, Quaker parochialism and its political foundation in the proprietary government clashed with the emerging intellectual cosmopolitanism of the metropolis of Philadelphia and with the political needs and aspirations of the non-Quaker majority in the backcountry. Quaker unwillingness (out of religious scruple) to cooperate with Braddock had been one of his chief sources of difficulty, and after the defeat it exposed the Pennsylvania frontier to Indian ravages. Behind the religious conflict, there was political tension between the Quaker proprietors, the non-Quaker citizenry, and the democratic intellectuals led by Franklin and his circle. Thomas Barton preached a sermon on Braddock in

1755 that reflects these tensions, as well as an interest in philosophical issues arising from the progress of French physiocratic thought and deism in
the cosmopolitan intellectual circles of Philadelphia. Franklin was Barton's
publisher, and William Smith, provost of Franklin's college, penned an introduction.

Unanimity and Public Spirit was the title of Barton's sermon, and his
part of the work pleads for political unanimity and a proper respect for the
liberties of the people. Although Braddock's defeat was the occasion of the
sermon and although its political message was made necessary in part by
the government's failure to support the war, Smith's philosophical speculations turn the reader's attention to the broader implications in the American situation. Ostensibly speaking on the "Duty of Ministers," he expresses
the environmentalist and evolutionary theory of history that, as we have
seen, characterized the thought of Franklin, Locke, and the French physiocrats. In the primitive past, "every one was his own priest and king."
Affairs were governed by natural reason, and faith was the result of a simple, inherent wisdom, such as the American primitives exhibit. The Indians, however, need not be taken as perfect models for emulation, since
each community may have a particular *"Genius"*: we are all "Creatures of
God, but also . . . members of a particular community." The role of ministers, then, should be to "light up . . . and . . . exalt our Country's *Genius*." [6] That genius, for Smith, consists in our ability both to create a political unity out of diverse elements through the application of republican
principles and to conquer the western wilderness by the plow and the
sword.

Thus Smith and Barton, like Chauncy, use the Braddock defeat as the
starting point for an essay in nationalism. All three associate national identity with the effort of colonizing and conquering the wilderness. But where
the New Englanders emphasize the military side of conquest — fighting
the Indian on his own ground and in his own style — the Pennsylvanians
emphasize the natural evolutionary processes that make conquest inevitable. Furthermore, they employ their concept of natural law as justification
for a carefully articulated political program of national unity and republican democracy.

Of all the colonies, Pennsylvania produced the most generally appealing assessment of the meaning of the war and the most viable image of the
American hero. The lines of communication linking the colonies to one another and to Europe all crossed in Philadelphia; and writers like Franklin,
Barton, and Smith could draw with greater ease on the literary traditions
of England, New England, and the South than these sections could on one

another's traditions. Hence they could have broad appeal. Organized colonial resistance to the postwar Stamp Act, which some regard as the first step toward the Revolution, centered around Philadelphia, which was also the jumping-off point for the last expeditions against the western Indians and a point of reentry for repatriated Indian captives. Philosophically, Philadelphian intellectuals drew on the radical Puritanism of the Quakers and the new rationalism imported from France and Britain.

All of these factors led to the production in Philadelphia of one of the most significant studies of wilderness life and warfare, William Smith's *Historical Account of the Expedition Against the Ohio Indians* (1765). Smith was provost of Franklin's College of Pennsylvania and a prominent member of Philadelphia's intellectual elite; he published theoretical and practical tracts on education, history, liberty, the Stamp Act, and emigration. This book was ostensibly written to advocate new methods of fighting Indians and new procedures for establishing settlements in the wilderness, as well as to give an account of Bouquet's adventures. But the work implies much more. It suggests that the proper way to live in America is to imitate the Indian and, conversely, that the Indian's patriotism, independence, and love of liberty make him the model of the ideal American. Although Smith's primary sources were the journals of Bouquet and his officers, he also drew on traditional and contemporary materials relating to the Indians and Indian warfare. The structure of his book resembles, in several important ways, that of the Puritan sermon-narrative; yet the materials are secular, and the image of the Indian is of course antithetical to that created by the Puritan. The wilderness seems, by turns, the Puritan chaos and the pastoral Arcadia. The popularity of the book in America and Europe was notable. It was first published in 1765 by William Bradford, a major printing house in a city that had become the publication and distribution nexus of the colonies. It was reprinted in London in 1766, was bound with the popular edition of Robert Rogers's *Journals* in Dublin, 1769, and appeared in French in Paris (1768, 1769) and Amsterdam (1769).

Bouquet's campaign was directed against Pontiac, who, after the French defeat, united the western tribes against the English and nearly drove them back over the mountains. Smith's book is in two parts. The first, by himself, is a brief introduction to the circumstances preceding the campaign, the march westward, the victory at Bushy Run, the treaty negotiation, and the return of the white captives. Following these is a long dissertation on the Indians and a plea for systematic imitation of the Indians by the military and the western settlers. This section was composed by a soldier on the expedition, Thomas Hutchins, later chief geographer of the

United States, who had gone on the expedition "for his own improvement." (The phrase echoes the terminology of Cotton Mather's and Mrs. Rowlandson's captivity narratives, but Hutchins was clearly more concerned with military efficiency than with the salvation of his soul.)

The description of Indian warfare and the landscape of the wilderness, with which the first part of the book is concerned, resembles closely the Calvinist image of the wilderness. One might expect this, since the account was drawn from the reports of the foreign-born Bouquet, to whom the wilderness was as alien as it had been to the first Puritan settlers. What is striking is that, despite the fact that their perceptions of the wilderness are the same, Bouquet, Hutchins, and the Puritans draw strikingly different conclusions from them. Bouquet portrays the American war as war carried to its ultimate logical development; compared to it, European war is a species of civilized amusement. The American war has a horrid, unpalliated reality, which in a European war one can at times avoid perceiving or suffering:

> Those who have only experienced the severities and dangers of a campaign in Europe, can scarcely form an idea of what is to be done and endured in an American war. To act in a country cultivated and inhabited, where roads are made, magazines are established, and hospitals provided; where there are good towns to retreat to in case of misfortune; or at the worst, a generous enemy to yield to, from whom no consolation, but the honour of victory, can be wanting; this may be considered as the exercise of a spirited and adventurous mind.

By contrast, American wars are

> a rigid contest where all is at stake, and mutual destruction the object. . . . [In] an American campaign everything is terrible; the face of the country, the climate, the enemy. There is no refreshment for the healthy, nor relief for the sick. A vast unhospitable desart, unsafe and treacherous, . . . where victories are not decisive, but defeats are ruinous; and simple death is the least misfortune which can happen to them.[7]

It is not hard to imagine Edwards or Mather employing this language to describe the spiritual warfare between sin and goodness. Yet the analogy occurs neither to Bouquet nor to Smith.

Rational adjustment to this type of war is shown as the secret of Bouquet's success at Bushy Run. Instead of refusing to enter the wilderness, he follows Church's example and takes his tactics from the Indians. In Hutchins's section of the book (which advocates the forming of a "ranger" corps) this adjustment to the wilderness becomes a kind of virtue as well as a necessity. The section begins with an account of the Indian way of life, emphasizing its independence, and concludes with a program for training white soldiers according to the premises of Indian military discipline. It is interesting, in view of the existence of Rogers's rangers, that Hutchins chose to call his proposed corps "hunters" rather than "rangers." The choice suggests the close affinity between the hunter and warrior in any Indian war — an affinity that was to characterize the symbolic figure of Daniel Boone, when he emerged as the myth-hero of the American frontier.

Hutchins sees the faults of the Indians — their supposed laziness and their preference for hunting over the agrarian life — but he portrays them as Rousseauistic patriots, loving liberty more than ease and believing in a religious discipline that puts them in harmony with their world, rather than setting them against it:

> The love of liberty is innate in the savage; and seems the ruling passion in the state of nature. His desires and wants, being few, are easily gratified, and leave him much time to spare, which he would spend in idleness, if hunger did not force him to hunt. That exercise makes him strong, active and bold, raises his courage, and fits him for war, in which he uses the same stratagems and cruelty as against the wild beasts; making no scruple to employ treachery and perfidy to vanquish his enemy.[8]

The savage, as here described, needs only a bit more "sentiment" and fellow feeling — and a library for his leisure hours — to make him the ideal republican citizen. Hutchins draws further implicit parallels between the Indians' love of independence and private property and the colonists' sentiments in the current crisis over parliamentary taxation:

> Jealous of his independency and of his private property, he will not suffer the least encroachment on either; and upon the slightest suspicion, fired with resentment, he becomes an implacable enemy, and flies to arms to vindicate his right or revenge and injury.[9]

The Indians' defects and advantages are in part racially inherited. Their lively senses and cleverness in woodcraft give them advantages in the woods, while their "racial" lack of "common feelings of humanity" renders them monstrous in war. Their acquired advantages — those qualities which they have gained from their life in the wilderness and from their discipline of adjustment — are all depicted as positive and "good":

> [They] have been inured to bear the extremes of heat and cold; and from their infancy, in winter and summer, to plunge themselves in cold streams, and to go almost naked, exposed to the scorching sun or nipping frosts, till they arrive to the state of manhood. Some of them

destroy the sensation of the skin by scratching it with the short and sharp teeth of some animal, . . . which makes them regardless of briars and thorns when running thro' thickets. Rivers are no obstacles. . . . They either swim over, or cross them on rafts or canoes, of an easy and ready construction.[10]

Their powers of physical endurance and their ability to either find food or endure hunger and thirst on a long campaign are matched only by their spiritual or mental qualities of patience and woods sense:

> By constant practice in hunting, they learn to shoot with great skill . . . and to steal unperceived upon their prey pursuing the tracks of men and beasts, which would be imperceptible to an European. They can run for a whole day without halting. . . . They steer, as if by instinct, thro' trackless woods, and with astonishing patience can lie whole days motionless in ambush to surprise an enemy, esteeming no labour or perseverance too painful to obtain their ends.[11]

They are ascetics, Puritans with a pagan religious zeal: "Plain food, constant exercises, and living in the open air, preserve them healthy and vigorous." [12] Their methods in war are perfectly suited to their environment. They do not form columns but snipe at them from the trees; they retreat if attacked but perpetually surround and harass slow-moving troops, compelling them to run or to fight an invisible enemy.

Hutchins does not propose that white men become thorough Indians. The "white" qualities of intellect and sentiment are too precious to be sacrificed for mere prowess. But he does suggest an adaptation of the white, a disciplining to the Indian life as a means of hardening the European into a competent ranger: "It is not . . . to be expected . . . that those light troops can equal the savages in patience, and activity; but, with discipline and practice, they may in a great measure supply the want of these advantages, and by keeping the enemy at a distance afford great relief and security to the main body." [13]

Hutchins's prototypal Euro-Indian American hero only gradually took hold of the American imagination. Negative associations with the Indians remained strong, and the traditions of the Indian-war and captivity myths determined that white-Indian relationships should still be defined in terms of violence. In Europe, however, the image of the Anglo-Indian caught on rather quickly. One reason for this was the traditional association of colonials and Indians, which had been employed for more than a century by satirists like Ned Ward, Ben Jonson, and Jonathan Swift. Now, however, the Anglo-Indian or proto-Christian Indian was seen as an admirable rather than a ridiculous or debased figure. This was partly because of the appeal of the Indian as an exotic but more because of the fashionable notion of the good savage and the natural nobility of man, fostered by Enlightenment philosophy. Americans on the make in Europe — like Robert Rogers of the rangers in 1765 and Capt. Gilbert Imlay of the revolutionary army at the century's end — could cut a swath in Parisian or London society and obtain political influence and favors by playing on the European romanticization of the Indian. Rogers (as we have seen) offered himself to the British public as a white man acculturated to the Indian's world, a man trained from birth as a ranger of the wilderness, finding his life's work in Indian warfare in the Indian's manner. To obtain the position he desired as governor of Michilimackinac, he emphasized the "English" half of his nature by publishing a tragedy in verse, with an Indian chief — one of his own former enemies — as its hero.

Rogers's Indian play, *Ponteach, or the Savages of America* (London, 1766), translates the ideas expressed in Hutchins's tract on the Indianization of the American fighting man into conventional European literary terms. It also updates many of the Puritan traditions about the Indians and the Indian wars by humanizing and even lionizing the savage. Rogers had already written his Indian war narrative — the *Journals* of his rangers' exploits in the last French and Indian War, included in which was a ranger manual like that sketched by Hutchins. On the conclusion of that war, he came to England, hoping to be named governor, of the western post of Michilimackinac at the nexus of the Great Lakes. The Indian play, the *Journals*, and the landscape description in his *Concise Account of North America* — all published between 1765 and 1767 — were written in order to portray Rogers himself as the great hero of the war and the expert of experts on Indian ways and character, as well as a cultivated man capable of expressing himself in the style and form of an English man of letters. For these reasons he made *Ponteach* a strange blend of fact and fantasy about the Indians, drawing both on actual experience and on conventional English and American images of the Indian. He violated English conventions just enough to create a sense that his knowledge and experience were deeper than any Englishman's, but not enough to confuse his audience or strain their credulity. The persuasiveness of his works is perhaps attested by his success in obtaining the appointment.

Rogers's own attitude toward the Indians was what one might expect of a frontiersman: personal contempt for the savages as a race, mingled with admiration of their ability as warriors. In his *Journals* he expresses disgust at having to address them with diplomatic courtesy.[14] In *Ponteach*, however, the Indians are the heroes. Ponteach emerges as a kind of Arthurian figure, and the Indian comes to represent a symbolic distillation of actual or potential American virtues. Rogers's view of the whites is correspondingly reversed. The virtues of the white pioneer, as expressed in his *Concise Account*, are those of the arcadian shepherd mixed with those of Rousseau's good savage: simplicity, moderation, and contentment within life's natural limitations: "These people, of any upon earth, seem blessed in this world: here is health and joy, peace and plenty; care and anxiety, ambition and the love of gold, and every uneasy passion seem banished from this happy region." [15] In *Ponteach* the whites (with a single female exception) are unrelievedly evil.

When *Ponteach* opens, the arcadian time has already passed for the Indians, although they preserve its memory. The intrusion of the English and French is one source of the decline of the Indian arcadia. The more intrinsic cause lies within the Indian himself, in the conflict between his stoic ethic and the unruly passions of his untempered, uncivilized heart. This dichotomy, it will be recalled, was precisely that used by the Puritan captivity and war-narrative writers to distinguish Puritans from Indians. Rogers, however, employs the Indian as symbolic spokesman for the traditionally conceived Euro-American, thus altering his symbolic function from that of antagonist to that of hero. In so doing he plays both on the traditional European association of colonist and Indian and on the new tendency of colonial writers to portray themselves as "Indianized." Accepting the logic of his Indian symbolism, Rogers uses the term *Christian* as an insulting epithet throughout the play, making it synonomous with cheat, hypocrite, and lecher.

The first scene is a dialogue between two white traders, who discuss the technique and rewards of cheating Indians in a fur trade and who practice their technique on a half-drunken brave. In the second scene a pair of white hunters, Orsbourn and Honnyman, complain that the Indians "kidnap all the Game," a crime traditionally attributed by the Indians to the whites. Orsbourn and Honnyman engage in a bloodthirsty dialogue on their hatred of Indians, which reveals them as potential murderers and cannibals: "Hell seize their cruel, unrelenting Souls! . . . . I abhor, detest, and hate them all, / And now cou'd eat an Indian's Heart with Pleasure." [16] Again, these are attributes traditionally imputed to the Indians as signs of their evil nature. Honnyman and Orsbourn complete the image by murdering two Indians from ambush and stealing their furs, without experiencing the least pang of conscience: "I'll strip this Fellow's painted greasy Skull. / . . . . It's no more Murder than to crack a Louse." [17]

When Ponteach and his chiefs come to the English officers, Colonel

Cockum and Captain Frisk, for justice, Rogers (like Thomas Morton) contrasts the hypocrisy of the British with the tolerance and virtue of the Indian.° The contrast is carried through in the scene in which Ponteach accepts treaty gifts from three governors, Sharp, Gripe, and Catchum, who have already engrossed the best of the gifts for themselves and their friends. This trio are caricatures of the Puritan merchant, miserly and hypocritically pious. "Christian charity begins at home," says Gripe, "I think it's in the Bible, I know I've read it." Sharp justifies the taking of graft: "Thus dictate Nature, Instinct, and Religion." Gripe replies (with a direct reference to the Puritan sermon): "We've heard the Doctrine; what's the Application?" [18] By contrast, Ponteach's speech is both open and honest:

> If honourable Peace be your Desire,
> We'd always have the Hatchet buried deep,
> While Sun and Moon, Rivers and Lakes endure,
> And Trees and Herbs within our Country grow.
> But then you must not cheat and wrong the Indians,
> Or treat us with Reproach, Contempt and Scorn;
> Else we will raise the Hatchet to the sky
> And let it never touch the earth again.[19]

After he has been cheated, Ponteach's words echo Shylock's speech in a demonstration of the Indian's humanity and his liberality of mind: "We see, we hear, we think as well as you, / . . . But I call no Man bad till such he's found." [20]

The sins of the Christian become more apparent as we get into Ponteach's camp. Chekitan, one of Ponteach's sons, is in love with the fair Monelia, daughter of a neighboring chief. Meeting with his love, he seeks to embrace her, but the chaste creature will not suffer it. She has, she tells him, "rebuffed a British officer's attempt to stain . . . my Virtue," and she will scorn him if he behaves like a "Christian lover." When he swears his love, she warns him not to swear a "Christian Oath" but to be an Indian and prove his love by virtuous action.[21] Rogers here employs Indians with the traditional virtues of Europeans — a feeling for sentiment, chaste virtue, love of honesty — as devices to belabor Europeans and Christianity. Here is an extreme form of the Rousseauistic vision of the primitive man as a proto-European. Rogers knew better, but in *Ponteach* he was writing for Europe and not America. In his *Journals* he refers to the Indians with contempt as "savages."

Further evidence of Christian perfidy is the attempt by the Catholic

----

° Rogers also includes an "authentic" Indian war dance, complete with masks — an unconscious echo of Morton's "Revels."

priest of the tribe to rape Monelia. The priest has previously been seen working in conjunction with the tribe's conjuror to promote the war and leading the realistic war dance at the council fire. "I must, I can, and will enjoy you now!" cries the priest. "You must! You shan't, you cruel barbarian Christian," replies Monelia. Chekitan leaps to her rescue, which provokes the usual sentimental scene. Monelia murmurs: "Oh I am faint — You have preserv'd my Honour / which he, foul Christian, thirsted to destroy." The priest responds by claiming he has a special dispensation to "quench" the fires of love when the need becomes great. Chekitan is furious: "None but a Christian could devise such lies! / . . . Every Christian is a Foe to Virtue." [22] The villain of the piece is Chekitan's brother, whose name is of course a Christian one: Philip. It is he who murders Monelia, out of jealousy of his brother, and is finally killed by the maddened Chekitan.

Ponteach's honesty sets him off from the Christians in the play, but Rogers also sets Ponteach off from Chekitan, whose European-like thralldom to the sentimental passions of the heart Ponteach finds unmanly and degrading. His own virtues are consciously drawn from those of the Roman Stoic: equanimity before catastrophe and devotion to order and the public good. Here Rogers suggests the outlines of the ethic that the Indian did, in fact, apparently derive from nature — an ethic which strongly suggested that of ancient Romans, to writers predisposed to find the roots of European virtues in primitive man. Thus when the captured Honnyman and his wife are tied to the torture stake for burning, Ponteach frees the woman and the children because "they have not wrong'd us; can't do present Mischief." [23] It is Philip, the son with the Christian name, who enjoys torturing captives.

When Ponteach shows the body of the murdered Monelia to Chekitan, he primes him with a stoic injunction: "Be not alarm'd my Son, the Laws of Fate / Must be obey'd; She will not hear our Dictates." [24] Chekitan, however, is unmanned by the sight, goes mad, and kills Philip, then himself. His final speech reveals him as the slave of a particular passion, a man with no sense of inner order and no belief in the fated order of the world:

> Monelia's dead — The World
> Is all unhing'd — There's universal War —
> She was the Tie, the Centre of the Whole
> . . . .
>
> Where next, Monelia, shall I bend my Arm
> To heal this Discord, this Disorder still,
> And bring the Chaos Universe to Form? [25]

Ponteach, who never loses his sense of universal form, measures his sons' fall against this classic standard:

> My Sons, my Name is gone;
> . . . .,
> Are more than murder'd, more than lost by Death.
> Had they died fighting in their Country's Cause,
> I should have smil'd and gloried in their Fall;
> Yes, boasting that I had such Sons to lose
> . . . .
> But thus to die, the Martyrs of their Folly
> Involv'd in all the complicated Guilt
> Of Treason, Murder, Falsehood, and Deceit,
> Unbridled Passion, Cowardice, Revenge,
> And every Thing that can debase the Man
> . . . .
> This is too much.[26]

"Unbridled Passion" was the nemesis of Puritan soldiers in the wilderness, as well as a stoic anathema: yet here the Puritan and stoic judgment is voiced by an Indian. Ponteach goes further and sets aside his private passion of grief for the public good, a model of republican virtue: "But I'm too far — 'Tis not a Time to grieve / For private Losses, when the Public calls." [27]

The extent of Rogers's departure from pre-Enlightenment European convention can be suggested by comparing his Indian play to Dryden's Indian tragedies of a century earlier. Like Rogers, Dryden ennobles the Indian by viewing him as a fit subject for heroic tragedy. But it is quite clear that Dryden's Indian settings are employed simply to lend an exotic air to the proceedings. The city of Zempoalla in Dryden's and Howard's *The Indian Queen* (London, 1664/65) might as well be Moorish "Aureng-Zebe" for all the resemblance it or its people bear to their American counterparts. Montezuma, the Aztec hero-king, steps to the footlights at the play's end to declare: "You see what shifts we are enforced to try, / To help out wit with some variety." Its sequel, *The Indian Emperour* (1667), also treats the Spanish conquest of Mexico in the terms and conventions of Augustan tragic drama. The Indians are moved by conventional passions of love and honor, not torn between the symbolic opposites of stoicism and unrestraint that give Rogers's play its psychological tension and its applicability to the cultural anxieties of the colonial English. Where Rogers's Ponteach affirms the stoic ethic at great emotional cost, Dryden's Montezuma is destroyed for failing to live by the ethic of romantic passion. Expression of feeling, not its restraint, is Montezuma's virtue: "For those, that here on earth their passions show / By death for love, receive their right below." [28]

Dryden's conquistadores greet the newfound land in the conventional terms of the chivalric romance and the arcadian myth. Conquest of the New World will bring them renewed strength as men and as lovers. It will also renew the strength and fortunes of Christianity and the Spanish nation. America is the Old World, Europe, purified and regenerated.

> On what new happy climate are we thrown,
> So long kept secret, and so lately known;
> As if our old world modestly withdrew,
> And here in private had brought forth a new?
> . . . .
> In Spain, our springs, like old men's children be
> Decayed and withered from the infancy:
> . . . .
> Here Nature spreads her fruitful sweetness round,
> Breathes in the air and broods upon the ground
> . . . .
> Methinks we walk in dreams on Fairyland,
> Where golden ore lies mixt with common sand.[29]

"Conquest and love" give the conquerors rights in the land; in the course of the play it becomes clear that New Spain is their proper home and that the Indians are unworthy of it. Just as ore is discovered in the common sand, so the earth of a New Spain has been found, mingled with Indian dust. At the war's end the Indians depart for a land without gold, where they hope the Spaniards will not follow them and from which they will no longer sally to trouble the Spaniards in their inheritance. To the golden men they leave the golden land.

Rogers's Ponteach, on the other hand, is clearly the rightful possessor of his soil. His characteristic personal virtues are drawn from the land. He is native to it; all others are intruders. Where Dryden's Guyomar, heir to Montezuma, leaves the golden land for a wasteland that is his proper home, Ponteach retires to the wasteland simply to recruit his forces. Like Arthur's retreat into westward Avalon, his withdrawal is temporary, for he is the once and future king of the New World:

> Ye fertile Fields and glad'ning Streams, adieu,
> . . . .
> I am no more your Owner and your King.
> But witness for me to your new base Lords
> That my unconquer'd Mind defies them still;
> And tho' I fly, 'tis on Wings of Hope.
> Yes, I will hence where there's no British Foe,
> And wait a Respite from this Storm of Woe;
> Beget more Sons, fresh Troops collect and arm,

And other Schemes of future Greatness form;
Britons may boast, the Gods may have their Will.
Ponteach I am, and shall be *Ponteach* still.[30]

Rogers's employment of the Indian as the symbolic embodiment of characteristically American virtues makes the fate of his works useful as evidence of the degree of acceptance this image of the American hero found in America and England. His three books were published frequently in Europe and not at all in the colonies. The *Concise Account* appeared in London in 1765 and in Dublin in 1769 and 1770; the *Journals* appeared in London in 1765 and twice in Dublin (both editions dated 1769). In 1767 a novel, *The Female American*, followed Rogers's lead in equating the Indian with all the virtues and offering a white-Indian woman as a prototypal American hero. The heroine and putative author of the novel was Unca Eliza Winkfield, supposed descendant of a match between a Virginia-born captive and a proto-Christian Indian princess. Unca is educated in England, is shipwrecked in an attempt to return to Virginia, and successfully converts a tribe of Indian cannibals to Christianity before she is rescued by her future husband. This novel was not reprinted in America, however, until well after the Revolution. Rogers's works, because of his Tory stand in the Revolution, were not published in his native land until he was more than a century in his grave.

The American rejection of Winkfield and Rogers is difficult to square with the distinct trend toward general acceptance of the Indian as a kind of model American. In 1773, for example, the Boston Tea Party rebels adopted Indian dress in executing their raid, and the militia at Concord and Lexington fought the regulars in the Indian manner. The first Democratic-Republican political club (founded in New York City in the 1790s) was named after the legendary statesman of the Five Nations, Tammany (Tamanend). The Whiskey Rebels of 1794 likewise adopted Indian war paint at their meetings and stated their case in a mock "Indian Treaty," employing the Indian as a symbol of their independence, courage, and defiance of authority in devotion to principle.[31] In 1767, however, American readers were not as prepared as the British were to accept the absolute, unqualified equation of Indian and American virtues employed by Rogers and Winkfield. Developments within the Colonial literary genres reflect more accurately the pace of American adjustment to the idea of Indianization.

Captivity and/or Adoption

As we have seen, the literary genres of the Colonial period developed around particular kinds of colonial experience. Most prominent among the secular genres were narratives of travel and exploration, of Indian fighting, of captivities (with the closely related genre of religious literature that concerned missionary efforts among the Indians), and of attempts to establish new settlements. Between 1620 and 1750 each of these narrative genres developed particular conventions through repeated and various usage. These conventions were shaped both by the actual experiences of the narrators and by the overall Puritan, middle-colony or southern frame of mind. This process of development did not end with the relaxing of Calvinist hostility to literary fiction in New England and the concurrent development of literary presses and large reading publics in the other colonies. On the contrary, these two developments led to an increased demand for more (and more sensational) narrative literature derived from American experience, as the continuing growth of American almanacs and periodicals (rich in narrative and anecdote) and the persistent popularity and increased variety of works in the traditional genres suggests. More "authentic" narrative was wanted for publication than could have been supplied by fortuitously appearing Mary Rowlandsons, equipped with both genuine experience and the skill to tell their own stories. The result was a tendency toward fictionalization of narratives, beginning with secondhand recastings of authentic experiences and ending with the fabrication of imaginary adventures.

This process led to a gradual acceptance of literary forms as valid vehicles for statements about the American experience. At the same time, it led to the emergence within each narrative genre of prototypal "American heroes," serving as participants in the narrative or as personas of the narrator. The Indian war narratives — the genre preferred by American writers — developed such a prototype in Smith's image of the American soldier-hero as an Indian-like "hunter." The Indian-study treatises, travel and exploration narratives, and captivity narratives underwent a similar development between 1765 and 1790.

The gradual dominance of literary forms and a literary attitude toward the narrative art meant that correspondingly less value was placed on direct experience with the frontier, or even on an acquaintance with reliable secondhand information. The literary author is permitted to work in the realm of his own imagination. Since his aim is to be plausible, rather than necessarily truthful, he can pay more attention to his audience's conventionalized conception of reality than to the thing itself. Where the Puritan chronicler had to work from experience or recorded fact as seen through the sharply focused lens of his theology, the writer of the late eighteenth century could work from a more diverse heritage of myths, philosophical premises, literary forms, and conventions. This diversity made possible a more direct approach to the expression of individual vision and experience in forms that were explicitly literary. The Indian war narratives, for example, had been based on genuine experiences which seemed to follow a formulaic pattern of cultural conflict and reconciliation (in peace or in death) between Indian and Christian. Missionary treatises and studies of Indian life, on the other hand, had developed a conventionalized image of the Indian as an incipient Christian. Writers of fiction, poetry, and drama in the latter half of the eighteenth century — both American and European — worked from these conventionalized portraits, eschewing exploration of the reality for exfoliation and development of the images inherent in their own minds. An early result of this exercise of the literary imagination was the development of a standard, distinctly mythlike narrative for each genre. Each of these narrative types suggested a particular approach to the experience of America and the figure of an American human hero appropriate to that experience. Ultimately these several generic visions and literary forms merged in the narratives relating to the Boone legend.

The early narratives of travel and exploration had acquired distinct literary conventions in the same way that the earliest captivity narratives did — through similarities in the actual experiences of generations of travelers and explorers and through the operation of the Puritan mind on literary materials. Where the captivities defined the relationship between whites and Indians, the accounts of the first explorers of New England and of the first Puritan planters dealt with the relationship between man and the land or the natural world. The typical narrative begins with an image of the happy, peaceful life in England and the intervention of some spirit or force — love of adventure or the malice of prelates — that impels the narrator to his voyage. He embarks on the sea, which tests his mettle with a fierce tempest, lands in the New World, and is further tested by the hostility of the climate and the natives. He perseveres, trusts in God, and is vouchsafed a vision of his future success, which he shares with his reader by way of encouraging him to come out. This pattern of events expresses the psychological anxieties which the Puritans experienced in emigrating: the tempest at sea and the hard times ashore served as self-mortifications or purification rites, making them worthy of their future success (and, perhaps, of their happy return to England). These conventions, like those of the captivity narratives, were employed by secular-minded writers in the early eighteenth century. Two English satirists, for instance, Ebenezer Cooke and Edward Ward, follow the pattern only to mock it. They show their protagonists fleeing merry England to escape the bailiff or paternity charges, heaving hilariously into the scuppers during the tempest, and railing at the climate and the natives as soon as they step ashore.

The colonists, however, had more liking for works that treated the form with a seriousness appropriate to its underlying significance. Such a work is Jonathan Dickenson's account of his shipwreck and travels in Florida in the latter part of the seventeenth century, an account which melds the genres of the travel and the captivity narrative. Dickenson is the human hero of the catastrophe, the leader of the party in its trials and its eventual rescue. In good Puritan fashion, he gives all the credit to God and effaces himself in the presence of Robert Barrow, the great Quaker missionary who is with the party. The title suggests the thesis of the account: GODS PROTECTING PROVIDENCE MAN'S SUREST HELP AND DEFENSE *In the times of the greatest difficult and most Imminent danger; Evidenced in the* REMARKABLE DELIVERANCE *Of divers Persons, From the devouring Waves of the Sea . . . And also From the more cruelly devouring jawes of the inhuman* CANIBALS OF FLORIDA. . . . It was first published in Philadelphia in 1699, became a best seller for its time (more than two thousand copies within a year), and was frequently reprinted into the nineteenth century.[32]

As the narrative begins, Dickenson, his wife, and their infant son are sailing from the West Indies to Philadelphia when a tempest arises that wrecks them on the Florida coast. Immediately they fall into the hands of the Indians, whom Dickenson styles "Canibals" on the basis of tradition rather than the evidence of his eyes. Although the Indians mistreat and rob them from time to time, they also aid them in their rescue. Their humanity toward Dickenson's child is particularly striking:

> [The] Casseekey's wife having a young child sucking at her breast gave it to another woman, and would have my child; which my wife was very loath to suffer; but she would not be denied, took our child and suckled it at her breast viewing and feeling it from top to toe.[33]

> The Indian women would take our child and suckle it, for its mothers milk was almost gone that it could not get a meal; and our child, which had been at deaths door from the time of its birth . . . began now to be cheerful. and have an appetite to food.[34]

Later Mrs. Dickenson has an opportunity to return the favor. Despite this intimate exchange, Dickenson persists in seeing the Indians as subhuman, comparing them to animals dwelling in a hideous wilderness. His presence among them is providential or accidental, and his whole desire is to return to civilization.

Although Dickenson's account continued to be popular, changing attitudes toward the Indian and the landscape produced significant changes in the genre. In the second decade of the eighteenth century William Byrd, as we have seen, portrayed himself as an heroic surveyor-naturalist, exploring the wilderness by choice and comparing that exploration to sexual union. The surveyor-naturalist, who enters the wilderness in the name of science and civilization, became an increasingly acceptable type of mediating figure. John Bartram's accounts of his explorations gave him an admirable reputation in both Europe and America; and Jefferson's *Notes on the State of Virginia* (1781) — a geographic, political, and naturalistic description of the colony — was the making of his great reputation in European letters. Jefferson's descriptions, as of the Natural Bridge and the Potomac River Gap, abstract the narrative movement of the travel or exploration narrative, reducing it to a visual image. Instead of describing a character moving through the several stages of a narrative, he carries the reader's own eye and sensibility through an analogous sequence of impressions, experiences, and sensations.

The philosophical charge of Jefferson's descriptions sets them above those of men like Rogers, who employed Rousseauistic imagery in an unsystematic way, simply as a device for rendering themselves and their product appealing to prospective buyers. Jefferson adopts as his vision neither the pastoral nor the sublime extreme. Rather, he combines the two into a vision of a land which both excites and soothes the soul, which stimulates the mind with terrors and drama and sates it with bounty and beauty, which exhibits both the ruinous force and the creative power of time and nature. His description of Virginia's Natural Bridge is the most characteristic: he views the bridge from two points of view, one of which harrows him with sublime terror, while the other soothes him with visions of harmony. Both experiences, he suggests, are necessary to a true sense of the land and its meaning:

> The *Natural Bridge,* the most sublime of Nature's works, . . . is on the ascent of a hill, which seems to have been cloven through its length by some great convulsion. . . . Though the sides of this bridge are provided in some parts with a parapet of fixed rocks, yet few men have the resolution to walk to them, and look over into the abyss. You involuntarily fall on your hands and feet, creep to the parapet and peep over it. Looking down from this height about a minute, gave me a violent headache.
>
> If the view from the top be painful and intolerable, that from below is delightful in an equal extreme. It is impossible for the emotions arising from the sublime to be felt beyond what they are here; so beauti-

ful an arch, so elevated, so light, and springing as it were up to heaven! The rapture of the spectator is really indescribable.[35]

It is the contrast between terror and order that gives Jefferson this emotionally rapturous sense of the beauty of his land. His description of the Potomac Gap also combines the pastoral and sublime visions of American nature and hints at the fundamental peculiarity of American landscape. Because it so openly shows the marks of natural forces and processes, the American landscape contains symbols of the whole motion of time from creation to conclusion. For Europeans like Volney, the presence of human ruins marked the passage of time and the natural rise and decay of human empires and civilizations; a shattered temple was the memento mori, the symbol of human tragedy. But the American "ruin" was not man-made but God- or nature-made; it intimated the waxing and waning of the world itself, over geological epochs of time. Thus Jefferson uses an item of landscape as his memento mori, his symbol of the threatening aspect of America, and a symbolic equivalent of the Puritan captivity which reminds man of his bondage to sin and death.

The change is significant. A death symbol in the landscape can be sought out and figuratively embraced and accepted willingly by a man, while a captivity is an undesired experience, with the power to make him a ruin. Jefferson's death reminders humble and terrify the soul, but they are rendered as positive forces by their juxtaposition with the pastoral, promising element in the landscape. What emerges is an experience of the destructive and creative powers of the land — a sense of the land which is based on its realities and which is neither despairing nor naïve. Thus his Potomac Gap landscape is composed of both shattered rocks and serene, distant skies. It begins with a view of the destructive force of the rivers:

> The passage of the Potomac through the Blue Ridge is, perhaps, one of the most stupendous scenes in nature. You stand on a very high point of land. On your right comes up the Shenandoah, having ranged along the foot of the mountain an hundred miles to seek a vent. On your left approaches the Potomac. . . . In the moment of their junction, they rush together against the mountain, rend it asunder, and pass off to the sea.

This vision immediately evokes the sense of the vast sweep of the current of time:

> The first glance of this scene hurries our senses to the opinion, that this earth has been created in time, that the mountains were formed first, that the rivers began to flow afterwards, that in this place . . . they have been dammed up by the Blue Ridge . . . and have formed

an ocean which filled the whole valley; that continuing to rise they have at length broken over at this spot, and have torn the mountain down from its summit to its base. The piles of rock on each hand, . . . the evident marks of their disrupture and avulsion from their beds by the most powerful agents of nature, corroborate the impression.

But this vision of nature's destructive force does not dizzy or upset the viewer on his peak, for he is able to comprehend the scene as a natural metaphor of the course of American history, from threatful present to promising future:

> But the distant finishing which nature has given to the picture, is . . . a true contrast to the foreground. It is as placid and delightful as that is wild and tremendous. For the mountain being cloven asunder, she presents to your eye, through the cleft, a small catch of smooth blue horizon, at an infinite distance in the plain country, inviting you . . . from the riot and tumult roaring around to pass through the breach and participate of the calm below. Here the eye ultimately composes itself; and that way, too the road happens actually to lead.[36]

Thus for Jefferson the ideal experience of America is one which enables a man to immerse himself temporarily in the wild landscape and then to emerge on a high plane of thought, from which he can analyze the significance of the spectacle below him.

The captivity narratives underwent a development analogous to that of the exploration narratives from Dickenson to Byrd and Jefferson. Captivity or the undertaking of a mission had been for the Puritans the only acceptable terms on which white and Indian could live together in the wilderness. Just as the idea of seeking greater intimacy with the natural landscape emerged in the exploration narratives, the idea of accepting greater intimacy with the Indians gained ground in the captivity narratives written between 1750 and 1800. Indeed, the very nature of the captivity narrative began to alter, until the line separating captive from Indian blurred and the captive provisionally accepted adoption into the Indian tribe. Accounts of Indian traders and diplomats (like James Adair and Henry Timberlake), who had lived with the Indians on terms other than those of captive or missionary, merged with the captivity narratives. Finally, as the narratives became more overtly fictional in response to the changing demands and tastes of the reading public, the Indian's symbolic function was heightened and altered, both to make him a fit brother or consort for his Christian counterpart and to make more comfortable the Christian's acceptance of that brotherhood. The captivity experience itself became an experience of adoption or initiation into the Indian's world.

Robert Eastburn's and John Maylem's captivity narratives of 1758 reflect some of these changes in the genre and suggest the direction its development was to take. Eastburn's narrative ought to have been very much in the tradition of Mary Rowlandson and John Williams. The narrative was solicited by Gilbert Tennent, who promoted the Great Awakening in the middle colonies and was a colleague of Jonathan Edwards in the attempt to promote revival in New England. Tennent's preface to the narrative, however, is not at all like those affixed to Mrs. Rowlandson's and Hannah Dustin's. No doctrine is developed, no theological issues are underscored. Tennent simply vouches for Eastburn's veracity and piety, and hopes the reader will find the narrative "entertaining and improving." Eastburn himself employs some of the traditional devices of the missionaries, drawing unfavorable comparisons between Indian piety and Pennsylvanian backsliding. The difference lies in the fact that Eastburn's Indians are, not converts to Protestantism, but either Catholics or downright pagans. His observation that they have "made better use of a bad Religion than we of a good One" thus smacks of a kind of cultural relativism.[37] And although his outbursts against his sinfulness and that of his people are what one has come to expect in captivity narratives, they have a more rhetorical than theological function here. He employs these expostulations as an effective literary device, adding dramatic value and a novelistic air of immediacy to the account by shifting quickly from the past tense in the expostulation to the present tense in recording his adventures.

John Maylem's *Gallic Perfidy* (Boston, 1758) is even more overtly literary, since it casts the captivity as a long narrative poem. Maylem recounts his experiences after the fall of Fort William Henry to the French in 1757, when the Indians, in violation of the surrender terms, attacked and massacred the British troops and their families as they marched out of the fort. The poem roughly approximates the sermonlike narrative form favored by writers of captivity narratives. It begins with a thesis that is suggested by the title, proceeds to a narrative, and concludes with an exhortation. Yet Maylem's values are clearly those of the Enlightenment, his standard of morality is the "laws of Nature," and his view of wilderness horror is more akin to that of sublime painters than to that in the Puritan martyrologies.

The poem begins with a statement of Maylem's theme or thesis:

> I mean to sing but Breach of plighted Faith,
> And Violation of the sacred Laws
> Of Nature and of Nations.[38]

He takes a negative view of the Indians, as did Buffon and de Pauw; but the sign of their degeneracy for Maylem is, not their closeness to primitive nature, but their violation of the natural laws of human kindness. Echoes of Mather and Hubbard creep into his portrayal of the Indians, indicating the persistence of Puritan imagery. He calls them "Hell's swarthy Allies,"

> With Visage foul, and horrid awful Grin;
> Red, black and green besmear'd their mighty Fronts,
> With snaky Braids, and dreadful Ornament,
> And pitchy Feathers platted on their Hair;
> Obscene and naked, daub'd with various Paints,
> . . . .
> Like Fiends of Hell, or worse (if possible)
> With fearful Yell, to raise the Hell below
> To th' Assistance of the Hell within 'em,
> Rush on their unforwarn'd defenseless Prey.[39]

Yet in his invocation to the muse, Maylem calls on God to fill his own heart with that same "Hell" and fury that motivates his Indians:

> Ye Powers of Fury lend
> Some mighty Phrensy to enrage my Breast
> With Solemn Song, beyond all Nature's Strain! [40]

This sentimental egocentricity — so antipathetic to the Puritan ethic of self-abnegation — makes Maylem's own sensibility and emotional response the central theme of the poem, eclipsing its ostensible subjects (Indian barbarity, French treachery, and the moral confrontation between English-Christian virtue and the hellish fiends of the wilderness). We are as much aware of Maylem's struggle to master his emotions long enough to write the poem as we are of his struggle with the savages:

> My lab'ring Muse swells with the raving God!
> I feel him here! my Head turns round! 'twill Burst! [41]

> My Numbers fail me! Oh! it is too much!
> But up, my Soul, and take another View.[42]

Maylem's landscape is no more a realistic notation than are the hellish landscapes of Bradford and Mather or the pastoral vision of Wolcott. Rather, it is a landscape designed to evoke in Maylem's persona the sublime emotions his egotism requires. Symbols of spectacular decay and destruction abound: blasted pines, bogs, mountains that appear splintered by a mighty force, serpents, and toads — the whole seeming to be an "Exile of the Damn'd." [43] Cannibalism is imputed to the Indians, who "ript up the Bowels" of a prisoner, gobbled them, and "swill'd the Blood." [44] Yet Maylem never echoes the Matherian dictum that if the wilderness is hell, Christians ought to avoid it; rather, he declares his intention to return as an explorer, once English victory has restored order by purging the forest of its demons. Nor do his powerful sensibilities render him incapable of independent action. Although he praises, in a formulaic way, the "stupendous Love of God to Man" (as evidenced in his being spared the stake),[45] his final prayer is addressed not to God but to the English generals, of whom he begs only sufficient force to go and harry the Indians and explore and enjoy their country:

> O Chief in War! of all (young) *Albion's* Force,
> Invest me only with SUFFICIENT Power;
> I (yet a Boy) will play the Man, and chase
> The wily Savage from his secret Haunts;
> Not Alpine Mounts shall thwart my rapid Course,
> I'll scale the Craggs, then, with impetuous Speed,
> Rush down the Steep, and scow'r along the Vale;
> Then on the Sea-Shore halt; and last, explore
> The green meanders of eternal Wood! [46]

Maylem, like most writers in Europe and America, valued the order and form of civilization. As a frontiersman of sorts, he recognized the incongruity between the reality and the pastoral vision. He did not reject the American wilderness, however, even though it did not prove amenable to pastoralization. Rather, the uses section of his poem emphasizes his desire to live in the wilderness. Yet Maylem — as his second poem, *The Conquest of Louisbourg*, reveals — could not find a hero who could properly embody this dual vision of America. Instead, he here chooses George II and the elder Pitt as his heroes, and he concludes with the savages being chased out of their "Eden" and replaced by the symmetry of civilization:

> Now a smooth Surface all along is seen,
> And white Tents harmonious intervene
> With gay Decorum to enhance the Shew.[47]

Both Eastburn and Maylem preserve one cardinal feature of the traditional captivity narrative in regarding the Indians as fiends incarnate and opposing them to the worthy English and Anglo-Americans. Benjamin Franklin's *Narrative of the Late Massacres* (Philadelphia, 1764), written contemporaneously with the violent outbreak of Pontiac's "rebellion," reverses the traditional roles of Indians and whites in recounting the massacre by the Paxton Boys of some Moravian Praying Indians in Pennsylvania. Here it is the white frontiersmen who behave like fiends, violating natural law in their disregard of age, sex, and innocence and breaking a treaty which dates to Penn's time and has been rigorously adhered to by Indians and Quakers. The Indians are described in terms usually reserved for the good Quakers of Enlightenment mythology:

> [They] have lived many Years in Friendship with their White Neighbours, who loved them for their peaceable inoffensive Behavior. . . . Of these, Shehaes was a very old Man, . . . an exceeding good Man . . . being naturally of a most kind, benevolent temper. Peggy was Shehaes's Daughter; she worked for her aged Father, continuing to live with him, though married, and attended him with filial Duty and Tenderness.[48]

Here the Indians represent the classical customs of hospitality, simplicity, benevolence, filial piety, and human kindness. The whites, on the other hand, are butchers and scalp-takers:

> On Wednesday, the 14th of December, 1763, Fifty-seven Men from some of our Frontier Townships, who had projected the Destruction of this little Common wealth, came . . . armed with fire-locks, hangers, and hatchets. . . . These poor defenseless Creatures were immediately fired upon, stabbed and hatcheted to death! The good Shehaes . . . cut to Pieces in his Bed. All of them were scalped and otherwise horribly mangled.[49]

The revolutionary hero Ethan Allen, writing an account of his captivity with the British in 1778, makes a further change in the personages of the captivity drama, all but replacing the Indian fiend with a British fiend. Allen was captured by the British and Indians in a foolhardy attack on Montreal in 1775 and was exchanged after three years in Canadian, English, and American prisons. He begins his narrative with the formulaic phrases of the traditional captivity narratives, declaring his work to be a true "narrative of the extraordinary scenes of my captivity, and the discoveries which I made . . . of the cruel and relentless behaviour of the enemy" toward captives. Allen is first seized, according to this account, by a typical captivity-narrative Indian:

> [A] savage, part of those head was shaved, being almost naked and painted, . . . came running to me . . . with more than mortal speed (as he approached near me, his hellish visage was beyond all description, snake's eyes appear innocent in comparison of his, his features extorted, malice, death, murder, and the wrath of devils and damned spirits are the emblems of his countenance).[50]

Among the British he is treated with cruelty, mocked, and derided; and his patriotism (rather than his religious faith) is severely tested. Instead of replying with homilies in the manner of Mrs. Rowlandson, Allen vaunts the superior character of his countrymen. At length, after long starvation and privation in the prisons and hulks of New York, he is liberated. His first act is to declare his discovery of the hellish, devilish nature of the British, beside whose actions those of the Serpent himself would be deemed merciful.[51]

Franklin and Allen, like the Puritans before them, are projecting the forces that threaten their society onto the captors and assailants in the captivity myth; Franklin merely substitutes the unruly lower classes of the frontier for the Indians, and Allen substitutes the European enemy. In both cases the Indian remains an enemy, but he now shares that role with others, who are seen as being in many ways more inimical to the colonies. Franklin's choice of villain is remarkably like that of the Puritans, who emphasized the tendency of the frontiersmen to degenerate and of the "better classes" to remain pure.

William Smith's account of the return of the Indians' captives after Bouquet's campaign reveals a similar bias, but it also makes significant changes in the return motif that was so essential to the captivity narrative. Mrs. Rowlandson and her sisters, throughout their stay with the Indians, dreamt only of returning to civilization; the thought that they might remain forever in the Indian camp was the source of their deepest despair. Nor did the Puritan ministers who "improved" their narratives treat with any sympathy at all the suggestion that one might marry and remain among the Indians. Smith makes much of the conventional pathos in the return of the captives:

> [There] were to be seen fathers and mothers recognizing and clasping their once-lost babes; husbands hanging round the necks of their newly-recovered wives; sisters and brothers unexpectedly meeting together after long separation, scarce able to speak the same language, or, for some time, to be sure that they were children of the same parents! . . . feelings of a very different nature were painted in the looks of others; — flying from place to place in eager enquiries after relatives not found! trembling to receive an answer . . . ! distracted with doubts, hopes and fears, on obtaining no accounts of those they sought for! or stiffened into living monuments of horror and woe, on learning their unhappy fate! [52]

However, he sees equal pathos in the separation of the captives from their Indian masters, husbands, and adopted parents, who had grown to love their white captives:

> They delivered up their beloved captives with the utmost reluctance; shed torrents of tears over them, recommending them to the

care and protection of the commanding officer. Their regard to them continued all the time they remained in camp. They visited them from day to day; and brought them what corn, skins, horses and other matters, they had bestowed on them, while in their families; accompanied with . . . all the marks of the most tender affection.[53]

One young brave exposes himself to death and torment at the hands of the frontiersmen by accompanying back to the settlements his most beloved captive — a young woman for whom, as Smith euphemistically puts it, "he had formed so strong an attachment as to call her his wife." Smith goes so far as to admit that the action might make the brave "a figure even in romance." [54] This implicit acceptance of the Indian and his way of life would have been impossible for the Puritans.

Although Smith does not say so in this initial view of the scene, further examination of the Indian treatment of their captives — and of the captives' response to their return to civilization — reveals that many captives preferred the Indian life. This had always been a tendency on the frontier and was greatly feared by the Puritans, as we have seen. But in the traditional exhortation, Cotton Mather and his colleagues usually were careful to distinguish those frontiersmen who lived *like* Indians from those who actually *became* Indians. The latter are rarely, if ever, mentioned before 1750. In 1765, however, Smith acknowledges this phenomenon, though he finds himself hard put to explain the great appeal of the Indians' way of life for certain Americans. Part of his answer he finds in the Indians' "humanity and tenderness" when not enraged by liquor or the desire for revenge. "When they once determine to give life [to a captive], they give every thing with it, which, in their apprehension, belongs to it." To women who are willing they give husbands, to children parents, to warriors wives and arms; no women "need fear the violation of [their] honour." Nor do they feel less affection for adopted members of a family than for those belonging to it by blood: "Every captive whom their affection, their caprice, or whatever else, leads them to save, is soon incorporated with them, and fares alike with themselves." [55] But these reasons are not, to Smith's mind, sufficient to explain why many adults and children preferred to remain Indians. The children, who had been weaned away from civilized habits in their years of innocence, he can excuse. The adults astonish and frighten him:

> But it must not be denied that there were even some grown persons who shewed an unwillingness to return. The Shawanese were obliged to bind several of their prisoners and force them along to the camp; and some women, who had been delivered up, afterwards found

means to escape and run back to the Indian towns. Some, who could not make their escape, clung to their savage acquaintance at parting, and continued many days in bitter lamentations, even refusing sustenance.[56]

Although Smith goes beyond the traditions of the capitivity and Indian war narratives in admitting that an Indian might love a white child or woman, he cannot countenance the converse. This love of whites for the Indians must therefore be a sign of degeneration. Significantly, Smith (like Franklin) gives a class-oriented interpretation of the source of their degeneracy:

> For the honour of humanity, we would suppose those persons to have been of the lowest rank, either bred up in ignorance or distressing penury, or who had lived with the Indians so long as to forget their former connections. For, easy and unconstrained as the savage life is, certainly it could never be put in competition with the blessings of improved life and the light of religion, by any persons who have had the happiness of enjoying, and the capacity of discerning, them.[57]

Henry Timberlake, a Virginia lieutenant and negotiator with the Cherokee, carries the argument a step beyond Smith. Writing in 1765 of his mission to the Cherokee (a confederation somewhat like that of the Five Nations of New York), Timberlake finds the Indian way of life is, in some special respects, more improving than that of his own society. Like Smith, he dwells on the love of Indian mistresses for their English soldier-loves, finding in their fidelity further proof of the sense of sanctity with which an Indian woman regards her marriage, in which she is at least equal and perhaps superior to her white counterpart.[58] Their government as Timberlake describes it is a "mixed" democracy and aristocracy. (Clearly he has Locke's definitions in mind, and perhaps Colden's Iroquois as well.) Their method of succoring the poor is infinitely superior to the English dole and almshouse. Their fierce enmity in war is matched by the full friendship with which they regard Timberlake on the conclusion of peace, and this contrasts strongly to the continued bigotry and suspicion of the whites. Indeed, Timberlake — obviously a member of the "better classes" in Virginia — returns from his embassy to grow disillusioned with his countrymen, partly because of their suspicion of him as an "Indian-lover" and their refusal to pay him for his service. When the Cherokee offer him refuge from the persecutions of society, Timberlake seriously contemplates accepting asylum among them, despite the possibility that a renewed Indian war would lead to his proscription as a traitor:

> The Indians expressed the highest . . . grief for my misfortunes; all the recompence they could offer, was an asylum in their country,

which I declined; since their murmurs . . . convinced me they would not fail at their return to spirit up their countrymen, to vindicate their right by force of arms, which would infallibly have been laid to my charge, and I perhaps be reputed a traitor to my country. My circumstances, however, are now so much on the decline, that when I can satisfy my creditors, I must retire to the Cherokee, or some other hospitable country, where unobserved I and my wife may breathe upon the little that yet remains.[59]

He died, however, shortly after the narrative appeared.

Timberlake's presence in the Indian camp and his long stay with them were the result of his own choice and his profession of military diplomat — not the result of a providential calling, as in the narratives of captivity and Indian missions. The diplomat joined the Indian trader and the naturalist-surveyor as new images of men (perhaps heroes) whose intimacy with the Indians' world was psychologically acceptable, even laudable. Their opinions about the Indians, although differing sharply from the traditional views, were likewise acceptable.

James Adair, an Indian trader, picks up where Timberlake and Smith leave off. His treatise of 1775, *The History of the American Indians*, revives the old speculation that the Indians are the ten lost tribes of Israel and systematically justifies it by comparative philology and anthropology of a rather dubious sort. Adair relies chiefly on analogies between biblical religious customs and political practices and those employed by the Indians. In so doing, he establishes the same scriptural grounds for Indian government that Puritan sages had claimed for their Bible commonwealth. Moreover, Adair's Indians share with the English Israel the common root of descent from a chosen people. Indeed, the Indians' claim, being founded on blood rather than on postnatal conversion, is the better.

This investment of the Indians with a symbolic mantle out of Puritan mythology and Lockean thought is typical of the tendency of American writers, in the latter part of the eighteenth century, to become more overtly literary in their depiction of the frontier. This necessarily entailed a heightening of symbolism and an inflation of rhetoric and pathos for the purpose of playing on the sentiments of a literary audience. Eastburn does this skillfully, as does Smith in his account of the captives' return, but they are essentially reporters rather than artists. The writer of literary fiction works primarily from the materials of his own consciousness (and perhaps his unconscious mind as well). This consciousness, as it applies to literary endeavors, is shaped by literary and social conventions, as well as by personal experience and psychological factors. Thus all literature partakes of the nature of myth, since it embodies the consciousness and memory of both individuals and the society in a traditional, imagination- and sentiment-stirring form. As American writers moved deliberately toward the writing of fiction in the traditional genres of the captivity, Indian war, and travel narratives, the mythological elements in their subject tended to emerge more sharply from their background. The artistic pursuit of the Puritan profession of systematic introspection is partially responsible for this, a tendency which became increasingly important once literature itself became a profession in America after 1800. In the last decades of the eighteenth century, however, the emergence of archetypal motifs was primarily a result of the conventionalization of the literary genres and the abstraction of their narratives into formulaic patterns that no longer needed to have reference to actual experience.

The most important early example of this mythlike form of narrative is a fictionalized captivity by a writer whose pseudonym was Abraham Panther. His narrative, purporting to be an account of an interview with a genuine captive, was published under numerous titles and enjoyed great popularity and wide circulation. It was almost certainly a source for Charles Brockden Brown's Gothic captivity novel, *Edgar Huntly*. First published in Middletown, Connecticut, in 1787, it was reprinted that same year in New York City and in a popular almanac in Norwich, Connecticut. Between 1790 and 1814 it was reprinted in Bennington, Rutland, Putney, and Windsor, Vermont; New York City; New Haven; Leominster, Massachusetts; and Augusta, Maine — some sixteen times in all. The narrative itself is a blend of the sentimental romance, Hannah Dustin's captivity, *Sir Gawain and the Green Knight*, and archetypal motifs as ancient as human mythology (including the Indian myths of the sacrifice of the corn god). Like the Edwardsian revival sermon, it employs symbols drawn from the experience and traditions of its audience to evoke in that audience the sensations and emotions of a quasi-religious experience.

The narrative is cast as a letter, describing the discovery of the captive by the author and including her own version of her story. The narrative begins with the author and a companion wandering deep in the wilderness, in Indian country. They are surprised to hear a voice, which may be either human or bird, singing from a thicket. They cross a brook, climb a hill, and discover a large dell, with a cave at one end and "a most beautiful young Lady" sitting before the cave mouth singing. After swooning and being revived, she tells her story of her star-crossed love for her wealthy father's clerk, their elopement to the frontier, and her lover's brutal murder by Indians. She herself escapes from the Indians and becomes lost in the wilderness. On the fifteenth day of her wandering, an Indian "of gigantic figure" surprises her, succors her, and takes her to the cave. He insists that she share his bed, and when she refuses, he binds her and gives her till sunrise to choose between love and death. She bites the bark withes that bind her, takes up the Indian giant's sword and hatchet, and dispatches him (as Hannah Dustin did her captors) with a blow on the head.

Her disposal of the body, and the results of that disposal, are somewhat extraordinary for a young lady of good breeding, although (the author suggests) they would not be so for a priestess of some "abominable" Indian cult:

> I then cut off his head and next day, having cut him in quarters, drew him out of the cave about half a mile distance, when, after covering him with leaves and bushes, I returned to this place. . . . I here found a kind of Indian corn which I planted and have yearly raised a small quantity. . . . here have I existed for nine long years. . . .[60]

Her murder and mutilation of the giant thus lead to her discovery of the corn and her decision to remain in the wilderness alone for an indefinite period. Her eventual return to her father's house is marked by a similar pattern of events. After being reconciled with the aged, ailing man, she watches him die also and inherits his wealth and lands.

The *Panther Captivity* offers several levels for interpretation. In its overall form it follows the classic pattern of the captivity narrative, save that sentimental passion replaces religious passion as the motive for the girl's desertion of the parental home. Moreover, the desertion is here an explicit part of the tale, rather than an implicit part of the psychological and social background. The tale begins with the girl safe and happy under the paternal roof, until the strong motive of love forces her to violate the filial bond by moving to the wilderness. The Indians visit the lovers with punishment in the form of captivity. The girl resists further sexual temptation, preserves her virtue, serves a term of exile and abstinence, and is restored to the parental domain. The Puritan myth of reconciliation with a deified father is counterpointed by the primitive fertility rites in which the girl engages with the giant. The giant dies, and she discovers corn in consequence. Moreover, her ordeal by Indian captivity, the sexual temptation of the giant, and the heroic act of slaying him have prepared her — made her worthy — of living in the giant's world and possessing his corn, land, and weapons. Likewise, her term of penance makes her worthy of replacing her dying father when she returns to his land.

The ritual slaying of a vegetation god, like the ritual coupling of the king-hero and the earth goddess, was a primitive ceremony aimed at restoring fertility to the soil. In some instances, the slaying of the king or tribal father might be enacted as a fertility rite, the king's body going to fertilize the ground and his potency and powers passing to the new generation, his heir. Several Indian tribes had a corn ritual much like the girl's slaying of the giant, but these were not printed until the nineteenth century, when Heckewelder's and Schoolcraft's compendia of Indian mythology appeared. Longfellow's *Song of Hiawatha*, based on Schoolcraft, contains a ritual slaying of the corn god that is remarkably similar to the action in the *Panther Captivity*.[61]

The author of the *Panther Captivity* may or may not have been acquainted with Indian legends, which were not widely available in print before 1787. (Since the author's identity — and hence his degree of acquaintance with the Indians — is unknown, this particular problem is insoluble.) He does, in any case, employ mythic motifs that have been part of literary mythology for ages. The confusion of the girl with a singing bird at the beginning of the narrative, for example, is a mingling of human and bestial natures typical of myth literature. The cave in the dell bears a peculiar resemblance to the chapel of the Green Knight in *Sir Gawain and the Green Knight*. The narratives too are similar. The Green Knight is a giant, who asks Gawain to cut off his head; when Gawain complies, the giant picks up his head and rides off laughing. When next they meet, the head is restored, and the green giant is whole. Gawain is forced to undertake a quest for the green chapel to submit himself to the Green Knight's sword. The knight tests Gawain, preparing him to be worthy of a final test. Sexual temptation by the knight's wife is the most important feature of that test, which Gawain passes by abstaining from taking her. The Green Knight's powers and coloring mark him as a kind of earth god, whose annual sacrifice is necessary to the maintenance of the crops and the renewal of spring; thus he insists that Gawain come to him at the turn of the year. It is impossible to say whether the author of the Panther narrative was acquainted with Arthurian myths. The most important point is that any writer who involves his imagination in the literary exploitation of such mythy matherial as the captivity narratives seems bound to uncover the archetypal patterns concealed deep beneath the conventionalized surface form of the narratives.

Although derived from a Puritan genre, the *Panther Captivity* was nationally popular because its strange and exotic action touched chords of memory and anxiety of which the readership was perhaps only partly aware. The tension between the traditional captivity pattern, which em-

phasizes filial reconciliation, and the fertility-myth pattern, which emphasizes the preparation of the new generation to destroy and replace the old,
expresses many levels of human and colonial anxiety in a single, emotionally evocative, symbolic drama. On the level of universal human psychology, this tension between the two patterns expresses the dilemma of all
men coming of age, inheriting their parents' world, and replacing their
sires as the shapers of that world. In the particular context of colonial history, it expresses the alternatives open to the American generations: (*a*) to
be reconciled with Europe and the culture of the first founders, or (*b*) to
acculturate, to adapt to the Indian's wilderness. The earlier generations
clung to their heritage (the Puritans most ferociously), as the captivity narratives reveal; later generations, as we have seen, tended toward acculturation. The *Panther Captivity* chooses neither alternative and excludes neither; rather, it expresses the full mind of the colonists by containing both
alternatives and weaving them into a unified, convincing drama. The heroine of the capivity is prepared for, or initiated into, the life of the Indian
giant and attains the right to his domain; but at the same time she is initiated into the Indian's world and prepared to inherit from her blood father
in the civilized world.

Although it fulfills most of the requirements for myth-literature, the
Panther Captivity was not in fact the version of the American myth that attained the widest currency in America and Europe. John Filson's account
of the adventures of Daniel Boone, published three years earlier, was far
more effective in impressing on the American and European mind a particular image of an archetypal American hero. But although the figure of
Boone proved more compelling, the narratives that gave him his stature
operated through the same means as the Panther narrative. They appealed
to the emotions, memories, and anxieties of their readers through the construction of a symbolic drama (whose terms are drawn from American narrative traditions and more fundamental archetypes) in which the dilemmas
of the human psyche and the American culture are resolved.

American Hero-Types in the 1780s

The desires of European readers, by contrast, could be more easily satisfied by a clarification of their preconceived notion of the variety of
American "types." Unity — dramatic, mythological, or cultural — was not
essential to the success of a European attempt to mythologize America, to
find an appropriate image for the new nationality. Crèvecoeur's *Letters
from an American Farmer*, published in 1782, has a particular interest in

this connection, since it was written by a man who belonged to both the French and American cultures, the former by birth, the latter by adoption and temporary residence. His book is useful at this point as a summary compendium of the variety of American heroes, as seen by both Europe and America. In addition, it suggests the nature and extent of the vocabulary of symbols on which the creators of the Boone legend were able to draw for their version of an American myth.

Crèvecoeur's *Letters* are a kind of epistolary fiction. Their ostensible author is a persona, behind whose features Crèvecoeur himself is very thinly disguised; the other correspondents, whose letters the "American farmer" passes on to his "English acquaintance," are also fabrications. The book is artfully constructed to lead the reader into agreement with Crèvecoeur's central thesis that human characters and the characters of religious and political institutions are the products of particular natural environments. Since nature is assumed to embody the principles of natural morality, a people like the Americans, who benefit from both wild, untrammeled nature and civilized arts, are bound to exhibit the rudiments of both superior characters and superior institutions.

The first letters set the reader within Crèvecoeur's frame of reference. The American farmer attempts to give his European friend a full account of his nation, humbly expressing his sense that his productions will be too rudely simple for a sophisticated man of letters, but relying on his natural gifts rather than the refinements of art. Crèvecoeur thus establishes the first point of his argument by reference to convention: Americans live close to nature and are natural, while Europeans live far from it and are artful. The simplicity of the American is not offered up for the European's amusement, as in the satires of Ward and Cooke. Rather, by having his farmer speak at times in the Quaker manner, Crèvecoeur reminds his reader that the good Quaker of Voltaire exalts simplicity of life into the highest of religious virtues. The description of the life of the farmer himself (in the second letter) underlines the simplicity and naturalness of his situation. He all but weeps with happiness when he views his peaceful farm, his happy animals, his snug hearth, and his wife suckling their babe before the fireplace. From the behavior of his cattle and bees he draws moral and political lessons of great pith, such as a scholar or philosopher might wear out the catalogues for and never discover.[62]

Having thus evoked the myth of the good Quaker, he proceeds to a systematic discussion of the question "What is an American?" For Crèvecoeur, the answer is to be found by observing the way in which the environment of America works on the characters of its people. Acculturation

— the process by which the diverse races of Europeans have become unified into a single, international nationality — is therefore the first of his major themes. These are people whom Europe has betrayed, and since their environment has turned them out and America has taken them in, they have naturally exchanged their European for American characters. Crèvecoeur himself is an example of this proto-American, but to point up the process, he resorts to fiction again. He recounts the tale of "Andrew the Hebridean," a Scotsman who emigrates to America and, after trials and misadventures, prospers in the virtuous bucolic profession. His fortunes are improved and his character is strengthened anew by this change of identities and initiation into a new life.

Within the ranks of the acculturated Americans, however, the varieties of American environment provide a variety of types. In the coastal cities, the accessibility of trade routes to the ports of Europe inclines men naturally toward commerce and the arts. Outside the commercial cities dwell the farmers, whom Crèvecoeur styles "the true Americans." [63] These are conceived in terms of the good Quaker image propounded by Voltaire. The whalemen and fishermen of the New England coast are included in this class, since they are farmers of the sea. Crèvecoeur uses the Quaker whaling island of Nantucket as the type and image of a community established along lines suitable to the notion of the good Quaker. The Nantucketers have derived their republican form of government from their natural response to the necessities imposed on them by the environment of the island, not from any art. As a result they have prospered — and prospered righteously by any standard:

> [The] first founders knew nothing either of Lycurgus or Solon; for this settlement has not been the work of eminent men or powerful legislators, forcing nature by the accumulated labours of art. This singular establishment has been effected by means of that native industry and perseverence common to all men, when they are protected by a government that demands but little for its protection; when they are permitted to enjoy a system of rational laws founded on perfect freedom. The mildness and humanity of such a government implies that confidence which is the source of the most arduous undertakings and permanent success.[64]

The Nantucket Quakers, abandoning a rich continent to farm a sterile sandbank and the fertile sea, have dared and attained what no comparably established group of European fishermen, dwelling on the borders of a monarchy, could have imagined.

Very different are the denizens of the frontier. "Men are like plants;

the goodness and flavour of the fruit proceeds from the peculiar soil and exposition, in which they grow." [65] As the Puritans noted, the frontiersmen had long been rooted in the Indian's soil and partaken of the Indian's sacramental dish. Crèvecoeur sees the frontiersmen as lawless, idle, irreligious, rude, and barbarous because they are removed from the area of commerce and government and plunged into the midst of savage men and beasts. Man dwells there, not as a peaceful Quaker, but "in a perfect state of war." He becomes merely a carnivorous "animal . . . of a superior rank, living on the flesh of wild animals"; and "eating of wild meat, whatever you may think, tends to alter their temper." [66] The steps of this alteration follow the pattern dolefully sketched by the Puritans. The pioneer farmers fall under the spell of the woods because of "proximity" and the constant intrusion of wild plants and animals into their gardens and fields. The hostile environment compels them to arm and become hunters, like the Indians; and "once hunters, farewell to the plow." Personal and social degeneration follow:

> The chase renders them [like the Indians] ferocious, and gloomy, and unsociable; a hunter wants no neighbour, but rather hates them. . . . In a little time their success in the woods makes them neglect their tillage. . . . Their wives and children live in sloth and inactivity . . . they grow up a mongrel breed, half civilised, half savage, except nature stamps on them some constitutional propensities.[67]

Crèvecoeur thus invokes the classic bugbear of colonial mythology — the half-breed, the white Indian. He takes pains, however, to point out that the tendency of such men to "degenerate a little" is, all things considered, less widespread than it might be, because of the influence of Quakers and Moravians, who settle the frontier in congregations rather than as family clans or single individuals. Moreover, his "bad people" are described not as half-Americans but as a blend of the Indian and the European (echoing the symbolism of Allen's captivity narrative):

> Thus our bad people are those who are half cultivators and half hunters; and the worst of them are those who have degenerated altogether into the hunting state. As old ploughmen and new men of the woods, as Europeans and new made Indians, they contract the vices of both; they adopt the moroseness and ferocity of a native, without his mildness, or even his industry at home.[68]

For a white man, the pursuit of hunting is a fall from grave into "licentious" pursuits. Crèvecoeur says with Cotton Mather: "After this explanation of the effects which follow by living in the woods, shall we yet vainly flatter ourselves with the hope of converting Indians? We should rather begin with converting our back settlers." [69]

For the Indian, the natural product of the woods, the pursuit of hunting is a custom that necessity and ignorance have imposed on him. Even though he cannot escape the defects of character and society that follow from his environment and hunting economy, he cannot be held to blame for them. Further, like the Euro-Americans he has acquired certain admirable attributes from his contact with the New World. Crèvecoeur, like any writer of the period dealing with America, must somehow work the character of the Indians and the closeness of the "new American race" to the Indians into his story. He approaches the problem through the European figure of the good savage and two of the conventional heroes whose evolution we have been tracing, the naturalist-surveyor and the captive adopted by the Indians.

William Bartram, "the Celebrated Pennsylvania Botanist" is Crèvecoeur's naturalist-hero. He recounts an interview between "Bertram" and a fictitious Russian gentleman, Iw—n Al——z, and begins by invoking the name of the original good Quaker, "the simple but illustrious citizen . . . *Penn*." Like Penn, Bartram is a Quaker and entertains his guest with Quaker simplicity. His house seems "small but decent," and "every disposition of the fields, fences, and trees seemed to bear the marks of perfect order and regularity, which in rural affairs, always indicate a prosperous industry." [70] Bartram, although he rambles extensively abroad, even among the savages in the wildest parts of the South and West, never neglects his husbandry. To the Russian, as presumably to the Indian, he brings the Quaker virtues of simplicity, industry, humility, and contentment with the gifts of the Creator. To make the picture complete, Bartram exhibits his only "vanity," if it can be called that: a coat of arms, revealing that he is of gentle lineage and (one can imagine the satisfaction of Crèvecoeur's Paris audience) of French ancestry on the paternal side. Like that other Pennsylvania "Quaker" so loved by the French — Benjamin Franklin — Bartram is a kind of ideal American figure, mediating between the highest refinements of European science and art and the simplicity of manners and morals of the American good Quakers and husbandmen. Similarly (although Crèvecoeur does not emphasize the point), he mediates between the wilderness and civilization, sallying into its precincts to gain knowledge for the more perfect pursuit of farming.

Crèvecoeur's last letter, "Distresses of a Frontier Man," brings his book to an ominous close. War, the ultimate insanity of civilization, threatens his rural haven with destruction. In desperation the American farmer prepares to flee back to the barbarous world of man's prehistoric origin — the world of the Indian camp. Like the seventeenth-century Puritan emigrating to Massachusetts, he does not submit to this exile and potential degeneration willingly; he is compelled to it by the natural motive of self-preservation. Crèvecoeur employs this chapter as the ultimate characterizing stroke in his portrait of the American farmer. His response to the evils of civilization is not to withdraw behind the hedge of civilization; rather, his sufferings determine him to move still more deeply into the land. The solution to the problems and distresses of living in a wilderness America is, not a return to Europe, but a move outward to a frontier less trammeled by Europe and civilization.

Crèvecoeur's farmer seeks to acquire the Indian's sense that the hardship of life on nature's frontiers is as "right" for the improvement of the soul as life in civilization. He seeks to acquire the qualities of mind and heart that mark the good savage — an ability to derive from harsh nature a stoic code of personal and public ethics; a natural, humane morality; and the power to hold himself and his passions in hand with great dignity and nobility under the most sordid and painful physical circumstances. The farmer lacks this self-possession before his removal. He portrays himself as sentimentally overwhelmed by the terrors of his situation:

> When, oppressed by painful recollection, I . . . contemplate my situation, and the thousand streams of evil by which I am surrounded, . . . I am convulsed . . . some times to that degree, as to be tempted to exclaim — Why has the master of the world permitted so much indiscriminate evil throughout every part of this poor planet . . . ? I bring that cup to my lips, of which I must soon taste, and shudder at its bitterness. What is life then, I ask myself, is it a gracious gift? No, . . . we are born to be victims of diseases and passions, of mischances and death: better not to be than to be miserable. Thus impiously I roam, I fly from one erratic thought to another, and my mind . . . is ready sometimes to lead me to dangerous extremes of violence.[71]

His reaction at this point is precisely that of the Puritan captive, faced with the alternatives of resignation to Providence or crying out against God for imposing the trial upon him. But where the Puritan sees hope in the possibility of rescue from the Indians, Crèvecoeur's farmer sees hope in the Indian himself. The Indian offers an image of man inured to terrors and hardships by discipline, a free soul bound only by his own nature, yet living in a society which admits its members "more ease, decency and peace than you imagine: where, though governed by no laws, [they] yet find, in uncontaminated simple manners all that laws can afford." This is precisely the encomium that Crèvecoeur's Iw—n Al——z bestows on the good Quaker, John Bartram. Like Bartram, the Indian is a symbol of redemption for the frontier man: "Yes, I will cheerfully embrace that resource, it is an holy inspiration." [72]

Despite his warnings against the degeneration undergone by those who eat the "wild meat" of the Indian hunter, the distressed frontier man does not fear that his own children will lose their European nature and become Indians. In the Indian camp one is free to be what one chooses. Although his children will have to learn Indian skills, so as not to seem out of place in their chosen environment — and although he himself will have to "hunt with the hunters" — it will be possible to avoid the "imperceptible charm of Indian education" that might "give them such a propensity for that mode of life, as to preclude their returning to the manners and customs of their parents." The remedy is to turn his family again to the sacred calling of the farmer: "to employ them in the labor of the fields as much as I can. As long as we keep ourselves busy tilling the earth, there is no fear of us becoming wild; it is the chase, and the food it procures, that have this strange effect." [73]

Yet within Crèvecoeur's breast another vision of the woods life is discoverable — one in which the life of the hunting Indian is a romantic substitute for the farmer's labor. The frontier man emphasizes that he does not seek a temporary haven in the wilderness, nor to live among the Indians without being touched by them. Previous white observers of the Indian "went there to study the manner of the aborigines; I to conform to them, whatever they are; some went as visitors, as travelers; I as a sojourner, as a fellow hunter and labourer. . . ." [74] Crèvecoeur consequently places a very different interpretation on the choice by some captives to stay with the Indians from that offered by William Smith in 1766. (For that matter, it also contradicts what he himself has said in "What is an American?") The captive's choice was freely made:

> The Indians . . . gave them their choice, and without requiring any consideration, told them, that they had been long as free as themselves. They chose to remain; and the reasons they gave me would greatly surprise you: the most perfect freedom, the ease of living, the absence of those cares and corroding solitudes which so often prevail with us; the peculiar goodness of the soil they cultivated, for they did not trust altogether to hunting. [75]

Those who dwell among the Indians are not the dregs of society. On the contrary, they may have intelligent grounds for their choice. Since it is freely chosen, the life of the Indian "cannot be . . . so bad as we generally conceive it":

> There must be in their social bond something singularly captivating, and far superior to anything to be boasted of among us; for thousands of Europeans are Indians, and we have no examples of even one of those Aborigines having from choice become Europeans! [76]

In short, Crèvecoeur's Indian village is simply a more extreme form of that New World society into which he symbolically inducted Andrew the Hebridean. Freedom, ease of living, easy admission to the full rights of the citizen, the advantage of a society that has been freely and rationally chosen and not thrust on one at birth — all await the "immigrant" to the Indian world.

Crèvecoeur's Indians in this last chapter bear no resemblance whatever to the Indians of his earlier chapters, and his genial attitude toward the Europeans who become Indians is nowhere else to be found. The adoption of Indian ways is roundly condemned in "What is an American?" Crèvecoeur there declares that whites who merge with the Indians are not "true Americans" but merely the base forerunners of others who will remain true to the ideal type. For Crèvecoeur himself, the idea of seeking refuge among the Indians was unthinkable. His natural impulse was to flee to the salon rather than the wigwam; when the proximity of revolutionary armies made his situation precarious, he abandoned his family and bucolic retreat and fled to New York, London, and ultimately Paris. His great book, like the letters with it, was addressed to Europeans and first saw print in Europe. The Indians of his last chapter are simply another portrait in his gallery of American "types." They are drawn to suit the conventional image of the good savage. If this image contradicts the values implicit in the other conventional portraits, those of the farmer and the good Quaker, Crèvecoeur and his audience remain untroubled. Unlike the Americans, they had no need to approach or deal with him firsthand.

Similarly, European readers had no psychological or social need for a single, unified vision of the American character and experience — no need to reduce that experience to coherence and create a national myth capable of evoking a sense of patriotism and common national destiny. A portrait gallery of American types, with any number of internal inconsistencies and contradictions, could content the Europeans as well as a single myth. In fact, the flexibility of interpretation that a gallery of heroes made possible suited their various requirements far better than any single type could have done. In some contexts, as Crèvecoeur demonstrates, it was well to portray the hunter, whether Indian or white Indian, as a degenerate type. In others, it was politic to show him as the repository of virtues lacking in the war-making civilizations of Europe. The frontier man's turning to the Indians is clearly meant to be taken as a desperate measure (like that of Timberlake), one which no Christian ought to take save under the direst necessity; but the step itself, since it puts the European more firmly within the natural environment, need not necessarily degenerate him. With his superior wisdom and strength of character, he can derive strength from the Indian's world without becoming, like the Indian, a solitary hunter and nomadic wanderer in the wilds.

Here is the gesture which reveals the extent of colonial acculturation to the American wilderness from Puritan to revolutionary times. The characteristic American gesture in the face of adversity is seen to be that of immersion in the native element, the wilderness, as the solution to all problems, the balm to all wounds of the soul, the restorative for failing fortunes. If the woods hold terrors, embrace them as signs of nature's power and God's. Do not flee from them, but master them, and make them your own powers. And if this requires that you become an Indian, then do so. It is this gesture that characterizes the legend of Daniel Boone, whose adventures among the Indians and in the wilderness made him the hero of a nationally viable myth of America. Moreover, it was as a hunter that Boone achieved his heroic stature among Americans, while Europeans persisted in regarding that type in Crèvecoeur's terms, as the most degenerate form of American character.

The resolution of a multiplicity of individual and cultural problems, of a variety of ambivalent literary and mythological traditions, and of a gallery of particular hero types into a single dramatic unity is the essential element in the creation of a viable national myth. The need for a symbolic hero, so evident in the writings of Wolcott, the "Lovewell balladeer," and the eulogists of Braddock and Wolfe, would have to be satisfied by this myth, as would the desire for a coherent expression of the new sense of national (and sectional) identity — a sense spoken to by Chauncy's eulogy of the New England soldiers' superiority to the British and Virginians, by Allen's linking of the British with the Indians as hostile aliens to an American way of life, and by Franklin's and Smith's substitution of class, sectional, and environmental distinctions for the racial and cultural distinctions that had been the basis of the early Indian war literature. To succeed in America, such a myth would have to combine the heroic attributes of the several hero types that had already emerged from the several genres of Colonial writing: the explorer, the naturalist-surveyor, the farmer, the military hero (ranger or soldier), the captive partially adopted by the Indian, and the hunter of beasts and men.

CHAPTER 9

Narrative into Myth:
The Emergence of a Hero
(1784)

> There was, thank God, a great voluptuary born to the American
> settlements against the niggardliness of the damming puritanical
> tradition; one who by the single logic of his passion, which he
> rested on the savage life about him, destroyed at its spring that
> spiritually withering plague. For this he has remained since buried
> in a miscolored legend and left for rotten. Far from dead, however,
> but full of a rich regenerative violence he remains, when his history
> will be carefully reported, for us who have come after to call upon
> him.
>
> William Carlos Williams, *In the American Grain*

IN 1784 John Filson, a schoolmaster turned surveyor and land speculator,
returned from two years in Kentucky. In Wilmington, the metropolis of his
home state of Delaware, he published *The Discovery, Settlement and
Present State of Kentucke*, an elaborate real-estate promotion brochure designed to sell farm lands in the Dark and Bloody Ground to easterners and
Europeans. Sales resistance was likely to be high. The Revolution had just
ended, and the bloody Indian wars which had decimated the Kentucky settlements were still sputtering out in petty raids and secret murders. Thus
Filson faced the classic problem of writers about the frontier since Underhill's time: how to portray the promise of the frontier without destroying his own credibility by glossing over the obviously perilous realities of
the pioneer's situation.

Filson attempted to persuade his audience by composing, as an appendix to that book, a literary dramatization of a hero's immersion in the
elemental violence of the wilderness and his consequent emergence as the
founder of a nascent imperial republic. In "The Adventures of Col. Daniel
Boon" Filson created a character who was to become the archetypal hero

of the American frontier, copied by imitators and plagiarists and appearing innumerable times under other names and in other guises — in literature, the popular arts, and folklore — as the man who made the wilderness safe for democracy. The Boone narrative, in fact, constituted the first nationally viable statement of a myth of the frontier.

A myth is a narrative which concentrates in a single, dramatized experience the whole history of a people in their land. The myth-hero embodies or defends the values of his culture in a struggle against the forces which threaten to destroy the people and lay waste the land. Myth grows out of the timeless desire of men to know and be reconciled to their true relationship to the gods or elemental powers that set in motion the forces of history and rule the world of nature. In the case of the American colonies, whose people were not native to the soil, this desire took the form of a yearning to prove that they truly belonged to their place, that their bringing of Christian civilization to the wilderness represented the fulfillment of their own destiny as children of Jehovah (rather than a perversion of that destiny) and of the land's destiny as the creation of God. (This yearning, common to all the colonies, was most clearly and intensely articulated by the Puritans.)

Filson's narrative, then, to qualify as myth, would have to draw together all the significant strands of thought and belief about the frontier that had been developed in the historical experience of the colonies, concentrate those experiences in the tale of a single hero, and present that hero's career in such a way that his audience could believe in and identify with him. Moreover, the tale would have to be constructed in such a way that it could grow along with the culture whose values it espoused, changing and adjusting to match changes in the evolution of that culture. Otherwise the tale would lose that essential quality of seeming to be drawn from the original sources of cultural experience. Ultimately, Filson's tale would have to dramatize convincingly the interdependence of Boone's destiny, the historical mission of the American people, and the destiny appointed for the wilderness by natural law and divine Providence. The evidence suggests that the Boone legend first put before the public by Filson did, in fact, fulfill these requirements.

John Filson and the Structure of "Kentucke"

Filson's achievement raises some important questions about the sources of myths, the reasons for their success in particular cultures, and the processes by which narrative becomes myth. Was Filson's myth an artful fabrication, or was it simply a fortunate coincidence of the circumstances of Boone's career and the pattern of American history? How aware was Filson of his role as myth-maker? How did he transmute the plain experiences of his own and Boone's lives into the visionary and prophetic utterance of *Kentucke*?

The details of Filson's life before 1784 are shadowy and vague. Even the date of his birth is uncertain, although his most recent biographer (John Walton) estimates it as 1753. He was a schoolmaster in Brandywine, Pennsylvania, and apparently spent the years of the Revolution in his schoolroom, since no record of military service by him has come to light. Other details of his background can be pieced together from the little that is known of his family and career, his personal library, and the literary sources and values inherent in his book. The Puritan Calvinism of the Great Awakening seems to have influenced him through his family, who were New-Side Presbyterians and supporters of the revivalism of the Tennents. But his writings indicate a profound interest in French and American deism — and, in fact, a preference for the concept of natural law and the religion of reason espoused by Jefferson and Franklin and by the French naturalist Buffon.[1]

In literature Filson apparently felt drawn to the melancholic sentimentality of early Romantic fiction. His personal library contained an old, pocket-sized anthology of fictional confessions, *Admonitions from the Dead*, "steeped in the romantic spirit of the late eighteenth century." [2] Walton speculates that Filson thought of himself as an exemplar of the somewhat necrophilic Gothicism that these epistles from the grave embody. He offers as evidence a pencil and ink-wash sketch of a man, apparently a self-portrait of Filson (who was a skilled draftsman), that appears on the flyleaf of Filson's copy of the book:

> So sepulchral is the aspect of the man that he could well be one of the spirits whose admonitions are included in the book. The face is neither handsome nor prepossessing, and the mournful eyes bespeak a hopeless despair. Incongruously, the man is a dandy. Stiffly bound up in a high-buttoned vest, a cravat, and a coat in the style of pre-Revolutionary France, this melodramatic little man bears slight resemblance to the stereotype of the American frontiersman.[3]

It is hard to justify so detailed a character analysis on the basis of an untitled drawing by an artist of limited ability. But one of the major themes of Filson's Boone narrative is, in fact, the ability of the wilderness to redeem man by liberating him from melancholy. Filson's portraits of frontiersmen dwell on stoic patience and temperate passions as heroic virtues.

He decries excessive emotionalism and melancholy preoccupations as destructive of man's ability to resist the brutalizing forces of the wilderness. His own end, as we shall see, may have been due to his failure to overcome the melancholic side of his own nature.

　The outlines of his career can be briefly stated. After spending the Revolution in the peace of a Pennsylvania schoolroom, he suddenly left for Kentucky in 1782 for reasons which are difficult to determine. Walton rejects the notion that Filson might have been suspected of Tory or neutralist sympathies; he speculates that land hunger drew him to the West. It is certainly true that as soon as Filson arrived, he began to lay claim to large tracts of land.[4] It also seems likely that Filson anticipated publishing some kind of study of Kentucky, for he began surveying land for a map and questioning the inhabitants on details of Kentucky history not long after his arrival. He also returned to the classroom, teaching school at Lexington in 1782 and returning to found an "academy" there after the publication of his book. Although *Kentucke* made a hero of the poorly educated backwoodsman Boone, Filson's prospectus for his academy emphasizes his belief in the necessity of a town-centered education as a means of saving the Kentuckians from becoming boorish "recluses." [5] Even in the Boone narrative, he puts classical allusions and references to city life into the mouth of the old hunter, in order to impress us with the civility of the hero's mind.

　Despite his training and cultural pretensions, Filson was not a professional dude, come to mock the frontiersman for his ignorance. While in Kentucky he sought a second education in the knowledge of the wilderness, and his acquaintance with frontiersmen was as large as he could make it in two years of almost constant travel. He spoke to all the prominent pioneers and made his name a byword for inquisitiveness.[6] His guide on surveying trips was Daniel Boone, and they grew close enough for Filson to credit Boone as the first person to whom he confided his plans for the book.[7]

　Filson's background thus gave him a broad, if not profound acquaintance with the major intellectual currents that had determined the evolution of America's vision of the frontier — Puritan Calvinism, deism, and the basic tenets of the physiocrats. His use in *Kentucke* of the conventions of form and attitude common to the writings of the Puritans and the philosophes suggests that he had access to their writings and carefully adapted them to the requirements of his own literary ideas. His knowledge of the frontier and respect for the ideas of frontiersmen like Boone gave his book a grounding in the dynamic and still-growing body of frontier legends that were being created by men living in the wilderness itself. His reading and

his intellectual interests enabled him to embody the frontiersmen's vision
in terms acceptable to intellectuals of the American and European Enlightenment and to early Romantic literary figures.

Filson also possessed the literary skill to weave these various sources
into a coherent pattern, imparting a mythic quality to the central Boone
narrative by making it refer to a broad range of literary, philosophical, and
cultural traditions. *Kentucke* roughly follows the sermon form favored by
the Puritans, in which narrative passages are set within a logical framework as circumstantial demonstrations of the truth of the author's thesis.
But where the Puritan form relies on a carefully articulated process of abstract logic to convince the reader, Filson's book relies on a narrative-like
movement of images resolving themselves into a dramatic unity. Boone's
initiation into the wilderness becomes the reader's own experience, as each
chapter of the book carries him deeper into the wilderness, into a more intimate knowledge of the life of the pioneer and the Indian. This quality of
narrative unity helps to give the Boone narrative its aura of myth by making it easier for the reader (and prospective settler) to identify with Boone
and to accept Boone's adventures archetypal of the frontier experience.
Because he was so careful in working out the context in which the Boone
narrative was set, Filson was able (in the narrative itself) to concentrate
wholly on the drama of Boone's character development and the enriching
of his wisdom and sensibilities. Thus later writers were able to take the
Boone narrative out of its original context and use Boone's character to
sanctify their own visions of the West, and the Boone myth was able to
grow and change with the development of American culture.

The structural plan and argument of *Kentucke* are modeled on those
of the Puritan narratives and histories. But where the traditional sermon
form begins with a biblical text, Filson takes the map of Kentucky for his
text. His plan is to develop the meaning inherent in the land in much the
same way that the Puritan sermon exfoliates the meaning in the biblical
passage. The map itself is watermarked with a plowshare and the words
"Work & be Rich." By holding the map up to the light, the alert reader
can thus see behind the pattern of the map the substance of Filson's doctrine. He develops this thesis in greater detail in the preface and in the
opening section, which treats the history, politics, and natural history of
the province.

Like Jefferson and the physiocrats, Filson reads nature as a Bible in
which facts imply moral judgments or grounds for prophecy. Thus the con-
figuration of Kentucky, the richness of her soil, and her location at the
headwaters of the Ohio suggest the prophecy that whoever holds Kentucky

holds the key to western empire. At the same time, the facts of Kentucky's natural endowment suggest that nature itself has intended (hence sanctioned) the imperial role for those who hold Kentucky. One moral drawn from nature is, therefore, the recommendation of a specific policy to the federal government: gain control of the rivers, beginning with the Ohio Valley.

In addition to imperial power, nature in Kentucky induces the growth of admirable institutions among those who emigrate thither. The growth of political democracy among the inhabitants is seen as the product of a happy conjunction of their preparation by Anglo-American political institutions and the environmental advantage of rich farming soil. The Kentuckians' background makes them capable of forming social organizations, and their soil enables each farmer to be relatively independent and self-sustaining.

Filson augments the impact of this physiocratic vision of the land by throwing a romantic and mysterious aura over many of the details of his landscape. He emphasizes exotic natural formations, such as the great limestone caves, and exotic plants and animals peculiar to Kentucky or the western hemisphere. He also emphasizes relics of past civilizations, mysterious sepulchres of unspeakably ancient human bones, which imply that America has seen the rise and fall of unknown empires. Mingled with these images of Kentucky's exotic present and mysterious past are brief, matter-of-fact treatises on agronomy, local history, and the laws of land tenure. These treatises foreshadow Filson's utopian vision of western agrarian democracy and contain hints that Kentucky will be the seat of an American republic-empire in the West. Throughout we see his imagistic logic at work, creating in the reader's mind a series of associations which connect agronomy with utopia, Indian wars with the establishment of empire, and all aspects of Kentucky with Romantic images of beauty and mystery.

These first chapters also introduce the two themes which will create a dialectic within Filson's narrative-like structure: history and geography — the efforts of men to impose their will on the land and their submission to its conditions. These conflicting themes are eventually resolved in a succession of semiprophetic statements which offer a single, coherent vision of the interdependence of the people's will and the land's requirements. Thus the first section concludes with an assertion that geographic advantages and the settlers' political and economic necessities will determine American domination of the Mississippi Valley. Similar prophecies follow the Boone narrative and the essay on the Indians, each new conclusion voicing a more sweeping vision of American glory.

The Boone narrative, which is the next section of *Kentucke*, epitomizes Filson's method of proving his thesis and justifying his affirmative prophecies through dramatic action rather than abstract logic. The narrative presents Boone as the embodiment of the historical purpose of the American frontiersmen, and his adventures are arranged to bring him into close acquaintance with the dual nature of the wilderness. Filson here repeats his dialectic structure in the conflict between Boone's will and the conditions of the wilderness, leading ultimately to a reconciliation of man and land. In addition, the Boone narrative is a stylistic and thematic antithesis of the first section on history and natural history. The narrative takes us back through the landscape we have been viewing as objective scientific observers, showing it to us this time from the highly subjective point of view of a white frontiersman who is emotionally committed to exploring Kentucky and developing its resources. Where the first chapters dwelt on the bounty of the soil and the peaceful growth of democratic institutions, the Boone narrative deals with war, famine, loneliness, and destruction.

The Boone narrative provides Filson's sermon-form structure with its reasons, its circumstantial justification of doctrine. Boone undergoes a series of initiations which give him progressively greater insights into the life of the Indians, the peculiar necessities imposed by the wilderness, and the natural laws which govern life. Through his attempts to interpret these initiations, Boone attains a higher degree of self-knowledge and self-discipline and an ability to impose his own order on both the wilderness and the settlement. The conflict between the influence of the wilderness environment and the creative postulations of Boone's mind is finally synthesized in Boone's concluding vision of Kentucky as a potential utopia and of himself as the chief architect of its triumph.

The dialectic of the Boone narrative thus follows that laid down in the first section on history, government, and natural history — a dialogue or conflict between the men and the land of Kentucky, resolved by a visionary statement prophesying the direction of their common destiny. In the opening section this visionary statement is merely a policy recommendation (domination of the river valleys). In the Boone narrative the dialectic is resolved by a venture into social theory and metaphysics. Apparently Filson means us to view the process of Boone's spiritual awakening as a Rousseauistic allegory in which the instinctually perfect republican citizen is seen emerging, by natural processes of perception and experience, from a primitive world.

The history of the Indian, which is Filson's next subject, is the thematic antithesis of the Boone narrative, showing the power of nature to destroy a people's capacity for civilized sentiment and social forms. In the partial transcript of a treaty negotiation that begins the section, Filson (unlike his Puritan forebears) allows the Indians to speak for themselves, revealing both natural dignity and oratorical gifts along with a great moral weakness: "God made the white flesh masters of the world . . . and we all love rum." [8] Like his French and Puritan predecessors, Filson discusses the origins of the Indians, dwelling on each of the "idle" speculations put forth by various American and European scholars. But he is less interested in scientific debate than in developing a series of images and associated ideas about the Indians that will contribute to his fictive picture of Kentucky. Before he has done with his theorizing over Indian origins, he has populated an apparently primitive continent with lost races of Carthaginians and Viking Danes, as well as the medieval Welsh. He returns to the ancient sepulchre full of bones, at which he glanced in his opening chapters, and discovers mines of potsherds and the remains of an ancient fortification of a style unknown to the present inhabitants. Filson believes that he has discovered in America the picturesque "ruins of empire" which Volney employed as symbols of the rise and decay of great civilizations. The implication of these speculations is that the Indians represent the remnants of a fallen or degenerated race. The American landscape, which is the scene of Boone's renewal of hope and moral strength, has also been the scene of a great failure.[9]

The Indian — for Filson, as for the Puritans and for Buffon and de Pauw — represents a memento mori, a warning of the power of the wilderness to kill man's better nature. Like Boone, the Indian is the product of a wilderness environment, but his politics lack the inner controls, the self-restraint, necessary to the citizen of an ideal republican democracy. The Indian is an instinctive democrat but without a sufficient sense of civic responsibility and of the need for law. Lacking the sentiment which binds Euro-American societies together, the Indians are unnecessarily cruel and revengeful in war, prone to mindless rages, and lacking in a proper sentimental feeling for white and Indian woman.[10] Thus Filson implies that the Indians, because of their defective racial character, failed to learn from the Carthaginians and Welsh the improved customs and institutions of civilization. Hence they may not be destined (as Rousseau suggested they might be) to emerge from the wilderness to live as good Quakers and dutiful republicans. The course of their evolution rises only briefly toward civilization before curving backward to savagery.

While Filson implicitly sees the Indians as racially inferior to the white Americans (and therefore as a people whom it is right to displace), he never condemns them with the moral rancor of a Mather. Anthropological and historical "research" are invoked as proofs of the defects of Indian society, but the moral premises inherent in Filson's analysis are tacitly assumed rather than articulated. With Colden and Rousseau, Filson uses the Indian as proof that the natural man instinctively works toward the ideal in morals and government. But like his great predecessors, he is aware that despite this basic worthiness, man's history is one of decline from freedom to oppression, from purity to corruption of social relationships and institutions. If they are unable to learn from the historical experience of European man, the Indians will simply repeat Europe's historical degeneration and so become increasingly intolerable to the progressive society on their borders. Filson and his readers, standing between the Indian image of man's natural potential for good and the European image of civilization's historical failures to realize that potential, have the opportunity to shape their own future with full awareness of their possibilities for good and evil.

Filson finally restores the reader to a sense of his own place, his own difference from the Indian, by returning him to a figurative mountaintop from which he can again view the whole scene objectively. Filson's "Conclusion" completes the cycle of experience that *Kentucke* traces. We end as we began, outside the wilderness; but because we have experienced the wilderness way of life with the Indian and the frontiersman, our perception of the landscape has been enriched. The "Conclusion" corresponds to the uses section of a sermon, but it offers neither the ethical imperatives of the Puritan application nor the practical advice with which narratives like William Smith's concluded. Instead, it resolves the dialectical tensions of the book with another imaginative prophecy — a visionary statement of the idea of manifest destiny, which makes a coherent synthesis of geographic necessities and American historical aspirations, just as Boone's evocation of a pastoral utopia imagistically reconciled (or at least terminated) the conflict between Indian and white man, wilderness and pioneer.

The "Conclusion" is a novelistic rather than a logical one, depending as it does on the recall of images that have acquired some emotive power through their use in the earlier chapters of the book. Filson imperceptibly slips into the pose of addressing the reader as if he were already a citizen of Kentucky, receiving the encomiums of history, rather than merely a prospective emigrant. The language blends the spiel of the land promoter with the idealism of the Declaration of Independence and the ironic view of European civilization characteristic of Rousseau and Voltaire:

> This fertile region, abounding with all the luxuries of nature, stored
> with all the principal materials for art and industry, inhabited by vir-

tuous and ingenious citizens, must universally attract the attention of
mankind, being situated in the central part of the extensive American
empire . . . where nature makes reparation for having created man;
and government, so long prostituted to the most criminal purposes, establishes an asylum in the wilderness for the distressed of mankind.[11]

In this Enlightenment utopia, the guardian spirits are those of the good
Quaker Penn (the exponent of brotherhood), Washington (the defender of
liberty), Locke (the rationalist and preacher of toleration), and Lycurgus
(embodying the republican spirit of ancient Rome). Filson's peroration
links Kentucky directly to the notion of the new Eden, the antithesis of the
Dark and Bloody Ground, the wilderness:

> In your country, like the land of promise, flowing with milk and
> honey, a land of brooks and water, of fountains and depths, that
> spring out of valleys and hills, a land of wheat and barley, and all
> kinds of fruits, you shall eat bread without scarceness, and not lack
> anything in it. . . . Thus your country, favoured with the smile of
> heaven, will probably be inhabited by the first people the world ever
> knew.[12]

This conclusion anticipates Whitman's call for a "new race of men" in
America; and the phrase "the first people the world ever knew" suggests
both a race of unquestioned superiority and a race closely resembling the
idealized primitive man of Rousseau.

The "Conclusion" is not in itself extraordinary, despite the fact that it
anticipates so many motifs of Jacksonian culture and politics. What sets it
apart from other descriptions of America as a new Eden is the fact that the
final vision of paradise is seen growing out of a savage combat and a descent into the wilderness and the world of the Indian. Filson does not attempt to convince his reader of the truth of his vision by eliminating horror
from the landscape. Rather, through the medium of the Boone narrative,
he conducts his readers through an experience of a range of "wilderness"
emotions and sentiments, hoping to awaken in the reader the sense that
only on the frontier could he completely utilize all the emotional and intellectual powers that make him a man. In this Filson stands with both
Mather and Jefferson: he says that in the wilderness man is subjected to
the naked power of the gods that rule the forces of nature. The effective-
ness of Filson's presentation hinges on the degree to which his reader is
emotionally convinced that Boone was a real man, a hero produced by his
intimacy with the wilderness, and that his experience could therefore be
duplicated to some extent by any man emigrating to Kentucky.

Filson's Boone Narrative

"The Adventures of Col. Daniel Boon" is the key to the immortality of Filson's vision of the West and of the fame of his hero, Daniel Boone. This chapter of *Kentucke* proved far more popular than the rest of the book. It was lifted out of its context and reprinted as a separate pamphlet, in anthologies of Indian war narratives and captivity narratives, and in popular literary periodicals in both Europe and the United States. It became the vehicle by which Filson's version of the frontier myth was transmitted to the literary giants of the American Renaissance and to the European Romantics. The narrative crystallizes everything that Filson had to say about the West, echoing his vision of its utopian future and paralleling the narrative movement into the wilderness that *Kentucke* as a whole follows. The Boone narrative does not state Filson's ideas explicitly (this is left for the "Conclusion"); the ideas are implicit within the drama of its events. This structuring of the book permitted Filson to concentrate on the depiction of Boone's character and allowed later writers to change the context in which the narrative was set, in accordance with changing interpretations of the frontier. For this reason, and because Boone himself was the sort of figure who continued to generate popular legends, the Boone narrative finally proved pregnant of more meanings than its author could have intended.

The Boone narrative, though ostensibly Boone's own narration of his adventures, is actually Filson's careful reworking of Boone's statements and of the legends that Filson had heard about Boone from his fellow frontiersmen. The narrative is a literary myth, artfully contrived to appeal to men concerned with literature; it is not folk legend. Filson selects incidents for portrayal and breaks into the strict chronology of events in order to establish in his reader's mind a sense of the rhythm of Boone's experience and to emphasize certain key images and symbols that define the meaning of Boone's experience. Boone's "Adventures" consist of a series of initiations, a series of progressive immersions that take him deeper into the wilderness. These initiations awaken Boone's sense of his own identity, provide him with a natural moral philosophy, and give him progressively deeper insights into the nature of the wilderness. Each immersion is followed by a return to civilization, where Boone can apply his growing wisdom to the ordering of his community, and by a momentary interlude of meditation and contemplation, in which Boone can review his experience, interpret it, and formulate the wisdom gained from it. As a result of these rhythmic cycles of immersion and emergence, he grows to become the commanding genius of his people, their hero-chief, and the man fit to real-ize Kentucky's destiny.

Filson casts Boone's adventures as a personal narrative, developed by the Puritans as a literary form of witness to an experience of God's grace. "The Adventures of Col. Daniel Boon" combines the conventions of form and substance of three types of personal narratives — the conversion nar-rative of the type written by Jonathan Edwards in his "Personal Narra-tive"; the narrative of personal triumph in battle, as written by Mason and Church; and the captivity narrative, the account of ordeals suffered at the hands of the wilderness's human children, the Indians. But Filson revolu-tionizes the Puritan forms by substituting nature or the wilderness for Je-hovah as his symbol of deity. The impression conveyed by the Puritan per-sonal narrative is that of a tightly closed, systematic, intimate universe, bound together by explicitly articulated, organic bonds between God and man — a universe manageable in size but containing all important things. The wilderness is the realm of chaos, impinging on the ordered cosmos but somehow outside the world protected by God. Filson, however, substitutes all of the wilderness landscape, its ambiguous and even hellish elements as well as its pure and paradisiacal qualities (its wigwams as well as its settle-ments), for the Word of God in the symbolic universe of Boone's personal narrative. He thus expands the boundaries of that universe to include the wild continent as an integral and vital part of the divine plan for the regen-eration of man. At the same time, by retaining the individual experience as the central focus and source of perspective in his narrative, he preserves the sense of organic unity and order that the Puritan form possessed.

The Boone narrative begins with an account of and an apology for the hero's motivation for leaving his family and moving to Kentucky. The ac-count is carefully calculated to overcome the objections made by oppo-nents of emigration from Increase Mather to Buffon. If a man is civilized, why would he leave society for the savage solitude of the forest? And if he is not civilized, how can he be set up as a hero for civilized men to emu-late? Boone's justification is largely pragmatic: the final results of his act are good, whatever his motives. He creates a new society through his emi-gration, and he does not destroy the existing society by leaving it. He re-turns in the end to his family. Thus the trinity of values on which Anglo-American society is based — social progress, piety, and the family — is in-voked at the outset as the basic standard for judging Boone's actions. But Filson reinforces this defense by having Boone present himself as a man nurtured in the values of the eighteenth century, so that he can further jus-tify his emigration by appealing to the "divinities" of natural religion —

natural law, human reason (and the desire for knowledge), and divine Providence:

> CURIOSITY is natural to the soul of man, and interesting objects have a powerful influence on our affections. Let these influencing powers actuate, by the permission or disposal of Providence, from selfish or social views, yet in time the mysterious will of heaven is unfolded, and we behold our own conduct, from whatever motives excited, operating to answer the important designs of heaven. Thus we behold Kentucke, lately an howling wilderness, . . . rising from obscurity to shine with splendor, equal to any other of the stars of the American hemisphere.[13]

This passage provides a major insight into the pattern of experience that is rhythmically repeated throughout the Boone narrative and the whole of *Kentucke*. Boone enters the wilderness in a state of innocence and naïveté, unsure of his own motivations and of the ultimate outcome of his adventures, but trusting in the strength of his own character and the goodness of nature to create ultimate good out of present confusion. This trusting immersion in the wilderness ultimately results in the attainment of self-knowledge and an understanding of the design of God — a state of awareness which Boone attains when he is able to stand above his experience, view it from outside, and exercise his reason upon it in order to reduce it to its essential order.

This pattern of experience is followed in the first crucial section of the narrative, in which Boone is initiated into a knowledge of the wilderness of Kentucky. With four friends, he enters Kentucky in 1769, after a fatiguing journey and "uncomfortable weather as a prelibation of our future suffering." The naïve hero is exposed to a series of experiences that give him direct knowledge of both the terror and the beauty of Kentucky. His arrival is a pastoral idyll, in which the wilderness appears to be the bucolic retreat of a divine country squire. Even the buffalo are compared to domesticated cattle. Behind the picture of peace there is a bare suggestion that the violence of man may disrupt the natural harmony: "The buffaloes were more frequent than I have seen cattle in the settlements, browzing on the leaves of the cane, or croping [*sic*] the herbage on those extensive plains, fearless, because ignorant, of the violence of man." [14] But Boone himself is as ignorant of the threat as are the buffalo.

Boone's description of the wilderness has a peculiarly neoclassic flavor about it, with nature appearing as an artful landscape designer and master gardener, the creator of the well-wrought forest. At another level nature is Boone's hostess, welcoming him into a formal garden planted with an eye

toward elegance of form and color, with animals provided apparently for
the amusement of the guests:

> We . . . passed through a great forest, on [*sic*] which stood myriads
> of trees, some gay with blossoms, others rich with fruits. Nature was
> here a series of wonders and a fund of delight. Here she displayed her
> ingenuity and industry in a variety of fruits and flowers, beautifully
> coloured, elegantly shaped, and charmingly flavoured; and we were
> diverted with innumerable animals presenting themselves perpetually
> to our view.[15]

In the eyes of Filson's Boone, the beauty of wild nature lies in the extent to
which it imitates cultivated nature and implies that civilization is itself the
crown of natural evolution.

Into this idyllic and civil landscape the violence of man intrudes,
catching the innocents unaware. Boone and one companion are captured,
their other friends driven off, their camp and furs plundered. The two men
manage to escape their captors and return to camp, where they find
Boone's brother Squire arrived before them. This coincidence provides
Boone with an opportunity for one of those philosophical asides in which
he finds the essential meaning of his experience and derives from that
meaning a practical wisdom. In this case he discovers that friendship and
human society are balm for the hurts inflicted by human enmity and evil:
"[Our] meeting so fortunately in the wilderness made us reciprocally sensible of the utmost satisfaction. So much does friendship triumph over mis-
fortune . . . and substitute . . . happiness in [its] room." [16] Soon his companion is killed by Indians, and Boone and Squire are left alone in the
wilderness. Yet he can still maintain his cheerfulness and confidence, indulge in civilized conversation, and articulate a stoic philosophy of asceticism and self-control:

> Thus situated, many hundred of miles from our families in the
> howling wilderness, I believe few would have enjoyed the happiness
> we experienced. I often observed to my brother. You see now how lit-
> tle nature requires to be satisfied. Felicity . . . is rather found in our
> own breasts than in the enjoyment of external things . . . it requires
> but a little philosophy to make a man happy. . . . This consists in a
> full resignation to the Will of Providence, and a resigned soul finds
> pleasure in a path strewed with briars and thorns.[17]

Boone's initiation into knowledge of the wilderness cannot be accomplished, however, while even one civilized amenity remains to him. He
must be stripped to the barest essentials for survival, in order to meet nature directly and without encumbrances. Thus, when their supplies run

low, Squire returns to the settlement, leaving Boone with no trace of civilized life except his rifle — "without bread, salt or sugar, without company of my fellow creatures or even a horse or dog." The dark elements in the wilderness have all but subdued the light. Death has nearly triumphed over life, loneliness has succeeded companionship, and melancholy passions have all but toppled the controlling power of "philosophy and fortitude." [18] But at this point the narrative takes a sudden turn, and Boone's melancholy is converted into a vision of the beauty and order of nature, which strengthens his spirit and gives him the determination to settle permanently in Kentucky.

Boone's melancholy takes the form of a morbid introspection, a dwelling on the insecurity of his position and his separation from his wife and family. This melancholy nearly destroys him and is overcome only when the beauty of the natural landscape forces him to turn his eyes outward. In the Puritan narrative of life in the wilderness, salvation depended on the opposite process. The Puritan needed the sense of insecurity to make vivid his dependence on God, and he pursued a course of rigorous introspection precisely in order to develop that sense of personal weakness. Where the protagonist of the Puritan captivity, yearning for God's felt presence, hearkened to a voice from the church or from his Bible, Filson's hero hears the voice of God calling him deeper into the wilderness. Filson's God makes himself apparent through the landscape, and the Word of God becomes apparent to the reader as the landscape alters Boone's attitude gradually from gloom to light and peace. Boone ascends from the wilderness to a commanding height, from which he can view the wilderness at a distance and (figuratively) take in the whole vista of Kentucky. The scene serves to comfort him, as biblical texts comforted the Puritan:

> One day I undertook a tour through the country, and the diversity and beauties of nature . . . expelled every gloomy and vexatious thought. Just at the close of day the gentle gales retired and left the place to the disposal of a profound calm. Not a breeze shook the most tremulous leaf. I had gained the summit of a commanding ridge, and, looking round with astonishing delight, beheld the ample plains, the beauteous tracts below. On the other hand, I surveyed the famous river Ohio that rolled in silent dignity, marking the western boundary of Kentucke with inconceivable grandeur. At a vast distance I beheld the mountains lift their venerable brows, and penetrate the clouds. All things were still. I kindled a fire near a fountain of sweet water, and feasted on the loin of a buck, which a few hours before I had killed. The sullen shades of night soon overspread the whole hemisphere, and the earth seemed to gasp for the hovering moisture. . . . I laid me

down to sleep, and I awoke not until the sun had chased away the night.[19]

This scene is the crisis of the book, for from this first initiation into the knowledge of nature Boone derives the "philosophy and fortitude" and the vision of future paradise in Kentucky which enable him to emerge from the later ordeals he must face. The scene is crucial to the successful operation of the narrative as a myth, since it is here that the human hero achieves communion with the gods of nature.

Filson's method of conveying this special relationship between man and God through the mediation of nature differs substantially, however, from that used by his cultural ancestors, and this change signifies an important shift in Americans' conceptions of their place in the wilderness. Filson's symbolism is implicit in his landscape and is communicated to the reader only in terms of Boone's changed perception of the objects around him. Both Edwards in his *Personal Narrative* and Jefferson in his descriptions in *Notes on Virginia* isolated the elements of divinity or of natural law which are present in the landscape and described them explicitly to the reader. To Jefferson such scenes were the basis for theories of natural evolution and geologic change. Edwards prepared for his vision of God in nature by reading his Bible, and he gained his first insights from a text ("I am the Rose of Sharon and the Lily of the Valleys"), rather than from a direct view of nature. It was only after he had read his Bible that the appearance of nature altered for him and there seemed to be "a calm, sweet cast, or appearance of divine glory, in almost every thing." The God in Edwards's landscape is a transcendent being, whose nature makes itself apparent in the landscape but whose essence is not the landscape. And where Filson's Boone does not mention "God" once in this description (as if to imply that nature is God enough), Edwards noted each of the several specific aspects which make up God's nature, his "excellency, his wisdom, his purity and love," and his biblical role as "the Redeemer." [20]

Boone's (or Filson's) vision is closer to the Indian vision of nature (as expressed, for example, in the conversion of the Sioux priest Black Elk), in which the seeker or hunter achieves a sense of kinship with all nature and nature's creatures and, through this natural kinship, a kinship with the gods. However, there remains a vital difference between Boone's and Black Elk's visions. In Filson's account, nature is not as concretely seen as in Black Elk's. Conventions of landscape portrayal intervene, to give Filson's descriptions a slightly abstract quality; and where he does go into detail, in the sections on Kentucky flora and fauna, the tone is scientific and impersonal. Boone appreciates the wisdom and moral intention of the God of nature through his intimacy with the landscape; for Black Elk, the intimacy is so intense that the gods become his grandfathers, the beasts his brothers and sisters and gods by turns, and he himself both god, man, and beast. Later writers, such as Timothy Flint and Fenimore Cooper, who developed the implications of Filson's narrative to their ultimate point, came closer to expressing in convincing and evocative terms the character of this hunter's vision of man's and God's places in the cosmos. Filson's vision is still bound to the conventions of description favored by the landscape artists and writers of the early Romantic period. God's nature becomes apparent through man's perceptions of symbolic relationships within the real world, rather than through direct supernatural revelation or mystical insight. These patterns of symbolic relationship in the natural world are then interpreted with a high degree of artifice, of intellectual plan, as in Jefferson's "Natural Bridge" and "Potomac Gap." [21]

The spiritual impact of Boone's experience (as Filson sees it) is to make him the perfect stoic — patient as an Indian, indifferent to danger, fearless, and content to live as the wilderness demands, by hunting and hiding in solitude. Moreover, Filson enables him to articulate his philosophy in a series of maxims and observations on social order and personal self-reliance. He does not, like a painter, leave the meaning implicit in his symbolic experience. Rather, he draws applications from his experience as a Puritan would, deriving practical standards of behavior and judgment. Thus he generalizes from his own stoic calm: "How unhappy such a situation for a man tormented by fear, which is vain if no danger comes, and if it does, only augments the pain. It was my happiness to be destitute of this afflicting passion, with which I had the greatest reason to be affected." Nothing in nature can hold fear for him now: even the "prowling wolves" and their "perpetual howlings" merely "diverted my nocturnal hours." But human institutions could never create in him this sense of inner peace and self-possession. Boone rejects both the comforts of civilization and the commercial values which characterize established urban societies like that of England: "I was surrounded with plenty in the midst of want. I was happy in the midst of dangers and inconveniences. In such diversity it was impossible that I should be disposed to melancholy. No populous city, with all the varieties of commerce and stately structures, could afford so much pleasure to my mind, as the beauties of nature I found here." [22]

Before Filson's Boone moves deeper into the wilderness, his "second paradise," [23] he returns to the East to tell his family and friends his vision of the West and to convince them to organize a settlement in Kentucky.

This return marks the end of Boone's first initiation into the wilderness and starts him on another series of initiations, which will make him a political and military leader capable of organizing and defending a civilized community in the wilderness. His first attempt ends in failure, when Indian attacks and the difficulty of the season force his emigrant caravan to turn back to the settlements on Clench River. Boone's meditation on this failure calls up a vision of the mountain pass in which disaster has overtaken the party. As in the earlier landscape, this description is a blend of symbols which define the divine truth implicit in the scene. But where the earlier description saw nature as a pastoral realm of order and promise, the description of the pass is more akin to sublime than to pastoral painting. Disproportionately huge rocks, shattered by wind and water — images of ruin and destruction and human weakness — embody a vision of the dark power of nature. The vision calls up in Boone a sense of the mortality of all natural things, the geologic cycles by which mountains rise and fall and the convulsions in which the civilizations of men are destroyed: "The aspect of these cliffs is so wild and horrid it is impossible to behold them without terror. The spectator is apt to imagine that nature had formerly suffered some violent convulsion; and that these are the dismembered remains of the dreadful shock; the ruins not of Persepolis or Palmyra, but a world!" [24]

The theme of this section of the narrative is the antithesis of the first. Nature is now seen as uncontrolled and callous of human sentiments and concerns. The institutions of man, though subject like Persepolis and Palmyra to natural decay, offer the only hope of succor and moral order. The wild disorder of the natural scene is contrasted with a little fable of the social contract. Boone, having been aided by his countrymen at Clench River, sets aside his own plans and instead serves his people as an officer in Lord Dunmore's War of 1774. As a consequence of this service, Boone becomes a partner of Henderson's Transylvania Company and takes a party west to survey the Wilderness Road and establish the settlement of Boonesborough on the Kentucky River. In the rest of this section of the narrative, Boone experiences a series of similar initiations into the various societal arrangements and value systems then contending for mastery in the West.

The narrative continues to suggest that sentiment is the bond which seals the social contract. Filson has Boone mention pointedly that his wife and daughter were the first white women to settle in Kentucky, as if this is the sign of civilization. Sentimental concern for women and children, as Filson points out in his discussion of Indian "Manners," is the quality which distinguishes the white from the Indian society. Thus it is inevitable that one of the tests in Boone's initiation into the responsibilities of civilized leadership should involve the rescue of three young girls (including his own daughter) from the ungentle hands of Indian raiders. This incident was to be developed in elaborate detail by many later writers of the Romantic period — Cooper in *The Last of the Mohicans* and other of the Leatherstocking tales, Imlay in *The Emigrants*, and Brown in *Edgar Huntly* — but Filson treats it rather briefly. He was not, after all, writing a novel; it was enough for his purposes to suggest that the Indians had no sentimental regard for the female and that Boone did. An audience raised on captivity narratives could fill in the blank spaces from memory.

The differences in social values between the frontiersmen, the Indians, and the commercial civilization of Britain and the eastern states are clarified for Boone in the course of his capture by the Shawnee, his march with them to the British Fort Detroit, and his adoption into the tribe. Like the hero-victim of the captivity narrative, Boone is tempted to turn apostate and become a Shawnee or British subject. His captivity forces Boone into acquaintance with the serpent in his garden of Kentucky. If he adopts the standards of the British or the Indians, Boone will incur a second fall of man; he will prove himself a new Adam with the identical weaknesses of the old. The Indians represent a fallen race, a people who have failed to realize the arcadian possibilities of the land and their own human capacity for civilized behavior. The white scalp-buyers and renegades like Simon Girty, against whom Boone was later to fight, also succumb to the evil temptation of the wilderness and realize their potential for evil and inhuman rapacity, rather than sentiment and humanity. Boone resists the temptation to become an Indian or a scalp-hunter because he brings to his ordeal the mind and heart of an eighteenth-century gentleman-philosophe (albeit in rudimentary form).

For the Puritan, resistance to temptation depended upon the degree to which man subordinated his will, intellect, and emotions to the revealed Word of God. In the conversion experience and the captivity narrative, this sentiment of subordination is evoked by an unanticipated and overwhelming providential event, which mere reason proves incapable of predicting or fully explaining. Heart, mind, and spirit are regenerated or created anew, and the premises of reasoning as well as the motives of willful action are so altered by their purification as to be unintelligible to the unregenerate. The mind and heart of Filson's Boone, on the other hand, are sequentially rather than apocalyptically educated. His reasoning mind accumulates and analyzes a continually accreting store of experience, both immediate or personal and traditional or historical. Where the Puritan is saved from sin by the infusion of sudden grace in an uninformed (or misinformed) spirit, Boone is saved by the power of his mind and the growing store of experience on which his reason operates. In Filson's work, this contrast between Boone's rationalism and the Puritan insistence on a mystical immediacy of revelation as ways of approaching knowledge of God appears as a contrast between Boone's rational and the Indian's mythopoeic and superstitious apprehension of nature.

After his capture, Boone is carried by the Indians to Fort Detroit, where Governor Hamilton treats him "with great humanity" and offers the Indians "one hundred pounds sterling" to release Boone. A group of English gentlemen, disturbed by Boone's situation, offer him a purse of money for his "wants." In these brief incidents Filson sketches a caricature of English social values. Hamilton and his fellow gentlemen are courteous and generous to the captive, but at the same time they are engaged in buying scalps and captives from the Indians. Their values are largely commercial, and their valuation of Boone is purely monetary. The Indians, on the other hand, have none of this British hypocrisy. They refuse the price offered for Boone, despite the fact that it represents a king's ransom. Similarly, Boone refuses the offer of a purse because to accept it would be inconsistent with the honor of an independent man ("I refused, with many thanks for their kindness; adding, that I never expected it would be in my power to recompense their generosity").[25] While the Indians do not offer Boone money for his comforts, they recognize his worth as a man and a hunter and adopt him into the tribe as an equal. Where the British are hypocritical in their courtesy, the Shawnee are affectionate and loyal within their family bonds. They accept their adopted brother as virtually a blood member of the tribe:

> I . . . was adopted, according to their custom, into a family where I became a son, and had a great share in the affection of my new parents, brothers, sisters, and friends. I was exceedingly familiar and friendly with them, always appearing cheerful and satisfied as possible, and they put great confidence in me.[26]

Yet Boone remains superior to the Indians: he masters their technique of living, without surrendering his consciousness of "white" social values or his personal philosophy of self-reliance and self-restraint. Thus he plays cleverly on the childish vanity of his adopted brothers and stays clear of their jealousy of his skill with a rifle:

> I often went a hunting with them, and frequently gained their applause for my activity at our shooting matches. I was careful not to ex-

ceed many of them in shooting; for no people are more envious than they in this sport. I could observe, in their countenances and gestures, the greatest expressions of joy when they exceeded me; and when the reverse happened, of envy.[27]

Boone can become as intimate as an Indian with the conditions of wilderness life, engage in long solitary hunts, and even allow his soul to be harrowed by the terrors of the wilderness landscape without succumbing to the Indian's debilitating religious terror. His prowess and his dispassionate, calculated personal diplomacy quickly make him one of the most prominent and respected braves in the tribe:

> The Shawanese King took great notice of me, and treated me with profound respect, and entire friendship, often entrusting me to hunt at liberty. I frequently returned with the spoils of the woods, and as often presented some of what I had taken to him, expressive of duty to my sovereign. My food and lodging was, in common, with them, not so good indeed as I could desire, but necessity made every thing acceptable.[28]

If Boone is allowed the liberty of hunting by himself, why does he not immediately seek his freedom? The question was to perplex many later writers, who assumed that Boone stayed because he found the Indian life very much to his liking. Filson does not explain the considerations which in fact determine Boone on staying with the Indians for a long period of time, but most likely they are pragmatic. Boone is fairly deep in Indian country and would run very grave risks in escaping by himself because of the winter season and the scarcity of game. Later he becomes aware that an assault on Boonesborough is being planned, and he waits to spy out the Indians' plans as they mature. In addition, he needs time to lull the Indians' suspicion of him. Filson's reasons for omitting Boone's motives for staying were based on literary considerations: to detail Boone's calculations would have vitiated Boone's initiation into knowledge of the Indian way. In order for Boone to know the Indians' life, he has to be truly immersed in it, accept (however temporarily) all of its assumptions and manners, and set aside the moral and political predilections of his own people. During the course of his life with the Indians, the values that belong to Boone as a white frontiersman gradually assert themselves, and this is a sign that his acceptance of the Indians has been simply another step in the larger initiation into his knowledge of himself and his own people's essential values. In the world Filson creates for Boone, knowledge and values proceed always from experience. Only when experience is completed does Filson's hero formulate its philosophic meaning.

The first sign of Boone's awakening sense of his true nature is his observation that the Shawnee lands have great potential for farming: "I hunted some [for the Indians], and found the land, for a great extent about this river, to exceed the soil of Kentucke, if possible, and remarkably well watered." He sees the land as a husbandman, not simply as a hunter, a perception which sets him off from the Indians. His sentimental feeling for his family's situation, another sign of his difference from the Indians, revives when he notes the gathering of an army of warriors, armed and painted "in a fearful manner" for an attack on Kentucky. Boone's reaction to these perceptions is swift: he makes his escape, despite the season, and returns to Boonesborough after a foodless march — a sort of purification ordeal-by-hunger.[29]

On his return Boone first leads the settlers in their successful resistance to a prolonged siege by four hundred Indians and eleven French Canadian officers. Then he makes a circuit to Carolina and back to retrieve his wife and family, who had returned to their home thinking Boone was dead. The events of this section reveal Boone's ability to apply the knowledge of Indian psychology, the wilderness environment, and the principles of political organization which he has gained in his several initiations. Boone's skills include his leadership of a reconnaissance raid deep into Indian territory around the flank of the approaching army, the clever diplomacy by which he delays the Indians' attack, and his grasp of military measures to thwart their attempts to undermine the palisade. (Despite the fact that the French were about to enter the Revolution on the colonial side, the Indian-Canadian army flew French colors next to British as they marched against Boonesborough, a fact which Filson's Boone notes without comment. Apparently the French of Canada regarded the British as temporary allies in their continuing struggle against the Anglo-Americans of the thirteen colonies.)

Boone's triumph over the Indians is only temporary, and after his return from Carolina he and his colony face the darkest period of their history. In this last adventure in the narrative Boone receives his final test, his final initiation into self-knowledge and the wisdom and power of leadership. The prowess which he has gained in his initiations into the knowledge of nature and the techniques of Indian war is not enough to make him leader of a civilized community. Simon Girty and Alexander McKee, the two "abandoned [white] men" who lead the next Indian assault on Kentucky, have as much prowess as Boone; but the civilized leader must possess those sentiments and sympathies which are at the basis of social cohesion, and these qualities the renegades have abandoned. In his last ordeal, as Boone experiences the depths of defeat and personal misery, his powers of rational control are all but overthrown by the tragedies which overtake his family and his nation. The land itself, as if in sympathy with the state of Boone's soul, goes through a period of barren fruitlessness and famine. It renews its vigor only when Boone renews his powers of self-control and his hopeful vision of the future.

The dark chapter begins with a disastrous hunting expedition. Boone and his brother, hunting food for the settlers, whose grain and corn crops have been ruined by Indian raids, are attacked by Indians. The brother is killed, and Boone himself is hunted through the woods by the Indians and their hunting dogs. The paragraph which recounts this misadventure ends with the observation that "winter soon came on, and was very severe." Thus Filson directly associates Boone's personal tragedy with the state of the land. The severity of the winter and the Indians' attacks force the settlers to abandon their reliance on the products of husbandry — corn and wheat — and turn to hunting buffalo for their sustenance like the Indians. But the Kentuckians have a philosophy which enables them to resign themselves to hardship: "Being a hardy race of people, and accustomed to difficulties and necessities, they were wonderfully supported through all their sufferings, until the ensuing Fall, when we received abundance from the fertile soil." [30] The Puritans were wont to claim that they were "wonderfully supported" in their sufferings; but where the Puritans' support came from the transcendent Jehovah, the Kentuckians' support derives from their belief in their own hardihood and in the coming renewal of the land's fertility. The Kentuckians thus adopt the philosophy which their culture hero Daniel Boone discovered in his first initiation into the wilderness.

With the coming of spring all the powers of darkness seem to gather for a last effort at destroying Kentucky. In 1782 the Indians and their British masters were to make a last effort to throw back the frontier and render invalid all American claims to the West. While Boone (in Filson's account) is apparently unaware of the threat to the nation at large, he knows that the year will see Kentucky saved or destroyed. To prevent the settlers from planting the corn that could carry them through another dark winter, the Indians send numerous raiding parties ahead of their main army and inflict a series of defeats on the settlers. Under McKee and Girty all the tribes of the Ohio country gather against Kentucky, as in Puritan times French officers mustered all hell and Canada against New England. Their rage and bloodthirstiness are excited to fever pitch by the monstrous sadism of the renegades, men who had abandoned both those human sympathies and sentiments which mark the civilized man and the tribal loyalties which ennoble the Indian.[31]

McKee and Girty are Boone's antitypes, men who have experienced the same initiation into the wilderness that Boone underwent but who were degraded by the experience. They embody all the negative, evil possibilities inherent in the emigration to the wilderness. At the climactic Battle of Blue Licks, Boone and the renegades meet head on, and the result is a tragic setback for Boone and his countrymen. Filson's account of the battle is brief and incomplete; he neglects to explain how so canny a frontiersman as Boone comes to fall into Girty's trap at Blue Licks, although such an explanation would certainly have enhanced his hero's reputation for prowess. Filson is not interested here in showing us more of Boone's skill. Instead, the Battle of Blue Licks gives him an opportunity to show Boone under the stress of strong passions and at last victorious over them. This is Boone's decisive struggle between the newly awakened sentiments of grief and his philosophy of rational self-control and attention to duty.

According to Filson's account, the Kentuckians under Boone and two other militia colonels, Todd and Trigg, pursue Girty's army on its retreat from an unsuccessful siege of Bryant's Station and assault a small party, on the other side of Licking River, which they take to be a rear guard. But this small rear guard is bait for a trap, which Girty springs when the Kentuckians cross over. (In historical fact, Boone and his fellow colonels were not deceived by the ruse. They had decided against attacking; but when Major McGary went berserk with battle-madness and precipitated the assault, Boone and the others could only join in and make the best of a desperate situation.) The Indians fire from their hiding places in brushy ravines on the riverside hills, and "an exceeding fierce battle immediately began, for about fifteen minutes, when we, being overpowered by numbers, were obliged to retreat." Among the dead are Colonels Todd and Trigg and Boone's second son, killed at his father's side at the height of the assault. Sixty-seven other Kentuckians are killed and seven captured; four of the latter are tortured to death "in a most barbarous manner, by the young warriors, to train them up to cruelty." [32]

The horrid details of the assault and the retreat do not emerge till Boone returns to the field some days after the battle, with Logan's relief force, to bury the dead. Then the terror and grief of his recollections shake him, and the "dreadful scene" before him is made still more poignant by the fact that his son lies among the mutilated dead:

> [We] returned to bury the dead, and found their bodies strewed everywhere, cut and mangled in a dreadful manner. This mournful

scene exhibited a horror almost unparalleled: Some torn by wild beasts; those in the river eaten by fishes; all in such putrified condition, that no one could be distinguished from another.[33]

Yet from this scene of desolation new hope is born. As in Rogers's *Ponteach*, the hero's powers of reason triumph over grief by subordinating his emotions to the moderate level necessary for an efficient discharge of his duties. He accompanies Clark's punitive expedition against the Shawnee towns and, as he sees again the land that he found so fertile even in his captivity, he experiences a revival of his hopes for its agricultural development. His ordeal and Kentucky's are over.° Both have emerged wiser in the ways of the wilderness, better able to organize and control their own affairs, and emotionally awakened to the bonds of sympathy and sentiment that hold civilization together.

Boone signifies his emergence in a concluding review of his adventures, in which he interprets the meaning of his part and projects a vision of the future. It is in this "Conclusion" that his ultimate character as a hero emerges. The section vaguely resembles one of those "improvements" that Cotton Mather attached to Hannah Dustin's captivity narrative, but its substance is not abstractly philosophical or theological. Filson has Boone recount his vision in a series of images and incidents drawn from the drama of his experiences. The symbols which give meaning to this vision derive their primary significance from the narrative alone, not from some biblical or other source outside the narrative. This self-contained quality and the fact that Boone's philosophic principles are voiced primarily as perceptions and experiences (rather than as abstract lessons or messages) make the Boone narrative the nearest approach in the eighteenth century to a truly novelistic treatment of the myth of the frontier.

Boone begins his concluding statement with a text, drawn from the words of an Indian chief rather than from the Bible: "To conclude, I can now say that I have verified the saying of an old Indian who signed Col. Henderson's deed. Taking me by the hand, at the delivery thereof, Brother, says he, we have given you a fine land, but I will believe you will have much trouble settling it." [34] Witnessing to the truth of this prophecy, Boone laments his losses and troubles, the hardships he has suffered at the hand of nature and the Indians. But the lament, like each of Boone's initiations, ends with a vision of the good that arises from the cruelties and hardships of the wilderness:

° Just as the sorrow of widowed women and the death of children in battle signify the dark moment of Kentucky's history, the renewal of Kentucky's hope and commitment to civilized, agrarian values is heralded by Filson's tale of a woman's successful defense of her home in Crab Orchard against an Indian attack.

My footsteps have often been marked with blood, and therefore I can truly subscribe to [Kentucky's] original name [Dark and Bloody Ground]. Two darling sons, and a brother have, I lost by savage hands, which have also taken from me many horses and abundance of cattle. Many dark and sleepless nights have I been companion for owls, separated from the chearful society of men, scorched by the Summer's sun, and pinched by the Winter's cold, and instrument ordained to settle the wilderness. But now the scene is changed: Peace crowns the sylvan shade.[35]

Boone's lament bears a close resemblance to Mary Rowlandson's concluding plaint, dwelling on the sleepless nights, the loneliness, and the discomfort experienced in the wilderness sojourn. But where the Puritan Mrs. Rowlandson believed that her captivity represented God's intention to chastise her and make more taxing the settlement of the wilderness, Boone claims that he is "an instrument ordained by God to settle the wilderness." Even in suffering, Boone is essentially the hero, the man of power.

The Boone narrative establishes its meaning through a rhythmic repetition of a single pattern of experience, reinforced by an imagistic connection between the state of Boone's mind and the state of the real landscape. This pattern of experience constitutes the essence of Filson's "myth." It begins with a total immersion of Boone in an experience of the wilderness, continues with his tasting both the promise and the terror of the Indian's world, and culminates in his achievement of a deeper perception of the nature of the wilderness and of his own soul and his assertion of rational control over his environment. The reader is led to assume that the result of this assertion of control will be to realize, through agrarian cultivation, nature's inherent power to sustain civilization. But in the narrative itself this result is seen only through Boone's perceptions of the land. It is the imagistic logic of literature that leads the reader unconsciously to draw a causal connection between Boone's perception of Kentucky's promise and the realization of a western arcadia. If Boone sees Kentucky as paradise, one feels, then it really is (or may really become) a paradise.

What is extraordinary about Filson's handling of this literary logic is that he portrays Boone's arcadian vision of the West as emerging from a thorough grounding in the evils and hardships of the wilderness, implying that these very evils are productive of the highest good for Boone's character and consequently for the character of the Kentucky settlements. The passage in which he describes his "footsteps" as "marked with blood" is followed by a vision of peace:

What thanks, what ardent and ceaseless thanks, are due to that all-superintending providence which has turned cruel war into peace, brought order out of confusion, made the fierce savages placid, and turned away their hostile weapons from our country! May the same Almighty Goodness banish the accursed monster war, . . . rapine, and insatiable ambition. Let peace, descending from her native heaven, bid her olives spring amid the joyful nations; and plenty, in league with commerce, scatter blessings from her copious hands.[36]

To Filson this vision represents Boone's realization of his true character and his true vision of the West. As a hero of the Enlightenment, enamored of peace and order, Boone views the promise of the West as dependent on its ability to produce an agrarian arcadia, cultivated to a symmetrical and orderly beauty, offsetting the sublime and terrible picture of what convulsions man and nature are capable of producing. Beyond the liberty to delight in this promise in "peace and safety . . . with my once fellow-sufferers," to enjoy the gratitude of his countrymen for his services, and to contemplate the prospect of Kentucky's becoming "one of the most opulent and powerful states of North America," Boone requires nothing further of nature. With this statement his narrative concludes.

The Boone Narrative as Myth

Myth, as I have defined it, is a narrative formulation of a culture's world view and self-concept, which draws both on the historical experience of that culture and on sources of feeling, fear, and aspiration (individual and universal/archetypal) deep in the human subconscious and which can be shown to function in that culture as a prescription for historical action and for value judgment. The adoption by the national reading public of the myth of Daniel Boone implied their acceptance of a certain myth-scenario of interaction between themselves, their land, and the dark races belonging to their land. In Filson's legend and in the myth that grew out of it, the roles and characters of hunter and husbandman are ambiguously equated through the association of the hero's career of seminomadic wandering, violence, and opportunity-seeking with the agrarian imagery and morality expounded by Jefferson and Crèvecoeur. Implicit in this ambiguity is a scenario of national progress in which the land and its resources are to be "cultivated" through their quick exploitation and given their "improved" value by speculation and in which the Indian is to be redeemed through the expropriation of his land, physical removal to desert and inhospitable regions, or (if necessary) extermination.

In view of these consequences, it is necessary that we understand the bases of the Boone myth's appeal, as well as the processes by which it gained credence as a national myth. Filson was not the first writer to offer a hunter and warrior of the frontiers as an image of American heroism. However, he was the first whose efforts met with a positive, general response throughout the several sections of the country over an appreciable period of time. Filson's success depended in part upon the existence of an intercolonial book trade which had not been available to Benjamin Church, Roger Wolcott, or the eulogists of Captain Lovewell. But the practicality of wide distribution merely facilitated the circulation of a work whose potential for success as myth was different from that of any generic predecessor. The reasons for its impact can be summarized:

1. Filson convincingly portrays his hero as a contemporary man, extraordinary in his skill and fortitude but still believable, a great man rather than a semidivinity. Moreover, he portrays a living man, whose continuing adventures could be reported by others to confirm and develop Filson's image of him.

2. Boone's adventures are shown as instances relevant to a range of metaphysical, moral, and historical questions that the enlightened reader would be sure to regard as having the highest level of philosophical and social importance.

3. The narrative, drawing on two levels of mythology, supports its rationalization of the westward movement by basing it on the deepest unconscious assumptions of the culture about its place, destiny, and value in the world. The first level is that of culture-bound mythology, as expressed in the several genres of Colonial narrative which had earlier functioned as a myth-literature. The second is that of archetypal myth, which Filson unconsciously evokes.

Filson's generic predecessors had each lacked one or more of these basic elements. Thomas Morton had portrayed himself as a hunter and Lord of Misrule, invoking the ancient British myths of Robin-Hood/Robin-Wood; but his very success in conveying this image of himself put him drastically out of step with the dominant population of the colony, the Puritans. Benjamin Church's book was prophetic in its depiction of a hunter hero gaining initiation into a symbolic kingship of the woods through his killing of an Indian ruler, but the work lacked the kind of unifying philosophical and moral framework Filson provides for Boone. (Most of the reprints of Church's book appeared in the early nineteenth century, after the popularity of hunter heroes was well established.) The "John Mason" of Wolcott's epic and Prince's narrative was an anachronism at his appearance, and Mason, like Captain Lovewell, was a purely local hero in a war of concern to New England alone. Although Robert Rogers was a hero in a war of significance to all the colonies, his adventures too were not given a moral or symbolic dimension; and his works, like Crèvecoeur's, were not published for American consumption. (His later career as a Loyalist, unlike Boone's, utterly destroyed his image as an American hero.) The captivity narratives in their heyday had possessed all the needed qualities to such an extent that they virtually overcame the disadvantages of the rudimentary book trade, appearing everywhere but the South. But captivities lost some of their impact as the demand for an image of emergent American power and dominance grew.

Part of Filson's success can be attributed to his conscious artistry in altering and ordering his raw materials for literary presentation. He departed in a number of ways from the facts of Boone's career in order to fit him into the necessary mold of hunter-husbandman-philosophe. Boone was fifty years old when Filson met him, the patriarch of a large and still-expanding family and the possessor of a great reputation among his fellow frontiersmen. To characterize him as a novice receiving his initiation into the ways of the wilderness, Filson had to suppress the facts that Boone was in his late thirties when his "Adventures" began, that he had long been familiar with the conditions of life in the wilderness, and that he had already developed the mental attitude and physical prowess needed for survival. But Filson was also fortunate in that the real Boone's character and activities contributed to the legend's credibility — over the next forty years of Boone's (and the legend's) life — in large and even small ways.[37] By an uncanny coincidence, Boone's personal history embodied the symbolic patterns of Voltaire's and Rousseau's imagery: Boone was born of good Quaker parents in Pennsylvania and was formally adopted by the good savages of the Shawnee nation. His personal philosophy of life apparently combined the Indian love of hunting, personal freedom, and combat with the Quaker's scrupulous morality, disapproval of cruelty and waste, and gentleness toward the helpless. It was part of the legend that developed early in his life that he killed neither Indian nor animal, except when compelled by necessity, and that he took no scalps.

Filson's portrayal of Boone as a hunter-husbandman is accurate as far as it goes, but it falls short of depicting Boone's real attitude toward farming. Although Boone did stake out and work a subsistence farm in the manner of the physiocratic yeoman, he never did fit into the yeoman's mold. He was primarily a hunter and trapper, who cleared only as much of his land as was needed for kitchen crops and a little salable tobacco to keep his family fed during his long absences. Most of the wealth the Boones had came from the bales of deer and beaver skins he brought back from the wilderness. Skins provided a substantial but unsteady source of income, and Boone supplemented his pelt money by serving as a guide to surveyors like Filson, bidding for government war contracts, serving in the militia and the Virginia legislature, and speculating a bit in land.[38] But he was not content to make a place for himself in the middling classes of the frontier. He became the business partner of Col. Richard Henderson, a land speculator who owned a vague grant from the Cherokees and attempted to establish a personal empire in Kentucky. Henderson provided the capital and organized support for a settlement; Boone was to explore the ground, lay out divisions of land, and lead the settlers west. Boone claimed land for himself, his family, and his near relations on a baronial scale, intending to take advantage of the rise in land values when western emigration finally began to fill up the Dark and Bloody Ground. Until then he hoped to use his vast claims as a personal hunting park, rich in deer, beaver, and buffalo.[39] As these large claims suggest, Boone was not without a good share of unyeomanlike vanity — a sense of personal grandeur that was fed by the legends of his fellow frontiersmen and later by the international reputation he acquired through Filson's book.

Unfortunately for Boone's business projects, his financial shrewdness was never proof against his boundless enthusiasm for the western land and the freedom from social restraints and obligations which it offered. After returning from his exploration of Kentucky for the Transylvania Company, he found that the British had tightened controls on emigration, making it impossible for Henderson to support an attempt at settlement. Despite the lack of the promised backing, Boone's impatience to return to Kentucky impelled him to attempt the settlement alone. It was a sign of his high reputation that his neighbors followed him in the venture — and continued to follow him, even after their first attempt to cross the mountains was turned back by the Indians.[40]

In addition to his enthusiasm for free land, hunting, and the chance of wealth, Boone was motivated by a mild but definite hostility to the civilization represented by the eastern settlements. Filson portrays this hostility in the terms of Jefferson's *Notes on Virginia*, as a dislike of the commercial values and clutter of an urban mercantile civilization. For the real Boone the terms were somewhat simpler: he disliked the complexities of legal obligations and involvements that attended landownership in those litigious days. As the Puritan sought the pure and unadulterated gospel, Boone sought the simple and uncluttered freehold — the ownership of land based on personal discovery and use of the land's resources. Even his baronial claims were less important to Boone than freedom from the pettifogging intervention of lawyers and sharpers between a man and his land. When strangers from the East challenged the validity of his leases or sued him for surveying claims so poorly that they wildly overlapped, he refused to become involved in litigation. He surrendered his lands to all claimants, sold what was left, and went west to Missouri, where he became the "Syndic" or governor of a Spanish province and dispensed law himself to his fellow settlers, most of whom were relatives of his. Even in the West he was bothered by the knowledge that old debts still tied him to the settlements; and to cut these ties, he returned to Kentucky with the proceeds of years of hunting and paid off every man who claimed Boone owed him a debt. He asked no questions of the claimants, and his pockets were emptied by the time he had made the circuit of Kentucky and his old hometowns in the East — but he was free of his last bonds to eastern society.[41]

Although Boone was by no means a well-educated man, there is no reason to suppose that his attitude toward the settlements was simply the product of his economic resentments. One of his favorite books was *Gulliver's Travels*, a copy of which accompanied him on one of his early exploring trips. Lulbegrud Creek in Kentucky got its name when his reading of the book aloud was interrupted by an Indian attack. Boone and his comrades beat off the attack, and one of Boone's companions remarked that they had taken care of the "Lulbegruds," referring (somewhat inaccurately) to the inhabitants of a city in Swift's Brobdingnag. The creek name immortalizes the hunter's witticism. After the publication of Filson's book, Boone went so far as to model his public statements on Filson's characterization of him. His famous remark about leaving Kentucky because he needed more "elbow room" was probably Boone's little jest at an overly inquisitive tenderfoot, who obviously expected to find in him an archopponent of civilization. The irony of his remark lies in the fact that he was then on his way to take up his post as Syndic of the Femme Osage District — hardly the occupation of a man opposed to society per se.[42]

The most distinctive trait of Boone's character was his love for the wild land. He reveled in the pleasures of discovering new trails through the wilderness, of recording a good day's hunt by carving his name on a tree, and of naming creeks and geographic features after particular experiences of his own. Thus he gave Dreaming Creek its name because he had had a peculiarly impressive dream while sleeping beside it. He seemed to enjoy the idea that his name and experiences would become permanently identified with the land, and on his return to Kentucky from Missouri he spent some time hunting up his initialed trees and uncovering the letters that had grown into the bark.[43] The most significant of the legends that had gathered around Boone before Filson met him centers on this sense of identification with the land and constitutes an eighteenth-century Kentucky equivalent of the primitive divine king and sacred marriage myths, in which a tribal hero meets and cohabits or weds with an avatar of the feminine nature spirit, thus insuring renewed life to both tribe and land.

This legend concerns Boone's courtship of his wife, Rebecca Bryan. He was fire-hunting one dark night, stalking the forest with a blazing torch whose light was supposed to attract a deer to his stand. The deer would have to be killed by a shot aimed between the two points of reflected firelight that would mark its eyes, because the animal would be otherwise invisible. After a long wait Boone saw the double gleam and prepared to fire, but some intuition stayed him. He moved toward the gleams, pushed aside the brush, and discovered Rebecca, who turned and fled home. According to the legend, she told her family she had been scared by "a painter," or panther, and soon afterward Daniel came courting.[44]

The outline of this legend closely follows the primitive rituals which were derived from the divine king myth. The king, whose health was supposedly interdependent with the fertility of the land, had to engage in a ceremonial sexual union with the goddess of the woods to induce a renewal of fertility after the barrenness of winter. Often this ceremonial union took the form of hunting some animal deemed to be the goddess's avatar. Out of this primitive myth grew the Greek and Roman myths of metamorphosis, in which gods become animals, virgins become trees, and young men become stags. There is an American Indian love chant which hinges on this same myth of metamorphosis:

> Early I rose
> In the blue morning;
> My love was up before me,
> It came running up to me from the doorways of the Dawn.
>
> On Papago Mountain
> The dying quarry
> Looked at me with my love's eyes.[45]

Boone and his doe/spouse conform to this archetype, which thus offers an implicit vision of Boone as the divine king, the hero whose body and spirit nourish the land and enable it to fulfill the role destined for it by the law of nature.

Equal in importance to the fact that the archetype is invoked are the characterizations of the participants in the mythical event, for the nature and direction of the shift in American attitudes toward the wilderness can be measured by the progressive changes in the sexual imagery of the white man–wilderness confrontation. For Bradford and Mather the wilderness is the proto-renegade's "strange bride" or a male captor-violator of female avatars of Christian culture. For Edwards nature is the male thunder god or the sweet spirit that murmurs to Sarah Pierrepont as she walks amid "groves and fields." For Boone the spirit of nature is feminine, and his relation to it is that of panther to deer, hunter to prey, sexual aggressor to coy, amenable victim — and both are beings of the wild.

The fire-hunt legend was well known to the Boones themselves, and they often repeated it to their children (who refused to believe it). Yet this legend and others which show Boone as the wild, lonely hunter were neglected or omitted by Filson. (Later, western writers like Timothy Flint and Romantics like Fenimore Cooper rediscovered them and worked them into the literary versions of the Boone myth.) Filson wished to retain the idea that Boone's hunting trips initated him into a deep intimacy with the powers of nature and that the health of his spirit was essential to the realization of nature's plan for the Kentucky land. Being committed to the philosophy and pastoral imagery of physiocracy, he would have wished to deny that the wild, man-shy spirit of the deer symbolized nature in Kentucky or that the symbolic hero of the American frontier had the lonely, restless spirit of the hunting panther, rather than the virtuous placidity of the yeoman.

Filson made other important alterations of the facts in his new images of Boone, Rebecca, and wilderness. Rebecca underwent the most considerable change. In life a strong and intelligent woman, she stood almost as tall as Daniel Boone, who was himself over the average in height. It was she who held their large family together while he vanished on long hunts, which might last a season or a couple of years. When he was taken by the Shawnee and presumed dead, she packed up her family and moved it east to Carolina by herself through Indian country at the height of the Indian wars. When he grew old and was attacked by rheumatism, she accompanied him on hunts, helped him kill game, and was accounted a fair shot.[46]

Filson all but eliminates Rebecca Boone from his account. She appears only as "my wife," never by name, and no attention is paid to her considerable accomplishments as provider and protector. She first appears in Boone's meditation on his loneliness during the first exploration of Kentucky; in this passage the thought of his family far away in the settlement inclines him to melancholy, and he has to put aside the sentiment. Next she appears as the "first white woman" to stand beside the Kentucky River, a symbol of the establishment of civilization on the river and of the settlement's weakness and exposure to the savagery of the wilderness. She does not appear again until after Boone has returned from his Shawnee captivity and beaten off the Indian attack on Boonesborough. Then the reader learns that she has returned to Carolina, heartbroken over the thought of his death. For Filson, Rebecca is simply a generalized "amiable Spouse," subject to the conventional weaknesses of the sentimental heroine, suffering deprivation and heartbreak without acquiring (in the narrative) a personality of her own.

Even in Filson's account, Boone's wife remains a symbol of the spirit of nature. But where the folk myth emphasizes her wildness and freedom and shyness of man, Filson's myth emphasizes her civilized qualities, her conformity to the conventional idea of woman in Anglo-American society — a morally strong but physically weak creature in need of a hero's protection, a victim suffering dutifully under physical discomfort and the pangs of womanly sentiment, so completely identified with her role as wife and mother that she has no identity independent of her social role.

Two opposed visions of nature are thus embodied in these two versions of Rebecca's character. The folk legend, accepting the wilderness for what it is, deifies its wild qualities. The Filson legend, following the Jeffersonian view of natural law, sees civilization (female spirit allied to male power) as the inevitable product of natural law, the realization of its inherent purpose or design. For Filson, as for Jefferson, the God who created nature was an artist, and within the fabric of the wilderness the symmetry of purpose and design could be perceived. Therefore civilization, the ultimate embodiment of design and symmetry, was immanent in the wilderness for the Jeffersonian, just as a nature goddess or earth mother was always invisibly present in the woods for the Indian or pagan. By the same token, Boone's self-realization — the discovery of identity which is the outcome of his initiation — involves (in Filson's account) his discovery of the husbandman and agent of civilization within the husk of his hunter's identity. In the primitive initiation ceremony, on the other hand, the novice Indian brave would spend an appointed exile in the woods, discover the hunter and the warrior within his effeminate boy's body, and take as the totem or symbol of his identity the panther rather than the plowshare.

This brings us to the third crucial element in the efficacy of Filson's narrative as an American myth: the resemblance between the structure of the Boone narrative and that of the archetypal hero myths which are found in all human cultures. This resemblance confirms the mythological credibility of the real Boone: only a true hero could evoke a response whose pattern is drawn from such profound levels of the human mind. At the same time, the legend's resemblance to the archetype helps to assure its continuing viability. The archetypal hero myth narrates a journey into the kingdom of death for the purpose of extracting some power or secret (a "boon") which will enable man to dominate his mortal fate. Although the pattern of the quest is archetypal, the symbolic items employed and the personages met during the quest vary from culture to culture, and a limited number of alternative paths to ultimate triumph or defeat are exhibited. The particular varieties of the archetypal hero myth — or *monomyth*, as Campbell terms it — are virtually infinite; but the structural formulas of the myths are virtually identical, since the myth is created as a response of the human psyche to the condition of mortality. All men fear and seek to overcome the death that arrives for all things that are born or created: men, families, kingdoms and tribes, dynasties, religions, the planted crops in the fields, the woods that grow, bear fruit, and die. The hero myth is based on a universal world-perception and a universal anxiety inherent in the human mind and situation.

The archetypal hero begins in a state of innocence or unawareness of the powers that are latent in himself and in his environment. He worships gods but does not know their true power. Then something arises to trouble this state, and he embarks on a quest. The motive for the quest varies: in Campbell's formulation of the archetype, the hero is "lured, carried away, or else voluntarily proceeds to the threshold of adventure." At the threshold of the "dark land" in which his adventure will be played out, he is challenged by a "shadow presence." He may conciliate the presence or fight and defeat it, either way passing alive into the underworld; or he may be defeated by it and pass into the underworld either as one of the dead (as did Christ) or as a captive of the power. The crossing of the threshold takes many forms, as does the shadow presence. The passage may be a battle or a sea voyage. The opponent may be a "brother" of the hero, a reflection of some dark power within himself that he must conquer.

The dark world beyond the threshold is "death's dream kingdom," resembling in many respects the hidden world of the human unconscious as well as that of the afterlife. It is peopled with "unfamiliar yet strangely intimate forces" that either aid the hero or impose a series of tests and initiatory ordeals upon him. After a supreme ordeal, he gains the object of his quest, the fire or other boon which embodies the power or light of wisdom he has come seeking. Depending upon his personal qualities and his relationship to the divine powers (as revealed in the manner of his passing the various tests), the culmination of the hero's quest is one of several alternative triumphs. He may attain sexual union or "sacred marriage" with the earth goddess, her priestess, or an avatar; he may become reconciled with a paternal divinity; or he himself may become divine or semidivine (apotheosis). If the gods are unfriendly, he may steal the goddess-bride or the boon and flee with it to the threshold of his own world. There he again experiences transformation, is reinitiated into his old world, and becomes the agent of its restoration or renewal.[47]

Filson's Boone narrative fits the archetype rather closely. In the first cycle of adventures, Boone begins by dwelling on a peaceful farm. Curiosity and the spirit of adventure lure him willingly to the threshold of Kentucky. After preliminary struggles with the Indians and his own melancholy fears, he descends into the western wilderness, which (as we have seen) is archetypal of the unconscious hidden mind, the kingdom of dreams, death's Valhalla. He submits to the ordeal of captivity and battle with the Indian presence and is initiated in the wilderness life by means of hunting the deer. He tastes the land's sweetness and returns with his vision to the world of his past, there to quicken the frontiersmen's ambition and aspiration. Next, in the captivity cycle of his adventures, he leaves the peaceful island of Boonesborough to hunt deer and salt, is carried over the threshold of the Indians' world in defeat and captivity, is initiated and adopted into the tribe, resists a series of temptations that test his character, and returns with the new wisdom to become the war chief of his people. His return is at once a resurrection (his wife has thought him dead) and a transformation (he has become a hero and chief). In a final test, he goes forth to battle, is plunged into misery and despair by his son's death, but returns to the land of death to retrieve and appropriately inter his son's body. He emerges with renewed strength — a superhuman strength from which his land and people will draw sustenance and which they will employ to achieve peace and to establish their settlements in the land (apotheosis).

Equal in importance to its resemblance to the monomyth is the resemblance in structure between the Boone myth and the other myths that had developed out of the particular anxieties and experiences of the American colonists and had found expression in the conversion narratives, the captivity narratives, and the discovery-emigration narratives. The Boone narrative draws on the traditional beliefs, evocative symbols, images, and narrative structures of these earlier myth forms, reconciling their contradictions of value and inconsistency of subject matter. At the same time, Filson alters their character by absorbing them into the myth of the hunter and warrior. The narrative of Boone's adventures recapitulates the experiences portrayed in the several narrative genres of Colonial literature about the frontier: Boone is sequentially the emigrant, the explorer, the captive, the convert, the hunter, and the hero. In each case, the protagonist of the narrative lives in an initial state of innocence on a (literal or figurative) island of sheltered light, walled in from the dark power of the sea or the wilderness, unaware of the powers within himself and in the God of this world. This passive state of happiness is disrupted, in the convert's case, by his discovery of the corruption in his native island (England); in the captive's case, by Indians who symbolize the sinful potential of his own soul and who drag the protagonist across the threshold and into the wilderness. In all four myth forms, the journey leads to the discovery of a dark land and the illumination of the dark land in the protagonist's own soul. For Boone, as for the captive, the emigrant, and the convert, it is necessary that he abandon family ties to embark on the quest. The trial of his ability to bear and justify this disruption of family — as well as the deaths of other relatives and companions during the adventure — is the most important test in his ordeal. In each case the protagonist achieves a return from the land of his quest, bearing a message or a gift that will enlighten and redeem his people.

There are, however, crucial departures from the earlier myth forms in Filson's myth of Boone the hunter. The captive, emigrant, and convert are either lured or abducted into their adventures; each is thrust unwillingly into the hero's role by Providence. Boone openly avows that his motivations are chiefly "curiosity" and a love of adventure. Unlike the Puritan, he does not deny the lure of the wilderness or succumb to that lure as a sinner to temptation. Rather, he reads in that lure the call of nature to his nature, and he follows the lure to its source as a hunter follows the track or scent of deer. The Kentucky forts are a new version of the theme of the walled gardens or islands of the West. The precolonial vision saw the West as a cluster of paradises in miniature, thrust above a dark ocean; the Puritan saw his settlement in the forest as a beleaguered island of light in another kind of sea. In Boone's Kentucky there are many isles of refuge, not all of them walled. Boone moves freely from walled fort to Indian town — and even into the formless ocean of the forest itself, to discover the power to make a refuge within his own mind. Thus the commanding ridge, like the fort or the town, is for Boone in effect a blessed isle.

The conclusions of the earlier myths and the Boone myth also differ. The culmination of each cycle of the Boone narrative is always an act of creation — the attainment of a new heroic identity for the hero, the establishment of a settlement, the saving of the harvest. The structure of *Kentucke* as a whole emphasizes this pattern by its arrangement into descriptive, narrative and prophetic sections. In the other myth narratives, this kind of creation myth is suppressed. The hero does not follow the wilderness spirits (the Indians or beasts) as the hero-lover does his goddess; and the end of the conversion or captivity experience resembles a "reconciliation with the father-creator" rather than a "sacred marriage" (to use Campbell's terms). A new self is created in these narratives, and the hero does bring light to his people; but because the motive, the path or method, and the conclusion or goal of his quest are different, the light he brings is different from that brought by Boone the hunter. The significance of the difference is suggested by the changes which the rest of Filson's *Kentucke* makes in the classic pattern of the emigration narrative. Instead of positing reconciliation with the Old World through an actual return to Europe or through the re-creation of a renewed Europe in the New World, he prophesies the creation of a new race and a new nation through a more profound penetration by the Americans into their wilderness continent.

It was Filson's implicit vision of Boone the hunter as the central figure in a creation myth that later chroniclers and commentators emphasized in dealing with the theme of Boone's career and the development of the nation. But although Filson's account was the first published work to express this vision, it did not by any means originate it. Since the pattern is archetypal, it is no surprise to find myths of the primitive Indians and folk tales of the frontier contemporaries of Boone that embody essentially the same vision. What is remarkable is the degree to which the American legends strike through the conventions of literary mythology and Christian theology to expound the myth in its simplest, most primitive terms. A comparison of one of the Indian myths, the fire-hunt legend that circulated among Boone's contemporaries, and the Filson narrative suggests a fundamental kinship in the minds of the Indian, the American frontiersman, and the middle-colony schoolmaster.

The creation myth of the Delaware Indians begins with the people dwelling in an underworld beneath a great lake. One of their heroes discovers a hole through which he journeys to the surface, crossing the threshold of the womblike underworld into the realm of his quest. On the surface he spies a deer, hunts, kills, and eats it, and returns with its meat to the underworld. His people find the meat so good that they follow the hero out through the hole to where they can "enjoy the light of heaven" and populate the world. The Mohawks had a similar legend, in which the people live under the earth until the hero Ganawagahka discovers the hole, finds the deer, and brings it back to the people. "And the favourable description he had given them of the country above and on the earth, their mother, concluded it best for them all to come out; and accordingly they did so, and set about planting corn, &c." [48] The imagery in both accounts emphasizes that the deer hunter's quest is a metaphor for human birth and the birth of the human race. The Mohawk version adds a second element — the discovery of the mother-goddess, the earth, and of the sacred marriage that produces crops from her body. The pattern of both myths relates closely to Campbell's version of the monomyth: one of the standard motifs to depict the hero's crossing of the threshold of adventure is that of a journey through the night over seas or large bodies of water. The analogy between this pattern and that of the trans-Atlantic emigration narrative, the ancestor of Filson's discovery-emigration narrative, is also readily apparent.

The fire-hunt legend and the Filson version of Boone's career recast the pattern of the emigration narrative in such a way as to develop or emphasize its resemblance to these primitive creation myths of the Indians. The fire-hunt folktale is the more overtly mythical of the two; its symbolic elements and dramatic events are presented with primitive clarity. Boone is hunting at night, afloat (by some accounts) on a large pool of water or (by others) at rest in a clearing. He sees two gleams of light in the darkness and, in his innocence, believes them to be those of a deer. He is tempted to shoot but restrains himself, sensing a mystery. He pursues the deer and discovers that it is, not a deer at all, but a woman. The tale culminates in his marriage to the woman and the commencement of his heroic career. Thus, like the Mohawk hero, the Boone of the folktale follows the track of the deer into a new plane of existence and acquires the power to sow seed and reap the fruits of the earth as a hero and king. But instead of the quasi-sexual violence and cannibalism of the Delaware deer-hunting creation myth, the Boone tale culminates in sexual union, which sublimates the violence and blood hunger of the ritual hunt.

The Filson narrative does not touch on these psychologically uneasy grounds; it does not play with the loaded issues of sexual desire, violence, and literal or figurative cannibalism. Boone dwells in a peaceful river valley below the mountains until the call of nature to his spirit summons him to leave the valley and cross the mountain threshold. He discovers a gap in the ridges and through it enters the Dark and Bloody Ground. Assailed by real Indians and by the melancholy fantasies of his solitary, kinless soul, he hunts a deer and brings it to the top of his "commanding ridge." There he kills the deer and discovers the beauty of the landscape, whose power works on him to chase his melancholy. Strengthened and renewed by the sweet meat of that land, he returns through the gap, reveals the beauty and plenty of the land to his people, and leads them back through the mountains into the land of Kentucky.

It is striking that the American myth of the hunter so closely resembles the creation myths of the Indians. This resemblance becomes even more striking when one notes that it represents a distinct departure from the European mythology of huntsmen and sacred beasts. There the hunter, at least in the Christian era and in several pre-Christian cultures, has traditionally been regarded as an accursed being. His pursuit of beasts makes him bestial — a figure of lust, rapacity, and materialism. Esau, Nimrod, and Ishmael were proscribed in the Bible as "hunters." One of Dionysos' names was Zagreus ("Great Hunter"), which was interpreted by early Christian scholars as symbolizing "insatiable incontinence." The Norse mythology and the Arthurian legends deal frequently with the figure of the "accursed hunter"; the Greeks' Orion and Actaeon also come to mind. Most significant is the Christian tradition in which the hunter is regarded as deserting the central, spiritual quest in order to pursue ephemera on "the endlessly turning periphery of the wheel of phenomena." [49] This was precisely the light in which the Puritans of the seventeenth century and Europeans of the eighteenth century regarded the colonists' pursuit of life in America.

The American Indian hunting myths have not the slightest tinge of moral disapproval of the hunter. The escape of the Indians from the underground and their spreading out over the face of the earth are not, as in the Judaeo-Christian Eden myth, a fall from grace and an enforced exile from a womblike garden. On the contrary, only when the Indian has escaped into the light can he perceive and love his good mother-goddess, the earth. For Boone and his predecessor Church, as for the Indian, the hunting of the beast is an initiation into a higher state of being.

This American rejection of the European and Christian myths of the hunter and movement toward that of the Indians suggests a shift in the colonists' attitude toward their land and perhaps toward their own hidden minds and passions as well. But the colonists were not Indians born, and although they became like the Indians in some ways in the process of acculturation, they did retain the traditions of European mythology — particularly the traditional opposition in European hunter myths between the active, physical life of the hunter and the life of contemplation essential to the saint and the intellectual. Acceptance of the hunter as the archetypal American hero reversed these values. It meant adopting the hunter's anti-intellectualism, his pursuit of the material and ephemeral, and his love of exploit and violence for the sake of their blood-stirring excitement — a love akin to the insatiable incontinence dreaded by Puritans. It is significant that Franklin, Jefferson, and other intellectual leaders of the nation-building epoch portrayed America's natural genius as essentially materialistic and practical, rather than theoretical, and as active rather than contemplative. This symbolic rendering of the American character was sharpened and exaggerated by succeeding generations. Jefferson's belief that democracy is best run by intellectual aristoi, in whom the man of affairs is tempered by the man of contemplation, gave way to the radical democratic belief of the Jacksonians, who held that any man competent to practice his personal affairs is competent to administer those of the nation.[50] Similarly, Filson's contemplative Boone gave way to the violent, garrulous, slaughter-loving hunter-buffoon, David Crockett.

It is vital to note that of these three analgous versions of the hunter myth, Filson's artifice-ridden version — the one furthest removed from the original, primitive, experiential source — was published first. Later generations, exploring the nature of the frontier hero in search of his sources and motivating principles, unearthed the Indian myths and the fire-hunt legend. The former were published in the first decade of the nineteenth century by Father Heckewelder and became one of Fenimore Cooper's sources. The latter first appeared in the 1830s in Timothy Flint's popular biography of Boone. The kinship of the American frontier hero and the Indian, on a spiritual or mythological plane, was thus increasingly emphasized as the initial image of Boone was developed by Filson's imitators. In effect, the literary exploitation of Filson's myth took the form of a progressive clarification of those archetypal patterns and symbols which Filson had obscured beneath fashionable artifice. This literary evolution reflected a popular preference for a primitive, mythopoeic mode of perceiving America and all things and persons pertaining to America. When American fiction emerged in the nineteenth century, the heroes of epics, novels, and tales devoted to illuminating the American condition would be seen embarking on quests very like those of Filson's and Flint's Boone, Heckewelder's Indians, and the Puritan captives. Brockden Brown's Edgar Huntly, Cooper's Leatherstocking, Melville's Ishmael, Hawthorne's Reuben Bourne, Thoreau at Walden — each embarks on a quest that takes him, figuratively or literally, back in time into a primitive world and downward into his own consciousness, until the basic or primitive core of the psyche is revealed.

Ultimately, then, the efficacy of Filson's narrative as (in Wheelwright's term) a consummatory myth depended on its synthesis of archetypal elements with the various forms of culture-bound myth that had developed out of the historical experience and literary interests of the colonies. Its power within its own immediate time and place of appearance, however, derived from less profound sources as well. Filson employed most of the fashionable conventions and devices available to him, placing his hero in several different frames of reference, offering the reader any one of several ways of identifying with his hero and interpreting his adventures. This variety was the secret of its immediate popularity; and popularity was the only guarantee of its seeing print frequently enough to impress its image gradually on the established literary conventions and habits of thinking. It could be read by a conservative New Englander as an echo of the traditional Puritan myth of the soul's regeneration; yet it also paralleled the Rousseauistic vision of man redeemed by contact with primitive nature, and it anticipated the myth of the American Adam that would preoccupy the writers of the Romantic period.

As a hero, Boone himself displays a wide range of qualities. After his first initiation into the laws of nature, he achieves the stoic resignation to circumstance that characterizes the idealized image of the Indian on which Rogers drew in creating Ponteach. After his successive initiations into the social orders of the Anglo-American frontier (the British at Detroit and the Shawnee), he emerges as a close parallel of Wolcott's Governor Winthrop: well versed in political lore, wise, tactful, shrewd in war and diplomacy, and able to lead men with skill and good sense. The tragic events of the latter half of the narrative make him for the moment a sentimental hero, related to the Puritan victim-hero of the captivity narratives, to Rogers's Chekitan, and to the Romantic hero of the sentimental novel. As Boone's character changes, so does the landscape. At first it is a neoclassical arcadia, a pastoral paradise of artful symmetry and contrived beauty. When harsh reality breaks in, it acquires the violent disorder of the sublime landscape, anticipating the tortured Alpine landscapes of Byron.

From this welter of apparently contradictory images, a definite pattern does emerge. The picture of the western landscape which is ultimately left with the reader fits into neither the pastoral nor the sublime vision of nature. Like Jefferson in his description of the Virginia landscape, Filson blends images of order and disorder in his depiction and allows the eye to move toward his images of peace and order through a landscape littered with images of death and destruction. The character of Filson's Boone, similarly, lies somewhere between the brutality of the savage and the passive orderliness of the good Quaker. Like Filson's "Savages" and the later Romantic hero, Boone seeks in solitude a personal contact with the elemental forces of nature that are immanent in the landscape. But where the savages and the Romantic become devotees of the primitive passions engendered by contact with wild nature, Boone abstracts a code of natural laws from the wilderness and brings these laws and his own passions under the control of his own civilized reason. These laws turn out to be synonymous with the virtues of the republican citizen: if he and his people would survive and prosper in the world, they must be self-disciplined, reasonable in response to their environment, respectful of the female, and fierce in both personal independence and tribal or patriotic loyalty. Even the base Indian (as William Smith and Colden also tell us) attains to virtue by his obedience to these laws; the Euro-American may attain utopia through them.

Although Filson's Boone has the Romantics' emotional rapport with nature, trust in intuitive wisdom, and ability to feel strong passions, his greatest need is for order. Thus he modulates his passions to the controllable level of sentiments by the exercise of reason. Although moved by the "ruins . . . of a world" which greet him in his first attempt to cross the mountains, Boone, like the Hudson River school painter, is more moved by the sunlit vistas from his sweet spring on the mountaintop. Great passions are necessary to his realization of his full potential for human feeling; but in order for him to attain heroic stature, he must restrain his passion, forget private grief, and attend to the public good.

For Filson, Boone's solitary hunting trips are, not ends in themselves, but means to a social end. Solitude has value in the Boone narrative only insofar as it contributes to the ultimate creation of a better society; hunting is noble only insofar as it clears the way for husbandry. Sentiments are of use only because they lead to self-knowledge and consequently to a higher quality of self-restraint. Here Filson echoes the Puritan insistence on self-restraint and attention to duty and opposes the Romantic tendency to luxuriate in strong passions, in images of darkness and chaos, in the symbolic toppling of ancient dynasties, worlds, and gods. The lesson of the frontier experience was that the maintenance of civilization against the powers of the wilderness was possible only through complete knowledge of one's own capacity for good and evil and of the wilderness's inherent threats and promises. Too much preoccupation with darkness would have weakened Boone's ability to resist the terrors of his environment and construct a viable social order. He had to retain a positive vision of a perfected civilization as his final goal. In this concern Filson's Boone prefigures that peculiar sense of social place, mission, and obligation that informs the characters of Cooper's Leatherstocking tales and the works of Emerson, Whitman, and their generation. Even in the darker writers of the American Renaissance, like Hawthorne and Melville, who did not put forward positive visions of an ideal America, the sense of obligation to society or civilization appears as a feeling of spiritual malaise or guilt for having pursued art into an antisocial wilderness of darkness, chaos, and blood.

Like Crèvecoeur's study of American character, Filson's Boone narrative offers a kind of composite portrait, containing many possible hero types — some themselves expressing antithetical values — within a single figure. Filson's Boone, however, is more hunter, warrior, and wanderer than he is farmer, while Crèvecoeur's farmer enters Boone's world only by compulsion. Filson's hero is also more clearly personalized than Crèvecoeur's posturing farmer; he is, after all, based on a living man. Nevertheless, as of 1784 Europe and America have each accumulated a gallery of stock figures and melded them into a composite image of an American hero, though each took a very different path in refining that composite into a single archetype. For the Americans it was the hunter who proved the most appealing figure. Writers working in the frontier vein gradually brought that figure forward and explored and described the depths of significances of his mind and heart.

Boone's personal myth continued to grow, as the old hunter continued to pursue his seasonal hunting and exploring expeditions until he was well into his eighties. Filson ceased to control his version of the myth not long after he had written it, and the literary version of the myth embarked on a long career of modification by European rationalists and Romantics and by American spokesmen for the northeastern, southern, and western sections of the new nation. Several distinct but related variations resulted, the peculiar emphasis and direction of each determined by the cultural needs and prejudices of the different sections and intellectual periods. Through them all, two major themes persisted: the Filsonian vision of the frontier hero as an untutored republican-gentleman-philosophe and the folk vision of Boone as the mighty hunter, child of the wilderness, and exemplar of values derived from sources outside Anglo-American civilization.

Having begun to propagate his vision by distributing copies to Washington and the diplomat Barbé-Marbois — and through the latter to Jefferson, the French court, and the Parisian intellectuals — Filson gathered his belongings and returned to Kentucky.[51] True to the principles of his book, he attempted to assert rational control over the affairs of Kentucky by establishing an educational academy and laying out the site of a new metropolis called Losantviville (later renamed Cincinnati). On a journey down the Wabash he was ambushed by the Indians but escaped by an exercise of the woodcraft he learned from Boone. In the end, however, the terrors of the forest prevailed over his powers of reason and self-control. On a surveying expedition in 1788 his party tangled with a roving band of Miamis. Apparently the Kentuckians were mutinous and insisted on attacking the Indians against the advice of Judge Symmes, their leader. There was a skirmish, a retreat, and a nagging pursuit by the Indians, which caused the Kentuckians to break up and desert the main body. Somewhere in the Miami country, Filson's blue devils of melancholy and sentimental terror found him again. "Poor Filson . . . had no rest after [the battle] . . . for fear of the Indians, and at length attempting to escape to . . . the Ohio, he was destroyed by the savages." [52] When he died, his book had already gained a hearing in Paris and London and in the literary press of the former colonies.

CHAPTER 10

Evolution of the National Hero:

Farmer to Hunter to Indian
(1784–1855)

> . . . fair Europe's noblest pride,
> When future gales shall wing them o'er the tide,
> A ruddier hue and deeper shade shall gain,
> And stalk, in statelier figures, o'er the plain.
> . . . .
>
> The sage, the chief, the patriot, unconfined,
> Shield the weak world and counsel for mankind.
>
> Joel Barlow, The Vision of Columbus

THE power of Filson's myth lay, not in an ability to alter existing conceptions of the frontier drastically and suddenly, but in the ease with which it could be assimilated to such preconceptions and made to adjust to new fashions, conceptions, and ideological requirements. In England, France, and Germany and in the several sections of the United States where the Boone narrative captured public attention, it became a barometer of developments in cultural history. In each case, the image of Boone was made to serve as the embodiment of local values or cultural assumptions and as the vicarious resolver of the dilemmas that preoccupied that culture. In the development of these variant images of Boone we can trace the emergence of American national consciousness, the process of cultural differentiation that finally divided the Euro-Americans from the Europeans.

This process of cultural differentiation is visible on two levels — in the content of the variants of Filson's myth (that is, their treatment of the Boone figure) and the manner in which the variants were printed and distributed (that is, the way in which they reached their audience). It is at the latter level that major differences appear earliest. In Europe the Boone narrative became the literary property of various intellectual coteries and went through various metamorphoses as a result of the arguments and rec-

onciliations among them — arguments arising from the philosophical de-
bates of the French Enlightenment and later from the social crisis of the
French Revolution. In America the narrative was seized upon by the popular press as ideally suited to the requirements of its audience: an American
tale, at once entertaining and relevant to the American concern with cultural self-definition. Most important to the Americans was the supposed reality of Filson's hero's adventures, for it was felt that a truly independent
American culture could only emerge from the dialectic between the people and the reality of their unique environment. The Boone figure would
have to conform credibly to what their literature had already taught them
about the wilderness and to whatever new knowledge arriving from the
West might teach them. In Europe the reality of the West was less important than the dialectic of liberals and conservatives, revolutionaries and
reactionaries. The figure of Boone was merely a convenient symbol, an
Emile in buckskins.

The Boone Narrative in Europe, 1785–1800

The Americanist coteries of Paris were chiefly responsible for the
wide currency of Filson's hero in Europe and for the conventionalized
image of Boone that characterized pre- and early revolutionary literature.
The Americanists met to discuss the politics, geography, and natural history of the new world which Crèvecoeur, Franklin, and the Battle of Sara-
toga had rediscovered to them. They also circulated American manuscripts
and books among themselves and published volumes by American authors,
as well as studies of America by their own members. Through Franklin's
contacts with these circles, French advice and promises of aid had reached
Philadelphia during the Revolution; and conversely, the wise sayings,
scientific speculations, and liberal political philosophy of this supposed
good Quaker were transmitted through the coterie to the court and the political reformers among the upper classes.[1] Personal recommendation of
Kentucke by influential Americanists and their correspondents was the key
to its success in France (and later in England and Germany). The book was
enthusiastically recommended to Ambassador Jefferson, and the Comte de
Vergennes by Barbé-Marbois, the young French diplomat in America
whose queries had led Jefferson to write his much-acclaimed Notes on Virginia. By the time Jefferson arrived in Paris, Kentucke had begun to make
the rounds of the Americanist salons. Crèvecoeur, a lion of the salons as
the inimitable Cultivateur Américain, sponsored a translation of the work

by Parraud in 1785 and used Filson's material in his own "Esquisse du Fleuve Ohio" in the 1787 edition of the *Lettres*.[2]

The coterie atmosphere assured *Kentucke* a sympathetic hearing by the intellectual and to some extent the political elite of France. The Americanist salons were presided over by some of the most brilliant women in Parisian society, among them Madame d'Houdetot, the former patroness of Rousseau, who was also intimate with Crèvecoeur. Members of the circle included political leaders and leaders-to-be like Lafayette, Brissot, Mirabeau, and Condorcet; du Pont de Nemours, Jefferson's friend and later an emigrant to America; Buffon, who had propounded a theory of American biological degeneration; Houdon, sculptor of an heroic bust of Washington; and La Rochefoucauld d'Anville, the philosophe to whom Crèvecoeur particularly addressed a copy of *Kentucke*. The encyclopedist Demeunier, on the advice of Crèvecoeur and Jefferson, used *Kentucke* as a source for his American articles; and the poet André Chenier began composing an epic called "l'Amérique" inspired largely by Filson's Boone narrative.[3] It is worth noting that the circle included all those figures for whom the idea of America was of metaphysical or, at any rate, philosophical importance, whether they were degenerationists like Buffon or Rousseauistic philo-Americans like Chenier. In this circle, discussion of the idea was of more immediate import than attempting to determine the reality.

The editorial preface to the Parraud translation defines the limits of French interest in Filson's work and perhaps in the American frontier in general. The translation is an accurate one, but the title is strategically altered to imply a connection between *Kentucke* and the two canons of Americanist writing, Jefferson's *Notes on Virginia* and Crèvecoeur's *Lettres d'un cultivateur américain* (of which *Kentucke* is said to be the sequel). Parraud's preface characterizes Boone as the civilizing force in the forest and as a philosophe manqué, whose home-truth sayings, derived from experience in "nature" (which may be a different thing from "wilderness"), are akin to the admired homilies of Franklin. His heroic deeds and hardships do not, for Parraud, constitute adequate reason for an intelligent reader to interest himself in the account; it is Boone's sayings that offer important *"matière à réflexions."* The extent of Boone's civilizedness is, of course, measured by the extent to which his presumably naïve moral-philosophical speculations resemble those of French philosophes.[4]

In addition to philosophic homilies, Filson had made Boone utter his most evocative descriptions of the wilderness landscape, thus making a love of the Indian's world one of Boone's chief distinguishing characteristics. Parraud minimizes this aspect of Boone, seeing him more as another version of the *cultivateur américain* than as the solitary hunter and the adopted Shawnee. Boone's solitary sojourn, so crucial to his spiritual awakening in Filson, is for Parraud a time of desolate "abandonment" by society. Here Parraud's commitment to Rousseau leads him into incongruity. On the one hand, he is disposed to lament the sad fate of the vanishing red man ("les Naturels," rather than "les sauvages") and to see in them a naïve, prelapsarian democracy. On the other hand, he is committed to progress, to the replacement of the Indians by the Quaker farmers of America and the more stable republicanism that they represent. Thus he juxtaposes a sentimentalization of the Indians' plight with a glorification of one whom he characterizes on his title page as chiefly engaged in annihilating them. Moreover, in order to emphasize Boone's civilizedness, his amenability to Parisian philosophy, Parraud eliminates from the character of Boone the real signs of spiritual affinity between the American frontiersman and "les Naturels." [5] To be sure, American writers stumbled over a similar dilemma in their perception that the achievement of true title to the wilderness seemed to require both the adoption of Indian lifeways and perspectives (Boone's vision) and the pragmatic elimination of the real Indians from the scene (Boone's victory). The difference between American and European responses to the dilemma is that the Americans, of necessity, had to adapt their conceptions and literary formulations to the solution of real problems, while the Americanists could content themselves with manipulating "Col. Boon," "les Naturels," and "les bons Quakers" as emotive counters in philosophic or political argument.[6]

The extent to which European intellectuals were committed to their American fantasies is revealed in their response to Gilbert Imlay, an American scoundrel and adventurer who made a career as a conspirator, speculator, and man of letters by playing on Americanist predilections. Imlay dramatized himself as the incarnation of Emile in buckskins — tender of sentiment but savage of judgment, experienced in wilderness life but able to hold his own in polite society. He apparently came to Paris directly from Daniel Boone's Kentucky, fulminating wrathfully against the old order, adopting every liberal cause as his own and his nation's, evincing the proper degree of anti-Europeanism to ingratiate himself with the revolutionary intellectuals. This talent for adapting his character to flatter the prejudices of those around him enabled him, for brief periods, to gain influential positions, first with the political leadership of Kentucky and later with revolutionary politicians in Paris. His intellect likewise reflected this chameleon quality, which made his books catchalls for current myths, images, and ideologies.

Imlay's first book was tremendously popular and influential throughout the 1790s and was frequently reprinted. Called *A Topographical Description of the Western Territory of North America*, it was derived largely from Filson's *Kentucke* (which Imlay reprinted verbatim in a later edition) and consisted of letters written by an American to an English friend (as in Crèvecoeur's *Letters*), contrasting American virtue and European vice. His second, an epistolary novel, *The Emigrants* — written with his mistress, the feminist Mary Wollstonecraft — was a fictional treatment of the subject matter of the Boone narrative, in which Imlay appears as the Romantic hero and natural aristocrat Arl—ton, the rescuer of female Europe from infidel hands. These works provided Imlay with the intellectual and sentimental credentials that gained him an entry into intellectual and political circles in Paris.

There was more to him than met the eye. He had been a lieutenant in the Continental army during the Revolution, emigrating to Kentucky at about the same time as John Filson. On the way west he promoted himself to captain, and it was by this title that his Kentucky acquaintances knew him. He began buying land and borrowing money even before he arrived, and he continued to file claims on land from 1783 to 1786. By that time he was heavily in debt to most of the state's leading citizens (including Daniel Boone) and quite unable to make restitution. In 1786 he fled Kentucky, leaving his affairs in the hands of Judge Sebastian and General Wilkinson, the military commander of the West. Like Filson, Imlay had served as a deputy surveyor, and after his flight to Europe he promoted himself again, this time to "commissioner for laying out lands in the back settlements." [7] In view of his later connection with French plans for an invasion of Spanish Louisiana, Imlay's close connection with Wilkinson and Sebastian is highly suspicious: both men were agents in the pay of Spain and might have been bought to the French cause. Imlay went out of his way to sell Wilkinson to the French by giving laudatory accounts of his Indian campaigns in the *Topographical Description* and by dramatizing him as the noble General W. in *The Emigrants*.

In 1790 Imlay appeared in Paris and formed close connections with the Americanist circles there. He became acquainted with Mary Wollstonecraft through a mutual friend, Helen Williams, who may also have been Imlay's mistress. Miss Wollstonecraft at first saw Imlay as exceedingly conceited, lean, and awkward in appearance. Later he seemed "an alert, personable man of liberal opinions who seems to have been cultivating the impression that, more than most Americans, he was an unspoiled child of nature, an incarnation of Rousseau's Emile." [8] The imposture worked; she became his mistress, bore him an illegitimate daughter, and even went on an obscure "secret mission" to Sweden in connection with a political or business intrigue of his. She also introduced him to Joel Barlow, Crèvecoeur, Paine, the German editor Forster (who printed German editions of Imlay and Filson), and through another of her friends to Brissot, the Americanist leader of the Girondists. Imlay worked this last connection hard, and after the appearance of his book in 1792 he was accepted by Brissot as an expert on western affairs. At Brissot's instigation he prepared two reports on the West for the government. In them he urged an immediate French descent on New Orleans, offered to serve on the expedition, and promised that sympathetic American democrats (perhaps under George Rogers Clark) would flock from the woods to aid their fellow republicans. The fall of the Gironde scotched these plans and made Imlay a suspect character to the terrorists.[9]

Mary Wollstonecraft's aid was more helpful in getting Imlay's literary works a sympathetic hearing by the Godwin circle. Nor was the response limited to critical acclaim.[10] Imlay's work stimulated attempts by French and English liberals to establish pastoral utopias in the wilderness. Brissot's vision of a new French empire on the Mississippi was strongly colored by his vision of an agrarian commonwealth, derived from Crèvecoeur, Filson, and Imlay's two reports.[11] The pantisocratic community projected by Coleridge and Southey was inspired by Rousseau and the Revolution but got its specific direction from the *Topographical Description*, which first led them to consider the Ohio River as a settlement site. From *The Emigrants* they took a model constitution and a set of marriage laws (which had been drawn by Imlay from Mary Wollstonecraft's *Vindication of the Rights of Women* and Filson's abstract of the laws of Kentucky) and an image of the terror of Indian wars, which led them to reject their original enthusiasm for the Ohio and settle on the peaceful Susquehanna.[12] Southey was strongly influenced in his writing by Imlay and Filson, publishing *Madoc* (an epic based on Filson's "Welsh Indians") and the dirgeful "Songs of the American Indians" in 1805.[13]

But his treatment of Miss Wollstonecraft showed the same lack of integrity as his business dealings in Kentucky and his treasonable proposals to Brissot. He enjoyed the prestige of their liaison, was flattered by the love of so intelligent a woman, and even proposed marrying her and moving to that utopian plantation in the West that the two of them had imagined in *The Emigrants*. Her brother Charles, an associate of Coleridge and the pantisocratic utopians, actually went to choose a likely site for such a colony. But Imlay never informed her of the impossibility of his returning to

Kentucky, just as he kept her in the dark on his intrigues with Brissot. Although he allowed her to use his surname, the marriage was never formalized, and he deserted her in 1796 after the birth of their daughter Fanny. The infamy of this desertion, publicized by Godwin in his memoir of Mary (whom he married), together with the collapse of his political intrigues, drove Imlay out of those circles whose favor he had so assiduously cultivated and into virtual nonentity until his death in the Isle of Jersey in 1828.

The *Topographical Description* had been the key to Imlay's self-promotion, and it proved to have a certain amount of staying power as an influence on European ideas of America, being frequently reprinted. In it Imlay portrays an America that is at bottom physically and intellectually amenable to conventional European preconceptions, while rhetorically seeming to challenge or criticize Europe. He contrasts the "simple manners and rational life of the Americans . . . with the distorted and unnatural habits of the Europeans"; but he attributes the latter, not to any congenital weakness of civilization, but to "universally bad laws" and the dominance of monarchs and established priestcraft. He evokes the Emile in buckskins stereotype very effectively, if simplistically: "We have more of simplicity, and you more of art. We have more of nature, and you more of the world. Nature formed our features and intellects very much alike; but while you have metamorphosed the one, and contaminated the other, we preserve the natural symbols of both. You have more hypocrisy, we are sincere." [14]

Where Filson tried to deal with processes and realities — with the evolution of Boone's character and culture through experiences involving hardship, solitude, and an apprenticeship to savagery — Imlay (like Parraud) needs only to deal with fixities, conventional images, and conclusions. Europe is decadent, progress in America moves on unchecked. The dark elements described by Filson are omitted from Imlay's picture. Here the landscape is uniformly arcadian, and the frontiersmen and their families are seen picturesquely celebrating seasonal labors and festivals like the bogus shepherds and shepherdesses of Louis XVI's Versailles. Imlay also exaggerates Filson's tendency to describe the beauty of natural objects in terms appropriate to the discussion of works of art or craft. Where Filson vaguely implies that some Hand has given his flowery vales their proportion, symmetry, variety, harmony, and color, Imlay completely urbanizes the scene by comparing nature's work to that of a "florist" and the mountains and cloud banks to city skylines and Pope's Temple of Fame. Where Filson describes Kentucky's progress by contrasting wigwam and settler's cabin, Imlay draws an invidious distinction between the "squalid stations" of the settlers and his own pastoral villages.[15]

Imlay's inherent Europeanism is even more to the fore in *The Emigrants*, which for all its American setting is addressed entirely to current European concerns (the woman question, the difficulties of class structure, the complications of romantic love). Imlay's American hero is a "natural aristocrat," with the emphasis on the latter term; his frontiersman is a woods-wise but socially inferior rustic. The plot revolves around the transplantation of two English gentlewomen to the New World and their rescue from Indian captivity and European intrigue by Arl—ton.[16] Civilization, for Imlay, is essentially European in nature, subject to debilitating seizures of effeminacy and to artificial manners, but for all that characterized by sensitivity, intelligence, sophistication, and artistic sensibility. The marriage of English Caroline to Arl—ton will mellow and cultivate both the "natural aristocrat" himself and the rude land he represents. Imlay, the ostensible critic of all things European, becomes like Parraud a manipulator of conventional symbols for a narrow and self-absorbed segment of the European population.

Early Influence of the Boone Figure in American Writing

The evolution of the image of the frontier hero in America during this period differed in character, direction, and literary process from the evolution of the American image in Europe. Boone's Indian-like exploits proved more attractive to American publishers and editors than the *matière à réflexions* that intrigued the French. Nor was the developing American myth shaped by the fluctuating sympathies of a volatile coterie. It was based, rather, on a popular literature that had a distinct sense of its audience, a set of traditions and narrative genres, and a marked bent toward conscious myth-making within those genres. European enthusiasm for the hunter and the proto-Indian in Boone never really developed, despite the suggestive ending of Crèvecoeur's *Letters*; and as the French Revolution turned toward terrorism and demagogy, the liberal enthusiasm for the American Emile in buckskins markedly waned (although the belief in the reality of such a figure remained fixed). In contrast, the tendency in American writing from 1790 to 1805 was for Boone the hunter and explorer to permeate the scene and breathe his spirit into most attempts at fabricating an American hero. Even the character of Parson Weems's George Washington — the George of the cherry tree — received his initiation into manhood in the Daniel Boone manner, as an Indian fighter and explorer.

Just as American writers diverged from Europeans in their portrayal of exemplary American heroes and values, they went their separate way in literary forms and values. The Europeans preferred standard genres as vehicles for dealing with America vis-à-vis Europe. Conventionalized American types could be opposed to Europeans for a variety of literary purposes — to shed light on the philosophical and political issue of the natural rights of man; to add a new variation to the traditional pastoral opposition between nature and art; or to add a new type, the woolly American, to the gallery of social comedy that already included the lecherous French fop, the stingy Scot, and the hot-tempered Irishman. American writers copied European forms to some extent, but until the turn of the century, most popular writers persisted in working the old veins of the captivity narrative. These traditional genres were developing into vehicles for fiction; and as they did so, they tended to bring to the surface the peculiarly American archetypes that had been hidden within the body of Colonial literature.

The American fiction which developed out of this literary heritage differed in many respects from European literature, primarily (as Richard Chase has said) in its greater preoccupation with myth and the probing of the psyche, but also in its attempt to formulate popular visions of the American character and its destiny. Literary characters, to be believable as *American* heroes, would have to be rooted in the wilderness soil, rather than among the refinements of European civilization, and their admirable qualities would have to reflect the virtue of American soil, rather than the triumph of European manners over American barbarism. This distinction appears sharply if we look ahead to Cooper's portrait of Leatherstocking. Cooper's hero has the admirable stoic qualities of Imlay's Captain Arl—ton — the tender heart and the hard, practical, moral head. But where Imlay attributes his hero's tender sentiment to the gentle tutelage of society and his rough, practical morality and hardness of head to the wilderness, Cooper attributes the better qualities of both head and heart to the workings of nature in pure solitude and the moral biases to Leatherstocking's societal education (among Indians and whites).

This divergence of American and European literature was partly a result of the literary trend toward myth-making that had already marked each of the narrative genres of Colonial literature. The direction of this trend, however, was itself determined by developments within American society. European visions of the American character failed not only for literary reasons — Europeans were insufficiently sensitive to the archetypes that Americans recognized as paradigms of their historical experience — but also for social and political reasons. They did not speak to the Americans' need for heroes whose characters and values would be relevant to the chaotic society of a half-created nation.

The French view of America as a stable political and social entity was unrealistic. Where the French saw a Franklinian republic firmly based on natural law, there was in fact a great creative and destructive flux of political ideas, in which no law, natural or statutory, was held so sacred that it defied the questioning of angry or ambitious men — men who had literally created the republic with their own hands. Where Parraud saw a national character type in Filson's Boone, with his admirable but strictly limited natural intelligence, there was in fact a conspicuous lack of any national self-image or culture hero. Where the French saw the frontier through their hazy dreams of a reasonable, benevolent nature and of the establishment of an imperial utopia in Louisiana, Americans were forced to deal with the harsh realities of the West — the savagery of frontiersmen and Indians, the hardships of the wilderness, and the conflicting land claims of the states, the Spanish, and the British. Almost all the states owned conflicting claims in the West, and the Confederation government had to reconcile these claims; yet before the Northwest Ordinance could be passed in 1787, there had to be some sort of national agreement on the proper role and character of an American national government. As a prominent landowner and politician, Boone was deeply involved in those practical problems.

The presence of British forts in the West and of French and Spanish agents in Kentucky and Tennessee pointed up the connection between the international problem posed to the American nation by the war in Europe and the government's stance toward the western territories. Indian wars, abetted by British agents, continued into the 1790s, and the tribes were powerful enough to maintain themselves in the field and threaten America with the specter of an independent Indian buffer state under British protection along the Canadian border. In 1786, George Rogers Clark fought an inconclusive campaign against the Indians, and in 1790 General Harmar was beaten by the Indians in Ohio. Gen. Arthur St. Clair, with most of the regular army of the United States, was ambushed and routed in 1791 by Indians in the Ohio country and lost nine hundred men. American power tottered in the West, while British, French, and Spanish agents schemed for territorial advantages and bought the services of prominent Americans. Included among the latter were General Wilkinson, commander of the American army in the West, who was an agent in Spanish pay, and General Clark, who accepted a French commission as major general and proposed to lead American soldiers against Spanish New Orleans to seize it for France (an intrigue in which Imlay may have been involved). Boone himself accepted the syndicship of a Spanish province. Former Vice-President Aaron Burr attempted to detach the western states to form an independent commonwealth.

The French Revolution and the Indian-harried West together formed a complex dilemma, the solution of which hinged in part on the choice of a national self-image. Were we to be republican revolutionaries from the wilderness, sacrificing life, treasure, and national interest to support the good cause among the more important nations of Europe? If so, Clark's filibustering in Louisiana for the benefit of France was an heroic act — the child of nature rendering service to the parent civilization of the Age of Reason and the hope of man. Or were we primarily interested in the exploration of the West and the exploitation of our potential for national power, rather than in political ideology, the Age of Reason, or the wars of Europe? America, half-formed in government and uncertain in will, cast up heroic images symbolizing solutions to her dilemmas. Washington was one, of course, with universal appeal; but local heroes like John Stark of New Hampshire, Israel Putnam of Connecticut, Ethan Allen of Vermont, and Daniel Boone of Kentucky had equally significant followings in the legend and literature of their own localities and served their people as legislators and political leaders as well.

The treatment of Filson's Boone by American editors and literary pirates between 1784 and 1794 is one index to the national conception of its western hero. In 1786 John Trumbull of Norwich, Connecticut, published a pirated version of Filson's Boone narrative, which was copied and reprinted in popular periodicals, pamphlets, and anthologies for the next fifty years.[17] Trumbull altered Filson's text, deleting all the philosophizing that intrigued the French and emphasizing the image of Boone as a man of action, as distinct from a man of thought and feeling. The Boone that emerges is a kind of Kentucky John Stark or Israel Putnam — lacking, of course, the former New England ranger's education, formal military rank, and relative sophistication and breadth of view in matters of morality and national policy. The New England editor also subordinated the realities of the frontier to the literary conventions and cultural preoccupations of the East. Where Parraud drew his image of Boone from the theories of the Enlightenment philosophes, Trumbull drew his from the conventional image of the West that had emerged in the Indian war literature of the last century and a half — an image in which some of the realism of long experience on the frontier mingled with the optimism of the visionary pioneer and the despair of the Puritan. The French were interested in the narrative as evidence confirming the intellectual predilections of a coterie. Trumbull was interested in printing and selling a pamphlet on the popular subject of western adventure, and he catered to the public's taste for the sensational and its desire to define the character of the westerner in familiar terms.

Trumbull attempted to satisfy his audience's demands by binding the Boone narrative with the captivity narrative of Mrs. Frances Scott, an account drawn from current newspapers. He thus combined two major forms of Indian war writing, the Indian war narrative and the captivity narrative, the tale of man's conquest of the wilderness and the tale of woman's victimization by the wilderness. To Boone's narrative are reserved those images which reflect the beauty and promise of the West and the courage and prowess of the frontier hero. All of Filson's dark landscapes and passages of melancholy or philosophic meditation are deleted, leaving only the image of an Edenic Kentucky and an adventurous, uncontemplative Daniel Boone. Mrs. Scott's narrative, on the other hand, contains only those images of the West which reflect its terror and its harshness. She is presented as an all-but-helpless female, sentimentally contemplating the spectacle of her own piteous destruction. Is Boone so much the man of action that he is blind to the fate of females in his hunter's Eden? No editorial attempt is made to reconcile the two visions of the frontier: hunter and captive are simply left in dramatic opposition, and the true image of the West is presumed to lie somewhere between the two. This juxtaposition of the captivity narrative and the Indian war narrative anticipates by a decade the beginnings of Romantic fiction about the wilderness, in which the human hero of the Indian war narrative steps directly into the captivity narrative to rescue the maiden in distress.

Trumbull's pamphlet reflects the persistence of the two main lines of myth about the frontier — the hopeful, outward-looking, woods-loving, realistic view typified by the works of Underhill, Church, Rogers, and Filson; and the pessimistic, inward-looking, fantasy-ridden view put forward in the sermon narratives of Mather and Hubbard, the Puritan captivity narratives, and later the Gothic fiction of Brockden Brown. Given the strength of the captivity tradition, any account which failed to acknowledge this darker aspect of the frontier would probably have failed to convince a New England audience of its accuracy. Subsequent New England editions led to the emergence of a characteristic format for New England revisions of the myth. The popularity of Trumbull's rough-and-ready, dephiloso-phized Boone is attested by the frequency with which his text of the narrative was reprinted in various American cities and towns and by its wide service as a basic source for more ambitious works on the trans-Appalachian West which now began to appear. Its literary influence was widespread; it affected all the traditional genres of Colonial writing and the conceptions of the wilderness experience which these genres purveyed.

Evidence of Filson's hero's effect on American expectations can be seen in the exploration narratives published after 1784 by William Bartram and the pseudonymous Alonso Decalves. Bartram, the son of that John Bartram whom Crèvecoeur so admired, had accompanied his father on naturalist explorations in the southeastern colonies in the 1760s and 1770s. He published his narrative in 1791, seven years after the publication of *Kentucke*, and his record bears the distinctive markings of the mind of Filson's Boone. There are frequent echoes of Filson's phraseology, but more significant is his sharing of Boone's expectation of receiving wisdom from the wilderness and his consequent willingness to submit himself to experience in it. Like Boone he is open to spontaneous impressions that reveal, without mental striving, great nature's message. His treatment of the Indians is particularly worth noting, since it differs sharply from the attitudes evinced by his father, who (Crèvecoeur notwithstanding) tended to find the Indians somewhat repulsive in person.

William Bartram's strange meeting with an Indian in the Florida woods begins with a persuasive echo of Filson's scene on the "commanding ridge." The time of day, state of the sky, and weather are described just as Filson describes the "level of Kentucke": "It was drawing towards the close of day, the skies serene and calm, the air temperately cool, and gentle zephyrs breathing through the fragrant pines; the prospect around enchantingly varied and beautiful. . . . The gaily attired plants which enamelled the green had begun to imbibe the pearly dew of evening; nature seemed silent, and nothing appeared to ruffle the happy moments of evening contemplation." Into this scene an Indian intrudes, armed and painted, frightening Bartram, who has no time to flee. Resigning himself to Providence, Bartram hails the Indian as "Brother" and greets him as a friend. He then experiences what he believes to be an insight into the Indian's mind, which he reports as follows: "White man, thou art my enemy, and thou and thy brethren may have killed mine; yet it may not be so, and even were that the case, thou art now alone, and in my power. Live; the Great Spirit forbids me to touch thy life; go to thy brethren, tell them thou sawest an Indian in the forests, who knew how to be humane and compassionate." Bartram later discovers that the Indian was a notorious murderer, who only the day before had been beaten by the whites. He draws from his experience the principle that man has an innate moral sense, which renders the Indian truly our brother and equal in all save education and experience of the world.[18] Thus, like Boone, Bartram descends into the wilderness, finds a kindred spirit in an Indian, and emerges with moral wisdom.

More profound than even the discovery of brotherhood with the Indian is the discovery by later writers that the Indian woman answers the longing of the American male soul for its missing, better half. Byrd toyed with the notion, and the makers of folktales about Boone involved him in a tale of hunting and ritual marriage to a wild creature. Alonso Decalves, pseudonymous author of *New Travels to the Westward, or Unknown Parts of America*, offers a case history of such a marriage, that of the captive Dutchman Vandelure, who refused to return to civilization and leave his Indian bride. The narrative of Vandelure's captivity is based on fact; the rest of the book is absolute fiction. Decalves employs all the conventional motifs and incidents of the exploration narrative, reducing the archetypal formula to its bare bones and setting this romantic image of Indian marriage at the penultimate point of its protagonist's quest. His chief interest is not in creating (like Filson) an ideal American hero nor in detailing information on the natural landscape and deriving philosophical generalities (as does Bartram). Rather, he fastens on the sensational and sentimental possibilities in the sequence, simply because it is what his public expects of a frontier tale. In thus reducing the experiences of the explorer, naturalist, and surveyor to their basic elements, Decalves focuses his reader's attention on a model pattern of a frontier experience.

As in the *Panther Captivity*, this employment of the formula as the basis for literary fiction emphasizes its archetypal elements without analyzing or explaining them. The journey of Decalves and his companions follows the archetypal pattern of Filson's Boone narrative and of the other quests outlined by Campbell. The party are urged on by curiosity and a love of adventure; they cross a wasteland to the threshold of adventure, a mountain pass so high that they nearly die of cold and low oxygen. On the other side of the gate they are confronted by a monster, which they hunt and kill:

> He was eight feet seven inches long from one extremity to the other; had short, thick and very smooth hair, of a dark yellow, rather inclining to green, with rows of spots a bright vermilion. His belly inclining to be red with spots of a black colour. This dress, as the reader may suppose, appeared really beautiful; but his armour was terrible, having a mouth full of the most pointed teeth, and uncommon tusks. His claws were long and sharp, in the form of a cat; but in full propor-

tion to his body; . . . and a tail about two feet long with a small brush on the end; and appeared to be a formidable fellow, and one that would be dangerous to engage.[19]

The hunt leads them to the discovery of a tribe of Indians of an equally remarkable appearance: "What particularly drew my attention, was a noble disinterested countenance . . . [and] a regular articulate sound of the voice when they spoke that seemed more like the language of civilized nations than that of savages." The king of the tribe, Knipperdoling, is likewise a regal and imposing personage, equal in dignity to any European monarch and possessed of a palace far more luxurious in its artistic decoration than any European king's.[20] The green fur of the monster and green ostrich plumes adorn his person and his palace.

The lands about the royal capital are fruitful and productive farmlands, tilled by freemen. Among them dwells Vandelure, the Dutch captive, with his Indian wife and half-breed son. The adventurers offer to restore him to civilization and provoke a violent conflict of sentiments in the Dutchman's breast. The scene that ensues fulfills the prophecy of William Smith in 1766 that the sundering of captives from their Indian spouses would be a fit subject for romance, though Smith himself never dreamed of writing it. Decalves, writing thirty years later, notes the same ambivalence in the white captive:

> On the one hand was a native country, parents, connections, religion, and a civilized world, whose customs and manners all men are tenacious of: on the other, a wife, for whom he had conceived a tender regard, and an offspring of his body in a promising son, were powerful motives in his virtuous mind.

To Smith such vacillation was the sign of a degraded mind and lower-class origins. Decalves takes this objection in stride and answers it by exalting the virtuous nature of the Indian woman and the nobility of Vandelure's soul:

> Here the reader will say, perhaps, that this was not of a very delicate taste, to set a value on an Indian wife, that should overbalance the powerful incentives he had to leave her. I will give his answer in his own words, viz. "That he had solemnly swore before God, to be her husband, and notwithstanding he cared but little about the God in whose pretended presence he swore, yet he absolutely gave up his heart to her in that ceremony, and in the presence of the Christian God, and therefore thought it sacred." And it is my opinion, that there never was one of the fair sex in a state of nature, who had so much true sense of virtue, modesty and becoming decency: and at the same time so engaging address as this woman.

Nonetheless, Vandelure concludes to go with them. He is only turned from his course by his inability to cause his wife pain by telling her he will leave her — so deep is his affection. In portraying the scene, Decalves does not palliate the nature of the Dutchman's choice; rather, he emphasizes that the choice confirms Vandelure in a true marriage to an unmixed Indian and involves him in miscegenation. Yet he clearly admires the choice:

> The next day, having his half Indian boy in his arms, and walking about his room, we observed he looked melancholy on his wife; he suddenly burst into tears and said, "I can't, I can't, I never will leave my wife and this dear child." This he uttered in Dutch, so that his wife could not understand him; and she never had heard that he had an inclination to leave her.[21]

Just as the concept of the nature of this frontier experience changed, so the concept of the American hero changed to produce one capable of wresting the greatest advantage from that experience. Bartram, the naturalist and philosopher, had the intellectual equipment to draw the necessary lesson from his meeting with the Indian. Decalves, the adventurer and romantic, was capable of dealing with the assaults of monstrous beasts and weather and of appreciating the significance and value of a marriage between Indian and white.

The development of the captivity narrative in this period reflects a similar change. Alexander Henry, an Indian trader captured during Pontiac's Rebellion, portrays his real captivity in terms that reflect a similar sympathy for the Indian life. Henry, whose narrative was published in 1809, was spared by his captors because of his friendship with Wawatam, a notable person in the tribe. Wawatam had adopted Henry as his "son and brother" before the rebellion and had tutored him in Indian ways and language. After the capture of Fort Michilimackinac, Wawatam intervened to save Henry from his angered fellow tribesmen. Yet Wawatam was no "good Indian." He had known of the conspiracy against the whites and did not betray the Indians to them. Although he rescued the Englishman for whom he felt a strong regard, he participated in a cannibal feast on the bodies of Henry's countrymen. Henry implies that Wawatam offered some of the "English broth" to him, and there is reason to suppose that, on this occasion or some other, Henry succumbed to cannibalism. One of the chief features of his long narrative is the recurrence of the notion of cannibalism, among hostile and friendly Indians alike, and even among Canadians during a time of starvation.

Wawatam is portrayed with a sympathetic objectivity that does not blink either his savagery or his virtues. Henry's description of Wawatam returning from the cannibal feast reflects the trader's understanding of Indian customs and psychology:

> After an absence of about half an hour, he returned bringing in his dish a human hand, and a large piece of flesh. He did not appear to relish the repast, but told me, that it was then, and always had been the custom, among all the Indian nations, when returning from war, or on overcoming their enemies, to make a war-feast, from among the slain. This, he said, inspired the warrior with courage in attack, and bred him to meet death with fearlessness.[22]

Yet Henry cannot leave Wawatam without "the most grateful sense of the many acts of goodness . . . , nor without the sincerest respect for the virtues which I had witnessed" in Wawatam's family.[23] During his captivity he strove to gain Wawatam's respect as a hunter and to help provide the family with food, often at the risk of his life. His account of Wawatam's farewell reflects the mutuality of their regard, the extent to which the white man and the Indian had "adopted" each another:

> My father and brother (for he was alternately each of these,) lit his pipe, and presented it to me, saying, "My son, this may be the last time that ever you and I shall smoke out of the same pipe! I am sorry to part with you. You know the affection which I have always borne you, and the dangers to which I have exposed myself and family, to preserve you from your enemies; and I am happy to find that my efforts promise not to have been in vain." [24]

Even allowing for some exaggeration on Henry's part, the scene is a highly significant one in the literature of Indian captivities. Never before had the relationship between captor and captive been portrayed in this manner, outside of a few literary romances by Europeans.

A sense of shared sympathy and even shared education with the Indian was no longer an automatic bar to a hero's entrance into the American pantheon. Indeed, such sympathy and education now became a prerequisite of sorts. One of the most popular of the adopted-Indian heroes was Col. James Smith, an Indian fighter, politician, and religious enthusiast who had been captured by Indians shortly before Braddock's defeat and held for six years. In 1799 Colonel Smith published an account of his captivity and adoption by the Indians, in which life among the Indians becomes the basis of his later heroism as an Indian fighter. Further, he offers a description of Indian discipline and tactics that will, he hopes, enable his countrymen to share the benefits of his experience by learning to imitate the Indian art of warfare. Thus, like himself, all America will derive the prowess necessary to heroism from intimate knowledge of and sympathy with the Indian.

Smith's captivity reflects the increasing American identification with the Indian and with the frontier hunter who lives as an Indian. The captivity, unlike Mrs. Scott's, recounts his adoption into the tribe and the relative ease of his life among them. He gives a detailed account of the "baptism" that cleansed him of his "white blood" and acknowledges that he was moved by the Indians' faithful adherence to the promise of the ceremony that he would be as a son of their blood. The account is written, he declares, not to warn the whites not to become like the Indians, but rather to exhort them to imitate the Indians' way of fighting in the wilderness. It is only laziness — an unwillingness to accept rigorous discipline — that keeps the Americans from such imitation, not any innate contempt for Indian ways. After all, we have borrowed language, food, and weaponry from them in the past.[25] Thus Smith berates his countrymen in the language of Cotton Mather ("rigor and discipline") in urging them to become more like the Indians, and he refers to a tradition of shared experience with the Indians, rather than to a European past.

Smith declares that his close experience with the Indians has made him master of their tactics, and (in a later edition) he provides a treatise on the Indian mode of fighting and techniques of imitating them with white soldiers. "Were only part of our men taught this art, . . . I think no European power, after trial, would venture to shew its head in the American woods." [26] He offers his own career in evidence of his claims, for the adopted captive later became a leader of frontier militia and a noted Indian fighter. Impatient of legalities, he led the vigilante Black Boys in reprisal raids against Indians and gunrunning traders, aping Indian vendetta-justice. He was arrested several times and was tried at least once for murder, but freed. He also raided a local jail in 1769 to free some of his imprisoned cohorts. Thus the captive of Puritan tradition becomes, in Smith's account, a combative, self-willed hero, deriving power values and independence of mind from intimacy with the Indians.

Parson Weems reaped the fruits of the literary development stimulated by Filson. Like Filson he was concerned with fabricating a hero to be a model of the ideal American. His choice of hero was more ambitious than Filson's; it was Washington himself. But Weems drew heavily on the heroic pattern of Filson's Boone and on the climate of expectation in which the literary personas of Boone, Bartram, Decalves, and Smith approach their experiences in the wilderness. Like Filson, Weems drew together many strands of the literary tradition, many genre heroes, in composing his own hero's portrait. The result was so successful a piece of myth-making that its subject's reputation has been hard put to live it down. But the moral fables that Weems inserted in the biography — to the horror of scholars and the delight of the righteous — are less integral a part of his portrait than his account of Washington's formative experiences in the wilderness, his initiation into manhood as a surveyor, explorer, and Indian fighter in the Boone mold.

The young Washington enters the wilderness on an errand for the governor of Virginia, confronting with his untutored courage "one immeasurable forest, from time immemorial the gloomy haunt of ravening beasts and of murderous savages," soundless save for the "hiss of rattlesnakes, the shrieks of panthers, the yell of Indians and the howling tempests." His temperament, trained in the pastoral settings of his native Virginia, is patient and sympathetic; his mind operates through "intuition" to adjust to the wilderness and grasp at policies for overcoming it. His self-possession derives in large measure from his profession as surveyor, a "simple, harmless employment" (like that of John Bartram in Crèvecoeur's letters) "which more than any other, tends to tranquillize the mind." [27] Boone, it will be remembered, was also a surveyor.

Once the French and Indian War breaks out, Washington leaves diplomacy and surveying for the role of soldier. He conducts an unsuccessful campaign against the French at Fort Duquesne, which ends in his surrender to them at Fort Necessity. This inglorious affair, actually the result of the unskilled Washington's impetuosity and blundering, becomes a Thermopylae in Weems's account, as Washington with his small band of heroes stands firm against hordes of attacking savages. Washington in Fort Necessity, like Boone in Boonesborough, is an explorer and wanderer of the woods who has come home to defend his island-fort against a sea of wilderness troubles. The parallel becomes still more evident in Weems's account of Washington's role at Braddock's defeat. The scene he paints is in the lurid tradition of the captivities and of Boone's account of Blue Licks. Braddock's British regulars are seen as incapable of self-defense in these circumstances, fighting in the open against an invisible enemy:

> Such sights of their bleeding comrades, had the enemy been in view, instead of depressing would but have inflamed British blood with fiercer thirst for vengeance. But alas! to be thus entrapped in a dreary wild! to be thus pent up, and shot from behind rocks and trees, by an invisible enemy, was enough to dismay the stoutest hearts.[28]

Braddock's men see the wilderness just as Puritan historians of King Philip's War, like William Hubbard, saw the Indian's chosen battleground — as a swamp, a mire, in which mind and body become tangled and imprisoned. In such terrain the English soldier is justified in refusing battle; but Washington, leading Braddock's Virginia auxiliaries, is, like Benjamin Church and Boone, in his element there. Because he knows the Indian's mode of fighting, the foe is not "invisible" to him; he can find and fight him with his own skills and weapons. Weems emphasizes the parallels by speaking of Washington as the commander of a group of "rangers," who deliberately and successfully ape the savages:

> Happily, on the left, where lay the deadliest fire, Washington's rangers were posted; but not exposed like the British. For, on hearing the horrible savage yells, in a moment they flew each to his tree, like the Indians; and like them, each levelled his rifle, and with as deadly aim.[29]

The Indians charge and are again met with their own tactics and weapons, as Washington's "rangers" interpose themselves between the Indians and the stricken British army:

> [F]aithful to their friends, Washington's rangers stepped forth with joy to meet the assailants. Then rose a scene sufficient to fill the stoutest heart with horror. Burning alike for vengeance, both parties throw aside the slow-murdering rifles, and grasp their swift-fated tomahawks. Dreadfully above their heads gleams the brandished steel, as with full exerted limbs, and faces all inflamed with mortal hate, they level at each other their last decisive blows. . . . Here falls the brave Virginia Blue, under the stroke of his nimbler foe — and there, man on man the Indians perish beneath the furious tomahawks, deep buried in the shattered brain.[30]

Weems is, of course, fictionalizing here, drawing on the ranger mystique to grace his hero. Washington was in fact the leader of uniformed troops of the provincial military establishment. But Weems follows the legend through: the British officers and soldiers fail, and Washington and the rangers alone remain to ward off disaster, as the regulars refuse Washington's call to rally. Similarly, after the battle the government refuses Washington's call (so like Benjamin Church's in 1676) to invade the Indian country, revealing again the depth of division between the wisdom of the frontiersman-hero and the policy of townsmen and Europeans.

Literary Nationalism and the Divergence of European and American Images of American Hero Types

Weems's study of Washington is the most significant, but far from the only example of an American political hero associated by his panegyrist with the pattern of Boone, the explorer, hunter, warrior, and adopted Indian. Where the Europeans began with the rough, unpolished image of Parraud's Boone and evolved from it the polished American of Captain Arl—ton's ilk, Weems begins with one born to the American purple as a Virginia plantation-lord (or rather, in Crèvecoeur's imagery, a planter-husbandman) and traces his conversion into an American hero through a baptism by fire and terror in nature's wilderness. This divergence of American and European images of the American character carries with it the implication of a more profound divergence of cultural, political, and literary values. The divergence was accentuated by the European revulsion against the romanticization of the natural man and the savage Americans that followed the excesses of the French Revolution. Americans, equally appalled by the strife in Europe, pictured themselves standing against a decadent Europe.

The causes of the change in European (and especially French) attitudes lay in the catastrophic disruption of the evolution of the European Enlightenment by the Revolution, the Terror, and the Napoleonic aftermath. German, French, English, and American rationalists had spent more than a century evolving a philosophy in which human behavior and natural laws were nearly reduced to a series of reasonable, comprehensible, power-bestowing formulas. Then, at the political crisis of the Enlightenment, even as the revolutionaries' Feast of Reason was instituted in place of the Mass, unreason triumphed. The dark people ran mad in the streets of Paris; the good and wise of the nobility were slaughtered; the ideal of a universal reign of peace and order was drowned in a wave of imperial nationalism. Lavoisier and Chenier died with Louis, Marat, and Robespierre. The French democracy called a despot to the throne, and the republic of the West fought by the side of perfidious Albion against their brother republicans of France. The image of the good savage had expressed the Enlightenment's faith in the essential goodness and reasonableness of the natural man; but the savages of France, given freedom to express their will, proved passionate and bloody-minded.

The disillusion of the intellectual elite with their own philosophy extended to America — that imaginary country which had for decades served as the stage on which their philosophic principles, in symbolic dress, acted out the drama of reason. Even the most devoted Americanists, like Crèvecoeur, began to employ the "degenerate" image more frequently than any of the other stock images of the American character. Americans, once the social lions of Paris, were out of favor in the salons. French travel-

ers no longer doted on the good Quakers and the pious yeomanry but casti-
gated American materialism and the philistine coarseness of her civilization. Nor could the travelers praise American liberties, since fear of French
radicalism had led to the Alien and Sedition Acts and the popular and
official harassment of French diplomats and tourists.

In 1785 Parraud had offered Daniel Boone as the ideal specimen of
the natural philosopher and a sensitive portrayer of landscape, the flower
of frontier civilization. Scarcely a decade later, Talleyrand described his
journey to the frontier as "travelling backward over the progress of the
human mind" and characterized the frontiersman as a boor, insensitive to
the natural wonders around him: "The American woodsman is interested
in nothing; any sensitivity is foreign to him. Those branches yonder arched
by nature, that lovely clump of foliage, that bright spot of color lighting up
a dark part of the wood, . . . all that is nothing, it means nothing to him.
His only thought is of the number of strokes it will take him to chop down
the tree." [31]

Crèvecoeur's *Journey into Northern Pennsylvania and the State of
New York*, published in Paris in 1801 and translated into German in 1802,
reflects the new European hostility toward America and suggests some
possible reasons. In his *Letters from an American Farmer*, Crèvecoeur had
written as a naturalized American to a European, answering questions a
European might ask and thus subtly applying the experience of America to
the perplexities of Europe. Although he preserves this fiction in the *Journey* by posing as "an adopted Oneida," he actually writes as a European
visiting America, his mind filled with the troubles of France. The conversa-
tions that take place on the journey begin with an American situation, but
they turn quickly and without much hesitation to European affairs. Instead
of prophesying for Europe in the light of American history, he criticizes
America (and his adopted Oneida kinsmen) in the light of European history. The character types who appeared in the first book are reconstructed
here, but their forms have hardened. Where "the Americans" had earlier
been a people capable of infinite change, adjustment, and improvement,
they are now rigidly defined in terms appropriate to the European class
struggle. The Indians and the white frontiersmen become equivalents of
the French Jacobins: savage, revengeful, philistine. Never having known
the refinements of the truly civilized classes, they quickly degenerate
under the compulsions of their environment into beasts, becoming superstitious, irrational, intemperate, and untrustworthy. Civilization is represented, not by a good Quaker Bartram, who mediates between all worlds,

but rather by a purebred Frenchman, living in exile from his war-torn country as a means of reproaching her for her savagery.

Crèvecoeur's first book had ended with his persona contemplating the seeking of a refuge among the Indians. In the *Journey* he offers an example of one man who did, a Scotchman living among the Winnebagos. The section contains several echoes of the Boone narrative, suggesting that Crèvecoeur regarded the Long Hunter as a white man who chose to live as an Indian. Crèvecoeur contrasts this character with that of another exile, a European youth who has fled from the disordered violence of Europe to find peace as an independent farmer on the frontier. In effect, Crèvecoeur splits the original character of Boone into two variant forms — the Indian-like hunter, able to maintain his identity among savages but unable either to preserve the Indian's culture or to aid the advance of agriculture; and the gentleman farmer, educated in Europe and bent on establishing civilization in the wilds.

The Scotchman's expatriation among the Indians, involuntary at first (he is a political refugee), has become voluntary because of his fear of the disordered and unnatural state of postrevolutionary Europe. The Revolution seems to him a shocking signal of coming convulsion in the New World as well, and he views the wilderness as a temporary "tranquil port in the shelter of storms." Like Filson, he sees the basis of America's present felicity in the triumph of the values of the freeholding farmer: love of independence, desire for self-sufficiency, and willingness to gain these ends through patient cultivation of modest landholdings. This decent desire for economic self-sufficiency is contrasted to the Jacobin principle of unbridled ambition and license, which is "extremely attractive to the multitude; because men, always discontent with their lot, hope to better it in the midst of tempests and tumults," and which results inevitably in social degeneration. The Winnebago-Scot points out that his fellow Winnebagos are as much afflicted with Jacobinic passions as the rabble of Paris, as much prone to drunkenness, rage, and bloody vengeance, as much impatient of leadership and "fond" of liberty. "This liberty pushed to excess . . . appears to me . . . to be a great evil, since it sterilizes the seeds of reproduction while inspiring in these nations an invincible aversion to a sedentary life of cultivation which would increase their strength and multiply their number." [32]

The Indians' love of "democracy," Crèvecoeur observes, coupled with their unfortunate predilection for the hunting economy, creates among them a single racial type in which intelligence and reason are debased and dominated by the passions and fears of the nomadic hunter. "Racial level-ling," a consequence of their political leveling, thus imposes on all members of Indian society the character type of the "least perfectable" type of man.[33] The point of Crèvecoeur's argument is that the results of Indian leveling are identical with those of Jacobin leveling: in both cases, even the better sort of man who joins the Indians/Jacobins becomes himself degraded, no matter what his personal attainments. Thus Crèvecoeur's Winnebago-Scot echoes Boone's philosophy of asceticism, simplicity, and self-restraint; but he lacks the truly civilized man's desire for earning and owning property. This proprietorial desire, evinced by both the real Boone and Filson's hero, is the antithesis of and the antidote for the Faustian ambitions of the levelers, Jacobins, and revolutionaries. Lacking this urge for the freehold, the exile is powerless and impotent, able neither to protect the Winnebago way of life nor to improve it.

The Winnebago-Scot is Crèvecoeur's final formulation of the hunter half of Boone's personality, the quality in his being that enables him to immerse himself thoroughly and with some gusto into the life of the Indian and the solitary hunter. The Indian himself, although superior to the "common herd of Europeans" because of the virtues inculcated by nature in a society shaped by natural necessities, is "empty" of mind and therefore static, imperfectible, doomed to decline and extinction. Moreover, the Indian's degeneracy has become a fixed racial trait, one that can infect even whites and white cultures who adopt the savage economy and life-style.[34]

Hope for mankind lies not with the Indians or the Jacobins but with the intellectual aristocracy, whose American equivalent is the gentleman farmer — in this work, the young Frenchman who has exiled himself to that half-savage continent. Through this noble expatriate, Crèvecoeur voices again the agrarian philosophy of *Letters of an American Farmer*. Cultivation of the soil is said to bring man into harmony with nature and, at the same time, to create a humanized and civilized natural environment, free from the terrible compulsions of the wilderness, on the one hand, and of the European city or court, on the other. The farm is utopia in microcosm, where the natural conditions of agrarian labor create a patriarchal government, whose "king" is also a philosopher and a husbandman, a good shepherd. Missing from this reprise of the earlier book is the emphasis on the uniquely Anglo-American character of this utopia's conditions of life, process of evolution, and social and philosophical antecedents. The heroes of the *Letters* and the personas-correspondents are all Anglo-Americans; in the *Journey*, emphasis is laid on the French character of the most admirable of its protagonists and on the wisdom he has derived from his unfortunate experience of French history and politics.

That this shift in his depiction of the American farmer signalizes a change in Crèvecoeur's politics is borne out by his introduction to the *Journey*. Here his literary rejection of the symbolic natural man, and of the idea that America is a melting pot in which free individuals may create new identities and a new society through the agricultural development of the wilderness, is seen to coincide with a rejection of Revolutionary democracy and internationalism in favor of Napoleonic despotism and nationalistic expansionism. In a modern European nation-state (and by extension an American one) only a hero-leader is capable of suppressing and redirecting the Jacobinic savagery that is latent in all men. In his preface he pays tribute to Washington, to whose leadership America owes the good fortune of having had a revolution without a terror. In creating a portrait of Washington as the archetypal American hero, Weems had compared him to the hunter-explorer Boone. Crèvecoeur, on the other hand, compares him with Napoleon Bonaparte, who healed the wounds of civil strife by suppressing democratic anarchy: "Freed from the chaos and horror of one of the most appalling revolutions that has ever drenched our land in blood, in fear and trembling even now at the memory of those laws of exile, expropriation, servitude, and disgrace, from which by a miracle the vision and the courage of a young man (Napoleon Bonaparte) of thirty-one has just delivered us, we are now like the sailor who watches with mingled feelings of fright and gratitude from the harbor he has safely entered the reefs he has had the good fortune to avoid." [35]

A study of the United States by the scholar-traveler Volney, written in the same period, carries the implications of Crèvecoeur's argument one step further. Since the premises on which the old image of American virtues was based have been discredited, the nation established on those premises must likewise be a monstrous creation. Volney rails at the folly of denominating the United States a nation, emphasizing its motley amalgamation of incompatible races and physical environments:

> By simply tracing their history, laws, and language, I proposed to detect the error of those who represent, as a sort of new-born race, as an *infant nation,* a mere medley of adventurers from all parts of Europe. . . . They have shown less frugality and order in their expenses, less integrity in their transactions with strangers, less public decency, less moderation and forbearance in their factions, less . . . discipline in their seminaries of education than most of the old nations of Europe. . . . [The] character and principles of their leaders have deplorably degenerated.[36]

Like Crèvecoeur, Volney traces the origin of American degeneracy to racial and environmental causes. But where Crèvecoeur, in his first book at least, made much of the fluidity and flexibility of the American character, Volney sees it as fixed in its divisions — the easterner turning naturally toward Europe and civilization, which he seeks to imitate; the westerner turning to the Indian and going native, or degenerating into a state of Jacobinic partisanship and anarchism.[37]

This distinction between the backwoods and the maritime sections of the country was in some measure justified by the facts. American writers like Timothy Dwight, Joel Barlow, and Hugh Henry Brackenridge found it necessary to refute assertions of American disunion and degeneracy by seeking out and exalting images of a national character. Dwight's epic poem, *Greenfield Hill* (New York, 1794), typifies this spirit of literary nationalism and, at the same time, reveals its dependence on a worked-up "controversy" with "spokesmen" for Europe. Although written by a member of the social and intellectual elite, it also reveals the dependence of Dwight and the other nationalistic poets of the Federalist school on the popular literary heritage of the Colonial period — a heritage that differed widely from Puritan New England to cosmopolitan New York to Quaker Pennsylvania to slavocratic Virginia. Images of a national character, as men of Dwight's generation conceived it, were derived from traditional conceptions of their own section's best character. Thus Dwight's ideal American is a New England farmer, whose historical experiences and qualities of mind and heart are generalized and who is allowed to move freely from New England and the maritime provinces into the woods.

The theme of the American's life in Greenfield Hill — whether he be Indian or Christian — is self-transcendence, progress toward a higher state of being through greater adjustment to the natural laws manifested in the American landscape. In this way Volney's bugaboo of "degeneration" is avoided. Dwight's American farmers live in a pastoral, nearly perfect present, the pleasure of which is enhanced by the memory of past trials; but the chief source of their happiness lies in their vision of an imperial future, in which the moral, natural sway of the American English will replace that of the corrupted European English through all the world.

The overall structure of the poem reinforces this emphasis on future progress and the overcoming of a dark, tumultuous past. The poem consists of seven books, the first two of which portray the present state of rural America in general ("The Prospect") and Greenfield in particular ("The Flourishing Village"). The past dominates the next two books: the first recounts the destruction of Fairfield by the British in 1779, and the second, the destruction of the Pequots by the Americans in 1638. This progressive movement into the past involves some drawing on the conventions of the captivity and Indian-war narrative genres, the cumulative effect of which is to point up the strong parallel between the savagery of the then-uncivilized Indians and the tyrannous British. The fifth and sixth books move from the distant past to the present again and detail the advice of a clergyman and a farmer to the townsmen. Although they speak in the present, their concern is in fact wholly with the future. They distill imperatives for future action out of the idyllic present and the memory of the dark past. These imperatives are viewed prophetically as accomplished fact by the poet himself in the last book, "The Vision," which portrays the utopian future of the nation.

From the start, Dwight deliberately molds his poetry to support a controversy with English character and English ideas of America. In his introduction he states his intention to "imitate . . . the manner of . . . many British poets"; in particular, he seems to have Goldsmith's *Deserted Village* in mind as a model. Greenfield, however, is the antithesis of Goldsmith's village, whose inhabitants have left cot, field, and barn to wander in the world, some to the dismal jungles of America:

> . . . a dreary scene,
> Where half the convex world intrudes between,
> Through torrid tracts with fainting steps they go,
> Where wild Altama murmurs to their woe.
> Far different there from all that charmed before,
> The various terrors of that horrid shore.
> Those blazing suns that dart a downward ray,
> And fiercely shed intolerable day;
> Those matted woods where birds forget to sing,
> But silent bats in drowsy clusters cling,
> Those poisonous fields with rank luxuriance crowned.
> Where the dark scorpion gathers death around;
> . . . .
> Where crouching tigers wait their hapless prey,
> And savage men more murderous still than they;
> While oft in whirls the mad tornado flies,
> Mingling the ravaged landscape with the skies.
> Far different these from every former scene,
> The cooling brook, the grassy vested green,
> The breezy covert of the warbling grove,
> That only sheltered thefts of harmless love.

Dwight's poem begins with a vision of Greenfield that refutes Goldsmith's view of the landscape and of the consequences of emigration and progress. Greenfield is a flourishing, not a deserted village, populated by independent yeomen rather than tenants and cotters:

How bless'd the sight of such a numerous train
On such small limits, tasting every good
Of competence, of independence, peace,
And liberty unmingled; every house
On its own ground, and every happy swain
Beholding no superior, but the laws,
And such as virtue, knowledge, useful life,
And zeal, exerted for the public good
Have rais'd above the throng. For here, in truth,
Not in pretence man is esteem'd as man.[38]

Dwight contrasts this image with that of the European villager, one cipher in a lumpish mass, "scarce raised above the brutes," worn down by the dull "horsemill round" of drudging, unrewarded labor. America is pastoral and orderly, Europe ruined and chaotic — a deliberate, direct reversal of the traditional view of America as the kingdom of riot, disorder, and degeneration. The demons of hell arise, not to dance like Indians around an American fire, but to weep for the Europeans whose plight is more miserable than their own, under the sway

Of silly pomp, and meanness train'd t'adore;
Of wealth enormous, and enormous want;
Of lazy sinecures and suffering toil. . . .[39]

In Matherian strain, Dwight rails against the "foul theaters," the farcical and idolatrous churches, and the foppish concern for apparel. The moral for Americans is clear: reject Europe, turn to the simple and natural conditions of American life, and live by the laws inherent in those conditions. He denies Volney's assertion that cultivated America is a European "backwoods" that must look east for improvement rather than west to degeneracy. "Ah then, thou favor'd land, thyself revere!" [40]

Emigration to the frontier is not a source of weakness to Dwight's Greenfield, as it is to Goldsmith's deserted village. There is no sharp division, such as Volney cites, between the east-looking town and the west-looking backwoods. Movement between these regions is easy. Since the American pioneer is not driven from his home by fear or want, he brings to the wilderness the virtues of Greenfield Village and becomes an agent of progress. The frequency of emigration to the woods is a sign of cultural vitality and activity, the antithesis of the stagnation of the European village. Like Boone, Dwight's pioneer enters the woods in the name of progress and in the hope of achieving self-transcendence through his actions. The wilderness itself, breathed upon by "gales of Eden cheer," is a warm, fruitful, abundantly endowed land, waiting impatiently to assume the plowed fields and white churches of a New Greenfield, a copy of its utopian forebear. The contrast between village and waste or empty lands in Europe is treated with the imagery traditionally reserved by European and Puritan writers for the American forests. In particular, he turns Goldsmith's imagery against Goldsmith's cause:

> Ah, dire reverse! in yonder eastern clime
> . . . the bewilder'd traveller, forc'd to roam,
> Through a lone forest, leaves his friends, and home;
> Dun evening hangs the sky; the woods around
> Join their dun umbrage o'er the russet ground;
> At every step new gloom enshrouds the skies;
> His path grows doubtful, and his fears arise:
> No woodland songstress soothes his mournful way.[41]

The reversal of landscape imagery is complemented by a reversal of the traditional characters of Americans and Europeans. In "The Burning of Fairfield," the English play the role traditionally reserved by the Puritans for the Indians. They assault the town, burn it, disrupt families, and kill and torture without regard to age or sex. Volney and Crèvecoeur, in disquisitions upon the Indians, refer frequently to the traditional hallmark of wilderness degeneracy — the fact that the Indians live in a state of incessant war and reject the notion of a society of freeholding farmers. Dwight accepts the values implicit in the tradition, but he reverses the roles of Americans and Europeans. The former become conservators of the bourgeois-farmer tradition, while the latter become anarchic, almost Jacobin, and certainly "savage" assailants of the freeholders. Even the Indians, to Dwight, are capable of improvement, of self-transcendence. "Peace . . . and truth" can "illumine the twilight mind" and turn them from the warpath and the scalping raid.[42] It is in Europe, not in America, that incessant warfare remains a way of life and, indeed, becomes more markedly characteristic of all nations. Hence it is the Europeans who are in process of degenerating into a savage, Indian-like state:

> See war, from year to year, from age to age,
> Unceasing, open on mankind the gates
> Of devastation, earth wet-deep with blood,
> And pav'd with corpses; cities whelm'd in flames;
> And fathers, brothers, husbands, sons, and friends,
> In millions hurried to th' untimely tomb;
> To gain a wigwam, built on Nootka Sound.[43]

The Puritan destruction of the Pequots is another matter. The Puritans burn the Pequot village as the British burn Fairfield, but their motives differ, and thus the consequences of their actions differ. The Puritans attack in response to the murderous, malicious assaults of the savages. They first attempt to maintain peace with the Indians and bring them the light of progress and religion; when peaceful means are bloodily rejected, war is their last and sole alternative. Their warriors slain in a romanticized battle, the remaining Pequots become reconciled to the English or else fade away into some forest limbo. Regret that war should have been necessary, rather than rejoicing in a righteous victory, is the appropriate American reaction. Dwight calls on America to "Indulge, my native land! indulge the tear,/ That steals, impassion'd, o'er a nation's doom." The Indian ought to be as near to us as "each twig, from Adam's stock," and Dwight calls upon the vanished chiefs to witness that his humble rhyme is in tribute to their valor and memory, as well as to the triumph of the Americans.[44] Reconciliation, not eternal division, ends Dwight's Indian war. The fight against the British, on the other hand, confirms the departure of the Americans from the downward path being followed in Europe. Ultimately, however, the spread of American liberty — triumphing by revolution in China, Peru, and even old Europe — will bring a reconciliation of the New World and the old similar to that between American and Indian.

Joel Barlow goes further than Dwight in seeking to mediate between Indian and settler, savagery and civilization, and in identifying the American national spirit with the figure of the Indian. He even suggests a figurative mingling of bloods as the key to the emergence of a new, Americanized race of independent, patriotic heroes. In *The Vision of Columbus* — first published in 1787 and later revised and offered as an American *Iliad* — Barlow begins with a portrait of Indian savagery and bestiality that appalls his visionary hero. In the poem, Columbus falls into a reverie on a Mount of Vision, and has his great destiny revealed to him by a divine "Guide." Columbus's "Guide" explains (in the environmentalist vein originally favored by Crèvecoeur) that man takes his coloration of skin and temperament from the soil he dwells on, the food he eats. The American land, left without the refinements of artful, intelligent cultivation, has grown distempered; and the Indians, after some initial progress toward civilization, have consequently degenerated:

> From earth's own elements, thy race at first
> Rose into life, the children of the dust;
> These kindred elements, by various use,
> Nourish the growth and every change produce;
> . . . .
> And, while unchanged the efficient causes reign,

Age following age the unvaried race maintain.
But where crude elements distemper'd rise,
And cast their sickening vapours round the skies,
Unlike that harmony of human frame,
Where God's first works and nature's were the same,
The unconscious tribes, attempering to the clime,
Still vary downward with the years of time. . . .[45]

The dominance in human affairs of consciousness — the intelligent, reasoning, artificing aspect of the mind — could alone have saved the Indians from decline. In the course of the vision, this element is infused into the New World through the settlers, who bring with them the arts and philosophy of cultivation. Yet these men gain something in return from the soil, which counteracts the servility and tolerance of tyranny which they have inherited from the overcultivated soil of Europe. Barlow glories in the notion that the settlers will acquire the darker complexions and the physical stature of the Indians and will imbibe likewise their passion for freedom and their patriotism. He even hints at a blood mixture that will lighten the savage as it darkens the settler.

A dread sublimity informs the whole [of the landscape],
And wakes a dread sublimity of soul.
    Yet time and art shall other changes find,
And open still and vary still the mind;
The countless swarms that tread these dank abodes,
Who glean spontaneous fruits and range the woods,
Fix'd here for ages, in their swarthy face,
Display the wild complexion of the place.
Yet when their tribes to happy nations rise,
And earth by culture warms the genial skies,
A fairer tint and more majestic grace
Shall flush their features and exalt the face;
While milder arts, with social joys refined,
Inspire new beauties in the growing mind.[46]

As the white man awakens the Indian to the light of "social" arts and beliefs and the glories of order and cultivation, the Indian awakens the white man to undreamed-of possibilities for human power and vigor. He offers not only physical strength and beauty but also a renewal of the imaginative powers of the mind, too long crabbed by scholastic artifices:

. . . fair Europe's noblest pride,
When future gales shall wing them o'er the tide,
A ruddier hue and deeper shade shall gain,
And stalk, in statelier figures, o'er the plain.
While nature's grandeur lifts the eye abroad

O'er these dread footsteps of the forming God;
Wing'd on a wider glance the adventurous soul
Bids greater powers and bolder thoughts unroll;
The sage, the chief, the patriot, unconfined,
Shield the weak world and counsel for mankind.[47]

In case the reader has missed the point, Barlow provides a footnote: "The complexion of the inhabitants of North America, who are descended from the English and Dutch, is evidently darker, and their stature taller, than those of the English and Dutch in Europe." [48]

The succeeding books of the poem demonstrate further that the discovery of America and its progressive development was the single great cause of the ending of the Dark Ages and the opening of the Renaissance and Reformation. A fictive history of the Inca Empire and the Emperor Capac indicates that native culture had progressed to a point where it rivaled that of ancient Greece when it was destroyed by rapacious, Catholic Spain.

Barlow's attitude toward the Indian is traceable to his politics. Unlike Dwight, Barlow was a Francophile and a libertarian of the Paine-Jefferson rather than the Adams school. It is true that *The Vision of Columbus*, despite its republican fervor, was dedicated to Louis XVI only two years before his overthrow by republican rebels — but only because Barlow naïvely saw in Louis's aid to the American Revolution a resemblance between the absolute monarch and the liberal *noblesse* who patronized Voltaire, Rousseau, and Crèvecoeur. Barlow's environmentalism and his notion of blending European and Indian to achieve an American national character can be traced to the romanticized image of the natural man that was so fashionable in eighteenth-century Paris. The same influence (as we have seen) played on Jefferson, Filson, and Crèvecoeur. Yet Barlow's image of white-Indian unity goes much further than any of these — further even than Crèvecoeur in the "Distresses of a Frontier Man," when he contemplated fleeing to the Indians; certainly further than the Crèvecoeur of the *Journey*.

The contrast between Crèvecoeur's Napoleon and Weems's Washington, as between Crèvecoeur's Indian and American and those of Dwight and Barlow, suggests the nature of the divergence of American and European culture between 1784 and 1800. Each writer affirmed similar values in art, politics, and morality, but each denied that the national character of the other was capable of realizing those values. Although their aspirations were similar, the American and the European faced different realities, different cultural and environmental influences, and therefore developed different styles for portraying and for pursuing the good life. The European intellectual, whose antecedents and best audience were among the social elite, when faced with the rise of middle-class commercialism and the radicalism of the lower classes, felt his world grow less beautiful and his power to control affairs grow weaker and more restricted. Liberty and equality in 1750 had meant freedom for Voltaire; in 1800 it meant freedom for some back-alley Robespierre or Marat. American intellectuals of the Barlow-Dwight stripe faced similar terrors in the wild Indian, who stalked the woods and the literature of the West, and later in the figure of the coarse, ungainly, Jacksonian politician and his artisan–coonskin–small farmer constituency. But just as the literary tradition of the Indian wars blended images of terror and hope, so the western land posed possibilities of power and beauty and of the improvement of the frontiersmen and Indians themselves. Thus Dwight and Barlow could view the expansion to the frontier (and even some degree of figurative Indianization) as a source of future power, while Goldsmith and Volney regarded it as a bleeding of the state and debasement of the race. Thus Weems could portray Napoleon as envying Washington — the frontier surveyor and commander of Braddock's rangers — for the permanence of the "empire" he has founded, while Crèvecoeur was praising Washington for merely approaching (in far easier circumstances) the accomplishment of Bonaparte in bringing order out of chaos. The conception of abstract virtue is the same in both paeans: order is valued above chaos, even democratic chaos, and empire is taken to be the final expression of a nation's virtuous power, rather than a corruption of a democratic ideal. Yet the imagery (and hence the potential for imaginative mythological extrapolation) in which the hero is presented is different. Weems's Washington is a natural product of the life of a free people in the Indian wilderness; Crèvecoeur's Napoleon is a transcendent figure, arriving from outside the world of revolutionary Paris to impose order.

The postrevolutionary European writer could hardly help despairing of the Enlightenment's dream and deserting it for Burkean conservatism, Napoleonic despotism, or Romantic irrationalism. The American writer did not have to despair of the older dream, since the availability of cheap land seemed to offer the hope that the American people could enjoy the progress derived from the awakened ambitions of middle- and lower-class people without suffering a breakdown of the Constitution or of the principle of rule by the "natural aristocracy," which were the political and social legacies of the Age of Reason. To be sure, the negative possibility also existed, as both Dwight and Barlow feared. In 1794, for example, the Whiskey Re-

bellion in western Pennsylvania, provoked by an excise on locally produced whiskey, raised the spectre of an American social revolution akin in
its program and vindictive spirit to that of the French Revolution, then at
the height of its Terror and its radicalism.

Hugh Henry Brackenridge's *Incidents of the Insurrection* — drawn
from the Whiskey Rebellion, in which he played a key role as deflector of
violence and mediator of differences — invokes the old Puritan association
of hostile Indians with rebellious commons in the new terms appropriate to
the era of Robespierre and Marat. Brackenridge was a man of letters as
well as a barrister; before the American Revolution he had collaborated
with Barlow on *The Columbiad*, an attempt at writing a national epic that
was the germ of Barlow's *Vision of Columbus*. Like Barlow, Brackenridge
was a Democrat, favoring the liberal republicanism of Jefferson over the
more conservative notions of Federalists like Dwight. Jeffersonian Franco-
philism notwithstanding, Brackenridge saw in the Jacobin spirit a profound
threat to the civil peace and, ultimately, to the republican government of
the United States. Nor was he an uncritical believer in the wisdom of the
common man, as his satirical novel *Modern Chivalry* reveals. While he believed that the people can only be ruled by their free consent, his *Incidents
of the Insurrection* suggests that they must occasionally be manipulated by
wiser heads to give their consent to the best measures. The basis of social
authority, for his Jeffersonian intelligence, rests or ought to rest in the ability and wisdom of the chosen rulers — their belonging to the open-ended
"natural aristocracy" of merit and achievement — rather than in their
mere position or power. Yet the principle of social order, that men ought to
consent to be governed, remains; and he invokes traditional imagery to
support his argument with the power of popular mythology.

Brackenridge first facetiously raises the association of rebels and Indians in a speech to a mob, in which he compares the government-rebel negotiations and an Indian treaty. An insurrectionist pamphleteer takes him
seriously and sets forth his party's position in a mock "Indian Treaty," with
the insurrectionists in the role of the put-upon natives. Brackenridge (who
moves among the rebels like Boone among the Indians, feigning brotherhood while working for the protection of his community, Pittsburgh) at
one point thinks of joining the rebels, whom he terms "Sans Culottes"; but
after an artfully rendered internal debate, he decides that to do so would
require him to advocate secession and alliance with the British, the de-
tested Spanish, the "banditti of the borders," and the "Indians from the
woods." Thus he specifically invokes, in a negative context, the image of

the Indian and white Indian as an expression of the Jacobin spirit of the lower classes.[49]

American writers, then, shared with disillusioned Europeans like Crèvecoeur a perception of the danger to even a (presumably) liberal and rational social order in the Jacobin spirit of 1793 and — later in American history — in the complex of social and political movements known as Jacksonian democracy. Whether Federalist or Republican, they likewise shared the traditional vocabulary of images in which the Indian functioned as a symbol for the internal and external forces threatening social order. However, in composing their national epics, they tended to emphasize the second and more hopeful association of the Indian with the natural potential for goodness in man, reserving the negative association for political (or, in the case of Brackenridge, satiric and political) prose.

Beyond the realm of literature, the Indian figure likewise possessed a dual character — as the despised nemesis of the frontier towns, hated and hunted by the trans-Appalachian pioneers; and as the occasional symbol of parties in revolutionary (or merely partisan) opposition to the established government, expressing the depth of the opposition's alienation from the existing order. Examples of the latter use, already cited, include the Boston Tea Party (for which the insurrectionists dressed as Indians), the Jeffersonian Tammany Club (named for a legendary Iroquois chief), and the adoption of Indian guise and mock–Indian-treaty propaganda by the Whiskey Rebels (who, by and large, were far more hostile to the continued presence of real Indians in their vicinity than to the central government). The emphasis given to this positive association with the Indian distinguishes American from European treatments of the West at this time. As we shall see, there was a strong tendency in American works for the emphasis on the Indian as an exemplar of republican virtue to increase, while the image of the European (as in Dwight's "Burning of Fairfield") ceases to connote civilization at its best.

A reciprocal disenchantment, a reciprocal turning away, thus marks the intellectual relations between the New World and the old at the century's turn. Mutual hostility was one symptom; but even those of one world who retained affection for the other tended, like Crèvecoeur, to see that other world solely in terms of conventional symbols. Crèvecoeur and Volney used negative stereotypes of the American character as rhetorical devices in speaking of European problems. Romantics like the young Chateaubriand and Byron, speaking for a more radical political viewpoint, employed favorable stereotypes. Neither school of thought had much interest in plumbing the reality of the American character. American writers, impelled by a cultural need for accurate self-definition, began to work out the dilemmas inherent in conventional formulations of the frontier experience and to seek clearer definitions of the "realities" of America and American experience.

Epic Poetry and the Evolution of Hero Images

The direction of that exploration emerges when we examine the several attempts of American writers to compose a national epic. In 1813, Daniel Bryan of Virginia issued *The Mountain Muse*, which departs drastically from the patterns of thought and hero imagery set by the Puritans Wolcott and Tompson and their successors Dwight and Barlow. Bryan's poetic technique and his point of view are distorted by conflicting pressures: the attraction/repulsion for Europe and European art, on the one hand, and for the wild frontier, on the other. Stylistically, his poem blends elements of the European and American traditions in proportions that are characteristic of the era. His effusive introduction marks him as an imitator of what he fancies are European literary fashions. His scheme of social and moral values resembles those of New England's Dwight and France's Volney: civilization is the chiefest good, the society of men preferable to exile and solitude, refinement better than barbarity, and Christians better than Indians. Dwight had declared his literary independence of Europe by investing America with all those pastoral virtues he and his European fellows so esteemed in the abstract. Byran carries Dwight's vision a step further: if the American farmer is an ideal man and his society is the manifestation of progress, then the hunters who precede the farmers are the agents of progress — or better still, representatives of the Heroic Age of the progressive civilization.[50] Thus he chooses for his hero a man whom neither Dwight nor his European models and fellows could have tolerated as a representative of the best in Christian humanity: Daniel Boone, Daniel Bryan's kinsman by marriage.

Yet despite his choice of a hero and his Americanism, Bryan is no more a leveler than Crèvecoeur. His Boone is an aristocrat in buckskins, a sentimental Romantic in his regard for picturesque scenery, but a man of the Enlightenment — or, more precisely, of the reaction of the heirs of the Enlightenment against the Revolution — in his fear of the lower classes and his insistence on moderation, prudence, and progressive refinement in human and national affairs. In his introduction Bryan is moved to admonish the "Sons of Poverty" not to "despise *prudent* industry" in their urge to imitate Boone's delightful preoccupation with "lonely rambles and simple amusements." [51] Heroes may hunt and fight with Indians, since it is the necessity of their roles; but for common men to mingle with savages and ape their ways is dangerous, productive of degeneration. Thus Bryan echoes the conservative thought of Filson, Crèvecoeur, and the Puritans: the woody solitudes are dangerous for those whose psychological or religious hold on civilization is weak and whose acceptance of the duties and pleasures of social men is not complete.

Bryan's epic roughly follows the story of Filson's Boone narrative, emphasizing and elaborating the sentimental incidents and the philosophic soliloquies of the original. Bryan makes two significant additions to the narrative: a prologue, in which he creates an artificial pantheon of deities to inspire and sustain the hero Boone, and a Romantic interlude involving the rescue of a maiden from the hands of white brigands. The pantheon testifies to his indebtedness to the Enlightenment. Religion, Beauty, Enterprise, and Zeal are the "Guardian Seraphs" of the human spirit; and their chief human agents are "Newton, Hershel, Locke and Reid," exponents of theistic science and the "Common-sense" philosophy. Like the Puritan historians, Bryan abbreviates history to emphasize the critical nature of his hero's accomplishments. The poem begins "immediately subsequent to the transformation of Chaos into Order" by the deities and their human agents, and Boone's "adventures" are destined to make the triumph of enlightened order secure. Before electing Boone as their ultimate hero, the Guardian Seraphs build themselves a Roman forum, or "Firmamental Hall," atop the Alleghanies, embellished with a "magnific dome" and other classical ornaments.[52] The building of the dome is symbolic of their intention to reform, refine, and exalt the human spirit by enabling Americans to civilize the rude wilderness of Kentucky:

> When nought but Beasts and bloody Indians dwelt
> Throughout the mighty waste, and Cruelty
> And Death and Superstition triple-leagued
> Held *there* their horrid reign, and impious sway;
> The Guardian Seraphs of benign REFORM
> With keen prophetic glance the worth beheld
> Of the immense expanse, its future fame,
> Its ponderous moment in the golden scales
> Of Freedom, Science, and Religious Truth,
> When by Refinement's civilizing hand
> Its roughness shall all be smoothed away.
> . . . .
> "O yes! companions in the joys of bliss!
> We will refine, exalt and humanize
> Th' uncivilized Barbarians of the West." [53]

Although he serves the bright gods of the Enlightenment, Bryan's Boone is a Romantic at heart. Characteristically for both a Puritan-captivity and a sentimental-romance hero, his first accomplishment on the road to his goal of a refined and civilized Kentucky is to aid in the rescue of the forlorn maiden and reunite her with her lover. The rescue motif had always been an important part of frontier literature, from the Puritan captivity narratives to the Romantic treatments of the West by Imlay, Chateaubriand, and Charles Brockden Brown. In all of these works the kidnapped girl symbolizes the values of civilization victimized by the Indian wilderness. Bryan's kidnappers, however, are white brigands rather than Indians — a broad hint at Bryan's antipathy for the coarse frontiersmen of reality, recalling the strictures against the ambitious "Sons of Poverty" in the preface. Only the noble Boone, the noble savages of Kentucky, and the lovers exhibit the saving grace of Romantic sentimentality.

Bryan exhibits throughout the work a desire to portray Boone and his Indian foes as the purest types of Romantic hero and Romantic villain, and he does not permit reality or even probability to intrude on his dream. In our first view of him, Boone is seated, like Byron's Childe Harold or Chateaubriand's René, on the brink of a hideous abyss, enraptured with his own thoughts, lost in contemplation. As Bryan puts it, the angel "on the holy Battlement espied / in Contemplation's solemn stole enrobed, / The high-souled Hunter." [54] The angel first inspires Boone's fancy and grants him a vision of the divine throne that sends him into a trance. Then the angel invigorates his reason and transmutes his vision into a sense of his civilizing mission. The landscape, in the worst Romantic manner, reflects the turmoil in the hero's soul:

> Along the ragged precipice he saw
> The lightning's rifted path. Each flickering breeze
> That swept the grey-brow'd turrets, seem'd to shake
> The elevated mass.[55]

This passage is in fact an elaboration of Filson's "commanding ridge" scene, in which his Boone undergoes a similar conversion experience. Bryan has personified Filson's natural landscape with fictive deities, thus restoring the pre-Filsonian vision of passive man receiving grace or revelation from an authoritative universe. After receiving this revelation, Boone feels justified in taking action. The hero prepares for his journey, enraptured with the vision of "Refinement's golden file with smoothing sweep / . . . Embellishing a dark Barbarian World!" [56]

Bryan's determination to make Boone a thoroughly acceptable Ro-

mantic hero leads him to embellish every hint of sentiment in Filson's original. Where Filson's hero merely notes that he "left [his] peaceable habitation," Bryan draws out Boone's farewell to his wife to the point of agony.
Rebecca Boone becomes the sentimental heroine, helpless before the pain
of strong emotions and the fear of loss. Her farewell speech would have
been more appropriate in the mouth of Imlay's English Caroline:

> "My Boone!" She cried,
> And press'd him to her groaning breast; "My Boone!
> How can you leave your Home, your Wife and Babes,
> . . . .
> My God! the horrid thought I cannot bear!
> How shall I rest in peace when dangers watch
> To take away my dear Companion's life?
> How, when the dreadful, silent, solitude
> Of dark and cheerless Night surrounds my Bed;
> When Fancy's gloomy spectres flit along
> My dreary chamber, and your bleeding Corpse
> By grinning Savages or glare-eye Beasts
> Before my *sleepless* eyes is rudely drag'd;
> How then shall I support my sinking heart? [57]

Boone is well-prepared with an answer. Filson's hero had gone west with
only his curiosity to impel him and with few preconceptions about his mission; only after he had submitted to the initiatory ordeal of experience did
he achieve the wisdom to see the divine purpose behind his actions.
Bryan's hero, having (unlike Mary Rowlandson at the time of her family's
disruption) received prior revelation, needs no initiation, no tutelage by
the wilderness. He has all his answers before he goes:

> My bosom's dearest love!
> The splendors, titles, honors, wealth and power,
> And all the glittering garniture of the earth
> To me are trash . . .
> . . . .
> . . . The sovereign law of Heaven
> Requires, that man should oft the sweets forego
> Of loved Society, Companions, Friends,
> Relations, Children, tender Wife and all!
> To tread th' adventurous stage of grand emprise!
> To scatter knowledge through the Heathen wilds,
> And mend the state of Universal Man! [58]

In his desire to fit Boone's experience into his strange Romantic-neo-
classic mold, Bryan transforms the crucial scene on the commanding ridge
into a frontier equivalent of an evening at a London theater or the Paris

Opera. The wild scenery of the original becomes an artificial stage, filled
with all manner of clever props, onto which nature sweeps in evening
gown and tiara, bowing to Boone in his balcony box and disdaining the
groundling Indians shuffling through the canebrakes:

> And oft the princely Pinnacle he scaled
> Of a smooth Hill, which o'er the green campaign
> In airy pride, and conic grandeur tower'd:
> He there in wondering contemplation gazed,
> On various God-proclaiming scenes, which shone
> In glorious fulgour far as eye could roll.
> He *thence* great NATURE'S THEATER beheld
> In all its pomp and splendid scenery cloth'd,
> Herself the Mistress of the grand DISPLAY
> And the distinguish'd HEROINE-ACTRESS too!
> Her curtain with the opening dawn she drew,
> And myriad strains of plausive Melody
> Her entrance on the gorgeous stage proclaimed! [59]

No conversion or change of heart occurs here: Boone's sense of self has
been acquired before he confronts nature in the wild. Elsewhere, while
bowing to the glamour of civilization, Bryan loyally echoes Filson's
Boone's disdain of the city. But it is clear that Bryan's hero does not miss
the city's theatric pomp because he has it in the wilderness; and the loving
accumulation of detail in Bryan's portrait of the rejected city suggests that
this is simply a rhetorical device, a bow toward the convention of viewing
America as the natural world and Europe as the artificial.[60]

Bryan's portrait of the noble savage is no less conventionalized and
dreamlike. His account of Costea, the kidnapper of Boone's daughter and
her two friends, reveals Bryan's lack of concern with the reality of his uncle's career and the life of the real West. Costea is a noble savage of great
pride, bravery, and innate honor:

> He was a Chief in Manhood's vigorous prime:
> Of stature lofty, straight and dignified —
> Strong, Muscular, and springy were his limbs;
> And haughty elevation marked his step.
> . . . .
> Such was the Savage Chief, on whom alone
> The Captive Maids for tenderness relied.
> Nor was their *feeble* confidence misplaced;
> His mandatory frown each look forbid
> Or freedom, that might shake with dread their breasts,
> Or wound their Modesty.[61]

The real Indian involved in the kidnapping was Hanging Maw — a middle-aged brave who, if his Indian name means anything, was gross of belly, rather than lofty and elevated in appetite and stature.

Bryan was not so much interested in truth as in creating an image of the western Indian as a fit subject for enlightenment and subjugation by the refining power of civilization. Boone, during his period of captivity with the Shawnee, makes this philosophy clear in a dialogue with Chief Montour. The Indian tells Boone his tribe's most important legend, the tale of the war between the Indians and the Mammoths, the old Titans of America. The war pitted the physical prowess of the Indians against the physical terrors of the monster Mammoths, until the war ended in the near extermination of the latter. The result of the strife is a lasting enmity between the Indians and the last surviving Mammoth, who roams the woods unseen, terrifying the Indians by his threat to avenge the downfall of his people and his gods. The Indian religion, the Indian attitude toward the land, is shaped by this primitive fear of the Mammoth. Boone offers an alternative tale, the epic of man's discovery of scientific knowledge and the civilized arts, which have enabled the whites to triumph over their fears and the necessities of nature, to "adorn and dignify the social sphere / Of polish'd Man." Now philanthropy, science, printing, agriculture, "and social Love in sweet profusion pour / Along Refinement's pleasure-blooming Vales." Mountour, struck to the heart by this vision of a world so much finer than his own, "Mourn[s] the rueful destiny that drown'd / In blood and gloom the Indian intellect." He pines to death very shortly thereafter.

In Bryan's poem it is not the simple yeoman but Boone the hunter who is the agent of progress in the American wilderness. It is the hunter who first brings the values of Dwight's Greenfield farmers to the Indian's world. This movement from Dwight's "epic" to Bryan's suggests a development in national acceptance of its frontier heroes as representatives of American virtues. In the next major attempt at a national epic, Longfellow's *Hiawatha*, this development is completed. Here the American hero is a full-blooded Indian, and events are drawn directly from Indian mythological sources. Longfellow's poem thus completes a series of epics that began with Tompson's apocalyptic *New Englands Crisis*, in which the Indians were devils visiting God's judgment on the passive Saints of backslidden New England by means of fire, death, and the ordeal of captivity. In Wolcott's *Brief Account of the Agency . . . of John Winthrop*, the Puritans were not victims but heroes, righteously exterminating barbarians in the name of English Christianity and civilization, in battles smacking more of the Greek epics beloved by the neoclassical eighteenth century than of the humility of the Puritan seventeenth. In Dwight's *Greenfield Hill* the hero is no longer even nominally a European, nor is he either captive or avenger. He is an American farmer, native to his soil, moving freely between his independent farm, his ordered village, and the promising wilderness. Bryan's Boone is still more attracted by and acclimated to the wilderness, a hunter rather than a farmer. Yet he too is justified in his wilderness-going by his role as a precursor of farmers (the true "refiners" of nature's design). Longfellow's hero is still more a child of the wilderness, an aboriginal American, an Indian; and although Hiawatha too is shown as a prophet of the triumph of agriculture, the hero's connection to that triumph is seen as an outgrowth of Indian myth and mysticism, rather than (as in Bryan) the confrontation of a correct and righteous view of nature (Boone's) with an incorrect and essentially unrighteous one (Montour's).

Although the epic, as a genre in American literature of this period, is generally a production of elite or high-culture artists and addressed to the middle and upper levels of the reading public (as the explicit pretension to the grandeur of classical models suggests), its stock of themes, symbols, and myths is so obviously drawn from antecedents in the popular literature that we can read these epics as extensions and exaggerations of tendencies at work in the literary imagination of the entire culture. Indeed, the popularity of Longfellow in his epoch, and the relative lack of the high/low culture distinction in Puritan literature of Tompson's time, suggest that the epics of these two authors may be considered as much a part of mass culture as of an elite subculture.

Changing Views of the Indian

Hiawatha is expressive of Americans' desire for a sense of kinship with the Indians as fellow natives of the soil. However, before such expression could be achieved, the image and the actual person of the Indian had to undergo a final stage of evolution. Between 1800 and 1845 the last hostile tribes east of the Mississippi were either reduced to insignificant numbers or removed to lands beyond the great river. The Five Nations (now six) were humbled, placed on reservations, and reduced to dependence. The Cherokee for a time were suffered to live in their own country, where they adjusted to the ways of the Americans, adopting a written alphabet and an agrarian economy and educating their chiefs in white schools. The Boudinots, chiefs of the southern Cherokee, were lawyers and scholars, fluent in English as in their native tongue. The discovery of gold on Cherokee land provided the impetus for white land-hunger, and in the 1820s the state of

Georgia attempted to force the Indians from their land. The case became a cause célèbre, putting the views of men like Dwight (who held that the Indian's savagery was the result of his economy and condition, rather than racial inheritance) to the test. Although the Supreme Court decided in favor of the Cherokee, President Jackson refused to prevent Cherokee removal, and the Indians were forced to march from Georgia to the Oklahoma deserts, robbed of their land and carefully accumulated property.

Indian removal revealed a number of contradictory elements in the American attitude toward the native Americans. Westerners like James Hall, who were relatively sympathetic to the Indians and portrayed them in a reasonably attractive light in stories of the West, regarded Indian removal as a desirable necessity. Racial hostility between whites and Indians, they felt, would always make close relations impracticable. Moreover, by living close to the whites, Indians would lose their native, pristine culture and acquire debased forms of white religion — and white vices. This argument was drawn directly from the pro-Indian literature of the 1780s and 1790s, which asserted that the Indians were innocent children of nature, natural democrats who degenerated on prolonged contact with the whites. Hall's argument also reconciled this argument to the contradictory assertion of that period — that the Indian was a latent Christian, requiring only the healing touch of refinement to "whiten" and civilize him. (Even a Moor could be "blancht" in three generations, William Byrd had said.) According to Hall, the Indian's virtues were his only while he remained pure; they perished when he mingled with the whites. Left to their own devices, the Indians would naturally evolve toward Christianity and cultivation; white interference, whether persecution or attempts to hurry them along the road, were unnatural and hence doomed to harm more than help.

Hall was a westerner, one of a people whose experience with the Indians was more recent and unhappy than that of the Cherokees' eastern friends. But although those easterners took a different stand on the specific question of Indian removal, their values and their image of the Indians' proper place in America were essentially the same as Hall's. In 1829 a pamphlet appeared in Boston under the pseudonym of William Penn — a name calculated to evoke images of the good Quaker and his long peace with the Indians — which stated the Cherokees' case. According to the writer, Jeremiah Evarts, the Indians' case hinged on questions of title. Certainly the Indians held their land by the right of original possessors; but the charge against them was that they had forfeited their right by not cultivating the land and, instead, pursuing the chase as a means of subsistence. It was this very argument that had cost Daniel Boone and other frontiersmen their land: the law required that a man "improve" his land, not simply enjoy it as a hunting park, and improvement meant agriculture. Evarts did not set himself against this principle; he simply denied that it applied to the Cherokee, who had become farmers.[62] Were they hunters, like the primitive Indians, their title might not be so clear. As it was, their life was identical with that of Greenfield Village:

> They are at present neither savages nor hunters. It does not appear that they ever were mere wanderers, without a stationary residence. At the earliest period of our becoming acquainted with their condition, they had fixed habitations . . . [and were] in the habit of cultivating some land near their houses, where they planted Indian corn, and other vegetables. From about the commencement of the present century, they have addicted themselves more and more to agriculture, till they now derive their support from the soil, as truly and entirely as do the inhabitants of Pennsylvania and Virginia. For many years they have had their herds, and their large cultivated fields. They now have, in addition, their schools, a regular civil government, and places of regular Christian worship. They earn their bread by the labor of their own hands, applied to the tillage of their own farms; and they clothe themselves with fabrics made at their own looms, from cotton grown in their own fields.

Yet the continuance of this idyllic condition depended on their being segregated from the society of white Americans:

> The assertion of the Cherokees, that their present country is not too large for a fair experiment of the work of civilization, is undoubtedly correct. The wisest men, who have thought and written on this subject, agree . . . [that] no tribe of Indians can rise to real civilization and to the full enjoyment of Christian society, unless they can have a community of their own; and can be so much separated from the whites, as to form and cherish something of a national character.[63]

Thus Evarts concurred with Hall in the opinion that separation of the Indians from white America was the prerequisite of progress for the Indians as for the whites. The sympathetic Evarts argued for the continuation of a segregated Indian establishment in Georgia and would have had its size undiminished to keep separation practicable. Hall simply argued that such separation was possible only if removal was effected. The two agreed in principle, though differing in policy, just as Dwight and Crèvecoeur had agreed on the virtues of the conservative freeholder and divided on his locus, nationality, and methods of government.

Once the threat of real Indians was removed from proximity to American civilization and banished to the frontier, the mythicization of the Indian could proceed without the problems and complexities arising from the realities of Indian-white relations. Indian virtues could be symbolically exaggerated and Indian values accepted as valid for American society, without being rudely checked by some savage outbreak near at hand. The conventional roles of the captivity mythology could even be reversed and the Indians seen as a pathetic alien minority in an "indigenous" white America. Moreover, the Indian's removal cast a tragic aura about his vanishing person that appealed to Romantic sensibilities. Whether by the natural processes of evolution, or by warfare with the whites, or by the ravages of white vices acquired through intermixing, or by forcible assimilation into the culture of his white "captors," the primitive Indian was clearly doomed. The rise and fall of his culture, like that of the Romans and Greeks, provided an image of the historical process which the new imperial republic was now entering. The replacement of the primitive Indian by the white settler confirmed the Americans' belief in the progressive nature of historical process, even while it reminded them that all mortal things are transitory and doomed. Moreover, the expansion of the nation into the Far West brought the Americans into contact with a very different group of Indian cultures, far more nomadic and barbaric, far less sophisticated in their forms of government, far more brutal to captives than the eastern tribes. Rape, for instance, was virtually unknown in the Indian wars of the East, since women captives were wanted for adoption as brides. The western tribes had no taboo against rape and, in fact, made it part of their celebrations of triumph, along with the torturing and sexual mutilation of male captives.

Thus, even as the Indians disappeared from the East, interest in their antiquities and traditions increased. When Indians had abounded, most works dealing with them described them in the context of particular problems. The missionaries discussed their character and religion solely to establish their aptness or inaptness for conversion. Soldiers studied them with a view to mastering their technique of warfare, revival preachers with a view toward their fitness as symbols of divine displeasure, political pamphleteers with the aim of using Indian polity to justify particular political programs in terms of natural law. As the last Indians were "removed" beyond the borders or pushed (quickly and slowly by turns) towards extinction, more thorough and objective treatments of their lifeways were undertaken, with the aim of preserving their own images of themselves and the wilderness. The most famous compilations were those of Heckewelder and Schoolcraft, both of whom lived with the Indians and gave accounts of Indian mythology. The former served as a source for Cooper, the latter for

Longfellow. These works brought to the public the Indians' primitive mythology and made it available to writers of every stamp, from significant artists to the literary hacks who filled popular magazines and compiled anthologies.

Even before Heckewelder and Schoolcraft, American writing about the frontier had showed a marked fascination with mythlike tales and archetypal structures. The mythology surrounding hunters like Boone, in particular, had shown strong resemblances to Indian myths — a result of spontaneous developments in American writing, rather than a deliberate use of Indian sources. Once the Indian sources became available, however, they were deliberately mined for mythic materials in a manner analogous to Cotton Mather's mining of biblical materials. The influence of such efforts became evident between 1820 and 1850 — in the series of Indian biographies and histories that appeared between 1830 and 1850; in the sudden, surprising currency given to the old myth that the Indians were the ten lost tribes of Israel; and in the emergence in the 1820s of a viable literary mythology of the Indian in "Indian dramas" like Stone's *Metamora*, in Irving's biography of King Philip in the *Sketch-Book*, and in Eastburn's and Sands's *Yamoyden*. Interest in the Indian's past coincided with a renewed interest in the Colonial literature in which the relationship of whites and Indians was the central subject matter, resulting in the issuance of new editions of the narratives of Church and Filson and the more famous captivities.

B. B. Thatcher's two-volume *Indian Biography*, published in New York in 1834, is typical of the reassessment of the historical Indian (and incidentally contains a Filson-based sketch of Indian-fighting Boone). Thatcher is all on the side of progress and settlement; but like Filson's Boone he sympathizes with the Indian's love of his land, his patriotism, loyalty, and courage, his stoic temperament and contentment with the simple life. Thatcher regrets the "prejudices" of white chroniclers who have failed to give the Indian character its due. His account of King Philip's War draws heavily on Church, with whom he is much in sympathy, save in the captain's barbarity toward the body of the slain Philip — denying Philip burial, calling him "beast," and mutilating his body. Church's behavior toward Anawon, however, is praised by Thatcher. Thatcher concludes that since the Indians are all rapidly vanishing, it is possible, laudable, and safe to give Philip his due (although this involves Thatcher in a small paradox): "He fought and fell, — miserably, indeed, but gloriously, — the avenger of his own household, the worshipper of his own gods, the guardian of his own honor, a martyr for the soil which was his birth-place, and for the proud liberty which was his birthright." [64] In short, Thatcher's Philip is a kind of Indian George Washington in a doomed, mistaken cause.

Such ennobling comparison was not reserved solely for long- and safely dead Indians. Within a year of the conclusion of the Black Hawk War, the autobiography of Chief Black Hawk himself appeared in print, apparently taken from his own dictation by an army interpreter. The work begins with a letter (printed in both English and the transliterated tongue of the Sauk and Fox) addressed to General Atkinson, Black Hawk's conqueror, and through him to the American people, reminding them of the Indians' past glory and of the tragic decline that time visits on the proudest of nations:

> SIR, — The changes of fortune, and vicissitudes of war, made you my conqueror. When my last resources were exhausted, my warriors worn down with long and toilsome marches, we yielded, and I became your prisoner. . . . The changes of many summers, have brought old age upon me, — and I cannot expect to survive many moons. . . . I am now an obscure member of a nation, that formerly honored and respected my opinions. The path to glory is rough, and many gloomy hours obscure it. May the Great Spirit shed light on your's — and that you may never experience the humility that the power of the American government has reduced me to, is the wish of him, who, in his native forests, was once as proud and as bold as yourself.
>
> BLACK HAWK[65]

The editor of the autobiography, in his "Advertisement" or foreword, presents Black Hawk in the character of hero and patriot:

> It is presumed no apology will be required for presenting to the public, the life of a Hero who has lately taken such high rank among the distinguished individuals of America. In the following pages he will be seen in the characters of a Warrior, a Patriot, and a State-Prisoner — in every situation he is still the Chief of his Band, asserting their rights with dignity, firmness, and courage.[66]

It had taken King Philip nearly a century and a half to receive sympathetic treatment by an American biographer. Black Hawk received not only sympathy but an accolade and a place in the pantheon of American heroes within a year of his strife with the Americans. The speed with which the frontier experience was assimilated into the national mythology had, by this evidence, accelerated so fast that there was hardly a break between the event and the mythologizing of the event. Moreover, the writer or editor engaged in composing the legend or mythologizing the facts could now take the Indians' point of view as his own. Heckewelder and

Schoolcraft listened to Indian accounts of the creation and the gods and interpreted their vision for the whites. Thatcher's *Indian Biography* is an attempt to write a history of America as seen by the Indians. Black Hawk's autobiography reduces both that history and that religio-mythological vision to a single dramatic encounter and allows an Indian hero to tell the entire tale himself.

Like the historians of the Puritans, who also fancied themselves an "original" people (through spiritual rebirth), Black Hawk begins his tribal history with an account of the creation and the genesis of the tribe. The life of the tribe, its ceremonial corn dances, and its rites of marriage are reported in detail and are invested with an air of the idyllic that may be due as much to the translator's affection for convention as to Black Hawk's own memory. His outcry against the whites is undoubtedly genuine — and remarkable in its complete accordance with the belief of Evarts and Hall that the Indian is better off when separated from the white man:

> At this time we had very little intercourse with the whites, except our traders. Our village was healthy, and there was no place in the country possessing such advantages, nor no hunting grounds better than those we had in possession. If another prophet had come in our village in those days, and told us what has since taken place, none of our people would have believed him. What! to be driven from our village and hunting grounds, and not even permitted to visit the graves of our forefathers, our relations, our friends? . . . how different is our situation now, from what it was in those days! Then we were as happy as the buffalo on the plains — but now we are as miserable as the hungry, howling wolf in the prairie! . . . Bitter reflection crowds my mind, and must find utterance.[67]

This association of the Indian with qualities symbolic of American virtue is most clearly evident in the spate of literature written to demonstrate that the Indians were the ten lost tribes of Israel. This had been one of the earliest speculations about Indian origins, dating back to the accounts of the first discoverers — Samuel Sewall, Daniel Gookin, and other proponents of Indian missions in Puritan times had adhered to this belief — but the first American work to examine the proposition in any great detail was Adair's *History of the American Indians* (1775). Between 1800 and 1850 the idea caught on, and innumerable works were published for and against it. The idea became so much a part of the American canon that it figured in the "revelation" vouchsafed to Joseph Smith and became a most persuasive tenet of the Mormon religion he originated.

One of the first of these "ten tribes" works was Elias Boudinot's *Star in the West* (Trenton, 1816). Like the works of Thatcher and Black Hawk,

Boudinot's book inverts the traditional symbolic roles of whites and Indians. Here the whites are persecutors and the Indians are strayed members of the Chosen People, whose title to descent from Israel is clearer than that of any European tribe. Boudinot, caught up in the millenarian enthusiasm of the Second Great Awakening, anticipates the imminent second coming of Christ to redeem his people Israel. If the Indians are, in fact, the lost tribes, the awakening and conversion of the Indians is to be worked for and hopefully expected. Moreover, the Indians will provide a sign or an omen foreshadowing the coming of Christ to them and their Hebrew brethren. Perhaps Christ himself will come from among them, a star in the West answering and fulfilling the promise of the original star in the East that led the kings to Bethlehem:

> A very bright and portentous Star having arisen in the East, making glad the hearts of God's people and urging the friends of Zion to unusual and almost miraculous exertions in spreading the glad tidings of salvation among the distant nations of the earth; the compiler of the following sheets . . . can no longer withhold the small discovery which has been made of a rising Star in the West, from the knowledge of those who are zealous and anxious to behold the returning Messiah . . . which star may in the issue turn out to be the *Star of Jacob,* and become a guide to the long suffering and despised descendants of that eminent-patriarch, to find the once humble babe of Bethlehem.[68]

The idea was flattering to American nationalism, which had recently accepted a symbolic association of the two American races, native red and native white. In the Romantic period, such speculation cast a charm of antiquity over a landscape bare of spectacular Roman ruins. And to a people nourished on the lore of the Puritans and the exhortations of revivalistic preachers, the association of anything American with the biblical Promised Land and Chosen People was bound to meet with sympathy.

The theory quickly became popularized and entered into the American popular mythology by the usual routes. Editors did not deem it essential to conduct research among the Indians themselves; instead, they relied wholly on the early published material by Adair, Colden, and Boudinot. Much of this early material was simply a kind of wishful speculation, but later editors accepted it as gospel truth and built a myth-convention on that foundation. Ethan Smith's *View of the Hebrews* (Poultney, Vermont, 1823) was probably the most popular of these works and certainly the most influential, yet most of it is simply a plagiarism of Adair and Boudinot, combined with Smith's own exhortations. Israel Worsley's *View of the American Indians* (London, 1828) is in turn a plagiarism of Smith and of

Smith's quotations from Adair and Boudinot. Once the convention was established, it gave a shape to the speculations of more intelligent writers, the direction of whose research was determined by their acceptance of the ten tribes theory as the chief problem and investigative starting point. Thus John McIntosh's *Origin of the North American Indians* (New York, 1844), despite some field research by the author, reiterates the notion of the biblical descent of the Indians. McIntosh, however, stops short of the ten tribes theory. He subscribes, rather, to the theory that the Indians are either the sons of pagan Magog or (more likely) the sons of Japhet, Noah's son.

It was Joseph Smith who transmuted the speculations about Indian origins into an epic which had the mythic power to evoke in numbers of Americans a religious sense of belief and conviction. *The Book of Mormon*, which Smith wrote or (as he claimed) translated, has as its theme the settlement of America centuries before Christ by the ten lost tribes (emigrants from overseas, like the Puritans), their division into "dark" and "light" folk, and their destruction in centuries of civil war. The last battle of the war took place on Hill Cumorah, where the white folk, who had cleaved to the righteous ways of their ancestors, fell before the dark folk, who had fallen into idolatry. The experience of this dark people, their acquaintance with the resurrected Christ (who visited them), and their prophecies relating to the nature of a true church and the coming of Messiah were inscribed on golden plates by Moroni. The plates were then buried beneath the hill of Cumorah until, in the fullness of time, the American-English came from overseas, settled in the land, and became worthy of a new and special revelation.

The Latter-Day Saints who followed Joseph Smith were thus required to consider the Indians their brothers and to endeavor to restore to them the light they had long lost, so that they might become "a white and delightsome people." The racial and religious conversion of the Indians was a major concern of the Mormons after their emigration to Utah, as it had been (at least in theory) of the Puritans after their emigration. Moreover, the Mormons tended to associate themselves with the Indians as brothers in persecution, sharing grievances against the "Gentile" government of the United States.[69]

The appeal of Smith's epic for his audience of farmers and frontiersmen in New York State, and later on the Missouri and Illinois frontiers, lay in its exaltation of America by associating it with Zion and the Chosen People. This exaltation was reinforced by Smith's explicit claim that America, because of its virtues and its departures from the debaucheries of the Old

World, was deserving of — and had in fact received — a special revelation from the Almighty. Although Smith's statement of the ten tribes theme was the most elaborate, complex, and detailed — and, in the long run, the most convincing to a considerable American communtiy — its values were shared by many Americans of the Romantic period. Eccentricities of doctrine, not belief in the Hebraic origins of the Indians, made the Mormons the objects of persecution and exile.

Hiawatha: The Indian as American Hero

The inversion of traditional Indian-white relationships and the Romantic association of the Indians with those characteristic virtues acquired by the Americans in their transit from the Old World to the new made the use of the Indian as a symbolic American hero practicable as a literary device. In 1848 Elbert Smith published an epic poem entitled *Ma-Ka-Tai-Me-She-Kia-Kiak; or Black Hawk, . . . A National Poem . . .* , in which the character of natural patriot given him in the *Autobiography* is linked with that of the white civilizers who come to perfect his land. A more influential and enduring use of the Indian as a national hero is Longfellow's *The Song of Hiawatha* (1855). Longfellow relied on this association of white with red Americans in offering his epic to those "who love a nation's legends" and the wilderness landscape of United States and to those who admit at least their human kinship with all men, however savage:

> Ye whose hearts are fresh and simple,
> Who have faith in God and Nature,
> Who believe, that in all ages
> Every human heart is human,
> That in even savage bosoms
> There are longings, yearnings, strivings
> For the good they comprehend not,
> . . . .
> Listen to this simple story,
> To this Song of Hiawatha![70]

Longfellow's attitude toward his subject is mixed. On the one hand, he offers Hiawatha as a godlike hero, embodiment of all the savage virtues and most of the Christian ones. On the other hand, he cannot deny that only through the conquest of Hiawatha's people and country by the white man have Christianity and civilization been brought into the Indian solitudes. This ambivalence is paralleled by his technique in composing the poem. In creating an epic, Longfellow wished to convey to his reader a

sense of the primitive, mythopoeic perception that characterizes the first
narrative poetry of any people. America, in its coming-of-age as a nation
and an empire, seemed in a state comparable to that of Homeric Greece or
the Rome of Virgil, requiring an epic poem to sum up and crystallize the
world view and historical experience of the people. Unlike the Greeks and
the Romans, however, America was the creation of human artifice as much
as of natural evolution; its people were, not a single tribe, but a mixture of
emigrants from all over Europe at various stages of acculturation. The epic
poet, like the writers of the Declaration of Independence, seemingly had
to create a nation and a people by verbal fiat.

The chief distinguishing feature of this people was the fact that their
heritage had, through long years in the wilderness, become a mixture of Indian and European. Thus Longfellow turned to the mythologies of both
primitive America and primitive Europe for his subject matter and his literary forms, borrowing the Indian legends compiled by Schoolcraft for his
story and the verse form of the Finnish epic *Kalevala* for his meter. Similarly, the meaning of Hiawatha's heroic career became, in Longfellow's
hands, a blend of Indian and European values. Hiawatha is both the Prometheus of his people and the prophet who prepares them for assimilation
into the greater, Christian people who will succeed them in the land. The
Indian legends are seen to embody the seed kernels of Christianity, and the
growth of Hiawatha reveals the slow, organic growth of Christian principles out of savage soil.

After the proem and invocation to the reader, the poem begins with
an account of the Manito's visit to the earth, his gift of the calumet, or
peace pipe, to the Indian tribes, and the careers of his sons, the four winds.
Mudjekeewis, the lecherous and fickle west wind, begets Hiawatha on the
daughter of Nokomis (as Zeus begot Dionysos on Semele). Reared from
childhood as a hunter and given magic gifts by the wise old squaw Nokomis, Hiawatha begins a series of quests by journeying to the home of his father, the west wind, to revenge his mother's death. Like the heroes of the
Norse, Greek, and Roman legends, he seeks a boon in the world of the gods
that will benefit his people, and he emerges from his combat against his father with a divine power. The theme is later repeated in his fight with the
divine Mondamin: from the buried corpse of Mondamin the corn, clad like
the god in green feathers and golden hair, springs up. Other exploits lead
Hiawatha (Beowulf-like) to the bottom of a lake, where he battles the
Great Sturgeon, and to a far land across black, serpent-filled swamps to
wrest the pearl-feather (a magic talisman not unlike the golden bough)
from its giant possessor.

The most important quests and ceremonies in the epic are those that relate to Hiawatha's power as a demigod of fertility, his power to make the land rich. In Longfellow's hands the sexual elements of the fertility myth are romanticized and made fit for the drawing room. More significantly, they are subsumed into the scheme of American values suggested by Dwight and others, in which the virtues of the agrarian life, not those of the hunter and adventurer, are supreme. Hiawatha's quests, like those of Filson's Boone and Bryan's Boone, are not ends in themselves. The ends they envision are those which will make the people permanently happy and prosperous; and as Hiawatha discovers, such permanent bliss can come only through agriculture and a Christian spirit.

The first step of Hiawatha's quest for the greatest of boons, the power to do all men great good, is his visit to his father, which gains him the ear of the gods. The next step requires him to fast in solitude and pray to the gods for aid. Wandering alone and hungry, on the threshold of death, he views the wild beasts and plants, and cries: "Master of Life! . . . Must our lives depend on these things?" In answer the Manito sends Mondamin, who greets Hiawatha as a friend and bids the starving warrior rise and wrestle with him for three nights. On the last night he promises that Hiawatha shall slay him and is then to bury him with a certain ceremony in the earth. Mondamin, like the Green Knight, is dressed in the colors of vegetation: his feathered dress is long and green, and his long hair golden. Hiawatha fights and slays him and buries him in the manner required; and within a season, Mondamin is resurrected as the corn, clad in green and with golden, silky hair. Like Jacob, father of the biblical Chosen People, Hiawatha has wrestled three nights with an angel of the lord and gained a boon thereby. To make his power for good secure, Hiawatha, like Jacob, must found and father a people; like Jacob he goes to seek a wife.

Minnehaha, or Laughing Water, is Hiawatha's bride; and like the water, she makes the soil of the cornfields fertile, insuring a good crop. Nor is her power simply agricultural: her ceremonial fertilization of the cornfields becomes, in harvest time, the source of fertility in the maidens of the tribe. Minnehaha discovers her power only after the consummation of her marriage to Hiawatha, and she begins the ceremony at his command:

> Once, when all the maize was planted,
> Hiawatha, wise and thoughtful,
> Spake and said to Minnehaha,
> To his wife, the Laughing-Water:
> "You shall bless to-night the cornfields,
> Draw a magic circle round them,

> To protect them from destruction,
>
> . . . .
>
> In the night, when all is silence,
> In the night, when all is darkness,
>
> . . . .
>
> Rise up from your bed in silence,
> Lay aside your garments wholly,
> Walk around the fields you planted,
> Round the borders of the cornfields,
> Covered by your tresses only,
> Robed with darkness as a garment.
> "Thus the fields shall be more fruitful . . ." [71]

Minnehaha does as she is bidden and walks naked around the fields in the nighttime. At the next harvest, the women go to "strip the garments from Mondamin" and wrestle with the corn god among the stalks:

> And whene'er some lucky maiden
> Found a red ear in the husking,
> Found a maize-ear red as blood is,
> "Nushka!" cried they all together,
> "Nushka! you shall have a sweetheart,
> You shall have a handsome husband!" [72]

Hiawatha's power, however, is not permanent. Natural decay weakens his powers, which were perhaps more limited than they first promised (he and Minnehaha have no son). In a great famine his wife, priestess of the corn, dies, and Hiawatha next appears as an old man, sadly foreseeing the doom of his people. In his final prophecy he remains true to the philosophy he has all along espoused — that men should live in peace and till the soil as farmers. His people's doom will come on them because they will forsake the ways of Hiawatha. The newcome white men, by contrast, will live up to Hiawatha's teachings better than Hiawatha's own people. Their wisdom, gleaned from natural sources like Hiawatha's but also from the superior light of revelation, will make them more powerful fertility gods than Hiawatha: "Whereso'er they tread, beneath them / Springs a flower unknown among us, / Springs the White-man's Foot in blossom." [73]

The Indian spirit, exemplified by Hiawatha, remains after the tribes have declined to illuminate the special nature of the New World to the Christian exiles who will come to it. Hiawatha stands in the same relation to the white man that Mondamin stood to Hiawatha: he dies and, in dying, gives the land to the white man's keeping, along with the gift of his knowledge of how to hunt and cultivate the land. The gift of Christianity to the Indian, which plays so prominent a role in early writings on the Indians, is almost wholly absent from the poem. The relationship of missionary to Indian is here inverted: it is the Indian who teaches and partially converts the white man, making the born European into a new, American man.

Hiawatha's career also suggests to the white man the proper relationship man must maintain between the forest world and the agrarian world, between hunting and agriculture, between solitude and society. In all his lonely quests, Hiawatha bears in mind that his purpose is a social one; even in his wooing of the forest-goddess/woman Minnehaha, personal passion is linked with the social passion. The consummation of his marriage is not an isolated act of passion in deep woods far from men's haunts; it is a social event, culminating in Minnehaha's blessing of the fields with her body. When the white men arrive, they will have less need than Hiawatha to exile themselves in solitude. They will reap the benfits of Hiawatha's lonely quests in the gifts of corn and agricultural technique they take from their benefactor. Solitude — the physical and moral isolation of the individual in the wilderness — is (as Longfellow sees it) the Indian's appropriate milieu, the environment in which he is most himself. Hiawatha's social passion and agrarian religion are more appropriate to the white men who will succeed him than to his own people, who are unruly and selfish during his life and disobedient after his death. In this judgment Longfellow misses the central qualities of Indian tribalism: a psychology of tribal solidarity which pervaded the universe, converting beasts and deities into kinfolk, and an ethic of sacrifice for the tribe which was generally so strong as to permit wide latitude for individual action without endangering the solidarity and order of the body politic. What was solitude to a white observer was a peopled dwelling to the Indian.

Longfellow carries to its logical conclusion the paradoxical premises at the heart of the Boone myth: that the American hero is simultaneously hunter and farmer, wanderer and citizen, exploiter and cultivator. Hiawatha's mingled passion for society and solitude, for agriculture and hunting, sets him somewhere between the two races and cultures, making him a spiritual half-breed or, more accurately, a mediating figure between mythological conceptions of the old and the new Americans — like Daniel Boone. Longfellow heightens the contradictions inherent in the hero-figure by making explicit the American tendency toward identification with the (mythological) Indian, by taking his hero from a well-known collection of Indian legends, and by presenting him in the poem as an exponent of the Indian way of life and mythopoeic consciousness of the wilderness world. At the same time, he emphasizes those aspects of Indian myths and lifeways that indicate a tendency toward cultivation and improvement of nature. That it is the ideal of cultivation (and its implicit connotations of general progress and uplift) that is for Longfellow the chief justification of Hiawatha (and the line of hunter heroes of whom he is the latest expression) is evidenced by the conclusion of the poem, in which the Indian hero is seen as accepting the displacement of his race in the favor of his gods by the whites — an acceptance inconceivable to any hero of a truly tribal mythology. The dual character of Hiawatha is thus a part of that useful ambiguity about the character and historic role of the developers of the American frontier that permitted contemporary writers to see the displacement of the Indians and the exploitation of their land as an aspect of their cultivation and improvement.

CHAPTER 11

Society and Solitude:
The Frontier Myth in Romantic Literature (1795–1825)

Seen from a palace stair
The wilderness was distance; difference; it spoke
In the strong king's mind for mercy, while to the weak,
To the weary of choice, it told of havens where
The Sabbath stayed, and all were meek,
And justice known a joke.

Some cast their crowns away
And went to live in the distance. There was nothing seemed
Remotely strange to them, their innocence
Shone in the special features of the prey
They would not harm. The dread expense
Of golden times they dreamed

Was that their kingdoms fell
The deeper into tyranny, the more they stole
Through Ardens out to Eden isles apart,
Seeking a shore, or shelter of some spell
Where harmlessly the hidden heart
Might hold creation whole.

Richard Wilbur, "Castles and Distances"

THE divergence of the European and American myths was a function of the difference in the psychological needs and environmental conditions under which the two cultures labored. In Europe the French Revolution, the Napoleonic Wars, and the foreshadowings of the Industrial Revolution destroyed the old order, the social arrangements by which its moral structure had been sustained, and the philosophic premises that had supported it. The resultant chaos offered two possibilities for literary action. A writer might seek to reestablish some vision of order by the literary manipulation of conventionalized figures representing the old values and principles: the man of reason and order triumphing over the savage or Jacobin (passion) and rescuing beauty from brutish hands. Or the writer might ally himself with revolution by inverting the morality play, giving the hero's role to the man of feeling, equating art with passion rather than rational order, and seeking beauty in ardor rather than symmetry. In either case, the writer would be preoccupied with the problem of Europe and, in attempting to solve it, would be working with the vocabulary of images and character types then current, among which were the American, the savage, the good Quaker, and Daniel Boone. American types, if not examined too closely or realistically, could still serve occasionally as symbolic confirmations of European cultural values, as they had for Voltaire and Rousseau.

In America, the frontier myth was continually reshaped and revalued by the ongoing process of adjustment to American conditions. Forced by their situation to deal with frontier realities (as Europeans were not), Americans found it difficult to maintain unaltered the conventionalized images of the wilderness and its people that were the mainstays of European literature about the New World. Even the established society of the coast, which was both physically and psychologically distant from the real frontier and therefore capable of fantasizing it, was bound to deal with the political and social problems the West presented and with the west-going impulse of people from the older settlements. Moreover, where the European stood amid the ruins of an established society and used its fragments to build a new house, the American felt himself to be the creator of something new and unprecedented. Where the European craved confirmation of older values, the American saw himself as exploring new moral grounds, returning to the primary sources of value for a new beginning, a new creation of the moral universe. Thus the American could not be satisfied, like the European writer, with simply employing the "American" conventions: he had to explore thoroughly the depths and the consequences of his myths.

The resulting difference between the European and American approaches to the myth of the frontier was that which divides (to use Wheelwright's terminology) the romantic from the consummatory myth. The former is based on the use of conventionalized images and figures, drawn from a myth tradition, to invoke traditional values and sentiments. The American myth-maker, in order to satisfy the demands of his audience, had to turn to consummatory myth-making in his approach to the frontier. He had to reevoke the primary, mythopoeic consciousness of the people in order to establish a new faith, a new sense of cultural identity, a new basis for moral order.

European Romantics employed American types to dramatize social and abstractly philosophical issues. Attitudes toward these types varied from writer to writer, according to his political allegiance, and even within the works of a single writer, according to the philosophical purpose of each work. There was, in general, more hostility toward America than there had been in the prerevolutionary days or the Americanist days; and America's attack on France during its republican phase, followed by her support of Napoleon against a relatively democratic Britain, augmented the disillusionment of liberal intellectuals like Crèvecoeur. There was a new spirit of "critical realism" toward America, which meant in practice the deliberate denigration of all those facets of America that the Americanists had romanticized. Yet, at the same time, writers like Chateaubriand and Byron were painting America in more attractive colors than any Rousseauist of the previous generation. Chateaubriand in particular portrayed an Indian chief who was a courtier at Versailles, sensitive to the beauties of civilization; yet outside his fiction he expressed the same contempt for American coarseness and philistinism as his anti-American contemporaries, Volney and Talleyrand. Thus the Europeans, developing conventionalized images out of older conventions, moved further from the realities of the frontier and closer to a definitive American fantasy, in which (paradox or no) both the degenerate and the pastoral America were real.

Americans also cultivated the fictive element in their traditional genres of frontier writing, employing the motifs of initiation, hunting, and captivity as the formulaic bases for literary genres. Like the Europeans, they also used frontier types as masks for philosophic principles and social values. But their sources of frontier material were being continually refreshed by new waves of narratives from the new frontiers; and their cultural need made their writers treat the frontier tale as a drama of evolving consciousness, as well as a confrontation between social types. It was therefore inevitable that the movement of the American literary mind during the Romantic era should be, figuratively and to a degree literally, a movement toward the Indian. The consummatory-myth maker, by definition, seeks to reachieve the kind of mythopeic consciousness which the Indian possessed — or, at least, which was traditionally associated with the Indian in European and American writing. This parallels the corresponding tendency (noted in the preceding chapter) to see the Indian as an American hero, even as the unique symbol of American virtues.

The literary consequences of the European-American divergence can be seen in the frontier novels of Chateaubriand and Charles Brockden Brown. Brown, considered America's first professional man of letters, was a spokesman for literary nationalism in the ideological controversies of the day; that is, he advocated the use of American materials in literary fiction. In practice, he employed such materials as the wilderness landscape and the Indians, and he drew on both the traditional action literature of the frontier and the soul-exploring narratives of Puritan popular literature. Most important, he approached these materials simultaneously, with the introspective and mythopoeic bias of vision that was to distinguish subsequent American writing. Chateaubriand, in contrast, used American types as shortcuts to express philosophic judgments on the course taken by postrevolutionary France. The only mind he considered worth examining was that of his European hero.

The lives of the two men suggest some of the causes of the variation, not only in their literary methods, but also in the social and philosophic values each spoke for. Brown was a product of the American popular press, whose literary forms and inclinations grew out of the New England printing-bookselling trade of the late seventeenth century. Narratives like Mrs. Rowlandson's, the fictional Abraham Panther captivity, and Filson's Boone were the staples of that press, which met the popular demand by issuing them in separate pamphlets or within the covers of popular magazines. Brown was a magazine editor and writer by profession and inclination. Captivity narratives and accounts of Indian warfare and travel and exploration were his stock in trade; and he prospered as a political pamphleteer for the Francophile Jeffersonians by his knowledge of the tastes and capacities of his audience. Although he read widely in European fiction, especially in Gothic romances, he read with an eye on his needs as an editor and the demands of his American audience.

His opposite number, François-René de Chateaubriand, was a product and servant of the intellectual coteries of Paris, a young member of the liberal *noblesse* of prerevolutionary France, and a moderate republican who, like Chenier, opposed the extremism of the Terror, the execution of the king, and the substitution of established "atheism" for established Catholicism. His early development was shaped by the philosophical controversies of the Enlightenment, the intellectual and sentimental quest for a viable religious faith and a life's purpose (which he equated with an active role in political affairs). At the age of seventeen he began preparing for the priesthood, then changed his mind and took a nobleman's place in the army. He fancied himself a disciple of Rousseau until the Revolution. Disgusted with revolutionary excesses and out of favor, he left France for

America in 1791, ostensibly to search for a Northwest Passage, but more probably to visit the primitive scenes theoretically beloved by his mentor Rousseau or to take the American "Grand Tour" vicariously described by Crèvecoeur. His tour was brief but productive. From the notes of his American journey he drew material for his novel, *Les Natchez*, and a travel book. He used material from these two larger works repeatedly in other books on Christianity and government published during his career.

Chateaubriand first gained literary fame through the publication of "Atala" and "René," two fragments of *Les Natchez*. "René" appeared in 1802 as part of his work on Christianity, although the bulk of his "American" books had been written in London in the 1790s. His youthful radicalism and discipleship to Rousseau had now been exchanged for a legitimist position in politics and a liberal Catholic stance in religion. The change purportedly was sparked when his criticism of the church in *Essai . . . sur les révolutions* (1796) greatly saddened his dying mother, but he had always been romantically inclined to faith, as his early thoughts of the priesthood suggest. The publication of *Génie du Christianisme*, in which "René" appeared, marked his return to the fold and gained him temporary favor with Napoleon, who had just reestablished the Catholic church. His legitimism soon dissipated that favor, but it insured him a career as diplomat and foreign minister after the return of the Bourbons.

Thus, in composing their works, Brown and Chateaubriand drew on antithetical experiences and traditions. Behind Brown was the inchoate mass of myth-literature of captives, hunters, warriors, and explorers — the literary given of any popular American writer and his audience in 1799. Behind Chateaubriand were the theories and illusions of Rousseau, Crèvecoeur, Parraud, and the Americanist coteries and the few American books favored by that circle. To Chateaubriand, America offered an exotic setting for the symbolic drama of a Romantic novel pitting reason against passion, savagery against civilization, rebellious anarchism against respect for order and precedence. America was for him a fantastic landscape of unknown powers, in which almost anything in or out of human imagination might be expected to occur. Moreover, this exotic setting had already acquired a traditional and accepted role in French literature as an image of pure nature — a world in which God's law and nature's law act upon the individual directly, without the mediation of civilization. The workings of God and his meanings are there more clearly exposed to sight, and there the human soul is free to bring into the light the darkest yearnings of the most hidden recesses of the psyche. Chateaubriand had been to America and traveled in the West. In his youthful enthusiasm for Rousseau he had discovered Imlay's book on the West and his edition of Filson's *Kentucke*, and he had read and annotated both books extensively. Yet his portrait of America owes almost nothing to what he may have really seen on a western tour or learned from a careful reading of Boone or Imlay. It owes everything to the Romantic dream of a world made terrible, lovely, and exotic by love and melancholy — the lyric transformation of commonplace nature into something alien and strange.

Chateaubriand's recasting of excerpts from Filson's Boone narrative (in the Imlay edition) is typical of his approach to his subject. He rewrote several of the landscape descriptions, emphasizing or adding picturesque elements, but retaining certain characteristic phrases from the original.[1] Boone's view from the commanding ridge particularly struck Chateaubriand, who enthusiastically endorses the life of the savage and the hunter and declares that Boone's experience is proof that man, in his happy natural state, is active rather than contemplative, adventurous rather than intellectual. In the original scene, the melancholy Boone is redeemed from a dark night of the soul by the vision of Kentucky from the ridgetop. He has killed a buck and is preparing to eat it on the mountaintop, hard by a spring of sweet water. He muses on the simplicity of his needs and his ability to retain internal felicity despite external discomforts. Chateaubriand restates the passage as a series of abstract propositions for living the good life, rather than as a dramatic moment in the narrative of either a hero's or a real frontiersman's life. He retains the elements of Filson's scene — the dead animal, the spring, the meditation on the simplicity of man's real needs and the happiness of the hunter's life — but he pluralizes and generalizes them:

> Pourquoi trouve-t-on tant de charme à la vie sauvage? Pourquoi l'homme le plus accoutumé à éxercer sa pensée s'oublie-t-il joyeusement dans le tumulte d'un chasse? Courir dans les bois, poursuivre des bêtes sauvages, bâtir sa hutte, allumer son feu, apprêter soi-même son repas auprès d'un source, est certainement un très grand plaisir. . . . Cela prouve que l'homme est plutôt un être actif, qu'un être contemplatif, que dans sa condition naturelle, il lui faut peu de chose, et que la simplicité de l'âme est un source inépuisable de bonheur.

> Why do we find so much charm in the savage life? Why does the man most accustomed to the exercise of the mind forget himself joyously in the tumult of the chase? To run through the woods, pursue the savage beasts, build one's hut, light one's fire, prepare oneself one's own repast near a spring of water, is certainly a great pleasure. . . . This proves that man is rather an active than a contemplative being, that in his natural condition he needs few things, and that simplicity of soul is in itself a source of inextinguishable happiness.[2]

As his early enthusiasm for Rousseau waned, he exchanged this hypothetical view of America for another. By the time he turned to the writing of *Les Natchez,* his attitude toward the Indian and the hunter had completely reversed: "Je ne suis point, comme Rousseau, un enthousiaste des Sauvages." [3] *Les Natchez* (including "Atala" and "René") was written to demonstrate his new belief that "thought makes the man" and that one cannot change life or identity simply by changing his condition. These American tales dramatize Chateuabriand's contention that the qualities of human nature which divide classes and races are immutable and ought to remain so and that when rebels — French Jacobins as well as hostile Indian "subjects" — attempt to alter this relationship, tragedy is the result. The tales "Atala" and "René" are told by their protoganists, the Indian Chactas and the French exile René; but they are framed by the observations of a third-person narrator, who applies the messages of the tales to his own situation and that of other Europeans who wander in strange lands and schools searching for new wisdom.

Brown's concerns and methods are quite different. The incidents related in the narratives of Indian warfare and captivity have for him a meaning in themselves that requires no framing of abstract philosophy. He declares in his introduction to *Edgar Huntly* that such incidents have special significance for Americans and, in fact, embody an essential and characteristic quality of the national experience, wholly different from anything in the ken of European man:

> America has opened new views to the naturalist and politician, but has seldom furnished themes to the moral painter. That new springs of action and new motives to curiosity should operate, that the field of investigation, opened to us by our own country, should differ essentially from those which exist in Europe, may be readily conceived. . . . It is the purpose of this work to profit by some of these sources; to exhibit a series of adventures, growing out of the condition of our country, and connected with one of the most common and most wonderful diseases or affections of the human frame.[4]

Brown's projected exploration of this American experience and the "wonderful" disease or affection — that is, psychological state — which he associates with it is undertaken in the name of national glory. Like Dwight, Brown intends to measure his work against the accepted European models, in this case the Gothic romance. The purpose of such romances is that of "calling forth the passions and engaging the sympathy of the reader." For such evocative purposes, "the incidents of Indian hostility, and the perils of the Western wilderness, are far more suitable [than European incidents or milieus], and for a native of America to overlook these would admit of no apology." [5]

Brown's purpose, then, is to employ incidents of Indian warfare and captivity as a means of engaging the sympathies of his American reader in Edgar Huntly's nightmarish discovery of the darkness and depth of his own hidden mind. His intention is essentially the same as that of a Puritan composing a personal narrative of a conversion of captivity; he even calls himself a "moral painter." He differs only in that his protagonist is a fiction, at most a persona of the author, most likely an utter fabrication. Like the protagonist of the Puritan confession, Edgar Huntly is a hero isolated in space and time; his acts relate essentially to the drama of his self-discovery and only tangentially to social conditions and issues. This treatment of Indian-war and captivity incidents as self-evidently significant, almost sacred — together with the emphasis on introspection, psychological probing, and confession — sets Brown's work apart from the romances of Chateaubriand.

Chateaubriand's *Les Natchez* is addressed to the problem of Europe. The conflict between Indian and white is seen as an analogue of the strife between democratic anarchism and the rational love of order. Like the Wordsworthian Romantics (whose political evolution parallels his own), Chateaubriand finds both passion and reason admirable within the proper spheres. But when passion presumes to rule in the realms that are better left to intellection — that is, in national politics, the relations between classes, religious faith, and marriage — the result is conflict and catastrophe. Thus when Atala and René attempt to "marry" the worlds of passion and reason, savage and Christian, they waste away and are destroyed.

Les Natchez is the story of an Indian rebellion against the French colonists at the mouth of the Mississippi in the eighteenth century. The chief characters are René, a young French exile (and Chateaubriand's namesake) living among the Indians, and Chactas, the patriarch of the tribe. The two men are united by their experience with forbidden and doomed love. "Atala" is Chactas's tale of a tragic, youthful love affair with a Christian Indian maiden. "René" is the young Frenchman's soliloquy, in which he recounts the Werther-like sufferings he is experiencing because he has fallen fatally in love with his sister, who has taken the veil. The two figures are in fact doubles. Chactas is an Indian who has lived for some time among the glories of French civilization before being restored to the forest; René is a product of French civilization but has become an exile among the Indians in order to escape that civilization and its discontents. Both aspire to forbidden marriages, pagan Chactas with Christian Atala, and René with his sister. Both are thwarted by women whose virtuous nature leads them to prefer death (in Atala's case) or the chaste prison of a nunnery to consummation of the forbidden union. The "marriage metaphor," which had long been employed to characterize the colonists' acculturation to the Indians' world, here functions in its traditional manner: the union of Christian and pagan is regarded in the same light as incest.

Like the figure of Daniel Boone, Chactas and René are mixed characters, blending traits of both white and Indian — Christian reason and restraint, and Indian passion. The image of Boone sketched by Enlightenment writers like Parraud, Chenier, and Crèvecoeur portrayed these antithetical inclinations of character as balanced within Boone's nature, with reason offsetting passion and sociability the hunger for solitude, to make an ideal type. In the old Chactas these elements are likewise in balance, although the equilibrium is achieved only as a result of the tragic events in "Atala." Thus, in narrating his tale, Chactas echoes Boone's philosophy of self-restraint and of respect for women and for the attributes of superior civilization. Chateaubriand describes him as "un Sauvage demi civilisé," not only acquainted with "les langues vivantes" but also conversant with the classical "langues mortes d'Europe." [6] He does not willingly leave his woods for France, which might imply a refusal to acknowledge his natural limitations, but is carried there a captive. Once in the court of Louis XIV, respect for superior civilization compels him naturally to emulation, but it also confirms him in his belief that his proper sphere is the forest and not the castle. Like Filson's Boone, Chactas has the best of two worlds. He confesses that he has seen "civilization at its highest point of splendor," basked in the rays of the Sun King's smile, attended fêtes at Versailles, and participated in the production of Racine's noble tragedies and in the funeral rites of the cleric-philosopher Bossuet. At the same time, he has remained "the patriarch and the love of the deserts" of America.[7]

But although Chactas's experiences ennoble him, they also render him, in effect, impotent. This becomes clear as he recounts his earlier love for Atala, the embodiment of those virtues and civilized values inherent in Christianity. It was the Indian passion for hunting that first tempted him to leave the patriarchal tent of his adopted white "father" Lopez and led him into captivity to the tribe of Atala, who is Lopez's half-breed daughter (which implies that Chactas's passion, like René's, is incestuous) and a Christian. Atala, touched by the young captive's plight, rescues him and flees with him into the woods. The solitude and natural beauty of their situation, the handsome features of young Chactas, and the heat of her own natural emotions tempt her to succumb to her love for Chactas. He at first mistakes her for the embodiment of his pagan equivalent of the Virgin, then for the Maiden of Last Loves — a girl given to a captive before he is about to die. His natural impulse is to make love to her, whether she be priestess or maiden, since this is the response appropriate to an Indian versed in his people's mores and rituals. He discovers, however, that she is a Christian and has been sworn by her dying mother to remain virgin at all costs.

As the spell of the wilderness acts on Atala, destroying her restraint, the spell of her Christianity works on Chactas. It awakens his power of sentiment, sensitizes him to the beauties of Christianity, and leads him to an appreciation of the benefits that flow from a belief in the Christian god, even in the midst of privation. Thus he takes from a Christian maiden the kind of knowledge and power of self-restraint that Filson's Boone gained from the wilderness. But the union of Chactas and Atala is never to be, for she poisons herself rather than succumb to her own love for Chactas. (The good French priest who attends her bemoans the fact that, in her Indian ignorance, she made such an impious vow.) Chactas's love for Atala will not permit him ever to love again within his own tribe, and so he is rendered effectually impotent, a king with no heir to perpetuate his rule of his people. He worships Atala's memory, worships remembered Paris, and fails to civilize his tribe or to prevent them from rebelling against the civilized French.

If Chactas speaks for Filson's Boone's philosophy of self-restraint, René speaks for his passionate, "Indian-like" love of solitude and the dark woods. Chateaubriand's descriptions of René's astonished joy at the sight of the wilderness closely paraphrase passages from Filson. Filson's Boone says: "I had gained the summit of a commanding ridge, and, looking round with astonishing delight, beheld the ample plains, the beauteous tracts below." Chateaubriand alters "ample plains" to "desert," in accordance with his hero's civilized prejudices. Otherwise, the feeling is identical: "Les magnifiques déserts du Kentucky se deploient aux yeux étonnés du jeune François." [8] In the opening scene of "René," Chactas, René, and the tribe's French priest view a Kentucky landscape which, despite Chateaubriand's ill-informed alteration of geographical features, is recognizable as yet another borrowing from Filson's "commanding ridge" scene. In the original, Boone sees

> on the other hand, . . . the famous river Ohio that rolled in silent dignity, marking the western boundary of Kentucke with inconceivable grandeur. At a vast distance I beheld the mountains lift their venerable brows, and penetrate the clouds.[9]

Chateaubriand's alterations increase the color and picturesqueness of the original but retain its mood, its general composition, and much of its language:

> Vers l'orient, au fond de la perspective, le soleil commençoit à paroître entre les sommets brisés des Apalaches, qui se dessinoient comme des caractères d'azur dans les hauteurs dorées du ciel; à l'occident, le Méschacèbé rouloit ses ondes dans un silence magnifique, et formoit la bordure du tableau avec une inconcevable grandeur.

> Toward the east, at the far end of the prospect, the sun was beginning to appear above the jagged peaks of the Appalachians, which seemed like figures of azure in the golden heights of the sky; to the west, the Mississippi rolled its billows in magnificent silence and marked the border of the scene with an inconceivable grandeur.[10]

Chateaubriand associates Boone's initial love of the wild landscape with René, the Rousseauistic exile and Romantic "anarchiste" who has chosen to live in the wilderness rather than France. While there is no doubt that Chateaubriand created in René a sympathetic embodiment of his own youthful enthusiasms, René is clearly a man doomed by a mistaken philosophy of Rousseauistic environmentalism. Instead of examining his own soul, curing its melancholy and incestuous passions, and disciplining it to works of Christian love and the cultivation of beauty, René pursues gloom, solitude, and freedom from the obligations of civilization in a new environment. His sensitive soul, which would have made him a poet in Europe, dooms him to perpetual discontent amid the material bounty and merely sensual pleasures of living in the Natchez village with his Indian bride, Celuta. His weakness, not his strength, takes him into his exile. In his first disappointment, he had considered entering a monastery, but his "inconstance naturelle" turned him from the path of discipline, and he decided to wander instead. Like Byron's Harold he went to Italy, seated himself on the brink of Mount Etna's crater, and indulged in *Weltschmerz*. Now he describes himself to Chactas and the priest as a passionate youth, feeling himself always seated on the lip of a symbolic volcano, an abyss — suffering for the suffering people below, but remaining alienated from them. In his dream-ridden state, the world seems "immense" and crushing when reality breaks into his fancies; but it remains "imperceptible," invisible, and unreal when he is in the grip of melancholy reverie. When he is "awake," he can neither dominate nor control reality nor make his poetic dreams relevant to it. He can only appeal for the sympathy of his friends and indulge in sentimental "cris de coeur." [11]

His reactions to the solitude of the forests are mercurial, rather than temperate like those of Boone. This inconstancy of passion, as Chateaubriand reminds us in "Atala," is a quality of the Indian's character and a source of its weakness. Civilized men ought to resist extremes of sentiment, and Chactas's strength of character largely derives from his intimacy with civilization. The Romantic René, on the other hand, willfully makes himself a savage, even before coming to America, through his destructive preoccupation with his own passions. René's first reaction to solitude corresponds to Boone's. Boone found himself "many hundred miles" from his family, but he "believe[d] few would have enjoyed the happiness [he] experienced." [12] To René the scenery and the absence of his friends, parents, and beloved give a sense of superabundant vitality.[13] But this swiftly changes to boredom, and his old disgust with life returns with renewed force. His heart is unquiet and furnishes discontent rather than felicity to his mind.

> Hélas! j'étois seul, seul sur la terre! Une langueur secrète s'emparoit de mon corps. Ce dégout de la vie que j'avois ressenti dès mon enfance revenoit avec une force nouvelle. Bientot mon coeur ne fournit plus d'aliment à ma pensée, et je ne m'apercevois de mon éxistence que par un profond sentiment d'ennui.

> Alas! I was alone, alone in the world! A subtle languor possessed my body. This disgust with life that I had felt since my childhood returned with a new power. Soon my heart could furnish no more nourishment for my thoughts, and I was only aware of my existence because of a profound sense of boredom.[14]

Having tasted civilization to the point of satiety, René flees to nature; when nature in turn disappoints him, he learns that man cannot gain happiness by changing his external condition through emigration.[15] The bloody failure of the Natchez revolt teaches him that revolution is equally useless for bringing improvement to the human condition. His discontent with the life close to nature is symbolized in his growing disaffection with Celuta, the female embodiment of Indian culture. Although she pleases him and satisfies his physical desires, she is a creature of material beauty, lacking the ethereal charge of his lost French beloved. She represents the overwhelming physical reality which, in America as in Italy, breaks into his dreams and dooms them to futility. He had desired freedom and a woman, and he found both in America, but his soul is still unsatisfied. Once again, happiness follows disgust in recurring cycles. Celuta, the beautiful child of the forest solitudes, pleases him, but he seeks instead to recover his lost forbidden dreams:

René avait desiré un désert, une femme et la liberté: il possèdait tout cela, et quelque chose gâtait cette possession. Il aurait beni la main qui du même coup, l'eut débarrassé de son malheur passé et de sa félicité présente, si toutefois c'était une félicité. Il essaya en vain de réaliser ses antiques chimères: quelle femme était plus belle que Celuta? Il l'emmena au fond du forêts, et promena son indépendance de solitude en solitude; mais, quand il avait pressé sa jeune épouse contre son sein au milieu des précipices, quand il l'avait égarée dans la région des nuages, il ne recontrait point les délices qu'il avait revées.

René had desired a wilderness, a woman, and freedom: he possessed all this, and something spoiled that possession. He would have blessed the hand that would, at one stroke, have rid him of his past unhappiness and his present felicity — even if this was, nonetheless, a felicity. He tried in vain to realize his old chimerical dreams: what woman could be more beautiful than Celuta? He led her into the depths of the forests and walked in independence from solitude to solitude; but, when he pressed his young bride against his breast in the midst of the precipices, when he made her stray with him into the region of the clouds, he did not find the ecstasy of which he had dreamed.[16]

Only one ending is possible for René and Celuta. The Indian girl's tribe has been destroyed in the rebellion. The young Frenchman's rebellion against his people has made him a permanent outlaw, and his disillusion with Indian life has long since become obvious to both himself and Celuta. They join in a double suicide, leaping into a cataract, and leave behind a daughter to tell their sad tale. Thus René's rebellion against civilization, his marriage of white and Indian qualities, and his preference for the sensual muse of the wilderness, rather than the spiritual one of Europe, lead to his progressive degeneration in both body and spirit. Chactas's attempt to marry civilized and savage passions likewise leads to a physical degeneration — he is sexually and politically impotent — but at least the civilized savage has taken some quantity of the true light into his soul by way of compensation. The ending of both heroes is that which convention would lead a European audience to expect as a consequence of rebellion and the passionate attempt to breach the fixed limits of race and class.

Chateaubriand's characterization of Chactas thus typifies the European Romantic's technique for creating an "American" character. In order to make him interesting, Chateaubriand says he found it necessary to make him a Frenchman in red skin and eagle feathers, indistinguishable from the sentimental René, save in his humble respect for French civilization.[17] America offers conventionally accepted symbols for the man of nature and an exotically wild natural backdrop for the drama, and Chateaubriand is consciously employing them as literary devices. He does not succumb to the spell of his own poetry and mistake the mirage for the reality. He "knows" that the Indian is a brute, the frontiersman an ignoramus, the life close to nature oppressive to the mind and destructive of poetic intelligence; and he expresses these ideas implicitly through the drama of René's destruction. The American wilderness is incapable of producing a new Adam or an Emile. The value of pursuing the adventures of Chactas and René lies in our awakening to the destructive potential of Romantic anarchism, savagism, passionism.

Chateaubriand's view of the consequences of the wilderness amalgamation of Christian and Indian traits is typical of European (or at least Continental) thinking at this time. Volney, in his book of American travels, draws the same conclusions far more explicitly, associating the degeneracy of American life with its affinity for the Indian. An American writer like Brown had an entirely different tradition to draw on in creating literary Indians and settlers — a tradition derived from long experience on the frontier, from captivity narratives and Indian-war narratives like those of Rowlandson, Church, and Filson, and from the assertive nationalism that made Indian disguise a mark of national distinction for the Tea Party rebels in 1773 and the Whiskey Rebels in 1794.

That Brown was aware of the nature of his controversy with Europe is manifested in his footnotes to his translation of Volney, where he argues against the Frenchman's anti-American stereotypes. Of Volney's comments on the "degeneration" of American political leaders and institutions and on the "hypocrisy . . . inexperience and insolence" of the national character, Brown says: "These are topics, on which his prejudices as a Frenchman, and as a vain and captious mortal, would have abundant opportunity to show themselves." Of Volney's great distinction between the proto-European coastal provinces and the Indian backwoods and his idea that America is to Europe as the backwoods are to the maritime provinces, Brown observes caustically: "Volney draws large inferences from a trivial circumstance." Volney observes that French settlers who fell for American pamphlets on the glories of the frontier have degenerated in health and fortune in that savage environment. Brown querulously attributes their leanness to a constitutional propensity (the result of French birth), rather than a spare diet.[18]

Their most interesting disagreement concerns the Indians, whom Volney attacks and Brown defends — an inversion of the eighteenth-century disagreement between French Rousseauists and American "realists." Volney states that the term *Indian* is inapplicable to the American natives, who could more appropriately be termed *sauvages*. Brown correctly notes that this substitutes a pejorative value-term for a proper name: "The French *sauvage* answers . . . to the English *savage*, which is applied to persons or actions which we want to stigmatize as wicked and cruel, and is given to men in the rudest state of society, only when we allude to their ignorance or ferocity." [19] Parraud, in his French translation of Filson some twenty years before, had referred to the Indians as "les Naturels." Volney's preference is symptomatic of the change in French thought in the intervening years.

To Volney's mind, the Indian is fatally limited by his racial heritage. The Americans, caught in the Indian's world, have been infected with the same germs of anarchism, arrogance, and violence. In rehashing the arguments about the spiritual consequences of the hunting rather than the pastoral economy, Volney employs the ambiguous term "American *hunter*," which (in the context) may be taken as a reference to both the Indian and those white Americans who, under environmental pressures, take up his ways:

> The American *hunter*, who had daily occasion to kill and eat the slain . . . has imbibed, of course, an errant, wasteful, and cruel disposition. He is akin to the wolf and the tyger. — He unites with his fellows in troops, but not in fraternities. A stranger to property, all the sentiments springing from a family are unknown to him. Dependent on his own powers, he must always keep them on the stretch: and hence a turbulent, harsh, and fickle character; a haughty and intractable spirit, hostile to all men.[20]

Crèvecoeur writes in a similar vein in *Letters from an American Farmer* and the *Journey*, even declaring that the hunter's love of solitude makes the Indian incapable of rooting his affections to the soil of his birth. While this was certainly true of white frontiersmen, the Indian's attachment for the soil had long been proverbial; indeed, it formed the keystone of the Romantic image of the Indian in the novels of Chateaubriand. Clearly, both Crèvecoeur and Volney identified the Anglo-American with the Indian, fusing the negative stereotypes of both peoples.

Brown denies that the Indian is unchangeable, his character fixed by racial inheritance. Habits and conditioning make each man what he is, and the characteristics that develop from conditioning cannot be inherited. Change the education and circumstances of the Indian child, and he will not be a savage like his fathers before him. Volney's remarks, says Brown, are the result of ignorance and prejudice: "Volney is an enthusiast against the savages, and is as zealous to depreciate, as Rousseau was to exalt their character." [21] For the American, a sympathetic but critical realism is the necessary approach to this symbolically most important of questions.

Brown offers a far more complex version of the frontier experience, charged with troubling ambiguities that suggest unexplored significances hidden deep within that experience. Like Chateaubriand, he brings Europeans, Indians, and colonists together on his American stage, but their relationships are not seen simply in terms of the conventional conflict between civilized and savage types.

Edgar Huntly centers around the dreams and adventures of the title character, whose name suggests a kinship with the frontier hunters. Huntly himself denies the aptness of the name and disavows any skill or pleasure in hunting. Yet events prove him a compulsive hunter, a skilled tracker, a crack shot, and if not an experienced then an inspired Indian fighter. His denial of his name suggests something about the nature of his character and the strange events of his story: Huntly is only half aware of, and guiltily terrified by, his powers and capabilities. Like the more obviously "possessed" Mercy Short, Huntly has seen his natural parents massacred by Indians and has acquired from the experience an extreme aversion to the sight of savages. The extremity of his aversion, however, cloaks a fascination with the crime which, in the course of the story, comes to suggest an obscure sense of guilt in that primal murder — not unlike the guilt that overwhelmed Mercy Short.

The tale begins with another murder, that of his saintly and paternal friend Waldegrave. Horrified and fascinated by the crime, Huntly revisits the murder scene to see if he can discover clues to the murderer's identity or perhaps surprise him returning to the scene of his crime. Strangely, he chooses the nighttime to take up his vigil — indeed, he shows a great preference for wandering alone in the night over any daylight activity. Beneath the great, ancient tree under which the murder was perpetrated, he discerns the half-naked figure of Clithero, a mysterious Irish immigrant, digging what seems a grave or a treasure trove. A second time he follows the entranced Clithero, who is in fact a somnambulist, to a rocky dell and cave very much like that described in the Abraham Panther captivity. As in that narrative, a strange change of identity between man and animal takes place. Clithero enters, and some time later "an animal leaped forth, of what kind I am unable to discover." [22]

Impulsiveness is Huntly's besetting sin. At first he wishes to take vengeance on Clithero; then he relents and forces from Clithero a confession. The Irishman is a sleepwalker, driven by an insane sense of guilt for having, through an awful combination of "gratitude" and monstrous conceit, seemingly murdered in her bed a woman who had been his benefactress and adopted mother. Some days after the confession, Clithero disappears. Huntly's response is characteristic: he attempts to hunt him down, to track him like an animal through the woods. He has already been strangely drawn to Clithero, and his embarking on the hunt carries this sense of kinship to its ultimate point: the hunter identifies himself with the beast he is hunting, becomes one with the thing he wishes to kill. (Thus Church assumed King Philip's regalia at the end of his hunt, and Boone married the woman whom he had mistaken for a deer during his fire hunt.) Huntly's quest brings him to the rocky dell and cave where Clithero had previously hidden himself and where Huntly had previously mistaken him for the mysterious animal that leaped out of the cave. As in the archetypal pattern of the Boone narrative, the dell in the hills and the cave are (in terms of Campbell's monomyth) the threshold of adventure. When Huntly crosses it, he enters a dark world in which identities shift and blend, and beasts and men interchange shapes and qualities.

On his first crossing, he passes through the cave's impenetrable darkness and comes to an open place atop the mountain, divided in the middle by a chasm through which a stream dashes itself. Huntly, like Filson's Boone, is enchanted by the contrast between the terror of the pass and the beauty of the view from his commanding ridge and by the fact that he beholds the scene in perfect isolation and solitude:

> The summit was higher than any of those which were interposed between itself and the river. A large part of this chaos of rocks and precipices was subjected, at one view, to the eye. The fertile lawns and vales which lay beyond this, the winding course of the river, and the slopes which rose on its farther side, were parts of this extensive scene. These objects were at any time fitted to inspire rapture. Now my delight was enhanced by the contrast which this lightsome scene bore to the glooms from which I had lately emerged. . . . There was a desolate and solitary grandeur in the scene. . . . A sort of sanctity and awe environed it, owing to the consciousness of absolute and utter loneliness. . . . Since the birth of this continent, I was probably the first who had deviated thus remotely from the customary paths of men.[23]

No sooner has he said this than he beholds on the other side of the torrent the savagely attired Clithero, who spies him, turns, and just as magically disappears.

Huntly, if he will continue to pursue his double, must pass another obstacle, the torrent. He does so by felling a tree across it, but his exploration is fruitless. He returns home, then comes a second time to the cave and surprises Clithero asleep; but fearing to wake and confront him, Huntly leaves food by his side and leaves to investigate the mysteries of Clithero's trunk and diary. A third time he returns to the threshold and crosses the chasm on the felled tree in search of Clithero. As in his first visit to the dell, he is assailed by an animal who guards the threshold (Campbell's "dragon" or "shadow presence"). On this occasion the beast is a grey panther, whom Huntly calls "a savage," thus associating the beast with both the Indians and, by extension, the now half-wild Clithero. Although he claims to be no hunter, Huntly dispatches him with a tomahawk, and the beast falls into the chasm. Clithero is nowhere to be seen. Huntly returns home and falls asleep. When he awakens, he is no longer in his bed but plunged in a cold, mysterious darkness that is pierced by no single ray of light. In his sleep he has again passed the threshold: he has become a sleep-walker, like Clithero, and has fallen into the deep pit in the cave.

The nature of Huntly's quest begins to become clearer. Clithero, his double, represents that dark quality of Huntly's own nature which is moved by irresistible passions and impulses and which prefers nighttime and solitude to the genial day and healthy companionship. Like Clithero, Huntly is now living the dark dreams that move beneath the conscious mind. That these dreams are potent with crime and violence we know from Clithero's career and from his association with the panther-"savage." Now that we know Huntly is a sleepwalker, the possibility arises that his fascination with Clithero and the murder of Waldegrave is prompted by a secret identification with the murderer. In his sleep Huntly may have murdered saintly Waldegrave, as Clithero apparently slew his benefactress. Huntly has been carried, without conscious will, into a kingdom of darkness by dark impulses in his own character. The parallels between his plight and Mercy Short's "captivity to Spectres" or Mrs. Rowlandson's captivity to the Indians are obvious. They are rendered more so by subsequent events.

The first peril Huntly confronts appears in the same guise in which Rebecca appeared to Boone on the fire hunt: two eyes gleaming like coals in the darkness. These are the eyes of a panther, apparently the mate or double of the one slain earlier by Huntly, but quite possibly something more mysterious. Huntly had seen traces of only one panther previously and assumed he had rid the cave of its denizen when he slew it. After slaying this beast too, he wanders lost in the cave until he finds himself near an entrance. He perceives at the cave's mouth "four brawny and terrific figures" — Indians in war paint — and a white maiden bound captive among them. Again his thoughts run to the notion of a captivity to strange powers: "Had some mysterious power snatched me from the earth, and cast me, in a moment, into the heart of the wilderness?" [24]

Huntly rescues the girl and kills the Indians after the manner of Boone and Imlay's Captain Arl—ton, employing the Indians' own weapons and techniques of ambush to effect it. Pursued by a second party of Indians, Huntly flees with the girl to an abandoned hut, leaves her prostrate, and goes to seek food with an Indian's rifle. With horror he discovers that it is his very own piece, a weapon bearing unmistakable devices to identify it. He concludes that the Indians have massacred his family and that his "ancient dwelling" is now "polluted with blood." [25] Like Clithero, Huntly has apparently been bereaved of his adoptive family by an unnatural murder. Clithero knows himself the perpetrator of the unfilial deed, but Huntly has no idea what his own implication in the murder may have been: at the very least, his sleepwalking has taken him away from home just when he would have been most needed. Again, Huntly's psychological plight raises echoes from the literature of the American past. The Puritan captivity narrative had developed largely as a device for dealing with the anxiety of the Puritan emigrants, an anxiety that expressed itself as a feeling of guilt for having separated themselves from the parental household. Huntly, pursuing the gloomy Clithero of his nature, fears he may have committed — while in some sleepwalking revery — a similar crime against his adoptive parents.

Buried still deeper is the memory of his natural parents' murder by Indians and the aversion to savages which he developed after the discovery of that crime. The child Huntly had been unable to save his first parents; now the man Huntly, because of his obsessive sleepwalking-search for Clithero, had been unable to save the second parents. Is the repetition of this pattern a signal of the presence of some malignant power? Or is Huntly himself dream-willing these crimes? Are the Indian devils really the devils of his mind, or are they symbols of his calling? Is he another Clithero? Before he can pursue this train of thought to its end and discover the nature of his kinship with Clithero, the Indians attack him and mortally wound the girl. Once again his nature has led him to desert a woman and a hearth in order to seek revenge and destruction. He fights with despair in his heart, slays the Indians, but is himself wounded and falls in a deathlike faint.

When he awakes, he is again alone. A party of white men has rescued the girl and left him for dead among the Indians. Again he is afflicted with the sense that he is wandering in "death's dream kingdom," as much as in the wilderness. This is enhanced by his discovery that the hut he has been defending is that of Old Deb, an Indian witch known locally as Queen Mab. He is at the nadir of his quest in the underworld, having suffered a symbolic death and resurrection in the chamber of a fairy queen. Now he must achieve his return. Alone, he begins to retrace the river trail back across the mountains toward his home. Before he can recross the threshold, another transfer of identity takes place. Huntly sees beyond the river a party of men whom he assumes to be Indians but who are in fact his friends searching for him. They in turn mistake him for an Indian, since he is on the side of the river where the war parties were most expected. The scene parallels Huntly's earlier sighting of Clithero across the torrent, but now Huntly stands in Clithero's place. Huntly and his friends, laboring under the mistake of identities, attempt to kill each other, and Huntly escapes by plunging into the stream. Once again it becomes clear that in crossing the threshold to the dream kingdom in quest of Clithero, Huntly has become strongly linked with the violent Irishman. He has become a hunter and a killer, like the panther, and is here mistaken for an Indian.

Tattered and savage-looking, Huntly bursts into the house of a neighbor, demanding to be told the horrible truth about his family — that all are dead as he has imagined them. His friend regards him as a madman and demands to know "what has filled you with these hideous prepossessions." [26] His uncle and adopted father is indeed dead, but not murdered. Rather, he has fallen in battle against the Indians, a victim of his own courage. It seems as if Huntly can at last awake from the guilt and horror of his wilderness dream. His friend clarifies the mysterious passage of his captivity and journey, his being left for dead at Queen Mab's hut, the mistake of identities at the river. The friend even holds out hope for Huntly's doomed soul-fellow, Clithero, whose patroness was not slain by him but is still alive and married to a good friend of Huntly's in New York. Like Huntly, Clithero has but dreamed that, like a savage Indian, he had slain his parent.

Eager to tell Clithero of his redemption, Huntly seeks him out, only to find that, more even than himself, his dream-double has fallen prey to the savages and lies "mangled by the tomahawk in a shocking manner." Despairing of his cure, Huntly tells Clithero that his deed against the lady was not fatal and leaves him to the ministrations of some Indian hags, who doctor him with herbs and dark incantations. To Huntly's surprise, Clithero recovers and disappears in the night to seek out the benefactress and reenact the ancient, bloody dream of matricide. Huntly, infatuated by his need to redeem his dark Clithero, has given him the woman's address and, in effect, put the hunting wolf onto the scent. For Clithero can never change his nature now: "Common ills are not without a cure less than death, but here all remedies are vain. Consciousness itself is the malady, the pest, of which he is only cured who ceases to think." Clithero declares to Huntly that he will seek her out only to ascertain that she is alive and well and his crime expiated, yet he hints of a "malignant" fate that impels him to bloody deeds.[27] Disturbed, Huntly writes to his friend to warn him of the danger to his wife, giving all particulars.

The besetting sin of impulsiveness — or perhaps some obscure, darker motive — prompts Huntly to send this letter. He knows that the wife, a woman weakened in health by her experience with Clithero and now about to bear a child to Huntly's friend, may easily open the letter and read it, yet the knowledge slips his mind. During the friend's absence Huntly's letter arrives, and the woman opens it. The friend, writing to Huntly, describes the consequences: "Terror could not assume a shape more ghastly than this. The effects have been what might have been easily predicted. Her own life has been imminently endangered, and an untimely birth has blasted my fondest hope. Her infant, with whose future existence so many pleasures were entwined, *is dead*." [28] So Huntly accomplishes the deed that Clithero dreamed, committing violence against that very woman whom Clithero had wronged. Huntly, not Clithero, strikes down the woman and the child in her womb by a rash, unthinking deed.

Thus is the riddle of Huntly's hunt for Clithero unriddled. Like the mythic hunters of Indians, he has become the thing he hunts. His fascination with Clithero is but the obverse face of his aversion for the savages who murdered his natural parents, the embodiment of his unacknowledged sense of guilt. His search in the physical wilderness is likewise a mask for his inquisition into his own mind and soul. His search for the guilty Clithero is an unconscious search for his guilty self. His nightmares of guilt, in which he fears that a malign and unknown fate has made him unwillingly the instrument inflicting multiple miseries upon his several families (his natural, adoptive, and surrogate parents), turn out to have been obscure, unconscious wishes. Although the Indians murdered Waldegrave and Clithero's visit prostrated his friend's wife, Indian and Clithero are in some sense the mere realizations of Huntly's dream wishes. The confusion of Huntly's identity with that of Clithero and the Indians is now revealed as the clue to the character of Huntly's malady. Had he seen the answer sooner, achieved self-knowledge, recognized the Clithero and the savage within himself, he might have avoided the deed. The friend points for him the lesson he ought to have learned from his Indian captivity: "Be more circumspect and obsequious for the future." [29] For Huntly, Clithero's choices are now open. He can become reconciled with his new consciousness; or he can reject it and, driven by remorse, go mad, to be cured of "consciousness" only by death. The "consciousness" that Huntly, at the end of his captivity, must contemplate is essentially that of the Puritan captive. Despite all the good will in the conscious mind, man is moved by secret impulses to evil. Like Clithero, we are both blood-guilty Indians and helpless captives to Indians.

Huntly's quest is a hunt for his identity from among the choices offered him by the American wilderness — that symbolic equivalent of the tangled mind of man. His adventure is psychological as much as physical and is shaped by archetypal myth patterns and a mythlike confusion of animal and human identities. These questions of psychology are not resolved in the novel. What Huntly may make of his discovered identity also is not revealed, but anything is possible. Like Boone, he may become reconciled with the wild beast he has hunted; like the Puritans, like Clithero, he may try in vain to exorcise the features of that dark visage that have, as an inevitable result of his living in the world, become mingled with his own.

In Chateaubriand's novel the qualities of psychological light and darkness are played against each other in a symmetrical pattern, like the conflicts between civilization and savagery, order and rebellion, society and solitude. The ending is clear and pat: the savage life is destroyed, and the white man who sought savage ways perishes by his own hand. The movement from sin or error to the fatal consequence or punishment is clear and direct. For Brown there is no symmetry, no clear conclusion. Huntly's situation remains full of possibilities for further illumination, an unmeasured variety of possible truths. Indian warfare takes place in a tangled jungle, and even the victorious fighter can never shake the mire of it from his feet or the spell of it from his consciousness. No "ending" is possible, since the dark Indian and light Christian within us can never be wholly disentangled. Only the nature of their interrelatedness, their intimacy, can be clarified through further exploration.

American literature in the next half-century continued that hunt for intimate knowledge of the Indian face of nature, while European literature rested content with its stereotypes. The power and fixity of these stereotypes is attested by their adoption by men like Byron, whose politics differed radically from the anti-Jacobin reversionism of Crèvecoeur, Talleyrand, Chateaubriand, and Volney and by their persistence in European thought into the twentieth century. Byron's *Don Juan* contains (in canto 8) a brief interlude in which the character of Daniel Boone is offered as an alternative to the horrors of civilized warfare experienced by Juan in the siege of Ismail. Byron falsifies the most obvious details of frontier reality in order to create a symbol appropriate to a poetic assault on the European establishment, just as Chateaubriand did in order to defend it.

Like the innocent maid Haidée, solitary child of the Edenic island where Juan had earlier found refuge from the criminality of society, Byron's Boone symbolizes the opposition of nature to the evils of civilization. He lives free of crime, "happiest amongst mortals," the patriarch of an "unsighing people of the woods," enjoying the "lonely vigorous, harmless days / Of his old age in wilds of deepest maze." They are "simple . . . not savage," but therefore they are not noble and tragic like Juan. (Byron's humorous rhyming of "buck, he" and "Kentucky" implies a kind of irony or patronization.)[30] Byron's Boone — derived from Filson, from Bryan's epic poem based on Filson, and from the newspaper accounts that the intrigued Byron sought out[31] — becomes nothing more than the good Quaker, the pious, pacifist (he hunts only for food) yeoman of the tradition. This favorable portrayal of Boone was, however, the only European treatment to be immediately republished in America. In 1823 it was bound with Filson's narrative and other material on Boone in an edition probably used as a source by Simms and Cooper.

The persistence of the European stereotype is attested by the critique of Chateaubriand's "American exoticism" published by Gilbert Chinard in 1918. Latter-day Rousseauists, enamored of the old ideals of popular revolution, were holding up the figure of Boone as an alternative to the conservative wisdom of Chateaubriand, reviving the image of Emile in buckskins. Chinard took the challenge seriously enough to attempt a defense of Chateaubriand against Boone, of the *philosophe en chambre* against the *philosophe en forêt*. Finally he reduced it to a question of differences in style: Chateaubriand's is elegant, witty, and full of poetic insight, while Boone's is "astonishing" in its vigor and "firmness" but essentially "rude and barbaric." From this Chinard concluded that Boone had been severely handicapped by having read "only the Bible" (like those good Quakers) and essentially brutalized by his intimacy with the Indians (since, says Chinard, he did not hesitate to scalp his enemies and display the hair as a trophy).[32] Chinard thus employed in his argument all of the vocabulary of stereotypes current in the writings of Crèvecoeur and Chateaubriand — the good Quaker, Emile in buckskins, the savages. He even continued in the delusion, foisted by Filson on Parraud and Crèvecoeur, that the style of the piece is that of Boone himself.

The original European versions of the Boone myth had been shaped by the prejudices, political problems, and literary predilections of the prerevolutionary generation of Imlay, Parraud, Crèvecoeur and Chenier. Byron and Chateaubriand drew their images of the West from these earlier treatments, rather than from contact with the frontier. In much the same manner Chenier had, in the 1780s, adapted his vision of the frontier to suit the fashions and conventions of the Paris coterie, borrowing from second-hand illusions rather than firsthand realities for the creation of his myth. Byron and Chateaubriand, writing within the closed circle of a European literary tradition, eliminated from their portraits of the West all those realities which did not suit their aesthetic needs. Like a dog chewing its own tail, the European myth of the frontier fed only on the symbols and images created by the original myth-makers.

In America, continuing contact with real frontiersmen and Indian problems kept the realities of the frontier in the public consciousness. American writers had to shape their myths to suit their audience's growing knowledge of that reality, but they could renew the power of their images by employing the new legends which continued to emanate from the West. Although they wished to domesticate the literary traditions and conventions of European Romantics, American writers had their own complex tradition to draw on — the dual vision of the good and evil aspects of the frontier which had been developed in the writing of Indian-war and captivity narratives in the last century and a half.

In the European mythology, whether in a pro- or anti-American phase, the frontiersman and the Indian symbolize the presumed preoccupation of Americans with the mere materials and commodities of the world, in preference to the pursuit of higher values and the cultivation of the finer things of the mind and spirit. The European Romantic hero envies the frontiersman's condition as he might envy that of the babe in the womb or the mystic drowned in the maternal sea of his vision. His envy is a literary device, intended to demonstrate the poet-hero's own capacity for sentimental agony, his sensitivity. So great are the sentiments of René and Juan that they yearn to be relieved of them at any price. If turning savage will bring contentment and peace to tumultuous thoughts, all is well; if not, peace can still be found in the bosom of death. They yearn to share Boone's contentment with his mere circumstances, yet this very yearning marks them as discontented, and this discontent makes them Boone's superior as poets and heroes. They are truly involved in the tragic drama of life, the great issues of existence, the spiritual flux of history, and the ethereal music of the spheres. The noble poet-hero embodies human aspiration; the frontiersman speaks at best for provincial, dull peace and at worst for a stultifying complacence.

In the American Romantic mythology the reverse is true. The man of action is as much the poet and hero as are noblemen like Don Juan and René. His natural education, in fact, makes him their moral superior, since his lonely quests in the woods are as productive of spiritual good as those of the poet-exile and are perhaps of greater practical value to society. For René and Don Juan the wilderness is an escape from the reality of society, where riddles lie waiting for solution and where their real responsibility as heroes lies. For Edgar Huntly and Boone the path into the wilderness is the path of self-discovery and (for Boone at least) of social duty — the path that leads them into greater involvement in reality in all of its moral ambiguity and psychological complexity.

CHAPTER 12

The Fragmented Image:
The Boone Myth and Sectional Cultures (1820–1850)

As [civilization] approached, the wild animals of the forest (like the aboriginals) receded, and to enjoy the society of the latter, in preference to that of his fellow-countrymen, Colonel Boone found himself necessitated to follow their example.

C. Wilder, in Filson's *Life of Col. Boone*

In an age of chivalry — during the Crusades — Boon would have been a knight-errant, equally fearless and gentle.

William G. Simms, "Daniel Boon"

The Indian way of life is the way of his heart, . . . giv[ing] scope to the exulting consciousness of his own appropriate and peculiar power.

Timothy Flint, *Indian Wars of the West*

THE myth of the hunter that had grown up about the figure of Filson's Daniel Boone provided a framework within which Americans attempted to define their cultural identity, social and political values, historical experience, and literary aspirations. To some extent the experience of each of the great sections of the country — the trans-Allegheny West and Southwest, the Old South, and the Northeast — was common ground. Each section had, in its turn, been settled by emigrants seeking a change of fortune in a new land. Each had had to make radical adjustments to a new environment, sacrificing some qualities of its parent culture in order to survive in the new environment. Each had had to establish itself in the face of natural hardships, Indian hostilities, and British oppression. Each had had to discover and express its new character in literature. Daniel Boone, Washington, Franklin, and Jefferson were heroes to the whole nation because their experiences had reference to many or all of these common experiences. "The Hunters of Kentucky," a popular song that swept the nation in 1822–28, helped elect Andrew Jackson as President by associating Old Hickory with Boone, the hero of the West.

Within this general pattern of national history, each section also had its own peculiar social and economic makeup, and its own history of relations with the Indians; hence each evolved its own special version of the national myth. As the poetry of Dwight reveals, a New Englander's version of the American hero was likely to be a representative of his section's virtues, and the same can be said for the South and West. The rising power of the West and the simultaneous growth of liberal social and political reform movements reinforced the traditional association of the frontiersmen with the radical democrats, or "Jacobins." For the proponents of the so-called Jacksonian democracy, this state of affairs made idealization of the westerner easy. For the opponents of radical democracy, the anxious older states and the conservative classes of the Northeast and Old South, the association of Jacksonian frontiersmen with the Jacobins resurrected images fraught with terror — the white Indian, the Indian rebel, racially degenerate and politically unstable, who had haunted the dreams of the Puritans; and the rebellious Negro who bedeviled the South. The roots of these sectional differences went back further than the political squabbles of the Jacksonian era. The South, Northeast, and West had each had a different relationship with the Indians and with Europe — the two poles of the American experience — and each had developed a different literary tradition, through which its experience could find expression.

The character of political and class tensions varied from section to section. In the West the conflict was between the men-on-the-make — farmers, speculators, and manufacturers, who sought to exploit the land and the law for the maximum personal profit — and the wealthier speculators who held their debts. In the plantation South the economic situation was less fluid. There the chief problem was maintaining order in an unstable political and economic situation that set impoverished planters against their slaves and against the poor whites, who had been excluded from the best lands by the dead hand of plantation economics. In the Southwest, democracy took a form similar to that in the free-state West, save that ownership of slaves became the goal of the man-on-the-make; its achievement was the mark of a man's attainment of full equality with the best in American society. The Northeast's turn toward commerce and manufacturing made that section sensitive to the challenges to its economic power posed by the other sections and by Europe. This resulted in a different set of internal tensions: those between employer and employee (aggravated by the influx of immigrant labor) and between established men of commerce and finance and the ambitious newcomers to their field.

In European mythology, the frontier hero symbolized American materialism. The Buffon-Raynal conception of America as a continent of degenerated species was echoed by the assertions of Talleyrand that Americans were philistines, ignoramuses, obsessed with engrossing land and turning profits. Even the more favorable Romantic views of America emphasized materialism. Byron's "General Boon" symbolized material prosperity, circumstantial freedom, and physical well-being; Chateaubriand's Chactas and Celuta were physically beautiful, physically free of the problems and obsessions of civilized men. Both Byron and Chateaubriand were somewhat patronizing toward these figures, even while they admired them, and Crèvecoeur's *Journey* frankly presented the pioneer farmers and hunters as members of the lower class. In the social disorder of Europe in the revolutionary and Napoleonic periods, these conventional literary images came to represent specific social classes. For men like Crèvecoeur and Talleyrand, the wildness and unruliness of the frontiersman, his devotion to materialism, and his disregard of traditional values made him a symbolic equivalent of the Jacobin, the lower-class radical. The poet-hero, on the other hand, was usually represented as liberal of mind and noble by birth and natural gifts — a representative of the enlightened *noblesse* of prerevolutionary days.

In America the social tensions of the Jeffersonian period (1800–24) made the European Romantic interpretation of the western myth seem relevant to the American situation. Since Puritan times, one dominant theme in the Indian-war literature had been the moral condemnation of the frontiersman as an irresponsible fugitive from the social responsibilities and moral duties of civilization. The fear of cultural dissolution lay behind the original Puritan condemnation, as it did behind the hostility of the ruling-class intellectuals of Europe. The shifts in the economic and political balance of power between classes and sections in America brought this same fear to the older states and the propertied and privileged classes who had previously dominated business and government. The demands of class-conscious interest groups — the small farmers, businessmen, and laborers who advocated universal suffrage and more liberal land-rent and debt-interest policies — suggested the Jacobin image to the older merchants and the squirearchy. These class-oriented demands for reform coincided with the rise of the West to a new position of political and economic strength — a rise which was due in large measure to the draining off of the eastern population to the frontier. The Virginia-Kentucky nullification crisis of 1796 and the real links between members of the Jefferson party and revolutionary France reinforced the association of Jacobinism, the West, and the radicals of the East.

Yet this association did not produce a simpleminded rejection of the West as a land of degeneracy and riot. In addition to the antifrontier tradition, the literature of the Indian wars had also transmitted a tradition in which the frontier represented the field on which America would realize her full potential, her ability to create a superior civilization. Cultural anxieties and the competition of sectional interest groups fostered a sectional divergence in the interpretation of this historical mission and hence of American character. Writers in each section attempted to create a rationale of American history in which the history and the cultural attitudes of their own section would emerge as the moral quintessence of the American national experience. But despite their differences, writers in all the sections focused on the frontier and Filson's Boone myth in posing the problem of national character and mission.

The coastal states, being not only closer geographically to Europe than those of the West but also longer settled and more thoroughly cultivated, seemed to be at a stage of civilization more closely approximate to that of Europe. The northeastern states in particular were drawn to Europe through their extensive commercial and intellectual contacts there. The relatively urbanized Northeast still stood in much the same relation to Europe and to the West as it had in the earlier period, serving as a mediator between frontier barbarism and the cultivation of Europe, a middleman bringing civilized amenities to wild Indians and frontiersmen and the virtues of natural democracy to corrupt Europe.

The western view of the East, on the other hand, was much like the eastern view of Europe. The East was the area of civilization, the home country from which westerners had emigrated and whose ways they had rejected in favor of those the wilderness had impelled them to adopt. New York was the Nineveh to which western evangelists like Charles G. Finney came, preaching against the intellectual Pharisees. Just as the emergence of national consciousness in the eastern states prompted men like Dwight to overtly reject "Europeanism" in literature, so western writers like James Hall and Timothy Flint rejected eastern characterizations of western heroes and adopted their own. Since their experience with Indian troubles was most recent, the ambivalence of their attitudes toward the Indians was more pronounced than that of eastern writers. In the South the dependence of the southern way of life on Negro slavery gave a peculiar twist to their evolving sectional mythology. Southern fears took the form of a triune image in which was mingled the blood of the red savage, the black rebel, and the white Jacobin.

The results of these differences can be seen in the variations which each section composed on the theme of Daniel Boone. Western writers emphasized his powers as man, exalting the image of the solitary, antisocial hunter to heroic proportions and rejecting the sentimental, philosophic Boone of Filson. In the East, Boone became either the embodiment of western Jacobinism and racial degeneracy — a white Indian — or else was cleaned up and given some specious social graces to make him fit for the company of his civilized betters in the eastern pantheon. In the South, Boone appeared in historical romances either as a disguised aristocrat, more noble than the herd of savages and white renegades about him, or as a humble subordinate to some more aristocratic hero representative of southern virtues.

The paths of literary and cultural influence leading to these sectional variations of the Boone myth can be traced in the lines of the book trade that tied the sections to one another and to Europe. New York and Philadelphia formed the axis of this book trade. European works reached the West and South through this center, and western and southern works passed through the hands of axis distributors before circulating through the rest of the nation and Europe. Writers in New England, the West, and the South who sought a wider readership brought their works to the axis for publication and distribution. The geographic poles of the trade were also the poles of thought about the frontier. On the one hand was the West itself, the source of personal narratives and oral folk-legends about the West and of whatever knowledge of the real frontier the other areas possessed. At the other extreme was Europe, the source of still other fantasies — whether hostile or friendly — about a West which was imagined with either fear or longing.

The publication history of the Boone narrative from 1793 to 1824 offers some insight into the nature of this literary interaction between the sections and its effects on sectional attitudes toward the West. In 1793 Imlay's edition of *Kentucke* appeared in New York. It was coupled with his own Romantic interpretation of the West in the *Topographical Description*, which painted Kentucky as a Godwinian utopia of liberty, pastoral economy, and rampant freedom for the development and pursuit of Romantic love. Copies of this New York edition passed along the main lines of the New York book trade into the West and New England. In 1812 Imlay's edition was used as a source for Humphrey Marshall's *History of Kentucky*, published in Frankfort, Kentucky. Many subsequent histories and anthologies of Indian war narratives published in the West between 1812 and 1848 cited Imlay's edition as a source. In 1809 or 1810 Henry Trumbull had published the Boone narrative in the first edition of his *Discovery of America*, which became the most popular anthology of Indian war tales in the period. The first edition appeared in Brooklyn, New York, but all subsequent editions save one were published in New England, most of them in the Boston area. Although Trumbull's text of the narrative may have been drawn from the edition published in 1786 by his kinsman and teacher, John Trumbull of Norwich, he also borrowed from *Kentucke* the "Minutes of the Piankashaw Council," a chapter which had not been reprinted in any American edition of the work save those of Filson in 1784 and Imlay in 1793. This circumstance — coupled with the fact that Trumbull's "Proposals," or advertising bill, for his book listed Imlay's narrative of the Scott-Wilkinson expedition in the abstract of contents — suggests that Trumbull's source was the New York edition of 1793. Thus the New Englander Trumbull drew on both the literature of his section and that imported through the axis in creating his portrait of the Indian wars.

Once the narrative had circulated to writers in the West and New England, it was edited to render it useful as a justification of each section's attitude toward the frontier. In New England, Trumbull used it to justify the thesis that expansion of the frontier beyond present limits would destroy the orderly fabric of society and government. Westerners like James Hall took the opposite viewpoint, influenced by the oral mythology of Boone the hunter which had been created by the hero's fellow frontiersmen. Hall offered the Boone narrative as proof that the early pioneers had heroic qualities of mind as well as of body. His *Letters from the West* (1822–28) presented Boone as a typical specimen of the class of frontiersmen — brave, adventurous, restless, delighting in danger and strife more than in the garnering of material wealth. Both Hall's western image and Trumbull's New England antiimage were then disseminated through the axis. Hall's letters, some of which were originally published in his Shawneetown, Illinois, newspaper, were sent east in 1823–25 for publication in the Philadelphia *Port-Folio*, a literary gazette. In 1828 they appeared as a book in London. Trumbull's anthology had reached the West before Hall's letters reached Philadelphia: in 1821, Samuel L. Metcalf used several items of the anthology in his own collection of Indian war narratives. Metcalf also published the Boone narrative, using the text of Imlay's 1793 edition rather than Trumbull's expurgated version, in order to counter eastern doubts of the western hero's intellectual capacities.

In 1823 and 1824 the East-West-East pattern of influence which these works represent again focused in New York, in an edition of the Boone narrative published by "C. Wilder." Wilder brought together in a single pamphlet the John Trumbull text of the Boone narrative (from the Norwich, 1786, edition), a fragment of an admiring treatise on the Indians from Metcalf's anthology of frontier heroics, a contrasting editorial condemnation of Boone's character as "Indian-like," and Byron's eulogy of Boone. Wilder's edition thus presented within a single volume the several traditional strains of national and sectional interpretation of the myth without attempting to integrate them. By juxtaposing all the versions of the myth — from Byron's Romantic Boone to Wilder's racially degenerated Boone — the New York editor in effect formulated it as a literary and cultural problem. In this form it became a source for more probing questions about the character of the frontier hero and for literary examinations which were intended to replace sectional prejudices with a true national vision of the American frontier. Ultimately, Wilder's edition became an important source for Cooper and Simms, whose novels sought to unify and reconcile the conflicting traditions. Simms devoted his efforts to making the Boone myth amenable to the emerging world view of the slaveholding South.

From this general pattern of circulation,[1] certain patterns of cultural interaction between the sections are discernible. The axis and the West seem to have engaged in a constant exchange of literature on Boone and the West: the axis cities acted as a middleman or cultural broker between the sections and ultimately nurtured the publication of works which combined and integrated the views of all the sections. The South's dialogue with the West was conducted primarily through the axis during most of the nineteenth century. After the West itself, the literary presses of the axis had the most ready access to literature derived directly from the oral mythology of the frontiersmen — works like Hall's sketches and the later tales of McClung (1832) and Flint (1833). The influence of European Romantics, especially during the early years of the nineteenth century, was weakest in the West because of that section's immersion in the realities of the wilderness and the natural difficulties which impeded the distribution of books in the area. Not until 1819, with the publication of the *Western Review* by Boston-born W. G. Hunt, was a systematic effort made to acquaint western readers with Scott and Byron.

The South's literary ties to Europe had always been close, and upper-class southern writers like Byrd of Virginia and Cook of Maryland had taken English poets and novelists for their models, while their New England brethren were working the vein of their own seventeenth-century Puritan sermon-form and personal narrative. Since literature there was more the pastime of an elite class than a popular one, the South did not develop a popular periodical press of the kind prevalent in New England and later in the Northwest. Thus the South lacked that background of quasi-literary, protomythological personal narratives that was the seed ground of literature in the Northeast and West. The differences are discernible in the works of Dwight and Bryan. Even though the New Englander was working with reference to European models, the books of his poem took on the traditional genre forms of New England popular literature — the captivity and Indian war narratives and the sermon. Bryan too had European models, but he had no American ones. Hence *The Mountain Muse* was a more consistent imitation of traditional epic narrative poetry as practiced by Milton and Scott. Although Bryan could only ape his models ill, he was more dependent on them than was Dwight.

For the southerner, imitation of English narrative poetry and later the historical romance was second nature. Southern writers turned to European writers and adopted their literary forms as the primary vehicles of their imaginative writing about the frontier, or else they eschewed fiction altogether and wrote histories. For the easterner and later the western writer there were intermediate forms, partway between history and fiction — short narrative forms that enabled a writer to turn experience into instant literature. In these spontaneous literary outbursts, the writer's imaginative reconstruction of an event was relatively free of the conventional restrictions of plot and characterization, and thus hidden emotions and the patterns of archetypal myths often emerged with surprising clarity.

The northeastern states had long had a native printing and bookselling trade and had early developed a market for popular fiction. A strong and distinct literary tradition had, as we have seen, developed in this section even before independence — a tradition sustained primarily by quasifictional personal narratives written for the local audience. Works in this tradition derived from a speedy transmutation of an actual event in the wilderness into literature and myth. The growth of Philadelphia and New York into the printing-distribution axis of America made the Northeast the literary marketplace and clearinghouse of the nation. The South, during the Colonial period, had lacked a native literary press and audience and tended to depend on the London presses for the publication of its own literary works. London was also the chief source of its literary readings, and its preferred authors were European. For these reasons, and because of the low literacy rate relative to New England, the South did not develop the plant or the audience capable of sustaining a popular literary press and developing a distinct literary tradition independent of European literary concerns. The West, where printing and bookselling were trades of recent origin, depended on two sources for its literature. The first source was the eastern presses. The second, which became increasingly important during the nineteenth century, was the popular journals and newssheets published in various large western towns, which drew on the oral traditions of the frontiersmen to fill their pages with sensational tales and sketches. These strong oral traditions, the folk myths of the frontiersmen, were thus translated into print before their heroes were dead and with only the briefest of gaps between the ostensible occurrence of each mythic event and its recording.

Western Versions of the Myth

The emergence of western writers in the 1820s and 1830s, coinciding with the West's emergence as a political and economic power in the nation, is perhaps the most important literary event of the period. It added a new viewpoint to the traditional controversy between Europeans of the Buffon-Raynal or Rousseauistic schools and eastern proponents of the myth of the American farmer. The effect is comparable to that of Indian fighter Benjamin Church's entrance into the lists of Puritan literature, setting the point of view of an active frontiersman against the secondhand histories of the townbred clergy. The difference is in the scale of literary events: Church contributed a single book, while the western writers of the 1820s and 1830s filled popular periodicals, anthologies, pamphlets, and books in every section of the country with western material. Like Dwight in the 1790s, they were highly conscious of their national and sectional distinctiveness vis-à-vis Europe and the effete East. Although they began by imitating eastern writers in both form and attitude, a distinct western viewpoint gradually emerged.

Daniel Boone's reaction to Bryan's *Mountain Muse* suggests the prevalent western attitude toward literature. Boone is reported to have told a visitor that such productions "ought to be left till the [subject] was put in the ground" and that he deeply regretted he "could not sue [the author] for slander." [2] His reaction would have been shared by most Kentuckians. The language of the poem was affected, highfalutin, and the depiction of the West bore no resemblance to reality. Like the Puritan literary censors, the western public wanted "realism" along with its sensational tales of violence and bravery.

Like the South, the West lacked a body of published literature treating the frontier in terms of a distinct set of traditional symbols and attitudes. Unlike the South, however, the West had only loose connections with the printers and poets of Europe. European books reached the West only after passing through the New York–Philadelphia axis, and western authors had always gone to the axis, rather than to Europe, to seek publication in the days before literary printing began in the Ohio Valley. Whatever literary ties the West had, bound it to the literature of the Northeast, where the Romantic influence was diluted by Yankee skepticism and Puritan symbolism. The literary background of western writers like Hall and Flint was derived from eastern sources, and western writers with ideas of reaching a national public kept the eastern audience in mind. The closeness of the nineteenth-century westerners to the early pioneers and to the remnants of the primitive wilderness and Indian tribes also augmented their disinclination for Romantic fantasies about their section.

These circumstances made for a strong vein of realism as well as uncritical admiration in the oral mythology that grew up in the West around pioneers like Boone. This oral tradition did not envision heroes wrapped in the "solemn stole of Contemplation" or enraptured with Romantic "fancies." Westerners admired men of action and prowess, men who knew how to live like Indians, fight like Indians, think like Indians, and take scalps like Indians. A real hero was one who could beat the Indians at their own game, live on less food, kill more animals, and even take more scalps. This is not to say that the westerners saw themselves as barbarians, devoid of all interest in establishing a stable civilization. (Trumbull and his readers admired the Puritan fathers, without wishing for a return to the rule of the old ministers and magistrates.) The environment of the wilderness had made it essential for men to imitate the Indians in order to survive and build. If some of the founding fathers of the West were renowned chiefly for their skill in destroying trees, men, and game, others were respected for their skills in settlement-building and lawmaking.

Just as the demise of the northeastern tribes had led to the romanticization of the leading figures of the colonial wars, so was there a noticeable shift in the development of later legends as the West became more fully settled and the worst days of the Indian troubles passed. New England legends had focused on the drama of the captive, the civilizer, and the vanishing noble red man, but Western mythmakers gave greater prominence to the hunters and fighters than to the less violent heroes. These men were the unique property of the West, symbolic of her sectional distinction. The

East was the land of the lawyer and the merchant; the West was home to
the crack shot, the hunter and Indian fighter. This vision of western distinctiveness was eventually embodied in the song "Hunters of Kentucky"
(1822), which won the West for Andrew Jackson in 1828 and confirmed a
symbolic unity of interest between the frontiersmen and the reform-
minded "radical" classes of the East.

Literary printing in the West began before the cult of the hunter replaced the worship of the pioneer gentry in the oral mythology of the section. The earliest literary periodicals — the *Western Monthly Review*, the
Western Monthly Magazine, and W. G. Hunt's *Western Review* — were
section-conscious in their choice of materials and their advocacy of specific
political and economic policies.[3] Hunt's magazine most accurately
reflected the temper of the time in its blend of literary miscellanies from
European reviews and novels, practical essays on farming, and accounts of
the Indian wars written by participants. Hunt was an easterner from Boston and a prominent publisher in Lexington, Kentucky, and Cincinnati.
Around him gathered many of the intellectual leaders of the West, including Horace Holley, president of Transylvania College, and Samuel L. Metcalf, or Metcalfe, a noted chemist and editor of a volume of Indian war
narratives. Hunt's magazine brought the tales of the frontiersmen into
print for the first time, and Metcalf's anthology collected many of these in
convenient book form.[4] Together these works constituted the first systematic attempt to bring the oral legends into literature. Like the Puritan personal narratives, these were more or less factual accounts. With such material as this circulating among his friends and neighbors, with the actual
heroes living within visiting distance, the western reader did not need the
trappings of poetry or fiction to make the tales seem real. Where the southern interpretation of Boone grew out of the Romantic fantasies of Bryan,
the western versions grew (like the earlier Puritan versions) out of the oral
tradition and the early personal narratives, such as those collected by Metcalf.

Samuel Metcalf (1798–1856) compiled his anthology while finishing
his medical studies at Transylvania College. He called his book *A Collection of Some of the Most Interesting Narratives of Indian Warfare in the
West* and drew his accounts primarily from the pages of the *Western Review* and Trumbull's *Discovery of America*. The featured item in the collection was Filson's Boone narrative, supposedly the most considerable
piece of writing by any Indian fighter. Metcalf reprinted the whole of Filson's original text, probably from one of the remaining copies brought west
by Filson in 1785 or from an edition of Imlay's *Topographical Description*

(New York, 1793). The narrative therefore stood out from the other anec-dotes, both as a literary performance and as a character sketch of the mind of the West. The only comparable entry was Col. James Smith's sympa-thetic treatise on the Indians, and this account was later attributed to Boone in pirated versions of Metcalf's text.

Metcalf's introduction marks him as one of the admirers of the "civi-lized" rather than the "hunter" hero. He frequently echoes Filson and Imlay in his admiration for the growing civilization and refinement of Ken-tucky: "Where lately stood a few dismal, smoky cabins, surrounded by woods and cane brakes, are now to be seen fertile fields, flourishing or-chards, blooming gardens, elegant and commodious cities, houses, popu-lous and refined cities." He disclaims all evil intentions toward the Indians and pleads for tolerance and understanding of their plight. Above all, he insists on the authenticity of his sources: "Nearly all the facts have been furnished by persons who were immediately concerned in the transactions which they described." [5]

The search for a sectional identity, however, turned the literary ac-complishment of Metcalf's Boone into a handicap. Boone was distin-guished from his fellow Indian fighters in the anthology by the superiority of "his" literary style and intellectual sophistication. The West demanded an image of its average man, its common man, its typical character. To the extent that he seemed more sophisticated, more intellectually aristocratic, Boone was unsuitable as a frontier culture-hero. The religious revival that swept the West and made it the source of a national religious revival was largely responsible for western antiintellectualism. Between 1821 and 1827 Horace Holley fought and lost his battle to keep Transylvania College in-tellectually liberal. In his study *The Frontier Mind*, Arthur K. Moore calls his defeat the West's symbolic "rejection of Athens," the city of philoso-phers, as its ideal. This rejection was echoed in the rejection of Filson's Boone by western writers, who either denigrated Boone as a too fastidious "aristocrat" among frontiersmen or altered his character to remove all traces of the contemplative, sentimental, Filsonian philosopher.

These trends in western thinking did not fully mature until the 1830s, but by 1822–25 the alteration in the western vision of Boone began to be apparent. In 1819 Judge James Hall of Illinois began publishing a series of "Letters from the West" in his newspaper office at Shawneetown. In 1822 he was invited by the publishers of the *Port-Folio*, a literary periodical in the axis city of Philadelphia, to become a regular contributor. Among the letters published by the *Port-Folio* was a sketch of Daniel Boone, drawn from Filson's account and reworked in accordance with Hall's own views on western character. This letter and others written for the series were eventually published as a book in London in 1828.[6]

Hall's views of the West were shaped by his desire to please both his own western audience and the literary audiences of the East. As a westerner he wanted to portray the West with absolute realism, faithful to both fact and spirit; at the same time, he coveted a literary reputation in the cities of the East and Europe. He was skillful or fortunate enough to achieve a little of both. His western stories and sketches were popular in the East because of his touches of Romanticism and in the West for the occasional realism with which he depicted western badmen like the Harpes. In *Letters from the West* he was chiefly concerned with defining the distinctive characteristics of the westerner through portraits of types. Rough boatmen, pioneers, hunters, generals, and Indians were all sketched with relative accuracy.

Letter 15, titled "The National Character," paradoxically consists of an elaborate differentiation between the character types of the various sections of the country. The first Americans had a distinct character, says Hall, which they derived from Britain; but life in various sections has altered the manners and appearance of the original stock, and the only common trait retained is that of patriotic opposition to Britain and all other rival powers. In New England "the soil is not rich and the population is dense. The mass of the people are, of course, laborious, close and frugal." They are usually moral and upright family men, but they are given to *"Yankee tricks"* and are "up to every thing." In Virginia the character of the people changes: "Most of the gentlemen are *born gentlemen;* they are wealthy, and receive liberal educations; from their cradles they despise money, because they are not in the habit of seeing those with whom they associate actively engaged in the pursuit of it." Slavery gives them leisure to cultivate their minds and indulge their sentiments and enables them to enjoy the pleasures of life and to be princely in their hospitality.[7] The western character owes much to the Virginian, since most of Kentucky's settlers came from the Old Dominion.

But these sectional characters, Hall asserts, are not fixed or immutable. Removed from his home to the West, the American of New England or Virginia adjusts; his spiritual resilience, martial disposition, and physical strength enable him to grow up to the requirements of the new land. His manners change, Yankee and Cavalier qualities blending together, and he becomes a devotee of honor and hospitality while retaining his characteristic American faith in liberty and hard work. Thus the West is the ground on which the essential qualities of the American character emerge from the crust of habit and custom built up in the more settled East.

Hall chooses Filson's Boone as representative of the western character. In Letter 16 he sketches Boone as "the chief . . . individual of a class peculiar to the United States," the "Back-woodsman." In Hall's account, Boone is born in the rich and peaceful country of the East, where the path to quick riches is both broad and easy. Unlike the frugal New Englander or the luxurious planter, Boone disdains monetary gains. He goes west for the pure love of adventure and excitement and revels in the exercise of his skill and the discovery of new lands. As devoid of selfishness as of softness, he depends on no arm but his own for sustenance:

> The first settlers of this country . . . were men whose object was not gain, but who appeared to have been allured by the very difficulties which discouraged others. . . . The American who takes a retrospective view of the early history of his country, must regard with admiration the sturdy woodsman, who, as the pioneer of civilization, . . . made smooth the road for others; but he will find him an isolated being, professing tastes and habits of his own, and voluntarily supporting hardships, peril, and privation, without the usual incentives or the ordinary rewards of courage.[8]

Hall's Boone symbolically turns his back on a civilization which, as Hall himself suggests, is a veritable Golden Age of agricultural plenty and abundant wealth. His values are not those of his eastern forbears; they are unique. He loves the wilderness for its wildness, the danger for the joy of overcoming it. "Boon himself [is] the very prince of hunters," exalted above the speculators and half-savage renegades who follow in his footsteps by the purity of his motives. Although he lives apart from civilization's Golden Age, he is an exemplar of heroic virtue reminiscent of classical epic heroes. Although he flees the society of the East, he carries his wife and family with him to provide the amenities of human society. Moreover, his wife is a true daughter of the wilderness, able to share her husband's enjoyment of the West and to make her own way through its dangers:

> If many of the heroes of Greece and Rome, derived immortal fame from a single act of heroism, how much more does Boon deserve it, whose whole life presents a series of adventures of the same character . . . ? Nor did he suffer and conquer alone; his wife accompanied him to the wilderness and shared his dangers; during his captivity . . . she returned with her family to her father's house in North Carolina, braving the toil and perils of a journey through a wilderness of immeasurable extent and gloom.[9]

)

In Hall's portrait Rebecca Boone finally receives her due. She is the symbol of the civilization of the new West, as Caroline was Imlay's symbol of refined European culture and Mrs. Rowlandson of imperiled Puritan virtue.

Hall's own desire for recognition in the literary capitals of the East led him gradually away from his early attempts at realism. His sketch of Boone appeared in the *Western Magazine* in Cincinnati in 1833, as did his *Sketches of History, Life and Manners in the West* in 1834 and 1835. Both works, however, were purportedly objective studies of history and not works of literature. In the *Sketches* Hall remained faithful to his original characterization of Boone as the type of the common man of the West: "He was [not] an eccentric man, nor did he stand in a class by himself. His character and adventures are studied and admired . . . because he was a complete and admirable specimen of [his] class." But even here a hint of Hall's preoccupation with the literary values of the East intrudes with his assertion that "the adventures of these bold explorers are full of romantic interest." [10]

Although his native Cincinnati was well on the way to becoming a major publishing center for the West at this time, Hall went to Philadelphia to have his fiction collected in book form — a clear indication of his desire to reach an eastern as well as a western audience. In his short story "The Backwoodsman," he blended romantic themes and motifs with a few touches of "authentic Frontieriana." The tale, which recounts the kidnapping of a young maiden by Indians and her rescue by a figure who is certainly Daniel Boone, opens at a camp meeting in one of the settled districts of the West. Thus the tale begins squarely in the midst of the distinctive civilization of the West during a "peculiarly Western" religious ceremony, the camp revival. To underscore the characteristic nature of the revival, Hall injects a bit of humorous western dialect (in patronizing italics): "It took a *powerful chance of truck* to feed such a *heap of folks.*" He loyally defends the superior virtue of his section by saying of the camp meeting: "It was thus our first parents worshipped their Creator in Paradise, and thus the early Christians assembled in groves and secluded places." [11] But he emphasizes the "picturesque" quality of the spot, rather than its austere harshness, and his worshipers are not harrowed and "slain" by preachers of hell and damnation. Instead, the scenery makes their hearts "romantic," their minds "elevated and refined." Having thus interpreted the revival meeting in terms of Romantic conventions, he can appeal to those same conventions in describing his hero and heroine: "It is unnecessary to inform the erudite reader that the young lady, who was just turned seventeen, was beautiful and interesting, and her lover tall and handsome." Needless to say, during her captivity, "her bodily afflictions were light in comparison with the gloomy anticipations of her mind." [12]

Her rescuer is Daniel Boone, but a Boone adapted to the tastes of Hall's eastern audience. He repeats the major characteristics first sketched by Filson: the contemplativeness of Boone's nature, his contentment with simple things, his amiable disposition, his love of the wilderness, and his enjoyment of the companionship of friends and family at the hearthside. The only alteration offered by Hall is "an archness . . . about the eye, which showed that its possessor was not deficient in humour" — a quality conspicuously lacking in Filson's original. Yet even this trait is rather a reflection of Leatherstocking's rustic irony than the broad humor of later western heroes. Hall's eastern Boone is not, however, the same lover of wildness and excitement that was offered in *Letters from the West*. This new Boone seeks the wilderness "in the same spirit in which the philosopher retires to the seclusion of his closet." [13] He seeks knowledge and the solitude necessary to philosophic meditation, rather than adventure. Nature is, not his loving adversary, but a metaphorical book from which he reads intellectual and moral abstractions:

> [He came to Kentucky] to enjoy unmolested the train of his own reflections, and to follow without interruption a pursuit congenial with his nature. Though unacquainted with books, he had perused certain parts of the great volume of nature with diligent attention . . . and without having any knowledge of the philosophy of schools, he had formed for himself a system which has the merit of being often true, and always original.[14]

Hall, like Filson and others before and after him, thus attempted to reassure Europe and the East that the wild woodsmen of the West learned nothing harmful in the woods and, indeed, became better and more Christian citizens, not outlaws and white Indians. Their religion was not pagan but, rather, like that of Adam and Eve or the primitive Christians; and if their philosophy of life was, like Boone's, distinctive and original, it was still "true," that is, free of moral error and evil result. But eastern opponents of the "new men" of the West in politics and economics were not convinced by Hall, nor were western audiences sympathetic to his well-scrubbed Boone. The gentleman-philosopher image did not jibe with the reality of western life or with the self-image which westerners coveted for themselves.

John A. McClung's *Sketches of Western Adventure* (Maysville, Kentucky; 1832) measures Boone by the standards of a self-identified westerner — standards in which the virtues of the gentleman-philosopher do not figure at all. McClung's standards were those of his audience, and throughout the text he keeps those standards before his readers by means of a running argument with eastern interpretations of frontier character. This points up his own presumed fidelity to sectional values and styles. McClung presents the West as the realm of violent adventure, in which a man's courage, prowess, and intelligence are proven in a struggle for survival against the wilderness and the savages. His aesthetic theory demanded "realism" (or at least a semblance of it), fidelity to historical truth, a wealth of exciting incident, and an accurate and sympathetic portrayal of the characters of real frontiersmen. He demanded little in the way of characterization of individual Indians but insisted that the race be treated with due attention to its savagery and treachery as the great antagonist of his frontier heroes. He declares his admiration for Cooper's *Last of the Mohicans* because it presents "a minute detail of *all the circumstances*" of its hero's adventures; but he scorns the "extraneous" plot material, the scenery descriptions, and the Romantic treatment of the Indians.

McClung's portrait of Boone presents him as a man of action rather than thought, a man of simple rather than subtle speech, a participant in thrilling combats rather than a sensitive landscape-painter. He ridicules Filson's portrait of Boone for its overemphasis on Boone's sensitive reactions to the landscape, and he terms those descriptions "gaudy and ambitious sketches of *scenery* which swell the bulk of the piece" and "neither excite . . . nor gratify curiosity." Filson is condemned for having done scant justice to his material, creating an artificial "barrenness of incident" in a career filled with exciting adventures. No amount of "flashy description" can compensate for this obscuring of the truth. If the reader finds his own treatment "dull," says McClung, he may blame Filson.[15]

In purifying and westernizing Filson's Boone, McClung emphasizes Boone's passion for hunting, solitude, and excitement. Where Filson's Boone was sensitive to the natural order in the wild beauty of the forest, where the Romantics' Boone admired its picturesqueness, McClung's Boone chiefly delights in the absence of all touches of order and civilization. He enjoys his loneliness and the hardships and dangers of the land: "The wild and solitary grandeur of the country around him, where not a tree had been cut nor a house erected, was to him an inexhaustible source of admiration and delight; and he says himself that some of the most rapturous moments of his life were spent in these lonely rambles [although] he sometimes lay in canebrakes, without fire, and heard the yells of the Indians around him." [16]

McClung admired in Boone, Simon Kenton, and other heroes of the *Sketches* all those qualities which southern, eastern, and European writers emphasized when they sought to portray the frontiersman as the foe of civilization. Just as Hall emphasized the absence of all traces of eastern commercialism from his portrait of Boone, so McClung sought to disparage Boone's pretentions to philosophic insight or literary accomplishment. Let the hunter stick to his rifle and tell only true stories of his hairbreadth escapes; leave literature to the dudes, who come to dress rough truth in the trappings of spurious poetry. McClung actually condemns Boone for falling victim to the literary blandishments of the East, mocks his literary interest and desire for fame in the East as unworthy of his hunter's vocation. He compares Boone, the strong champion of the West, to Samson, shorn of his strength by the artful temptations of an effeminate civilization: "The written account of his life was the Delilah of his imagination. The idea of 'seeing his name in print,' completely overcame the cold philosophy of his general manner, and he seemed to think it a masterpiece of composition." [17] McClung's own admiration, as the rest of the text makes clear, was reserved for men who read less and took more scalps.

McClung's interpretation was undeniably popular. Western audiences admired the prowess of his bold and sometimes bloodthirsty heroes, seeing in them a confirmation of the vigor and skill of their section. Eastern audiences appreciated the sensational narratives and could also read in them confirmation of their own conception of the westerner as a man of rough habits and violent disposition. The book was first published in Cincinnati, the chief publication-distribution center in the Ohio Valley, in 1832. It was also issued in the same year in Maysville, Kentucky, and in Philadelphia, which still shared honors with New York as the literary publishing capital of the East. A fourth edition appeared that same year in Dayton, Ohio. Subsequent editions appeared in Maysville in 1836, 1839, and 1844 and in Cincinnati in 1836 and 1839. Thus the book enjoyed a wide circulation, its nine editions being issued in the most important publishing center of the West, the second most important in the East, and two additional cities in the West.

The West's preference for the image of Boone the hunter over Boone the philosopher is not difficult to understand. The West was preeminently the land of opportunity for men on the make. Boone himself had seen the West in these terms when he carved out a baronial land grant for himself and speculated unsuccessfully in land. Everything in the West was a commodity or a resource — something that could be mined, cultivated, or exploited for profit. A farmer could leave bad land for good and settle a few western acres long enough to make a few crops; then, if the soil were depleted or the market for a cash crop fell, he could sell out and move on. Land could be "farmed" without a plow by a speculator clever enough to buy it cheaply before the rush of emigration came. Trees were timber; animals were hide, tallow, and meat; and in the Southwest, Negroes were livestock rather than men.

Behind the economic motives and aspirations of the westerners were more subtle impulses of fear and of hope. Like the Puritans they conceived of their movement to a new land as a means of achieving a new life, in a spiritual as well as an economic sense. The revival spirit was strong in the West, as it had been in New England in the seventeenth century and the Great Awakening. Like the Puritans, the western emigrants feared the changes that their new environment might induce and the dark impulses it might discover within them. They feared the unfamiliar surroundings; the threat of Indians; the thick, encumbering woods that isolated them from their past and their kind. However, they differed from the Puritans in some crucial respects, not the least of which was their possession of a store of historical knowledge, derived through legend and literature, of the experiences of their predecessors in the wilderness, which provided precedents for their life in the forest that their ancestors had lacked. More crucial than this was the belief of the new frontiersmen that their own individual prowess, their associated power, and the efficacy of their time-perfected technological gear (axe and rifle) made them able to contest with the forces of the natural wilderness as an equal antagonist.

The growth of this confidence is the central theme of the evolution of the literature of human frontier heroes out of the Puritan literature of human subjection to God and natural forces. The conditions of survival in the wilderness and the terrors of settlement there had changed little, but the response of the settlers to the terror and the promise of the wilderness had changed greatly. The consequences of this development were every bit as disastrous for the Indians and forests of the new West as for the old Puritan frontier, but the motives of destruction differed. Where the Puritan cleared the country in the name of converting heathendom to an exemplary Christian commonwealth, the heirs of Daniel Boone did the same in the name of "getting ahead" (or merely "getting on") and of self-realization through the prideful display of individual prowess and independence of social or other external restraints. They turned on the woods and its creatures with violence, destroying that which they had come to save from barbarism and to bring under cultivation. Trees were hewed down for the sake of destruction; animals were hunted for the pride of destruction as much as the lust for profit. Indeed, the two emotions went hand in hand: the hunter and the western entrepreneur, the man-on-the-make, were essentially the same in their attitude toward the world and their fellows. Both relied on material success on a massive scale to prove the power of their manhood in a threatening world. The speculator proved his value by engrossing more profitable land than his competitor; the hunter, by killing more beasts or cutting down more trees than any three men in the county. The first felt that he had demonstrated his superiority to the poverty of his origins, the second that he had asserted his power over the obstacles put in his way by nature.

The reality of this link between the spirit of the free hunter and that of the speculating protocapitalist can be verified by examining the careers of the legendary Mountain Men, those semibarbaric figures who cut a swath in the popular literature of the nineteenth century. They were usually viewed by the fastidious as filthy white Indians and by the romantic as an heroic, but only temporarily free, alternative to the money-and-status society of the East. Yet the hard evidence indicates that the Mountain Men shared the Jacksonian passion for upward mobility and self-transcendence through capitalist endeavor: "many Mountain Men lived for the chance to exchange their dangerous mountain careers for an advantageous start in civilized life." A study of the careers of 446 Mountain Men (45 percent of the total) reveals that only 5 remained trappers until retirement (182 were killed at the work). Of the 154 whose subsequent careers are fully known, all adopted "civilized" careers, ranging from the somewhat arcadian careers of farmer and rancher to the more urban careers of politician, artisan or mechanic, shopkeeper, and the like. (One became a horse thief, a far more social occupation than trapping, since it requires neighbors.) [18] Thus the Mountain Man was, not an alternative to the money-and-status religion of Jacksonian America, but an idiosyncratic and extreme expression of its values.

The sectional character of the western hero is in fact a radical departure in *style* and *mode* of economic operation, which conceals a basic affirmation of social values widely (if not universally) held by the rest of the nation. This does not diminish the significance of the differences in sectional myths, where divergences of style and imagery reflect real differences in sectional self-images, political attitudes, and approaches to economic activity. It does in part explain the national popularity achieved by sectional and even "local color" heroes in a time of intersectional political rivalry; and it illustrates the role of myth as a way of expressing a national ideology in locally accepted terms.

The most perfect embodiment of the western "style" was Col. David Crockett of Tennessee, a frontier hero of indubitable backwoods origin, whose national reputation was manufactured by Whig politicians to offset the appeal of the Democrats' "Old Hickory" Jackson. Crockett learned, like the fictional Simon Suggs, that it was "good to be shifty in a new country." [19] His early years were spent wandering from farm to farm on the frontier, with intervals of militia service, Indian fighting, speculation, and hunting. He had a gift for gab that opened politics up for him as a potential field of speculation, and he answered the Whig desire for a figure who could offset Jackson's claim to represent the westerner and (by association) the common man. For a while, the image worked so well that Crockett was a presidential possibility. He doomed himself when he stepped out of character, opposing Jackson on bills dear to the western heart, such as Indian removal.

The sources of the Crockett myth are difficult to unravel. In one sense he is a product of the eastern stereotype of the frontiersman as lowbrow and clown. In another he is clearly a product of western popular literature — a clown whose apparent simplicity masks a cleverness that is superior to city wit and a human sensitivity more profound than the effusive sentimentality of the city, for all its being concealed under a bantering, ironic manner. Crockett (or his ghost writer) portrays the colonel's eccentricities and pursuits as examples of the highest heroic virtues and, at the same time, emphasizes that Crockett is the representative man of his section.

Crockett's life, as he presents it in *A Narrative of the Life of Col. David Crockett* (Philadelphia, 1834), is a sequence of exploits in which he gradually grows from poor frontier farmer to war hero to successful politician to successful speculator to successful hunter. His failures are also exploits — chances for him to demonstrate his resilience, his ability to resist the hard knocks and scramble back to his feet. His vocations of hunter, politician, and speculator blend into one another until they seem different phases of the same quest, the same picaresque movement from the bottom to the top of the social heap. After a successful trapping season, he comes to town to sell his peltry, passes a few words with some local politicians, and is immediately drafted for the legislature. Between political campaigns he engages in a successful lumber speculation and, without pause for breath, embarks on an epic bear hunt. It is in the bear hunt that he is most himself. Politics and business do not involve as much of his passion or his talent, since they do not provide the same opportunity for concrete engagement with an antagonist. In the bear hunt the forces opposing him, keeping him from his desires, become tangible. They can be met in direct, open combat and vanquished. The triumph is more satisfying because the struggle is physical rather than cerebral, and the slain bear is more tangible and permanent evidence of his prowess than any set of paper profits or votes on a tally sheet. The source of Crockett's satisfaction with politics lies in his association of vote-getting and hunting, as when he belabors the metaphor of the canvass as a bear or "coon" hunt.[20]

Crockett dwells with great pleasure on the act of killing itself, the moment in which he has most clearly asserted his power over the beasts of the forest:

> I pursued on, but my other hunters . . . killed the bear before I got up with him. I gave him to them, and cut out again for a creek called Big Clover, which wa'n't very far off. Just as I got there, and was entering a cane brake, my dogs all broke and went ahead. . . . I listened awhile and found my dogs was in two companies, and that both was in a snorting fight. I sent my little son to one and I broke for t'other. I got to mine first, and found my dogs had a two-year-old bear down, a-wooling away on him, so I just took out my big butcher, and went up and slap'd it into him, and killed him without shooting. . . . In a short time, I heard my little son fire at his bear; when I went to him he had killed it too. . . . We pushed on . . . and . . . found that we had a still larger bear than either of them we had killed, treed by himself. We killed that one also, which made three we had killed in less than half an hour. . . .[21]

Sheer quantity comes to delight the colonel, for once the repeated killing is done, he has only the bears' bodies as testimony to his deeds. The "105 bears" are neither more nor less to him than the profits he realizes (or attempts to realize) on his lumber and other business speculations, or the votes he garners as he "stalks" the hustings. They are quantifiable indicators of the degree of his prowess, symbols of great deeds of skill. Women — those Puritan symbols of Christian values and civilization — play no ameliorating role in Crockett's universe. His wives (he had three) do not figure prominently in his narrative; they appear chiefly as conquests of a hunt, as do bearskins, votes, and a powerful reputation in the community.

The implications of the Crockett figure were fully elaborated in the writings of the "southwestern humorists," a group of popular writers who devoted their works to the delineation of the character and life-style of the denizens of the southern Appalachian and trans-Appalachian frontier. Their works pretend to realism in their preoccupation with the low life of the settlements, their scruffiness of appearance, the queer cracker-dialect spoken by the inhabitants, and the rude manners and base concerns of the people, whose primary aims in life seem to be fighting, getting drunk, and swindling or befooling their neighbors or visiting "dudes." The attitude of these writers toward their subjects is simultaneously patronizing and admiring. They recognize rudeness when they see it, being (like the respected reader) men of literacy and feeling; yet they are also struck by the simple force of their heroes' characters and by the tremendous skill with which they conduct their worldly business.

In works of this genre — works like A. B. Longstreet's *Georgia Scenes* (1835), G. W. Harris's Sut Lovingood stories (collected in 1867), and Johnson Jones Hooper's *Some Adventures of Captain Simon Suggs* (1846) — the confidence game is so often played by the hero that it becomes his self-defining activity and a metaphor for all forms of social (and, as Melville's *The Confidence-Man* suggests, metaphysical) transactions. The hunter-prey drama is enacted within a social framework in which the clever hero "euchres" a dupe, playing upon his ignorance or on the vainglory of his dreams and ambitions. Typical targets are fops and pretentious tenderfeet, preachers, schoolteachers, sheriffs, the hero's own father, and local men of property — all symbols of respectability, social position, and authority whom the hero's skill sets at naught.[22] On the other hand, the hero is glad to take advantage of the credulity he finds among the wretched of the earth, chiefly poor farmers, Negroes, and Indians.[23] Only occasionally does he meet a fellow swindler whose powers are equal to his own, and their confrontation becomes an exercise in virtuosity.[24] The hero who, in one incident, stands for the power of the skilled individual to transcend and defy the limitations of social class and order is seen, in the next, engaged in bilking the already bilked and dispossessing the already dispossessed.

The paradox of social values inherent in the southwestern hero's behavior is matched by the contradiction in his creator's (and his audience's) attitude toward him. The tone of the stories is at once patronizing and genuinely fascinated. Distance is established between the hero and the author, whose language reflects higher social position, yet there is an effort to explain and even justify the hero's crudeness of manner as directness or pithiness born of hard experience.

Both the social and the stylistic paradoxes of the southwestern heroes can be resolved if we recognize that the language of the confidence man is an exaggerated and stylistically eccentric version of the more respectable languages of American commercial expansionism — the "Language of Anticipation," as Daniel Boorstin calls it, of the "Boosters" and land promoters engaged in western development; the language of speculation; the language of the Jacksonian men-on-the-make, arguing against the dear-money policies of the Bank of the United States and the creditor classes and for a loose, expansive, mobile currency; the language of Manifest Destiny used to persuade the nation of the necessity of imperial expansion.[25] The aura of the free hunter which surrounds Crockett, Suggs, and Lovingood makes romantic and palatable the essentially commercial and exploitive character of their ambitions and activities, just as the Indian trappings of the Mountain Man concealed his essentially Jacksonian character. The southwestern hero's ethic is the hunter's: get what you can from the territory, then move on, relying on the bounty of nature to repair the waste of timber or game and to provide those who have been defrauded with the opportunity to renew their fortunes.

But however similar in economic motive the commercialism of the Crocketts and Suggses might be to that of northern capitalists like the Vanderbilts and Southern new-rich planters like Jefferson Davis's family, they differed in political aims and methods according to the economic development and mythology of their sections. The patronizing tone taken by the writers of southwestern tales toward their heroes was a device for defusing and denigrating the threat to older vested interests implicit in the rise of the western states to economic power and political consciousness. Indeed, it was the Whig opposition to Jackson that gave birth to the stereotypical southwestern hero, Davy Crockett; and Hooper's *Some Adventures of Captain Simon Suggs* begins with a barbed comparison of Jackson and Satan.[26] However, the same work might serve in the West as a defiant satire on easterners and eastern manners (a literary echo of Jackson's "war" on the Bank of the United States), and the images of western scruffiness might be glossed as a mannered and deliberate inversion of eastern values. Certainly the image of the westerner conveyed by the Crockett-Suggs type of story is identical with that painted by Talleyrand of the frontiersman as an insensate boor, incapable of seeing anything more in a grove of trees than an opportunity to cut down more of them in an hour than his neighbor. Like Talleyrand, American writers of conservative sympathies (like Fenimore Cooper) associated this type of western hero with demagogic politics, Jacobinism, philistinism, savage anarchy, and disrespect for social position and private property.[27] In the West the same type of hero — common in origin and speech, materialistic, and skilled in all the arts of hunting and speculative economics — was presented as the quintessential representative of local spirit and virtu.

Timothy Flint: The Indian Kinship
of the Western Hero

In developing their myths of the hunter, writers of both the West and the East stumbled on the dilemma inherent in traditional interpretations of that necessary symbol, the Indian. Since Puritan times, the Indian had been associated with precisely those traits of character that now composed the virtues of the frontier hero: skill in woodcraft, independence of social restraint, crudeness of manner and origin, materialism, hostility to social order, and rebelliousness. With the gradual vanishing of the Indian populations east of the Appalachians, it became possible to romanticize the Indian as the noble savage and to employ him as a symbol of American libertarianism and independent patriotism. This romantic tendency did not in any substantive way alter the policy of the nation toward actual Indians, as the removal of the Cherokee from Georgia suggests; nor did it alter the fundamental conviction of the nation that the Indians were a race doomed by constitutional and institutional weaknesses to diminution, assimilation, extinction, and replacement by the civilization of the whites. In literary terms, however, it became possible for a writer like Cooper to transfer the burden of the negative "Indian" qualities from the red man to the common borderers and squatters — the vengeful, clannish Bush family in *The Prairie*, for example. In contrast Cooper's Indians, though doomed to extinction, are upright, moral, proud, and occasionally aristocratic.

For the western writer aiming at achieving a national recognition for himself, for his literary creation, and for the culture of his section, the problem was a complex one. He was cut off from the vocabulary of eastern romanticism, in which heroes might be identified with the symbolic noble savage, by the nature of his section's recent and continuing engagement with the task of despoiling and suppressing the Indians. He was likewise faced with the presumption that, as a man of the frontier, he and his heroes were quasi Indians themselves, embodying those negative qualities traditionally associated with Indians. The western writer logically had to reject the Indian as a model of his own character; but his chosen myth of the hunter pointed up the strong affinities between the red and white hunters of the West.

Given a choice between the effeminacy and incompetence of eastern dudes and the masculine prowess of the Indian, the westerners had chosen the latter. Their justification of this choice had, however, to be couched in terms that would effectively vitiate if not resolve the paradox of their attitude toward the Indian. Sut Lovingood and Simon Suggs suggest one method of handling it: they play their tricks on dudes and redskins alike, proving themselves superior to both. Or they achieve their fame by killing Indians, then use their achieved position to argue against the latter-day efforts at robbing the Indians of land or liberty — like Benjamin Church's resistance to the enslavement of surrendered Indians and Crockett's protest at the removal of the Cherokee. A more profound and basic method, which subsumes both the Suggs and the Crockett approaches, is that of defiantly converting the resemblance into a virtue, adopting as heroes men whose crude, boastful, materialistic manner is the very antithesis of eastern notions of heroic gentility. Like the Puritans and easterners of the early republic, westerners found it easiest to define their identity by setting themselves off against other groups, describing what they thought they were by satirically repudiating what they were not or by inverting the ostensible values of their cultural opponents.

The literary consequences of the westerners' attempt to find a nationally viable image of their sectional virtues can be seen in the writings of Timothy Flint and Benjamin Drake. Flint was a popular writer-journalist in Cincinnati, which had recently emerged from the status of frontier station to that of urban center. Like Hall, Flint was a self-appointed interpreter of the West to the East, and his early works were historical and geographic studies aimed at increasing the store of accurate information available about his section. Like Hall, he owed much to the literary and intellectual heritage of the East, having been educated for the ministry at Harvard.[28] His several treatments of the Boone legend were attempts at presenting the authentic virtues of the western character in terms that would be equally acceptable in Cincinnati and Philadelphia. Although he presents Boone as sympathetic to the Indian and enamored of the Indian life-style, he embeds this savage spirit within a character of essential gentleness, manifested as courtesy toward women and a refusal to indulge in excesses such as scalping. The qualities of character that easterners found threatening in their earlier ideas of the Indian and their current ideas of the Jacksonian westerner were ameliorated by abstraction. The Indian's and the confidence man's delight in sheer skill becomes, in Flint's portrayal of Boone, an instance of professionalism analogous to the disciplined delight of an artist or a preacher in his calling. The activities of the hero are firmly established in an historical setting (and thus limited in time). Various incidents are invested with an aura of mythic mystery and treated explicitly as legendary, which increases their evocative power and relevance to the traditions of other sections while defusing the social threat implicit in the image of the real contemporary westerner.

Flint treated the Boone myth directly in three works published between 1828 and 1833 in Cincinnati: a study of the geography and population of the Mississippi Valley, *Indian Wars of the West*, and *Biographical Memoir of Daniel Boone* — the last being the first full-dress biography of the hero. Flint drew on the available sources with a thoroughness not equaled by any predecessor. He mined newspaper files for incidents and first-person accounts of historical events, interviewed Boone's surviving family and friends, and gathered folk legends about Boone from the people of his section. It was Flint who first put into print the fire-hunt legend that is so crucial to any understanding of Boone as a myth-hero. In composing his books, Flint employed the conventional forms of western popular literature artfully. In *Indian Wars* his central theme is the conflict between Indians and whites and the adaptation of the whites to Indian ways. The book is a series of dramatic incidents linked by theme and common characters — in effect, an anthology of popular narratives and hero tales, put together in such a way that they seem a unified narrative. In the Boone biography the theme is that of a single representative man's development into a western hero through his pursuit of the art and religious discipline of hunting.

At the outset of *Indian Wars* Flint draws a sharp dividing line between the savages and the white frontiersmen. He admits that "the white borderers have too often been more savage, than the Indians themselves," and have often committed "aggression" upon the Indians. But viewing the whole of western history, he finds that the racial characteristics of the white and the Indian place the greater burden of crime on the Indian's shoulders, in the proportion of "a hundred to one." The whites are "a race more calculating, more wise, with ampler means," while the Indians are characterized by "the instinct of gratuitous cruelty or a natural propensity to war as a pursuit." [29] Although the whites enjoy, with the Indians, the thrill of the chase, they have not the same gusto for human slaughter. Thus their kinship is limited. The whites accept the sublimation of the warlike passions in the Indian discipline of hunting; but unlike the Indians, their blood is not so heated by the chase that it leaps for the fuller expression of the bloody passion in war.

Flint sees the experience of his western heroes in terms of archetypal structuring patterns. In his study of the Mississippi Valley, he retraces the course of Boone's adventures, without reference to the hero himself, as a kind of general pattern of western experience, an archetype cast as a folktale at a campfire:

The narrations of a frontier circle, as they draw round their evening fire, often turn upon the exploits of the olden race of . . . pioneers,

. . . who wore hunting shirts, and settled a boundless forest, full of panthers, and wolves, and bears, and the more dreadful aborigine Savages. Not a White man within a hundred miles — a solitary adventurer penetrates the wilderness, and the strokes of his axe resound in the forest.

The Indians find him out, ambush, and imprison him. A more acute and desperate warrior than themselves, they wish to adopt him, and thus add his strength to their tribe. He feigns contentment — uses the Savage's instructions — outruns him in the uses of his own ways of management, but watches his opportunity, and, when their suspicion is lulled, and they fall asleep, he springs upon them, kills his keepers, and bounds his way into unknown forests, pursued by Savages and their dogs. He leaves them all at fault — subsists many days upon roots and berries, and, finally, arrives at his little clearing. . . . In a pallisade, three or four resolute men stand a seige of hundreds of assailants — kill many of them — and mount calmly on the roof . . . to pour water on the fire which burning arrows have kindled there — and achieve the work amid a shower of balls.[30]

For the sake of emphasizing and dramatizing the archetypal quality of the experience, the teller exaggerates the violence of the events and the odds against the hero. In much the same way, Flint embroiders his material on Boone, adding his own inventions to newspaper accounts, the Filson biography, and the oral legendry.

Boone appears in *Indian Wars* as the representative westerner, the initiator of a virtually new species of man. His chief distinguishing characteristics are his love of wild nature and his emulation of the Indian hunter:

He stands at the head of a remarkable class of people, almost new in the history of the species, trained by circumstances to a singular and unique character, and in many respects dissimilar to that of the first settlers on the shores of the Atlantic. The thoughts of these backwoodsmen expatiated with delight, only when they were in a boundless forest, filled with game, with a pack of dogs behind them, and a rifle on their shoulders. Yet as much as their character seems dashed with a wild recklessness, they were as generally remarkable for high notions of honor and generosity, as for hardihood, endurance, and bravery.[31]

Flint takes pains to distinguish the western from the eastern pioneer and to emphasize the difference in sectional characters. The westerner is a true Romantic in his disdain of the artificiality of traditional education; he relies instead on spontaneous emotion, intuition, and instinct, his natural "quickness of apprehension." These same qualities mark him as a Christian of the revivalistic or evangelistic stamp, relying on an inner light rather than on stagnant tradition for his moral justification. His intuition gives him the spiritual necessities of life — "a stern firmness of decision, strength of character, self-possession" — which fit him for "self-command and self-dependence." Thus, without recourse to Puritan theology, the frontier hero embodies all the virtues most needed by the Puritans in the wilderness. Beyond these simple necessities, the frontiersman needs nothing. He is as content as Filson's Boone with fresh water and unsalted deer meat and no bread or strong drink.

But Flint, still generalizing the character of Boone, carries his portrait beyond Puritan limitations. Boone's admirable, restrained character finds its truest expression in the Indian arts of the chase and ambush:

> A Nimrod by instinct and physical character, his home was in the range of woods, his beau ideal the chase, and forests full of buffaloes, bear and deer. More expert at their own arts, than the Indians themselves, to fight them, and foil them, gave scope to the exulting consciousness of the exercise of his own appropriate and peculiar powers.[32]

This "exulting consciousness" finds its purest expression when Boone is living the life of the Indian in the Kentucky wilderness, exercising his skills of woodcraft. Thus Boone's Indian captivity becomes the pivotal experience in Flint's account of his career, just as the "commanding ridge" scene formed the turning point in the career of Filson's Boone — the point at which the hero realizes the nature of his own powers and discovers his true relation to the wilderness.

Flint's account of Boone in *Indian Wars* follows the sequence of Filson's narrative, with a single exception. Flint shifts Boone's Indian captivity to an earlier point in the narrative, where it replaces the "commanding ridge" scene. In the Romantic manner, Filson's Boone experienced spiritual regeneration and discovered his life's mission by perceiving divinity in the natural landscape. (There are similar scenes in Imlay's novel of the West, in Byron's *Childe Harold*, in Goethe's *Werther*, and in Rousseau's *Confessions* and *Emile*, as well as in Crèvecoeur and Jefferson.) Flint's Boone realizes his identity through his adoption into the life of the Indian tribe. Flint, striving to express an archetypal pattern, generalizes this part of Boone's life, as he generalized the captivity pattern in his book on the valley. In the process, he makes the outline of Boone's career fit the captivity-escape pattern:

> He fights [the Indians] in numerous woods and ambushes. His companions fall about him. He is one of those peculiar persons, whom destiny seems to have charmed against balls. . . . At length he is taken. But the savages have too much reverence for such a grand "medicine"

of a man as Boone, to kill him. He assumes such an entire satisfaction
along with them, and they are so naturally delighted with such a
mighty hunter, . . . that they are charmed, and deceived into a confidence that he is really at home with them, and would not escape if
he could.[33]

Through his emotional response to the natural landscape, Filson's Boone
discovered a sympathy between his human heart and the mind of the Enlightenment's reasonable, civilized God of nature. Flint's Boone, by contrast, discovers that "the Indian way of life is the way of his heart." His satisfaction with the Indian life is not entirely feigned. Flint goes so far as to
suggest that Boone's affection for the Indian tribe is nearly equal to his
love for his family and for the culture of Boonesborough: "It is almost one
thing to him, so that he wanders the woods with expert hunters, whether
he takes his diversion with the whites, or the Indians." Like any artist or
devotee, he feels most akin to those who share his craft, his calling, and his
passion. Even his religious "creed" does not contain many more "articles"
than those of "his red rival hunters." [34]

In Flint's *Biographical Memoir of Daniel Boone*, this element of violence and conflict is muted and sublimated into the slow process of his
hero's initiation into the calling of the hunter. The account, published
under various titles, first appeared in Cincinnati in 1833 (along with *Indian
Wars*), was issued in a second edition the following year, and became one
of the most frequently reissued and widely circulated accounts of Boone's
life. Flint employs Filson's narrative again, but he now goes into far more
detail on Boone's exploits and his preparation for heroism, basing his account on his own researches among Boone's family and acquaintances. The
oral tradition surrounding Boone's life is, for the first time, systematically
collected and presented, with the evidence, as a unified whole. Flint's
study seems a deliberate attempt to express a myth of the West in terms of
a symbolic confrontation between the hunter and the hunted — between
the solitary Boone and the Indian, the wild animal, and the spirit of the
wilderness itself. He repeatedly insists that Boone's pursuit is an "art," a
"discipline," a religious "calling" or vocation.

Boone is first presented in his early youth, already exhibiting the traits
of character that will later make him unique among men. Flint presents
him as a man without a past or an ancestry, a figure wholly independent of
the limitations of heredity and history:

> The ancestors of Boone were not placed in positions to prove,
> whether he did or did not receive his peculiar aptitudes [as] a legacy
> from his parents, or a direct gift from nature. He presents himself to

us as a new man, the author and artificer of his own fortunes, and showing from the beginning the rudiments of character of which history has recorded no trace in his ancestors.[35]

Thus Boone is the perfect type of the self-made man. Indeed, he represents an exaggeration of that figure to mythic proportions, springing from the womb an independent and all-but-matured hero. He begins as a man free of inherited traits or traditions, and he remains throughout his life the "author and artificer" of his own destiny, his own identity.

This disinclination to accept any modification of his character that is not of his own choice or making becomes evident when he confronts the problem of education by tricking and exposing the schoolmaster to ridicule. Traditional schooling is not for him; the hunt is his classroom, and the animals he pursues are his teachers. Because of this rejection of traditional schooling, Boone becomes in Flint's eyes a kind of western bard. He is described as "essentially a poet" whose métier is action rather than versification.[36] Boone's real education and his initiation into the life of the wilderness begin when, as a man, he escapes from the schoolroom and pursues his other study more deeply.

This early initiation culminates in the fire hunt, in which Boone stalks a deer which metamorphoses into the woman he will marry and is himself mistaken for a panther by the wild, shy girl. Flint portrays the hunt as a kind of ritual. Although forbidden by game laws, the nocturnal fire hunt is pursued by the more enterprising local youths. It serves as a local manhood ritual, testing the youth's ability to successfully deal with the powers of nature and the powers of society. Only by matching strength and skill with the adults of the tribe and the laws they make can the boy attain full equality with them. Only when he has proved that he can successfully break the law will his obedience to it have moral significance. Flint reinforces the implication that the fire hunt is a ritual by emphasizing the nocturnal setting, the extralegal nature of the act (which sets Boone outside the bounds of commonday life), the mysterious nature of the "metamorphoses" and of the impulse that causes Boone to withhold his fire from the deer/woman, and the fact that the incident has become local legend. Thus Boone is portrayed as a semidivine, heroic lover of the wild and free wilderness spirit, whose acts of love are the acts of the hunter. The spirit of the wilderness rewards the faithful lover, making him a wife out of the substance of a wild creature. Boone's departure for Kentucky, in Flint's account, follows immediately upon his consummation of his marriage to Rebecca. Having married the avatar of the wilderness spirit, he is ready for the great quests of his heroic career.

The fire hunt clarifies the symbolic relationship between Boone and his wilderness world. His relation to his beloved is that of hunter to prey, "painter" or panther to "deer." His act of worship and love is the violent act of the hunter; but it is Boone's restraint of that act — his sublimation of the hunter's passion in that of the husband, priest, and artist — which enables him to achieve his symbolic marriage with the female spirit of the wilds. In a similar way, his sublimation of the passion for war in the passion for hunting enabled him to resist degeneration into savagery during his captivity in *Indian Wars*. Once he has exhibited this power of self-restraint, free expression in his "art" is permitted him, and he begins to paint violent tableaux with his rifle for a brush. Boone kills a bear, a panther, and a deer in extraordinary circumstances or with an incredible marksmanship; he kills two Indians with one bullet; he picks off the chief of his opponents. The peculiar mingling of love and violence that was implicit in the fire-hunt myth of his courtship of his wife becomes his characterizing trait. He destroys the wilderness and the game by the very acts which reveal his love for them. He admires the Indian as an adversary, but his combats ensure that his character as Indian fighter will die with the achievement of victory. Thus his imitation of the Indian becomes the means by which he brings progress to the West and destroys the basis for his own lifeway.

Flint's biography of Boone ultimately becomes a justification of the life of the hunter, a life that is regarded as representative of the western character. Hunting is not simply a necessity for Boone. If it were, he might have become like the Indians, whose dependence on the chase made them unamenable to Christian feelings and progress. For Boone hunting is at once a "luxury" and "indulgence" and a form of religiously disciplined art. Flint describes it as a "profession" — a discipline in which Boone demonstrates, like any other artist, his "tact and superiority," his powers of discrimination and selection, and his power to control his materials, create events, and impose his will on his subject. Flint does not deny that Boone fled from civilization in order to pursue his art — but, he asks, is there any shame in the scholar's seeking a quiet study, the saint a cloister, the holy hermit a desert, or the painter a picturesque site for his easel and exotic pigments for his palette? [37] (Flint's allusion wrings a significant pun out of Rebecca's identification of Boone as a "painter.")

Flint carries the myth a step further and applies it to the character of the whole American nation, as well as of the West. He cites the works of Byron, Bryan, and Cooper as proof that the image of the hunter has charms for all enlightened men and especially for Americans. "Even in cities," the mainstays of civilization, men seek to practice this "natural" profession of hunting at every opportunity. The businessman and politician are hunters in their daily lives, and all desire the clean, uncomplicated expression of the hunting passion in the actual chase of a beast. Every American shares with Boone the love of the chase, the conflict, the kill.[38] His acts demonstrate his peculiar combination of love for the wild country and the urge to destroy, digest, and remake it in his own image. In Boone's decency of behavior and gentleness of outward manner there are overtones of the traditional image of the good Quaker and of the gentle warrior depicted by Chenier, Chateaubriand, Byron and Parraud. But Flint's hero is far more active. He is simultaneously a passionate devotee and lover of the wilderness. He is not simply a man who, by unfortunate circumstances, must hunt game and kill Indians to survive. He is a professional killer, a solitary acolyte perpetually sacrificing and consuming his god.

Changing Images of the Indian in the West

Flint's vision of the Boone figure provided a model of the western hero capable of satisfying many if not all of the expectations of both the popular, southwestern-humor-oriented audience of Davy Crockett and the eastward-looking audience of the more respectable James Hall. Flint's Boone mediates between symbolic savagery and civilization, combining the gentleness and self-restraint of Hall's backwoodsman with the professional prowess and independence of the Indian and the southwestern hunter. We can appreciate the nature of Flint's accomplishment by noting its effect on the image of the Indian in western writing. For westerners the Indian was paradoxically both their racial antagonist and the symbol of their defiance of the East, their wildness and freedom, their independence of customary restraint. Their literary reconciliation to identification with the Indian, exhibited in Indian biographies and other works of the 1840s and 1850s, takes the form of a systematic association of certain Indian heroes with the character of Flint's Boone. They reject eastern models of reconciliation with the symbolic Indian — the association of Indians with farmers and patriots in Thatcher and Evarts, the linking of images of the noble savage and the childlike innocence of Leatherstocking in Cooper — in preference for Flint's hero. Such alteration of the Indian's image in no way altered the westerners' conviction that the Indian constituted an obstacle to progress on the frontier and that he must be removed from his land and sent into the desert places of the Far West. In both East and West, the adoption of a favorable mythology of the Indian coincided with the rapid disappearance of real Indians from the local scene.

Prominent among the western contributions to the literature of Indian biography is Benjamin Drake's *Life of Tecumseh*, published in Cincinnati in 1841. The history of Tecumseh's Shawnee, like that of Black Hawk's Sauk and Foxes and Evarts's Cherokee, is made to resemble American history in microcosm. For Bostonian Evarts, this history is essentially that of a progressive movement from a pagan culture based on hunting to a Christian culture based on farming. Salvation comes to the Cherokee when they accept from the white, chosen people the gift of Christianity. For Drake history has a different pattern. Tecumseh is seen as a tragic hero — admirable because he holds unswervingly to the traditions and beliefs of his race; tragic because, for that same reason, he is doomed to defeat by the whites. Evarts's view of history envisions a reconciliation of the races through the destruction of the Indian's racial integrity. Drake's history is a clash of irreconcilable opposites, each with an identical tradition in which it appears as the chosen race and each emigrating from a distant pole to converge on the West. By a tragic paradox the very similarity between Indian and American history, which suggests the spiritual kinship of westerner and Indian, is the source of their historical division and conflict.

Tecumseh and his brother, the Prophet, are seen as preachers of an Indian revival, red-skinned Puritans in manner and message. The similarities between Tecumseh's account of the Indian's fall from grace and that expounded by white revivalists could not have been lost on Drake's audience. The Shawnee hold themselves born, like Greek Athena, from the brain of God — unlike other Indians, who believe themselves native to their soil. They do not believe that they have emerged from under a mountain or lake, as Heckewelder reports of the Delaware; rather, they report themselves as having emigrated from another land. Like the Israelites from whom the Christians trace descent, they are divided into twelve tribes; and like the Israelites, they periodically receive prophets, who warn their kings of impending doom and turn them to the righteous path. Like the Christian Americans, the Shawnee are said to believe in the fall of man. Originally they were the favored and chosen people of the Master of Life, "who was himself an Indian," and the other races were inferior. The Shawnee were made of the brain of God, the French and English of his breast, the Dutch of his feet, and the "long-knives" or Americans of his hands. The Shawnee were given a promised land (Ohio) to dwell in, while the inferior peoples were cast out beyond "the stinking lake" (the Atlantic).

Tecumseh and his brother, the Prophet, describe the fall of the tribe in the Jeremianic terms of Cotton Mather preaching to the New English: "They became corrupt, and the Master of Life told them that he would take away the knowledge which they possessed, and give it to the white people, to be restored, when by a return to good principles they would deserve it." Thus the whites appear (as the Indians had appeared to the Puritans) in the guise of divine justice and punishment for sin: God has given the Indians into the hands of these white devils for punishment and regeneration. Tecumseh's message and prophecy are apocalyptic: "These things will soon have an end. The Master of Life is about to restore to the Shawanoes both their knowledge and their rights, and he will trample the long-knives under his feet." [39]

Drake shifts his point of view back and forth between that of the Indian and that of the white man. The wars between them are seen as the result of provocations by the vile classes of whites, who pollute the frontiers with whiskey, debauch and cheat the Indians, incite them to revenge, and thus set off the cycle of raid and counterraid that quickly escalates to war. The courage, daring, and tactical genius of the Indians are praised most highly, and the accolade given to American troops is for besting the Indians with their own skills and weapons. Thus there is a blending of character qualities that crosses racial lines: the frontiersmen and the Indians share a common heroism that transcends political and economic differences. Violence accomplishes what a peaceful love could not: Indian and white man are reconciled in the bond that unites the victim with his killer, the prey with the hunter.

Tecumseh, the great hero of the Shawnee, embodies this truth in his own career. His education is portrayed as identical with that of Flint's Boone. Like Boone, he is from his youth a leader, particularly delighting in the martial sports that were to be his vocation as a man. Like Boone, he blends humanity with the love of violence and protests against the burning of captives, despite its traditional acceptance by his tribe. If he differs from Boone, it is only in one important respect: Boone was free to choose the life of the hunter as his profession, whereas Tecumseh is compelled to it by circumstances. Therefore Tecumseh, unlike Boone, is subject to and tolerant of the Indians' fanaticism and earthy passions. With this exception, they are brothers in spirit. Drake describes hunting as Tecumseh's "favorite amusement" — a phrase repeatedly applied to Boone in virtually every work about him. Like Boone, Tecumseh achieves his leadership over his people through his hunting exploits:

> The parties took to the woods, and at the end of the stipulated time, returned with evidences of their success. None of the party, except Tecumseh, had more than twelve deer skins; he brought in upwards of thirty — near three times as many as any of his competitors.

From this time he was generally conceded to be the greatest hunter in the Shawanoe Nation.[40]

Like Boone he pursues hunting for its own sake, not for mere material profit. Hunting is a means of fulfilling social duty. It is the true role of a man in his tribe:

> The love of property was not a distinguishing trait of his character; on the contrary, his generosity was proverbial. . . . He loved hunting because it was a manly exercise, fit for a *brave;* and, for the additional reason, that it gave him the means of furnishing the aged and infirm with wholesome and nourishing food.[41]

The shared identity of Boone and Tecumseh seems at odds with the assertion that the two are representative heroes of antithetical cultural poles, one of which must be annihilated if the other is to survive. Yet the paradox is itself the essence of the myth of the hunter, in which each man kills the thing he loves, and the thing he loves is both his darker self and his necessary other half (anima).

> On Papago Mountain
> The dying quarry
> Looked at me with my love's eyes

says the Indian chant. In the act of seeking and struggling with this other self, one's own identity is created and confirmed. Thus Benjamin Church takes his new identity from the trophies of the dead King Philip, Boone weds the deer-woman, and Melville's Ahab hunts whales on a leg made of whalebone.

Preeminent among such heroes in the western political pantheon was Sam Houston, the George Washington of Texas, a figure who bridges the gap between Boone and Tecumseh. In an autobiography, published anonymously in 1855 as a ploy in his campaign for the Presidential nomination, Houston describes himself as the "Hunter, Patriot and Statesman of Texas." Stress is laid on his frontier background, and an affinity for the Indians is among his virtues. In his teens, he says, he left his family and civilization itself to live as an adopted Cherokee, for "he preferred measuring deer tracks, to tape . . . he liked the wild liberty of the Red men, better than the tyranny of his own brothers . . . running wild among the Indians, sleeping on the ground, chasing wild game, living in the forests, and reading Homer's Iliad withal." The description makes him sound like a blend of Boone, Tecumseh, and Thoreau, with perhaps a touch of the classical hero implied by his carrying the *Iliad* as his sole tie to Euro-American culture. This sojourn of some years among "the untutored children of the

woods" was not a mere boyish holiday but "a necessary portion of that
wonderful training that fitted him for his strange destiny." In the Indian
camp "he was initiated into the profound mysteries of the Red man's character, and a taste was formed for forest life, which made him, many years
after, abandon once more the habitations of civilized men, with their cold-
ness, their treachery, and their vices, and pass years among the children of
the Great Spirit." [42]

Years later, after a failed marriage has blighted the ambitions engendered by his early success in Jacksonian politics, "he determined instantly
to resign his office as Governor, and forego all his brilliant prospects of distinction, and exile himself from the habitations of civilized men." Houston
defends this as "a resolution more likely to have been begotten by philosophy than by crime." Thus he follows through on the program of "going
back to the Indians" that Timberlake and Crèvecoeur had ironically or
sentimentally toyed with at the end of the previous century. He returns to
the Cherokee, now displaced to Oklahoma, and when the call to Texas
comes, he has been living for three years as the chief's adopted son. Houston leaves "his wigwam" for Texas, and the passage makes an interesting
contrast to Boone's setting out for Kentucky from his "peaceful habitation." Houston's starting point for regeneration and the rise to fame is the
wilderness, not the farm or town. Nor does he regard his Indian proclivities
as idiosyncratic and only to be justified (as in Boone's case) by his extraordinary powers of "philosophy" and self-restraint. Rather, they are presented as typical of a new, heroic race of empire builders: "These hunter-
legislators, these squatter-founders. . . . A young hero-people, a new
Rome, coming out of the forests, walking in light, clothed in strength." [43]

For Houston the image of the American hero is that of the white Indian. It is certainly the image he chooses to project of himself in his campaign biography, and he attempts to persuade his reader that he is, like
Flint's Boone, not unique but representative of a new class of men. That he
is consciously invoking the positive myths of the Indian is reflected in his
speaking of his translation from Tennessee to Cherokee Oklahoma as his
"return to the forest" — although Oklahoma is a land of grassy plains and
open spaces.[44]

In the world of the western writers, Boone, Tecumseh, and Houston
represent a set of cardinal virtues. They are generous as well as diligent in
their trades and pursuits; they do not seek to amass property but consume
or give away all that they take. Their values emphasize individual initiative
and reliance on one's own forces. Progress is equated with the remaking of
one's individual fortune and one's individual spirit. The self-made man is

perpetually engaged in a bustling strife of self-transcendence, making a new identity (or, as western revival preachers said, a new soul) as he might make a new fortune. Divested of its rhetorical trappings, however, this western figure appeared in the East in a nightmare guise. Boone's contempt for property and generosity suggested the attitude of the spendthrift, the reckless speculator, the "cheap money" man, always angling to defraud the creditor of his due. The protean qualities of the self-transcending westerner, seen with a cold eye, were taken as signs of political and emotional instability, a tendency to disorder, a belief that men might escape the just consequences of flouting civil and divine law. And for the South and the Northeast, the western resolution of the problem of American kinship with the Indians was not acceptable. It too readily equated the American character with the radical democratic, Jacobinic spirit traditionally associated with the Indian. It made figures like Jackson politically powerful symbols around which the radical sentiments of eastern workers and reformers could coalesce.

Eastern Responses to Western Heroes

The traditional division of the seaboard states into New England, the middle colonies, and the Old South had some value as a description of sectional divisions in the East. The middle colonies — or, more specifically, Philadelphia and New York City — were the hub of the nation, the main entry ports for European goods and literature and the distributors of such things to the other sections. Of all the seaboard states, New York and Pennsylvania had the closest literary ties to the West, since they lay at the terminus of the main routes of commerce and since they contained substantial tracts of wilderness and recently settled territory themselves. The axis cities were also the centers to which New England writers with aspirations to a national reputation brought their works. The resemblance between the popular literary tradition of the West and that of New England derives in part from the fact that the axis distributors made money by transmitting literature from New England to the Northwest and back again. This circumstance reinforced the links forged by the patterns of emigration: when New Englanders emigrated, they followed the Erie Canal–Great Lakes route to the West.

The impact of the West and its literature on the New England mind was therefore strongly felt. New England's reaction to the West was shaped by its political and social tensions but complicated by its longstanding commitment to bring civilization and Christianity to the wilderness. The dilemma was much like that of the seventeenth and eighteenth centuries, in which the Puritans were torn between their vision of the promise of America and their fears of cultural dissolution. New England was economically weak as the nineteenth century began, and it only slowly gained a position of relative economic security. The states were small in size, and their populations, which had been ample enough in the eighteenth century, were no longer growing as quickly as the population of the western and middle states. The errand into the wilderness was valid in the small area of New England, but the West was too vast, capable of absorbing too many people and changing them into hunters and half-Indians.

In literature, the New England reaction fell into traditional patterns. Its writers dealt with the West through the old literary genres of the war narrative, the captivity, and the travel or emigration narrative. One of the most popular practitioners of this New England art was Henry Trumbull, a kinsman of John Trumbull of Norwich and author-editor of *History of the Discovery of America*, the most popular anthology of Indian war narratives in the nineteenth century.[45] The anthology first appeared in Brooklyn, New York, and Norwich, Connecticut, in 1810 and was extensively edited and added to over the next half-century, appearing at various times in Boston, New York, and Trenton. The thesis of this work, implicit in the ordering of the various articles, is that the true flowering of America was in the days of the Puritan triumph over the Indians; that all before that epoch was a strife between pagans and papists for material booty; and that the annexation of the transmontane West, motivated by materialistic greed, caused Americans to overextend themselves in the wilderness, dissipate their power, and purchase a series of horrid defeats.

Three types of Indian war narratives are used to convey this message. The first third of the book is an account of the greed-motivated Spanish conquest of the Aztec and Inca empires, written by Trumbull himself. The second part, also by Trumbull, deals with the Indian wars of New England and the triumph of Puritanism over King Philip. The last third of the book consists of accounts by various hands of the British and American defeats in Indian warfare west of the mountains, beginning with an adaptation of Filson's Boone narrative. A running commentary by Trumbull, plus certain editorial changes in the articles, constitute the only explicit links between the pieces. In subsequent editions of the anthology, the last section on defeats was enlarged until it accounted for virtually half of the text.

Like Filson, Trumbull begins with a preface in which he defines a motive for the discoverers of a New World. Filson, bowing to the values of the Enlightenment, cited "Curiosity" for knowledge of God's world as Boone's chief motive. Trumbull omits this passage and substitutes for it a Calvinist vision of human selfishness and depravity:

> To the avarice of mankind, and the enterprise of the Portuguese, we owe the present abundance of the gold, the silver, the precious stones, and the rich manufactures. To that same avarice we owe the discovery of the New World, the idea of whose very existence was for a long while held so absurd, that the love of gain itself could not prompt men to the undertaking.[46]

Thus Trumbull, like the Romantics, associates materialism with the aspirations of the frontiersmen, the explorers and adventurers who are the vanguard of civilization in the wilderness. But his tradition is Calvinist, and his heroes are the militant divines and pious soldiers who imposed a religious order on the material chaos of the New World. Where the Romantic admires passion and indulgence in a variety of intense emotions, Trumbull admires the orderly and restrained habits of the Puritans. The ruling metaphor of his work is the contrast between the "symmetry" of Puritan law and life and the "monstrous," disproportioned, American world of nature-gone-wild:

> Let us for a moment, contemplate the situation of this country . . . [before 1620] — an almost impenetrable forest, abounding with Savages and beasts of prey! — the vast trees that grew up to the clouds so encumbered with plants that they could scarcely be got at — . . . the human race, cloathed with the skins of . . . monsters, fled from each other, or pursued only with intent to destroy. . . . But our Forefathers landed, and very soon changed the face of *New-England.*

Essential to their achievement of "symmetry" is the destruction of the Indian — a task which Trumbull sees, with Mather, as a holy crusade:

> [They] destroyed or dispersed a horde of fierce and blood thirsty *Savages* — they introduced order and symmetry by the assistance of the instruments of art . . . and thus the new world like the old became subject to man.[47]

The focus of Trumbull's anthology is the section dealing with New England's triumphs. The chapters on the conquest of Latin America serve to emphasize the piety and asceticism of the Puritan fathers by dwelling on the imperial opulence of new and old Mexico and Peru and on the blood orgies of the pagans and the Inquisition. The defeats of the western armies, recounted in the last third of the book, are also used to point up the differences between the conquest of New England in the name of God and the conquest of Kentucky for wealth and power. Within the section on Indian wars before 1765, Trumbull's entire concern is with the New England wars. No mention whatever is made of the Carolinian wars against the Cherokee in 1760–62, the Yamasee war of 1715, or the Jamestown massacres. To Trumbull the history of the American attempt to establish a nation in the wilderness is the history of the Puritan conquest and transformation of the Indian's world.

Trumbull's version of the Boone narrative is in the final section of the anthology, dealing with the Indian wars of the West. The major theme of the section is the defeat and destruction of the whites, climaxing the incredible hardships and dangers of western settlement. Although Boone succeeds in surviving the Indian wars, the reader is forced to conclude that America has reached her farthest limit in Kentucky. No longer does God make victory relatively easy, as he did in the days of the Puritan fathers. Trumbull presents Boone in the context of numerous accounts of defeat, implying that Boone's accomplishments have been achieved with the last strength rather than the renewed energy of civilization. The power of God and of civilization, which sustains Boone, has reached its limits in his settlements; to extend its sphere of action farther from the center of society would weaken it to destruction.

Trumbull uses a text of the Boone narrative which is virtually identical with that of John Trumbull's 1786 Norwich edition. In both versions Boone's philosophical and sentimental meditations are deleted, to emphasize the man of action in Boone and weaken the traces of intellectual sophistication in his character. Where Filson shows the frontiersman as an exemplar of civilized virtues, John and Henry Trumbull portray a man of minimal cultivation or education, resembling the truly civilized man as the shadow represents the body.

Trumbull's Boone does represent civilized values, although these have been weakened through long exposure to the wilderness. Three textual alterations made by Henry Trumbull in his 1811 edition suggest the nature of this weakening process. In the original (Brooklyn and Norwich, 1810) editions of his anthology, he copied the ending of John Trumbull's edition of the Boone narrative with the words: "Peace crowns the sylvan shade." In the later editions he eliminates this phrase and ends on a more pious note with Boone's assertion that "I have been . . . an instrument ordained to settle the wilderness." By eliminating the reference to the attainment of peace, Trumbull implies that the war with the Indians has not yet been resolved. At the same time, he suggests a kinship between Boone and the Puritans, who also battled in the name of God. But Boone is a weakened son of the Puritans, subject to unmanly terrors, a helpless witness to unspeakable atrocities. In Filson's original portrait, Boone viewed nature's loveliness from his "commanding ridge" and achieved an inner sense of peace and resignation. Trumbull's Boone is allowed no such resolution. After the account of Boone's view from the ridgetop, Trumbull inserts the words: "At a distance I frequently heard the hideous yells of Savages." Fear, not felicity, is the result of Boone's wilderness ordeal. Finally, Trumbull adds a touch of sensational heightening to Filson's original account of the settlers' sufferings, as if to emphasize the overwhelming power of Indian evil in the West. Filson recounted an attack on Ashton's Station, in which the Indians killed one man and carried off a Negro slave. In Trumbull's 1811 edition, this passage is drastically altered. No men are killed, but the Indians are said to have "ravished, killed, and scalped a woman and her two daughters near Ashton's Station." [48]

The publication history of Trumbull's anthology spans nearly forty years and suggests that his persistent association of the West with defeat and terror gradually made his book a distinctly New England document. The first edition appeared in Brooklyn and in Norwich in 1810. Since New York was a major publication and distribution center, works published there circulated widely throughout the areas it served: the New England towns along the Sound, the Hudson Valley, and western New York. Although Philadelphia was still dominant in literary publishing for the South and West, New York had begun to make inroads in these sections as well. However, after these two editions and a Trenton edition in 1812, Trumbull's book did not appear outside of New England. In New England it was first published in Trumbull's home town of Norwich. It went through two editions there in 1810, a third in 1811, which contained several important textual changes, and a fourth in 1812. In 1817 Trumbull took the work and his shop to Boston, where all subsequent editions appeared — in 1819, 1822, 1828, at least once in every year from 1830 to 1836, and in 1840. In 1841 the title was changed to *History of the Indian Wars*, and under that title it was reissued in 1844 and 1846–48. In 1840, in Boston, Jerome Van Crowninshield Smith published *A Condensed History of the Wars with the Indians*, which substantially reproduced Trumbull's 1840 edition. Despite Boston's reputation as the hub of the universe, books published there did not circulate widely even in New England at that time; New England authors who sought circulation usually went to New York publishers. The book's popularity within this restricted area was considerable, however, and its reputation was fairly high. In the 1820s Samuel G. Drake listed it as one of the standard texts on the Indian wars. It is a virtual certainty that Cooper, who was educated in the southern New England area and who read Indian war books avidly, was acquainted with an early edition of the work. But while its influence could be felt in national literature through the medium of Cooper, its influence as a cultural document remained purely sectional. Trumbull's portrayal of Boone as a latter-day Puritan — victimized and all but defeated by the terrors, Indians, and renegades of the West, but still holding to his belief in God's power — suited New England's traditional conception of its own relationship to the frontier and gave little scope to later conceptions of the frontiersman as hero.

Trumbull elaborated on this concept in a pamphlet, published at Providence in 1817, 1819, and 1824, called *Western Emigration: Journal of Doctor Jeremiah S[im]pleton's Tour to Ohio*. The work, cast as a "fable" or a fiction, is a tract denouncing emigration to the West. Trumbull draws on all the conventions of the "come-outer" Puritan emigration tracts — as well as Mather's antiemigration sermons — and turns them against the new "Land of Promise." The motives for emigration, by this account, are born of man's darker, wilder nature. They chiefly consist in an irrational restlessness, an indisposition to be content with enjoyment of God-blessed New England, not unlike Adam's and Eve's discontent with the Garden. Instead of power and wealth, emigrants find ruin and death, the wastage and dissipation of vigor. In Trumbull's eyes, the emigration impulse is not simply Adamic but essentially Faustian. It reflects a desire for all kinds of temporal power. "Wealth and popularity" that can, as in Crockett's case, be turned to political advantage are the obvious aims of this "wild and chimerical pursuit," but Trumbull also speaks of the emigrant as seeking " 'the philosophers' stone' in this boasted 'Land of Promise.' " Happy are those who return, before irremediably ruined, to their ancestral home, to take up again the frugal and industrious life of New England and enjoy the benefits of the "unrivalled" society of Puritan Christians.[49]

Simpleton expects the West to be another "Garden of Eden," abounding in docile game and fruitful soil. He expects to survive by hunting until his first crop is made, but he finds the life of the hunter too full of surprising reverses: "While you are *ambushing* a Bear or Buffaloe, in fond expectation of making a meal of one of *them*, one or the other may lie in ambush with as fond expectation of making a meal of *you!*"[50] This is, in fact, the outcome of Simpleton's own "hunt" for a bargain in land and a life of ease. The speculator from whom he thinks to take his trophy entraps him, as he says, far more easily than he could have snared an animal.

Simpleton's ambitions to be great in the West depend for their fulfillment on the sparseness of the western population:

> Retir'd from the *world* as a body may say,
> I am Captain and Colonel of all I survey,

All within my power to controul:
A *Farm* of Three Hundred Acres I've here,
If with pick-ax I pick up an acre a year,
How long will it take me to pick up the whole!
High ho! deedle-dum day! [51]

Through Simpleton, Trumbull mocks the western fondness for military titles — a trait remarked by most European travelers as a symptom of the
upstart nature of the westerner, his insolent desire to equal and surpass his
betters by fair means or foolish. Simpleton's aspirations in this line have
dire consequences. His fortune and health are ruined. Moreover, he exposes the females of his family to the physical and psychological hardships
that, as a Christian and a civilized man, he ought to have kept far from
them. These are entirely the result of that solitude that Simpleton has
sought in order to overstep his rank and station.[52]

Simpleton's sin consists in having willfully sought the solitude of the
wilderness, embarked on a quest or hunt for some prize in the woods. Daniel Boone and Davy Crockett, being far more ambitious hunters, were
therefore far greater sinners. Their active pursuit of the Indian's amusement of hunting and their refusal to return to the civilized fold were taken
as signs of their racial degeneracy. This denigrating view was held by a
number of eastern writers. Thus Washington Irving's *Astoria* (1836) prophesied that those who settle in the Great Plains will become a "mongrel
race" of brigands.[53] C. Wilder, who edited and published an important edition of Filson's narrative in 1823, spoke mockingly of Boone's "prejudice"
in favor of the Indian and his dislike of "D——d Yankees," implying that
Boone was a white Indian, the product of a spiritual marriage with the barbarous spirit of the wilderness.

Wilder's edition was important because it brought together several
sectional versions of Boone's character — the John Trumbull text of Filson's narrative, an account of Boone's career from western sources, the Indian war treatise on tactics by former captive James Smith (erroneously attributed to Boone), Wilder's own sarcastic critique of Boone, and Byron's
effusive eulogy from *Don Juan*. The book itself, which appeared in Brooklyn in 1823 and was pirated in Providence by Henry Trumbull in 1824,
testifies to New York City's importance as a literary marketplace, tying the
West, the South, New England, and Europe together. It suggests that New
York editors and writers were subject to a broader spectrum of influences
than those of the other sections and that New York publishers were "the
discoverers and interpreters of American literary taste and . . . the chan-
nel through which the taste of the South and West moved, to influence

. . . the production of literature on the coast." [54] From the compendium of images of Boone offered by Wilder, writers could choose those images that suited the stereotypes of western character which had evolved from the social conditions of their particular sections. South Carolina's William G. Simms, for instance, preferred the Byronic image of a noble, aristocratic Boone, while New Englanders elected that offered by Wilder in his own contribution to the mélange — the image of a white-Indian renegade.

The text of the Boone narrative used by Wilder is that employed by John Trumbull in 1786 and later by Henry Trumbull in his famous anthology. This text omits most of Boone's philosophical and mental speculations, leaving the impression that he was a man of action, rarely a man of thought. Hunting is his "chief amusement," rather than his dire necessity or his art. To reinforce this barbaric adventurousness, the editor attributes to Boone the remarks made by James Smith in his treatise on the Indians. This treatise had been published along with the Boone narrative in Metcalf's anthology, and the vague wording of the title page of Metcalf's book seemed to indicate that Boone had written the treatise. Wilder apparently saw Metcalf's edition and amalgamated the accounts of Boone and Smith. However, he did not use Metcalf's text of the Boone narrative, in which the philosophical pretensions of Filson's original were retained intact.

Wilder shared Trumbull's hostility toward the West, and he vented his anger on Boone. His editorial comment on Smith's Indian treatise is typical:

> By the foregoing the reader will perceive how greatly prejudiced was Colonel Boone in favor of the tawny inhabitants of the Western wilderness, whose manners and habits he did not hesitate to declare to the day of his death were far more agreeable to him than those of a more civilized and refined race. [55]

Smith's treatise, which is the immediate occasion for this editorial rancor, is hardly an apology for the Indians. Like most realistic treatments written by frontiersmen, it recognizes the Indians' prowess and urges its imitation by white soldiers. Its most positive evaluation of the Indians is its recognition of their intense love of the wilderness land, a love in which Smith finds nothing objectionable. But Smith's treatise is included by Wilder in a sketch of Boone's later career, ostensibly written by a kinsman of the hero living in Cincinnati. The attitude of this putative relation is indicated by his assertion that "the great object of the Colonel appears to have been to live as far as possible from every white inhabitant" in order to pursue his barbaric amusements without hindrance. Wilder interprets this sentiment as a sign of active hostility toward his own racial traits, a deliberate and degenerate preference for the Indian over the white. His reaction to Boone's "elbow room" remark exactly parallels that of Increase Mather to the same expression one hundred and fifty years before.[56] Wilder has Boone state his sentiments in the terms most offensive to his audience:

> It was frequently remarked by him, that while he could never with safety repose confidence in a Yankee, he had never been deceived by an Indian, when he had once declared himself friendly disposed; and that so far as his own experience would enable him to judge, he would certainly prefer a state of nature to a state of civilization.[57]

This section is followed by the editor's commentary quoted above and then by an account of Boone's death, in which Wilder's irony is apparent:

> Considerable search found the poor old man stretched lifeless on the ground near one of his traps. Beside him stood his faithful dog, pawing and smelling of the dead body of his master. Nor would he quit it until forced to.
>
> It was supposed that the death of this extraordinary man was occasioned by a fit of apoplexy.[58]

For apoplectic rage, as Wilder has insinuated, was Boone's characteristic reaction to the encroachments of civilization.

Despite the ironic tone of this passage, Wilder appends Byron's eulogy without editorial comment. This is especially surprising, since Byron's view of Boone's "peaceful and harmless" old age contradicts his own. The net impression left by the book is that of an unresolved problem in point of view. Is the reader to accept the prowestern and pro-Indian statements of Boone and Smith, or the critical strictures of the easterner, or the effusive admiration of the English Romantic poet? Wilder did no more than suggest his own choice in the pamphlet. Even the excerpt from Smith's treatise on emulation of the Indians in warfare is allowed to speak for itself before Wilder imposes on it his editorial judgment that it indicates Boone's anti-white bias. The American elements that make up Wilder's book are drawn from the West and the middle states as well as from New England. They are written by participants like Smith; clever editors like Metcalf, Filson, and Trumbull; and outright fantasists like Byron.

The image of Boone in England and in the several sections of the United States had been fixed and stereotyped under the pressure of literary conventions and social conditions. By juxtaposing these stereotypes, Wilder helped to unfix the image of the hero, to make him problematical and thus provoke deeper investigation of the Boone hero and his cultural implications. Moreover, Wilder couched the problem of Boone in literary terms, suggesting literary patterns of solution to the fledgling novelists of the 1820s and 1830s and making possible the merging of the myth-oriented popular works with the literary writing of the American Renaissance.

As Wilder's inclusion of Byron's eulogy suggests, New England's view of the West was not wholly negative. If the descendants of the Puritans felt something like their grandfathers' dismay at the threat of degeneration in the wilderness, they also had inherited the hope that impelled the early Puritans to emigrate. New Englanders continued moving west through upper New York State and into the Northwest Territory, where New England governments had reserves of land for their people. There was a crucial difference, however, between the New England emigrants and the Boones and Crocketts. Where the latter moved singly or in clans into empty districts, the New Englanders often moved as communities — or at least attempted to establish all the forms and institutions of their home villages in a prospective settlement before or during the process of moving in. In addition, the social radicalism of the Jacksonians gradually became respectable through its persistence in national politics, especially since the intellectual progress of New England made it a hotbed of enthusiasm for democratic reform movements. The results can be seen in the development of an alternative to the white-Indian Boone in New England and New York literature — an image of Boone as the protector of the social values cherished by the Puritans, rather than of the antisocial values so attractive to the European Romantics and westerners.

Development and Extension of Captivity Mythology

This positive image of Boone was most clearly expressed and permanently fixed in marble by Horatio Greenough in his "Rescue Group," commissioned for the national Capitol in 1838 and finished in 1851. The statue consists of five figures, dominated by a naked Indian brandishing a large tomahawk. His arms are spread and pinioned by a powerful, giant figure clad in a rough blouse and a strange hat, half helmet and half liberty cap. The two figures together make a single vertical column in the center of the statue; to their left is a hunting dog, and to their right is a woman huddled over her infant, shielding him from the hatchet. Proportions are strangely distorted: the woman is exceptionally diminutive when compared with the Indian, while the rescuer is so giantesque as to make the Indian seem adolescent. Yet the giant's whole purpose is centered on the small woman and tiny infant; it is for them that he exerts his strength. Without the least coaching from the sculptor, Greenough's work was popularly dubbed "Daniel Boone Protects His Family," testifying to the ubiquity of the image of Boone as the archetypal American hero. This was the aspect in which the successors of the Puritans could see Boone as a hero — as the rescuer in the framework of a captivity, not as the hunter in an open wilderness. In the former context, Boone's role as hero is determined by his relationship with social and Christian values, as represented by the woman and child. In the latter he is alone; the context is (to eastern eyes) dark and empty of all save dreams and fears; and the hero is embarked on a profound and solitary quest, with violence and strange marriage at its end.

Perhaps the most significant use of the captivity mythology was in the narratives of southern slavery published by the abolitionists between 1830 and 1860.[59] These narratives were largely personal accounts by escaped or freed former slaves, some of them genuinely autobiographical, some fictional, some the result of collaboration between the former slaves and white abolitionists. Given this variety of auctorial characters, the consistency of the narrative pattern from account to account is remarkable. The black slave undergoes the classic captivity. He (or she) is born with a natural predisposition to Christian meekness, humility, and charity that, in Puritan times, would surely have been taken as a sign of indwelling grace and marked him as elect. The slave's circumstances, however, make it impossible for this Christian soul to realize itself. The slave system denies him (in most cases) the full benefits of "instituted worship," subjects him to the lusts and whims of a worldly master, and perverts his loyalty and willingness to work into the brutality of the overseer and the "laziness" and "carelessness" of the forced laborer. Like the white Puritan captive to Indians, the slave is in an alien environment, a Christian in hell. If he succeeds in hell's terms, he becomes like the devils around him (like the white-Indian renegade). If he fails, by being "shiftless," "thievish," or "careless," he falls into habits that any exponent of the Protestant ethic must regard as evil and in that way shares the devil's nature. There is nothing he can do but escape or "be redeemed" from his captivity.

The escape is often accompanied or preceded by a religious conversion. Discovering the sweetness of Christ, the slave perceives his master's distance from the white man's ostensible Christianity and recognizes his own sinfulness in cooperating with, admiring, and emulating his white master. In one of the best of these accounts, *Father [Josiah] Henson's Story of His Own Life*, this sense of sin — the necessary precondition for Puritan conversion — is accentuated by the fact that Henson has served as an overseer and, in an attempt to "be like his master," has prevented some of his fellow slaves from attaining freedom. Revulsion from sin frees the black soul of its spiritual bondage to slavery; the aid of Christian men frees his body as well; and the redemption of the soul is followed by the rescue of the body, as in the classic captivity of Mary Rowlandson. True to the pattern, the narrative ends with the reunion of the family group sundered by captivity.

In this slave-captivity narrative, the contemporary characters of black man, southerner, and abolitionist take on the mythic disguises of seventeenth- and eighteenth-century captivities. The black, like Mrs. Rowlandson and her fellows, is passive under the sufferings of exile, enforced servitude, and the rupture of the family. Father Henson, whose mother is sold away from him, accepts the tragedy as part of his lot and tries to be a "good nigger." The captive's and the slave's heroism is internal: they become true Christians under the stress of un-Christian circumstances. Physical rescue is an adjunct of this spiritual rescue and is most often effected, not by the captive's strength or intelligence, but by the power of an outside, semidivine agency. Father Henson frankly avows a sense of pride in his skill and courage, which enabled him first to make his escape from the South and then to return and aid other slaves to escape. Harriet Beecher Stowe, who based the character of Uncle Tom on Henson, found it necessary to eliminate this quality of Henson's character in order to make her protagonist more perfectly an embodiment of the Christian values of American society — values that had traditionally been embodied in the figure of the white female captive. She embodies the militant aspect of Henson in the figure of George Harris, whose pride and willingness to shoot his way to freedom are morally suspect and are rebuked both by the pacifism of the Quakers on the underground railroad and by the sentimental pleas of his Christian wife, Eliza.

Uncle Tom's Cabin acquires much of its force from its ironic inversions of the classic captivity-narrative situation, in which the dark people captivate the white. Nonetheless, it preserves the structures and moral biases of that mythology intact. The admirable qualities of Tom are those of the captive: passivity, persistence in Christianity in the face of torment, charity, sympathy, purity. As Mrs. Rowlandson moved from the mild bondage to vanity (in Lancaster) to a vision of the explicit bondage of her soul to sin (in the Indian camp), so Tom moves from the gentle servitude of Kentucky to the more drastic slavery of the Deep South. His qualities of character are, as William R. Taylor notes, "feminine" qualities, as these were seen in the literature of nineteenth-century America; and the archetypal protagonist of the captivity was either actually or symbolically female. Thus Wendell Phillips reports that at an abolition meeting a former slave failed to rouse the enthusiasm of the crowd until he had evoked an image of a black mother being whipped for protecting her child; and pictures and anecdotes in antislavery journals dwelt upon the persecution of female slaves in images and language which echo the captivity literature of the Mathers.[60]

The masculine qualities of intelligence, lust for power, strength, and the will and capacity to exploit are, in Mrs. Stowe's novel, the attributes of whites — not, as in the captivity myths, the attributes of "darks." George Harris is proud and violent because of his white blood and white appearance; Tom is described as a "pure African." The quintessential character of the white male exploiter is that of Simon Legree, a planter whose style of life and manners are those of a Simon Suggs or Sut Lovingood, whose ancestry is sharp-dealing Yankee, and whose current status is that of slave driver — in short, a figure who combines all the evils of exploitive commerce, as these were perceived in New England.[61] Significantly, Legree shares the characteristic attributes of the most evil figures in the captivity narratives. He is a monster of sensuality, with a craving for miscegenation; he is lazy, living by the labor of captives and women; he devotes his time to pleasure, profligacy, and hunting.

There are good planters as well as bad, but their goodness arises from their sharing the nature and, to some extent, the situation of the captive. Thus St. Clare is seen as an unwilling captive of the slave system, bound to it by spiritual weakness. As a man, he is more effeminate in his helplessness than Uncle Tom and therefore is still more to be pitied, according to the standards of the captivity myth.

The spectrum of southern character and motivation, both black and white, is reduced in this novel to the presanctioned, simple types of the captivity mythology. The real slave's complex motives for acquiescing in and rebelling against slavery, as expressed by Father Henson, are reduced in Uncle Tom to the ineluctable image of captive feminine Christianity. The slaveowner appears either as the white-Indian Legree (a latter-day Simon Girty), the courtier-gone-native Alfred St. Clare (an updated François Hertel), or the enervated Augustine St. Clare (a moral successor to the Canadian priests whose long sojourn with the dark Indians sapped their fiber and made them passive before the evils their flocks engaged in).

Mrs. Stowe's use of the captivity mythology is, however, not self-conscious, as is Cooper's use of frontier materials. Her falling into the idiom of the captivity myth — and her audience's response to that idiom — is apparently unconscious and characteristic. That this coincidence of mind between audience and propagandist significantly contributed to the success of abolitionist propaganda seems clear. But the success of the captivity myth in abolitionist tracts had its ill consequences as well, reinforcing as it did the tendency toward stereotyping of sectional characters and the oversimplification of the South's problem. The captivity myth's terms contained a pattern for solving that problem which was to prove ultimately destructive of the ends of abolitionism.

More obviously sinister was the revival of the captivity myth in the anti-Catholic propaganda of the nativist movement of the Jacksonian period. Playing on the traditional participation of the Catholic nunneries of Montreal and Quebec in the forcible conversion of Indian captives from 1689 to 1764, writers like Charles Frothingham told tales of Protestant maids being abducted and persecuted into conversion. Maria Monk's spurious account of the frauds, abductions, and sexual abominations of Montreal's Hôtel-Dieu was both a best seller and a cause célèbre. She and others mention the presence of "squaw-nuns" and Indian superstition in the convent. Frothingham's works were in part responsible for the destruction of Charlestown's orphanage and other Catholic institutions by Protestant mobs.[62]

The apparent revival of the captivity mystique was accompanied by the resurrection of most of the old Puritan narratives of captivity and disaster. In the 1820s, Samuel G. Drake of Boston began a series of reprints of Colonial narratives that continued to appear into the 1860s. Increase Mather's tracts on King Philip's War and the tracts of Saltonstall and Hutchinson were among those reprinted. The most popular single narrative was Drake's edition of Benjamin Church's narrative, but he set the old hero's tale in a framework of captivities, both current and traditional. In this guise the work was reissued thirteen times in New York, Boston, and Exeter, New Hampshire, between 1825 and 1846. Other collections of captivities and similar or related narratives were titled *Indian Captivities* (Boston, 1839), *Tragedies of the Wilderness* (Boston, 1846), *The Old Indian Chronicle* (Boston, 1836), and *Indian Biography*, which was reissued nine times between 1832 and 1845 under various titles and with numerous additions. Drake sometimes reprinted the narratives as he found them, but he sometimes composed versions of his own for the purpose of discovering the dominant themes and significances of the captivity experience. Like Flint in his abstraction of Boone's hunting expedition and captivity, Drake was detailing the pattern of an experience which he himself regarded as archetypal.

Among the most interesting of the reprints that appeared during this period (although not published by Drake) is the first American reprint (1831) of Robert Rogers's adventures, *Reminiscences of the French War* (1765). Rogers, out of favor because of his pro-British leanings in the Revolution, is here refurbished as an authentic New England hero, and his Revolutionary disservices are discounted. The editor of the volume, Luther Roby, is at pains to identify Rogers' Rangers with New Hampshire and the New England frontier. However, he acknowledges freely, and even with a touch of un-Puritanical pride, that Rogers's men fought in the barbarous manner of their enemies:

> They were . . . to fight the enemy according to his own fashion, and with his own weapons. . . . [If] they sometimes deviated from the usages of civilized warfare, in making use of the scalping knife, the barbarity of the enemy, the law of retaliation, and the emergency of the time must be their apology. They were compelled to fight the Indians upon their own terms.[63]

Obedience to the principle of retaliation, inherent in the captivity mythology, sanctifies their Indian-like mode of warfare. Frank acceptance of this principle, however, signifies the open adoption of a method of justice that had been traditionally associated with the "vengeful Indian" and, on that ground, condemned. Just as in Mather's treatment of the captivity to specters of Mercy Short, the need to combat the Indian becomes the excuse for adopting an "Indian ethic." The author of *Reminiscences* goes so far as to offer Rogers's example as a means of preserving American loyalty to Revolutionary principles, despite the fact that Washington proscribed Rogers as a British sympathizer.[64]

Reminiscences also includes a number of highly interesting captivity tales which reflect both the continuing power of the captivity myth, with its anti-Indian values, and the countertendency to accept initiation into the Indian's world as a precondition for American heroism. The story of William Moore, one of the rangers, involves a captivity of six years, during which Moore is compelled to eat (or at least mouth) the heart of a fellow captive and is then adopted as a son by the mother of an Indian Moore had killed. Thus killer and victim, captive and captor become reconciled. Like Boone, Moore "gained the affections of the Savages" during his protracted stay.[65] His partaking of the wilderness Eucharist seems not to have disqualified him for membership in the roll of those sanctified by captivity.

Even more striking is the narrative (included in Roby's book) of John Stark's captivity and later adventures. Stark, New Hampshire's great hero in the Revolution and a former ranger, was captured by the St. Francis Indians when a young man. His treatment among them is described in much the same manner as that of Boone. Like Filson's Boone, he gains their approval and adoption by a chief because of his bravery and refusal to do "Squaw's work." Like the Boone of Wilder's scurrilous account, Stark's experience leads him to contrast civilized with savage men to the advantage of the latter:

> They were pleased with his boldness, called him "young chief," and he was accordingly adopted as the son of their sachem. In the latter days of his life, he used to relate with much humour, the incidents of his captivity; observing that he had experienced more genuine kindness from the savages of St. Francis, than he ever knew prisoners of war to receive from any civilized nation.[66]

That Stark should be permitted to speak thus, in a narrative intended to portray him as an exemplary hero, is a sign of the changes in New England attitudes toward the frontier that had taken place since the Puritans. Still, it is worth noting that Stark's acceptance of Indian adoption is sanctified by the fact that he is a captive, not a voluntary renegade. (Even Crockett acquired an odor of sanctity after his captivity and martyrdom at the Alamo.)

Thus the captivity tradition held as strong in popular literature as in religious enthusiasm. In 1824, the same year in which Henry Trumbull's pirated version of Wilder's book appeared in Providence, two popular captivities were published in New England and New York. The response to these works suggests that the captivity pattern still expressed that section's conception of its relationship to the two extremes of American life and history — civilized Europe and the savage wilderness. The first of these works was Israel Ralph Potter's tale of his captivity in England, published by Henry Trumbull; the second, James Seaver's account of the Indian captivity of Mary Jemison, "the White Woman of the Gennessee." Both narratives are in the quasi-fictional form traditionally favored by American presses, but both were received as literature. Seaver's narrative sold as well as the novels of Scott and Cooper during the 1820s, and in the year of its appearance it sold better than either novelist. Potter's narrative, while less popular, became the basis for a novel by Melville.

Both narratives reflect the developments in the frontier literature of the preceding half-century, particularly the discovery that the marriage myth or marriage metaphor lies at the bottom of the captivity genre (and of the Indian-war and exploration genres as well). Potter and Seaver offer an inverted view of the marriage metaphor as Flint and Byrd had expressed it. Flint's Boone and Byrd's English colonists are renewed in strength by their marriage to the women of the wilderness. The marriages of Potter and Mrs. Jemison result in the prolongation of their exiles — their captivities are of fifty years' duration — and the intensification of their miseries. Like Wilder's Boone, the protagonists suffer a racial degeneration by their wedding of "American" and "non-American" qualities.

As in the traditional captivity narrative, Israel Potter and Mary Jemison represent the values of American society in an alien and hostile world. Their ordeals are a testing of their fidelity to those values and of the power of such fidelity to redeem the soul from its hellish bondage. Potter and Mrs. Jemison attempt to live by the remembered standards of American or Christian morality and social decency, and both (or their editors for them) express an acute awareness of the view society will take of their acts during their captivity. Both, however, are forced to adjust to their surroundings, and the power of American values in their daily lives weakens as memory grows faint. This necessary adaptation to their circumstances is most dramatically expressed in their marriages to representatives of the cultures that hold them captive. Ultimately, however, Mrs. Jemison and Israel Potter are redeemed from captivity and attain something like a proper place in their native society.

Potter begins life as an Indian trader and mariner, fights at Bunker Hill, and is captured by the British on a privateering foray. He is taken to England and, like Ethan Allen before him, attempts to serve his nation's cause as a spy and a spokesman for the American cause. His marriage to an Englishwoman and the birth of a son make it impossible for him to take passage to America with other returning captives at the war's end, for the American government will pay only for its own citizens, and Potter (like the Dutchman Vandelure in Decalves's narrative of the western Indians) will not desert the wife of his captivity. He is thus compelled to eke out a miserable living as a mender of old chairs — doomed to poverty, dependence, and social inferiority — when he might have lived as an independent yeoman on his own land in America. Ultimately, the death of his wife frees him, and he returns to America at the age of seventy to seek (unsuccessfully) a pension.

Mrs. Jemison's narrative closely parallels Potter's, but where the former soldier experiences the social hardships of a poor American in a class-oriented society, Mrs. Jemison experiences the profound psychological trauma of a helpless Christian soul in the clutches of the devil's people, the embodiment of all her dark impulses. Her psychological plight is far more severe than Potter's, since he is a mature man when captured and she is a young girl. Potter retains strong memories of his past, but she soon loses the memory of Christianity and the habits of white communities, retaining only the unhelpfully vague knowledge that she does not belong among her adopted people. Potter returns from Europe, but Mrs. Jemison never wholly escapes from the world of the Indian. Even though the tatters of her white inheritance still invest her in her captivity and enable her to end her days in respectability and relative affluence as the heiress of tribal lands, she retains a sense of guilt about her marriages. Her peace of mind is constantly threatened by the outbreaks of fratricidal and Oedipal violence within her family and by her own inability either to impose matriarchal order or to mollify by feminine suasion (in the manner of Mrs. Rowlandson).

Although Seaver's account closely resembles the traditional captivity narrative, he makes some important departures from the traditional images and value structures, which reflect the changing attitudes of New Englanders toward the Indians and their historic relationship to them. Seaver's treatment thus becomes a blend of self-contradictory and ambivalent ideas about the Indians and their merit relative to America and Europe. He gives a sympathetic account of the Indian myths of creation and Indian morality but decries Indian superstition. He appends numerous accounts of Indian and renegade atrocities but makes no attempt to conceal or explain away Mrs. Jemison's evident affection and admiration for her warrior-husbands and her attainment through them of a respectable financial position in New York State. Potter emerges from European captivity an old, broken, ruined man; Mrs. Jemison emerges with more wealth and position than she had before her captivity, albeit with severe psychological wounds. Potter's tale was retold by Melville, but even in that form it had a limited popularity. Mrs. Jemison's narrative was a best seller in 1824 and for many years thereafter; its sales, in fact, placed it on a par with the novels of Cooper and Scott.[67]

Seaver describes Mrs. Jemison, from whose lips he heard her narrative, as an extraordinarily active woman of fifty, whose behavior smacked oddly of both the cabin and the wigwam. Her complexion remained white, and she expressed emotion with a freedom and sensitivity not expected of an Indian or a white Indian. He makes much of her virtuous, industrious habits and stresses her Puritanical humility and plainness of dress. Although her wealth was sufficient for her to dress fashionably, she preferred her Indian clothes and rejected ostentation. Seaver puzzles over whether this is a result of her Indian habits or of the natural simplicity and austerity of her nature. Like an Indian, though, she was jealous of her rights and suspicious of white people: she kept a lawyer by her side throughout her interview with Seaver in order that she might not confuse her legal title to her lands by any unguarded word.

Potter's marriage in England involves him in the complications of social life, the conflicts of manners and classes. Mrs. Jemison's captivity in the wilderness involves her in psychological more than social complications. Early in her account she tells of her first marriage to an Indian, Sheninjee, a gentle man and a good provider for her and their children:

> Sheninjee was a noble man; large in stature; elegant in his appearance; generous in his conduct; courageous in war; a friend in peace; and a great lover of justice. He supported a degree of dignity far above his rank. . . . Yet, Sheninjee was an Indian. The idea of spending my days with him, at first seemed completely irreconcilable to my feelings: but his good nature, generosity, tenderness, and friendship towards me, soon gained my affection; and, strange as it may seem, I loved him! [68]

Not many years after their marriage, Sheninjee dies, and she is forced to remarry. Her next husband, Hiokatoo, is no such quasi Christian as Sheninjee but a war-loving, scalping, torturing red devil, renowned for his cruelty to the whites. This marriage plunges her into a deeper union with the true spirit of the Indian. The results for her family are disastrous: the sons of her two marriages are perpetually at each other's throats, and fratricide occurs twice. Her brood seems marked by the degeneracy associated with the frontiersmen. As if to corroborate this impression, Mrs. Jemison also experiences an untoward ingratitude from a white kinsman, a frontier farmer, whom she has befriended. But although her brood is degenerate and self-destructive, Mrs. Jemison and her second husband — the pure white and the pure Indian — emerge as admirable characters in her narrative. She states that she has refused an opportunity to return to her white family, preferring her family ties to the bloody Hiokatoo.

Mrs. Jemison clearly admires Hiokatoo for his courage and his power. Indeed, he emerges in the narrative as a kind of Indian Daniel Boone, preserving his sexual and martial powers until his death at the incredibly ancient age of 103. She says, admiringly, that although he was "an old man when I first saw him, he was by no means enervated. Like Boone, he was trained from the cradle as a hunter and soldier and was renowned as the performer of incredible feats of strength." Her description of him is strikingly like current descriptions of Boone, as well as Cooper's description of Natty Bumppo and Simms's portrayals of frontier types in "Daniel Boon" and *Guy Rivers*:

> Hiokatoo was about six feet four or five inches high, large boned, and rather inclined to leanness. He was very stout and active, for a

man of his size, for it was said by himself and others, that he had
never found an Indian who could keep up with him on [sic] a race, or
throw him at wrestling. His eye was quick and penetrating; and his
voice was of that harsh and powerful kind, which, amongst the Indians, always commands attention. His health had been uniformly good.
. . . And, although he had, from his earliest days, been inured to almost constant fatigue, and exposure to the inclemency of the weather,
in the open air, he seemed to lose the vigor of the prime of life only by
the natural decay occasioned by old age.[69]

Mrs. Jemison herself shares this strength of physical constitution and adds
to it the austerity of Puritan virtues. Like Mrs. Rowlandson among the Indians, she neither smokes nor drinks nor joins in dances or "frolics." [70] She
describes her situation in 1823 with a good deal of contentment; and wit-
tingly or unwittingly, Seaver's account of her words recalls both Byron's
image of the aged Boone seated in the midst of his happy brood of unspoiled "children of the woods" and Dwight's image of the free American
farmer on his own land — a revolutionary variation on the restoration
scene that concluded the captivity tales of the Puritans:

> I live in my own house, and on my own land. . . . Thus situated in
> the midst of my children, I expect that I shall soon leave the world,
> and make room for the rising generation. . . . If my family will live
> happily, . . . I feel as though I could lay down in peace a life that has
> been checked in almost every hour, with troubles of a deeper dye,
> than are commonly experienced by mortals.[71]

The Jemison and Potter captivities reflect the mingling of new positive attitudes toward the Indian and the West with the traditional patterns
that fear of the wilderness had always taken. They also reflect the emergence of distinct images of the wilderness and the Old World as alternative
models for American life. (The contrast between the Potter and Seaver
narratives also reveals the literary consequences of the divergent traditions
of European and American prose fiction — the former derived from the literary tradition of social drama, the latter from the Puritan personal-confes-
sion and captivity-narrative tradition.) The Old World exemplifies all the
social ills from which America had, with labor, attempted to free itself.
The New World of the wilderness is the realm of psychological terror, in
which the dreams that led Americans to break free of Europe take on tan-
talizing or nightmarish shapes. It is in the West that the answer to the riddle of American identity lies, for in Europe the rigid class structure and the
fixed stereotypes of established bigotry place narrow limits on the American's ability to realize and express his individual identity. Yet the social ri-
gidity of Europe has its reassuring qualities, providing a sustaining struc-

ture for the individual. The wilderness solitudes can as soon destroy the American as enable him to create a new self.

Typical of the New England tradition in frontier writing during this period is Catherine Sedgwick's *Hope Leslie* (1827). The plot itself plays numerous variations on the captivity theme; and it is clear from the epigraphs to her chapters that the author had read extensively in the Colonial histories of captivities and Indian wars (either in the original or in Drake's reprints), in the tracts of Indian missionaries, and in more recent studies of Indian life, as well as in the early Leatherstocking novels of Cooper. Her sympathetic treatment of the (vanished) Indians is typical of the trend already noted in connection with the pro-Indian biographies and the tentribes tracts of the 1820s and 1830s. Similar plots and attitudes appear in Lydia M. Child's *Hobomok* (1824) — in which, as in *Hope Leslie*, a white captive woman marries an Indian — James Eastburn's and Robert Sands's *Yamoyden* (1820), and the "Indian dramas" of the 1820s, of which Bird's *Oralloosa* and J. A. Stone's *Metamora* are typical examples.

The hero of *Hope Leslie* is Everell Fletcher, scion of an English family too fond of liberty to remain in England and too tolerant to be entirely comfortable in the Puritan coastal towns. With his mother and the Leslie sisters, Hope and Mary (his wards), he moves to the frontier in 1642, just after the conclusion of the Pequot War, and settles in the environs of Springfield. To the household is added Magawisca, daughter of the last surviving Pequot chief and now a servant to the victors. She is tall and aristocratic in bearing, "a wild doe from the forest," and between her and Everell a strong emotional attachment is formed. A similar affection grows between Mary Leslie and Magawisca's brother Oneco, then children of ten.

Magawisca is tormented by divided loyalties and affections. She is aware of her father's plan to avenge the murder and enslavement of his people by attacking the Fletchers, yet her affection for Everell and his mother runs counter to the ties of blood. Thus the key problem of the novel is posed: to which world does the American belong, English, or Indian, or some divided blend of the two? Magawisca cannot betray her father. He attacks, and Mrs. Fletcher and her daughters are murdered horribly on their doorstep, while Everell and Mary are bound and carried into captivity. Mary, too weak to travel, is saved and borne by Oneco. Magawisca attempts to assuage her divided heart by freeing Everell, but she fails. He is brought to a sacred mountain for sacrifice, and just when her father is about to slay Everell, in the very manner in which the English killed his own son and heir, she suddenly leaps from a thicket and interposes her arm. The chief's stroke descends; her arm is lopped off; she cries that this sacrifice has bought Everell's life; and the Indians, awestruck, allow the mourning Everell to escape, believing the girl is dead.

At this point a second narrative begins, and another character is introduced: Hope Leslie, sister of the captured Mary and the embodiment of all that is pure and good in Christian maidenhood. She replaces the remembered Magawisca in Everell's heart. Against her virtue (and simultaneously against the liberty of New England) a plot forms. It is led by a trinity of villains drawn from the bosom of New England tradition — Sir Philip Gardiner, a sensual, materialistic Englishman with the cold heart and calculating depravity of a European courtier; Thomas Morton, the famous debauchee of Merrymount, now grown old and suffering the physical consequences of his sins; and Jennet, the Fletchers' maid, an incarnation of all that was wrong with Puritanism, a bigot and persecutor of Indians and witches. The Indians, in Romantic contrast, are treated sympathetically. Their lust for vengeance and their cruelty are seen as instinctual and inevitable reactions, for which nature rather than their own souls is blamable. In this context their overcoming of nature in frequent acts of mercy and charity becomes more remarkable. The Indian hag Nelema cures a sick Englishman, though she has every reason to hate him and his race. Jennet responds by accusing her of witchcraft, since (to a mind unacquainted with Indian herb-skill) the cure seems to pass the bounds of nature.

To be sure, the plot against the virtue of Hope Leslie and the political liberty of New England fails — but not before Hope has gone through a series of trials in captivity. Magawisca returns, hiding her "deformity" beneath a robe, to spy out the land for her father and, incidentally, to reestablish contact with Everell. She brings with her Oneco and Mary, who, it now appears, have been married. Hope's reaction is intense: "At this first assurance that she really beheld this loved lost sister, Hope uttered a scream of joy; but when, at a second glance, she saw her in her savage attire, fondly leaning on Oneco's shoulder, her heart died within her; a sickening feeling came over her — an unthought-of revolting of nature." [72] This is, as Miss Sedgwick knows, the traditional Puritan revulsion against sexual marriage with the Indians. But Hope, apparently, is not wholly a girl of her time, for sisterly love overcomes her revulsion. Nonetheless, she is convinced of the superiority of her religion and culture and tries, by fair means and some casuistry, to win her sister back. For this the author rebukes her soundly, through the mouth of Magawisca.

At this moment the treacherous Gardiner intervenes and snatches Magawisca and Mary; Oneco grabs Hope and flees. The exchange of captivations offers a contrast that underlines the changes in the New England notion of Indian captivity. The English captives are persecuted and unjustly jailed; Hope, fleeing from Oneco, is nearly captured and raped by European pirates in Gardiner's pay. But the Indians treat their captive civilly and even kindly, with a natural respect for virtue.

It is the Indian heroine Magawisca who, at the conclusion of the novel, resolves the problem of divided love and loyalty that troubles Everell, Mary, and even Hope herself. It is she who informs Everell that love — even sibling love — between them is impossible, for they are too much bound by blood and experience to the fate of their severed races. When Everell offers to share the land with Magawisca and her people, she replies: "It cannot be. . . . My people have been spoiled; we cannot take as a gift that which is our own; the law of vengeance is written on our hearts: you say you have a written rule of forgiveness — it may be better if ye would be guided by it; it is not for us: the Indian and the white man can no more mingle and become one than day and night." [73] Earlier she has compared the coming of the whites to the "daylight" that chases away and destroys the "shadow" and its Indian people.[74] Magawisca, for all her racial pride (perhaps because of it), does exactly what the Puritan would have her do — refuse to mingle her blood with the white man's, preserving her racial integrity and his. As Magawisca says, the proper bride for Everell is Hope.

But the novel has a further message: it is possible for one to become wholly absorbed in the wilderness way of the Indian, to the extent that one loses all ties to the white world. This is the experience of the captive Mary, who has married Oneco. Miss Sedgwick violates Puritan psychology and aligns herself with the more radical environmentalists in asserting that Mary's proper place is now with her Indian husband and in seeing this acculturation in a positive light, rather than as a sort of degeneracy. It is Magawisca who explains this to Hope: "Both virtue and duty . . . bind your sister to Oneco. She hath been married according to our simple modes, and persuaded by a Romish father, as she came from Christian blood, to observe the rules of their law. When she flies from you, as she will, mourn not over her, Hope Leslie; the wild flower would perish in your gardens; the forest is like a native home to her, and she will sing as gayly again as the bird that hath found its mate." [75]

Thus, by means of the captivity, each of the characters finds his proper identity, his proper place in the world, his proper social milieu. For Everell and Hope, the social world of American Christendom is clearly appropriate; their doubles, Mary and Oneco, find the same bonds of social amity in the Indian villages. Only Magawisca, the divided heroine whose blood sacrifice redeemed Everell from the grave, remains unmated and solitary. But she herself dispels the notion that she must perish forlorn in a wilderness solitude. She has, as Miss Sedgwick notes, the God-making eye of the Indian, "whose Imagination breathed a living spirit into all the objects of Nature." When Hope fears that her mind will be "wasted in those hideous solitudes" of the wilderness, she replies: "Solitudes! . . . Hope Leslie, there is no solitude to me; the Great Spirit and his ministers are everywhere present and visible to the eye of the soul that loves him; Nature is but his interpreter; her forms are but bodies for his spirit. . . . Those beautiful lights . . . that shine alike on your stately domes and our forest homes, speak to me of his love to all: think you I go to a solitude, Hope Leslie?" [76]

Hope Leslie suggests both the continuing power of the captivity myth and the changes it had undergone since the days of Cotton Mather. The Romanticization of the Indian, the acceptance of the idea of white-Indian intermixing, and the use of the conventional Romantic-novel form set the book off from its literary ancestors. Yet the centrality of the captivity myth is still evident: captivity is the means for whatever acculturation the whites are permitted to undergo, the means to whatever reconciliation between Indian and settlers is possible. The alternatives posed to the characters are still the same: one can either succumb to the Indian spell or resist and reject it, seeking proper love objects among one's own people. But the book has a further suggestion to offer, regarding the proper approach of a white man to the wilderness. If (like Gardiner) the American enters the wilderness as a hunter of free land, wild beasts, and Indians, he will become like the thing he hunts — a creature wholly subject to animal impulse and the material world. If he enters as a captive, resisting changed circumstances and the temptations of strange marriage, striving always to preserve his white Christian heritage, his adjustment to the wilderness will not debase him and will require only minimal adjustments in his character and habits. Indeed, he may even be able, in the end, to impose his inherited culture on the wilderness he enters.

The power of the captivity motif to sanctify the marriage of the American and the wilderness can be seen in two poems dealing with the wilderness, Whittier's "Mogg Megone" and Bryant's "The Prairies." In Whittier's poem, the consequences of the hunter's life are tragedies — murder, betrayal, and miscegenation. In Bryant's, the experience of captivity is part of the natural process by which nations, like plants, flourish and decay; it is thus an important part of the revolutionary process called progress.

Whittier's tale revolves around the destruction of Norridgewock in the 1720s by New England rangers, who killed the tribal chiefs and the Jesuit missionary Sebastien Râlé, or Ralle. The villains of the piece are white renegades, John Bonython and Father Râlé. The former is an "outlaw" from New England, a hunter more disposed to the Indian than the Puritan life, who lives with his daughter Ruth in the Indian-haunted solitude of the woods. Ruth is the child of solitude, whose passions, innocent of any need for restraint, grow great in the emptiness of the wilds. She is seduced and betrayed by an English ranger, who deserts her, and abets her father in a plot of revenge. The Indian chief Megone is promised the white girl for his squaw if he will return with the Englishman's scalp. When he has enacted the Bonythons' revenge and comes to claim his bride and lusted-for bedfellow, Bonython makes him drunk. Ruth, more savage than her father, murders Mogg, then goes to confess to Father Râlé. The priest, whose evil designs against New England died with Mogg, rejects her and profanes his priestly role; in retribution, he perishes a coward during the English attack. Ruth flees into the wilderness and dies there. Such are the consequences of the life of solitude, the life of the wilderness hunter, for those whose appropriate sphere is social. The Indians are seen in a favorable light, praying with Râlé or tending their pastoral fields under his supposedly paternal care. The Indianized whites and the Indians suborned to serve white designs — the amalgamated figures — are the sources of evil. Whittier's tale is therefore a dramatization of the end psychological effects of Indian solitude on white sensibilities and of white culture on the Indians.

In Bryant's poem, the outcome of the captivity marriage is seen in more optimistic terms as the foundation of a new race. Bryant views the prairies, imagining them first as a "Garden" or "temple," then as a great ocean of land, a sea beneath whose earthy billows the bones of wrecked cities lie like shattered hulks. His realization of the oceanic quality of the prairie is accompanied by his immersion in an inward ocean of the mind, of reverie. In his dreams he sees the history of the first conquest of the continent, in which the conquering role now played by his own people is transferred to the present Indians, who come to destroy the native Mound Builders and lay their cities waste. The red men are utter savages, "roaming hunter-tribes, warlike and fierce," unlike the agrarian, "urbanized" Mound Builders. Some of the older natives remain as captives and are adopted into the tribe, where they mingle their blood with the red man's, disappearing with a lingering sense of regret into the less admirable life of their conquerors:

> Haply some solitary fugitive,
> Lurking in marsh and forest, till the sense
> Of desolation and of fear became
> Bitterer than death, yielded himself to die.
> Man's better nature triumphed then. Kind words
> Welcomed and soothed him; the rude conquerors
> Seated the captive with their chiefs; he chose
> A bride among their maidens, and at length
> Seemed to forget — yet ne'er forgot — the wife
> Of his first love, and her sweet little ones,
> Butchered, amid their shrieks, with all his race.[77]

Thus even in that rude time the social passions triumphed over the savagery and fear of solitude.

The cycle of things is, as Bryant says, repeated in the evolution and decay of all living things and all nations. The triumphant red man now relives the experience of the Mound Builder, and his hunting cry is replaced by the "domestic hum" of the bee and the Sabbath song of white maidens and Christian worshipers. In a sense, this corresponds to Cotton Mather's idea that the white triumph over the Indian was a retribution, a vengeance in kind on the Indians for past crimes. Bryant has mellowed the process by making it seem as natural as the ripening of fruit. The social passion triumphed when the Indians adopted the captive Mound Builder; when civilization shall have absorbed and assimilated the Indian's prairie and the remnants of his tribe, the cycle will be complete. This, at least, is the poet's dream, from which a "fresher wind" awakes him, "breaks my dream." Gone are the Mound Builder ruins and the visions of multiplied Greenfields covering the prairie like herds of white buffalo. Bryant is back in the real West: "And I am in the wilderness alone." [78] But now the solitude is simply physical, for on a spiritual or mental plane Bryant still stands amid the domestic bustle of future comers.

As the contrast between "Mogg Megone" and "The Prairies" suggests, the aura of the captivity narrative cast a sanctifying glow on whatever figures it touched, whether of Indian pagans or Daniel Boone, while the shadow of the hunter invested the ill-clad and worse-educated figures of the Davy Crocketts and Simon Suggses with a dark and threatening power for evil. As a protector of the family and rescuer of captives, Daniel Boone might play a hero's role; as a hunter and lover of wilderness solitudes, he was a threat to the existence of civilization. Early western accounts of Boone that were aimed at eastern audiences, such as Hall's "The Backwoodsman," played more or less successfully on the association of Boone with the rescue of captive Christian maidens.

After the furor of the Jacksonian advent had somewhat died down — and after the crisis of New England's feelings toward the West had passed from fear to patriotic approval — John M. Peck, a western Baptist minister, succeeded in placing Boone in the pantheon of American heroes that New England's Jared Sparks was then erecting in his multivolume *Library of American Biography*. Peck's *Life of Daniel Boon*, which appeared as volume 13 (Boston, 1847), portrays Boone as a domesticated being, the protector and conservator of American and Christian values. Peck's Boone is free of greed and the desire for social preeminence. His motivation for emigrating is not Faustian but rather a Puritanical dislike of the "fashions, and the oppressions of the rich in North Carolina." [79] The "rich" of Boone's time, however, are to be equated, not with the present upper classes, but with the tyrannical, monopolistic, and royalist aristocrats of prerevolutionary days. Boone abhors their economics as he abhors their un-Puritan periwigs, and his own economic aspirations are not unlike those of the Massachusetts merchants of the 1770s. Oppression forces him to an act of rebellion, compelling him to desert a model household for the wilderness. His action, however, is comparable to the colonials' declaration of their independence — a regrettable breach in good order made necessary by circumstances which Boone, like the Puritan captive or emigrant, is unable to prevent.

Peck elaborates on Filson's description of Boone's first home as a "peaceable habitation." Boone is described as a perfect family man and Rebecca as a model housewife: "His affectionate wife, who was an excellent household manager, kindly and quietly consented to this separation, and called into requisition her skill as a housewife in assisting to provide the necessary outfit." [80] Peck completely ignores the fire-hunt legend, which characterizes Rebecca as a spirit of the wilderness. He also ignores the evidence of her own considerable prowess as a hunter and pioneer, which had been brought forward by Hall in his account of Rebecca's return to Carolina during Boone's captivity. He gives Boone an efficient housewife for his helpmeet, a woman of great domestic virtue, rather than a wild and exotic wood nymph or a rugged pioneer matriarch.

This attitude is echoed in Peck's presentation of Boone's relationship to civilization and the wilderness. Flint presented Boone as delighting in the solitude and wildness of the woods; Filson showed him reveling in its picturesque and terrible beauty; McClung showed him enjoying the absence of all signs of human cultivation. Peck's Boone admires neither scenery nor wildness nor solitude. When he arrives in Kentucky, he is already very conscious of his role as a pioneer of civilization. Thus he experiences no great change of heart at the sight of the West. Peck shows him simply noting the lay of the land and avoiding the Indians during his first expedition. His captivity, which Filson represented as a stage in his initiation into the wilderness and which Flint's sketch depicted as the spiritual crisis of his life, is seen simply as an interruption in the real work of tilling the soil and laying the foundations of civilization. Boone's later emigration from Kentucky is ascribed by Peck to his unfortunate failures to maintain his rights by law. He is presented as a man driven from Kentucky by evil men, rather than as a willful exile from society.

The final chapter of Peck's biography contains the author's account of a visit to Boone and a eulogy on his character by Kentucky's Governor Morehead. Peck's own sketch is intended to dispel the old image of Boone as a coarse and violent Indian killer:

> In boyhood, he had read of Daniel Boon, the pioneer of Kentucky, the celebrated hunter and Indian fighter; and imagination had portrayed a rough, fierce-looking, uncouth specimen of humanity, and, of course, at this period of life, a fretful and unattractive old man. But in every respect the reverse appeared. His high, bold forehead was slightly bald, and his silvered locks were smooth; his countenance was ruddy and fair, and exhibited the simplicity of a child. His voice was soft and melodious. A smile frequently played over his features in conversation. . . . His clothing was the coarse, plain manufacture of the family; but every thing about him denoted that kind of comfort, which was congenial to his habits and feelings, and to a happy old age.[81]

Peck found him a representative of the "better class" of western pioneers—although not of the "best class." As a minister he found Boone's religious sentiments particularly interesting. He does much to render Boone's religious backgrounds and sentiments acceptably orthodox. He claims that Boone's father was "an Episcopalian," who "taught his children the rudiments of faith and forms of worship used in that church." (In reality, Boone's immediate ancestors were largely defrocked Quakers.) Peck found Boone himself "not destitute of religious sentiments," despite the fact that "a large portion of his life was spent without the influence of gospel ministry." Peck found him reverential toward his Creator, "moral, temperate, and chaste" of character, and free of "superstition" and "religious credulity." Unlike the "superstitious and illiterate" classes of the frontier, he "told of no remarkable dreams and strange impressions." Although he had always believed himself the instrument of his Creator, he was free of the wild messianism of some western zealots. He attributed his accomplishments as a pioneer, not to any foresight of his own, but to his simple pursuit of his duty.[82] In short, Peck's Boone is a humble, virtuous man, obeying his Creator's designs rather than seeking to create his own, and thus emerging as the most heroic of common men.

Governor Morehead's eulogy, which closes the Peck biography, carries Peck's characterization one step further. Morehead sees Boone as the type of the western hunter, who "came originally to the wilderness, not to settle and subdue it, but to gratify an inordinate passion for adventure and discovery; to hunt . . . ; to roam through the woods; to admire the 'beauties of nature;' in a word, to enjoy the lonely pastimes of a hunter's life, remote from the society of his fellow men." His sagacity was limited by his lack of education. He was "powerless to originate plans on a large scale," although adept at executing "the designs of others." Yet he was exempt from the "rude characteristic of the backwoodsman," from the lust for human murder, and from the lack of familial love that characterizes most solitary nomads.[83] Where Peck's account of Boone seeks to make Boone respectable in conventional eastern terms, Morehead's eulogy places Boone in his proper rung of society, above the run of his class but inferior to the true leaders of American society.

Southern Image of the Boone Figure

The South had been the slowest of the sections to develop its own literary printing and bookselling trade. Hence it remained dependent on English presses and productions for its literary fare and never developed a popular literature analogous to that of New England in the Colonial period. Where every Indian skirmish in New England (and later in the West of Hall, McClung, and Flint) produced a deluge of cheap books and magazine copy, southern Indian wars were less thoroughly reported and less intensely imagined. Whatever literature those wars produced appeared first in London and was then reimported to the South and circulated among the small literate population in the scattered towns and plantations. Where New England and middle-colony authors and printers could produce books with an exclusively American audience in mind, southern writers and their English publishers had to suit the tastes and interests of both English and American audiences. Moreover, the southern literary audiences were dominated, like southern politics and economics, by the semi-aristocratic planter class. During the Colonial period this class formed the bulk of the southern reading public, and their tastes in religion and literature ran more to the latitudinarian, rationalist philosophy and neoclassic literature of the Enlightenment than to Calvinist interpretations of the Indian wars. Their social position as rulers of a population of slaves, tenants, and marginal farmers reinforced their association of themselves with the liberal *noblesse* of prerevolutionary France and later with the nobly born or nobly constituted Romantic heroes.

During the Colonial period the New Englanders had created a considerable body of specialized literature on the Indian wars, devoted to the symbolic interpretation of their historical experience in the light of the violent conflict between Indian and settler. The lack of such a body of literature in the South restricted the southern author's artistic vocabulary and frame of reference to contemporary thought and current literary trends. Trumbull's interpretation of the West, to be sure, owed much to the current attitudes of New England conservatives toward the emerging states of the West. However, Trumbull was able to create (for his New England audience) the impression that his vision of history represented the culmination of the historical continuity of American experience. He accomplished this primarily through subtle allusions to the symbolism and terminology of the literature of Puritans like the Mathers. Having no such tradition, the southern writers had to create one through retrospective views of southern history, based inevitably on contemporary social and literary conventions.

It was perhaps this lack of a tradition of popular literature and lack of a prosperous popular press that cut the South out of the direct line of literary commerce that linked the presses of the axis cities with the mythogenetic sources of the West. Even southwestern humor, that distinctly sectional genre, found its chief journal (Porter's *Spirit of the Times*) located in New York; and writers of that school, seeking the wider circulation and fame that a book collection of their stories might achieve, tended to have their works printed in the axis.[84] Southern writers who engaged the subject of the frontier — William Gilmore Simms, James K. Paulding, Joseph P. Kennedy, and Robert M. Bird, among them — seem to have been responding to literary depictions of the West originating in the axis cities or in Europe, rather than to the original productions of western mythologists. The example of Daniel Bryan's *Mountain Muse* is instructive in this connection: a kinsman of the hero, presumably having access to the kind of folk material Flint made use of, he nevertheless composes his epic in incompetent imitation of Milton and Collins. Likewise, William Gilmore Simms, perhaps the best of the southern novelists, came to a literary consideration of the historical-mythological character of Boone long after he had begun practicing the art of writing historical romances about the "border." His portrayals of the southern frontier in *Guy Rivers* (1834) and *The Yemassee* (1835) are clearly responses to the literary West of Cooper, rather than the contemporary West of Crockett or the legendary West of Flint. Simms's contemporary, Robert Bird, specifically compares his own border romances with those of Cooper in the introduction to his *Nick of the Woods*. Not until 1845 did he deal directly with Boone and give evidence of acquaintance with sources outside of the genres of high-culture literature. His sources, even so, were secondhand: he cites Wilder's edition of the Filson narrative, a work originating in the axis and partaking as much of New England and of Europe as of the West. The essay on "Daniel Boon" appeared first in Simms's Charleston magazine, *The Southern and Western* [or *Simms'*] *Magazine*, which was to perish of a lack of audience that same year. It was also printed in the axis as part of an anthology of critical pieces by Simms called *Views and Reviews*.

Simms's treatment of Boone, following as it does his formulation of an image of the frontier in his novels, is interesting as an indication of the values southern writers brought to frontier material. In describing Boone, he disregarded Wilder's hostile assessment of the hero as a white Indian and presented him as a natural aristocrat with roots in the chivalric tradition of the South. As a Romantic nobleman, Boone is a fit representative of the South in its confrontation with the American wilderness and the Indian. Where Wilder condemned his hatred of "d——d Yankees," Simms admires him for his disdain of Yankee commercialism. Hall, McClung, and Flint made a similar judgment of Boone's character; but where the westerners substituted the love of hunting and adventure for a Yankee love of gain, Simms substitutes an aristocratic love of Romantic beauty and the chivalric ideal. He compares Boone successively to an inspired poet or painter, a crusading knight-errant, and a Romantic rescuer of captive beauty.

Where the western writers boasted that Boone was a common type of frontiersman — a notion with which Wilder ironically agreed — Simms seeks to portray Boone as an uncommon type:

> He was born a pioneer. It is useless to talk about training here. A man like Boon is as much the creature of a special destiny as the poet or the painter. He has his office appointed him — the mere influence of the community in which he is reared, though these may contribute to his passion, cannot at any time subdue it. In an age of chivalry — during the Crusades — Boon would have been a knight-errant, equally fearless and gentle. That he would have been a Squire of Dames is very uncertain — but he loved his wife, and risked his scalp more than once to rescue beauty from the clutches of the savage.

Boone's Romantic love of solitude and picturesque scenery motivates his emigration to the West:

His native mood prompted his adventure. He had an eye for the picturesque in nature, as is the marked characteristic in all very great hunters — characteristics of which Cooper has given us an exquisite ideal in Leather Stocking. His mind was of a contemplative character, and loved to muse undisturbed by contact with man, upon its own movements, as influenced by the surrounding atmosphere. A constant desire for change of scene and object, is the natural growth of a passion for the picturesque, and an impatience of the staid and formal monotonies of ordinary life.[85]

Later Simms pointedly compares Boone to Byron's Childe Harold.[86]

Simms's portrait of Boone suggests that what a southern writer wanted in a frontier hero was evidence of an innate nobleness of spirit, expressed not as some vague, natural moral sense but as a genuine gentility of spirit, of blood. The metaphors of this innate quality are aristocracy ("a knight-errant") and poetic or artistic genius ("poet" and "painter," lover of "the picturesque"). Both aristocratic nobility and genius are qualities unattainable by mere effort. Their possession comes either by blood inheritance or divine grace, and it sets the possessor distinctly and immutably above and apart from the mass of his fellows. Simms's Boone is the antithesis of the western confidence-man–hunter, whose pranks and swindles make him a leveler of social hierarchies. He is rather the promise that southern aristocracy, translated to the West, will retain its essential, its racial characteristics.

The derivation of this figure is both social and literary. Simms's debt to literary Romantics like Byron and Cooper is explicitly acknowledged. Other reasons for the fixity of the southern image of the western hero in this romantic guise can be found in the peculiar structure of southern society. The institution of slavery gave the South its own unique internal frontiers, where the territory of the whites was broken by the "savage" islands of the slave quarters. Beyond those borders lay a primitive world, peopled (for the white southerner) with nightmares of vengeful savagery and bloodlust or with fever dreams of forbidden eroticism. The southerner's relationship to his slaves was psychologically equivalent to the early Puritan's relationship to the Indians, with one qualification: the southerner's contact, especially his sexual contact, with the slaves was far greater than the Puritan's contact with the hostile Indian cultures on his borders.

These internal frontiers produced much the same attitudes in the South as in New England toward those who, literally or figuratively, overstepped the boundary between the kingdoms of light and darkness, civilization and savagery. If anything, southern hostility toward (or guilt feelings over) racial amalgamation grew more intense than New England's. The southerner's preoccupation with race spilled over into his conception of social classes as well and imparted something of the feeling of racial antipathy to the relations between poor whites and plantation "aristocrats" or nouveaux riches. Democratic leveling was seen as akin to racial treason, and this exacerbated the South's objections to the northern reformers.

The most important consequence of the southern tie to European literature was the southern writers' inability to deal with the West as a psychological problem of immense national significance. Unlike the New Englanders and westerners, they did not try to reconcile the Indian and American aspects of the frontier character or to confront the problem of the "marriage" of Indian and Christian through the hunting and captivity rituals. They did not treat the West, as Bryant and Whittier did, as a field for psychological exploration. Rather, they dealt with it as Potter dealt with England, as a stage for a conflict between rigidly defined social classes, each represented by distinct and unproblematic types. To the slaveholding South there could be no question of the degeneracy inherent in any form of race mixing. Any figure who blended Indian and white traits would be automatically suspect.

The South, however, did not share New England's antipathy for the figure of the hunter. For the southerner the idea of democracy was equated with the attainment of economic equality with his economic betters — a standard which he shared with Crockett and his ilk. However, where hard cash, profitable trade, or a successful sale of peltry defined prosperity and equality for Crockett, the possession of slaves was for the southerner the hallmark of success. Until a man owned slaves and cotton or tobacco land, he was of an ignoble, impoverished class. With slaves, he was the associate and ally of the wealthiest and oldest plantation families, even if he continued to live in a scruffy frontier cabin in the Mississippi or Alabama backwoods. Thus the Jacksonian impulse toward attainment of democratic "equality of conditions" was strongly associated in the southern mind with the twinned distinction of race and social class.

The South's literary bias toward the European tradition of social fiction was reinforced by these social and racial preoccupations of the planters and would-be planters. The consequences can be seen in the South's literary contributions to the American Renaissance. Where northeastern and western writers like Cooper, Hawthorne, and Flint delved deeper into the mythological and psychological problems and significances of the frontier experience and the quest for American identity in the Indian wilderness, southerners like Robert M. Bird and Simms were restricted to the conventional formulas of the historical romance, in which identity is predetermined by social position and the wilderness is a stage for social more than psychological conflict (although Bird's *Nick of the Woods* stretches those limitations considerably).

Thus between 1800 and 1845 a distinct version of the Daniel Boone type of American hero was developed in each section of the United States and in Europe. Each vision was shaped in part by the social conditions of the particular section, especially its class divisions and tensions, and by its proximity to the access routes to either Europe or the West. In the West these forces gave rise to the figure of Davy Crockett, who embodied the western ambition for self-improvement and the attainment of equality (equated with economic prosperity) and whose career reflected the concept of economics and politics as a hunt, in which he who bags the most and biggest prey is the best man. But the West also developed the almost mystical image of the hunter delineated by Flint, as a myth-hero whose deeds of violence and destruction are deeds of love that lead him to a marriage with the wilderness. The aura of sanctity that invests Flint's hunter, who is the hero of an Indian-like myth of sacred marriage and creation, is the source of the halo that for a time circled the fool's head of Crockett and made his entrepreneurial bear slaughter seem a kind of exalted American profession.

The westerners frankly exalted the figure of the hunter. They accepted both the Indian view of his creative function and, paradoxically, the traditional European view of his fatal limitation to the pursuit of transitoriness, of material and worldly things. In the new country of the West and Southwest the social-climbing ambitions of a Crockett were seen as admirable and necessary — in fact, the underpinning of society. This was equally true in the South, which depended for its existence on the expansion of slave territory by ambitious entrepreneurs. In New England, however, Boone was acceptable as a hero only if he could be assimilated into a society whose social, political, commercial, and literary traditions were Puritan in origin. In the context of its more firmly established institutions, a figure such as Crockett threatened social upset and perhaps anarchy. Most threateningly, such a figure represented the encroaching interests and beliefs of an alien outside world — the riotous, radical laborers of Europe and the powerful commercial competitors who ruled them; the western speculator and debt-ridden farmer, friends of cheap money and foes of protection for the fledgling industry of the East; and the southern planter, likewise the foe of protection and, moreover, the proponent of a repugnant system of chattel slavery.

The captivity myth best expressed New England's sense of its relationship to these people and forces. In the world view structured by that myth, the highest values are those represented by the passive, virtuous, Christian female. The male hero — her husband (or father) and rescuer — is physically stronger but morally weaker than she. The strength that gives him power over his adversaries is also the sign of his kinship with them, his latent tendency to become a man of action rather than of thought or feeling, his potential as a hunter. The hero's function is conservative, rather than creative or procreative. He resists change as he resists the temptation to sin; he protects the feminine avatar of the social virtues instead of seeking the woman of his dark, wilderness dreams. The hunter is the antitype of this conservative hero.

CHAPTER 13

Man without a Cross:
The Leatherstocking Myth
(1823–1841)

> True myth concerns itself centrally with the onward adventure
> of the integral soul. And this, for America, is Deerslayer. A man
> who turns his back on white society. . . . An isolate, almost selfless,
> stoic, enduring man, who lives by death, by killing, but who is pure
> white.
>
> You have there the myth of the essential white America. All the
> other stuff, the love, the democracy, the floundering into lust, is a
> sort of by-play. The essential American soul is hard, isolate, stoic,
> and a killer. It has never yet melted.
>
> D. H. Lawrence, *Studies in Classic American Literature*

By 1830 the popular literature of the United States and Europe had generated several stereotyped images of the frontier hero, Daniel Boone —
images that became conventionalized and fixed in the popular imagination.
These fixed images expressed a simple perception of "the American situation" as seen through the eyes of a westerner, a southerner, a New Englander or New Yorker, and an Englishman or Frenchman. The relation of
this symbolic hero to the surrounding peoples and natural conditions —
the Indians, the settlements, the wilderness — reflected the social philosophy and political and economic anxieties of each of these sections and nations. Such images were developed as responses to problems, as symbolic
means of reducing the complexities and ambiguities of the American situation to a simple, satisfying formula. This method of problem solving does
not proceed by the difficult path of study, experiment, argument, and full
intellectual and emotional engagement with a dark unknown. Rather, it replaces the troublesome and problematic facts of the real world with a
counterworld of pseudofacts. The reader is thus given a new world to perceive, more consistent than the real one and more in line with his own
hopes, fears, and prejudices.

Had the several communities that made up the United States been able to remain isolated from one another, these fixed images might have served as durable explanations of the ultimate nature of American history and only slowly been subjected to challenge. As the publication of Wilder's book indicates, the sections were not isolated; they were linked by a communications system whose nexus was the New York–Philadelphia axis. Here works on the frontier by westerners, southerners, Europeans, and New Englanders appeared side by side and even (as in Wilder's book) between the same covers. The juxtaposition of these variant views posed a problem for the reader: it offered him irreconcilable alternatives and thus engaged his intelligence in a deeper examination of the subject. Thus for the first American novelists of stature who dealt with the frontier — Cooper, Simms, and Bird — Wilder's book and others like it were primary sources. However, Wilder and his fellows did not attempt to explore the problems their works posed. Their interest in and knowledge of human psychology ended with an ability to assess and serve the popular taste. They neither knew nor needed to know the psychological factors which shaped that taste or the significance and consequences of the popular acceptance of a particular reading of the myth.

In relating the works of conscious artists like Cooper, Simms, and Bird — and of supreme artists like Hawthorne and Melville — to those of popular mythologists like Hooper, Flint, and Trumbull, we confront a number of critical problems. The concerns of the serious art-novelist go far beyond those of the purveyor of popular images, although he may take popular materials as his point of creative departure. Similarly, his powers of analysis and of composition enable him to see further into his material and extract more from it in the way of moral, social, and metaphysical meaning than do his purely commercial colleagues. Then too, within the ranks of serious artists there are important differences in talent and intellectual powers that affect the author's ability to get to the bottom of his material. Thus any discussion which emphasizes the bond between cultural history and popular mythology, on the one hand, and the works of a serious artist, on the other, risks oversimplifying the interpretation of those works. However, it is important for our understanding both of the individual works of art and of the culture that has produced them that we be able to see how such works relate to the living culture of their period, how they function within the mythology of their place.

That such works do function in the evolution of popular mythology is demonstrable, as a glance at the career of Cooper will show. His first group of Leatherstocking novels appeared in 1823–27 and derived their power from a blending of the literary conventions of English Romantic fiction with materials from the popular literature of New England and the new West. Cooper's novels themselves helped to provoke a further literary interest in the figure of Daniel Boone among western and southern writers. McClung's anti-Romantic strictures, Flint's meliorative combination of western roughness and eastern gentility in his Boone character, Simms's appropriation of and Bird's refutation of Cooper's view of the hunter and the Indian — all testify to the impact of Cooper's fiction on the popular mind of the time. His vision of the mythic hero became a figure in the popular imagination, to which all subsequent versions of the hero had perforce to refer, whether in emulation or denigration. As a consequence, his return to the series in 1840–41 yielded novels in which the author makes the reader aware of his own consciousness of having created a myth.

Cooper's preeminence among mythologizers of the American frontier derives as much from the manner in which he (and other artists of equal or greater power) approached the literary task as it does from his fortunate choice of subject matter. The purveyors of the popular fiction that had dominated American letters since Puritan times had generated myth-images and suggested the presence of archetypal patterns in frontier history. But they had relied on the feelings and prejudices of their audiences to supply the extra imaginative effort required to illuminate the significance of the tales and transmute them into articles of a mythic faith. (Alternatively, as in the Puritan sermon, they had restricted the force of the myth by imposing a moral interpretation and applying it simplistically to the solving of limited social problems.) Only the superior literary artists were capable of the imaginative effort necessary to perceive the fundamental ambivalences of desire and value that undergulfed the fixed features of the popular myth and to carry it forward in time to the point where its ultimate consequences and meaning revealed themselves. For the popular writers and their audiences, the presentation of the evocative myth-image was the end in itself. For the literary artists, the images were the bare beginning.

George C. Bingham's painting of Daniel Boone leading the settlers through Cumberland Gap into Kentucky exemplifies the fixed image of Boone and the patterns of association that had become conventionally associated with the hero in the first fifty years of the nineteenth century. As in Greenough's evocation of the captivity mystique in his "Rescue Group," Bingham's painting evokes the emotions traditionally associated with the frontier by visual references to the several streams of lore about the frontier and frontiersmen. He treats the problem of the wilderness visually, reconciling all ambivalences into a visual whole, while leaving the fundamental question of Boone's meaning for the American character unanswered. In this his approach is essentially the same as that of Wilder, Henry Trumbull, Abraham Panther, and those other writers of captivities and Indian war tales who offered their puzzling materials straightforwardly, with almost no perception that their tales had reference to fundamental problems of history, politics, and psychology.

At the center of Bingham's painting stands Boone himself, clad in yellow buckskins and with a rifle on his shoulder. He leads by the bridle a milk-white horse, whose lowered head is level with his own. Seated upon the horse, visually above Boone, is the Madonna-like figure of a woman, her head and body covered in a flowing, gray cloak or robe. The other women in the scene wear white bonnets, emphasizing the strangeness of her garb and thus underlining the association of the emigrant group with the Holy Family fleeing into Egypt. The woman's face seems mature; her expression is pensive and perhaps sad; her eyes look abstractedly downward. Boone's eyes look up from under thick, somewhat coarse black eyebrows, out of a craggy, coarse face. Behind the enigmatic pair come the rest of the settlers, a blend of quiet, domestic figures (a girl with a bonnet; an older man looking affectionately at a younger man, perhaps his son, who walks beside him) and harsh, crude figures in violent motion — most notably, a man frozen in the act of flailing a beast with his whip. The whole group forms a triangle in the lower center of the frame, with its apex at the bright face of the Madonna-like woman; its base points are a hunting dog and a dead tree. The group is framed by the mountain pass and by the sky, stormy overhead and calm in the eastern distance. Dead trees lean dramatically away on either side of the calm, stolid triangle of marching men and women, giving the impression that for all the quiet, repose, and order of the group, some latent force within them has blasted a breach violently through the hills.

Like Wilder's catchall edition of Filson, the painting is a collection of images, each one conventional and apparently self-explanatory — but the juxtaposition is productive of questions. What is the relationship of Boone to the Madonna-like woman? Clearly, Boone is no saint or aristocrat; the coarseness of his features belies such an interpretation. Visually, he is below her, just as the Boone hero in the captivity-oriented literature of New England and the stories and biographies of Hall and Peck was morally subordinate to the females he rescued. Yet there is a possibility that the two are man and wife, halves of a whole and not alternatives of passivity and force. What is the relationship of Boone to his fellow emigrants? The hunting dog to the left and the mustachioed hunter who walks beside Boone on the right are offset by the background figure of the farmer beating his animal with a whip. Clearly Boone has neither the brutish look of the hunter nor the brutal nature of the farmer who exploits and abuses animals. The domestic group behind Boone may be more closely associated with him; but like him, they bear weapons of conquest — albeit axes instead of a rifle. The images evoke the various schools of sentiment in regard to Boone's character, his class, his historical role, his profession (hunter or husbandman? explorer or settler?), and his moral significance as an archetype of the American character. But with the fixing of the image, the painter's interpretive power ends.

The literary artists of the American Renaissance attempted to set this picture in motion, to convert statuesque fixity into dramatic movement, and thus discover the ends or consequences of the American myth. They engaged their artistic intelligence in the study of the problem and the projection of solutions. In the process of making their own discoveries and projecting them into literary form, they created fictional versions of the myth that were capable of evoking a stronger sense of audience identification than had been possible for the writers of early popular literature.

Several factors shaped the course of development of literary myth-fiction in the 1840s and 1850s. Individual genius and the peculiarities of intelligence and sensibility that characterize individual writers exercised a more profound influence over this type of fiction than they had over the popular fiction of the eighteenth and early nineteenth centuries. In the popular fiction there had been no great or profound engagement of literary intelligence with a fundamental problem; in great or near-great literature, such engagement is the primary characteristic. The writer of popular captivities succeeded through his ability to see events just as the majority of his audience would like to see them. The literary artist enlists his audience's attention by showing him perceptions that he may not have achieved and thus surprising or violating his normal expectations. The literary intelligence, however, does not exist in a vacuum. Conventional notions of the proper form and function of literature help to shape the artist's perceptions, once he attempts to set them down in writing. Moreover, his perceptions, like those of his audience, are seen through the lenses of myth and tradition. Hence the factors that shaped the fixed images of Boone in the several sections also influenced the literary efforts of writers in those sections, conditioning the manner in which they set the fixed image in motion and the conclusions they drew about the end or consequences of the mythic drama.

Writers in the various sections and in Europe saw Boone in the context of the political and psychological problem of individualism, the conflict between "society" and "solitude" as images of the good life and the American way of life. The political and social factors that led them to frame the Boone myth in this way grew out of the economic and political evolution of Europe and America in the postrevolutionary, protoindustrial era. The movement for political democracy was complemented by the Romantic belief in the unfettered expression of self as the ultimate in literary and religious freedom. These in turn were paralleled by the drive of the entrepreneurial "new men" to make their way in the world without the artificial checks of establishments and institutions. In politics, religion, economics, and aesthetics, the central conflict was that between the individual and the collective entity, between the personal and the public or organizational will, between the right of the individual to solitude and unfettered expression and the right of society to impose order in the name of the public. In America the growth of the settled area and the decline of available land in the open wilderness reinforced the contrast between a world in which man was free to seek God and the good life in solitude and one in which his behavior was compelled by social necessities.

In a Europe recovering from the excesses of revolution and counterrevolution, extreme images of social regimentation and Byronic anarchism formed the poles of myth and fantasy about the Old World and the New. While Romantics like Byron might dream of a Boone-like solitude, they knew — as did their opponents — that society was the European's proper sphere of action. The European novel had, from its beginnings, been shaped by the conviction that character is best discovered or revealed in a social context, in which manners and class characteristics are portrayed with reasonable accuracy. In the American West, as we have seen, the solitude of the individual and his right to untrammeled freedom of movement and expression were the mythic ideal. The Northeast was more ambivalent, torn between the western and European views as it had been since Puritan times. The South, likewise, was torn between Europe and the West, but it inclined literarily to the former. New England literature traced its ancestry to the Puritans, whose literary ideals were embodied in the personal narratives in which a man, alone and unaided, confronts his God in the absolute solitude of his mind and the worldly wilderness. For the southern writer, whose purpose was to sustain and justify an elaborate social structure that blended democratic upward mobility with antidemocratic racism and class distinctions, no solitude could be absolute. Even in the empty wilderness, Simms's Boone bears with him the marks of his place in southern culture; he remains spiritually within the context of society and does not blend with the Indian wilderness. Thus the early literary fiction of the American Renaissance bears the same stamp of sectional culture as does the popular literature dealing with Daniel Boone.

The literary and intellectual consequences of these differences can be seen in the contrasts between the short tales of Hawthorne and the magazine fiction of the West and between the historical romances of Cooper, Simms, and Bird. The historical romance itself was a European literary form, and all three men adopted the form as practiced by Walter Scott. Scott's historical romances were the product of the rise of nationalistic enthusiasms in the late eighteenth and early nineteenth centuries and of the consequent Romantic vision of history as the dramatic clashing and final reconciliation of philosophical, moral, cultural, and racial opposites. The historical romance as practiced by Scott defined history in terms of the conflict between individuals representing nations and classes; and the definition of these class and national types was a primary interest of the writer. Reconciliation between the opposed groups was achieved through the revelation or discovery of a fundamental racial kinship between the parties. Thus the Scots and English in *Rob Roy* and the Saxons and Normans in *Ivanhoe* are reconciled through their common racial heritage of valor, nobility of mind, generosity of heart, and love for Christianity and the soil of England. The family ties that bind the chief characters of the historical romance provide the metaphorical structure of the work. The division within the family reflects the social disorder of the nation, and the achievement of a familial peace is the conclusion of both the social problem and the family drama.

Scott's historical romances were the most important European source for Cooper, Simms, and Bird (although Chateaubriand also had an important effect on Bird). Scott himself suggested the adaptation of his favorite genre to American history in the introduction to *Rob Roy*, in which he compares the conflict between Augustan England and wild Gaelic Scotland to the conflict between whites and Indians in America.[1] There were, however, certain problems native to America and American literature that Scott's formulas could not resolve. The question of racial kinship between the opposed parties was especially fraught with psychological tensions not present in Europe. For one thing, Americans were closer to their struggle with the Indian than Scott was to the era of English-Scottish warfare. The English and Scots had been historically reconciled and united. While the

Americans had become symbolically united with the Indian, sharing both his love of the land and his mythopoeic perception of his relationship to it, it was always difficult to acknowledge the kinship and to embrace the idea of a racial amalgamation.

For the American writer, the conflict of cultures meant the replacement or extermination of the Indian. The reconciliation of white and Indian could be seen only as the reconciliation of the hunter and his prey — a flash of sympathy and fellow feeling that caps the climactic moment when the long hunt ends and the kill is achieved. This myth of the hunter's path to the discovery of identity and to reconciliation underlay the literature that formed the American source material of Scott's American imitators. That literature was also characterized by a tendency to see the world in a mythopoeic manner and to borrow consciously from the mythology of the American Indians. Most significantly, it was a literature in which the Puritan personal-narrative tradition was strong. Hence it approached its subject matter, both the experiential or historical and the mythological, in terms of a confrontation between figures and their gods in isolation — both the physical solitude of the wilderness and the dark isolation of the psyche. The Scott novel treated man in his social context and revealed his hidden but immutable innate character through social interaction. What traditionally emerged from the American solitudes was the creation of a new character out of the old. The Puritan personal narratives were originally accounts of conversion, of the generation of a new and better soul from the broken shards of the former proud and sinful self.

The belief that a new nationality had been created in America, a new and better race of men, characterized the nationalistic fervors of the post-revolutionary and Jacksonian generations. This social fervor was the social expression of the belief (derived from the Puritans) in personal regeneration and unlimited self-improvement. The great emphasis on the theme of individual initiation into the life of the New World has at its roots the same dream of the re-creation of the self in a new image. This conversion, or self-creation, or initiation, is essentially a personal process, taking place within the individual. But in American society the experience of acculturation and of nation building made this individual experience a social one as well. All men, individually and collectively, were engaged in becoming Americans — in making a new, American identity for themselves and, by extension, for the whole culture.

This, at least, was the direction in which American literature had been moving at the time of Cooper's, Simms's, and Bird's emergence. The aesthetic poles of their world were defined, after the fact, by Hawthorne in his preface to *The House of the Seven Gables*. Hawthorne there opposes the "Novel" as a form to the "Romance." The former aims at verisimilitude and accuracy in depiction of manners; it is careful, in its attention to the limitations of its audience's mind, not to surpass conventional expectations in regard to human behavior. The romance, by contrast, aims at a psychological rather than a material or a social realism. It is based on an examination and depiction of the human mind and heart, with all their fantastic impulses and motivations — a vision that, though true, challenges the reader's perceptions instead of coddling them.[2] Cooper, Simms, and Bird stand somewhere between the two types, between the European concept of literature as a social and familial drama and the American concept of literature as a psychological drama with mythic implications that transcend social phenomena. In the course of his career, Cooper moved toward the latter model in his treatment of Leatherstocking. Simms and Bird, hampered by the South's dependence on European literary sources and models — and by the southern social mystique — did not stray far enough from their models. Although all three began with the same sources (Wilder's Boone anthology and the novels of Scott), Cooper delved more and more deeply into American and especially Indian materials and myths, while the southerners, after exciting preliminary explorations, limited themselves to the retailing of stable, sterile stereotypes.

The short fiction of Hawthorne and the early western writers is at the opposite literary pole from the historical romances of Scott, and these two types of writing frame the artistic development of Cooper and his southern imitators. The short story, as it appeared in American literary periodicals and anthologies, was the direct descendant of the Puritan personal narratives: brief, vivid tales which aimed at revealing both the nature of a fundamental change of character and the nature of God's will for man in an emotionally convincing, intensely concentrated drama. If the concerns of the novelist and the writer of historical romances derived from the conventions of social commentary and comedy, the concern of the short story — as Hawthorne and other Americans practiced it — was man in solitude, pursuing an inward quest in a realm that is empty of all but a few people, with the teeming social world of the novel thinly suggested on the tale's periphery.

The western writers, as we have seen, were very much in debt to the Puritan-born literature of the northeastern states, both for literary interest itself and for literary values and symbols. New England and New York were among the longest established colonies and had the longest and most copious history of literary effort; hence their literary forms and values and

their mythological conception of the American experience (with all attendant symbols and conventions) were fairly well formed by the nineteenth
century. In the new country of the West, where printing was more recent,
experience in the land shorter, and the population composed of recent emigrants from diverse areas and nations, neither sectional character nor sectional mythology nor sectional literary tradition was strongly formed. The
westerners had a unique view of their situation vis-à-vis the Indian, not
only because their experience was more recent than that of the East but
also because they lacked the Puritan's elaborate ideology about natural
man and his Indian avatar. Since their society was in the process of formation and since the population was in large part southern in origin and
slaveholding by conviction, they shared some of the South's preoccupation
with the definition of fixed social types, as well as the northeastern, myth-
oriented, personal-narrative tradition in literature and their own democracy of the upwardly mobile.

The contrast between Hawthorne and his western counterparts is that
between a writer working within the framework of an established tradition
of social values and mythic symbols and writers whose major task is to create a previously undefined conception of social character and the nature of
the American myth. Significantly, both Hawthorne and western writers
treat man's relationship to the wilderness in terms of the hunter myth.
Hawthorne's tales reflect a Puritan image of the wilderness as the land of
the terrible unconscious, in which the dark dreams of man impress themselves on reality with tragic consequences. The hunter becomes like the
beast he hunts; the would-be destroyer of bestial sin himself degenerates
into a Belial. Western writers like Flint and Thomas B. Thorpe take a
different view, an Indian rather than a Christian or Puritan view, of the
myth of the hunter. In their tales it is presented as a white American
equivalent of the Indian creation myths. However, the western writers
were only half aware of what they were doing and so failed to get beyond
the expression of the myth to an analysis of the myth's origin and consequences. Hawthorne, who was aware of both the nature of his literary tradition and the mythic or legendary content of his tales, developed the consequences of the myth more fully. Indeed, his moral and philosophical
concerns extend so far beyond those of popular hacks who used the same
or similar material that any analysis limited to his use of traditional frontier
myth-matter is bound to oversimplify the works. Still, it is clear that such
traditionary matter is a preferred point of departure for him, and his handling of it illuminates the ambiguities inherent in the popular mythology,
even though such illumination is but one aspect of his artistic concern.

Hawthorne's tales of the frontier employ the method of the personal narrative in its purest form. The hero's experience is always one of self-discovery and conversion, either from a sinner to a good man or from an innocent to a sinner. Although Hawthorne stresses the social virtues of fellow-love and domesticity, his heroes discover the importance of these values only through the confrontation of their isolated souls with a divine truth or reality. His vision of the wilderness is strongly influenced by that of the Puritans, as well as by the psychological theories of Romanticism. The wilderness is a screen on which the human mind and heart project images of secret guilts and desires. Because the wilderness is outside the realm of social order and convention, these desires become deeds and the dreams realities. True character emerges from the husk of social habit, to reveal the soul as either a white or a blasted ear.

Hawthorne was widely read in Colonial literature, and the symbolic vocabulary of that literature was his own. The Puritan association of the wilderness with religious fanaticism and Quaker radicalism appears in "The Gentle Boy" and "The Man of Adamant." The latter tale portrays the fanatic as one who seeks God in isolation, forsaking social duty and love to pursue his quest in an isolated cave, and as a result turns into the stone of the cave that he sought as a temple. In "The Great Carbuncle" the foolish and materialistic searchers for a jewel follow an Indian legend to its destructive conclusion in the forest; and the hero of *Septimius Felton* is enslaved to materialism by an Indian-brewed potion of immortality. Roger Chillingworth returns from the forest in the company of Indians, perfected by them in malice and black science, to wreak vengeance in *The Scarlet Letter*. In the latter tales, the early dreams of the New World as a source of both unending wealth and the perpetual renewal of life are symbolically dramatized and rejected.

Like Cotton Mather, Mercy Short, and Mrs. Rowlandson, Hawthorne associates the sensual delights of the pagan dance with both the dark denizens of the woods and the dark thoughts of the hidden mind. The man who enters the wilderness hunting for something he regards as truth or power is always led to a place where devils dance in a ring, inviting him to a Black Eucharist. The young kinsman of Major Molineux meets the devil in Boston, and the devil, dressed as an Indian, opens the young man's innocent eyes to reality in a hellish dance scene. The mob, dressed as Indians, are playing the part of rebels and Jacobins by humiliating the figure of paternal authority, Major Molineux.

In "Young Goodman Brown" the wilderness plays the role Cotton Mather feared it would play. It is the abode of a mocking devil of cynical realism, whose power is to reveal and make concrete for Brown the dark impulses and suspicions he has suppressed, thus teaching him the hollowness of civilization and religion and robbing him of the unquestioning faith that alone binds him to man, society, and God. Brown, whose sires massacred the Pequots and scourged Quakers, becomes like his sires the victim of the disintegrative forces of the wilderness. His self-restraint is overcome by the temptation to know what the wilderness has to teach him, and his hunt for "truth" leads him to the circle where the witches dance. Even his subsequent recantation of devilish knowledge and rejection of the wilderness lesson, which sends him fleeing back to the safety of his hedged enclave, leaves within his heart the seeds of disaffection planted by the wilderness experience. These make him a man of solitude within the social pale, self-contained and — in his denial of conjugality — without heirs and self-ending.

Hawthorne's tales are both critiques of and participations in the Puritan myth of the wilderness. Hawthorne sees that myth as a tale of man's fall and degeneration through the arbitrary grace of given experiences — not, as in Flint's tale of Boone, a myth of self-creation and self-renewal through the hunt. The hope of his protagonists is the captive's hope, that his ordeal will expiate his sin. It is not the hope of the hero that his trials will make him a king.

Hawthorne's most profound treatment of the hunter myth is "Roger Malvin's Burial." This tale illustrates the effect on the frontier myth of a superior artist's engagement with its materials. When contrasted with Thorpe's version of the hunting myth in "Big Bear of Arkansas," it suggests the nature of the different literary paths taken by eastern and western writers from their common source in Puritan personal narratives. The contrast between the myth of sin and expiation in "Roger Malvin's Burial" and the half-realized creation myth in "Big Bear of Arkansas" also defines the alternative views of the hunter myth that confronted Cooper and formed the basis of his problematical conception of the character of Leatherstocking.

In "Roger Malvin's Burial" the wilderness functions as the stage on which the guilt-ridden hero, Reuben Bourne, acts out his secret fears and desires. The wilderness is morally neutral, imposing hardships on the flesh but leaving the spirit free to choose between good and evil. The terror of Hawthorne's wilderness lies in its permissiveness, the scope which it gives to the darker impulses of man and the realization of evil dreams. Reuben Bourne, haunted by the guilt of having deserted Roger Malvin, his "second father," after both were wounded in Lovewell's Fight of 1725, attempts to flee from his guilt by emigrating to the farther frontier. But once he re-enters the wilderness, he is again alone with his soul. His guilt works outward into the realm of real action: he mistakes his son for a deer and kills him on the very spot where Malvin's bones lie unburied. Thus he expiates his symbolic parricide by actually sacrificing his son.

The tragic conclusion is the result of his own flawed character. Moral weakness had led him to think about deserting Malvin, even before the old man begged his "son" to save himself. That same weakness leads him to conceal from his wife Dorcas, Malvin's daughter, his vow to return and bury Malvin. Ultimately it leads him to flee his place in society and the penance imposed on his fortunes by his own guilty conscience. So long as he remained within the precincts of New England society, he enjoyed temporary safety from the terrible power of his own heart. Within society he married Dorcas and raised a son. But his guilt and the moral weakness that prevented him from confessing it forced him into a morbid introspection, which made him (like Boone) a neglectful husbandman, hostile to society and plagued by lawsuits. Thus egocentricity symbolically drove him into the wilderness of his own mind and heart. At last, following this impulse of his psyche, he seeks refuge in the physical wilderness and there confronts the image of his own guilty character. In destroying the image, he murders his son, his hope of physical and spiritual immortality and happiness.

The final scene of "Roger Malvin's Burial," in which Bourne unwittingly sacrifices his son in expiation of his guilt, offers an implicit critique of the western symbols and values expressed by the fire-hunt legend in Flint's account and in the oral mythology about Boone. In both scenes the hunter performs a quasi-religious act of violence in which he appeases the spirits that haunt the wilderness in which he lives. In the fire hunt Boone mistakes Rebecca for a deer and nearly shoots her. The illusory metamorphosis of Rebecca into a deer and Boone into a panther suggests the kinship between this legend and the primitive myth of the divine king, in which a hero-chieftain engages in a ritual hunt of an animal sacred to the goddess of nature. The hunt is a symbolic sexual union, which proves the vigor of the hero and restores fertility to the forest ruled by the goddess. Reuben Bourne's ritual sacrifice, however, ends his line. Instead of a symbolic intercourse with a goddess of fertility, Reuben's hunt becomes an act of self-mutilation, murdering his hope both for future happiness and for the immortality of fathering a line of sons. Like Chactas and René in the works of Chateaubriand, like Crèvecoeur's Winnebago-Scot, like the frontiersmen condemned by Cotton Mather as "breakers of the Hedge," Hawthorne's frontier hero is doomed to impotence, to childlessness.

Thorpe's "Big Bear of Arkansas" also treats the wilderness as a realm of mystery in which there is an interchange of identities between the soul of the hunter and that of his prey. In Thorpe's tale, however, this represents man's attainment of the creative power of nature, not his moral degeneration. The tale itself is told by the hunter in what is ostensibly his own choice of words and style, but the personal narrative is framed by Thorpe's account of his meeting with the teller on a steamboat. Thus the context of the tale is social. The teller is environed with sharply delineated social types, reflecting the diversity of classes, conditions, and nationalities of western society. In the eyes of the observing author, the teller of the tale himself is a social type of the backwoodsman; his class and condition are reflected in his dress, boisterous manners, and dialect. Admiration and condescension mingle in the author's attitude toward the speaker. He does not know what to make of him, whether he is a clown or a hero — just as the teller reveals that he himself was unable to decide whether the great bear he hunted was simply an outsized bear or some kind of avatar of mystic powers.

Jim Doggett, the backwoods teller of tales, bursts on the startled company in the steamboat parlor, making sounds like an Indian and calling himself "the Big Bear of Arkansaw." It is some time before we learn his given name, and he seems much to prefer his chosen one. It soon emerges that Doggett is a hunter by profession, in the manner of Flint's Boone. He hunts for the love of it and as a means of increasing his stature and powers in his own eyes and in the eyes of nature and her creatures. His motives are like Crockett's but without Crockett's calculation and greed. He rejects the idea that hunting is an "amusement" — a notion that eastern writers emphasized in portrayals of Boone. Rather, it is an art and a necessity, requiring selectivity in execution and purity of motivation. A man must hunt from spiritual or physical need, not simply for pleasure; and for feeding both belly and ego, petty beasts are to be eschewed in favor of the great beasts, the panthers and bears. A city dude, Doggett says, once asked him what "the principal game in Arkansaw" might be, and Doggett replied, "Poker, and high-low-jack." Animals are not "game" but "meat." "Game, indeed, that's what city folk call it; and maybe with em it means chippenbirds and shite-pokes; maybe such trash live in my diggins, but I arn't noticed them yet."[3]

Doggett unwittingly reveals that his hunting is a means of gathering into himself the incredible power of the wilderness in which he lives — the power to destroy and to procreate. Size and fecundity are the symbols of this power. Even the mosquitoes in Arkansas are, in Doggett's tale, heroic in size: "If they are large, Arkansaw is large, her varmints ar large, her trees ar large, her rivers ar large, and a small mosquito would be of no more use in Arkansaw than preaching in a cane-brake." Even the farmer must be a hero to master the fecund power of the wilderness, for the crops grow so quickly that *"planting in Arkansaw is dangerous."* [4] Doggett's own stature is appropriate to the setting; and he possesses, by his own account, a weapon of almost magical potency and a dog of equal powers. Moreover, he describes his use of weapon and beast in terms of the marriage metaphor that lies at the basis of the hunter myth. Tracking the bear requires that the hunter and dog know the bear's ways as the lover or seducer knows a woman's, and the attraction that brings the dog and hunter to the bear is compared to the universal human passion for marriage:

> That gun of mine is a perfect *epidemic among bear:* if not watched closely it will go off as quick on a warm scent as my dog Bowie-knife will: and then that dog — whew! why the fellow thinks that the world is full of bear, he finds them so easy. It's lucky he don't talk as well as think; for with his natural modesty, if he should suddenly learn how much he is acknowledged to be ahead of all other dogs in the universe, he would be astonished to death in two minutes.
>
> Strangers, that dog knows a bear's way as well as a horse-jockey knows a woman's: he always barks at the right time, bites at the exact place, and whips without getting a scratch.
>
> I never could tell whether he was made expressly to hunt bear, or whether bear was made expressly for him to hunt: any way, I believe they were meant to go together as naturally as Squire Jones says a man and a woman is, . . . "Marriage according to law is a civil contract of divine origin; it's common to all countries as well as Arkansaw, and people takes to it as naturally as Jim Doggett's Bowie-knife takes to bear." [5]

The tone of Doggett's self-praise seems to mark him as a buffoon, a braggart, a type of the western loudmouth. The mythic content of his speech seems simply the exaggeration of a typical "ring-tailed roarer" — until Doggett begins the tale of his greatest hunt and its mysterious course and consequences. Then both he and the narrator become fascinated by the mystery inherent in the events, and the mythic skeleton emerges more clearly from the color and furor of Doggett's rhetoric. "I will give you an idea of a hunt," says Doggett, "in which the greatist bear was killed that ever lived." His use of the passive voice sounds the first note of ambiguity: although he is the hunter, he does not say that it was he who brought about the bear's death. Someone or something unspecified was behind the hunt from the first.

Doggett first sees the bear's signs when he has grown somewhat jaded with the ease of bear hunting. So proficient has he become that the bears either surrender or leave the country. The size and power of this bear are surprises that upset his previous belief in the completeness of his bear-knowledge. In their first chase the bear outruns both man and horse, a circumstance previously "unknown to me as possible." Impregnable in his power, the great bear helps himself to a hog from Doggett's stock whenever he pleases. Doggett has miscalculated the power of the fecund wilderness. The bear is the visible embodiment of that power that makes the corn explode out of the earth like cannon shot and the mosquitoes grow big as hawks. He has too readily assumed his power to dominate the wilderness, and for this hubristic sin he suffers an exchange of roles with the bear. The bear becomes a haunting vision, an embodiment (like the Puritan Indian-devil) of the hellish powers of the wilderness. From a hero and hunter, Doggett has become a victim and virtually a captive besieged. "I would see that bear in everything I did: *he hunted me*, and that, too, like a devil, which I began to think he was." [6] Thus the first stage of the ultimate exchange of identities between wilderness beast and civilized man is achieved.

The next stage of the hunt invests the bear with a godlike nature and, at the same time, draws more emphatically the image of Doggett's kinship with the beast. Doggett and his hounds pursue the bear's trace and see him in the distance, climbing a tall, bare hill which is topped by a tree. Although the dogs snap at his heels, the bear's ascent is leisurely, and Doggett cannot decide if the dogs were either "a match for him this time in speed, or else he did not care to get out of his way." The hunter's response is to see the bear as a thing of beauty in his stately performance of his role and to respond to the perception of the beauty and appropriateness of the bear's actions with a surge of love for the beast: "But wasn't he a beauty though? I loved him like a brother." [7] Despite this love — or rather, under the aspect of the hunter myth, because of it — he still seeks to achieve dominance over the bear by killing him. The bear by this time has ascended the tree and seated himself in the crotch, and the dogs harry him there. The bear is clearly an embodiment of the power of nature; the image is that of the hanging god of primitive mythology and, by extension, of the crucifixion. The hanging and mutilation of the god or his priest and avatar was part of the ritual of fertility — of death and resurrection for crops, beasts, and men — as was the rite of sacred marriage. The presence of the archetype here suggests the godlike power of the bear and the significance of Doggett's hunt for him. Doggett seeks to master the power of nature, the power of fecundity and natural resurrection, of self-perpetuation. He wishes to assimilate the magic of the bear as he digests his meat.

The bear's next actions reinforce this impression of his godlike nature. He takes one shot square on his forehead and brushes it off, then "walked down from that tree as gently as a lady would from a carriage." Although the bear is masculine, Doggett momentarily thinks of his prey as feminine — as indeed it should be, in the myth of the hunter and his sacred marriage. The bear flees, swims a stream, and disappears into the brush of an island; then it reappears, is chased by the dogs, and is slain by the dog Bowie-knife, who is embraced by the bear in a loverlike fashion and falls "clenched together" with the bear into the water. Doggett fishes the drowned bear from the bottom of the stream, only to discover that the great bear has somehow created a she-bear and sent her out as a sacrifice while escaping himself.

The elements of the archetype embodied in the fire-hunt myth are all present here. The hunter and his victim confront each other in a wilderness above a pool of water. The symbolic environment of the hunt suggests that this is a quest into the unconscious for the vision of an anima, as well as a hunt in the wilderness for meat. The water and the wilderness both function as symbols of the unconscious; and the island — like the islands of the mystic western sea in prediscovery visions of America — is the place where the principles and elements of the subconscious, the sea, are objectified and made concrete. Doggett is frightened and senses that he is in the presence of some mystery, but he has no comprehension of its ultimate significance or consequences. His reactions are like his previous ones: he sees the bear as the embodiment of the devilish, dangerous spirit of the wilderness and himself as the bear's victim. At the same time, apparently offhandedly, he identifies himself metaphorically with the bear and its power of procreation: "The way matters got mixed on that island was onaccountably curious, and thinking of it made me more than ever convinced that I was hunting the devil himself. I went home that night and took to my bed — the thing was killing me. . . . I grew as cross as a bear with two cubs and a sore tail." [8]

Doggett now makes the ultimate commitment to the hunt — "to catch that bear, go to Texas, or die" — and prepares himself for an ultimate struggle. He no longer relies with overweening confidence on his own powers. Realizing his weakness before the powers of the forest, he makes himself ready for final battle, leaving nothing to chance. As if in response to this change of heart and to the hunter's newly acquired love and respect for the bear-god, the bear himself appears before the hunter, apparently offering himself for the kill. The bear walks toward him slowly, looming "like a black mist." Out of instinct the hunter fires, and again the element of mystery is complicated by the clownish nature of the hero, who "was tripped up by my inexpressibles, which either from habit, or the excitement of the moment, were about my heels." By the time he reaches the bear, the beast's groans and thrashings have ceased, and he lies dead. Doggett then goes into an extravaganza on his size and ends by calling him "a creation bear." [9] The allusion is to the creation in Genesis — "There were giants in the earth in those days" — but also to creation in general.

The bear, as Doggett half realizes, is the embodiment of the creative potency of the wilderness. That power, presumably, is now his, as his taking the identity of "Big Bear of Arkansaw" implies. But if Doggett is a god, he is an ignorant one, innocent of his own powers. He invites the company to warm their souls with liquor, in a vaguely Bacchic spirit, but there is no implication in the story that he is unwittingly inviting them to a kind of Eucharist or to the drunkenness that traditionally accompanied the rites of fertility and spring. Doggett remains troubled by the bear's last actions. He senses in the bear's submission some kind of fatality; but the character, motivation, or purpose of that fatality eludes him:

> But stranger, I never liked the way I hunted him, *and missed him.* There is something curious about it I could never understand — and I never was satisfied at his giving in *so easy at last.* Prehaps, he had heard of my preparations to hunt him next day, so he jist guv up . . . but that ain't likely. My private opinion is, that that bear was an *unhuntable bear, and died when his time come.*[10]

The author-listener too is moved by the sense of mystery. Doggett had said in starting that the tale would be "instructible" to him, as a younger man listening to an older and wiser. But the author also strikes wide of the mark. In the context of the steamboat-parlor society, Doggett is Doggett, an ignorant woodsman, and not the mystical big bear of Arkansas. Viewed under the aspect of Indian or other primitive mythology, Doggett's tale is a myth of initiation and of divine kingship. Viewed under the aspect of civilization and Christianity, it is "superstitious awe," resulting from the confrontation of a typical specimen of the ignorant "children of the wood" with "anything out of their everyday experience."

The same alternatives of vision divide Thorpe's hunter myth from that of Hawthorne. Hawthorne's Reuben Bourne suffers sexual mutilation and impotence in expiation for his guilt; his experience in the wilderness is a fall rather than an initiation, ending in decline of his powers and happiness. Thorpe's "Big Bear" gains the procreative power of the wilderness by merging his identity with that of its avatar, the bear; the result is a kind of elevation to heroic stature. Nor does Doggett lose his innocence as a result of the experience. On the contrary, he recovers lost innocence. Before the hunt he assumed himself to be powerful by virtue of the knowledge he had gained from worldly experience. After the hunt has proven the depth and strength of his power, he "knows" less, is sure of less, than when he began.

Doggett's motives in the final hunt likewise differ from Reuben Bourne's. In the Christian context of Hawthorne's tale, Bourne's motivation is Faustian. By seeking new land in the West, he thinks to escape from the consequences of sin and dominate the moral power that informs human life. The result is the destruction of his dream by an ineluctable reality and the retributive justice which, as the reflexive mirror of man's mind, it embodies. Doggett is at first Faustian in his hunting of the bear, but he is chastened to humility. He learns the limits of his powers in the struggle, comes to respect and love the strength that nature's avatar embodies, and will play out his proper role with all the appropriate means at his disposal — not in contempt but in love and respect, not in the expectation of success but with resignation to failure.

The Christian-myth context of Hawthorne and the Indian-myth context of Thorpe represent the halves of the dilemma inherent in American mythology. The Puritan and European tradition, in which the wilderness is a temptation to expression of the passions and consequent dissolution, is set against its polar opposite, the Indian myth in which the quest of the wilderness's beasts is the source of creative power. It was this dilemma that Cooper perceived and attempted to resolve in the Leatherstocking cycle.

The Leatherstocking cycle begins with *The Pioneers* (published in 1823) and concludes with *The Deerslayer* (1841). The first novel introduces the frontier hero, Natty Bumppo, in the social context of a frontier settlement in New York State — an idealized portrait of Cooper's own home in Cooperstown, New York. Natty is an old man on the verge of decrepitude, the representative of an admirable but vanishing breed of man, the Indian-like hunters of the first frontier. Natural and social necessity demands that he give way before the laws and the ways of settlement folk. In the last novel, Natty is a youth on the verge of manhood, embarking on his first warpath. Discarding the Christian name given him through baptism, he is seeking to make new names, new identities, for himself through his deeds as a hunter and warrior, for like the Indian he identifies with and takes his name from the things he hunts and slays. The Deerslayer's quest is enacted in conditions of almost perfect solitude, far from the settlements themselves, in the physical and psychological isolation of the dreamlike forest.

Leatherstocking, in the course of the cycle, passes from old age through death (in *The Prairie*, 1827) into a new youth. Thus the legend of Leatherstocking, as it unfolded for the American reader of 1820–45, was a myth of renewal and rebirth of the hero. Moreover, the movement backward in historical time to Leatherstocking's youth was accompanied by a movement toward a more mythopoeic conception of the wilderness, a greater use of Indian mythology, and a concentration of focus on the psychology of a single personality, such as had characterized the Puritan personal-narrative literature and made it capable of generating myth.

The seeds of this ultimate development can be found in *The Pioneers*. The structure of Cooper's first serious novel, *The Spy*, had been very much in the Scott tradition: an historically important conflict (the Revolution) between opposing components of a single race, mirrored in a family conflict. In *The Pioneers* Cooper turned from an obviously important conflict to a more subtle one, that between the Indian world and the white. He shifted his interest from the artificially re-created world of the Revolution to the world he had known in his youth. Instead of applying the techniques of Scott to American events, he was reexamining his own past and heritage, his own perceptions of and role in the creation of the new American world. This turn toward self-examination and the examination of the real frontier world of Cooperstown was accompanied by a deep interest in the mythology and character of the Indians and of the white men who lived with and came to resemble them. The narratives relating to Boone's life — certainly the Filson text in Wilder's and Trumbull's editions and probably Flint's studies in the 1830s — formed part of his reading and supplied incidents and images to several novels in the cycle. Certainly he was aware of the literature of Indian captivities that was a staple of Colonial and later New England popular literature. The capture of white women by Indians and associated villains and their rescue by Leatherstocking and his associates is the recurrent theme of the action in all the novels save *The Pioneers*. Perhaps his most important reading was in Heckewelder's study of Indian culture, history, and mythology. From Heckewelder he took what he believed to be myths expressive of the Indians' own conception of their history and an idea of the importance of their sense of spiritual intimacy with the land — an intimacy that gave them strength while it lasted but made them vulnerable to moral degeneration when the preemption of the land by the whites had displaced them.

Although he had immersed himself in American source materials while writing *The Pioneers*, Cooper was still very much under the spell of

Scott and of the myth of progress through conflict and Christian reconciliation which informed the historical romance. Thus *The Pioneers* first exhibits the characteristic formal division of the Cooper novel into a "plot" and the thematic Leatherstocking "saga." The plot, involving Romantic themes of star- and class-crossed love and family division, justifies the writing of the novel in terms of the literary conventions established in Europe and imported to the East. Its sources are essentially European, as are the attitudes it embodies. The Romantic heroes and heroines, and their foils or accomplices, are almost always stereotypes, two-dimensional stock figures from Scott or the novel of manners. The thematic saga, which has its origin in the quasi-fictional narrative literature of the colonies and in the Indian legends collected by Heckewelder, relates to the character development of the hunter-hero Leatherstocking and his Indian associates. The two parts of the novel interact at various points but are in many essentials independent. As the cycle approaches its culmination in *The Deerslayer*, Leatherstocking's personal narrative comes to dominate plot, and Leatherstocking himself becomes the single focus of the novel.

This formal ambivalence in the novel is not simply a result of Cooper's hasty writing and defective craftsmanship. The two formal elements grow out of different mythological antecedents, Indian and European, and these myths prove to be the sources of the central conflict in *The Pioneers*. The novel tells two stories — the reconciliation of the Temples and the Effinghams, families divided in the Revolution, through the marriage of Oliver Effingham and Miss Temple; and the destruction of the world of the primitive frontier, symbolized in the death of Indian John and the exile of Natty Bumppo. Oliver is Bumppo's friend and protégé and is rescued by him (with Miss Temple) from the climactic forest fire. But Bumppo's conflict with Judge Temple is unrelated to that which divides the Temples and the Effinghams. Bumppo wishes to live by the laws of the Indian and the hunter, killing meat for use only (unlike the settlers) but doing that whenever the spirit moves and in despite of game laws. The central conflict in the novel is, in effect, between two different modes of perception: that which regards Bumppo's conflict with Temple as the most significant struggle in the town, and that which regards the Effingham-Temple misunderstanding as most crucial. In the context of the Indian mythology which Cooper employs to characterize Natty and Indian John, the former is of ultimate significance; in the context of the conventions of the historical romance, the second is of more pertinent interest.

The conflict between these modes of perception is introduced in the lengthy tavern scene. Cooper paints the scene carefully, setting the reader within a group of townsfolk of various conditions and types in the convivial glow of the inn fire. When the scene has been well set, Leatherstocking enters and then Indian John. The theme of the scene is established by the discussion of the Indian's name. Bumppo calls him by his Indian name Chingachgook, or Big Serpent, the name he won through subtlety and valor on the battlefield. The others call him John Mohegan, the Christian name given him by the Moravian missionaries who banked the fires of his heart and converted his spirit, after the death of all his tribe and his son had broken it. From Christians he has also learned the use of rum, and his lust for this white-man's-poison wars with his knowledge that it unmans him, makes him unable to play the Indian's part of a hunter and warrior. In Chingachgook the mythologies of the Indian and the Christian are at war, and the final resolution of that conflict is the catastrophe of the narrative portion of the novel.

The conflict reveals itself as the scene unfolds. Bumppo sounds its first note when he replies to Judge Temple's advocacy of laws restricting hunting and woodcutting: "You may make your laws, Judge, but who will you find to watch the mountains through the long summer days, or the lakes at night? Game is game, and he who finds may kill; that has been the law in these mountains . . . and I think one old law is worth two new ones." [11] The context of the remark is crucial. Temple has just been talking of the Jacobin excesses in France, the lawlessness of the mob and the killing of the king. Bumppo's defiance in one sense associates him with the Jacobins as a revolutionary. From Bumppo's point of view, however, it is Temple who is the lawbreaker. Moreover, Temple and his like have killed the true king of America — Chingachgook, chief of the Delawares, whose spirit is drowned in a rum bottle. The host calls for drinks, and a song is struck up, but the color and sound are thin concealments of the gulf of violence, strife, and revolutionary overturn that has been revealed.

In proof of this, the Indian spirit of Chingachgook begins to rise; and as the whites roar out their drinking songs, he begins to sway and chant the song of his miseries, his triumphs, and his passion for revenge. Leatherstocking is the only man who understands what is happening. They offer him drink and call for a song, but he refuses: "I have lived to see what I thought eyes could never behold in these hills, and I have no heart left for singing. If he, that has a right to be master and ruler here, is forced to squinch his thirst, when a-dry, with snow-water, it ill becomes them that have lived by his bounty to be making merry, as if there was nothing in the world but sunshine and summer." Ironically, the men mock Leatherstocking as "blind" and offer him "spectacles" to see the world more cheerily.

They laugh at "how Old John turns his quavers" but pay no attention to the song they cannot understand.[12] As he sings, Chingachgook's manner changes. He ceases to be Indian John, although the others call him so, and begins to chant a song of war and battles:

> Mohegan was uttering dull, monotonous tones, keeping time by a gentle motion of his head and body. He made use of but few words, and such as he did utter were in his native language, and consequently, only understood by himself and Natty. . . . he continued to sing a wild, melancholy air, that rose, at times, in sudden and quite elevated notes, and then fell again into the low, quavering sounds, that seemed to compose the character of his music. . . . Mohegan continued to sing, while his countenance was becoming vacant, though, coupled with his thick bushy hair, it was assuming an expression very much like brutal ferocity. His notes were gradually growing louder, and soon rose to a height that caused a general cessation in the discourse.[13]

At this point Natty breaks in, admonishing him in the Indian language. Suddenly "Natty" and "Mohegan" become "Hawkeye" and "Chingachgook," as Leatherstocking cries, "Shed not blood!" Then the crisis passes; Chingachgook is again John Mohegan, and Hawkeye is the rustic Bumppo. The play on their names reprises the theme on which the scene began and emphasizes the conflict between the two worlds or modes of perception. In the Indian world the two are heroes of renown, Hawkeye and the Serpent; in the world of Judge Temple they are ignorant, undisciplined backwoodsmen, John Mohegan and Natty Bumppo.

The different modes of perception derive from different mythological views of history. To the Christian Temple, the settlement of Templeton and the conversion or destruction of the Indians are part of a providential plan, figured in the creation of man by Jehovah and in the commandments to replenish the earth and to gather the souls of men into Christ's church. To the Indian, the settlement of Templeton is a breach in nature, a violation of natural law that must culminate in tragedy. The Delaware creation myth is the tale of a quest and an initiation, not a fall from grace. The law inherent in that creation is the law of the hunter. The woods and its animals are free for all, owned by none; any man may seek his god or his prey there, checked only by the limitations of his own skill and discipline and the direct action of God through nature. Temple's law converts the hunting land to tillage and the savage hunter to the Christian farmer and merchant, who wring profit from the soil through speculation as much as husbandry. Hawkeye's law ordains, not the conversion of the land, but the adjustment of man to the land; not the breaking of the forest to man's will, but the submission of human will to the laws inherent in nature. Temple, to preserve valuable game, would forbid shooting does out of season. Hawkeye, moved by love and respect for the creatures of his world and a desire to see their species perpetuated, would withhold his fire voluntarily, without the check of law.

These differences derive from the polarity of their inherited modes of perception. Hawkeye and the Indians understand and can live independently by natural law because it is native to them. Temple and the settlers are from a different world and, since they lack the perceptions that would keep them obedient to natural law, must fabricate artificial laws to accomplish the same ends. Both Leatherstocking and Temple want to preserve the game, but their means and their motives differ. Where Temple urges economy in hunting out of a passion for regulated moderation in all things, Leatherstocking hunts both for food and for the spiritual satisfaction of participating in the necessary, ennobling rite of the kill. Thus when Temple concurs with Leatherstocking in disapproval of the townspeople's wasteful slaughter of the lake fish, the hunter denies the implied alliance with the judge: "No, no; we are not much of one mind, Judge, or you'd never turn good hunting grounds into stumpy pastures. And you fish and hunt out of rule; but to me, the flesh is sweeter, where the creater has some chance for its life." [14]

The depth of their difference is revealed through scenes in which each acts out his mythic heritage in an almost ceremonial fashion. Natty's last hunt precipitates the conflict between him and Temple and brings about the combined ending of the narrative and the plot. Natty, young Effingham, and Chingachgook have been sitting at their fire reminiscing, and Natty speaks of a view from a mountaintop overlooking the Hudson. The warmth with which he reports the scene recalls that of Filson's Boone, and Effingham remarks (as many did of Boone) that he has a remarkable sensitivity to nature. At that moment their reverie is broken by the baying of the hounds, who have started a deer. Dogs and deer explode out of the bushes, race through the camp, and plunge into the lake at its side. Although the game laws forbid hunting at that season, the Indian and the old hunter are so moved by the beauty and size of the beast that they cannot control the passion to hunt it, and they push off after it in a canoe. The hunt is long and arduous, Hawkeye and Chingachgook moving with the deer, adjusting their movements to his until they can feel the hunt as the deer feels it and so anticipate his movements. Then Effingham, whose scruples have been overcome by the excitement of the chase, slips a noose over the beast's head, and Leatherstocking reaches into the water to grapple the deer and slit its throat in the middle of the lake.

There is a ceremonial quality about the strange circumstances of this killing that gives it a mysterious and mythical air. The origin of the scene is in fact mythological, drawn from Heckewelder's account of the creation myth of the Delawares, Chingachgook's tribe. The people, according to this legend, lived under a lake until one of their hunters discovered a hole through which he saw a deer. He hunted the deer, killed and ate it, tasted in its flesh the sweetness of earth and the goodness of the goddess of nature, and brought his tribe out to people the earth. Leatherstocking and Chingachgook live in the world of this myth, acting out a primitive ritual of creation and the perpetuation of life in defiance of the white Christians' law. Judge Temple, however, sees in this rite the unchecked expression of personal will and passion, and he sees in the free expression of Bumppo's and John Mohegan's nature a threat to order and moderation. In the context of European Christian mythology, the lake hunt takes on far different significance. The legend of the hunting priest, or wicked hunter — with roots in Norse mythology or even in the Greek myths of Actaeon and Orion — portrays the hunter as a man who deserts religious discipline for the grossly materialistic, sex-linked passion of the hunt. According to the legend, a priest or abbot who had a love of the chase was saying Mass when his dogs bayed a deer, and the priest left the Holy Eucharist to partake of the savage Eucharist of the hunt. His punishment was to run "an endless chase, whirling across the plains behind his howling dogs, never to run down the quarry he so bootlessly pursues." The hunter is, in this view, guilty of "falling away from the center," from passive contemplation of the spiritual truth of a transcendent God, to a passion for mere transitory phenomena.[15] This is precisely the end Temple imposes on Leatherstocking, and in the final scene the old hunter vanishes into the West, surrounded by his baying hounds, in fruitless pursuit of an unrealizable dream.

The Christian society lives by control of the passions and bridling of the will — not, like the Indian society, by their expression. The deer in the lake excites passion in the hunter (as in the fire-hunt legend of Boone's marriage). In Jungian terms, the deer is like the anima, the feminine principle which the masculine mind has lost and which it seeks both within the mind and in the objective world. The water of the lake is both real and symbolic, the liquid element in which the desired object really appears and the symbolic element of the unconscious, the inward ocean. To the Indian the hunting ritual is his initiation into a symbolic marriage with the spirits of his world, the source of his procreative power. To the judge this ritual of creation is, like the eating of the apple in Genesis, a type of fall from grace. Thus Temple presides at the rite of trial in which Natty Bumppo is condemned to be exhibited in the stocks and publicly humiliated for his pride in setting self above society. The punishment demonstrates that the two worlds are irreconcilable. What is humility and reverence to Leatherstocking is pride and disobedience to Temple, and the latter is compelled by his belief in a fallen world and a Christian law to impose humility on the unregenerate hunter.

The climax of the tale comes on a hill called, significantly, The Vision. Bumppo, escaped from jail, rescues Temple's daughter from a forest fire and thus makes possible both the happy resolution of the Temple-Effingham plot and the catastrophe of the mythic narrative of the Indian's creation and doom. The deer hunt has also been fatal to the aged Chingachgook. He has suffered a mysterious hurt, some invisible internal damage, in the course of the deer's slaying. He sits atop The Vision, looking on the ruined wilderness and the prospect of the distant village, immersed in thoughts of death. The strange slaying of the deer has for him a ritual significance. In the archetypal myth, when the king of the woods (the male partner to the goddess in the ritual procreation or marriage) becomes impotent through age or disease, his land suffers with him. Only if the king surrenders his blood to the soil in sacrifice and passes his power to a successor can the homeopathic relationship between the people and their land be profitably maintained. Chingachgook has lost the power and dignity of his kingship; his sons and daughters are dead; and he is unable to produce another heir, since all the worthy women of his tribe have vanished. As the fire consumes the hill on which he sits, Chingachgook casts off the vestiges of Christianity and submits to his mutilation and sacrifice. But his blood is without an heir.

Cooper invests each event in the process of his dying with a ritual aura. The chief, with Effingham and Miss Temple, sits in a stone grotto by a pool with fire rising around him, "looking into the womb of futurity." The pool recalls the mythic function of the lake as a symbol of the creative essence of nature and is here explicitly associated with a feminine presiding spirit. The image of the "womb of futurity" reminds us of the possibility of sacred marriage between king and goddess which, for Chingachgook, has been foreclosed. Young Effingham reinforces our perception of the chief's impotence, his inability to engage in the sacred marriage, by recalling the chief's decayed physical condition and the mysterious hidden wound he received during the last hunt, which has seriously impaired his vigor: "He considers this as the happiest moment of his life. He is past seventy; and has been decaying rapidly for some time; he received some injury chasing that unlucky deer, too, on the lake. Oh! Miss Temple, that was an unlucky chase indeed." [16]

Chingachgook regards as happy a chance which Effingham regards as unlucky, because the Indian is immersed in the world defined by primitive myths of the sacred marriage and the sacrifice of the king. According to the morality implicit in those myths, the king whose vigor declines toward impotence must be ritually sacrificed to the goddess so that the natural world he has ruled will not follow him into death. For Chingachgook the death by fire is a consummation analogous to the death-in-love of sexual orgasm and the sacred marriage. However, to the Christian Effingham, who dreams of marriage to the chaste Miss Temple, the situation is appalling. At this crisis Effingham, who has been torn between love of civilization and the love of the solitudes which he shares with Bumppo and Chingachgook, makes his decision for society. But Chingachgook chooses the ways of his fathers, and for him the pain of death is nothing. Indeed, he revels in his torment as in the clasp of a beloved pleasure because his ability to bear the pain proves his manhood and gives value to his sacrifice.

Through the flames Effingham and Miss Temple see as in a vision the figure of Judge Temple, innocent of impending disaster, standing in his pastoral fields lost in contemplation, the embodiment of the virtues they have temporarily deserted in seeking the hunters on the mountain. Chingachgook sees another vision, that of his dead tribesmen calling to him from beyond the grave, their red faces appearing through the white faces that obscure his vision of the land like smoke. Even as Bumppo arrives to rescue the young couple, a powder horn explodes between Chingachgook's legs. Such sexual mutilation was a part of king-sacrifice rituals in primitive cultures.[17] Here it serves as symbolic confirmation of the termination of Chingachgook's kingly powers and the passing of the power of the soil to a new and better lord, Oliver Edwards/Effingham.

The final confrontation between the two worlds comes at the moment of Chingachgook's death. The minister asks "John" to make his confession of sin and humble himself before his Judge and Redeemer. Chingachgook replies with an Indian death song, a chant in praise of his own mighty deeds. The divine is shocked: "May Heaven avert such self-righteousness from his heart! . . . Humility and penitence are the seals of Christianity." But the minister speaks with a vision of death far different from the Indian's. Chingachgook sees in his death a return to the world of his youth, before the white man came, when Indians were the people of that place and when game was plentiful. In death his strength will be renewed, and he will be a king again, exercising a king's power in a new and better realm. Thus he sings of his deeds of blood and battle, not of his failings or his deeds of charity. His chant alternates with the irrelevant queries of the minister: "What says he, Nathaniel? does he recall the promises of the mediation? and trust his salvation to the Rock of Ages?" [18]

Now it is Leatherstocking who is torn between the Indian and the Christian visions. Where Chingachgook believes wholeheartedly in an afterlife where "he is to be young ag'in, and to hunt, and be happy till the ind of etarnity," Leatherstocking is uncertain. He knows that such a heaven is not appropriate to a member of the white race, yet he might wish for a heaven very like that of Chingachgook.[19] It is clear that for him neither myth is wholly satisfactory, that he is sui generis, neither white nor Indian, though he partakes of the nature of both. Chingachgook's end is signaled by a crash of thunder and lightning, and he dies in his homeland, looking into the setting sun. Leatherstocking has no home and, like the cursed abbot, is doomed to wander until his end on a fruitless quest for a faith and identity like those of Temple and Chingachgook. This, at least, is how the ending must be viewed under the aspect of the European Christian tradition. By the end of the Leatherstocking cycle, however, Natty has become young again. Thus from the viewpoint of Cooper writing the tales, or his first audience reading them, Natty would seem to have achieved an Indian heaven.

Cooper's ultimate concern in the Leatherstocking tales is the problematic character of the frontiersman — the troubling blend of European, American, and Indian elements that made him both a figure of promise and a nightmare to Cooper's contemporaries. The problem of vision that confronts Leatherstocking at the moment of Chingachgook's death is Cooper's way of portraying the psychological consequences of the white-Indian character of the frontier hero. It was not, like Wilder's image of a degenerated Boone, a means of answering the problem, but of posing it. Cooper devoted the rest of the cycle to attempting to resolve the problem. Leatherstocking's obsession with the question of his racial loyalties becomes increasingly pronounced. In *The Last of the Mohicans* (1826) he describes himself as "a man without a cross," [20] meaning that his blood is unmixed with Indian blood. The phrase, however, is ambiguous, since he is not a Christian and has no conception of being a member of a fallen race. Hence he neither identifies with the cross nor bears the cross of guilt, punishment, or expiation. Although Cooper never does resolve the problem, his attempts exercise a curious power over his writing, causing him to focus more intently on Leatherstocking, to deemphasize the stock characters from the genre of the historical romance, and to clarify and emphasize the mythological elements in the career of his hero.

The mythic function of the ocean, sea, or lake, for example, becomes progressively more clear in each novel of the cycle. In *The Pioneers* the lake is the source of the wilderness's teeming life, the refuge of its once innumerable birds and fish. The exploitation and depletion of the lake by the Templeton settlers dramatizes the role they play in destroying the sources of the natural, Indian life of the woods. Natty Bumppo and Chingachgook, by contrast, know how to appreciate and utilize the dark, fecund life-force inherent in the lake. They fish it in the appropriate manner; they sacrifice a deer in it; and Bumppo even resurrects the half-drowned body of Benjamin from it, thus converting near-death into a baptism to renewed life. (Benjamin later becomes fast friend and emulator of the hunter.) In *The Last of the Mohicans* the lake functions in the archetypal role of an inward ocean, the subconscious of the human mind. It is from the lake that Magua emerges to seduce the weakly Christian Montcalm to his plan of betrayal and blood. Still more significant is the reference of the Delawares to the real ocean, from whose shores they have been driven by the white men. The withering of the tribal seed and the untimely death of the heir of Chingachgook are seen by Tamenund and Chingachgook as consequences of the Indians' being cut off from the primal life-source.

In *The Prairie*, Cooper's concept of the significance of the ocean is still clearer. Here all the elements of landscape and situation that were present in *The Pioneers* are exaggerated and abstracted, that is, reduced to their simplest archetypal forms. The forest solitudes and lakes and the scattered clearings of *The Pioneers* have become an oceanic desert with islands of rock scattered across its heaving level. The transformation of lake into ocean and of settlement into island simplifies and enlarges them so that they resemble the landscapes of primitive myth. These images also serve to link the story with the early dreams and discoveries of America, when the New World was conceived as a group of strange islands in a barren sea. The wagons of the Bush clan that move across it are prairie schooners.

Thus both universal archetypes and the archetypal patterns in the American experience are invoked in *The Prairie*. Leatherstocking himself has grown to suit the landscape. In *The Pioneers* he was a decaying old man; in *The Last of the Mohicans*, a somewhat uncouth and bumpkinly subordinate to the Romantic hero of the piece. In *The Prairie* he appears as a protean figure, larger than life, alternately hidden and revealed by the landscape, materializing mysteriously as if out of the sun itself before the dazzled eyes of the half-dreaming Bushes:

> The sun had fallen below the crest of the nearest wave of the prairie, leaving the usual rich and glowing train on its track. In the centre of this flood of fiery light a human form appeared, drawn against the gilded background as distinctly, and seemingly as palpable, as though it would come within the grasp of any extended hand. The figure was colossal; the attitude musing and melancholy. . . . But imbedded, as it were, in its setting of garish light, it was impossible to distinguish its just proportions or true character.[21]

The Bush clan represent in an equally exaggerated form the values of the townspeople in Templeton (although not, presumably, of the good judge). They come fleeing from the consequences of crime and ill husbandry in the East. They are clannish, destructive, and bound by a rigid Old Testament code of vengeance that is little different from the Indian vendetta code. They are strongly associated with the Indian villains of the captivity myth, since they carry with them, as a prisoner and captive, a girl-woman who represents the Christian virtues of passivity, meekness, and gentility. She too, however, is an exaggerated type of the captive. Like the woman in Greenough's "Rescue Group," her size is disproportionately (perhaps preternaturally) diminutive. She is almost a freak of nature. The girl is, of course, rescued by Leatherstocking and her noble lover, and the Bushes are suffered to wreak their savage justice on one another. But the marriage of the captive and her lover — the Christian reconciliation that ought to climax the Romantic plot — takes place offstage. The ideal and just world of the paternal god Temple is nowhere present in this latter vision of the West; it is not one of the alternatives open to the hero. Offered a choice between the Bushes and the Indians, Leatherstocking's choice is not very difficult. His one regret is that the Christian world is no longer an alternative for him, but he is resigned to the fact. He disappears as he entered the novel, in a death scene not unlike that of Chingachgook. Having materialized from the life-giving sun at the novel's start, he gives up his ghost to the sun as it sets in the west at the novel's end.

Yet the riddle remains. He says as he dies that, unlike Chingachgook and Temple, he has never been a chief or king and that he dies without children or heirs, the last of his race. He has no idea of the life beyond as firm as either Temple's or Chingachgook's. There is a hint that a portion of his spirit is bequeathed to the Indian and white heroes, Hard Heart and Captain Middleton, suggesting that through him there is ground for a kind of reconciliation between the two worlds. Hard Heart suggests that his death may have the power of a king's sacrifice when he hails him as "just chief of the Palefaces." With this bare suggestion of a conclusion, Cooper leaves the Leatherstocking tales, only to return compulsively to the theme thirteen years later in *The Pathfinder* and *The Deerslayer*.

These intervening years are of crucial importance for our understanding of the relationships between Cooper, his sources, and his public — that is, the connection between the artist and the popular myths which inform his works, and the effect which the artist himself has on the mythogenetic mind of his audience. In the 1820s, Cooper had been an explorer of sources; by the time he returned to the wilderness with *The Pathfinder*, the character he had created had entered directly into the popular mythology of the South and West. In the South, Simms and Bird had written frontier novels that were responses — highly critical ones — to Cooper's statement of his vision. McClung, the popular western anthologist who rebuked Boone for his flowery Filsonian rhetoric, offered a vision of the westerner as man of pure action-and-instinct, which was likewise an answer to Cooper's portrait of the westerner as rustic philosopher and mystic. James Hall's romanticized stories of the frontier, in particular "The Backwoodsman," owed their characterization of the frontier hero to Natty Bumppo (wry humor, cool courage, sentiment) and their plot lines to *The Last of the Mohicans* (an alternation of captivities and rescues). Even Timothy Flint's characterization of Boone as the hunter-poet or hunter-priest can be seen as a development to its logical conclusion of Cooper's hunter. The artist, having drawn on the mythology of his people for his materials, makes a contribution to his culture's myth-history; and when next he turns to his mythic sources, he meets (among other realities) his own creations coming back toward him. The Natty Bumppo of the later novels reflects not only Cooper's own development of his original conception but also the light thrown on it by others who had built on the suggestions of his earlier novels.

In *The Deerslayer* Cooper returns to the sources of his hero's character and values in another attempt to resolve the ethical and racial dilemmas that make his hero's nature and destiny so problematical. The novel recounts Leatherstocking's initiation into the world of manhood, his moral testing and awakening. Again the conflict is between the worlds of Indian myth and of Christian-European myth, and the success and consequences of the young hero's initiation are measured against the standards of value inherent in both mythologies. The setting contains in developed form the same archetypal elements that dominated *The Pioneers* and *The Prairie*. The action centers on a lake in the distant wilderness (an ocean within an ocean), in the center of which is a man-made, stockaded island called the Castle. In the Castle live the Hutters — Old Tom, a former pirate, and his foster daughters, Judith and Hetty. Judith is passionate, headstrong, and sensual; Hetty is chaste, pure, and Christian, with an innocence of nature that seems born of a retarded intellect. Natty Bumppo, called Deerslayer, Chingachgook, and their friend Hurry Harry March come to the lake to warn the Hutters of an impending Indian war, but their quest also involves them with the Hutter girls in a romantic, ritualized round of captivities and rescues.

As in *The Pioneers*, the object of Deerslayer's hunt or quest is found in the middle of a lake, this time in a woman's shape rather than an animal's. As in the Indian creation myth, Deerslayer's hunt involves him in the possibility of marriage to the lady of the lake and forest. The success of his quest, in terms of the Indian myth, depends on the success of his romance with Judith. To emphasize this, Cooper mirrors Natty's situation in a subplot dealing with the romance of Chingachgook, the king who has come seeking his proper queen and destined mother of his heirs.

Deerslayer's quest is complicated by the fact that he knows himself to be neither a king nor an Indian by birth, but rather a Christian and a white man. The tensions within the Hutter family create problems for this side of Deerslayer's nature and complicate his desire to achieve manhood according to Indian standards. As their surname indicates, the Hutters' naming their home the Castle smacks of a desire to climb above their appointed station in life. This overweening pride is embodied in the darkly beautiful and passionate Judith, who is contemptuous of her father's pretensions and seeks to rise above him by becoming the wife or mistress of an officer at a British fort. By so doing she breaks the moral and social laws that are embodied in the meek and sympathetic Hetty. She, however, is a rather weak spokesman for the values she represents, since her Christianity depends on the utter innocence of her mind.

Deerslayer's problem — that of discovering or molding his own character or identity — is posed as a choice between myths. The Indian myth, represented by Chingachgook, if followed to its normal conclusion, would impel him to marry Judith. The values inherent in the European-Christian myth, represented by Hetty, would demand that he reject Judith because of the moral impurity of her nature and the fact that she has sinned with her British lover. The choice of Chingachgook's way is complicated by Deerslayer's discovery that the Indian's values are not completely his own — that the Indian's conscience sanctions scalping and the killing of women and children, while his own cannot. The choice of Hetty's way is complicated by the facts that she is a near-idiot and that her recommendations for action violate both the instincts and the experience of the hunter.

The values by which Deerslayer judges each of the alternative myths are not assumed a priori but are achieved by him through his initiation ordeals. He remains unaware of his gifts, of the character of his conscience and the nature of his passions, and of the limitations of his own nature, until he has passed through the test of experience. Deerslayer is portrayed as a man consciously seeking to create his own character through his deeds as a hunter. The quest involves him in the creation of a personal myth, a conception of his own character and destined role which sustains him like a religious faith and which (as Cooper frequently points out) makes him a myth-hero to American society at large. This last perception of Cooper's is an important one, since it touches the source of the American mythology of the hunter. The initiation experience of Deerslayer, set in the physical and moral isolation of the wilderness and in the psychological isolation of the hero's mind, is a paradigm of the historical experience of the whole nation in its acculturation to the Indian's America. Americans' response to their situation, as we have seen, was to create a myth, an intellectual construct charged with religious emotion that would explain and justify their situation. Filson and other writers of the Colonial period had created such myths without being conscious that the tremendous urge to create them was itself a primary characteristic of the historical experience of their culture. Cooper is aware of this and therefore makes his hero an initiate not only as a hunter but also into the art of myth-making. Deerslayer, Cooper tells us, will fulfill the promise suggested in Flint's portrait of Boone: he will be a poet whose words are deeds, whose poems are the deaths of sacred beasts.

The evolution of this character is conveyed in terms appropriate to the Indian and pagan rather than the Christian mythology. By emphasizing that the Indian mythology establishes the context for Deerslayer's action, Cooper strengthens the force and applicability of the Indian evaluation of Deerslayer's quest. His ultimate rejection of Judith, for reasons that are both Indian and European-Christian, thus appears as a profound revelation of the fatal limitations of Deerslayer's character. He will never wed, never consummate a union in either the Indian or the Christian myth of marriage, and thus will never attain the final prize of heroism, which is to become a "divine king," or the founder of a people or dynasty. The stages of Deerslayer's initiation are marked by the changes in his name and totem animal, for as the noble traits of his character develop and reveal themselves, Natty Bumppo becomes worthy of killing increasingly higher forms of animals. The metaphor of the hunt as a marriage of man and beast applies here: since the hunter becomes one with his prey at the moment of the kill, he must prepare himself to be a fit and equal opponent for it. In the kill itself, he assumes the powers of the thing he has dominated and slain and therefore takes his new name and character from his victim. Each new name thus reflects a newly revealed or achieved quality of character and is closer to being the true or authentic name that will express the initiate's whole and ultimate character.

Deerslayer himself clarifies the meaning of this motif in talks with Judith and Hetty. Judith asks him the English translation of Chingachgook's name and is told: "Big Sarpent — so called for his wisdom and cunning; Uncas is his ra'al name — all his family being called Uncas, until they get a title that has been 'arned by deeds." The deeds by which Deerslayer has earned his name were acts of violence and physical prowess. As his skill in violence progressively revealed itself, the Delawares among whom he was raised gave him the names of new totem animals. As he tells Hetty, who wants to know "all [his] names," his original name was Natty Bumppo, a humble name of simple, industrious, Christian people, which symbolizes his white heredity. The Delawares first named him Straight-tongue for his honesty, then Pigeon for his fleetness, and then Lap-ear for his skill as a tracker. When he became a man and owned his own rifle, he took his name from the animal he killed and was called Deerslayer.[22]

Part of Deerslayer's inner conflict is expressed in his attitude toward his names. If Uncas is Chingachgook's real name because he was born with it, then Bumppo is Deerslayer's real name, and that which he earns by deeds is less expressive of his nature. In *The Pioneers* the minister asked Natty if he and Chingachgook believed in the efficacy of works to change and convert a man's sinful natural being to that of a savable Christian. All the Christian learning of John Mohegan did not prevent his becoming Chingachgook at the crisis. Much the same question is at issue here: to what extent do the Indian deeds of Natty Bumppo make him an Indian? Is he really the mythic hero Deerslayer and Hawkeye or the low-class bumpkin Bumppo? The problem is the same as that in "Big Bear of Arkansas": is the hero clownish Jim Doggett or the man who has by hunting acquired the name and powers of the big bear itself?

Most of the events of Deerslayer's initiation seem to point toward his acceptance of his role under the aspect of the Indian myth. As Cooper describes him, he is a kind of priest of the woodlands, a figure out of primitive mythology or out of Flint's portrait of Boone as the hunter-acolyte of the forest, whose deeds of violence are contained by a moral spirit that transforms them into acts of devotion. The development of this religious discipline is one of the chief signs of Deerslayer's maturation through the experiences recounted in the novel. Cooper emphasizes this innate quality in the opening scenes of the book, in which the appearance of Deerslayer is contrasted with that of Hurry Harry. After noting the Indian source of the custom of assigning *"soubriquets,"* Cooper describes the dress and manner of the two men. Hurry Harry's arms and equipment are worn in a "careless, slovenly manner," reflecting his "indifference" to the figure he cuts before Indians and wild animals. Deerslayer, on the other hand, has arranged his appearance with "some attention to smartness and the picturesque," as if the wearer were attempting to measure up to some ideal standard of his own. "His rifle was in perfect condition, the handle of his hunting-knife was neatly carved, his powder-horn ornamented with suitable devices lightly cut into the material, and his shot pouch was decorated with wampum." [23]

These are the outward signs of a profound difference in their moral make-up, which is revealed through their subsequent actions in the book. Deerslayer is rigorously moral throughout, adhering firmly to his own code of honor in the teeth of the disapproval of his friends among both whites and Indians. Hurry Harry is honorable only so long as it is to his interest. When Judith Hutter rejects his suit, he deserts the Hutters. Deerslayer never contemplates deserting the imperiled family, even though he initially dislikes both Thomas and Judith Hutter. In an early encounter with a deer, Deerslayer reprimands Hurry for attempting to kill the beast out of season, when they were in no need of food. Hurry, who delights in killing for the joy of it, fails to understand Deerslayer's moral standard.

The fullness of this moral standard is only gradually revealed to the reader and to Deerslayer himself through the unfolding events of the novel. The incident of the deer and Deerslayer's refusal to accompany Hurry and Hutter in a raid against the Indian women and children are preludes to the most crucial episode of the narrative. In mortal combat with an Indian enemy, Deerslayer proves himself worthy to kill his fellow man and receives the name that is to become "as renowned as many a hero" of classical mythology. Just as his earlier name was taken from the thing he killed, so his new name, Hawkeye, is given him by his dying foe. The scene thus parallels the fire-hunt myth, in which Boone's goddess — Rebecca metamorphosed into a deer — names Boone "painter" or "panther" after the rituallike hunting incident has been completed. The Indian, le Loup Cervier (or the Lynx), fires at Deerslayer from ambush. Deerslayer, following the Indian practice of warfare, plays dead until the enemy exposes himself. But Deerslayer must remain true to his "white gifts," and he refuses to shoot from ambush.[24] Instead he stalks the Indian, tricks him into leaving cover, then announces his presence and calls for a peaceful parley. When the Indian breaks the truce and fires from a second ambush, Deerslayer's quickness of sight enables him to shoot through the concealing bushes and hit the invisible body of the Indian. Still true to his "white gifts," he brings water to his fallen foe and refuses to take the scalp.

> "Good!" ejaculated the Indian, . . . "good! young head; young *heart,* too. *Old* heart tough; no shed tear. Hear Indian when he die, and no want to lie — what he call him?"
> "Deerslayer is the name I bear now, though the Delawares have said that when I get back from this warpath, I shall have a more manly title, providing I can 'arn one."
> "That good name for boy — poor name for warrior. He get better quick. No fear *there* [tapping Deerslayer's heart] . . . — eye sartain — finger lightning — aim, death — great warrior soon. No Deerslayer — Hawkeye — Hawkeye — Hawkeye. Shake hand." [25]

Other ordeals test Hawkeye's new identity and further develop its strength. After being threatened by his Mingo captors with torture and then let off on a temporary parole, he is tempted to flee the area. His refusal to succumb to this weakness rises from that same vigorously stoic Indian morality that restrains him from shedding blood heedlessly. His successful passage of this moral ordeal gains him another totemistic emblem of his new manhood: Judith Hutter gives him Killdeer, a rifle of simple perfection in design and a mythlike reputation for accuracy. Just as the possession of his first rifle marked his attainment of the station of hunter and the estate of manhood, the gift of this mythic weapon marks his achievement of heroic stature (much as the armor of Hephaestos was given to Achilles on the eve of his heroic battle with Hector). In describing the weapon and the act of gift, Cooper underlines the symbolic significance of the act in terminology which strangely anticipates that used by Frazer in his discussion of the "Divine King," or "King of the Woods," myths in *The Golden Bough.* Hawkeye admires the rifle:

> "But this is a lordly piece, and would make a steady hand and quick eye the king of the woods."
> "Then keep it, Deerslayer, and become king of the woods," said Judith.[26]

Other analogies from pagan and early Christian myths are suggested by the scene, particularly the Arthurian legends of hero kings and knights receiving their legendary weapons from the Lady in the Lake. The origin of these myths is identical with that of the hunter myth, in which the hero seeks the anima, the quality of soul that will complete his half-formed identity and realize his potential for worldly power, spiritual attainment, and self-perpetuation through a dynasty of heirs. Measured by her actions in the novel, Judith is a redemptive woman. Her courage saves the Ark from the Indians; she offers herself to Deerslayer to entice him to violate his parole and refuse to return to face death at the hands of the Indians; and she goes herself to the Indian camp, disguised as a "goddess," to rescue him.

The whole strain of this archetypal myth is toward some form of sexual union between the male and female principles: the gift of the weapon itself signifies that the woman's function is to enable the predatory male to play the man's part. The problem that confronts the Deerslayer's emerging moral character is therefore couched in terms of the marriage metaphor. The psychological and emotional urges embodied in the archetypes of primitive myth, which inform our expectations of the life experience, seem to demand his marriage to Judith, his union with the anima. Indeed, she would make an ideal wife in the Indian's sense of the term, since she is strong and courageous in her own right and can deal with hardship and danger. But given the logic of the American frontier myth, as it had evolved from the Captivity Era through the Boone Era, Leatherstocking's celibacy and impotence are inevitable. His stature as an American hero depends on his uniting the characters of the hunter and the captive, since the captivity and the hunter myths *together* constitute the national myth of the frontier (and had done so since Filson at least).

Leatherstocking's submission to captivities in The Pioneers, The Prairie, and The Deerslayer is always a method of expiating the Indian sinfulness of his profession of hunter. It is a way of ameliorating his masculine force as a predator, of domesticating or at least restraining it within the moral bounds set by the feminine symbols of civilized culture. In The Pioneers it is the killing of the deer that Natty expiates in Temple's stocks. In The Deerslayer his killing of the eagle, a wanton act motivated by pride in his own prowess, produces in himself a moral revulsion that determines him to submit to Indian captivity; and it is this submission which finally breaks the eternal round of the novel, in which captivity and rescue alternate relentlessly. At the same time, the conflicting demands of the hunter's mystique and the captive's morality neutralize Leatherstocking and render him impotent, incapable of choice or marriage.

The conclusion of the novel reveals that although his blending of Indian and Christian qualities makes him a hero and a kind of saint, it ultimately prevents him from playing his proper role in either the Indian or the Christian frame of reference. His rejection of Judith in his final ordeal firmly establishes the moral foundations of his character that will make him a myth-hero. However, it also dooms him to childlessness, just as does Reuben Bourne's expiatory slaying of his son, and thus constitutes a kind of self-mutilation — especially since Judith is the lady of the lake who has given him his manly weapon. Under the aspect of primitive myth, Hawkeye's act of renunciation can be seen as a sacrifice to his goddess, although a futile and ultimately self-defeating one, with ritual rather than practical significance.

There is a version of the myth of sacred marriage in which the partner of the goddess is destroyed, immolated, or mutilated. Its structure is based, presumably, on the traditional conception of the blending of the sexes in sexual orgasm as a figurative death-in-love. Such a conclusion is, in terms of Indian mythology, as appropriate an ending for the hunter's quest as Boone's achieved marriage to the deer-woman. A legend of the Lakota or Sioux is relevant to this point. The legend recounts the means by which the calumet, or peace pipe, was given by the goddess of the earth to the people. The pipe itself symbolizes the unity of man with all the spirits of the earth — his blood relationship with the animals, the four directions and seasons, the maternal earth and paternal sky. It is both a weapon and a symbol of peace, an agent of destruction and a phallic symbol of fertility, in which a burnt offering of bark and herbs is made and consumed in a Eucharistic manner by the worshiper. Four ribbons hang from the stem, symbolizing the quarters of the universe, the seasons, and the four aspects of natural divinity — a black ribbon for the west, source of angry thunder and fertilizing rain; red for the east, source of wisdom and the morning; white for the north, whose winds cleanse and purify the land; and yellow for the south, source of the summer heat that makes things grow. An eagle feather symbolizes the One Spirit, who is the unity of all spirits, the all-fathering sky; it is also an admonition to the people that their thoughts should be as high as eagles' flight and the mind of their maker. A patch of buffalo hide symbolizes the earth and the brotherhood of man with all living wild things.

According to legend, the pipe was received from a mysterious white woman who appeared to two braves as they hunted for bison. One brave had lustful thoughts about her, while the other regarded her as sacred. To the first she said, "You do not know me, but if you want to do as you think, you may come." Delighted, "the foolish one went; but just as he stood before her, there was a white cloud that came and covered them. And the beautiful young woman came out of that cloud, and when it blew away the foolish man was a skeleton covered with worms." The goddess turns from the body of the lover she has consumed and instructs the other brave to tell the tribe of her coming and of her gift, which, she says, will enable the tribe to walk always in righteousness, cleave to a law that will make them strong, and be the source of a fecundity that will make them "multiply and be a good nation." She gives her gift, the calumet, and then turns into a white bison and flees across the prairie. Thus she reveals that she is the bison goddess, goddess of the earth, and that her gift is a sacred object — weapon, sceptre, and sacrament — that will make her chiefs true kings, her braves men, her women perfect mothers. But the necessary prelude to the gift is that moment of sexual union and sacrifice, in which the foolish young man gives life and manhood to the goddess, uniting her with mankind and enabling her to give her people the child- and nation-making gift.[27] Deerslayer's renunciation of sexuality is not preceded by any such prelude and thus ends in sterility rather than renewal of the life spirit.

Part of Hawkeye's motivation in refusing Judith's proposal of marriage is the mystical love of the wilderness that makes him seem a potential king of the woods and that, for him, is stronger than the urgings of the heart or passion for any human woman. Part of it, however, is simple Christian priggishness. Judith asks him if his decision is based on his belief in the aspersions cast on her character by Hurry Harry, and Deerslayer in part affirms this; yet to the reader Harry's judgment of any person seems gravely suspect. Although Judith may have succumbed to her vanity — although she may actually have fallen — she has been a redemptive figure, a would-be rescuer and life saver throughout the action. And she has certainly proved her ability to overcome pride and her repentance of sin by her humble proposition to the hunter. It is his concept of class distinction that divides them, and his refusal dooms her to a life of sin as Warley's mistress, while he goes on to live a life of legendary purity and integrity. This moral ambiguity renders the conclusion problematic and suggests that the apparently simple legend is quite complex. How are we to reconcile Hawkeye's reverence for all natural life (as evinced in his regret for killing the eagle out of pride)[28] with his treatment of Judith? Cooper does not answer the question, but his manner of posing it opens new roads for interpretation.

Hawkeye's ideas of race are similarly problematic. In the earlier Leatherstocking novels Cooper was careful to have Natty distinguish himself as white. In *The Deerslayer* the insistence that his original name, Bumppo, is white echoes the racial distinction. Indeed, as Deerslayer discovers his true character, he becomes progressively more conscious of his racial distinction, his "white gifts." This concept of racial difference, which the Romantics of Europe and America used as the basis of literary symbolism, had been a key element in the Indian war literature of the past. The opposition between civilization and the wilderness had of necessity been couched in terms of racial antagonism between Indian and white, and the "degeneration" of the white frontiersman was symbolized by his amalgamation with the Indians, his adoption of Indian traits. As a racial purist, Hawkeye is not given to the idea of marrying "a redskin." On the other hand, his way of life and his moral values make even white women unsuitable as mates; their natures are either too high for his manner of life or too low (in Judith's case) for his respect.[29] Thus he dies childless, like Reuben Bourne and like Chateaubriand's Chactas and René.

The code of the wilderness is also problematic. The hunter's violence, markedly sexual in its symbolic character, brings him into communion with the goddess of this world, the wilderness. Yet the violence itself and the consequent initiation into another identity violate the norms of European culture and of Christian morality and moralized sexuality. To accept wholeheartedly the wilderness marriage and Eucharist is to lose one's white soul; to hold back is to fail in America as an American. Leatherstocking's rationalizations save his purity but unsex him, render him permanently celibate. He is a purist in the related matters of morals and race. He will not mingle his blood with the Indians or with a woman whose character he sees as "dark" or morally compromised. He wishes to remain (what he calls himself at several points in the cycle of the novels) a "man without a cross." [30] To him this means in part a man without a crossing of Indian blood in his ancestry and with no desire to cross bloods in the future. It also implies his desire to preserve his pristine innocence: he is a man without a cross of sin to bear, a man exempted from the fall, a new Adam. Yet he is also, implicitly, a man beyond the pale of Christianity, a man without the Cross to guide him.

In *The Deerslayer* Cooper seems more aware of the irony in this racial attitude than he was in his earlier books. When Deerslayer muses on his white-Christian racial "gifts" while tending the dying Loup Cervier, the Indian's attitude is resentful, and Cooper seems sympathetic to that resentment:

> "My gifts are white, as I've told you; and I hope my conduct will be white also!"
> Could looks have conveyed all they meant, it is probable that Deerslayer's innocent vanity on the subject of color would have been rebuked a little; but he comprehended the gratitude that was expressed

in the eyes of the dying savage, without in the least detecting the bitter sarcasm that struggled with the better feeling.[31]

Thus even the spirit of innocence, so admired by Romantics of Cooper's own stamp, is put to the question by the artist in his pursuit of his hero's character.

Cooper's portrayal of the American character in *The Deerslayer* reduces that character to a series of artistically heightened, symbolic figures which are embodiments of ambivalences or problems, rather than of clear and simple truths. The "Big Sarpent" is wise, honorable, and cunning, brave in battle and admirable in rescuing his beloved from the Mingos — yet there is some doubt as to his Indian gift for marriage, and he may turn out as callous toward his squaw as the rest of his race. Although Judith Hutter has succumbed to the sin of pride and desired above her station, her ultimate fall is as much the result of Deerslayer's perverse purity as of her own weakness of character. Even the innocent Hetty Hutter is not a conventional ingenue: her virtue is the result of feebleness of mind, which renders her incapable of imposing her biblical morality on those around her. She is innocence reduced to impotence and near-idiocy. Interestingly enough, Cooper pointedly contrasts her to Deerslayer by distinguishing between her civilized "heart" and her "wilderness . . . head." Deerslayer is spoken of as having a "wilderness heart" and a "head" in which the reasoned discipline of civilization prevails.[32] Both are amalgamations of incompatible absolutes, and their innocence is doomed to ultimate impotence. (It is worth noting that this imagery reverses the French convention of Chenier, in which the tender heart is the product of civilized nurture and the hard head is the result of wilderness experience.)

Still, it is clear from the novel that the career and myth of Natty Bumppo — and by implication, the career of his mythic ancestor, Filson's Boone — has something to offer to civilized man, a set of values which is a result of long experience in the American wilderness. Supreme among these values is that of reverence for all life, which in Deerslayer's religion lies at the basis of all moral action. More significant is the fact that this value is derived from experience rather than from theory, for Deerslayer points out on a number of occasions his complete ignorance of the Bible. Moreover, the experience from which this basic principle has been derived is one that includes strife and violence, cruelty and hardship, loneliness and exile. Innocence, in the idiom of the Boone-Bumppo myth, is the prerequisite for deriving moral value from the wilderness ordeal; and this innocence consists in a completely receptive, open state of mind, a naïveté and absence of preconception in one's approach to experience. Moral truth emerges only when the hero totally immerses himself in his wilderness environment, forgetting (however briefly) his other ties and even his concepts of the differences between races and sexes, between body and soul, between man and god. Through this trusting immersion he discovers truths about himself and his world that were hitherto hidden to him; his discriminations are now more just, less the result of habit. In solitude and isolation his acts of war and hunting awaken him to his kinship with creation, to a sense of reality and of religious and social duty. His heart is cleansed of evil impulses, and his reason is clarified, strengthened, more dominant over his passions. This concept of the central drama of human experience is repeated throughout American literature and American culture, in the pietistic concept of conversion and the literary method of the Indian-war–personal-narrative tradition, as well as in Thoreau's experiment at Walden Pond and Whitman's journey through the jungle of "Myself." It is, at the same time, one of the universal themes of human literature.

William Simms's southern treatment of the Boone legend follows a distinctly different pattern. Like Cooper, Simms began by attempting to set the frontier hero in his proper place in the context of nineteenth-century society; but where Cooper increasingly plumbed the problematic nature of his characters, Simms's characters became more rigid sectional stereotypes. In the romantic novel *Guy Rivers* (1834) he created Mark Forrester, a cool-headed woodsman who serves as the rescuer and adviser of Ralph Colleton, Simms's Romantic hero. Forrester's character, like that of the Leatherstocking of 1823–27, is fundamentally decent but has been somewhat corrupted by too lengthy sojourns among the Indians:

> A better heart, or more honorable spirit lived not; and in spite of an erring and neglected education — of evil associations and sometimes evil pursuits — he was still a worthy specimen of manhood.

Simms is at pains to define Forrester's sectional identity, to present him as a type of southern character, a beneficiary of the southerner's racial advantages and spiritual gifts, despite his Indian-like mode of living:

> His face was finely southern. His features were frank and fearless — moderately intelligent, and well marked — the *tout ensemble* showing an active vitality, strong, and usually just feelings, and a goodnatured freedom of character. . . . With . . . a giant's powers he was seldom so far borne forward by his impulses as to permit of their wanton or improper use.[33]

Yet despite his good qualities, Forrester is not a true southern nobleman.

He lacks, like the Indian, a sentimental regard for the female. Ralph Colleton has nearly laid down his life for his love, but Forrester's one love is "a light rifle of the choicest bore; . . . which in time [the hunter] learns to love with a passion almost comparable to his love of a woman." [34]

Where Cooper turned from Leatherstocking's manners to a greater preoccupation with the larger implications of his character and values, Simms continued to work out the problem of the frontiersman's place in a social hierarchy. In *The Kinsmen* (1841), later called *The Scout*, he created Supple Jack Bannister, a vivid and realistic frontiersman who steals the reader's interest from the Romantic plot. Like Leatherstocking in the earlier books, Bannister is intended as the foil, assistant, and adviser to the noble hero. His dialect is heavy; the hero's is refined. Simms thus echoes the European distinction between the "Romantic" nature of aristocratic civilization and the coarseness of frontier American "reality."

Supple Jack and Mark Forrester assist the Romantic hero in his fight against evil members of their common culture — the Tories, the British, or Guy Rivers's outlaws. They do not represent southern culture in the great confrontation between civilization and the wilderness, between the South and the American frontier. Rather, they serve their noble masters against those forces within the nation at large which opposed the southern way of life. Thus Simms's use of the frontier hero marks a distinctly southern departure from the conventions of the Indian war narrative, in which such heroes traditionally stood for Anglo-American civilization against the destructive paganism of the savage. His departure reflects the emergence in the South of a feeling of sectional exclusiveness and alienation from the nation.

When Simms did need a hero to represent the South in the traditional Indian war confrontation, he created figures like Lord Craven of *The Yemassee* (1835) and the knight-errant Boone of his 1845 sketch. His sources for these figures were the same literary and social conventions that he had followed since *Guy Rivers*; unlike Cooper, he did not seek further enlightenment from the literature of westerners like Flint. His concerns were parochially restricted to the problems of southern society. The novel form in which he chose to work depended heavily on the existence of a contemporary audience's consensus on his concepts of social order, racial character, and relations between the upper and lower classes. While his ideas were certainly relevant to the aspirations of the South in his time, changes in social values in the South, as well as the other sections, made his social types seem increasingly dated. Lord Craven, for example, is a plausible portrayal of the ideal southern gentleman — conscious of his birth and intellectual superiority, but just and gentle to his inferiors; cultivated and civilized in habits and tastes, but able to hold his own in the rough-and-tumble of an Indian fight; a lover of tilled fields and the conversation of the towns, but able to live in the forest. His behavior in the novel, however, would have made it difficult for men not of Simms's social and political convictions to accept Craven as a hero. His open consciousness of superiority is distasteful at times, as is Simms's assertion that the common frontiersman wants nothing more than to find, to follow, and to worship such a leader.[35]

Simms's frontier heroes were created as final answers to the problem of the frontiersman's social place. Cooper's Leatherstocking, particularly in the later novels, poses more problems than he answers. His perceptions and beliefs question the values of society, and Cooper's tendency over the course of the cycle is to play down easy answers and let these questions stand out strongly. The reader of the Leatherstocking tales can develop an almost unlimited number of interpretations of the frontier hero, of American values, and of civilization in general from Cooper's problematic symbols. Simms's reader is restricted to the authorized interpretation of social type. The same distinction can be drawn between Hawthorne's tales of the frontier and R. M. Bird's *Nick of the Woods*, although Hawthorne is less flattering than Cooper in his vision of the frontier and Bird's Nick is a far more complex vision of frontier character than Simms's Mark Forrester. The significant differences between these four men are, not in their hostility to or love of the wilderness, but in their approaches to the definition of character, the problem of identity.

Simms and Bird approached the problem of identity in terms of the conventions of the Romantic novel. Each character represents a social or racial type. The true character of the Romantic hero is thinly obscured through the chicanery of a villain or the hero's own deliberate mystification, but both reader and hero are aware of the deception. Thus in Simms's *The Yemassee*, Lord Craven masquerades as Gabriel Harrison, a mysterious man of unknown rank and background whose personal worth makes him the natural leader of men who are unaware of his identity. In Bird's novel, Roland Forrester — the young "Knight of the Woods" — has exiled himself from Virginia after being cheated of his patrimony. During the course of the novel, his rights are vindicated, his identity is proven, and he returns to claim his plantation. The problem of identity for these heroes is an artificial device of Romantic fiction, rather than the fictional equivalent of a cultural and universally human problem. Both heroes are completely loyal to the social values of their class and culture; their triumph over adversity is a vindication of these values. They never seriously question the validity of their assumptions, and their moral judgments tend toward the simplistic. There is not much that either Craven or Simms can say for a character like the villainous Richard Chorley: he is simply a white renegade. The morbid passions of the young frontiersman Grayson, whose jealousy of Craven's success with the heroine Bess Mathews nearly drives him to outlawry, are attributed to his neglect of husbandry for the brooding solitudes of the forest.

Only two subordinate characters, Bird's Nathan Slaughter and Simms's Occonestoga, stand out against the conventionalized structure of these novels. Both are men torn between cultural standards, between opposed loyalties. Their character or identity is a very real problem for them, and their problem parallels the cultural problem of defining a national or sectional identity. The necessity for dealing with the problems posed by these characters brought out the artist in Simms and Bird. It stimulated them to touch on the profound doubts and questions that undergulfed the thin structure of social and literary convention.

Occonestoga is the tragic son of Chief Sanutee of the Yemassee. He is torn between his love for his father and his Indian heritage, on the one hand, and his admiration of the stronger, more advanced culture of the whites, on the other. As an Indian he is intellectually unequipped to analyze the source of the white culture's strength, and he succumbs to its evils before he can fully appreciate its true virtues. He becomes a disgraceful drunkard, aids English land-grabbers against his own tribe, and is therefore banished by Sanutee. Yet beneath this maudlin drunkard's self-pity there remains a spark of honor, a desire to serve his ideals. Occonestoga's dilemma lies in his inability to reconcile the opposing ideals represented by the two aristocratic rulers, Craven and Sanutee. Unfortunately for the novel, Occonestoga dies before the potential implications of his problem have been worked out.

A more promising work, and hence a more tragic failure, is Robert M. Bird's *Nick of the Woods* (1837). Bird's Nathan Slaughter is, potentially at least, a critical revision of the concept of the frontier hero as developed by Filson, his imitators in America and Europe, and Cooper. In the character of Nathan Slaughter, the Boone-like Quaker turned killer, Bird makes a profound comment on the Puritan character and the psychological consequences of the captivity mythology. As a southerner sharing his section's deep involvement with the psychology and symbolism of racism, he had a unique opportunity to shed an emotionally intensified light on the idea of the western character as a blend of Indian and white racial elements and on the consequences of that blending. Although he partly realizes this opportunity, he is fatally limited by the literary heritage of the South and the conventions of his chosen form. Like Cooper, his story is divided into a Romantic plot and a subplot dealing with the problem of the frontier hero; but where Cooper shifted his focus to the more significant problem, Bird's analysis of Nick of the Woods remains a subordinate, tangential theme in the Romantic story of Roland Forrester.

Bird apparently availed himself of most of the available source material on the settlement of Kentucky as preparation for his novel. He seems to have drawn on western popular fiction and on New England fiction in the captivity vein for many of the character types and attitudes employed in the novel. Filson was also an important source, and Boone's description of Kentucky from the commanding ridge is quoted with approval on the first page of the novel. Like Cooper, Bird was artist enough to make an original and perceptive synthesis of his sources in the character of Nathan Slaughter. Nathan is a Quaker, whose family has been murdered by Indians. The overwhelming grief he experienced has converted the pietistic passion of his radical Puritan sect into a fiery and implacable hatred of Indians. He becomes a hunter of Indians, murdering them by stealth, and mutilating their corpses by carving a cross on their breasts.

Curtis Dahl, in a modern edition of Bird, reports two antecedents for the character: James Hall's account of "The Indian Hater" (1832) and N. M. Hentz's *Tadeuskund: The Last King of the Lenape* (1825).[36] Hall's account (used by Melville in *The Confidence-Man*) defines a classic type of the frontiersman and border ruffian, with the same motivation as Nathan. Hentz's hero is a Quaker whose family has apparently been slain by Indians; in his passion for peace, the Quaker attempts to prove that the real murderers were white Indians and not Delawares. Hentz's work, published in Boston, thus reflects the traditional symbolism of his section. The Quaker and the Indian chief Tadeuskund represent the virtues of racial purity and self-restraint; the villains are renegades, and even the Indian-hater who assists the hero is regarded as a debased form of the species. Bird's originality lies in his synthesis of the western Indian-hater and the Quaker-Puritan and in his perception that within the rhetoric of Christian self-abnegation, which characterized Puritan and later New England writing about the captivities, lay the seeds of an overwhelming and barbarous retaliatory violence — exemplified in New England history by the massacres of the Pequot Fort (1638), the Swamp Fight (1676), and Norridgewock (1725). Boone had long since been portrayed, as his birth justified, as a Quaker hunter and Quaker warrior. Bird, who drew extensively on the literature relating to Boone, exaggerates the halves of this conventional character, heightening them into a conflict between the violently ambivalent inclinations of Nathan's nature.

Bird admits, in the preface to the 1853 edition of his novel, that it was written partly in response to the Romantic portraits of the West which Cooper and Chateaubriand had popularized. Cooper's contemporaries had seen his Natty Bumppo as a parallel for Daniel Boone, an heroic type of mediating figure linking the white and Indian worlds. Francis Parkman wrote admiringly of Leatherstocking and noted that the portrait accurately portrayed one of the best types of western character:

> There is something admirably felicitous in the conception of this hybrid offspring of civilization and barbarism, in whom uprightness, kindliness, innate philosophy and the truest moral perceptions are joined with the wandering instincts and hatred of restraint which stamp the Indian or the Bedouin. Nor is the character in the least unnatural. . . . Men as true, generous, and kindly as Leatherstocking may still be found among the perilous solitudes of the West. The quiet, unostentatious courage of Cooper's hero had its counterpart in the character of Daniel Boone; and the latter had the same unaffected love of nature which forms so pleasing a feature in the mind of Leatherstocking.[37]

In Cooper's and Parkman's eyes, Leatherstocking is a blend of essential Puritan or at least New England virtues with those of the Indian. His sensitivity to landscape and care of captive women reflect this blending of traits. To Bird, he is a blend of all that is perilous in both Yankee Puritanism and the Indian solitudes of the wilderness. Not Nathaniel Bumppo but Nathaniel Slaughter is his proper name.

Bird rejected Cooper's reading of Filson's Boone and adopted his own, which in most respects resembles the later portrait by Simms. Like Cooper and Parkman, Bird was struck by Boone's sensitivity to landscape and took it as a sign of his possession of the highest faculties of civilized man. These he naturally equated with the virtues of his own section, which he employed in creating his own conception of the frontier hero. The standards by which Bird judges a character's viability as a hero emerge in his discussion of Indian character in the 1853 preface. He dismisses the conceptions of "*Atala* and *Uncas*" as "beautiful unrealities and fictions merely, as imaginary and contrary to nature as the shepherd swains of the old pastoral school of rhyme and romance" — figures that were in fact their literary progenitors. In Bird's vocabulary, human virtue in its highest forms is expressed in the term "gentleman": "The Indian is doubtless a gentleman; but he is a gentleman who wears a very dirty shirt, and lives a very miserable life, having nothing to employ him or keep him alive except the pleasures of the chase and of the scalp-hunt — which we dignify with the name of war." [38]

Bird's own hero is a gentleman born, but he has been sent into exile through the chicanery of a scheming relative — one whose red inclinations lead him, characteristically, into a renegade's relationship with the hostile Indians who are harrying Bird's Kentucky. His name, Roland Forrester, suggests his character as Roland of the Forest, a knight-errant of the wilderness, whose ultimate desire is to prove his title to the family manor in Virginia and return there as its rightful lord. To do this he must overcome public doubts about his true identity. The revelation of his established character, as in *The Yemassee* — rather than the creation of a new character, as in *The Deerslayer* — is the point of the plot. Subordinate to Forrester are Ralph Stackpole, an Indian-hater and braggart of the Mike Fink–Davy Crockett variety, and Colonel Bruce, commander of the frontier station that is the focus of the action. Bruce is Boone with the hunter's glamor removed, a man who would have "been like a Nimrod" had nature not "extinguished the race of demigods" and heroic hunters. Although he dresses in Boone's buckskins, he is "otherwise a plain yeoman, endowed with gifts of mind appropriate to his station." He speaks in the coarse dialect of the frontier but knows his place relative to "the quality." [39] He is Boone domesticated (made a farmer, as a class type) from Filson's portrait of the hunter-husbandman. Forrester likewise is an embodiment of the highest values of mind and blood, the soul and moving spirit of civilization. He is an abstraction of the qualities of poet and philosopher in the character of Filson's Boone.

In the portraits of Forrester and Bruce, social and literary conventions lead Bird to split the character of the Filsonian hero into two parts, one genteel and intellectual and the other common and action-oriented. Where the Boone image symbolically reconciled the antitheses of the democratic-barbaric wilderness and stratified-refined civilization, Bird's novel restates the antithesis in terms of social stereotypes. The Forrester-Bruce pairing establishes an idealized microcosm of southern society in the wilderness, in which the natural aristocrat is the man of good birth and breeding and the man of lately achieved power is his natural subordinate. But in the character of Nathan Slaughter, Bird has abstracted the Indian-like qualities of Filson's hero; and in so doing, he has involved himself with psychological rather than social relationships and problems, with the consequences of solitude rather than those of society. Like the Puritans, Nathan blames himself for exposing his family to the wilderness. He seeks to exorcize a personal demon that haunts him in the shape of an Indian (Wenonga), and until he finally grapples with his archfoe, he contents himself with killing his avatars — any others of his race that may be hunted out. He kills his victims with peculiar cruelty and violence, hacking their skulls with his axe, scalping them, and carving a cross in their chests with his knife.

Nathan is the product of two solitudes. First is the psychological solitude of the Puritan believer, who stands always alone and unaided in the eye of God, humble and abnegatory before the light. Even as a Quaker, believing in an inner light rather than the cold light of a transcendent, inhuman Jehovah, Nathan is alone with his God and his conscience, suffering no figures or institutions to mediate the relationship. The second solitude is that of the wilderness, a solitude deepened and made more agonizing by the slaughter of his family and the years of lonely pursuit of his vengeance. Nathan appears in society dressed in the Indian-like garb of the hunter — a sign that he has become like the thing he hunts — but with the mien of a Quaker. His self-abnegation, in the context of a brawling frontier station, seems almost pathological to the viewer, and indeed it ultimately proves so. In society the force of Nathan's religion, with its passion for restraining and suppressing passion, comes violently to the fore, in reaction to his memory of the deeds he has been committing upon the bodies of his foes. In solitude, extreme abnegation reverts to extreme ferocity. The captive and victim becomes the bloody avenger. Nathan becomes more savage than the Indians.

In contrast to Leatherstocking, Cooper's "man without a cross," Bird makes it plain that Nathan bears a cross and also exhibits by his behavior a psychological cross between Indian and Christian. Both these crosses are figured in the one he carves in the flesh of his victims. Nathan Slaughter is called Nick of the Woods because he has become like the wilderness devil of the New England nightmares, Old Nick himself. Bird deftly turns the Puritan belief that the wilderness brings out the devil in man against the Puritan captivity mythology. By conceiving of themselves as being purely victims of the Indians, rather than the agents of their own troubles, the Puritans put the onus of their morally questionable acts on the Indians and justified their extermination of them. Nathan Slaughter's self-pity leads him into a similar moral barbarism, giving partial justification to a revenge that expresses the suppressed dark passion for violence inherent in all men.

In Bird's novel, as in Simms's, the literary and psychological insights that led to the creation of this problematic and significant character are be-

trayed by the social values and literary affectations inherent in southern social philosophy and the conventions of the historical romance. Both
Cooper and Hawthorne begin with a problem in the psychology of an individual which corresponds to the social and archetypal dilemmas faced (according to the tradition) by men in the wildernesses of the western world.
But they work away from the conventions of the historical romance and toward an involvement in the psychological, racial, and mythical concerns of
the American, Indian-war, personal-narrative tradition. This is not to imply
that either Cooper or Hawthorne was necessarily more realistic in his portrayal of details of frontier life or more daring in his concept of the frontier
character than Bird or Simms. Bird's Nick of the Woods is more complex
than any of Cooper's heroes, more intensely divided within himself, and
hence more dramatically interesting; and Simms's portrayal of Indian torture scenes and ceremonies is often more vivid and convincing than Cooper's.

What sets Cooper and Hawthorne apart is their presentation of the
wilderness experience as a search for values and identity, not merely as an
occasion for exhibiting the superiority of certain cultural assumptions and
class types. This approach to characterization led them into extensive exploration of the central metaphor in the myths of America since precoloni-
zation times — the association of the New World wilderness with the terrors and delights of the hidden mind. It also meant that their heroes' quest
for salvation through self-integration would recapitulate in dramatically
convincing form the experience of acculturation and change of character
undergone by American emigrants since 1620. Their method also led them
to use archetypal myths as well as paradigmatic American experiences and
to examine the consequences of both the American experience and the
American adoption of certain myths as their own. This last element — the
power to shed light on the consequences of the psychology represented by
the American mythology — is lacking in Simms and deficient in Bird, since
their most pointed commentary is devoted to defending the premises of
the artificial arrangements of southern society, rather than examining the
psychological grounds of those premises. Cooper, on the other hand, tends
more and more to abstract Leatherstocking and his world from social reality, to use the Leatherstocking world as a refuge from reality, where issues
might be resolved on a psychological and symbolic plane that could not be
resolved in fact (at least not in the way Cooper wished them to be resolved).

Cooper notwithstanding, the American hunter was not a "man without a cross," independent of the past history, present context, and future

consequences of his character and his acts. The year 1776 marked, not simply the birth of a new nation, but a new stage in a process of mythogenesis that reached back into the primitive dreams of the West which motivated explorers and colonists and into the psychological tensions which broke to the surface in the witchcraft delusion and in the mad massacres of the Pequots and the Narragansetts. American literature would have to come to terms with both its psychology and its history if it was to achieve and promulgate a more truthful vision of the American experience than Cooper, Bird, or Simms had done. For this purpose the literature of personal narrative, derived from the Puritans, offered better models than the formulaic historical romances of Scott. Moreover, if the mythic hero was to retain a permanent viability in American culture and to keep pace with his audience's increased experiences and perceptions of their situation in America, the knowledge or fear of these crosses and consequences would have to be incorporated in the figure of the hero.

CHAPTER 14

A Pyramid of Skulls

He turned back to the Indians, it is the saving gesture — but a gesture of despair. . . .

But this primitive ordeal, created by a peculiar condition of destiny (the implantation of an already partly cultured race on a wild continent) has a plant in its purpose, in its lusts' eye, as gorgeous as Montezuma's garden of birds, wild beasts and albino natives in wooden cages.

But he who will grow from that basis must sink first. . . .

However hopeless it may seem, we have no other choice: we must go back to the beginning; it must all be done over; everything that is must be destroyed.

William Carlos Williams, *In the American Grain*

SAM CROFT
THE HUNTER

A lean man of medium height but he held himself so erectly he appeared tall. His narrow triangular face was utterly without expression. There seemed nothing wasted in his hard small jaw, gaunt firm cheeks and straight short nose. His gelid eyes were very blue. . . . He hated weakness and he loved practically nothing. There was a crude unformed vision in his soul but he was rarely conscious of it. . . .

His ancestors pushed and labored and strained, drove their oxen, sweated their women, and moved a thousand miles.

He pushed and labored inside himself and smoldered with an endless hatred.

(You're all a bunch of fuggin whores)
(You're all a bunch of dogs)
(You're all deer to track)
I HATE EVERYTHING, WHICH IS NOT IN MYSELF

Norman Mailer, *The Naked and the Dead*

GREAT literature is at once the apprentice and the master of myth. Its sources are mythic, for its statements refer to the ultimate questions of human consciousness and human existence, and it employs metaphors appropriate to the experience of the writer and his audience, his culture, and his people. But the literary artist employs myth to probe both the bases of myth — that is, the psychology and history which gave birth to a specific myth — and the ultimate consequences of the acceptance of myth. The myth of the hunter, in the hands of second- and third-rank literary intelligences, became an informing structure in the popular literature and thought of the United States. But the ultimate test of its meaning as a conception of the American experience and as a basis for prophetic visions of national character and destiny lay outside the bounds of popular literature. Writers in subsequent years would not turn to Cooper, Simms, Bird, Timothy Flint, or T. B. Thorpe for their visions of the universe or their artistic models. They would look, rather, to writers who were less widely known and appreciated during their lifetimes, writers whose perceptions and manner of expression passed by a wider margin the bounds set by the norms of the popular vision. Although the fact is recorded in no contemporary journal, Thoreau and Melville completed the work Cooper had begun — Thoreau by describing an ethical system based on Deerslayer's experience of the wilderness, Melville by forging (at last) the American epic.

Melville and Thoreau are set apart from the other writers in this mythic vein by the superior quality of their literary talent and the greater depth of their intelligence and emotional sensitivity. But beyond these personal qualities, Thoreau and Melville share the advantage of a particular literary situation. Their predecessor Cooper had blazed several important trails for them, uncovered and employed many important sources of the hunter myth, and assimilated them into the metaphoric structure of his novels. Melville and Thoreau, although they employed many of the same sources, had the advantage of not being wholly dependent on them. Cooper had recognized the mythic function of popular treatments of the frontier and had made his consciousness of the mythic nature of his subject explicit in *The Prairie* and *The Deerslayer*. Melville and Thoreau could take Cooper's clouded vision of the archetypes and proceed to clarify them further and to develop hidden significances in their content that Cooper may have been blind to.

Thoreau: The Writer as Captive and Hunter

The affinities between Thoreau's usual persona and Leatherstocking are particularly striking. George Eliot, in an early British review of *Walden*, sees Thoreau in terms of the conventional European image of the naturally wise but undomesticated backwoodsman. Indeed, she conceives the Walden experiment as a Leatherstocking-like return to the Indian mode of life, a deliberate choice by Thoreau to become "a stoic of the woods." [1] Emerson, in his eulogy of Thoreau, cites as typical of the man his "jealousy" of cities and their "refinements and artifices." Most significantly, he recalls Thoreau's Boone-like disgust that "the axe was always destroying his forest." Emerson echoes (knowingly or unknowingly) the thoughts of Leatherstocking in *The Pioneers* and *The Prairie* when he quotes Thoreau as saying, "Thank God . . . they cannot cut down the clouds." [2] Emerson carries the analogy further, recalling that Thoreau expressed an Indian sensibility in his attitude toward nature, identifying himself with the beasts of prey or with the Indian hunters themselves. His impulse to the study of nature was, by Emerson's and his own account, a sublimation of the hunting passion:

> His determination on Natural History was organic. He confessed that he sometimes felt like a hound or a panther, and, if born among Indians, would have been a fell hunter. But, restrained by his Massachusetts culture, he played out the game in this mild form of botany and ichthyology. His intimacy with animals suggested . . . that "either he had told the bees things or the bees told him." Snakes coiled around his leg; the fishes swam into his hand . . . [he] took the foxes under his protection from the hunters. [3]

Thoreau conceived his life (as Flint conceived Boone's) as an extended initiation into the profession and art of the hunter. Flint declared that Boone's act of slaying a beast was a kind of religious devotion and a form of poetry, an artistic act symbolic of a world vision. For Thoreau the act of observation, the perception and assimilation of fact, was a kind of sublimated hunt; and the record of observed facts was a kind of symbolic poetry containing the seeds of a moral imperative. Before going to Walden, he had developed the germs of a system of values and a method of stalking life. In the microcosmic "wilderness" of Walden he tested and cultivated these and created for himself a symbolic vocabulary, in which the facts of observation could be identified with values and truths. After his return from the solitude of Walden, this vocabulary became the basis of his assault on the values and behaviors of society, a weapon and a talisman of vision — like the Indian calumet, Boone's vision of the "new Eden," and Deerslayer's Killdeer.

The informing metaphor of Thoreau's vision is the struggle between two modes of perception, that of the hunter and that of the farmer. Thoreau's farmer, unlike Crèvecoeur's, is the materialist, bound forever to the routine of plowing and profiting, getting and spending; his soul is "plowed under for compost." The hunter and the poet are free souls, whose purpose in life is neither to sow nor to reap but to perceive and to respond to all of life. To perfect their perceptions is their only ambition; to increase the depth and significance of their response is their only profit. These two kinds of vision correspond to the divided vision of the Leatherstocking tales, in which the Indian and the Christian — the mythopoeic and the rational or civilized — modes of perception are opposed. In Thoreau, however, the conflict is more purely internal and psychological. The proponents of the "civilized" or "farmer's" vision have to meet Thoreau on his own ground — the tangled wilderness of the mind — where their superior numbers, industry, wealth, and instruments of cultivation and destruction are of little use. Before going to Walden, he writes: "I must not lose any of my freedom by being a farmer and a landholder. . . . When the right wind blows or a star calls, I can leave this arable and grass ground, without making a will or settling my estate." [4]

At Walden Thoreau re-creates the experience of the Puritan and the western pioneer — the solitary hunter and sometime husbandman living on the frontier of civilization, the verge of absolute nature. Wildness and wilderness, he says in "Walking," are the essence of the West, and the West is the symbol of that which is essentially American. If the settled country of the East is still in essence American, a man should be able to play the pioneer there within the shadow of Athenian Boston. Thoreau's preliminary explorations of this symbolism, its implications, and its role in his own perceptions and experiences are recorded in the book he wrote at Walden, a retrospective account of a journey taken some years before: *A Week on the Concord and Merrimack Rivers*. The relived journey takes him through the districts of Massachusetts that had been harried frontier communities during the Indian wars of 1675–1745. As he passes down the rivers, two streams of perception are generated — one by the observed natural phenomena in the present moment of the journey, the other by the area's literary and historical past, embodied in the old narratives of the captives, Indian fighters, and Indian missionaries. Thoreau seems especially well acquainted with the narratives of Indian missionary Daniel Gookin, with Cotton Mather's captivity tales, and with the *Entertaining Passages* of that hunter of men, Benjamin Church, all of which are referred to, directly or obliquely, in Thoreau's book.

As the two streams — that of immediate perception and that of memory or historical-cultural tradition — begin to merge, Thoreau achieves the expression of a crucial metaphor for his whole mission at Walden, his approach to reality, his mode of perception. In the "Thursday" chapter, he equates the inspired perception of the poet and the disciplined perception of the naturalist and surveyor with the perceptions imposed on the mind of the frontiersman and hunter by his situation on the verge of the wilderness. In our agrarian's and land speculator's passion for expansion, we have thrust our borders "where we will on the *surface* of things," even to the Pacific. "But the lives of men, though more extended laterally in their range, are still as shallow as ever." The old frontiersmen have scratched the surface of the New World with plow marks from coast to coast, leaving behind them a society marred by the evil of chattel slavery, the slavery of social and financial ambition, and the imposition of a socially conventional-ized husk over the creative organs of perception. "We do not avoid evil by fleeing before it" — by moving laterally away from it as Leatherstocking does — "but by rising above or diving below its plane." [5] The new fron-tiers are within the present geographical bounds of American society, within the mind of man. They must be approached as the frontier hunter approached the wilderness: not in terms of civilized conventions, but as an unknown reality to be plumbed by total self-immersion in direct, simple, and unanticipated experience:

> The frontiers are not east or west, north or south, but wherever a man *fronts* a fact, though that fact be his neighbor, there is an unset-tled wilderness between him and Canada, between him and the set-ting sun, or, farther still, between him and *it*. Let him build himself a log house with the bark on where he is, *fronting* IT, and wage there an Old French war for seven or seventy years, with Indians and Rangers, or whatever else may come between him and the reality, and save his scalp if he can.[6]

Thoreau's approach to discovering Truth in the ambiguities of reality is that of the Indian hunter in his hunting of a sacred beast. He submits himself wholly to the necessity imposed on him by the nature of his envi-ronment, risking his scalp and life to the power of the wilderness. In re-sponse, the spirits of the wilderness may reciprocally risk something of their own life; they may relinquish something of their power and knowl-edge by permitting him success and unanticipated revelations in the con-summation of his hunt. Thoreau converts this hunting doctrine into an aes-thetic theory: the true poet is he who writes from an absolute and undeniable necessity, like the hunter who (in Leatherstocking's manner) hunts only for the satisfaction of the body's and the soul's hunger.

> There are two classes of men called poets. The one cultivates life, the other art; one seeks food for nutriment, the other for flavor; one

satisfies hunger, the other gratifies the palate. There are two kinds of writing, both great and rare: one that of genius, or the inspired, the other of intellect and taste, in the intervals of inspiration. The former is above criticism, always correct, giving the law to criticism. It vibrates and pulsates with life forever. It is sacred, and to be read with reverence, as the works of nature are studied.[7]

The literary method of the solitary and the hunter is the root of sacred literature. It is spontaneous and wild, of the nature of the poet's soul, not of his socially formed, socially oriented reason. It is also a dangerous activity, requiring a foray into a reality whose potentials of meaning cannot be anticipated. Therefore "we can never safely exceed the actual facts in our narratives." [8]

In proof of his method, Thoreau offers an "improvement" of Cotton Mather's account of Hannah Dustin's captivity and escape from the Indians. Mather had mined the account for all the symbolism and typological data it might possibly contain. He had approached it as a man composing a sermon on "Humiliation and Deliverance," and his perception of it was limited by his method of approach. Thoreau begins with facts, reconstructing the events of the narrative carefully and objectively. Where Mather luridly recounted the advent of the "raging Demons" and the horrid cruelties which their devilish nature led them to perpetrate. Thoreau reports simply that the Indians forced her to rise from childbed and go with them, that her husband and children had fled but she knew not where, and that "she had seen her infant's brains dashed out against an apple tree." [9] The apple tree is Thoreau's own subtle addition to the tale, a seed of metaphor and myth planted among apparently stable, established facts. The rest of the tale is told with equal economy. The Indians threaten Hannah and her female companion with being stripped naked and made to run the gauntlet. The women, stirred to resolution, rise secretly in the night, brain their captors with their own axes, and flee in terror. Then, with a return of reason, they return to the scene of slaughter to scalp their enemies as evidence of the deed. They reach home in safety and are awarded the bounty of fifty pounds. At this point Mather cried out at the justice of the retribution and pleaded for his parishioners to turn from pagan to more Christian ways. Thoreau makes no such obvious appeal for us to identify ourselves with the drama of Hannah Dustin, nor does he assert his own valuation of the meaning of her actions:

> According to the historian, they escaped as by a miracle all roving bands of Indians, and reached their homes in safety, with their trophies, for which the General Court paid them fifty pounds. The family of

Hannah Dustan [*sic*] all assembled alive once more, except the infant whose brains were dashed out against the apple tree, and there have been many who in later times have lived to say that they had eaten of the fruit of that apple tree.[10]

The last sentence, for all its spartan adherence to simple statements of fact, touches a tangled and complex mystery in the tale of Hannah Dustin. It begins with an image of the typical ending of the captivity narrative, the sundered family group reunited. The only missing member of the family is the infant, murdered on an apple tree, a permanent and abiding sacrifice to the wilderness. In the same sentence, however, we are told that people have "lived to say that they had eaten of the fruit of that apple tree." The fruit of the tree, in a figurative sense, is the sacrificed infant whose broken skull is the image most strongly associated here with the tree. The eating of the fruit of the tree thus seems a kind of Indian-cannibal Eucharist. The specification of the apple tree, reminiscent of the Eden tree, of man's knowledge and death, reinforces this impression. Interpreted with the most intense concern for symbolism, the infant is a type of Christ; the tree, the cross on which the little god is hanged; and the eating of the fruit, a sacrament that ties the living family group to its sacrificed, divine child. Thus the sacrament mythologically completes the reunion of the family required by the captivity narrative genre. Moreover, it serves to link the present dwellers in the land to the reality of that bloody revelation of wilderness by means of a sacrament in which the symbolic fruit is perceived as a scant covering, an insignificant palliation or sublimation, of the reality of infant blood and torment. It is a Eucharist, with real rather than figurative flesh and blood, a revision of the Eden myth in which the eating of the apple of knowledge is a sacrament rather than a sin.

Thoreau seems aware of the sacramental quality of this sympathetic reliving of the Dustin captivity. It leads him first into contemplation of the mythology of woman — the great archetypes of the feminine principle, mother goddess and anima. The history of the world, he reflects, is embodied in sixty generations of "old women," including Columbus's nurse, the Virgin, the sibyl, Queen Semiramis, and mother Eve.[11] The captivity and the exploration of the landscape thus illuminate two symbolic archetypes, woman and the wilderness. These two in conjunction symbolize a third component of divinity, the human unconscious, source of poetic genius and abiding place of the spirit of God in man. "The unconsciousness of man is the consciousness of God." To merge with this consciousness by sinking into the unconscious is the quietist mystic's path to sainthood. For Thoreau, however, the act of creation is, not a passive sinking into the unconscious, but a conscious hunter's foray into the "wilderness of the mind": "The talent of composition is very dangerous — the striking out the heart of life at a blow, as the Indian takes off a scalp. I feel as if my life had grown more outward when I can express it." [12] (He might as well have identified himself with the Indian who created the child-god by seizing him and dashing him against the tree.)

This insight emerges from a critical exfoliation of the narrative facts with which Thoreau begins. Nor is the sequence of ideas that follows the narrative unified by a structure of logical or narrative connectives. Like the narrative itself, the ideas generated by the narrative are offered as facts, as events for the reader to perceive. No explanation, no explicit justification or illumination of the underlying symbolism of the tale or of the associational logic of the exposition is given. The reader is left to make his own foray into the wilderness of Thoreau's intention, to make his own discovery and take his own scalps. The words on the page are as enigmatic and full of possibility as the events themselves. The symbolism we read into them, like the meanings Thoreau sees in Dustin's tale, may be an illusion imposed on reality by our own sensibilities. On the other hand, there may in fact be some truth inherent in the very nature of the objects or events.

The poet is the man of most prowess in such hunts, surprising truth in her cabin, capturing her, and forcing her to run naked the gauntlet of his intelligence. This grotesque image seems valid, since for Thoreau the Indian symbolizes the wild, spontaneous quality of poetic genius in the mind. To the civilized white man are left the lesser functions of the understanding — material calculation, experience rather than innocence of mind, and recognition of rational limitations rather than acceptance of the infinite possibilities of the mind and the passions:

> The white man comes, pale as the dawn, with a load of thought, with a slumbering intelligence as a fire raked up, knowing well what he knows, not guessing but calculating; strong in community, yielding obedience to authority; of experienced race; of wonderful, wonderful common sense; dull but capable, slow but persevering, severe but just, of little humor but genuine; a laboring man, despising game and sport; building a house that endures, a framed house.[13]

The Indian, who does not bind his genius to the soil by a plow, retains a transcendent buoyance of genius. He does not entail himself to the gods and the soil like the white man, but retains "the wary independence and aloofness of his dim forest life" and thus "preserves his intercourse with his native gods, and is admitted from time to time to a rare and peculiar society with Nature." [14] These flashes of communion with nature come to him because his relation to nature has remained free and spontaneous; he neither breaks his spirit to nature nor seeks to break nature's spirit to his own desires. Perception, rather than domination or calculation, is his forte:

> He has glances of starry recognition to which our salons are strangers. . . . It is true, there are the innocent pleasures of country life, and it is sometimes pleasant to make the earth yield her increase, and gather the fruits in their season; but the heroic spirit will not fail to dream of remoter retirements and more rugged paths. . . . We would not always be soothing and taming nature, breaking the horse and the ox, but sometimes ride the horse wild and chase the buffalo. The Indian's intercourse with Nature is at least such as admits of the greatest independence of each.[15]

The Indian's aloofness from his beloved nature permits him, in Thoreau's vision, a kind of transcendental and chaste relationship with "his mistress." Like the Indian, Thoreau wishes to have "garden plots . . . elsewhere than on earth, and gather nuts and berries by the way for . . . subsistence, or orchard fruits with such heedlessness as berries." [16] Thoreau reverses the seventeenth- and eighteenth-century convention in regard to the degeneration of hunters into savages through the overexcitement of their sexual passion for the goddess. In Thoreau's vision it is the farmer whose sexual relationship to the earth is obscenely intimate, and it is agriculture which leads to human degeneration:

> If [the Indian] is somewhat of a stranger in [Nature's] midst, the gardener is too much of a familiar. There is something vulgar and foul in the latter's closeness to his mistress, something noble and cleanly in the former's distance. In civilization . . . man degenerates at length, and yields to the incursion of more northern tribes.[17]

Civilized poetry is degenerate because it is removed from the wild, spontaneous sources of poetry in the natural, uninhibited genius:

> There are other, savager, and more primeval aspects of nature than our poets have sung. It is only white man's poetry. Homer and Ossian even can never revive in London or Boston. And yet, behold how these cities are refreshed by the mere tradition, or the imperfectly transmitted fragrance and flavor of these wild fruits. If we could listen but for an instant to the chant of the Indian muse, we should understand why he will not exchange his savageness for civilization.[18]

Thus his hoeing in the "Beanfield" of *Walden* is not the "farming" of mere "property" but rather an exploit, not unlike Deerslayer's killing of his name-animal. Thoreau says he hoes to learn (and so dominate or assimilate) the essential character (special power) of the plant, so that he may convert it into the stuff of "tropes and parables."

In *Walden*, written after his sojourn there, Thoreau applies this "Indian" literary method to an extended and complex examination of his own experience in the literary medium. The original title of the work, *Walden, or a Life in the Woods*, reveals Thoreau's conception of the meaning of his experience. It was a systematic attempt to live by the methods and in the manner of the hunter-poet, to place himself on the frontier between society and solitude, art and nature, civilized and primitive, written record and live observation, and to submit himself absolutely to the natural necessities imposed on man by unmediated nature. As in *A Week*, immediate experience and literary memory are his alternative means of grappling with reality. In *Walden*, however, the two are more closely interdependent, the literary allusions more fully assimilated to the free and natural perceptions of the observer, surveyor, and fisherman. The literary antecedents of *Walden* are concealed rather than exhibited.

Walden, a unique synthesis of several genres of Colonial writing, transforms the conventions of those genres into the basis of a myth and a symbolic language. The book is certainly in the vein of the personal narrative of conversion, since Thoreau's experience is that of "awakening." At the same time it is a discovery narrative, complete with the traditional paraphernalia of surveyor's measurements and lists of plants and animals. These, however, become the sources of the light that awakens Thoreau. The objects (plants and animals) that Thoreau names become the word-symbols in the vocabulary of the awakened mind — not bare emblems of value, like beasts in a fable, but the living incarnation and expression of the values themselves. They require observation and depiction, in contrast to the usual imposition upon objects of the conventional vocabulary of symbols. Like the captivity and hunter tales, *Walden* frames Thoreau's conversion or awakening as a sojourn or expedition into the solitude of the wilderness. Finally, it is a handbook or manual, detailing the methods and materials necessary to living the good life at Walden Pond.

The initial chapters on "Economy" and "What I Lived For" establish the scheme of values that Thoreau proves at Walden. They serve the same purpose as the prefaces and apologies attached by Puritan writers to their emigration tracts. These chapters also sound the first note of a thematic conflict which informs the structure of the book and unifies it. The conflict is that between the visions of the farmer and the hunter, of the man of society and the man of solitude, of the Christian and the Indian. Thoreau begins as a civilized man seeking some unknown "awakening" in the wilderness. He ends by acquiring the Indian's mode of perception — and this constitutes his awakening. He anticipates the conclusion in his opening paragraph:

> When I wrote the following pages . . . I lived alone, in the woods, a mile from any neighbor, in a house which I had built myself, on the shore of Walden Pond . . . and earned my living by the labor of my hands only. I lived there two years and two months. At present I am a sojourner in civilized life again.[19]

This paragraph establishes a tension between the solitude of Walden, where (he reiterates) he "lived," and the society of Concord, in which he is merely a "sojourner." The implication is that only at Walden did he feel himself fully alive. Subsequent paragraphs develop and extend the theme:

> I see young men, my townsmen, whose misfortune it is to have inherited farms, houses, barns, cattle, and farming tools; for these are more easily acquired than got rid of. Better if they had been born in the open pasture and suckled by a wolf; that they might have seen with clearer eyes what field they were called to labor in.[20]

Man's true task is to perfect himself, soul and body, by the only means available to him, that of his senses. Until he can see clearly—until he can train his perceptions to true vision—he is blind, imperfect, half-created. The poet who sees a farm gains more from it through his vision than the farmer through his toil and investments.

The chapter on "Economy" records the first steps of his self-initiation into the wilderness, in which he systematically strips himself of outworn or unnecessary physical and mental gear (an action which he compares to the Indian busk ritual) and prepares to grapple naked with naked truth. He frames this purification ritual as a discourse on business methods, reminding us of the link between the hunter's passion and the entrepreneurial passion exemplified in Davy Crockett. However, for all his talk of such civilized items as profit and loss, it is clear that his risk capital is the totality of his being — his emotions, beliefs, intellectual convictions, and knowledge, all of which are exposed to loss or ruin in the "transaction of business" at Walden.[21] Each item in the catalogue of necessities is carefully established through rigid analysis and a niggling attention to detail. Yet the very finickiness of that attention has the cumulative effect of investing his economy with the appropriate aura of mystery and ritual purification, preparing us for the revelations that will follow.

Opposed to the business metaphor of the first chapter, which characterizes the Walden experience in society's terms, is Thoreau's own, more mysterious postulation of his mission. Anticipating the method of the rest of the book, he states his own concept of his purpose obliquely, offering a kind of parable with symbolic animals. The animals, however, are treated like real, extant beasts, and although Thoreau's experience with them smacks of fable, he does not overtly illuminate the symbolism:

> I long ago lost a hound, a bay horse, and a turtle-dove, and am still on their trail. Many are the travellers I have spoken concerning them, describing their tracks and what calls they answered to. I have met with one or two who heard the sound, and the tramp of the horse, and even seen the dove disappear behind a cloud, and they seemed as anxious to recover them as if they had lost them themselves.[22]

The quest is thus described in terms of an Indian-like metaphor, in which the hunter tracks animals who are totems of his own identity. What their true character may be or what they signify he declines to reveal; but he must risk all for them, submit to the necessity of a dark quest or hunt, and hope at the end of the hunt for epiphany.

Increasingly, Thoreau identifies himself with the Indians. Speaking of his relationship to his fellow townsmen, he compares himself to those Indians whose frame of reference was so entirely different from that of the Christians who attempted to convert them that the very essence of Christianity communicated to them only served to make them more themselves:

> The Jesuits were quite balked by those Indians who, being burned at the stake, suggested new modes of torture to their tormentors. Being superior to physical suffering, it sometimes chanced that they were superior to any consolation which the missionaries could offer; and the law to do as you would be done by fell with less persuasiveness on the ears of those, who, for their part, did not care how they were done by, who loved their enemies after a new fashion, and came very near freely forgiving them all they did.[23]

This identification with the Indian involves both a mode of perception and the adoption of a scheme of ethics. While the achievement of the former is of major concern to Thoreau in *Walden*, the ethical consequences of that perception do appear, as in his acceptance of a brief jail term for civil disobedience (in the chapter called "The Village"). But the jailing itself is seen as the result of a failure in the townsmen's perception, their blindness, and is offset by the exercise of vision in the following chapter, "The Ponds." Here Thoreau's thoughts follow a distinctly Indian-like pattern, moving from the contemplation of immediate phenomena to the vision of their archetypes. Thoreau was not consciously aping the manner of the Indian myths, however; he was reachieving their mythopoeic mode of consciousness for himself by his own means and from his own motives.

In Thoreau's vision, the ponds whose surface and depth he measures become extensions of their oceanic archetypes, totems of ocean itself. Fishing thus becomes a means of linking the archetypal and the phenomenal worlds:

> I drifted in the gentle night breeze, now and then feeling a slight vibration along [the line], indicative of some life prowling about its extremity, of dull uncertain blundering purpose there, and slow to make up its mind. At length you slowly raise, pulling hand over hand, some horned pout squeaking and squirming to the upper air. It was very queer, especially on dark nights, when your thoughts had wandered to vast and cosmogonal themes in other spheres, to feel this faint jerk, which came to interrupt your dreams and link you to Nature again.

Sky and pond, like heaven and ocean, reflect each other and seem to be a single identity:

> It seemed as if I might next cast my line upward into the air, as well as downward into this element which was scarcely more dense. Thus I caught two fishes as it were with one hook[24]

— that is to say, a worldly and a heavenly "fish." In Christian mythology Jesus is both the fish and, through Peter, the fisher of men. Like Christ, the hunter-hero moves and mediates between the world of men and the underworld of the gods and is himself a part of both worlds.

This movement from finite measurement to the revelation of immeasurable depths and profundities within the finite bounds of Walden characterizes the movement of the whole book. What begins as an account of a "private transaction" becomes an archetypal experience like those of Filson's and Flint's Boone and Cooper's Leatherstocking. All the elements of the hunter archetype — the oceanic pool, the island solitude of the hunter, the interchanging of human, divine, and animal identities — are present. As in the Indian creation myths and Flint's fire-hunt legend, the culmination of the hero's experience is the attainment of a creative power. *Walden* ends with the resurrection of an insect egg from its apparent tomb in a table of post-Edenic applewood, a figurative spring which follows his chapters on winter. As if to emphasize that the seasonal renewal of life is the archetypal expression and essential meaning of his experience, Thoreau has earlier stated that he stayed at Walden another year and has implied that this account of one year-cycle may serve as a model, or archetype, of the whole.[25]

The hinge of this year-cycle is the sequence of experiences related in the chapters called "Baker Farm," "Higher Laws," and "Brute Neighbors." In the first of these Thoreau visits the farm of an Irish immigrant, the living embodiment of those values Thoreau had come to Walden to escape. Faced with the vision of the farmer's spiritual poverty, Thoreau reverts emphatically to the life of the hunter in "Higher Laws." Here he comes up against the central dilemma of the hunter myth, its sensual and erotic basis.

The chapter begins with a vivid image of the emotion of the hunter, a passion that so moves Thoreau that he identifies himself with a beast of prey:

> As I came home through the woods with my string of fish, trailing my pole, it being now quite dark, I caught a glimpse of a woodchuck stealing across my path, and felt a strange thrill of savage delight, and was strongly tempted to seize and devour him raw; not that I was hungry then, except for that wildness which he represented. Once or twice, however, while I lived at the pond, I found myself ranging the woods, like a half-starved hound, with a strange abandonment, seeking some kind of venison which I might devour, and no morsel could have been too savage for me. I found in myself, and still find, an instinct toward a higher, or, as it is named, spiritual life, as do most men, and another towards a primitive rank and savage one, and I reverence them both.[26]

The scene closely resembles that of the Delaware creation myth. In the legend, the people at the dawn of time were dwelling in darkness, in a hole under a pond or lake. A hunter, hungry for meat, chased a deer through a hole into the outer world and ate it. In the taste of the wild meat he discovered the goodness of his mother earth and consequently led his people forth to populate the land. Thoreau's reverence of his savage lust for the wild meat is of a kind with that of the Indian hero. As Thoreau says, it is not simple hunger that impels him but the desire to imbibe and assimilate the spiritual essence of the animal, its "wildness," its at-oneness with the wilderness of nature. He agrees with "the Algonquins" that, for some ages, "hunters are 'the best men.' " He himself abjures his fowling piece because he has no need of the flesh of birds and can know their essence better through disciplined observation than through killing them. The motivating impulse, however, is in both cases identical.[27]

In this lies the seed of a problem. If, as the title of the chapter postulates, there are higher laws that must be lived by, is not the emotion of the hunter ranked with the low and base? "I have found repeatedly, of late years, that I cannot fish without falling a little in self-respect." The hunter's emotion partakes of the sensual, and "all sensuality is one, though it takes many forms; all purity is one. It is the same whether a man eat, or drink, or cohabit, or sleep sensually. They are but one appetite."[28] Like

Cotton Mather, Thoreau perceives in the hunting of the beast an opportunity for the expression and release of the inner beast: "We are conscious of an animal in us, which awakens in proportion as our higher nature slumbers. It is reptile and sensual, and perhaps cannot be wholly expelled; like the worms which, even in life and health, occupy our bodies. Possibly we may withdraw from it, but never change its nature." [29]

Yet this sensuality, expressed in lust for the kill or sexual fever, is the source of the "generative energy," the creative power of man. To destroy it is to destroy man himself. What, then, is the alternative? For Whitman, working with the same type of perception in "Song of Myself," the answer was absolute freedom of expression. For Thoreau the answer is like that of Timothy Flint: the sublimation of the sensual procreative passion, the disciplining and training of it to acts of restrained and creative violence, as in the composition of poetry or the greedy observation of the birds. "The generative energy, which, when we are loose, dissipates us and makes us unclean, when we are continent invigorates and inspires us." [30] Chastity, then, is the hunter's salvation — for Thoreau as for Cotton Mather and Natty Bumppo — although this means a womanless, childless existence. It also means the renunciation of wild or other meat (the bread of the wilderness Eucharist), since meat-eating stimulates dark passion. Ideal chastity, however, is part of the acculturated American's ethic of solitude, as embodied in Leatherstocking. It enables the hero to submit to the Indian dark of the wilderness without becoming debased by sexual amalgamation. It is this aloofness from prolonged sensual intimacy with woman or nature which Thoreau, in *A Week*, had characterized as an Indian virtue.

Thoreau's form for partaking of the wilderness Eucharist is a chaste sublimation of the myth of sacred marriage, in which the union is figuratively, rather than overtly, sexual. As in the Indian creation myth, the discovery of this divine principle through the tasting of the wild meat produces both an emigration and a vision of the wilderness spirit — both, however, figurative rather than literal. At the conclusion of the chapter on "Higher Laws," Thoreau affirms his doctrine of chastity and self-restraint, speaking to a figurative and archetypal farmer and calling him to come away from his fields and, as a start, to "practise some new austerity, let his mind descend into his body and redeem it." [31] This passage suggests the direction of the next chapter on "Brute Neighbors," as well as echoing the Puritan conception of Christianity's relation to the wilderness.

In "Brute Neighbors" Thoreau seeks to observe and identify his animal neighbors, especially the loon whom he pursues on the surface of the lake. As the farmer passage suggests, the quest is both in the physical world and within Thoreau's own mind. The loon is a bird but also an emblem of the wilderness spirit of both the hunter and his goddess. The hunting of the loon, like the hunting of the deer in the lake by the Delaware hero or by Leatherstocking and Chingachgook in *The Pioneers*, involves the hunter in a mystery. The loon appears and disappears; the hunter attempts to adjust his sympathies and movements to the bird so as to anticipate him, but always the bird surprises expectation. As the hunt wears on, the bird's laughing cry becomes "demoniac," and after each triumph over his hunter "he uttered a long-drawn, unearthly howl, probably more like that of a wolf than any bird. This was his looning — perhaps the wildest sound that is ever heard here." The loon thus seems to embody the essence of that wildness Thoreau had sought to devour and assimilate. As if to confirm the impression that he is avatar of the antic spirit of his wild goddess, the loon turns the lake against his hunter: "At length . . . he uttered one of those prolonged howls, as if calling on the god of loons to aid him, and immediately there came a wind from the east and rippled the surface, and filled the whole air with a misty rain, and I was impressed as if it were the prayer of the loon answered, and his god was angry with me; and so I left him disappearing far away on the tumultuous surface." [32]

Since literal union between the hunter Thoreau and the goddess of the loon is unimaginable, Thoreau's union with that "generative energy" which brings man to woman and thrusts the insect out of the applewood table must occur in the realm of perception and intellection rather than sexual action. As a psychological hybrid of the woods and the town, Thoreau desires a balance between society and solitude, maintained in equilibrium by "chastity." "We need the tonic of wildness" without which "our village life would stagnate." Knowledge of the wild consists in a descent from civilized consciousness to primitive and even animal consciousness. The civilized mind bases behavior on the certainties of its knowledge, but certainty is limiting. "We must be refreshed by the sight of inexhaustible vigor," and hence we require something of the loon's and the Indian's vision, in which things are antic, chancy, "mysterious and unexplorable" — greater than we are, yet of our kind and make. Only by submitting to knowledge of the wildness, mystery, and animality of our world and our persons can we live by our higher laws: "Compassion is a very untenable ground. It must be expeditious. Its pleadings will not bear to be stereotyped," as they are amid the conventions of society.

The triumph of the hunt at Walden is thus intellectual rather than physical or mytho-sexual, ending with the acquisition of an Indian-like manner of perception, in which objects — animals, trees, rocks, clouds, water — become totally identified with their archetypes. Like Cotton Mather, Thoreau perceives archetypes in all phenomena. Unlike Mather he does not rhetorically or metaphysically divorce the archetypal from the phenomenal realm. The loon is not spoken of as the figure of a wild god, but he functions as one. Only at the conclusion of the experience is the vision explicable. Before we can interpret the tale of Hannah Dustin and the apple tree as a myth, the story must be plainly told. In his nature essays on "The Natural History of Massachusetts," "Walking," and "Wild Apples," description of the natural object comes to embody an inherent (but unstated) interpretation or value. He speaks of this spontaneous, uncerebral, unverbalized expression of the sudden knowledge of the meaning of things as "a more perfect Indian wisdom." [33]

The essay on "Wild Apples" is typical of Thoreau's post-Walden philosophy of "chaste intercourse with nature" and his new literary method. It also clarifies a symbol that functions importantly in both the Hannah Dustin tale in *A Week* and the insect resurrection in *Walden*. The apple in both cases can be associated with the Eden tree, although Thoreau is more carefully oblique about the metaphor in *Walden*. In the Dustin tale, the Eden tree that brought sin and death to man is identified with the cross of Christ; the resurrection of the insect from applewood can be seen as a type of man's salvation from the consequences of man's first fruits. In both cases the symbolic interpretation is left dark, a mystery for the reader to discover and illuminate for himself, following the tracks left by the author, as Thoreau followed the tracks of his bay horse, hound, and dove. In "The Wild Apple" the apple tree still functions as a type of the natural man; but here Thoreau's concern is to distinguish between various kinds of apple trees, according to their relationship with their American soil. Although he explicitly speaks of indigenous apples and imported varieties, he implicitly speaks of the process by which certain imported varieties have adjusted to the American wilderness. "*Our* wild apple is wild only like myself, perchance, who belong not to the aboriginal race here, but have strayed into the woods from the cultivated stock." More wild than this is the "native and aboriginal crab-apple," whose fruit is acid but good for rich, intoxicating cider and whose flowers are remarkable for their "delicious odor" and beautiful petals of mingled white and rose. This "half-fabulous tree" he calls "indigenous, like the Indians" — and like them beautiful in form, productive of intoxicating drink, seductive, and primitively noble, but acrid to a civilized palate.[34]

Even the Indians are said to have "welcomed" the emigrant apple, a richer and sweeter fruit, if a less seductively beautiful tree. But the true center of Thoreau's interest lies with "those backwoodsmen among the apple trees, which, though descended from cultivated stocks, plant themselves in distant fields and forests, where the soil is favorable to them." These, like Thoreau himself, have a strength naturally acquired through ages of contention with unmediated nature. Its apples are rarer, and it often fails of its fruit. Yet what fruit it does bear is sweeter than any garden-grown apple. This hybrid wilderness-farm tree is like Thoreau himself, or like fruitless Leatherstocking, in its paucity of heirs and its plenitude of sweet wisdom and virtue: "chastity" begets no children but many poems. Moreover, like poetry and myth, "every wild apple shrub excites our expectation, . . . somewhat as every wild child. It is, perhaps, a prince in disguise," the source of a dynasty of trees bearing "celestial fruit." [35] The symbolic language acquired in *Walden* is thus employed in "Wild Apples" to restate poetically the meaning at the heart of the *Walden* experience — a mythic assessment of Thoreau's own function as a figurative king of the wood or, rather, of his failure to fulfill the sexual role of the king.

Whitman, less cerebral than Thoreau and hence less inclined to maintain his chastity of mind and body, perhaps lived up to some of the implications of *Walden* better than its author. The sublimated spirits of place in the long hunt for identity in "Song of Myself" emerge as sexual beings, both male and female, whose mating is the sexual source of a new physical race as well as a new community of intellects (although Whitman also speaks of being "aloof" from his beloved, as well as absorbed in her). In *Walden*, Thoreau declares, "I do not propose to write an ode to dejection, but to brag as lustily as chanticleer in the morning . . . if only to wake my neighbors up." Chanticleer Whitman's "barbaric yawp," sounding like Indian war cries full of bloodlust and sexual threat over the rooftops of an assaulted town, was perhaps more dramatically effectual as a statement of identification with the Indian character and spirit of the wilderness and the erotic impulses of the subconscious mind.

Thoreau did, however, develop in detail the intellectual, ethical, and social implications of his vision. Implicit in the passage about the Jesuits and the Indians in *Walden* is the notion that when visions clash, philanthropy is useless to palliate the strife. The Jesuits, giving the golden rule to Indians who expected and desired only torment from their captors, simply confirmed them in their uncivilized practices. To the apostles of wildness and freedom, social compromise seemed as tangled and evil as the wilderness did to the men of society. In "Walking," written in 1850–51, the thematic opposition between society and wild solitude appears again. This time, however, Thoreau is not an advocate of moderation and mediation between Walden and the village:

> I wish to speak a word for Nature, for absolute freedom and wild-ness, as contrasted with a freedom and culture merely civil — to re-gard man as an inhabitant, or a part and parcel of Nature, rather than a member of society. I wish to make an extreme statement, if so I may make an emphatic one, for there are enough champions of civiliza-tion: the minister and the school committee and every one of you will take care of that.[36]

He portrays the hunt for the wild spirit in archetypal terms, recalling the early explorers' dreams of "Atlantis, and the islands and gardens of the Hesperides"; the sun itself becomes "the Great Western Pioneer." The goal of the quest is release and liberation of the imagination, expanding to take in a grander world as the hunter develops ever-augmenting strength in his search for bigger beasts. Not only does one's understanding broaden, but one's urge to joy increases, the spirit of delight in wildness that is akin to sensual passion. If such things are not realized, "to what end does the world go on, and why was America discovered?" Under this archetypal as-pect, "the West of which I speak is but another name for the Wild," the archetypal wilderness in which the impulses of the heroic age find expres-sion. Thoreau even dreams "that this was the heroic age itself." [37]

This assertion of belief in an archetypal West leads to a vision of what manner of man is appropriate to its conquest and how man may become worthy of the task. In essence, the heroic man is seen as a savage, tasting the milk or the blood of wild things, devouring raw flesh. The image of the wild Eucharist is reiterated again and again, in forms ranging from Romu-lus and Remus being suckled by a wolf to the Indians and Africans devour-ing raw antelope and reindeer, crunching bones for rich marrow:

> Give me a wildness whose glance no civilization can endure — as if we lived on the marrow of koodoos devoured raw.
> There are some intervals which border the strain of the wood thrush, to which I would migrate — wild lands where no settler has squatted; to which, methinks, I am already acclimated.

Not content with echoing Natty Bumppo, Thoreau extends the association of savage man and animal to the point of identification and (like Whitman) finds the idea of turning to the animals and acquiring a dark skin admira-ble:

> The African hunter Cumming tells us that the skin of the eland . . . emits the most delicious perfume of trees and grass. I would have every man so much like a wild antelope, so much a part and parcel of

nature, that his very person should thus sweetly advertise our senses of his presence, and remind us of those parts of nature which he most haunts. A tanned skin is something more than respectable, and perhaps olive is a fitter color than white for a man — a denizen of the woods. 'The pale white man!' I do not wonder that the African pitied him.[38]

The essence of this savage life is transferable to all walks of life. As in the case of Davy Crockett, it leads man to a perpetual discontent with things as they are, an immersion in a never-ending process of self-transcendence and renewal or conversion of spirit and fortune. Such a man, in Thoreau's vision, would be the most alive, his life a perpetual hunt along the frontiers between society and nature, past and future, illusion and truth:

> Life consists with wildness. The most alive is the wildest. Not yet subdued to man, its presence refreshes him. One who pressed forward incessantly and never rested from his labors, who grew fast and made infinite demands on life, would always find himself in a new country or wilderness, and surrounded by the raw material of life.[39]

The consequences of such activity are exhibited in the destructive career of Crockett and his heirs, who treated the woods as "raw material" for economic development. But Thoreau in his enthusiasm misses the significance of the remark that he himself "would be climbing over the prostrate stems of primitive forest trees" in the course of his wild progress.[40]

"Walking," developing the ideas of *Walden* to their extreme, offers a radical and revolutionary approach to aesthetics, ethics, and politics. The aesthetic doctrine of Whitman — enthusiasm for the sensuous apprehension of nature, even the smells of skinned animals and of hunters and their clothing; love of the tanned and rough over the pale and effete — is anticipated in "Walking." Implicit in Thoreau's aesthetic of wildness is Whitman's assertion of the primacy of the priapic urge in all things, all men, animals, natural forces, and cycles. In "Song of Myself" and the rest of *Leaves of Grass*, Whitman gives concrete expression to that which Thoreau suggests or implies but, because of his fastidiousness, fails to realize. Even the sharing of identity between Thoreau and the objects of his observation becomes part of the psychological pattern of the *Leaves*, particularly in poems like "There Was a Child Went Forth" ("And everything he saw, that thing he became").

Thoreau himself tried to behave as a living example of the ethical theory implicit in the worship of wildness. The man of solitude does not consult custom or law to know if his actions are moral; he consults nature and his own nature or conscience, since these are the only guides man is ever given. Hence his civil disobedience, his passive resistance to the demands of a law he believes to be unjust, since law itself is, to the man of solitude, an affectation rather than a necessity. His reaction to law and his motives for resistance are analogous to those of Leatherstocking in *The Pioneers*. Having no property, no stake in society, he desires no protection of social laws; requiring no protection, he deems himself free of the duty of obedience to those laws. To become a political revolutionary, however, is to exchange solitude for society and accept struggle on society's terms. It is, in effect, to sacrifice the chastity of self-restraint, self-discipline, and self-containment by a passionate involvement in a social rather than a natural wilderness. But like the heroine of the captivity narrative, Thoreau in his act of rebellion remains passive and therefore chaste, doing nothing to rescue himself but permitting himself to be rescued by some unknown and presumably gracious agent — the man who paid his bond and freed him from Concord jail. Thus he is at once spiritually involved in the war with darkness and aloof from its actual swamps and jungles. He descends into the social wilderness, but he does not bide with or marry the darkness.

Like "Song of Myself" and the Leatherstocking cycle, *Walden* is an attempt to achieve an American epic — a poem whose images and sequence will recapitulate the experiential and spiritual history of the New World as myth and as personal narrative. (Thoreau persistently begs comparison with Homer.) So Thoreau in *Walden* goes, like Boone and Leatherstocking, into a wilderness of the material world and of the soul, seeking a primitive truth; he becomes acculturated to the woods; and he is finally able to bring down truths the way an Indian snatches scalps (to use his own metaphor). However, this thematic affinity with the backwoodsmen is offset by the awareness that the wilderness of Walden is second growth, really a back lot of civilization, in which Indians and larger predators are no longer even memories but myths. Around the garden plot and the pond he calls *"Walled-in,"* the nineteenth century fumes and howls.[41] Like the exponents of America-as-Arcadia, he inhabits a *hortus inclusus* in a sea of troubles. Like the Matherian Puritans, he senses that his wilderness sojourn, which smacks of adventure, may also be seen as an exile, an imprisonment, a captivity; it is at least a sequestration. Thoreau acknowledges this strain of myth as well in his allusion to the night in Concord jail that was the starting point of "Civil Disobedience": in a society where men are slaves, the only place a "free" man may abide with "honor" is a prison or a "cell." Thoreau's hut at Walden is a metaphorical cell; and it is possible also to see it as a northern equivalent of the slave cabin, just as it is presented as a substitute for the wigwam. (*The Cabin and the Wigwam* was the title of a book by Simms.) Thoreau's American epic is the epic of the captive, in which the adventuring impulse turns inward and becomes a moral and psychological struggle against the forces that imprison the body and against the torpor of mind and spirit that bind the soul to Satan or (to use a term more appropriate to Thoreau) to death and "deadness."

"Moby-Dick": The American National Epic

Melville's *Moby-Dick, or the White Whale*, likewise attempts the achievement of an American epic, but Melville's direction is outward, and his voyager must go in company with others. Society and human history are inescapable. Representatives of all the races of men inhabit the island-universe of the *Pequod*, and all must participate in the quest for Moby Dick, although some are slaves, some are masters, and some have solitary visions of concord in the crosstrees. Thoreau is spiritually venturous in physical captivity or sequestration; Melville's heroes are captives in spirit, even as they prowl the oceans in search of Leviathan.

Like Cotton Mather, Melville is a student of mythologies; and through his use of mythic and biblical archetypes, his novel achieves that sense of the unity of the human and the archetypal or divine drama that is the essence of epic. Melville's typology, however, is greater than Mather's because his sources (like his intelligence) are more extensive and profound. He draws his symbols, not only from the Bible and the classics, but from the primitive myths of the Indians and the Pacific islanders, the lore of whalemen, his own experiences — and from Thoreau's best source, nature itself. He also draws extensively on the mythology nearest to the consciousness of his audience, the myths of the western pioneers and hunters, Andrew Jackson, Davy Crockett, and Daniel Boone. Where Mather tended to string his tales together, to scatter allusions broadcast and at random, and to tie typological analysis loosely to the framework of his histories, Melville succeeds in unifying and integrating several streams of mythology in a single, internally coherent, dramatic narrative. Mather's people tend to have their own light of character outshone in the superior glow of the archetypes they represent. Melville's heroes are first palpably human, and their symbolic significance is concealed — as in reality — behind the enigmatic and problematic mask of a human face. Mather's histories are analyses and reductions of events. Melville's narrative is itself a mystery, evoking in the reader a sense of the depth and complexity of life, an urge to seek for some truth or illuminating god-spirit among the tangles.

In *Moby-Dick* the American epic takes the form of a colossal hunt. All the elements of the hunter myth are developed to their archetypal extremes. The mythic characterization of the wilderness as a symbol of primal states of nature and of human consciousness had been distilled by Cooper (in the last Leatherstocking tale) and Thoreau into the image of the lake (Glimmerglass) or pond (Walden) — bodies of water which reflect the features of heroes and contain mysteries in their depths; sources of the forest's life and repositories of death's victims. In Melville's novel Glimmerglass/Walden becomes ocean itself; and Cooper's oceanic prairie and forest become metaphors by which Melville defines the vastness of his ocean and the relatedness of the *Pequod*'s hunt to the mythologized adventures of Boone and Leatherstocking. The object of his quest is likewise magnified. No deer or loon embodies in microcosm the spirit of a natural divinity, but Leviathan himself, a beast like an island or a continent in the middle ocean, a creature sometimes worshiped as the godhead itself. These expansions, which represent the ultimate development of the terms of the hunting myth, in fact restore original elements of the dream of the West that impelled the first discoverers — the dream of the mystic islands in the ocean-sea that hold both the possibility of eternal bliss and godlike power and the potential for utter death and damnation. In the end is the beginning.

This return to basic archetypal terms, however, does not imply a denial of the changes and developments of the hunter myth in America during the intervening years. Rather, the novel gathers together the variant strands and images of the myth and relates them to one another, to the central myth that underlies them, and to the history that has been shaped by the myth over the previous two centuries of American history. The myth of the hunter, as we have seen it develop in America, has centered on the theme of initiation into a new life, a new world, a new stage of manhood. This initiation has been variously imagined as a Puritan religious conversion, or as a cannibal Eucharist unifying the spirit of the white man with that of the Indian wilderness, or as a sacred marriage sexually linking the hero and the woods-goddess, or as a novice's or a boy's initiation into the mysteries and skills of the natural powers. Within each of these variants of the initiation theme, characteristic polarities and conflicts exist, centering on the difference between the Christian and the primitive-mythopoeic approaches to envisioning the wilderness and living in it. Each of these variants of the myth figures in Melville's novel, as does the central conflict of vision, and each is framed by the story of Ishmael's (the narrator-persona's) initiation.

Ishmael is a novice at whaling, and the voyage of the *Pequod* is his initiation into its lore and its arts. The reader is also entered upon a careful initiation into whaling, since Ishmael, like an old hand, carefully and patiently explains both the function and the mythology connected with the activities, gear, and tackle of the whaling trade. However, we are warned at the outset that this double initiation is not simply into the activity of the whaleman's life. "Meditation and water are wedded for ever," says Ishmael, in the chapter called "Loomings," [42] and the whaling voyage opens up for us not only the outward but the inward ocean as well. Before Moby Dick appears on the physical horizon — indeed, before Ishmael has even seen the seacoast or the whaler or heard the name of Moby Dick — the goal of the quest looms mysteriously in his mind:

> Chief among these motives was the overwhelming idea of the great whale himself. Such a portentous and mysterious monster roused all my curiosity. . . . the great flood-gates of the wonder-world swung open, and in the wild conceits that swayed me to my purpose, two and two there floated into my inmost soul, endless processions of the whale, and, mid most of them all, one grand hooded phantom, like a snow hill in the air.[43]

Ishmael's mind moves toward this prophetic vision, Melville suggests, by a mental process as instinctual and archetypal as that which draws men and streams down to the ocean that is their source and ending. Intellection is powerless to discover any adequate substitute for the sea-hunger. In deciding on a whaling voyage, intellectual "curiosity" is Ishmael's first motive, as it was Filson's Boone's. But, as with Flint's Boone, even before he has begun to satisfy that curiosity, the mythic form of his object begins to take shape in his mind. His image of the "processions of the whale" couches that vision in almost Indian terms: the group of creatures, appearing in a revery, are identified by their species name (not as individual, plural "whales"), and that species is headed by its archetypal grandfather in the shape of a solitary, unpaired, and unwedded whale, the phantom mountain-shape he later knows as Moby Dick.

Melville draws heavily on the island mythology that characterized both the prediscovery European myths of the West and the later images of island colonies in the oceanic forest. This imagery is also clarified and heightened by Melville to bring out its last significations. All great continents are but islands in the sea — enclosures of light, order, and peace in a dark, fundamental, all-creating, all-dissolving ocean. So the reasoning mind of man is an isolated enclosure amid the chaos of his emotions. Within that mind are ideas that are themselves like islands, offering intellectual refuge from the daily tragedy of existence — the dream-remembered, womblike haven of an innocent childhood, ruled and ordered by a maternal figure; or the dream-longed-for "Tahiti" with which the exiled soul stays its hunger for refuge, peace, and completion. To leave the maternal home for the life of a mature man, or to allow the soul to venture out of the secure solitude of the ego's mental Tahiti in search of human love, is to immerse oneself in the destructive element, to expose oneself to passion, degradation, and dissolution: "For as this appalling ocean surrounds the verdant land, so in the soul of man there lies one insular Tahiti, full of peace and joy, but encompassed by all the horrors of the half known life. God keep thee! Push not off from that isle, thou canst never return!" [44]

Each of the main characters in the novel is an islander of sorts — which is to say, in contradiction to Donne, that each man *is* an island. Ahab and Starbuck are Nantucketers, Stubb a Cape-Codder (nearly an island), Flask a Vineyarder, Ishmael from Manhattan, Queequeg a Polynesian, Tashtego a Vineyarder. "They were nearly all Islanders in the Pequod, *Isolatoes* too . . . not acknowledging the common continent of men, but each . . . living on a separate continent of his own." [45] Even the African Daggoo is an islander, for the continents themselves are but islands in the universal ocean. The whale himself, we are told, is often mistaken for an island.

What relationship can islanded man have with the ocean that sustains or, at a whim, destroys him? Crèvecoeur, in his study of Nantucket, suggests that man can farm the physical ocean as he cultivates the land, thus bringing it under the rule of his skill. Crèvecoeur offers the island of Nantucket as proof of what reasonable cultivation can produce. Melville, however, sees Nantucket as a product of man's mythically motivated confrontation with the irrational, oceanic forces of nature. Melville's brief history of Nantucket begins with an Indian legend about its discovery; and his Nantucketer is pictured as a man at home only on the sea, an absolute stranger to land, a man whose life and labor embody the island nature of all human life, both mental and metaphysical: "so at nightfall, the Nantucketer, out of sight of land, furls his sails, and lays him to his rest, while under his very pillow rush herds of walruses and whales." [46]

Not all men can live on such accepting terms with their island nature. The Negro cabin boy, Pip, deserted in the ocean, discovers his island nature with a vengeance. The vast oceanic universe enters his mind and devours it, drowning reason in an all-encompassing, ineluctable experience of cosmic reality:

> The sea had jeeringly kept his finite body up, but drowned the infinite of his soul. Not drowned entirely, though. Rather carried down

alive to wondrous depths, where strange shapes of the unwarped primal world glided to and fro before his passive eyes; and the miser-
merman, Wisdom, revealed his hoarded heaps; and among the joyous,
heartless, ever-juvenile eternities, Pip saw the multitudinous, God-
omnipresent, coral insects, that out of the firmament of waters heaved
the colossal orbs. He saw God's foot upon the treadle of the loom, and
spoke it; and therefore his shipmates called him mad. So man's insanity is heaven's sense; and wandering from all mortal reason, man
comes at last to that celestial thought, which, to reason, is absurd and
frantic; and weal or woe, feels then uncompromised, indifferent as his
God.[47]

Pip, in other words, has been mentally drowned in the primal, archetypal
realm (Moira). In that encounter he has perceived and been reconciled to
the cosmogonic powers and processes of the natural universe. But the god
he beholds is neither man nor demon. Rather, that god is figured in the
image of the teeming, nonhuman, unindividuated multitudes of the coral
insects, whose pyramided skeletons — piled by blind process, not purpose
— are the substance of the islands that are the orbs or worlds of the ocean-
universe.

Ahab, a man proud of his Promethean or Faustian reason, cannot be
passive in acceptance of reality, as Pip is. Always he seeks to impose his
reason — by imposing reasons — on the blank, unintelligible face of the
natural universe or the featureless front of the faceless whale.[48] Only the
whale is adjusted to his island nature and able to maintain some integrity
of soul in the chaotic sea. Moby Dick is apparently immortal in his solitude. Lesser whales, traveling in herds, build a kind of social order that
takes its pattern from the island-sea relationship. In "The Grand Armada"
the whalemen enter the "charmed circle" at the center of the whale herd:
while stricken and angered leviathans rage at the circumference, the cows
and calves and the amorous, breeding young swim in an "enchanted," enclosed, and protected island-pond. Even the bloody whalemen are moved
to sympathy. Queequeg is especially moved to pat the foreheads of the
young whales and Starbuck to scratch their backs with his lance. It is a
Nantucket vision of the earthly paradise.

The stages of Ishmael's initiation offer Melville an opportunity to develop his and his reader's symbolic vocabulary, making the novel as independent of exterior frames of reference as possible, making it an island of a
book — self-sufficient, self-explaining, and self-justifying like all myth.
Through Ishmael's observations, his actions, and his metaphorical descriptions of whaling activities and equipment, an elaborate structure of inter-
locking mythological and metaphorical systems or thematic streams is es-

tablished; and these are unified in the course of the observer's dual initiation into whaling and wisdom.

The American popular mythology forms one such stream of metaphor, linking the hunting of the whale to the mythology of explorers, hunters, and Indian fighters. Ishmael's Boone-like approach to the threshold of adventure has already been cited. His subsequent actions also smack of the frontier myth. Of all places to begin his quest, Ishmael chooses Nantucket because it was the primitive source of American whaling, the island from which "those aboriginal whalemen, the Red-Men, first sall[ied] out in canoes to give chase to Leviathan." [49] The ship Ishmael chooses to voyage in is the *Pequod*, named for the tribe massacred by the Puritans in 1638 and now the island and vessel of successors of both Puritan and pagan, united in a mutual quest. The captain of the ship, Ahab, is both Quaker and hunter, like Boone himself and like Bird's Nathan Slaughter. The object of his hunt, Moby Dick, has a forehead like "the prairie" and a hump like a buffalo. The whale's resemblance to the prairie marks him as the true avatar of the essential spirit of his element, for the sea is also called "prairie," "meadow," and "desert." As his hunter resembles Boone, so is Moby Dick, as chief of the order of solitary bull whales, compared with "moss-bearded Daniel Boone." The whalemen snatch their harpoons from the crotch as quickly "as a backwoodsman swings his rifle from the wall." The white whale is compared to the "White Steed" in the popular fiction of western magazines, and "your true whale hunter is as much a savage as an Iroquois." [50]

The use of this frontier metaphor, however, is not restricted to imagery and motif merely. The central concern of the epic is to illuminate the motives and consequences — the very nature — of the archetypal myths that undergulf these American legends. The frontier motif is therefore made to function as a subordinate aspect of the archetypal myths of the Eucharist and the sacred marriage and of Ishmael's gradual discovery of their presence and power in the world of the *Pequod*. The marriage metaphor is the more crucial of the two, since the cannibal Eucharist is a ritual sublimation of the mutual sexual absorption of hero and goddess. Both myths are essentially myths of fertility — of the procreation, preservation, perpetuation, and resurrection of human and animal life. Ishmael begins his quest because there is a winter, a "November" in his soul; he seeks the spring and the resurrection of life through his quest. In his vision the whales appear to him in wedded pairs, and in the first stages of his initiation he finds himself embracing the cannibal king Queequeg, wielder of a mighty harpoon, as bride embraces husband. The object of their quest is the sperm whale, whose very name suggests a titanic, phallic power of pro-creation. Queequeg's rescue of a fallen harpooneer from the sperm well of a severed whale's head is described as an act of rebirth, a resurrection of the fallen man from the womblike well of the whale's "tun." One of the most erotic scenes in nineteenth-century American literature is that in which Ishmael and his fellows bathe their hands in sperm oil to squeeze out impurities and experience an exquisite, sensual melting-together of characters and sympathies.

The nature and significance of cannibalism is slowly unveiled in a sim-ilar manner. The association of cannibalism and whaling seems, in the first marriage of Queequeg and Ishmael, simply to refer to the primitive basis of the whale- or man-hunting instinct. The discovery of the *Pequod* expands the motif. Her rig and appearance partake of the mysteries of Japan and Gothic Europe. Her decorations of whalebone, however, mark her as wor-thy of her Indian name. "She was a thing of trophies. A cannibal of a craft, tricking herself forth in the chased bones of her enemies." [51] The Pequot Indians, suppressed by the fathers of these Nantucketers, thus have their final triumph. As the Pequots decked themselves in scalps, so their white heirs (like Benjamin Church) deck their ship in the name of their slaugh-tered foe and make their ship a cannibal as well. The motif further unfolds its meaning in "Stubb's Supper," in which the mate eats a steak from the whale he has killed, imbibing its power with its flesh in the Indian manner. In so doing he associates himself with the sea-hounds, the obscene self- and fellow-devouring sharks who harry the stricken whales and, in their hun-ger-lust, pervertedly devour their own entrails when wounded.

The marriage and cannibal metaphors, and the mythic strains they represent, provide the context in which the problem of the great hunter-captain Ahab slowly reveals itself. The act of eating and drinking the body and blood in the Eucharist is meant as an act of love, uniting a worshiper with a beloved deity; the sacred marriage that consummates the hunt is likewise meant as a loving consummation. Hunters like Actaeon, Orion, and the unfortunate brave in the Sioux legend of the White Buffalo Woman — those who approach the hunt with lust or hatred in their hearts — are destroyed, and the rites of love are thwarted or consummated in an-nihilation. Ahab's hatred of the thing he hunts violates the ethic of the hunter myth, in which the hunter and the beast are lovingly to share and interchange identities. As in *Nick of the Woods*, the conflict is between the points of view represented by the captivity mythology of the Puritans and the hunting mythology of the Indians and frontiersmen. In the former man is either passive victim or agent of vengeance, either Quaker or slaughterer. In the latter he is the lover of the thing he hunts.

Ahab and his intended prey are doubles. Both have ribbed brows, wry mouths, and withered or stricken limbs. Both share an apparent spirit of conscious malice that goes beyond the natural, instinctual violence of whalemen like Starbuck and Stubb and of normal whales. The root of malice is in both cases the same: Ahab has been wounded and maimed by the whale, and the whale by whalemen. Both are driven into isolation, away from the normal life of marriage and begetting: Moby Dick is a solitary whale, Ahab leaves wife and babes to pursue his vengeance. Both share a common mystery or ambivalence in their nature. Ahab is both victim and hero, Quaker and killer, Christian and blood-lusting pagan. Moby Dick is similarly enigmatic and mysterious, both animal and spirit, unconscious and conscious in malice, instinctual and intelligent, the exile from the whale-herd's "charmed circle" and the rescuer of hunted females, the victim of men and the destroyer of men. Ahab identifies Moby Dick as being either the "principle" or the "agent" of the inscrutable but malicious power that rules the universe. Similarly, in his conversation with Starbuck in "The Symphony," he identifies his own case in these terms, torn between the idea that he is the "principle" in the quest and the willful controller of its action and the contrary idea that he is the "agent" of some outside force: "Is Ahab, Ahab? Is it I, God, or who, that lifts this arm?" [52] One thing only divides them: it is possible that the whale is, as Starbuck says (and as Pip's vision implies), a mere beast.

Ahab's pursuit of the whale with murderous intent is thus a compounded violation of nature. If there is no reasoning intelligence behind the events of life, then Ahab's quest is the projection of a madman's vision on the neutral face of reality, a denial of that "atheism" of the natural universe represented by "the Whiteness of the Whale." [53] If the associations that link Ahab and the whale are emblems of their common creaturehood (whether of an integral deity or of the soulless deities of Pip's vision), then the hunt is a symbolic fratricide; and since kinship suggests a fundamental sharing of identity, the hunt is also an act of self-destruction, so that the whale blood Ahab hopes to drink will perversely be his own. The choice that opens before him involves a choice of approaches to the beast. Will he come as a metaphysician-madman — a self-willed, self-devouring, perverted hunter-shark, bent on obscenity and evil — or as a worshiper and lover?

Melville binds the characters of Ahab and the whale by the cords of mystery, by involving us in the task of unraveling a riddle of appearance and reality. The chapters on the whale present no definitive view of him; rather, they view him from every conceivable viewpoint, portray him in every conceivable shape, denying none and accepting none. By the time the whale is sighted, his character has been established as protean and many-leveled. Ishmael has shown him to us as agent of God, as avatar of God, as God himself. He has also shown him as he appears to Ahab and to the objective scientist or the fact-minded Starbuck. Is the whale God, or avatar of the gods of the wilderness-sea, or simple beast, or projection of Ahab's own mind, avatar of the hunter's own soul? And if he is any of these, what ought Ahab's response to the whale be? If a God or avatar of a god, should Ahab not worship him? If an animal, should he not ignore him? If a projection of his own mind, should he not seek to comprehend and be reconciled to him?

The choice that confronts Ahab as the chase nears its end is couched in the terms of the marriage metaphor that has informed the structure of the epic. Under the aspect of this myth, Moby Dick is either an avatar of the nature goddess, embodying a principle of fertility, or else the objective correlative of the anima, the necessary feminine component of Ahab's own mind — or both at once. Ishmael, unfolding some more of his whale lore to the reader, gives us the features of Ahab and his dilemma reflected in the mirror of the whale world. The sperm whale is a creature of schools and societies, a *pater familias* and affectionate mate during his youth. But in his crabbed age, when wounds and years have weakened his procreative powers (thus enforcing the chastity prized by Thoreau and Leatherstocking) and declining vigor and health torment him, he becomes a solitary hermit. Melville expresses this in terms of the Boone myth and the myth of the hunter's sacred marriage: "Almost universally, a lone whale — as a solitary Leviathan is called — proves an ancient one. Like venerable moss-bearded Daniel Boone, he will have no one near him but Nature herself; and her he takes to wife in the wilderness of waters, and the best of wives she is, though she keeps so many moody secrets." [54]

The sperm whale at each stage thus has his appropriate mate, the younger in whale society, the older in a more mystical and mythological union with the goddess of nature herself, the earned result of a life spent in perfect accordance with the gifts of nature. Ahab, by this standard, is guilty of violating natural law. An aged, crabbed man, he has taken a young woman to wife, solacing himself for his time-bound decline in vigor as King David did, by taking young virgins to bed. Even so, she is a more appropriate wife for him than the whale or god or goddess he seeks; and his leaving her widowed when he still might be a true husband is a crime equivalent to a paternal whale's deserting his "harem." Enforced chastity (through age or isolation) or perversely motivated chastity converts Thoreau's "saving virtue" into corruption and destruction of the loving motives that should underlie the hunter's acts. Ahab seeks only to be wedded to Moby Dick by the binding cord of the harpoon line, but hate drives him, and he is fleeing from his true "haven" behind. He wants no communion with unknowable divine mystery, no wife with moody secrets. His purpose is to dispel mystery with cruel and metallic analysis, to "strike through the mask" of the whale and murder its symbolic essence. He has been wounded by the whale as by time, and his response to both wounds, both diminutions of his vigor, is violence, hatred, and repudiation rather than love. When, on the eve of the sighting of Moby Dick, Starbuck offers Ahab the choice between the image of his proper love, his wife, and the image of his hatred, Ahab hesitates. Then, looking into the mirroring sea ("meditation and water are wedded forever") to behold his own features, he declares for vengeance and destruction rather than love. All around him, sky and sea marry in a unity which (as Melville describes it) is a coitus of cosmic sexual principles.

The whale can be the source of either salvation or damnation to Ahab. As an avatar of the goddess of nature and the double of Ahab, Moby Dick mediates between the man and the divine. Ahab rejects the hope of a mediator and puts his faith in the direct confrontation of man and god in mortal strife, with salvation and immortality as the stake.

The identity of the whale, at which Ishmael has been hinting, is suddenly revealed. The whale appears to Ahab and the crew as the very vision and embodiment of the god and goddess of wilderness nature and of the dreams of the subconscious mind, which the Puritans so feared to release, express, or give opportunity to escape. The whale is at once masculine and feminine, a phallus and an odalisque, enticing and overwhelmingly erotic, recalling the fertility myths of the Greeks in which beast-gods mate with human virgins:

> A gentle joyousness — a mighty mildness of repose in swiftness, invested the gliding whale. Not the white bull Jupiter swimming away with ravished Europa clinging to his graceful horns; his lovely, leering eyes sideways intent upon the maid; with smooth bewitching fleetness, rippling straight for the nuptial bower in Crete; not Jove, not that great majesty Supreme! did surpass the glorified White Whale as he so divinely swam.[55]

Three times Ahab, seduced by this vision, assails the whale to kill it. On the third try the whale ceases to restrain its power and reveals its full majesty to destroy Ahab, ship, men, and all in universal catastrophe. On each day of the chase the alternative choice is renewed to Ahab — to cease his hatred of the whale, to lovingly accept and worship its power and the power it represents, and to give over the chase and return to his proper wife. Each day he declines that choice, seeing in the whale only the embodiment of the darker impulses of man and of nature — of Ahab and Ahab's God — that he wishes to obliterate. His response to the spirit of nature is that of the Puritan: he is either its captive and victim or the agent of a transcendent power that destroys it. He worships, not the whale or the god, but the wound they gave him; and he does not seek healing so much as vengeance. As a Puritan he perverts the hunter myth, thwarts its ritual purpose. For Ahab there is no consummation. Like the hunting priest, he follows the whale forever, accompanied by the sea-hounds, the sharks, who follow his boat on the last day of the chase and pursue him as he is towed behind the whale from the noose made of his own harpoon line.

Ahab sets himself against the current of the informing myths of nature and so destroys himself. But the Ahab impulse, the Puritan impulse, is as natural and inevitable a part of the nature of things as the hunter archetype itself. Ahab Puritanism seems unnatural under the aspect of primitive religion because it violates an ethic which, to the primitive mind, is inherent in nature. Such a judgment is equivalent to Cotton Mather's judgment on the "unnatural" behavior of the Indians, who violated the natural law inherent in the Christian view of the cosmos. Mather delighted in Captain Church's murder of "that great leviathan" Philip, in his history of the Pequot and King Philip wars, but Melville takes no similar delight in the whale's triumph over Ahab. The passion that drives Ahab, as Melville perceives, is as much and as natural a part of the human makeup as its opposite, the spirit that acquiesces in the fulfillment of mythic function.

The cannibals, Indians, islanders, and savages of the *Pequod*, the novice Ishmael, the Quaker Starbuck, the sensual Stubb, and the aggressive Flask are not alternatives to Ahab, as Cotton Mather is to King Philip, but rather specialized extensions of himself. Only Queequeg (and perhaps Mad Pip) stands as a possible alternative. Queequeg respects and loves whales and enjoys a relationship with them that conforms to the fertility mythology. Like Ahab, he bears a king's name and mind. Like Ahab, he is the double of the whale, for the fish is his totem signature and the tatooed sign of kingship that appears on his breast; the tattoos that cover his body are likened to the "hieroglyphics" that marble the skins of whales. Like Ahab he is the agent of the gods, the giver of divine gifts. But where Ahab's deeds or gifts are of death and violence, Queequeg's are of love and kindness. Ahab makes corpses out of the whales; Queequeg, rescuing the Indian Tashtego, dives into the spermy basin of the whale's head to bring a renewed and resurrected life out of that figurative womb. Yet even Queequeg is subordinated to the will of Ahab, not by compulsion after long antagonism but by Ahab's touching of a common chord in the nature of Queequeg as in all his fellows: "My cogged circle fits into all their various wheels, and they revolve." [56] Queequeg's active principle of love, like Starbuck's of dutiful, passive nonaction and Pip's mystical acceptance, is an element of Ahab's character, not an alternative to his character. Ahab himself is the best and fullest expression of the totality of the crew he binds to his will.

In this he is the true American hero, worthy to be captain of a ship whose "wood could only be American," [57] whose name could only be Indian. Like the American pioneer, he has bound men of God and men of nature, Christians and pagans, captives and captors, Chingachgook and Simon Girty, Boone and Mather, Mary Rowlandson and King Philip within the framework of a single, purposeful endeavor, a quest fraught with complex ironies. Indian and white, materialist and idealist, natural and artificial, passionate and intellectual, stoic and Platonist, Prometheus and Faust have all been amalgamated in a single vessel, bound into the wilderness of the world and of the human mind, to seek out and murder the very spirit and essence of world, mind, and wilderness.

For it is the essence of the real that Ahab seeks to destroy, devour, assimilate to himself, replace with his own being and intelligence. He speaks always of a "reasoning thing," a thing therefore like himself, behind the mask that is Moby Dick, behind the veil that hides the true face of nature's god. "Moby" Dick's name may refer us to Hamlet's Gertrude, the masked or "mobled Queen" (II.ii.506–8), who seems a loving wife and mother and may be a murderous jade. Yet, as Pip's vision tells us, this reasoning thing may be merely the wish of maddened Ahab, not a true vision: for the God that Pip beholds is "indifferent," insentient, compacted of an infinitude of deaths, just as the "orbs" or islands of the ocean are fabrications of the meaningless, redundant, undifferentiated, time-extended deaths of billions of "coral insects" — which is to say that God is indistinguishable from the nonhuman, unreasoning processes of the world-as-it-is. When Ahab confronts that reality in the blank forehead of the faceless whale, he and his ship are cracked like lice, or like bodies fallen at random into the heart of a huge dynamo. Ahab's Promethean-Satanic dreams and all the individuated existences so carefully accumulated in the foregoing chapters drop in a moment into the shapeless maw of the undifferentiating sea. The whale swims off, marked a bit more with obscure hieroglyphics, but with no recognition or memory of his victims' peculiar aims and identities. "Then all collapsed, and the great shroud of the sea rolled on as it rolled five thousand years ago." Nothing has changed of the eternal, divine processes of the world; but all that man has been here has collapsed, vanished in an apocalyptic holocaust, leaving only one mind to remember and carry the tale to us.

Literary Myth as Prophecy

The relationship of *Moby-Dick* to the popular myth-literature of the American nineteenth century is that of the consummatory myth to the romantic, or conventionalized, myth. In creating his epic, Melville reenvisioned the traditional myths of his culture, bringing their implicit structures of symbol and value to consciousness by extending and expanding the symbolic elements and by providing new contexts for and therefore new perspectives on the central themes of the hunter's adventure. Unlike the works of Flint, Cooper, and Filson — or even the narrative of Mrs. Rowlandson — Melville's presentation of mythic materials did not evoke a response of recognition or identification from the contemporary audience. Not until the early years of the twentieth century was the profundity of the novel's vision recognized and accepted. This suggests that what a mass audience expects from popular literature is a reflection of the images and symbols that are the outer emblems of its collective mythology, rather than a painful analysis or probing of the depths beneath the surface. Popular mythology serves as a gloss for the painful or troubling aspects of a people's history, providing an illusory solution of real difficulties through the interplay of sacred (or at least familiar and accepted) symbols and character types.

What *Moby-Dick* provides is a prophetic extrapolation of future history from the evidence of motivation and purpose inherent in national myths. Hence its recognition by critics like D. H. Lawrence in the 1920s as a vision of the doom of "white civilization" brought about by the western theology of idealism, by our devotion to material progress, and by our exploitation or repression of natural and human (particularly sexual) forces and impulses. Given the realization in history of certain of the possible meanings of Melville's novel, one can feel in reading *Moby-Dick* a sense of recognition similar to that felt by the readers of Mrs. Rowlandson or Filson or Cooper. Moreover, works such as this also provide us with the kind of moral perspective on our mythology that the skills of popular mythologizers of the Filson or the Crockett type are exercised to obfuscate or avoid.

The hero of the hunter myth is the representative of that spirit in us which demands that the frontiers of our knowledge and our control (the two go together) be ever extended into the unknown wilderness of the natural world, of the yet-unrealized possibilities of our destiny. His starting point is the commonday world, that part of reality which we know well and over which we have established our dominion and power. This world and its values are symbolized by the family, whose presiding deities are the paternal law of society and the maternal spirit of religion and Christian sentiment, represented by the white woman (wife or mother). In leaving this familial universe of order and safety, the hero implicitly or explicitly calls its values into question; and his action suggests that the lure of the unknown and the forbidden has more appeal to him than the social and religious affections.

His adventure is an initiation and a conversion in which he achieves communion with the powers that rule the universe beyond the frontiers and acquires a new moral character, a new set of powers or gifts, a new identity. The spirit that rules the wilderness is embodied in the native persons and animals of the wilderness, but it also is latent within the hero himself. Something below the level of his consciousness responds to the wilderness, recognizing an aspect of his own dream life in the lives of the wilderness creatures. The hero's mode of interaction with these beings is that of the hunt. He tracks them, learns from them the secrets of their skill, and brings to the surface that latent sympathy or consonance of spirit that connects him with his prey. But his intention is always to use the acquired skill against the teachers, to kill or assert his dominance over them. The consummation of his hunting quest in the killing of the quarry confirms him in his new and higher character and gives him full possession of the powers of the wilderness. Through the ordeal and discipline of the hunt and its culmination in violence, the hero has achieved a regeneration of the spirit akin to the Puritan conversion experience as expressed in the earliest American myth, that of the Indian captivity.

The captivity myth, however, originated as a preventive for the diseases of the spirit — Faustian ambition, impatience of social restraint, spiritual pride — which the Puritan colonists associated with the wilderness-goers, the hunters and the individualistic pioneers. Since the Puritan fear of the frontier and the frontiersman persisted (although with changing ideological biases), the values inherent in the captivity myth likewise persisted. The captive enters the wilderness unwillingly, passively; her purpose is to resist the temptations of the forest and prepare for her rescue by divine providence. Although bound to the wilderness, her spirit dwells on

the perfection of order and sanctity that is society. Although she is aware
of her unworthiness in the eyes of God, she at least has not been guilty of
breaking, by her own act, the circle of social order and sentiment that is
represented by the family. Measured by captivity-myth standards, the
hunter, in achieving his quest, runs grave moral risks. He has broken the
family circle by his own act. He becomes partly assimilated to the world
whose ways he is learning, the world of the Indian; and he may partake so
much of the flesh of wild, hunted things that he becomes like them. Or he
may so delight in the exercise of his newly acquired skills and powers that
his pursuit of them becomes a calling or profession, an activity that he regards as self-justifying or as a substitute for civil religion.

To avoid the moral disaster which threatens him, the hunter-hero relies on his own "natural" moral code or conscience and on the inevitable
intrusion of white females as settlers and as captives in the wilderness. Of
the two, the hunter's own code is the weaker. The basis of the code is prag-
matism: action is valuable only insofar as it is a useful response to real conditions. From Benjamin Church to Simon Suggs, moral abstractions which
do not conform to reality as the hunter experiences it, or which do not further the ends he has chosen, are treated satirically. What nominally prevents this code from becoming merely a glorification of egotistical oppor-
tunism is the ethic of self-restraint that accompanies it. The hunter
possesses a natural humility, a reverence for something greater than himself (God, nature) that checks the full expression of his will. He will kill
only when and only so much as practical necessity requires. Yet this check
is a precarious one, and even a paragon of self-restraint like Leatherstocking can occasionally kill an animal to test his own skill. As Lawrence says,
"Patient and gentle as he is, . . . self-effacing, self-forgetting, still he is a
killer." [58]

More certain salvation for the hunter is gained through his participation in the ritual drama of the captivity myth. As the rescuer of white
women captured by the Indians, the hunter reaffiliates himself with the
world of familial order which he had previously deserted. But participation
in the captivity myth alters his relationship to the wilderness. For the sake
of the captive and the values of society and Christianity which she represents, the hunter must exterminate the Indians who have taught him his
skill and establish a safe refuge for the captive by opening the wilderness
to settlement. He may not merge his identity with the wilderness so far
that he is truly *of* it. Hence his acquisition of the powers of the wilderness
creatures has disastrous consequences: he will use those powers, not to sustain the wilderness world, but to destroy it in the name of something

higher. At best (from the viewpoint of the wilderness) he will allow those powers and the vision that goes with them to die with himself by refusing to marry a woman of the wilderness and so to pass the powers down to a successor.

The rescue of the captive and the extension of civilization beyond the frontiers presents the hero with a dilemma. In saving the captive he has destroyed the conditions of life that made him a hero. Beyond this paradox lies the problem of how the hero truly values the different phases of his adventure and the different powers and beings with whom he interacts. If the ethic of the white woman is finally the only acceptable one, the impulse that originally led the hunter to seek the dark female spirit of the wilderness must be corrupt. The ethic of the white woman is the ethic of self-restraint and -abnegation; that of the wilderness is self-realization and -aggrandizement. The Indian is the human expression of the natural powers that rule the wilderness, and his character in the myth embodies the traits of the libido: sexual and conceptual energy, filled at once with creative and destructive potentialities. Is acculturation to the Indian's way of life consistent with defense of the moral principles of self-repression and self-denial?

The hunter myth resolves these dilemmas in the symbolic action of the killing of the beast. This is the moment at which all of the hunters — from Benjamin Church, through Daniel Boone and Davy Crockett, to Jim Doggett, Reuben Bourne and Ahab — ultimately realize their identity and achieve their power to dominate events. In that moment there is an exchange of identities or an acknowledgment of kinship between hunter and prey which symbolically reconciles them. This exchange of identities has been imagined in various ways. For Cotton Mather it took the form of the possession of the soul by the demonic forces of the heathen wild. For Benjamin Church the confrontation produced a literal exchange of costumes and roles with the slain Philip, signifying the assimilation of the Indian's powers by the white conqueror. For Jim Doggett the exchange is something never to be understood, an inexplicable reversal of roles between man and prey that leads him to say that he loves the bear like a brother and that he will kill him, die, or go to Texas. For each of these heroes, as for Cooper's Leatherstocking, the communion with the avatar of the wilderness spirit ends in the killing of that spirit. And although the hero takes his character in mythology from the deed, as Deerslayer gets the name Hawkeye from the Indian he kills, the deed itself makes inevitable the destruction of the hero's universe and the conditions that gave him his identity. Only in the fire-hunt legend of Flint's Boone is the outcome temporarily different, for in that instance the hunter restrains himself and the "prey" metamorphoses into a white woman.

It is this image of the hunter's self-restraint that is the most perplexing aspect of the myth. Certainly it is the most significant trait of Leatherstocking, the quality which keeps him from succumbing to the darker impulses of wilderness life. Yet there is a conflict between the ethic of self-restraint that he speaks for — when he insists on remaining true to his "gifts," when he refuses to marry Judith Hutter — and the idealized state of self-indulgence and escape from social order that his freedom from marriage bonds and social obligation or position and his association with Indians represent. As Lawrence notes, Cooper pays lip service to the ideals represented by the white woman but is most strongly attracted by the Leatherstocking-Chingachgook relationship in the freedom of the woods.

Moby-Dick suggests that the conflicts so charmingly resolved by the Leatherstocking tales and the fire-hunt myth are not so easily resolvable in actuality. Whatever gloss of spirituality, self-restraint, or sacred marriage the myth may cast over the scene, the fact remains that the hunter myth imagines the relationship between man and nature (or man and god) as that of hunter to prey; and the final expression of such a relationship is the domination, destruction, and absorption of one by the other. Only if there is true "marriage" between the two principals — that is, a mutual absorption and acceptance of each by the other, in which neither is destroyed — is the murderous quality of the hunter's communion purged. And the ethic implicit in the captivity myth demands that the wilderness be destroyed so that it can be made safe for the white woman and the civilization she represents. Hence the hunts that are undertaken in the service of this myth can end only in the exorcism or the destructive assimilation of the wilderness spirit. The marriage of the hunter and his prey is unrealizable as such because the defense of the captive requires that the wilderness spirit be rejected or repudiated. For Cotton Mather the rejection is explicit and takes the form of ritual exorcism. For Cooper and Thoreau the repudiation is implicit, expressed in the idea of the hunter's chastity, his withholding at the last the final resignation of himself and his social conscience to the mystery and power of the wilderness.

The hunter myth provided a fictive justification for the process by which the wilderness was to be expropriated and exploited. It did so by seeing that process in terms of heroic adventure, of the initiation of a hero into a new way of life and a higher state of being. Parrington addresses himself to this function of the myth in his discussion of Davy Crockett, whose true lineaments were concealed behind the "shoddy romance" of his myth:

> The real Davy was very far from romantic. . . . It was a slovenly world and Davy was pretty much of a sloven. Crude and unlovely in its familiar details, with its primitive courtships and shiftless removals, its brutal Indian campaign and fierce hunting sprees, its rough equality, its unscrupulous politics, its elections carried by sheer impudence and whiskey, the autobiography reveals the backwoods Anglo-Irishman as uncivilized animal . . . yet with a certain rough vigor of character. Wastefulness was in the frontier blood, and Davy was a true frontier wastrel. In the course of several removals he traversed the length of Tennessee, drinking, hunting, talking, speculating, begetting children, scratching a few acres of land to "make his crap," yet living for the most part off the country; and his last squatting place . . . was as primitive as the first. . . . He was a hunter rather than a farmer, and the lust of killing was in his blood. With his pack of hounds he slaughtered with amazing efficiency. . . . His hundred and five bears in a single season, his six deer shot in one day while pursuing other game serve to explain why the rich hunting grounds of the Indians were swept so quickly bare of game by the white invaders. Davy was but one of the thousands who were wasting the resources of the Inland Empire, destroying forests, skinning the land, slaughtering the deer and bear, the swarms of pigeons, the vast buffalo herds.[59]

It is this reality that the fiction of the Deerslayer (who kills only at need) served to conceal, when writers like Flint chose to wrap the western hunter in the mantle of Daniel Boone.

Two mythic associations made the Crockett figure acceptable as a symbol of American values — his association with the image of the self-restrained, professional hunter Boone through the invocation of hunting as his characteristic activity; and his association with the values of civilization, represented by the white woman and her male associate, the farmer, who together bring civilized value and progress into the wilderness. As Parrington says, Crockett is no farmer, no cultivator or improver of the soil; yet that is certainly what he pretends to be, and the pretense is supported by the mythic linkage of the hunter and the farmer as joint redeemers of the wilderness. But it is the *hunter* quality that sets the hero apart from the yeomanic herd and makes him the hero. Not the cultivator, but the *conquistadore* is the American Aeneas.

This confounding of the figures of the hunter-wastrel and the farmer-cultivator has had disastrous social consequences. It enables us to exploit and lay waste the land as a means of transforming and improving it and converting it into the ideal world of our dreams. It enables us to express our love of the land and its potential by destroying it. The key term is *improvement*. Mather "improves" the narrative of Hannah Dustin because the history, in its primitive human form, is useless to him. If he is to assimilate it, appropriate it for his own, either the story must be altered or he himself must be. The same term is used to describe what settlers must do to the wilderness if they are to achieve clear title to the land. Thus Boone and the Indians lose their land for failing to improve it, for enjoying it in its natural state. Crockett and his farmer-speculators, on the other hand, who planted one field of corn for one year that they might reap specie when they sold out the next, gained the absolute right to the property because they had demonstrably increased its value in money.

To a certain degree, the hunter myth sanctifies the activities of a Crockett as ends in themselves, independent of their function as part of the progressive extension of civilization and progress. Flint invests Boone's professionalization as a hunter, his love of the chase for its own sake and the sake of exercising his skills, with an aura of religious sanctity. Crockett and Doggett likewise see their hunting as a self-expressing and therefore as a self-validating activity. It is not the pelt money nor even the manufactured furred hats that prove the hunter's worth, but the killing of the animal. Such a hunter is not concerned with producing carcasses of beasts for the use of the population, whether for food or clothing. The sole uses of the creatures are as occasions for the exercise of his hunting passion and prowess, for it is this exercise that proves him a man. Thus Crockett is the progenitor of Dreiser's "Titan" and "Financier," Frank Cowperwood, for whom predatory business habits and the sexual exploitation of his victims' wives and daughters go hand in hand. It was Crockett's spirit that Tocqueville saw when he remarked the prevalence of ambition and the paucity of great or lofty designs in American society.

In a democracy based on the social equality of the upwardly mobile, perpetual motion is as important a sign of social importance as the possession of an established fortune. Indeed, the former is of more value, since stagnant or inherited wealth is, by the hunter's standards, a sign of lost vigor. The myth of the hunter, as seen by the Indians and by writers like Flint and Cooper, is one of self-renewal or self-creation through acts of violence. What becomes of the new self, once the initiatory hunt is over? If the good life is defined in terms of the hunter myth, there is only another hunt succeeding the first one. Thus Boone ultimately departs from Boonesborough, the cycles of departure and return continuing beyond the conclusion of the first, Filsonian hunts. Crockett, having failed in Tennessee, hunts for new animals, new enemies, new voters, and a new fortune in

Texas, only to die at the Alamo. The consequences are those suggested in the European myths of the accursed hunter: the abbott and his dogs, like the Greek Orion and Melville's Ahab, are doomed to pursue an ultimately unassimilable, unhuntable prey on the periphery of the cosmic round till the end of time. They do not escape the European heritage to achieve an Indian world in which the hunt completes the hoop of the world and joins man forever to the god of nature.

Believing in the myth of regeneration through the violence of the hunt, the American hunters eventually destroyed the natural conditions that had made possible their economic and social freedom, their democracy of social mobility. Yet the mythology and the value system it supported remained even after the objective conditions that had justified it had vanished. We have, I think, continued to associate democracy and progress with perpetual social mobility (both horizontal and vertical) and with the continual expansion of our power into new fields or new levels of exploitation. Under the aspect of this myth, our economic, social, and spiritual life is taken to be a series of initiations, of stages in a movement outward and upward toward some transcendent goal. We have traditionally associated this form of aspiring initiation with the self-transcendence achieved by hunters through acts of predation. The forces of the environment and the hidden or dark sources of our personal and collective past — factors which limit our power to aspire and transcend — become the things which, as hunters, we triumph over, control, and transcend. They become, under the aspect of the myth, enemies and opponents, who captivate and victimize us and against whom we must be revenged.

Leatherstocking refers to himself as "a man without a cross," meaning that his blood is unmixed with Indian blood and implying his new-Adamic innocence. The literary efforts to create an image of the American character, which tended to express that character in terms of the hunter myth, had since 1785 emphasized the idea that Americans were a new race of people, independent of the sin-darkened heritage of man, seeking a totally new and original relationship to pure nature as hunters, explorers, pioneers, and seekers. In fact, as we have seen, the American was far from being a man without a cross. His peculiar versions of the hunter myth revealed both the crossing of his consciousness with that of the Indian and the heavy cross of his European's and emigrant's heritage of anxiety. The consequences of his myth and the psychology that produced it led him, like Boone initialing trees or Nick of the Woods mutilating Indians, to carve the sign of his cross on all nature, all hunted beasts, all captive men. The seeds of many American tragedies are planted in the captive-and-hunter myth, the myth of regeneration through violence. Although communion with God and nature is the goal of the religious hunter, the passion for the hunt itself and the opportunity it offers to express suppressed urges and desires subvert and confuse the hunter's quest. Fear of those urges, intruding on the consciousness as Natty Bumppo's fear of marrying an Indian or becoming too like Chingachgook, leads the hunter-seeker to abhor the natural spirit he seeks as dark and evil. It thus converts the marriage-hunt into an act of murder, violation, repudiation, or exorcism. It converts the initiation into a fall.

The archetypal enemy of the American hero is the red Indian, and to some degree all groups or nations which threaten us are seen in terms derived from our early myths. Rebellious urban blacks, hippies, and the "youth culture" are recent examples. For most of our history, our most significant conflicts were the campaigns against the Indians, and most American wars against European or Mexican powers until 1898 were accompanied by wars with the Indians. The Indian wars were in many ways the characterizing event of American history, bringing into dramatic focus the forces contending for mastery of the opening continent.

In the mythology derived from the literature of the Indian wars, the Indian is the representative of a culture and a social order that offer a radical alternative to the established order of Euro-American society. His very existence, even as a symbol, poses the fundamental question: why should we order our lives in *this* way, since there is clearly an alternative? In this guise he appeared to the Puritans who suppressed Thomas Morton and to the fearful conservatives of the 1790s and the 1830s, who associated his savagery with Jacobinism and the philistine radicalism of the Jacksonian westerner. The Sons of Liberty who adopted Indian garb to dump the tea in Boston harbor and the westerners who identified their own prowess and independence with the Indian held similar ideas about Indian character, although their response was one of temporary identification rather than repudiation. So in the 1970s the Indian is chosen by the media and by young people in rebellion as a revolutionary symbol of the exploited poor of America and the third world and as a symbol of a utopian vision of a new, more "natural" political economy, a freer and more expressive form of love and worship.

Yet both the repudiators of and the identifiers with the symbolic Indian are dealing with myths of the Indian rather than with realities. The demise of the Indians is in part attributable to the compatibility of their hunting mythology with the economics of the fur trade, the buffalo-hide trade, and territorial ambition, which led many of them to aid the whites in

exploiting the resources of the land and displacing "hostile" tribes. Tashtego serves Ahab too. What differentiated the Indian hunter from Davy
Crockett was, not a racial antipathy for capitalism and trade, but a sense of
belonging to the world one exploited. In *Creative Mythology* Joseph
Campbell speaks of the conflict between the mythology of the hunter and
that of the shaman. The former provides the cosmology and ethic for a religion of world heroes, dominators, rulers, exploiters; the latter is the mythology of the saint and seer, the mystic adventurer in consciousness, who
experiences and suffers the universe, mastering it through sympathy rather
than power. The power of figures like Daniel Boone and the Hayowentha
of Iroquois legend lies in their combining the traits of hunter and shaman.
Boone is a Quaker as well as a killer; Hayowentha had been a cannibal
warrior but was converted to a belief in human solidarity and universal
peace by the mystic Deganawidah.

In the Indian cultures of the eastern woodlands a precarious balance
between the visions of the shaman and the hunter had been achieved, in
which the ideals, rituals, and poetry of the former sanctified the necessary
activities of the latter. Thus the Indian hunter mourned the death of the
animal he killed as he would that of a relative, and he thanked the creature's kin for serving his dire necessity. Believing a common life-spirit to be
immanent in all things, he could learn to respect and conform to the balance of natural relationships which sustains life. The Euro-American, having no such connection with the earth he possessed, destroyed the balanced world in an attempt to remake it in the image of something else, and
among the balances he destroyed was that which sustained the Indian in
his universe. The appeal of trade goods led the Indian to seek profit
through the sort of exploitative hunting and land transactions that destroyed the game and squandered the soil on which he lived. The white
mythology of the Indian dimly recognized that the Indian's feeling for nature was of a different quality from that of the colonist. Yet the mythology
insisted that the Indian's essential character was that of the hunter who exploits the land and that he was by nature opposed to the spirit of the
farmer who cultivates it. In fact, no such dichotomy existed for the wood-
land Indians, who were sometime farmers and who in any case envisioned
hunting as an appreciative cultivation of certain spirits inherent in nature.

Beyond this inaccurate appreciation of the Indian's economy, the mythology misconceived the nature of Indian society. The white hunter-heroes of the myth who are identified are men of solitude, men whose intense
privacy sets them temporarily or permanently against the social order.
The wilderness for them is an alternative to the obligations/protec-

tions/restrictions of civilization. They are, as Lawrence says, integral souls venturing outward in space and backward or forward in history; or as Melville puts it, *"Isolatoes,"* "fleeing from all havens astern." This image of the solitary hunter is, however, an imposition of a colonial vision of social conflict on the Indian. For the tribesmen, wilderness life, notwithstanding its requirement of hunting, was one of community rather than solitude. For the Indian the wilderness was home, the locus of the tribe that was the center of his metaphysical universe as well as his social existence. Even in moments of physical solitude, on a long hunt or a vision quest, the world community about him remained intact, for the gods and the wild animals were his fellows and his kin. The border of tribal solidarity extended out from the village center to the edges of creation. The white hunter was an alien, paradoxically achieving a sense of relation to the world through an ordeal of profound physical, moral, and psychological isolation from society. His destiny was personal rather than tribal; his moral obligation was to himself, his "gifts," and his racial character, rather than to his fellows and his environment.

In psychological terms, the Indian in our mythology functions as the image or symbol of the American libido — the primitive source of sexual, conceptual, and creative energy that lies below the level of psychological consciousness and is (according to Jung) the root of creative, religious, and erotic inspiration. In the myth of the hunter, this libido is variously symbolized as a brother or second (and darker) self (Chingachgook), a bride (anima: Magawisca, Boone's deer/woman, Ishmael's Queequeg, Judith Hutter), a male antagonist (animus: Church's Philip, Ahab's Moby Dick), and an ambivalent blending of two or more of these elements (Church's Annawon, Deerslayer's Loup Cervier, Jim Doggett's bear). Against these symbols of the power of the libido and of the nonconscious aspect of the psyche are ranged the powers of the conscious mind: reason, the power of will, the socially formed conscience. Conscience and reason are the attributes of the white woman of the captivity myth, and it is her function to turn the heroic will from its pursuit of the symbols of the libido and the unconscious to the service of society and society's God.

The attitude toward the libido and the unconscious expressed in the myth is ambivalent. On the one hand, it recognizes in the symbols of the libido the source of creative life-energy and of power in and over the natural wilderness. It dreamingly depicts the integration of the nonconscious with the conscious elements of the psyche in the various unions of anima and animus figures. Yet, at the same time, the myth recognizes that the full resignation of consciousness and will to the powers of the libido and the unconscious would threaten the safety and integrity of the conscious mind, the ego, and the will. If the will and conscience, formed to facilitate the progressive thrust and the moral order of society, are thus turned from their proper social objects and concerns, social disintegration may follow.

The symbol of the Indian expresses this deep-seated fear of the powers of the libido and the unconscious and, at the same time, historicizes it, relates it directly to the central problem of American colonization and expansion. In America the tension between the two aspects of the psyche surfaces in the "political reality" of cultural conflict between Indian and European civilization.[60] Thus the Indian is alternately the symbol of humanity's childhood and of the Golden Age of man's solidarity with God and creation and the lustful, cruel violator of American pastoral peace. He is both the victim (of the hunter) and the violator (of the captive). His character in the myth changes as the psychological requirements of the myth's audience alter with time and social change.

The terms of the hunter and the captive myths serve to conceal the reality of painful or perplexing historical situations and to provide illusory but emotionally satisfying solutions for real problems. Occasionally reality imposes a vision of itself in spite of all that mythology can do to conceal it. But in the case of the racial antagonists of white America — initially the Indians, later the blacks — it has been possible for us during most of our history to impose our vision on reality, to behave in accordance with our myths without suffering unduly for it. The most desperate consequences of the mythology were suffered by those who figured in it as useful symbols. The captivity mythology, for example, provided Harriet Beecher Stowe with a profound basis for appealing to the sensibilities of New Englanders on behalf of the captive black slaves. But the terms of that mythology required that the protagonist be essentially feminine in spirit, passive and ideally Christian. This image of the black slave may well have created false expectations among those who later interested themselves in the lot of the freedman and limited their capacity to deal with the reality of the post–Civil War South. Moreover, the captivity mythology could, during and after Reconstruction, be brought to bear with equal and perhaps greater power on behalf of the reestablishment of lily-white rule. The vision of Reconstruction purveyed in novels like Thomas Dixon's *The Clansman* (later made into the film *Birth of a Nation*) and in the Democratic papers of the 1870s had much to do with the termination of Reconstruction and the undoing of its reforms. That vision — which shaped our image of the period at least until the 1930s — is one of the white South, embodied in an aristocratic woman, captive in the hands of savage, lustful blacks and corrupt carpetbaggers and scalawags, the King Philips and Simon Girtys of their time and place.

Myth may do more than distort analysis of a given set of social or historical circumstances. Since it is a vision which combines both an appreciation of a putative reality and a value structure, myth provides a scenario for response to events whenever it is successfully invoked — as, for example, by Mather in the case of Mercy Short. Recent history suggests that a favorite occasion for invocation of the hunter and captive myths is that of the imperialistic adventure. The Indian wars of the post–Civil War period, particularly the war on the southern plains in 1867–69, were provoked, often deliberately and officially, by the whites in order to justify the expropriation of Indian lands for use by the railroads and their associated land companies. The essentially economic basis of the conflict was concealed behind a rhetoric which emphasized the need to rescue white captives, particularly women, from the brutal rapists of the plains.[61] Similarly, the Spanish-American War was presented as a vengeance for the massacre of the sinking of the *Maine* and for the rescue of American filibusters and Cuban guerrillas from Spanish concentration camps. The expedition to China in the Boxer Rebellion that won us our share of the Chinese market was nominally a mission to rescue the families of traders and diplomats besieged by maddened Oriental fanatics in the International City.

The most recent employment of the myth has been on behalf of escalating the war in Vietnam.[62] President Johnson, in his Johns Hopkins address of 1965, invoked the characteristic imagery of the captivity myth, in which the family — symbolic embodiment of social order, centering on the figure of the mother and child and associated with the cultivation of the soil — is assaulted by dark and savage forces from beyond the borders, aided by local renegades:

> First and most important is the simple fact that South Vietnam, a member of the Free World family, is striving to preserve its independence from Communist attack. Of course, some of the people of South Vietnam are participating in this attack on their own government . . . but Hanoi . . . is the heartbeat of the war.

> And it is a war of unparalleled brutality: Simple farmers are the targets of assassination and kidnapping. Women and children are strangled in the night because their men are loyal to the government. And helpless villages are ravaged by sneak attacks.[63]

Or, as John Filson put it: "The innocent husbandman was shot down, while busily cultivating the soil for his family's supply." [64]

Implicit in the myth is the rescue of the captive by the hunter, who will fight the enemy on his own terms and in his own manner, becoming in the process a reflection or a double of his dark opponent. Only self-restraint, self-abnegation, and a devotion to the concept of opening the forest to higher cultivation will save him from his fate. Thus President Johnson went on to emphasize that the war was undertaken not for worldly gain but for the rescue of the helpless and to offer a super-TVA-type development of the Mekong delta as a vision of the regeneration that might follow peace on American terms.[65] It is clear that this widely (if never universally) persuasive invocation of myths obscured both the nature of the conflict and the character of our participation in it, with grave military and social consequences. One officer aptly (and without irony) remarked at the time of the Tet offensive in 1968, "We destroyed the city in order to save it."

As Whitman says in "Song of the Broad-Axe," we are indeed one of the "lands of the make of the axe" and of its companion weapon-tool, the rifle. The orgiastic outbursting of creative energy which he imagines in that poem expresses itself in orgiastic destruction, by which trees are converted to lumber, ore to metal, and primitive conditions into an image of "the Great City." The love we have for the things of the world, the delight we take in them, goes hand in hand with our destruction and conversion of them, perhaps because the act of destruction itself somehow makes us believe in our manhood and godhood, our Ahab's power to dominate life and to perpetuate and extend ourselves and our power. The mythopoeic mode of reconciling historical parodoxes enables us to glory in this role, on the one hand, and to take the curse off our axe- and gun-work, on the other, by allowing us to identify with what is wounded or destroyed. In the captivity myth, the unfilial emigrant is reconciled with his family by identification with the suffering of the female captive and by his recognition that his masculine will to achieve in the wilderness world is the true cause of her suffering. But the vicarious suffering obtained through the captivity myth atones for the sin and permits the continuance of the emigrant's career.

In the hunter myth, the emigrant's sense of guilt for having broken the family circle by his departure is seen as the grounds for establishing a spiritual kinship with the Indians. But this kinship is justified in that it makes the hunter more effective as the destroyer of the Indian, as the exorcist of the wilderness's darkness. He comes to know the Indian only in the act of destroying him. Beyond this exorcism, there is further expiation in the fact that the destruction of the Indian makes the hunter obsolete. His final atonement with society may take the form of a voluntary exile (as in

The Pioneers) or a marriage with a white woman. With the Indian's vanishment, the dialectic of the hero's history ends, and the masculine rifle is hung on the wall above the feminine hearth.

But the cycle of the myth never really ends. The animal skins on the wall, the tree stumps in the yard, the scalp bounty money in the bank, and the pervasive smell of burning are proofs of what we have been; and they suggest that we still will play, in concept or action, the same role in dialectical opposition to a new Indian, a new social or political antithesis. As the captivities of Mary Rowlandson and Mercy Short suggest, rescue from dark events is never complete. Physical combat with and captivity to the dark forces (whether they are really dark or only imagined to be so) infects the mind itself with darkness. The hunters and the redeemed captives return from the forest to find the people still only restively pacified, still mourning the passing of a Golden Age of complacency, still anticipating new captivities and rescues. The struggle turns inward: Indians are discovered lurking in subversive forces within society itself, in the independence and aspiration of one's own children, in the recesses of one's own mind. A new captivity, a new hunt, and a new ceremony of exorcism repeat the myth-scenario on progressively deeper, more internal levels. Wars are followed by witch-hunts. Moby Dick is both a creature of external reality and an aspect of his hunters' minds. It has been said that men "make a waste land and call it peace"; and the desert is not simply that of a savaged landscape but of a tortured mind.

Our heroes and their narratives are an index to our character and conception of our role in the universe — Whitman's woodchopper, gaining mythic stature through the reduction of wilderness to planks and blocks, in the service of civilization and the soul; Ahab and the *Pequod* furnished in the "chased bones" of their prey, Benjamin Church decked in the scalps and royalties of the slain Philip; Leatherstocking accepting a mythic name from his slain Indian enemy; Davy Crockett grinning by a mountain of 105 bear-hides; Boone, whose rifle shots are prayer and poetry, an acolyte perpetually sacrificing to his god. The heroism in these figures consists for us in their method of achieving their goal. The trophies they are perpetually garnering have no material value; their sanctity derives from their function as visual and concrete proofs of the self-justifying acts of violent self-transcendence and regeneration that produced them. So the Indians (no less "American" than Crockett) garnered trophies as proofs and reminders of their battle valor and as kernels around which to build their names and the myth-tales of the tribe. In Vietnam it was called the body count.

Under the aspect of mythology and historical distance, the acts and motives of the woodchopper, the whale and bear hunter, the Indian fighter, and the deerslayer have an air of simplicity and purity that makes them seem finely heroic expressions of an admirable quality of the human spirit. They seem to stand on a commanding ridge, while we are still tangled in the complexities of the world and the wilderness. But their apparent independence of time and consequence is an illusion; a closely woven chain of time and consequence binds their world to ours. Set the statuesque figures and their piled trophies in motion through space and time, and a more familiar landscape emerges — the whale, buffalo, and bear hunted to the verge of extinction for pleasure in killing and "scalped" for fame and the profit in hides by men like Buffalo Bill; the buffalo meat left to rot, till acres of prairie were covered with heaps of whitening bones, and the bones then ground for fertilizer; the Indian debased, impoverished, and killed in return for his gifts; the land and its people, its "dark" people especially, economically exploited and wasted; the warfare between man and nature, between race and race, exalted as a kind of heroic ideal; the piles of wrecked and rusted cars, heaped like Tartar pyramids of death-cracked, weather-browned, rain-rotted skulls, to signify our passage through the land.

NOTES, SELECTED BIBLIOGRAPHY, AND INDEX

Notes

Chapter 1: Myth and Literature in a New World

1. See especially Benjamin T. Spencer, *The Quest for Nationality*, and Albert D. Van Nostrand, *Everyman His Own Poet*.

2. My discussion of myth and mythogenesis is based on the following works: Joseph Campbell, *The Masks of God* and *The Hero with a Thousand Faces*; Richard Chase, *The Quest for Myth*; James G. Frazer, *The New Golden Bough*, ed. Theodor Gaster; Carl Gustav Jung, *Psyche and Symbol*, ed. Violet S. de Laszlo; Claude Lévi-Strauss, *The Savage Mind* and *Totemism*; Lucien Lévy-Bruhl, *How Natives Think*, chaps. 1 and 2; Thomas Sebeok, ed., *Myth: A Symposium*; Alan Watts, *Myth and Ritual in Christianity*; and Joseph L. Henderson, *Thresholds of Initiation*.

3. See Carl Gustav Jung, "The Psychology of the Child Archetype" and "The Special Phenomenology of the Child Archetype," *Psyche and Symbol*, pp. 113–47; and Henry Nash Smith, *Virgin Land*, p. v.

4. See *Hero with a Thousand Faces*, pp. 3–25, 255–69, and Philip Wheelwright, "Semantic Approach to Myth," in Sebeok, *Myth: A Symposium*, p. 154.

5. See *New Golden Bough*, pp. xiii–82.

6. "Semantic Approach to Myth," pp. 154–68.

7. Ibid., p. 158.

8. Ibid., p. 159. See also *How Natives Think*, chap. 2; *Savage Mind*, chaps. 5, 6; and *Totemism*, passim.

9. See *Hero with a Thousand Faces*, p. 258.

10. See Claude Lévi-Strauss, "Structural Study of Myth," in Sebeok, *Myth: A Symposium*, pp. 84–85; see also "Semantic Approach to Myth," pp. 158–59.

11. Richard Chase, *The American Novel and Its Tradition*, pp. 243–46.

12. *Hero with a Thousand Faces*, pp. 245–46.

13. *Thresholds of Initiation*, pp. 10–13.

14. *Masks of God: Primitive Mythology*, quoted in *Thresholds of Initiation*, p. 13.

15. *Thresholds of Initiation*, p. 13; see *Psyche and Symbol*, pp. 10–22.

16. *Thresholds of Initiation*, chaps. 2, 9; *Hero with a Thousand Faces*, pp. 246–51.

17. "Semantic Approach to Myth," pp. 155–56.

18. Ibid., p. 156.

19. Ibid.

20. Quoted by Richard L. Greene in "Myth and Myth Criticism," unpublished manuscript, Wesleyan University, September 1967.

21. Quoted in Howard Mumford Jones, *O Strange New World*, pp. 14–15.

22. Bernal Díaz del Castillo, *Conquest of New Spain*, p. 413.

23. Kenneth Rexroth, "Classics Revisited LXI: Parkman's History," p. 35.

24. A full discussion of the phenomenon of white settlers becoming "Indianized" can be found in A. Irving Hallowell, "Backwash of the Frontier: The Impact of the Indian on American Culture," in Paul Bohannan and Fred Plog, eds., *Beyond the Frontier*, pp. 319–46; Peter Farb, *Man's Rise to Civilization as Shown by the Indians of North America from Primeval Times to the Coming of the Industrial State*, pp. 260–66; and Felix S. Cohen, "Americanizing the White Man," pp. 177–91.

25. *Hero with a Thousand Faces*, chap. 2; *Thresholds of Initiation*, pp. 3–8.

Chapter 2: Cannibals and Christians

1. Quoted in Wilcomb F. Washburn, ed., *The Indian and the White Man*, pp. 213–14.

2. D. H. Lawrence, *Studies in Classic American Literature*, p. 85; see also "Backwash of the Frontier," p. 345, and *Man's Rise to Civilization*, p. 261.

3. See *O Strange New World*, pp. 1–34.

4. *Hero with a Thousand Faces*, pp. 245–46.

5. Carl Gustav Jung, "Aion," *Psyche and Symbol*, pp. 1–22; Denis de Rougemont, *Love in the Western World*, books 1–3.

6. *O Strange New World*, pp. 36–37.

7. Ibid., pp. 11–14.

8. Michael Drayton, "For the Virginian Voyage," *Works* 2:363–64.

9. Richard Hakluyt, *The Portable Hakluyt's Voyages*, pp. 186, 189, 190, 195–96.

10. Ibid., p. 184.

11. See introduction by Genaro Garcia to Bernal Díaz del Castillo, *The Discovery and Conquest of Mexico*, pp. xiv–xv, 190.

12. Ibid., p. xxxiii.

13. Ibid., book 2; see also Hernando Cortés, *Five Letters*, pp. 31–133.

14. *Conquest of New Spain*, p. 413; see also *Five Letters*, pp. xlvi–xlvii, 243–86.

15. Edward G. Bourne and Julius E. Olson, eds., *The Northmen, Columbus, and Cabot*, pp. 59–66.

16. Leo Marx, "Shakespeare's American Fable," in his *The Machine in the Garden*, pp. 34–72.

17. Alvar Nunez Cabeza de Vaca, "The Narrative of . . . ," in Frederick W. Hodge and Theodore H. Lewis, eds., *Spanish Explorers in the Southern United States*, pp. 12–126.

18. Perry Miller, *Errand into the Wilderness*, pp. 1–15.

19. The following discussion of the American Puritans has, in its broad outlines and general conclusions, been shaped by the following works: Perry Miller, *Errand into the Wilderness* and *The New England Mind: The Seventeenth Century*;

Perry Miller and Thomas H. Johnson, eds., *The Puritans*; Edmund S. Morgan, *The Puritan Dilemma*, pp. 34–53, 155–84; Samuel Eliot Morison, *The Puritan Pronaos*; Richard H. Tawney, *Religion and the Rise of Capitalism*; and Max Weber, *The Protestant Ethic and the Spirit of Capitalism*.

20. William Bradford, *Of Plymouth Plantation*, p. 25.

21. Ibid., p. 26.

22. Ibid., p. 25.

23. John Bunyan, *Pilgrim's Progress*, ed. Louis Martz, pp. viii, 9–12. See also C. L. Sanford, "An American Pilgrim's Progress," in Hennig Cohen, ed., *The American Culture*, pp. 77–91.

24. *Pilgrim's Progress*, p. 9.

25. See *The Puritans* 1:86 and *Puritan Dilemma*, pp. 34–44, 176–86, 194–203. See also John White, *The Planters Plea*.

26. Thomas Shepard, "A Defense of the Answer," in *The Puritans* 1:121.

27. William C. MacLeod, "Celt and Indian: Britain's Old World Frontier in Relation to the New," in *Beyond the Frontier*, pp. 25–42.

28. The following discussion of the American Indian culture and the quasi as-similation of whites to Indian ways is based on the following works: Harold E. Driver, ed., *The Americas on the Eve of Discovery*; Felix S. Cohen, "Americanizing the White Man"; John Collier, *Indians of the Americas*; Jack D. Forbes, ed., *The Indian in America's Past*; Peter Farb, *Man's Rise to Civilization*; James G. Frazer, *The New Golden Bough*; George E. Hyde, *Indians of the Woodlands*; Roger C. Owen, James J. F. Deetz, and Anthony D. Fisher, eds., *The North American Indians; A Sourcebook*, pp. 1–119, 185–235, 529–605; Frank G. Speck, *Penobscot Man* and *A Study of the Delaware Indian Big House Ceremony*, vol. 2; John Tebbel and Keith Jennison, *The American Indian Wars*; Willard Walker et al., "The Indians of Maine"; Edmund Wilson, *Apologies to the Iroquois*; and Paul Bohannan and Fred Plog, eds., *Beyond the Frontier*.

29. *Big House Ceremony*, pp. 64–65.

30. Ibid., p. 65.

31. See Cadwallader Colden, *History of the Five Nations*, pp. xvi–xxi; A. A. Goldenweiser, "Iroquois Social Organization," in Owen, Deetz, and Fisher, *North American Indians*, pp. 565–76; and *Apologies to the Iroquois*, pp. 44–47. Contrast these with *The Puritans* 1:17–19.

32. *Big House Ceremony*, p. 27.

33. John G. E. Heckewelder, "History, Manners, and Customs of the Indian Nations," pp. 249–56.

34. Roger Williams, *A Key into the Language of America*, p. 138.

35. *Big House Ceremony*, pp. 145–53. The Iroquois myth of the creation of their league and its value system (righteousness, reason, and peace) is similar in pattern to the Christian formula, since it involves a fall and redemption. The hero Deganawidah gets the cannibal Hayowentha to turn from his evil ways and join the brotherhood of the people by the trick of peering secretly into Hayowentha's boiling kettle. Hayowentha, seeing Deganawidah's face reflected there and believing it to be his own, recognizes his brotherhood with humanity and is turned from can-nibalism. This leads to the creation of the Iroquois League for Peace. It should be noted, however, that this myth recounts the creation of man as a creature, not of

the earth, but of a system of social organization (*Apologies to the Iroquois*, pp. 132–34).

36. *Big House Ceremony*, p. 22. (The Iroquois counterpart of the Big House is the longhouse; the tribal name signifies "People of the Longhouse.")

37. Ibid., pp. 22–24.

38. The terms used in this discussion are drawn from those used by Joseph Campbell in his *Masks of God*, especially vols. 1 (*Primitive Mythology*) and 4 (*Creative Mythology*).

39. *Big House Ceremony*, p. 32.

40. A. Irving Hallowell, "Ojibwa World View," in *North American Indians*, pp. 210–23; see also *Black Elk Speaks*, trans. John G. Neihardt, p. 32. Speck, in *Penobscot Man*, recounts the myths of the origin of family groupings (Bear, Whale, etc.) within the tribe (pp. 212–49).

41. *Big House Ceremony*, pp. 50–51.

42. Ibid., p. 51.

43. See Jonathan Edwards, "A Treatise Concerning Religious Affections" and "Narrative of Surprising Conversions," *Works* 1:234–364, and his "Personal Narrative," *Representative Selections*, pp. 57–72; Thomas Hooker, "True Sight of Sin" and "Meditation," in *The Puritans* 1:292–314; and Perry Miller, *Jonathan Edwards*, pp. 133–63.

44. "Ojibwa World View," pp. 234–35; *Penobscot Man*, p. 237; Henry Timberlake, *Memoirs*, pp. 92–93.

45. "Americanizing the White Man," p. 177.

46. "Ojibwa World View," pp. 227–35; *Thresholds of Initiation*, pp. 32–38; *Black Elk Speaks*, pp. 166–80; and A. F. C. Wallace, "Psychoanalysis among the Iroquois," in *Americas on the Eve of Discovery*, pp. 69–79.

47. Winthrop D. Jordan, *White over Black*, pp. 89–91. Michael P. Rogin, "Liberal Society and the Indian Question," *Politics and Society* 1, no. 3 (May 1971): 269–74.

48. *Indians of the Woodlands*, pp. 203–4.

Chapter 3: A Home in the Heart of Darkness

1. Horatio Smith, *Festivals, Games, and Amusements, Ancient and Modern*, pp. 126–27; Phillip Stubbes, "Anatomy of the Abuses in England in Shakespeare's Youth, A.D. 1583," 6th series, nos. 4, 6, 12, pp. 140–46; Edmund K. Chambers, *The Elizabethan Stage* 1, chap. 8; 4:184–345.

2. Charles Francis Adams, *Three Episodes of Massachusetts History*, pp. 181–82; see also "Celt and Indian," pp. 40–41.

3. Charles E. Banks, "Thomas Morton of Merrymount," *Proceedings of the Massachusetts Historical Society* 58 (December 1924): 147–93.

4. Thomas Morton, "New English Canaan or New Canaan," pp. 11, 17–18, 38–40.

5. Ibid., pp. 21, 34–35, title page, 23–24, 82.

6. Ibid., p. 85.

7. Ibid., p. 82.

8. *Of Plymouth Plantation*, pp. 316, 319, 321, 404–12.

9. *New English Canaan,* pp. 82, 87–89.

10. *Three Episodes of Massachusetts History,* pp. 181–82; see also *Festivals, Games, and Amusements,* pp. 126–28.

11. Lewis Spence, *Myth and Ritual in Dance, Game, and Rhyme,* pp. 29–38; Joseph Strutt, *The Sports and Pastimes of the People of England,* pp. 339–42, 351–53.

12. "Anatomy of the Abuses," p. 149.

13. *New Golden Bough,* pp. 40–49; cf. p. 50.

14. Edmund K. Chambers ("The Mask," *Elizabethan Stage* 1:149–212) notes the folk origins of the masque in the May and Christmas games, thus illustrating the similarity of motivation in Puritan opposition to both drama and folk ritual. See also "Anatomy of the Abuses," pp. 140–50, in which the condemnation of masques and plays is followed directly by an attack on the May games and the Lord of Misrule. Frazer analyzes the May games in *New Golden Bough,* pp. 320–24.

15. *New English Canaan,* pp. 89–92; *Elizabethan Stage* 1:149–51.

16. *New English Canaan,* pp. 90–91.

17. Ibid., pp. 91–96.

18. *Of Plymouth Plantation,* pp. 205–6.

19. John Rolfe, "Letter of John Rolfe, 1614," in Lyon Gardiner Tyler, ed., *Narratives of Early Virginia,* pp. 239–44.

20. Connecticut, Colony of, *The Code of 1650,* p. 53.

21. *The Puritans* 1:64–79.

22. The structuring of Puritan sermons is readily apparent in their texts, since the several subdivisions were clearly labeled by the authors. See, for example, Jonathan Edwards, "Sermon Notes," *Representative Selections,* pp. 203–5. Cf. *Puritan Pronaos,* pp. 152–76.

23. William G. McLoughlin, "Pietism and the American Character," *American Quarterly* 17, no. 2 (Summer 1965):165.

24. Raymond P. Stearns, "John Underhill," *Dictionary of American Biography* 19:110–11.

25. John Underhill, *Newes from America,* pp. 12–13.

26. Philip Vincent, "A True Relation of the Late Battell Fought in New-England," pp. 33, 41.

27. Ibid., p. 41.

28. Ibid., p. 42.

29. Ibid., pp. 42–43.

30. *Newes from America,* pp. 9–12.

31. Ibid., p. 24.

32. Ibid., p. 26.

33. "True Relation," pp. 37–38.

34. *Newes from America,* pp. 19, 18.

35. Ibid., pp. 19–20.

36. Ibid., p. 20.

37. "True Relation," p. 34; *Newes from America,* p. 22.

38. *Newes from America,* p. 25.

39. "True Relation," pp. 34–35.

40. Ibid., p. 39.

41. Increase Mather, *A Brief History of the Warr with the Indians in New-England*, p. 48.

42. John Easton, "A Relacion of the Indian Warre," in Charles H. Lincoln, ed., *Narratives of the Indian Wars*, p. 10.

43. Ibid., p. 12.

44. Edward Wharton, *New-England's Present Sufferings*, p. 4.

45. N[athaniel] S[altonstall], *The Present State of New-England with Respect to the Indian War*, in *Narratives of the Indian Wars*, p. 40; John Tebbel and Keith Jennison, *American Indian Wars*, pp. 43–44.

46. Ibid., p. 40.

47. Ibid., p. 41.

48. *A Farther Brief and True Narration of the Late Wars*, p. 3.

49. Ibid.

50. *Present State*, p. 38.

51. *Brief History*, p. 1.

52. Ibid., pp. 1–2.

53. Ibid., p. 13.

54. Ibid., p. 20.

55. Ibid., p. 21.

56. Ibid., pp. 43–44.

57. Ibid., p. 47.

58. Increase Mather, *An Earnest Exhortation to the Inhabitants of New-England*, p. 1.

59. Ibid., p. 9.

60. Ibid.

61. Ibid., p. 5.

62. Thomas Wheeler, *A Thankfull Remembrance of Gods Mercy to Several Persons at Quabaug or Brookfield*, p. 29.

63. Samuel Nowell, *Abraham in Arms*, p. 11.

64. William Hubbard, *A Narrative of the Troubles with the Indians in New-England*, reprinted as *History of the Indian Wars* 1:24.

65. Ibid., pp. 52–53.

66. Benjamin Tompson, *New-Englands Crisis*, p. 1.

67. Ibid., pp. 10–11.

68. Ibid., p. 19.

69. *O Strange New World*, pp. 51–57.

70. Edward Johnson, *Johnson's Wonder-Working Providence*, ed. J. Franklin Jameson, p. 149.

71. *Present State*, p. 41; see also *O Strange New World*, p. 57.

72. *New-Englands Crisis*, p. 30.

Chapter 4: Israel in Babylon

1. *Newes from America*, pp. 19, 18.

2. See Roy Harvey Pearce, "The Significances of the Captivity Narrative." See also Robert William Glenroie Vail, *The Voice of the Old Frontier*, pp. 167–218, and Frank Luther Mott, *Golden Multitudes*, pp. 303–5.

3. See *Voice of the Old Frontier* for listings of editions of the Rowlandson and Williams narratives; see also *Golden Multitudes*, p. 303.

4. Jonathan Edwards, "Sinners in the Hands of an Angry God," *Representative Selections*, pp. 158–59.

5. Cotton Mather, *The Short History of New-England*, pp. [42–43]. (Page numbers are illegible.) See also Increase Mather, *A Brief History*, p. 9.

6. Deodat Lawson, *A Brief and True Narrative of Some Remarkable Passages Relating to Sundry Persons Afflicted by Witchcraft at Salem Village*, in George Lincoln Burr, ed., *Narratives of the Witchcraft Cases*, pp. 160–61.

7. John Williams, *The Redeemed Captive Returning to Zion*, pp. 173–74.

8. See Solomon Williams, *The Power and Efficacy of the Prayers of the People of God When Rightly Offered to Him*.

9. Mary Rowlandson, *The Soveraignty and Goodness of God, Together with the Faithfulness of His Promises Displayed: Being a Narrative of the Captivity and Restauration of Mrs. Mary Rowlandson*, in *Narratives of the Indian Wars*, pp. 166–67.

10. *Of Plymouth Plantation*, pp. 23–27; "Defense of the Answer," pp. 120–21.

11. *Pilgrim's Progress*, p. 23.

12. "Sinners in the Hands of an Angry God," pp. 155–56.

13. Ibid., pp. 162–63.

14. Michael Wigglesworth, "The Day of Doom," in Roy Harvey Pearce, ed., *Colonial American Writing*, pp. 233–34.

15. *Soveraignty and Goodness of God*, p. 120.

16. Ibid., p. 121.

17. "Sinners in the Hands of an Angry God," pp. 160–61.

18. *Soveraignty and Goodness of God*, p. 120.

19. *Pilgrim's Progress*, p. 23.

20. "Defense of the Answer," p. 121.

21. *Soveraignty and Goodness of God*, p. 133.

22. "The Day of Doom," pp. 248, 289–90.

23. Ibid., pp. 289–90.

24. *Soveraignty and Goodness of God*, pp. 120, 126.

25. *Pilgrim's Progress*, p. 11.

26. *Soveraignty and Goodness of God*, p. 121.

27. Ibid., p. 134.

28. Ibid., p. 149.

29. Ibid., pp. 166–67.

30. "Sinners in the Hands of an Angry God," p. 165.

31. *Soveraignty and Goodness of God*, p. 166.

32. Cotton Mather, *Humiliations follow'd with Deliverances*, pp. 48–49.

Chapter 5: A Palisade of Language

1. See Francis Parkman, *Count Frontenac and New France under Louis XIV*, chap. 11. See also *Puritan Pronaos*, p. 259.

2. John Wesley Hanson, *History of Gardiner, Pittston and West Gardiner*, pp. 23–24.

3. Increase Mather, *Remarkable Providences: Illustrative of the Earlier Days of American Colonisation*, pp. 116–18.

4. Cotton Mather, *Decennium Luctuosum*, in *Narratives of the Indian Wars*, pp. 243–47.

5. Ibid., p. 247.

6. Ibid., p. 206.

7. Robert Ratcliffe, *A Particular Account of the Late Revolution at Boston*, in Charles M. Andrews, ed., *Narratives of the Insurrections*, p. 197.

8. *Decennium Luctuosum*, pp. 207–13.

9. See Emma Lewis Coleman, *New England Captives Carried to Canada* 1:181–219. A. Irving Hallowell, "Backwash of the Frontier," in *Beyond the Frontier*, pp. 323–26. Willard Walker, comments at History Club Symposium on a reading of this chapter, Wesleyan University, February 1971.

10. Francis Parkman, *A Half-Century of Conflict*, p. 313.

11. Ibid., p. 126.

12. Cotton Mather, *Magnalia Christi Americana: Or, The Ecclesiastical History of New-England* 2:499.

13. Sebastien Râlé, "Letter to His Brother," in Reuben Gold Thwaites, ed., *The Jesuit Relations* 67:141.

14. Francis Parkman, *The Old Regime in Canada*, p. 127.

15. Cotton Mather, "A Brand Pluck'd Out of the Burning," in *Narratives of the Witchcraft Cases*, p. 259.

16. Emma Lewis Coleman describes one of many such cases in *New England Captives* 1:325.

17. *Decennium Luctuosum*, p. 292.

18. Ibid., pp. 277–78.

19. Ibid., p. 242.

20. George Lincoln Burr, in *Narratives of the Witchcraft Cases*, pp. 257–58.

21. "Brand Pluck'd Out," p. 259.

22. Ibid., pp. 264, 267.

23. Ibid., p. 261.

24. Ibid., p. 270.

25. *A Brief and True Narrative of Some Remarkable Passages*, pp. 160–61.

26. "Brand Pluck'd Out," p. 270.

27. Ibid., p. 271.

28. Ibid., p. 270.

29. Ibid., p. 269.

30. Ibid., p. 268.

31. "Psychoanalysis among the Iroquois," pp. 78–79.

32. Quoted ibid., pp. 72–73.

33. Ibid., p. 74.

34. "Brand Pluck'd Out," p. 274; *Soveraignty and Goodness of God*, p. 121.

35. "Brand Pluck'd Out," p. 270.

36. Ibid.

37. Robert Calef, *More Wonders of the Invisible World*, in *Narratives of the Witchcraft Cases*, p. 384.

38. "Brand Pluck'd Out," p. 287.

39. *More Wonders*, p. 353.

40. Cotton Mather, *The Wonders of the Invisible World: Observations as well Historical as Theological, upon the Nature, the Number, and the Operations of the Devils*, in *Narratives of the Witchcraft Cases*, pp. 219–20.

41. Samuel G. Drake, *Annals of Witchcraft in New England*, pp. 79–85, 112, 121, 170.

42. James E. Seaver, *A Narrative of the Life of Mrs. Mary Jemison*, pp. 182–84.

43. Epaphras Hoyt, *Antiquarian Researches: Comprising a History of the Indian Wars*, p. 179.

44. "Psychoanalysis among the Iroquois," p. 79.

Chapter 6: The Hunting of the Beast

1. Samuel Sewall, "Phaenomena," in *The Puritans* 1:376–77.
2. Thomas Shepard, "Autobiography," ibid. 2:472.
3. "Personal Narrative," pp. 59–60.
4. Ibid., pp. 60–61.
5. Ibid., p. 61.
6. *Jonathan Edwards*, pp. 3–34.
7. Jonathan Edwards, "Of Insects," *Representative Selections*, p. 3.
8. Ibid., pp. 9–10.
9. "Sinners in the Hands of an Angry God," pp. 164–65.
10. *Black Elk Speaks*, chap. 14.
11. *Magnalia Christi Americana* 2:500–2.
12. Edward Church, "The Life of Col. Church," in [Benjamin and] Thomas Church, *History of King Philip's War*, ed. Samuel G. Drake, p. xii. The authorship of the work is ascribed to Thomas Church by Vail in *Voice of the Old Frontier*, following the signature on the title page. The Library of Congress lists Benjamin Church as author and Thomas Church as editor. Editors of editions are inconsistent in ascribing authorship (see entries in the Selected Bibliography). It seems reasonable to list Benjamin and Thomas Church as joint authors, since Benjamin Church notes in the text ("To the Reader") that the work is composed by his son Thomas from his own "minutes" (presumably a diary or journal and copies of official correspondence).
13. Benjamin [and Thomas] Church, "To the Reader," *History of King Philip's War*, ed. Henry Martyn Dexter, [pp. i–iii, immediately preceding text]. All subsequent references are to this edition.
14. *History of King Philip's War*, pp. 69–71.
15. *Puritan Pronaos*, p. 194.
16. Increase Mather, "An Historical Discourse Concerning the Prevalency of Prayer," in *A Relation of the Troubles Which Have Hapned in New-England, by Reason of the Indians There*, reprinted as *Early History of New England: Being a Relation of Hostile Passages*, p. 245.
17. "To the Reader," *History of King Philip's War*, [p. ii].
18. Ibid., [p. iii].
19. "Historical Discourse Concerning the Prevalency of Prayer," p. 256.

20. *History of King Philip's War*, pp. 56–59.

21. Cotton Mather, quoted in George Howe, *Mount Hope: A New England Chronicle*, p. 44; *History of the Indian Wars* 1:148.

22. *History of King Philip's War*, p. 122.

23. "Historical Discourse Concerning the Prevalency of Prayer," p. 257.

24. *History of King Philip's War*, pp. 45–46.

25. Ibid., p. 28.

26. Ibid., pp. 33, 37–38; *History of the Indian Wars* 1:81.

27. *History of King Philip's War*, pp. 20–22.

28. *Magnalia Christi Americana* 2:497, 499.

29. F. O. Matthiessen, *American Renaissance*, p. 640.

30. *History of King Philip's War*, p. 42.

31. Ibid., p. 25.

32. *History of the Indian Wars* 1:87.

33. *History of King Philip's War*, pp. 73–74.

34. Ibid., pp. 80–82.

35. Ibid., pp. 97–98.

36. *History of the Indian Wars* 1:251, 268–69.

37. "Historical Discourse Concerning the Prevalency of Prayer," pp. 258–59.

38. *History of the Indian Wars* 1:263.

39. Ibid., p. 265.

40. *Magnalia Christi Americana* 2:499.

41. *History of King Philip's War*, pp. 151–53.

42. Ibid., pp. 149, 164.

43. Ibid., pp. 168–71.

44. Ibid., pp. 171–72.

45. *Big House Ceremony*, p. 65.

46. Ibid.

47. *History of King Philip's War*, p. 179.

48. *History of the Indian Wars* 1:276–78.

49. *Half-Century of Conflict*, p. 95.

50. *New Golden Bough*, p. 3.

51. Ibid., p. 194.

52. Ibid., p. 181.

53. *History of King Philip's War*, pp. 181–82.

Chapter 7: The Search for a Hero

1. Thomas Symmes, *Lovewell Lamented: Or, A Sermon Occasion'd by the Fall of the Brave Capt. John Lovewell*, reprinted in Frederic Kidder, "The Expeditions of Captain John Lovewell, and His Encounters with the Indians," p. 40. The second edition of *Lovewell Lamented* has the variant title, *Historical Memoirs Concerning the Late Fight at Piggwackett*.

2. Ibid., pp. 52–53.

3. Ibid., pp. 56–57.

4. "Song of Lovewell's Fight," in the "Expeditions of Captain John Lovewell," pp. 96–97.

5. "The Mournful Elegy on Mr. Jonathan Frye, 1725," in "Expeditions of Captain John Lovewell," pp. 99–101.

6. John Mason, "A Brief History of the Pequot War," ed. Thomas Prince, Collections of the Massachusetts Historical Society, 2d ser., 8 (1819):151.

7. Ibid., p. 144.

8. Thomas Prince, in *Brief History of the Pequot War*, p. 121.

9. Ibid., p. 125.

10. Ibid., pp. 127–28.

11. Ibid., p. 126.

12. Robert Rogers, *Journals of Major Robert Rogers*, p. 113.

13. Ibid., pp. iv–v.

14. George Chapman, Ben Jonson, and John Marston, "Eastward Hoe," in *Elizabethan Plays*, ed. Hazelton Spencer, p. 496.

15. Edward Ward, *A Trip to New-England: With a Character of the Country and People, both English and Indians*, pp. 3–9.

16. Ebenezer Cooke, "The Sotweed Factor," in Kenneth Silverman, ed., *Colonial American Poetry*, pp. 289–90.

17. Ibid., p. 301.

18. Ibid., p. 283.

19. Ebenezer Cooke, "Sotweed Redivivus," in "The Maryland Muse," ed. Lawrence C. Wroth, pp. 327–35.

20. [Thomas Shepard], "The Day-Breaking, If Not the Sun-Rising of the Gospell with the Indians in New-England," p. 17.

21. Henry Whitfield, "The Light Appearing More and More To-wards the Perfect Day," pp. 146–47.

22. John Eliot, "A Late and Further Manifestation of the Progress of the Gospel Amongst the Indians in New-England," pp. 269–72.

23. John Eliot and Thomas Mayhew, "Tears of Repentance: Or, A Further Narrative of the Progress of the Gospel amongst the Indians in New-England," p. 246.

24. "A Late and Further Manifestation of the Progress," p. 274.

25. Ibid.

26. *Tears of Repentance*, pp. 232–33.

27. Ibid., p. 229.

28. "A Late and Further Manifestation of the Progress," pp. 277–78.

29. David Brainerd, in James M. Sherwood, ed., *Memoirs of David Brainerd*, pp. 43, 62.

30. Ibid., pp. 59, 107.

31. Samuel Hopkins, *Historical Memoirs, Relating to the Housatunnuck Indians*, pp. 164, 167–80.

32. *History of the Five Nations*, p. vi.

33. Ibid.

34. Ibid., p. xvii.

35. Ibid., p. xx. See also Timberlake, *Memoirs*, p. 93.

36. *History of the Five Nations*, p. xvii.

37. [Corneille] de Pauw, *Recherches philosophiques sur les américains* 1:xi, 2, 34–35. See translation in "From the *Philosophical Investigations of the Americans*,"

in Henry Steele Commager and Elmo Giordanetti, eds., *Was America A Mistake?*, pp. 79–80, 100. See also Durand Echeverria, *Mirage in the West*, pp. 3–15.

38. F. M. A. Voltaire, *Lettres philosophiques* (1734), pp. 82–95.

39. Roger Wolcott, "A Brief Account of the Agency of . . . the Honourable John Winthrop, Esq; in the Court of King Charles the Second," *The Poems of Roger Wolcott*, pp. 32–33.

40. Ibid., p. 37.

41. Ibid., p. 52.

42. Ibid., p. 46.

43. Ibid., pp. 56–57.

44. Ibid., p. 66.

45. Ibid., p. 67.

46. Ibid., pp. 67–68.

47. Ibid., pp. 72–73.

48. John Woolman, *Journal*, p. 132.

49. Benjamin Franklin, *Autobiography*, p. 132.

50. Ibid., p. 133.

51. See William Byrd, *Histories of the Dividing Line Between Virginia and North Carolina*, ed. William K. Boyd, pp. v–xxxix; J. A. Leo Lemay, "Richard Lewis and Augustan American Poetry," *PMLA* 83, no. 1 (March 1968):80–81; and *Colonial American Poetry*, pp. 258–59.

52. See *Colonial American Poetry*, pp. 259–60.

53. *Voice of the Old Frontier*, pp. 92–314, and *Colonial American Poetry*, pp. 259–63.

54. *Colonial American Poetry*, p. 263.

55. *Histories of the Dividing Line*, pp. 2–3.

56. Ibid., pp. 3–4.

57. Ibid., p. 4.

58. Ibid.

59. Ibid., pp. 4, 120.

60. Ibid., p. 46.

61. Ibid., p. 50.

62. Ibid., p. 57.

63. Ibid., pp. 54, 92.

64. Ibid., p. 58.

65. Ibid., p. 291.

66. Ibid., p. 281.

67. Ibid., p. 202.

68. Ibid., p. 70.

69. Ibid., p. 59.

70. Ibid., p. 114.

71. Ibid., p. 116.

72. Ibid., p. 115.

Chapter 8: A Gallery of Types

1. *Golden Multitudes*, pp. 303–5.

2. Samuel Davies, *Virginia's Danger and Remedy*, pp. 7–8.

3. Ibid., pp. 9–11.

4. William Vinal, *A Sermon on the Accursed Thing that Hinders Success and Victory in War*, pp. 12–15.

5. [Charles Chauncy], *A Letter to a Friend . . . [on] the Ohio-defeat*, p. 9.

6. Thomas Barton, *Unanimity and Public Spirit*, pp. viii, x.

7. [William Smith], *Historical Account of Bouquet's Expedition Against the Ohio Indians* (reprint title), p. 19.

8. Ibid., p. 95.

9. Ibid.; Winthrop D. Jordan, *White over Black*, pp. 90–91.

10. *White over Black*, pp. 96–97.

11. Ibid., p. 98.

12. Ibid.

13. Ibid., p. 110.

14. Rogers, *Journals*, p. 91.

15. Robert Rogers, *A Concise Account of North America*, quoted in Dorothy A. Dondore, *The Prairie and the Making of Middle America*, p. 113.

16. Robert Rogers, *Ponteach: Or The Savages of America*, reprinted in Montrose J. Moses, *Representative Plays by American Dramatists* 1:123.

17. Ibid., p. 125.

18. Ibid., pp. 129–30.

19. Ibid., pp. 131–32.

20. Ibid., p. 135.

21. Ibid., pp. 155–56.

22. Ibid., pp. 174–79.

23. Ibid., p. 188.

24. Ibid., p. 196.

25. Ibid., p. 205.

26. Ibid., p. 206.

27. Ibid.

28. John Dryden, *The Indian Emperour*, in *Works* 2:345.

29. Ibid., pp. 325–26.

30. *Ponteach*, p. 208.

31. Hugh Henry Brackenridge, *Incidents of the Insurrection in the Western Parts of Pennsylvania* 2:6–8.

32. *Golden Multitudes*, p. 303; see also *Voice of the Old Frontier*, entries on editions of Dickenson.

33. Jonathan Dickenson, *Journal*, p. 12.

34. Ibid., p. 26.

35. Thomas Jefferson, *Notes on the State of Virginia*, p. 21.

36. Ibid., pp. 16–17.

37. Robert Eastburn, *A Faithful Narrative, of . . . his Late Captivity Among the Indians*, pp. 8, 43–44.

38. John Maylem, *Gallic Perfidy*, p. 7.

39. Ibid., p. 9.

40. Ibid., p. 8.

41. Ibid.

42. Ibid., p. 10.

43. Ibid., pp. 11–12.
44. Ibid., p. 15.
45. Ibid.
46. Ibid.
47. John Maylem, *The Conquest of Louisbourg*, p. 16.
48. Benjamin Franklin, "A Narrative of the Late Massacres, in Lancaster County, of a Number of Indians," *Papers* 11:48–49.
49. Ibid., p. 50.
50. Ethan Allen, *Narrative*, p. 21.
51. Ibid., p. 107.
52. *Bouquet's Expedition*, p. 76.
53. Ibid., pp. 76–77.
54. Ibid., p. 77.
55. Ibid., p. 78.
56. Ibid., p. 80.
57. Ibid., pp. 80–81.
58. Timberlake, *Memoirs*, p. 89.
59. Ibid., pp. 174–75.
60. *The Abraham Panther Captivity*, p. 172.
61. Chase S. and Stellanova Osborn, *Schoolcraft, Longfellow, Hiawatha*, pp. 144–45.
62. Michel Guillaume St. John de Crèvecoeur, *Letters from an American Farmer*, pp. 18–22.
63. Ibid., p. 51.
64. Ibid., p. 86.
65. Ibid., p. 40.
66. Ibid., pp. 42, 49.
67. Ibid., pp. 47–48.
68. Ibid., p. 49.
69. Ibid.
70. Ibid., pp. 77–78.
71. Ibid., pp. 203–4.
72. Ibid., pp. 205–7.
73. Ibid., p. 215.
74. Ibid., p. 223.
75. Ibid., pp. 208–9.
76. Ibid., p. 209.

Chapter 9: Narrative into Myth

1. John Walton, *John Filson of Kentucke*, pp. 31, 98.
2. Ibid., pp. 13–14.
3. Ibid., p. 20.
4. Reuben T. Durrett, *John Filson: The First Historian of Kentucky*, pp. 13–14; Walton, *John Filson*, pp. 24–27, 29.
5. Walton, *John Filson*, pp. 97–101.

6. Durrett, *John Filson*, pp. 15–16; Walton, *John Filson*, p. 28.

7. Durrett, *John Filson*, pp. 21–24; Walton, *John Filson*, p. 28. See John Filson, *The Discovery, Settlement and Present State of Kentucke*, p. 6; this work is cited hereafter as *Kentucke*.

8. *Kentucke*, pp. 85–86.

9. Ibid., pp. 95–96.

10. Ibid., pp. 105–6, 100–1.

11. Ibid., pp. 107–8.

12. Ibid., p. 109.

13. Ibid., pp. 49–50.

14. Ibid., p. 51.

15. Ibid., pp. 51–52.

16. Ibid., p. 53.

17. Ibid., pp. 53–54.

18. Ibid., p. 54.

19. Ibid., pp. 54–55.

20. "Personal Narrative," pp. 60–61.

21. *O Strange New World*, chap. 10.

22. *Kentucke*, pp. 55–56.

23. Ibid., p. 56.

24. Ibid.

25. Ibid., p. 64.

26. Ibid., pp. 64–65.

27. Ibid., p. 65.

28. Ibid.

29. Ibid., pp. 66–67.

30. Ibid., p. 73.

31. Ibid., pp. 74–75.

32. Ibid., p. 76.

33. Ibid., pp. 77–78.

34. Ibid., p. 80.

35. Ibid., pp. 80–81.

36. Ibid.

37. The following account of Boone's life is drawn primarily from the definitive biography by John Bakeless, *Daniel Boone: Master of the Wilderness*.

38. Ibid., pp. 405–6.

39. Ibid., p. 115.

40. Ibid., p. 67.

41. Ibid., pp. 344–46, 361–62, 405–6.

42. Ibid., pp. 55, 360.

43. Ibid., pp. 52, 404.

44. Ibid., p. 27; and Timothy Flint, *Biographical Memoir of Daniel Boone*, pp. 38–40.

45. "Love Song from the Papago," trans. Mary Austin, in Oscar Williams, ed., *A Little Treasury of American Poetry*, p. 14.

46. Bakeless, *Daniel Boone*, pp. 28–30.

47. *Hero with a Thousand Faces*, pp. 245–46.

48. "History, Manners, and Customs of the Indian Nations," pp. 250–51.

49. Juan E. Cirlot, *A Dictionary of Symbols*, pp. 146–47.

50. See Daniel Boorstin, *The Lost World of Thomas Jefferson*; see also Arthur K. Moore, *The Frontier Mind*.

51. Walton, *John Filson*, pp. 31, 41–43; Jefferson, *Papers* 7:568, 10:4–5.

52. Walton, *John Filson*, p. 117.

Chapter 10: Evolution of the National Hero

1. *Mirage in the West*, pp. 124–25, 144–45.

2. *Papers of Thomas Jefferson* 7:568, 10:4–5; Howard C. Rice, *Le Cultivateur américain*, p. 32.

3. *Mirage in the West*, pp. 144–45.

4. [Henri] Parraud, "Préface," in Filson, *Histoire de Kentucke*, trans. Parraud, pp. vii–viii.

5. Ibid., pp. iii–vi.

6. A fascinating example of these conventions as utilized in the thinking of a coterie poet is André Chenier's "L'Amérique." This long poem, based on Filson (who is mentioned in the text), consists of notes and fragments of verse that record Chenier's search in the vocabulary of stereotypes for a model of the hero suited to both the French Enlightenment and the Filsonian frontier. See André Chenier, *Oeuvres complètes*. See also *Mirage in the West*, pp. 125–67; Jean Fabre, *André Chenier*, p. 195; and *Cultivateur américain*, pp. 197–98.

7. Ralph L. Rusk, "The Adventures of Gilbert Imlay," *Indiana University Studies* 10, no. 57 (March 1923):6–13; Bakeless, *Daniel Boone*, p. 343.

8. Ralph M. Wardle, *Mary Wollstonecraft*, pp. 184–86.

9. "Adventures of Gilbert Imlay," pp. 17–21.

10. Oliver F. Emerson, "Notes on Gilbert Imlay, Early American Writer," *PMLA* 39, no. 2 (June 1924):437–38. For contemporary British reaction to the Imlay book, see the *Monthly Review* (London), August 1792, and *Critical Review* (London), 1793.

11. *Cultivateur américain*, p. 214.

12. "Notes on Gilbert Imlay," pp. 427–31; Sister Eugenia, "Coleridge's Scheme of Pantisocracy and American Travel Accounts," *PMLA* 45, no. 4 (December 1930):1075–77; *Cultivateur américain*, pp. 214–15; Gilbert Imlay, *The Emigrants*, p. 298.

13. For another source of Robert Southey's "Madoc," see Samuel Cole Williams, "Introduction" to Timberlake, *Memoirs*.

14. Gilbert Imlay, *A Topographical Description of the Western Territory of North America*, pp. 25, 151–52.

15. Ibid., pp. 29, 136–38, 56–57.

16. *Emigrants*, pp. 246–53. The rescue scene is an overelaborate reworking of Boone's rescue of his daughter; it may later have been copied by Charles Brockden Brown in *Edgar Huntly*.

17. In 1793–94 it appeared as a single volume in Vermont and in *Beers's Almanac* in Hartford. During the uproar over Shay's Rebellion on the Massachusetts frontier, it appeared in Carey's *American Museum* (Philadelphia, 1787), an ex-

tremely influential magazine whose list of subscribers included most of the intellectual and political leadership of the states (then in Philadelphia for the Constitutional Convention) as well as foreign diplomats accredited to the government (like Crèvecoeur). For a complete bibliography of the Boone narrative, its peregrinations, and its service as a source for other works about the frontier, see my *Emergence of a Myth,* appended material.

18. William Bartram, *The Travels of William Bartram,* pp. 44–46.

19. Alonso Decalves, *New Travels to the Westward, or Unknown Parts of America,* pp. 13–14.

20. Ibid., pp. 19–20.

21. Ibid., pp. 44–45.

22. Alexander Henry, *Travels and Adventures in Canada and the Indian Territories between the Years 1760 and 1776,* pp. 104–5.

23. Ibid., p. 161.

24. Ibid., pp. 161–62.

25. James Smith, *An Account of the Remarkable Occurrences in the Life and Travels . . . During His Captivity with the Indians,* pp. 160–61.

26. Ibid., p. 161.

27. Mason Locke Weems, *The Life of George Washington,* pp. 32–34.

28. Ibid., p. 43.

29. Ibid.

30. Ibid., p. 44.

31. Quoted in *Mirage in the West,* pp. 204–5.

32. Michel Guillaume St. John de Crèvecoeur, *A Journey into Northern Pennsylvania and the State of New York,* pp. 314–15.

33. Ibid.

34. Ibid., pp. 10–11, 14.

35. Ibid., p. xvi. Weems inverts Crèvecoeur's eulogy, quoting Napoleon's envy of the permanence of Washington's "empire" (*Life of George Washington,* p. 1).

36. Constantin F. C. Volney, *A View of the Soil and Climate of the United States,* pp. x, xiv–xv.

37. Ibid., pp. 17–18.

38. Timothy Dwight, *Greenfield Hill,* p. 12.

39. Ibid., p. 18.

40. Ibid.

41. Ibid., p. 50.

42. Ibid., p. 52.

43. Ibid., p. 19.

44. Ibid., pp. 104–5.

45. Joel Barlow, *The Vision of Columbus,* p. 53.

46. Ibid., pp. 54–55.

47. Ibid.

48. Ibid., p. 55.

49. *Incidents of the Insurrection* 1:34, 2:6–8, 101–2.

50. Daniel Bryan, "Introduction," *The Mountain Muse,* pp. 2–[6].

51. Ibid., p. [6].

52. Ibid., pp. 21–22.

53. Ibid., pp. 22, 30.

54. Ibid., p. 52.

55. Ibid., pp. 52–53.

56. Ibid., p. 54.

57. Ibid., p. 56.

58. Ibid., pp. 58–59.

59. Ibid., p. 131.

60. Ibid.

61. Ibid., pp. 164–66.

62. Jeremiah Evarts ("William Penn"), *Essays on the Present Crisis in the Condition of the American Indians*, p. 8.

63. Ibid., pp. 8–9.

64. Benjamin B. Thatcher, *Indian Biography* 1:176. See also Washington Irving, "Philip of Pokanoket," in *The Sketch-Book.*

65. Black Hawk, *Black Hawk: An Autobiography*, [p. 1].

66. Ibid.

67. Ibid., p. 89.

68. Elias Boudinot, *A Star in the West*, p. i.

69. Thomas F. O'Dea, *The Mormons*, pp. 22, 25.

70. Henry Wadsworth Longfellow, *The Song of Hiawatha*, pp. 7–8.

71. Ibid., pp. 177–78.

72. Ibid., pp. 186–87.

73. Ibid., p. 282.

Chapter 11: Society and Solitude

1. See Gilbert Chinard, "Notes sur la voyage de Chateaubriand en Amérique," *University of California Publications in Modern Philology* 4, no. 2 (10 November 1915):328; Thomas Walker, *Chateaubriand's Natural Scenery*, pp. 104–5.

2. Cited in "Voyage de Chateuabriand," p. 328. My translation.

3. François-René de Chateaubriand, "Atala," in *Les Martyrs; Atala; René; . . .* , p. 495. For a full discussion of the influence of the myth of America on Chateaubriand, see Gilbert Chinard, *L'Exotisme américain dans l'oeuvre de Chateaubriand.*

4. Charles Brockden Brown, *Edgar Huntly*, p. xxiii.

5. Ibid.

6. "Atala," p. 495.

7. Ibid., p. 503.

8. *Kentucke*, p. 55; "Atala," p. 504.

9. *Kentucke*, p. 55.

10. François-René de Chateaubriand, "René," in *Les Martyrs; Atala; René; . . .* , p. 558. My translation.

11. "René," p. 563.

12. *Kentucke*, p. 53.

13. "René," p. 566.

14. Ibid., p. 568. My translation.

15. See *L'Exotisme américain*, p. 214.
16. See ibid., p. 213. My translation.
17. "Atala," p. 510.
18. *A View of the Soil and Climate of the United States*, p. xxii.
19. Ibid., p. 352.
20. Ibid., p. 395.
21. Ibid., pp. 371–72, 399.
22. *Edgar Huntly*, p. 18.
23. Ibid., pp. 105–7.
24. Ibid., p. 180.
25. Ibid., p. 196.
26. Ibid., p. 256.
27. Ibid., p. 292.
28. Ibid., p. 307.
29. Ibid.
30. Byron, *Don Juan: A Variorum Edition*, 3:143–45.
31. Willis W. Pratt, "Notes," ibid. 4:177–78.
32. *L'Exotisme américain*, p. 98.

Chapter 12: The Fragmented Image

1. See my "Bibliography of Filson's 'Boone Narrative,' 1784–1848," *Emergence of a Myth*.
2. Bakeless, *Daniel Boone*, p. 394.
3. Ralph L. Rusk, *The Literature of the Middle Western Frontier* 1:272–73.
4. Frank L. Mott, *A History of American Magazines* 1:207, 312.
5. Samuel L. Metcalf, "A Collection of Some of the Most Interesting Narratives of Indian Warfare in the West," pp. 6, 8.
6. Randolph C. Randall, *James Hall*, p. 130.
7. James Hall, *Letters from the West*, pp. 239, 242–43.
8. Ibid., pp. 251–52.
9. Ibid., p. 259.
10. James Hall, *Sketches of History, Life and Manners in the West* 1:242–43.
11. James Hall, "The Backwoodsman," *Legends of the West*, p. 243.
12. Ibid., p. 252.
13. Ibid., p. 253.
14. Ibid., pp. 253–54.
15. John A. McClung, *Sketches of Western Adventure*, p. 45.
16. Ibid., p. 49.
17. Ibid., p. 86.
18. William H. Goetzmann, "The Mountain Man as Jacksonian Man," in Hennig Cohen, ed., *The American Culture*, pp. 64, 68–70.
19. [Johnson Jones Hooper], *Some Adventures of Captain Simon Suggs*, p. 13.
20. David Crockett, *Narrative of the Life*, pp. 167–70. This discussion of the character of the frontier hero is based on *The Frontier Mind*.
21. Crockett, *Narrative*, pp. 176–77.
22. See Hennig Cohen and William B. Dillingham, "Introduction," *Humor of*

the Old Southwest, pp. xii–xiii; Constance M. Rourke, *American Humor*, chaps. 2, 5; *American Renaissance*, pp. 635–45; *Some Adventures of Captain Simon Suggs*, esp. chaps. 1, 2, 5, 10; Augustus B. Longstreet, "The Character of a Native Georgian," *Georgia Scenes*, pp. 34–64; and Joseph G. Baldwin, "Sharp Financiering," in *Humor of the Old Southwest*, pp. 262–63.

23. See, for example, *Some Adventures of Captain Simon Suggs*, chaps. 1, 7.

24. See, for example, Longstreet, "The Horse Swap," *Georgia Scenes*, pp. 22–33.

25. Daniel Boorstin, *The Americans: The National Experience*, pp. 276–98.

26. *Some Adventures of Captain Simon Suggs*, p. 8; "Introduction," *Humor of the Old Southwest*, p. xi.

27. Henry Nash Smith, *Virgin Land*, pp. 64–76; Vernon L. Parrington, *Main Currents in American Thought* 2:222–37.

28. James K. Folsom, "Introduction" to Timothy Flint, *Biographical Memoir of Daniel Boone*, pp. 7–12; *Main Currents in American Thought* 2:162–64.

29. Timothy Flint, *Indian Wars of the West*, pp. 126–27.

30. Quoted in George Turner, *Traits of Indian Character* 2:140.

31. *Indian Wars of the West*, p. 359.

32. Ibid., p. 53.

33. Ibid., pp. 53–54.

34. Ibid., p. 54. See also the assertion in *Biographical Memoir* that even before he knew them, Boone had a "peculiar intuition" of their character.

35. *Biographical Memoir*, pp. 29–30.

36. Ibid., p. 63.

37. Ibid., p. 172; see also p. 63.

38. Ibid., p. 171.

39. Benjamin Drake, *Life of Tecumseh and of His Brother the Prophet*, pp. 21–22.

40. Ibid., p. 83.

41. Ibid.

42. Samuel Houston, *The Life of Sam Houston*, pp. 22–24.

43. Ibid., pp. 47, 64, 15.

44. Ibid., pp. 51, 62, 65.

45. Joseph Sabin questions whether Henry Trumbull was a real name or a pseudonym (*Bibliotheca Americana*). G. H. and M. C. Brown, *A Directory of Printing, Publishing, Bookselling, and Allied Trades in Rhode Island to 1865*, p. 170, gives the biography of a man of that name, with the same dates and locations of offices. See also Providence Typographical Union, *Printers and Printing in Providence: 1762–1907*, p. lxxxvi.

46. Henry Trumbull, *History of the Indian Wars*, p. 3.

47. Henry Trumbull, *History of the Discovery of America: of the Landing of Our Forefathers, at Plymouth, and of Their Most Remarkable Engagements with the Indians, in New-England* (Norwich, 1811), pp. iii–iv.

48. Ibid., pp. 118–25.

49. Henry Trumbull, *Western Emigration: Journal of Doctor Jeremiah S[im]pleton's Tour to Ohio*, pp. 3–4.

50. Ibid., p. 7.

51. Ibid., p. 15.

52. Ibid., p. 14.

53. Cited in *Virgin Land*, p. 205.

54. William Charvat, *Literary Publishing in America*, p. 37.

55. John Filson, "Life and Adventures of Colonel Daniel Boone" (1823), p. 26.

56. See chap. 3, note 6.

57. "Life and Adventures of Colonel Daniel Boone" (1823), p. 23.

58. Ibid., pp. 27–28.

59. See, for example, William L. Katz, ed., *Five Slave Narratives*; Josiah Henson, *Father Henson's Story of His Own Life*; Arna W. Bontemps, ed., *Great Slave Narratives*.

60. William R. Taylor, *Cavalier and Yankee*, pp. 287–92; Irving H. Bartlett, *Wendell Phillips*, p. 43. Also cf. *The Anti-Slavery Almanac*, 1840, p. 7, and "Decennium Luctuosum," pp. 212, 210.

61. *Cavalier and Yankee*, pp. 289–90.

62. Maria Monk, *Awful Disclosures*, esp. chaps. 6, 7, 9; Charles W. Frothingham, *The Convent's Doom*. Discussed in Ray Allen Billington, *The Protestant Crusade, 1800–1860*, pp. 345–67.

63. Luther Roby, ed., in Robert Rogers, *Reminiscences of the French War*, p. 4.

64. Ibid., p. 7.

65. Ibid., p. 146.

66. Ibid., p. 174.

67. *Golden Multitudes*, p. 305.

68. *Narrative of the Life of Mrs. Mary Jemison*, pp. 52–53.

69. Ibid., pp. 126–27.

70. Ibid., p. 150.

71. Ibid., p. 153.

72. Catherine M. Sedgwick, *Hope Leslie* 2:71.

73. Ibid., p. 230.

74. Ibid., p. 229.

75. Ibid., p. 233.

76. Ibid.

77. William Cullen Bryant, "The Prairies," *Poetical Works*, pp. 132–33.

78. Ibid., p. 133.

79. John M. Peck, "The Life of Daniel Boon," *Library of American Biography* 13:21–22.

80. Ibid., p. 22.

81. Ibid., pp. 186–87.

82. Ibid., pp. 188–89.

83. Ibid., pp. 195, 197, 198.

84. See "Introduction," *Humor of the Old Southwest*, pp. x–xi.

85. William Gilmore Simms, "Daniel Boon," *Views and Reviews in American Literature, History and Fiction*, p. 150.

86. Ibid., p. 155.

Chapter 13: Man without a Cross

The discussion of Cooper in this chapter owes much to the treatment of Cooper by Arthur K. Moore (*The Frontier Mind*), Henry Nash Smith (*Virgin Land*), and Leslie Fiedler (*Love and Death in the American Novel*).

1. Walter Scott, *Rob Roy*, p. vii.
2. See, in this connection, Richard Chase, *The American Novel and Its Tradition*, pp. 1–28.
3. Thomas B. Thorpe, "The Big Bear of Arkansas," *Humor of the Old Southwest*, p. 270.
4. Ibid., pp. 271, 273.
5. Ibid., p. 271.
6. Ibid., p. 276.
7. Ibid.
8. Ibid., p. 278.
9. Ibid., p. 279.
10. Ibid.
11. James Fenimore Cooper, *The Pioneers*, pp. 156–57.
12. Ibid., pp. 160–61.
13. Ibid., pp. 161–62.
14. Ibid., p. 270.
15. *Dictionary of Symbols*, pp. 146–47.
16. *Pioneers*, p. 426.
17. *New Golden Bough*, pp. 129–43.
18. *Pioneers*, pp. 436, 438.
19. Ibid., pp. 437–39.
20. James Fenimore Cooper, *The Last of the Mohicans*, p. 70.
21. James Fenimore Cooper, *The Prairie*, p. 8.
22. James Fenimore Cooper, *The Deerslayer*, pp. 129, 51–53.
23. Ibid., p. 3.
24. Ibid., p. 106.
25. Ibid., p. 116.
26. Ibid., p. 382.
27. *Black Elk Speaks*, pp. 2–5.
28. *Deerslayer*, p. 458.
29. *Virgin Land*, pp. 71–73.
30. *Last of the Mohicans*, p. 70.
31. *Deerslayer*, p. 115.
32. Ibid., p. 77.
33. William Gilmore Simms, *Guy Rivers*, pp. 58–59.
34. Ibid., p. 60.
35. William Gilmore Simms, *The Yemassee*, pp. 182, 184–85, 357.
36. Curtis Dahl, "Introduction" to Robert M. Bird, *Nick of the Woods*, pp. 16–18.
37. Francis Parkman, "James Fenimore Cooper," in Warren S. Walker, ed., *Leatherstocking and the Critics*, pp. 4–6.

38. *Nick of the Woods*, p. 32.
39. Ibid., pp. 46–47.

Chapter 14: A Pyramid of Skulls

1. George Eliot, "[An Early British Review]" (1856), reprinted in Henry David Thoreau, *Walden and Civil Disobedience*, ed. Owen Thomas, p. 265.
2. Ralph Waldo Emerson, "Thoreau," reprinted ibid., p. 280.
3. Ibid., p. 275.
4. Henry David Thoreau, *Journal*, 27 March 1841, *Works*, ed. Henry Seidel Canby, p. 9.
5. Henry David Thoreau, *A Week on the Concord and Merrimack Rivers*, pp. 261–62.
6. Ibid., p. 262.
7. Ibid., p. 319.
8. Ibid., p. 279.
9. Ibid., p. 275.
10. Ibid., p. 277.
11. Ibid., p. 278.
12. Ibid., p. 282.
13. Ibid., p. 54.
14. Ibid., p. 56.
15. Ibid., pp. 56–57.
16. Ibid., p. 56.
17. Ibid., p. 57.
18. Ibid.
19. *Walden*, p. 1.
20. Ibid., p. 2.
21. Ibid., p. 13.
22. Ibid., p. 11.
23. Ibid., pp. 50–51.
24. Ibid., p. 117.
25. Ibid., p. 211.
26. Ibid., pp. 139–40.
27. Ibid., pp. 140–41.
28. Ibid., pp. 142, 147.
29. Ibid., p. 146.
30. Ibid.
31. Ibid., p. 148.
32. Ibid., p. 157.
33. Henry David Thoreau, "The Natural History of Massachusetts," *Works*, p. 659.
34. Henry David Thoreau, "Wild Apples," *Works*, pp. 718–19.
35. Ibid., pp. 719, 722.
36. Henry David Thoreau, "Walking," *Works*, pp. 659–60.
37. Ibid., pp. 669, 671.
38. Ibid., pp. 672–73.
39. Ibid., p. 673.

40. Ibid.
41. *Walden*, p. 122.
42. Herman Melville, *Moby-Dick*, p. 2.
43. Ibid., p. 6.
44. Ibid., p. 276.
45. Ibid., p. 119.
46. Ibid., p. 63.
47. Ibid., p. 413.
48. Ibid., pp. 335–36, 344.
49. Ibid., p. 7.
50. See ibid., pp. 189, 289, 343, 392. For a full account of Melville's uses of frontier sources and images, see Edwin Fussell, *Frontier: American Literature and the American West*, pp. 256–80.
51. *Moby-Dick*, p. 69.
52. Ibid., pp. 534–35.
53. Ibid., pp. 194–95.
54. Ibid., p. 392.
55. Ibid., p. 538.
56. Ibid., p. 166.
57. Ibid., p. 564.
58. *Studies in Classic American Literature*, p. 59.
59. *Main Currents in American Thought* 2:178–79.
60. Violet S. de Laszlo, "Introduction," *Psyche and Symbol*, p. xxxi; Michael P. Rogin, "Liberal Society and the Indian Question," pp. 269, 273–74. Rogin suggests that the association of the Indian with libidinous and unconscious forces may derive from the conception of the Indian cultures as representing the "childhood" of the human race, as opposed to the "adult" or "mature" civilization of the whites. In this connection, see "The Psychology of the Child Archetype" and "The Special Phenomenology of the Child Archetype," and see *Hero with a Thousand Faces*, pp. 318–34.
61. See, for example, George Armstrong Custer, *My Life on the Plains*, pp. 165, 185, 189–90, 245, 247–53; and Charles J. Brill, *The Conquest of the Southern Plains*, esp. p. 246.
62. For a fuller discussion see my "Dreams and Genocide: The American Myth of Regeneration through Violence." See also "Liberal Society and the Indian Question," pp. 271, 312.
63. Lyndon Baines Johnson, "American Policy in Viet-Nam," in Marcus G. Raskin and Bernard B. Fall, eds., *The Viet-Nam Reader*, p. 344.
64. *Kentucke*, pp. 60–61.
65. "American Policy in Viet-Nam," pp. 348–49.

Selected Bibliography

Punctuation and capitalization have been regularized.

Abraham Panther Captivity, The. Edited by Robert William Glenroie Vail. Reprinted from the Norwich, 1787, edition. *The American Book Collector* 2 (August–September 1932): 165–72.

Adair, James. *The History of the American Indians: Particularly Those Nations Adjoining to the Mississippi, East and West Florida, Georgia, South and North Carolina and Virginia; Containing an Account of Their Origin, Language, Manners, Religious and Civil Customs, Laws, Form of Government, Punishments, Conduct in War and Domestic Life, Their Habits, Diet, Agriculture, Manufactures, Diseases and Method of Cure, and Other Particulars, Sufficient to Render it a Complete Indian System. . . .* London: Edward and Charles Dilly, 1775.

Adams, Charles Francis. *Three Episodes of Massachusetts History: The Settlement of Boston Bay; The Antinomian Controversy; A Study of Church and Town Government.* Boston: Houghton Mifflin, 1892.

Allen, Ethan. *The Narrative of Colonel Ethan Allen.* Edited by Brooke Hindle. Facsimile of the Walpole, N.H., 1807, edition. American Experience Series. New York: Corinth Books, 1961.

———. *Reason the Only Oracle of Man.* Introduction by John Pell. Facsimile of the Bennington, 1789, edition. New York: Scholars Facsimiles and Reprints, 1940.

Andrews, Charles M., ed. *Narratives of the Insurrections, 1675–1690.* Original Narratives of Early American History Series. New York: Barnes and Noble, 1943.

Andrist, Ralph K. *The Long Death: The Last Days of the Plains Indians.* New York: Macmillan, Collier Books, 1969.

Angoff, Charles. *A Literary History of the American People.* Vol. 1. New York: Alfred Knopf, 1931.

Antislavery Almanac, 1840, The. Boston: [no publisher], 1840.

Bakeless, John. *Daniel Boone: Master of the Wilderness.* New York: William Morrow, 1939.

Banks, Charles E. "Thomas Morton of Merrymount," *Proceedings of the Massachusetts Historical Society* 58 (December 1924): 157–93.

Barlow, Joel. *The Columbiad: A Poem.* 2 vols. Philadelphia: C. and A. Conrad, 1809.

————. *The Vision of Columbus: A Poem in Nine Books.* Hartford: Hudson and Goodwin, 1787.

Bartlett, Irving H. *Wendell Phillips: Brahmin Radical.* Boston: Beacon Press, 1961.

Barton, Thomas. *Unanimity and Public Spirit: A Sermon, Preached at Carlisle, and some other Episcopal Churches, in the Counties of York and Cumberland, soon after General Braddock's Defeat.* . . . Philadelphia: B. Franklin and D. Hall, 1755.

Bartram, William. *The Travels of William Bartram.* Edited by Mark Van Doren. Introduction by John Livingston Lowes. Reprinted from the Philadelphia, 1791, edition. New York: Barnes and Noble, Facsimile Library, 1940.

[Beverley, Robert.] *The History and Present State of Virginia, in Four Parts. I. The History of the First Settlement in Virginia, and the Government thereof to the Present Time. II. The Natural Productions and Conveniencies of the Country, Suited to Trade and Improvement. III. The Native Indians, Their Religion, Laws, and Customs, in War and Peace. IV. The Present State of the Country, as to the Polity of the Government, and the Improvements of the Land.* London: R. Parker, 1705.

Billington, Ray Allen. *The Protestant Crusade, 1800–1860: A Study of the Origins of American Nativism.* New York: Macmillan, 1938.

Bird, Robert Montgomery. *Nick of the Woods.* Edited by Curtis Dahl. New Haven: College and University Press, 1967.

Black Elk. *Black Elk Speaks: Being the Life Story of a Holy Man of the Oglala Sioux.* Translated by John G. Neihardt. New York: William Morrow, 1932.

Black Hawk. *Black Hawk: An Autobiography.* Edited by Donald Jackson. Urbana: University of Illinois Press, 1955.

Bohannan, Paul, and Plog, Fred, eds. *Beyond the Frontier: Social Process and Cultural Change.* New York: Natural History Press, 1967.

Bontemps, Arna Wendell, ed. *Great Slave Narratives.* Boston: Beacon Press, 1969.

Boorstin, Daniel. *The Americans: The Colonial Experience.* New York: Vintage Books, 1958.

————. *The Americans: The National Experience.* New York: Random House, 1965.

————. *The Lost World of Thomas Jefferson.* Boston: Beacon Press, 1960.

Boudinot, Elias. *A Star in the West: Or, A Humble Attempt to Discover the Ten Lost Tribes of Israel, Preparatory to Their Return to Their Beloved City Jerusalem.* Trenton: D. Fenton, S. Hutchinson, and J. Dunham, 1816.

Bourne, Edward Gaylord, and Olson, Julius E., eds. *The Northmen, Columbus, and Cabot: 985–1503.* New York: Charles Scribner's Sons, 1906.

Brackenridge, Hugh Henry. *Incidents of the Insurrection in the Western Parts of Pennsylvania, in the Year 1794.* 2 vols. Philadelphia: John M'Culloch, 1795.

————. *Modern Chivalry.* Edited by Claude M. Newlin. New York: Hafner, 1962.

Bradford, William. *Of Plymouth Plantation.* Edited by Samuel Eliot Morison. New York: Modern Library, 1967.

Brief and True Narration of the Late Wars Risen in New-England: Occasioned by the Quarrelsome Disposition, and Perfidious Carriage of the Barbarous, Savage and Heathenish Natives There, A. London: Printed for J. S., 1675.

Brill, Charles J. *The Conquest of the Southern Plains.* Oklahoma City: Golden Saga Publishers, 1938.

Bristol, Roger P. *Evans' American Bibliography: Supplementary Checking Edition.* Charlottesville: Bibliographic Society of the University of Virginia, 1962.

Brown, Charles Brockden. *Edgar Huntly: Or, Memoirs of a Sleepwalker.* Edited by David Lee Brown. New York: Macmillan, 1928.

Brown, Glenn H., and Brown, Maude C. *A Directory of Printing, Publishing, Bookselling, and Allied Trades in Rhode Island to 1865.* New York: New York Public Library, 1958.

Bryan, Daniel. *The Mountain Muse: Comprising the Adventures of Daniel Boone; and the Power of Virtuous and Refined Beauty.* Harrisonburg, Va.: Davidson and Bourne, 1813.

Bryant, William Cullen. *The Poetical Works of William Cullen Bryant.* Chronology of Bryant's life and poems and bibliography by Henry C. Sturges. Memoir of his life by Richard Henry Stoddard. Roslyn Edition. New York: D. Appleton, 1925.

Bunyan, John. *Pilgrim's Progress.* Edited by Louis Martz. New York: Holt, Rinehart, and Winston, Rinehart Editions, 1965.

Burr, George Lincoln, ed. *Narratives of the Witchcraft Cases: 1648–1706.* Original Narratives of Early American History Series. New York: Barnes and Noble, 1966.

Butler, Mann. *A History of the Commonwealth of Kentucky.* Louisville: Wilcox, Dickerman, 1834.

Byrd, William. *Another Secret Diary of William Bird of Westover, 1739–1741: With Letters and Literary Exercises, 1696–1726.* Edited by Maude H. Woodfin. Translated by Marion Tinling. Richmond, Va.: Dietz Press, 1942.

———. *Histories of the Dividing Line Between Virginia and North Carolina.* Edited by William K. Boyd. New York: Dover, 1967.

———. *A Journey to the Land of Eden and Other Papers.* New York: Macy-Masius, 1928.

———. *Natural History of Virginia: Or, the Newly Discovered Eden.* Edited and translated by Richmond Croom Beatty and William J. Mulloy. Richmond, Va.: Dietz Press, 1940.

———. *The Secret Diary of William Byrd of Westover, 1709–1712.* Edited by Louis B. Wright and Marion Tinling. Richmond, Va.: Dietz Press, 1941.

Byron, George Gordon, Lord. *Byron's Don Juan: A Variorum Edition.* Edited by Truman Guy Steffan and Willis W. Pratt. 4 vols. Austin: University of Texas Press, 1957.

Calef, Robert. *More Wonders of the Invisible World: Or, the Wonders of the Invisible World, Display'd in Five Parts; Part I. An Account of the Sufferings of Margaret Rule, Written by the Reverend Mr. C. M.; P[art] II. Several Letters to the Author, etc.; and His Reply Relating to Witchcraft; P[art] III. The Differences between the Inhabitants of Salem Village, and Mr. Parris Their Minister, in New-England; P[art] IV. Letters of a Gentleman Uninterested, Endeavouring to Prove the Received Opinions About Witchcraft; with Short Essays to Their Answers; P[art] V. A Short Historical Accou[n]t of Matters of Fact in that Affair. . . .* London: Nath. Hillar and Joseph Collyer, 1700.
    Reprinted in Burr, *Narratives of the Witchcraft Cases.*

Campbell, Joseph. *The Hero with a Thousand Faces.* New York: World, Meridian Books, 1949.

————. *The Masks of God*. Vol. 1: *Primitive Mythology*. Vol. 2: *Oriental Mythology*. Vol. 3: *Occidental Mythology*. Vol. 4: *Creative Mythology*. New York: Viking, 1959–68.

Carey, Mathew, ed. *The American Museum: Or, Repository of Ancient and Modern Fugitive Pieces, Prose and Poetical* 2, no. 2 (October 1787).

Chambers, Edmund Kerchever. *The Elizabethan Stage*. 4 vols. Oxford: Oxford University Press, 1961.

Chapman, George; Jonson, Ben; and Marston, John. "Eastward Hoe." *Elizabethan Plays, Written by Shakespeare's Friends, Colleagues, Rivals, and Successors*. Edited by Hazelton Spencer. Boston: Little, Brown, 1933.

Charlevoix, [Pierre François-Xavier] de, *Père*. *Histoire et déscription générale de la nouvelle France: Avec le journal historique d'un voyage fait par l'ordre du roi dans l'Amérique septentrionnale*. 4 vols. Paris: Chex Pierre-François Giffart, 1744.

Charvat, William. *Literary Publishing in America: 1790–1850*. Philadelphia: University of Pennsylvania Press, 1959.

Chase, Richard. *The American Novel and Its Tradition*. Garden City, N.Y.: Doubleday, Anchor Books, 1957.

————. *The Quest for Myth*. Baton Rouge: Louisiana State University Press, 1949.

Chateaubriand, François-René de. *Génie du christianisme et défense du génie du christianisme: Avec notes et eclaircissements*. Paris: Garnier Frères, 1891.

————. *Les Martyrs; Atala; René; Adventures du dernier abencerage; Poésies*. Paris: Chez Lefevre, Libraire. Chez Letendu, Libraire, 1838.

————. *Les Natchez*. Paris: Librairie de Firmin Didot Frères, 1844.

————. "Voyage en Amérique." *Oeuvres complètes*. Vol. 12. Paris: Pourrat Frères, Editeurs, 1836.

[Chauncy, Charles.] *A Letter to a Friend, Giving a Concise, but Just, Account, According to the Advices hitherto Received, of the Ohio-defeat, and Pointing Out also the Many Good Ends, this Inglorious Event is Naturally Adapted to Promote: Or, Shewing wherein it is Fitted to Advance the Interest of all the American British Colonies; To which is added, Some General Account of the New-England Forces, with What They Have already Done, Counter-balancing the Above Loss*. Boston: Edes and Gill, 1755.

————. *A Second Letter to a Friend, Giving a More Particular Account of the Defeat of the French Army at Lake-George, by the New-England Troops, than Has Yet Been Published, Representing also the Vast Importance of this Conquest to the American-British Colonies: To which is added, such an Account of what the New-England Governments Have Done, to Carry into Effect Their Design Against Crown-Point, as Will Shew the Necessity of Their Being Helped by Great-Britain, in Point of Money*. Boston: Edes and Gill, 1755.

Chenier, André. *Oeuvres complètes*. Paris: Librairie Delagrave, 1927.

Child, Lydia Maria. *An Appeal in Favor of that Class of Americans Called Africans*. Boston: Allen and Ticknor, 1833.

Chinard, Gilbert. *L'Amérique et le rêve exotique dans la littérature française au xviie et au xviiie siècle*. Paris: Librairie Hachette, 1913.

————. *L'Exotisme américain dans l'oeuvre de Chateaubriand*. Paris: Librairie Hachette, 1918.

————. "Notes sur la voyage de Chateaubriand en Amérique (Juillet-Décembre, 1791)." *University of California Publications in Modern Philology* 4, no. 2 (10 November 1915): 269–349.

C[hurch], [Benjamin and] T[homas]. *Entertaining Passages Relating to Philip's War, Which Began in the Month of June, 1675: As also of Expeditions More Lately Made Against the Common Enemy, and Indian Rebels, in the Eastern Parts of New-England; with Some Account of the Divine Providence Towards Benj. Church Esqr.* Boston: B. Green, 1716.

    The Library of Congress lists Benjamin Church as author and Thomas Church as editor of this first edition. Vail (*The Voice of the Old Frontier*) follows the title-page signature "T. C." in ascribing the work to Thomas Church. In his preface, Benjamin Church notes that the work was composed by his son Thomas from his own "minutes." It therefore seems reasonable to regard the work as a collaboration. See also the following entry and chap. 6, esp. note 12.

Church, [Benjamin and] Thomas. *The History of King Philip's War, Commonly Called the Great Indian War, of 1675 and 1676: Also of the French and Indian Wars at the Eastward, in 1689, 1690, 1692, 1696, and 1704. . . .* Edited and with an appendix by Samuel G. Drake. Exeter, N.H.: J. and B. Williams, 1829.

    Frequently reprinted; contains additional accounts of Church's life and of the Indian wars.

Church, Benjamin [and Thomas]. *The History of King Philip's War.* Edited, with an introduction by Henry Martyn Dexter. Boston: John Kimball Wiggin, 1865.

    Reprinted from the Newport, 1772, edition, itself a reprint of the original, *Entertaining Passages*.

Cirlot, Juan Eduardo. *A Dictionary of Symbols.* Translated by Jack Sage. Foreword by Herbert Read. New York: Philosophical Library, 1962.

Cohen, Felix S. "Americanizing the White Man." *American Scholar* 21 (Spring 1952): 171–93.

Cohen, Hennig, ed. *The American Culture: Approaches to the Study of the United States.* Boston: Houghton Mifflin, 1968.

————. *The American Experience: Approaches to the Study of the United States.* Boston: Houghton Mifflin, 1968.

Cohen, Hennig, and Dillingham, William B., eds. *Humor of the Old Southwest.* Cambridge, Mass.: Houghton Mifflin, Riverside Editions, 1964.

Colden, Cadwallader. *History of the Five Nations Depending on the Province of New-York in America.* Ithaca, N.Y.: Cornell University Press, Great Seal Books, 1958.

Coleman, Emma Lewis. *New England Captives Carried to Canada: Between 1677 and 1760 During the French and Indian Wars.* 2 vols. Portland, Me.: Southworth Press, 1925.

Coleman, John Winston. *A Bibliography of Kentucky History.* Lexington: University of Kentucky Press, 1949.

Collier, John. *Indians of the Americas: The Long Hope.* New York: New American Library, 1947.

Collins, Frank M. "Cooper and the American Dream." *PMLA* 81, no. 1 (March 1966): 79–94.

Commager, Henry Steele, and Giordanetti, Elmo, eds. *Was America a Mistake?:*

An Eighteenth-Century Controversy. New York: Harper and Row, Harper Torchbooks, 1967.

Connecticut, Colony of. *The Code of 1650: Being a Compilation of the Earliest Laws and Orders of the General Court of Connecticut; Also, the Constitution or Compact, Entered into and Adopted by the Towns of Windsor, Hartford and Wethersfield, in 1638–9; To which is added, Some Extracts from the Laws and Judicial Proceedings of New-Haven Colony, Commonly Called the Blue-Laws.* Hartford: Andrus and Judd, 1836.

Cooke, Ebenezer. "The Maryland Muse." Edited by Lawrence C. Wroth. *Proceedings of the American Antiquarian Society* 44 (1934).

Cooper, James Fenimore. *The Deerslayer: Or, The First Warpath.* New York: Harper and Brothers, 1926.

———. *The Last of the Mohicans: A Narrative of 1757.* New York: G. Putnam's Sons, 1907.

———. *The Pioneers.* Edited by Leon Howard. New York: Holt, Rinehart, and Winston, Rinehart Editions, 1959.

———. *The Prairie.* Edited by Henry Nash Smith. New York: Holt, Rinehart, and Winston, Rinehart Editions, 1964.

Cortés, Hernando. *Five Letters: 1519–1526.* Translated and edited by J. Bayard Morris. New York: W. W. Norton, 1962.

Crèvecoeur, Michel Guillaume St. Jean de. *A Journey into Northern Pennsylvania and the State of New York.* Paris, 1801. Translated by Clarissa Spencer Bostelmann. Ann Arbor: University of Michigan Press, 1964.

———. *Letters from an American Farmer.* Edited by Warren Barton Blake. New York: E. P. Dutton, 1957.

———. *Lettres d'un cultivateur américain addressées a Wm. S . . . on Esqr. depuis l'année 1770 jusqu'en 1786.* Paris: Chex Cuchez, 1787.

Crockett, David. *The Autobiography of David Crockett.* Edited by Hamlin Garland. New York: Perkins Book Co., n.d.

———. *Narrative of the Life of David Crockett of the State of Tennessee.* Philadelphia: E. L. Carey and A. Hart, 1834.

Custer, George Armstrong. *My Life on the Plains: Or, Personal Experiences with Indians.* New York: Sheldon and Company, 1874.

Davies, Samuel. *Virginia's Danger and Remedy: Two Discourses, Occasioned by the Severe Drought in Sundry Parts of the Country; and the Defeat of General Braddock.* Williamsburg, Va.: William Hunter, 1756.

Decalves, Alonso [pseud.]. *New Travels to the Westward, or Unknown Parts of America: Being a Tour of Almost Fourteen Months; Containing an Account of the Country, Upwards of Two Thousand Miles West of the Christian Parts of North America; with an Account of the White Indians, Their Manners, Habits, and Many Other Particulars. . . .* [No place or publisher], 1797.

Defoe, Daniel. *The Fortunes and Misfortunes of the Famous Moll Flanders, &c.: Who Was Born in Newgate, and During a Life of Continu'd Variety for Threescore Years, Besides her Childhood, Was Twelve Year a Whore, Five Times a Wife (Whereof Once to Her Own Brother), Twelve Year a Thief, Eight Year a Transported Felon in Virginia, at Last Grew Rich, Liv'd Honest, and Died a Penitent; Written from Her Own Memorandums. . . .* Edited with an introduction by Mark Shorer. New York: Modern Library, 1950.

————. *The History and Remarkable Life of the Truly Honourable Col. Jacque, Commonly Call'd Col. Jack: Who was Born a Gentleman, Put 'Prentice to a Pick-Pocket, Was Six-and-Twenty Years a Thief, and then Kidnapp'd to Virginia; Came Back a Merchant, Married Four Wives, and Five of Them Prov'd Whores; Went into the Wars, Behav'd Bravely, Got Preferment, Was Made Colonel of a Regiment, Came Over, and Fled with the Chevalier, and Is Now Abroad Compleating a Life of Wonders, and Resolves to Die a General.* Edited with an introduction by Samuel Holt Monk. London: Oxford University Press, 1965.

Demos, John. "Underlying Themes in the Witchcraft of Seventeenth-Century New England." *American Historical Review* 75 (June 1970): 1311–26.

de P[auw, Corneille]. *Recherches philosophiques sur les Américains: ou mémoires intéressants pour servir à l'histoire de l'espèce humaine.* 3 vols. London: [no publisher], 1776.

Díaz del Castillo, Bernal. *The Conquest of New Spain.* Translated by J. M. Cohen. London: Penguin Books, 1967.

————. *The Discovery and Conquest of Mexico.* Translated by A. P. Maudsley. Edited by Genaro Garcia. New York: Farrar, Straus, and Giroux, 1966.

Dickenson, Jonathan. *God's Protecting Providence Man's Surest Help and Defense in the Times of the Greatest Difficulty and Most Imminent Danger: Evidenced in the Remarkable Deliverance of Divers Persons, from the Devouring Waves of the Sea, Amongst which They Suffered Shipwrack; And also from the More Cruelly Devouring Jawes of the Inhumane Canibals of Florida; Faithfully Related by One of the Persons Concerned Therein; Jonathan Dickenson.* Philadelphia: Reinier Jansen, 1699.

————. *Jonathan Dickenson's Journal: Or, God's Protecting Providence, Being the Narrative of a Journey from Port Royal in Jamaica to Philadelphia, between August 23, 1696 and April 1, 1697.* Edited by Charles McLean Andrews and Evangeline Walker Andrews. Foreword and new introduction by Leonard W. Labaree. New Haven: Yale University Press, 1961.

A reprint of *God's Protecting Providence.*

Dickinson, John. *Letters from a Farmer in Pennsylvania, to the Inhabitants of the British Colonies.* Edited by R. T. H. Halsey from the London, 1768, edition. New York: Outlook Company, 1903.

Dixon, Thomas, Jr. *The Clansman.* 1905. Edited by T. D. Clark. Lexington: University Press of Kentucky, 1969.

Dondore, Dorothy Anne. *The Prairie and the Making of Middle America: Four Centuries of Description.* Cedar Rapids, Iowa: Torch Press, 1926.

Drake, Benjamin. *Life of Tecumseh and of His Brother the Prophet: With a Historical Sketch of the Shawanoe Indians.* Cincinnati: Anderson, Gates, and Wright, 1858.

Drake, Milton. *Almanacs of the United States.* 2 vols. New York: Scarecrow Press, 1962.

Drake, Samuel Gardner. *Annals of Witchcraft in New England, and Elsewhere in the United States, from Their First Settlement: Drawn up from Unpublished and Other Well-Authenticated Records of the Alleged Operations of Witches and Their Instigator, the Devil.* Boston: W. Elliot Woodward, 1869.

Drayton, Michael. *The Works of Michael Drayton*. Edited by J. William Hebel. 5 vols. Oxford: B. Blackwell, Shakespeare Head Press, 1931–41.

Driver, Harold Edson, ed. *The Americas on the Eve of Discovery*. Englewood Cliffs, N.J.: Prentice-Hall, 1964.

Dryden, John. *The Works of John Dryden*. Edited, with a life of the author by Sir Walter Scott. Revised and corrected by George Saintsbury. Vol. 2. Edinburgh: William Paterson, 1882.

Durrett, Reuben T. *John Filson: The First Historian of Kentucky*. Filson Club Publications, no. 1. Louisville, Ky.: Filson Club, 1884.

Dwight, Timothy. *Greenfield Hill: A Poem in Seven Parts*. New York: Childs and Swain, 1794.

Eastburn, James Wallis, [and Sands, Robert C.]. *Yamoyden: A Tale of the Wars of King Philip, in Six Cantos*. New York: James Eastburn, 1820.

Eastburn, Robert. *A Faithful Narrative, of the Many Dangers and Sufferings, as well as Wonderful Deliverances of Robert Eastburn, During his Late Captivity Among the Indians: Together with Some Remarks Upon the Country of Canada, and the Religion, and Policy of Its Inhabitants; the Whole Intermixed with Devout Reflections.* . . . Preface by Rev. Gilbert Tennent. Philadelphia: William Dunlap, 1758.

Echeverria, Durand. *Mirage in the West: A History of the French Image of American Society to 1815*. Princeton: Princeton University Press, 1957.

Edwards, Jonathan. *Representative Selections*. Edited by Charles Faust and Thomas H. Johnson. American Century Series. New York: Hill and Wang, 1962.

———. *The Works of President Edwards*. Edited by Edward Williams and Edward Parsons. 8 vols. London: James Black and Son, 1817. Two supplementary volumes were published in Edinburgh: Robert Ogle and Oliver and Boyd, 1847.

Eliot, John. "A Late and Further Manifestation of the Progress of the Gospel amongst the Indians in New-England. Declaring Their Constant Love and Zeal to the Truth: With a Readiness to Give Accompt of their Faith and Hope; as of Their Desires in Church to be Partakers of the Ordinances of Christ. Being a Narrative of the Examinations of the Indians, About Their Knowledge in Religion, by the Elders of the Churches." Reprinted from the London, 1655, edition. *Collections of the Massachusetts Historical Society*, 3d ser. 4 (1834): 261–87.

Eliot, John, and Mayhew, Thomas. "Tears of Repentance: Or, A Further Narrative of the Progress of the Gospel amongst the Indians in New-England: Setting Forth not Only Their Present State and Condition, but Sundry Confessions of Sin by Diverse of the Said Indians, Wrought Upon by the Saving Power of the Gospel; Together with the Manifestation of Their Faith and Hope in Jesus Christ, and the Work of Grace Upon Their Hearts." Reprinted from the London, 1653, edition. *Collections of the Massachusetts Historical Society*, 3d ser. 4 (1834): 197–260.

Emerson, Oliver F. "Notes on Gilbert Imlay, Early American Writer." *PMLA* 39, no. 2 (June 1924): 406–39.

Eugenia, Sister. "Coleridge's Scheme of Pantisocracy and American Travel Accounts." *PMLA* 45, no. 4 (December 1930): 1069–84.

Evans, Charles. *American Bibliography: A Chronological Dictionary of All Books, Pamphlets, and Periodical Publications Printed in the United States of America from the Genesis of Printing Down to and Including the Year 1820* [sic, but actually 1800]. *With Bibliographical and Biographical Notes.* 13 vols. Chicago: Blakely Press, 1903–59.

Evarts, Jeremiah ["William Penn"]. *Essays on the Present Crisis in the Condition of the American Indians: First Published in the National Intelligencer, Under the Signature of William Penn.* Boston: Perkins and Marvin, 1829.

Fabre, Jean. *André Chenier.* Paris: Hatier-Boivin, 1855.

Fagin, Nathan B. *William Bartram: Interpreter of the American Landscape.* Baltimore: Johns Hopkins Press, 1933.

Farb, Peter. *Man's Rise to Civilization as Shown by the Indians of North America from Primeval Times to the Coming of the Industrial State.* New York: E. P. Dutton, 1968.

Farther Brief and True Narration of the Late Wars Risen in New-England, Occasioned by the Quarrelsome Disposition and Perfidious Carriage of the Barbarous and Savage Indian Natives There: With an Account of the Fight, the 19th of December Last, A. London: Printed by J. D. for M. K., 1676.

Faulkner, William. *Absalom, Absalom!* Introduction by Harvey Breit. New York: Modern Library, 1951.

———. *Go Down, Moses.* New York: Modern Library, 1955.

Fiedler, Leslie. *Love and Death in the American Novel.* New York: Criterion Books, 1960.

———. *The Return of the Vanishing American.* New York: Stein and Day, 1968.

[Filson, John.] *The Adventures of Colonel Daniel Boon. One of the First Settlers at Kentucke: Containing The Wars with the Indians on the Ohio, from 1769 to 1783, and the First Establishment and Progress of the Settlement on that River: Written by the Colonel Himself: To which are added, A Narrative of the Captivity, and Extraordinary Escape of Mrs. Francis* [sic] *Scott. . . .* Norwich: John Trumbull, 1786.

      See Jillson, *The Boone Narrative.*

[———.] "The Adventures of Colonel Daniel Boon, One of the Original Settlers at Kentucky: Containing the Wars with the Indians on the Ohio, from 1769, to the Year 1783, and the First Establishment and Progress of the Settlements on that River. Written by the Colonel." In *Beers's Almanac and Ephemeris of the Motion of the Sun and Moon; and the True Places and Aspects of the Planets; the Rising and Setting of the Moon, for the Year of Our Lord, 1795. . . .* Edited by Andrew Beers. Hartford, 1794.

———. *The Discovery, Settlement and Present State of Kentucke: and an Essay Towards the Topography, and Natural History of that Important Country: To which is added, an Appendix, Containing, I. The Adventures of Col. Daniel Boon, One of the First Settlers, Comprehending Every Important Occurrence in the Political History of that Province; II. The Minutes of the Piankashaw Council, Held at Post St. Vincents, April 15, 1784; III. An Account of the Indian Nations Inhabiting within the Limits of the Thirteen United States, Their Manners and Customs, and Reflections on Their Origin; IV. The Stages and Distances between Philadelphia and the Falls of the Ohio; from Pittsburgh to*

Pensacola and Several Other Places: The Whole Illustrated by a New and Accurate Map of Kentucke and the Country Adjoining. Drawn from Actual Surveys. Wilmington, Del.: James Adams, 1784.

   Cited hereafter as *Kentucke.* See Jillson, *Filson's "Kentucke,"* and Metcalf[e], *"A Collection. . . ."*

—————. *Histoire de Kentucke, nouvelle colonie à l'ouest de la Virginie: Contenant, 1°. La Découverte, l'aquisition, l'établissement, la description topographique, l'histoire naturelle, &c. du territoire; 2°. La Relation historique du Colonel Boon, un des premiers colons, sur les guerres contre les naturels; 3°. L'Assemblée des Piankashaws au Poste Saint Vincent; 4°. Un Exposé succinct des nations indiennes qui habitent dans les limites des treize États-Unis, de leurs moeurs & coutumes, & des réflexions sur leur origine; & autres pièces; avec une carte; ouvrage pour servir de suite aux "Lettres d'un cultivateur américain."* Traduit par [Henri] Parraud. Paris: Chez Buisson, 1785.

[—————.] "Life and Adventures of Colonel Daniel Boone the First White Settler of the State of Kentucky: Comprising an Account of His First Excursion to Kentucky in 1769, Then a Wild Wilderness, Inhabited by no Other Beings than Savages — His Removal There with His Family in 1773, and of His Various Encounters with the Indians from the Year 1769 to 1782 Written by Himself; To Which Is Added a Narrative of the Most Important Incidents of His Life from the Latter Period until the Period of His Death June 27, 1821, at the Advanced Age of 90 Years — Comprising an Account of His Many Extraordinary Excursions and Hairbreadth Escapes, While in Pursuit of the Wild Beasts of the Forest, His Favorite Amusement Until the Day of His Death; Annexed is a Eulogy on Col. Boone and choice of life, by Lord Byron." Edited by C. Wilder. Reprinted from the Brooklyn, 1823, edition. *The Magazine of History with Notes and Queries* 45, no. 4, extra no. 180 (1932).

—————. *Reise nach Kentucke und Nachrichten von dieser neu angebaueten Landschaft in Nordamerika: Aus dem englischen ueberstetet* [sic]. Leipzig: Chr. Weigel, 1790.

Fitzroy, Alexander. *The Discovery, Purchase, and Settlement of the Country of Kentuckie. . . .* London: H. Goldney, 1786.

   A plagiarism of Filson's *Kentucke* (1784), but lacking the Boone narrative.

Flint, Timothy. *Biographical Memoir of Daniel Boone: The First Settler of Kentucky: Interspersed with Incidents in the Early Annals of the Country.* Reprinted from the Cincinnati, 1833, edition. Edited by James K. Folsom. New Haven: College and University Press, 1967.

—————. *The History and Geography of the Mississippi Valley: To Which Is Appended a Condensed Physical Geography of the Atlantic United States, and the Whole American Continent.* Cincinnati: E. H. Fleet, 1833.

—————. *Indian Wars of the West: Containing Biographical Sketches of Those Pioneers Who Headed the Western Settlers in Repelling Attacks of the Savages, Together with a View of the Character, Manners, Monuments, and Antiquities of the Western Indians.* Cincinnati: E. H. Fleet, 1833.

Forbes, Jack D., ed. *The Indian in America's Past.* Englewood Cliffs, N.J.: Prentice-Hall, 1964.

Fox, John. *Fox's Book of Martyrs: Or, The Acts and Monuments of the Christian Church; Being a Complete History of the Lives, Sufferings, and Deaths of the Christian Martyrs; from the Commencement of Christianity to the Present Period. . . .* Revised and improved by Rev. John Malham. New York: Oliver Wilson, 1828.

Franklin, Benjamin. *The Autobiography of Benjamin Franklin and Other Writings.* Edited by L. Jesse Lemisch. New York: New American Library, 1961.

———. "A Narrative of the Late Massacres, in Lancaster County, of a Number of Indians, Friends of this Province, by Persons Unknown: With Observations on the Same." Philadelphia, 1764. *The Papers of Benjamin Franklin.* Vol. 11. Edited by Leonard W. Labaree. New Haven: Yale University Press, 1967.

Frazer, James George. *The New Golden Bough.* Edited by Theodor Gaster. Garden City, N.Y.: Doubleday, Anchor Books, 1961.

Frost, John. *Border Wars of the West: Comprising the Frontier Wars of Pennsylvania, Virginia, Kentucky, Ohio, Indiana, Illinois, Tennessee, and Wisconsin; and Embracing Individual Adventures Among the Indians, and Exploits of Boon, Kenton, Clark, Logan, Brady, Poe, Morgan, the Whetzel's* [sic], *and Other Border Heroes of the West.* Auburn: Derby and Miller, 1853.

———. *Heroic Women of the West: Comprising Thrilling Examples of Courage, Fortitude, Devotedness, and Self-Sacrifice, Among the Pioneer Mothers of the Western Country.* Philadelphia: A. Hart, 1854.

——— ["William V. Moore"]. *Indian Wars of the United States, from the Discovery to the Present Time: From the Best Authorities.* Philadelphia: R. W. Pomeroy, 1840.

Frothingham, Charles W. *The Convent's Doom: A Tale of Charlestown in 1834.* 5th. ed. Boston: Graves and Weston, 1854.

———. *Six Hours in a Convent: Or, The Stolen Nuns.* 16th ed. Boston: Graves and Weston, 1855.

Frye, Northrop. *Anatomy of Criticism: Four Essays.* Princeton: Princeton University Press, 1957.

Fussell, Edwin. *Frontier: American Literature and the American West.* Princeton: Princeton University Press, 1966.

Goldsmith, Oliver. "The Deserted Village." *The Collected Works of Oliver Goldsmith.* Vol. 4. Edited by Arthur Friedman. Oxford: Oxford University Press, 1966.

Gookin, Daniel. "Historical Collections of the Indians in New England: Of Their Several Nations, Numbers, Customs, Manners, Religion, and Government, Before the English Planted There; Also a True and Faithful Account of the Present State and Condition of the Praying Indians. . . ." *Collections of the Massachusetts Historical Society for the Year 1792,* 1st ser. 1 (1806).

Hakluyt, Richard. *The Portable Hakluyt's Voyages: The Principal Navigations Voyages Traffiques & Discoveries of the English Nation Made by Sea or Over-land to the Remote and Farthest Distant Quarters of the Earth at Any Time within the Compass of these 1600 Yeeres.* Selected and edited by Irwin R. Blacker. New York: Viking Portable Library, 1965.

Hall, James. *Legends of the West: Sketches Illustrative of the Habits, Occupations, Privations, Adventures, and Sports of the Pioneers of the West.* Cincinnati: Robert Clarke, 1869.

————. *Letters from the West: Containing Sketches of Scenery, Manners, and Customs; and Anecdotes Connected with the First Settlements of the Western Sections of the United States.* London: Henry Colburn, 1828.

————. *Sketches of History, Life and Manners in the West.* 2 vols. Philadelphia: Harrison Hall, [1835].

Handlin, Oscar. *Race and Nationality in American Life.* Garden City, N.Y.: Doubleday, Anchor Books, 1957.

Hanson, John Wesley. *History of Gardiner, Pittston and West Gardiner. . . .* Gardiner, Me.: William Palmer, 1852.

Harris, George Washington. *Sut Lovingood: Yarns Spun by a "Nat'ral Born Durn'd Fool."* New York: Dick and Fitzgerald, 1867.

————. *Sut Lovingood's Yarns.* Edited by M. Thomas Inge. New Haven: College and University Press, 1966.

Hawthorne, Nathaniel. *The Complete Works of Nathaniel Hawthorne.* Edited by George Parsons Lathrop. 12 vols. Cambridge, Mass.: Riverside Press, 1883.

————. *Selected Tales and Sketches.* Edited by Hyatt H. Waggoner. New York: Holt, Rinehart, and Winston, Rinehart Editions, 1960.

Heckewelder, John Gottlieb Ernestus. "History, Manners, and Customs of the Indian Nations Who Once Inhabited Pennsylvania and the Neighbouring States." Edited by Rev. William C. Reichel. *Memoirs of the Historical Society of Pennsylvania* 12 (1876).

Heinsius, Wilhelm. *Allgemeines Bücher-lexikon: Oder vollständiges alphabetisches Verzeichniss der von 1700 bis zu Ende [1892] erschienenen Bücher, welche in Deutschland und in den durch Sprache und Literatur damit verwandten Ländern gedruckt worden sind. . . .* Leipzig: [no publisher], 1812–94.

Henderson, Joseph L. *Thresholds of Initiation.* Middletown, Conn.: Wesleyan University Press, 1967.

Henry, Alexander. *Travels and Adventures in Canada and the Indian Territories Between the Years 1760 and 1776.* New York: I. Riley, 1809.

Henson, Josiah. *Father Henson's Story of His Own Life.* Edited by Walter Fisher. Facsimile of the Boston, 1858, edition. American Experience Series. New York: Corinth Books, 1962.

Hentz, N. M. *Tadeuskund: The Last King of the Lenape.* Boston: [no publisher], 1825.

Hewatt, Alexander. *An Historical Account of the Rise and Progress of the Colonies of South Carolina and Georgia. . . .* Facsimile of the London, 1779, edition. Spartanburg, S.C.: Reprint Company, 1962.

Hodge, Frederick Webb, and Lewis, Theodore H., eds. *Spanish Explorers in the Southern United States: 1528–1543.* Original Narratives of Early American History Series. New York: Charles Scribner's Sons, 1907.

Hoffman, Daniel G. *Form and Fable in American Fiction.* New York: Oxford University Press, 1961.

Hoole, W. Stanley. *Alias Simon Suggs: The Life and Times of Johnson Jones Hooper.* University, Ala.: University of Alabama Press, 1952.

[Hooper, Johnson Jones.] *Some Adventures of Captain Simon Suggs: Late of the Tallapoosa Volunteers; Together with "Taking the Census," and Other Alabama Sketches.* Philadelphia: Carey and Hart, 1846.

Hopkins, Samuel. *Historical Memoirs, Relating to the Housatunnuck Indians: Or, An Account of the Methods Used, and Pains Taken, for the Propagation of the Gospel Among that Heathenish Tribe, and the Success Thereof, Under the Ministry of the Late Reverend Mr. John Sergeant. . . .* Boston: S. Kneeland, 1753.

[Houston, Samuel.] *The Life of Sam Houston: The Hunter, Patriot, and Statesman of Texas; the Only Authentic Memoir of Him Ever Published.* Philadelphia: John E. Potter, 1867.
    First printed for the presidential campaign of 1856.

Howe, George. *Mount Hope: A New England Chronicle.* New York: Viking Press, 1959.

Hoyt, Epaphras. *Antiquarian Researches: Comprising a History of the Indian Wars in the Country Bordering Connecticut River and Parts Adjacent. . . .* Greenfield, Mass.: Ansel Phelps, 1824.

Hubbard, William. *The History of the Indian Wars in New England from the First Settlement to the Termination of the War with King Philip in 1677.* Edited, with a biography of the author by Samuel G. Drake. 2 vols. Roxbury, Mass.: W. Elliot Woodward, 1865.
    Reprint of Hubbard's *Narrative of the Troubles* (see following entry).

———. *A Narrative of the Troubles with the Indians in New-England, from the First Planting Thereof in the Year 1607. to this Present Year 1677: But Chiefly of the Late Troubles in the Last Two Years, 1675. and 1676.; to which is added a Discourse about the Warre with the Pequods in the Year 1637.* Boston: John Foster, 1677.

Hunt, William Gibbes, ed. *The Western Review and Literary Miscellaneous Magazine. . . .* Vols. 1–4 (1819–21).

H[utchinson], R[ichard]. *The Warr in New-England Visibly Ended: King Philip that Barbarous Indian Now Beheaded, and Most of His Bloudy Adherents Submitted to Mercy. . . .* London: Printed by J. B. for Dorman Newman, 1677.
    Reprinted in Lincoln, *Narratives of the Indian Wars.*

Hutchinson, Thomas. *The History of the Colony and Province of Massachusetts-Bay.* Edited by Lawrence Shaw Mayo. Cambridge: Harvard University Press, 1936.

Hyde, George. *Indians of the Woodlands: From Prehistoric Times to 1725.* Norman: University of Oklahoma Press, 1962.

Imlay, Gilbert. *The Emigrants, &c: Or, The History of an Expatriated Family, Being a Delineation of English Manners, Drawn from Real Characters.* Edited by Robert R. Hare. Facsimile of the Dublin, 1794, edition. Gainesville, Fla.: Scholars' Facsimiles and Reprints, 1964.

———. *A Topographical Description of the Western Territory of North America. . . .* London: J. Debrett, 1792.

———. *A Topographical Description of the Western Territory of North America: Containing a Succinct Account of Its Soil, Climate, Natural History, Population, Agriculture, Manners, and Customs; With an Ample Description of the Several Divisions into which that County is Partitioned; to which are added, The Discovery, Settlement, and Present State of Kentucky, And an Essay Towards the Topography, and Natural History of that Important Country; By*

John Filson; To which is added, I. The Adventures of Col. Daniel Boon, One of the First Settlers, Comprehending Every Important Occurrence in the Political History of that Province; II. The Minutes of the Piankashaw Council, Held at Post St. Vincent's April 15, 1784; III. An Account of the Indian Nations Inhabiting within the Limits of the Thirteen United States; Their Manners and Customs; Reflections on Their Origin. 2d ed., with considerable additions. London: J. Debrett, 1793.

  This second edition adds the complete text of Filson's *Kentucke*, 1784, and other materials to the text of the London, 1792, edition of Imlay's *Topographical Description.*

——. *A Topographical Description of the Western Territory of North America.* . . . 2 vols. New York: Samuel Campbell, 1793.

  The text of the second edition (London, 1793) in two-volume format, with Filson's *Kentucke* as the second volume with a separate title page.

Irving, Washington. *Astoria: Or, Anecdotes of an Enterprise Beyond the Rocky Mountains. The Works of Washington Irving.* Vol. 2. New York: Thomas Y. Crowell, n.d.

——. *The Sketch-Book of Geoffrey Crayon, Gent.* Van Tassel Edition. New York: G. P. Putnam's Sons, 1895.

Jackson, Helen Hunt. *A Century of Dishonor: A Sketch of the United States Government's Dealings with Some of the Indian Tribes.* New York: Harper and Brothers, 1881.

James, Marquis. *The Raven: A biography of Sam Houston.* New York: Paperback Library, 1971.

Jantz, Harold S. *The First Century of New England Verse.* Worcester, Mass.: American Antiquarian Society, 1944.

Jefferson, Thomas. *The Life and Selected Writings of Thomas Jefferson.* Edited by Adrienne Koch and William Peden. New York: Modern Library, 1944.

——. *Notes on the State of Virginia.* New York: Harper and Row, Harper Torchbooks, 1964.

——. *The Papers of Thomas Jefferson.* Vols. 7, 10. Edited by Julian P. Boyd. Princeton: Princeton University Press, 1953, 1954.

Jillson, Willard Rouse, ed. *The Boone Narrative: The Story of the Origin and Discovery Coupled with the Reproduction in Facsimile of a Rare Item of Early Kentuckiana; to which is Appended a Sketch of Boone and a Bibliography of 238 Titles.* Louisville, Ky.: Standard Printing Company, 1932.

  The Norwich, 1786, edition of Filson's Boone narrative is reproduced.

——. *Kentucky History: A Check and Finding List of the Principal Published and Manuscript Sources of the General, Regional, and County History of the Commonwealth, 1729–1936.* Louisville, Ky.: Standard Printing Company, 1936.

——. *Rare Kentucky Books, 1776–1926: A Check and Finding List of Scarce, Fugitive, Curious and Interesting Books and Pamphlets, with Annotations and Prices Current Appended.* Louisville, Ky.: Standard Printing Company, 1939.

——, ed. *Filson's Kentucke: A Facsimile Reproduction of the Original Wilmington Edition of 1784, with Paged Critique, Sketch of Filson's Life, and Bibliography.* Louisville, Ky.: J. P. Morton, 1929.

Johnson, Edward. *Johnson's Wonder-working Providence: 1628–1651*. Edited by J. Franklin Jameson. Original Narratives of Early American History Series. New York: Charles Scribner's Sons, 1910.

Jones, Howard Mumford. *O Strange New World: American Culture, the Formative Years*. New York: Viking, 1965.

————. "Prose and Pictures: James Fenimore Cooper." *Tulane University Studies in English* 3 (1952): 133–54.

Jordan, Winthrop D. *White over Black: American Attitudes towards the Negro, 1550–1812*. Baltimore: Penguin Books, 1969.

Jung, Carl Gustav. *Psyche and Symbol: A Selection from the Writings of C. G. Jung*. Edited by Violet S. de Laszlo. Garden City, N.Y.: Doubleday, Anchor Books, 1958.

Katz, William Loren, ed. *Five Slave Narratives*. New York: Arno Press, 1968.

Kayser, Christian Gottlob. *Bücher-Lexikon . . . 1750 bis zu Ende des Jahres 1832. . . .* Leipzig: Ludwig Schumann, 1834.

Kidder, Frederic. "The Expeditions of Captain John Lovewell, and His Encounters with the Indians: Including a Particular Account of the Pequauket Battle, with a History of that Tribe; and a Reprint of the Rev. Thomas Symmes' Sermon." *Magazine of History with Notes and Queries* 2, extra no. 5, part 1 (1909).

    Also contains "The Mournful Elegy on Mr. Jonathan Frye, 1725," and "Song of Lovewell's Fight," as well as reprints of Thomas Symmes's *Lovewell Lamented* and *Historical Memoir*, for which see below.

Lawrence, D. H. *Studies in Classic American Literature*. New York: Viking 1961.

Lawson, Deodat. *A Brief and True Narrative of Some Remarkable Passages Relating to Sundry Persons Afflicted by Witchcraft, at Salem Village which Happened from the Nineteenth of March, to the Fifth of April, 1692*. Boston: Benjamin Harris, 1692.

Lawson, John. *A New Voyage to Carolina*. Edited by Hugh Talmage Lefler. Chapel Hill: University of North Carolina Press, 1967.

Lemay, J. A. Leo. "Richard Lewis and Augustan American Poetry." *PMLA* 83, no. 1 (March 1968): 80–101.

Levin, David. *History as Romantic Art: Bancroft, Prescott, Motley and Parkman*. New York: Harcourt, Brace and World, 1959.

Lévi-Strauss, Claude. *The Savage Mind*. Chicago: University of Chicago Press, 1966.

————. *Structural Anthropology*. Translated by Claire Jacobson and Brooke Grundfest Schoepf. New York: Basic Books, 1963.

————. *Totemism*. Translated by Rodney Needham. Boston: Beacon Press, 1963.

Lévy-Bruhl, Lucien. *How Natives Think*. Authorized translation by Lilian A. Clare. Introduction by Ruth L. Benzel. New York: Washington Square Press, 1966.

Lewis, R. W. B. *The American Adam: Innocence, Tragedy and Tradition in the Nineteenth Century*. Chicago: University of Chicago Press, 1965.

Lincoln, Charles Henry, ed. *Narratives of the Indian Wars: 1675–1699*. New York: Barnes and Noble, 1966.

Longfellow, Henry Wadsworth. *The Song of Hiawatha*. Boston: Ticknor and Fields, 1856.

[Longstreet, Augustus Baldwin.] *Georgia Scenes: Characters and Incidents, &c., in the First Half Century of the Republic.* Augusta, Ga.: [no publisher], 1835.

McClung, John A. *Sketches of Western Adventure: Containing an Account of the Most Interesting Incidents Connected with the Settlement of the West, from 1755 to 1794; Together with an Appendix. . . .* Louisville, Ky.: Richard H. Collins, 1879.

> Originally published in Maysville, Ky.: L. Collins, 1832.

McCorison, Marcus A. *Vermont Imprints: 1778–1820.* Worcester, Mass.: American Antiquarian Society, 1963.

McLoughlin, William G. "Pietism and the American Character." *American Quarterly* 17, no. 2 (Summer 1965): 163–88.

McMurtrie, Douglas C., and Allen, Albert H. *American Imprints Inventory Number 5: Check List of Kentucky Imprints, 1787–1810.* Louisville, Ky.: Historical Records Survey, 1939.

———. *American Imprints Inventory Number 6: Check List of Kentucky Imprints, 1811–1820.* Louisville, Ky.: Historical Records Survey, 1939.

———. *American Imprints Survey Number 38: Supplemental Check List of Kentucky Imprints, 1788–1820.* Louisville, Ky.: Historical Records Survey, 1942.

Mailer, Norman. *The Naked and the Dead.* New York: Modern Library, 1948.

Marshall, Humphrey. *The History of Kentucky: Including an Account of the Discovery, Settlement, Progressive Improvement, Political and Military Events, and the Present State of the Country.* Frankfort, Ky.: Humphrey Marshall, 1812.

Marx, Leo. *The Machine in the Garden: Technology and the Pastoral Ideal in America.* New York: Oxford University Press, 1964.

Mason, John. "A Brief History of the Pequot War." Edited by Thomas Prince. Reprinted from the Boston, 1736, edition. *Collections of the Massachusetts Historical Society,* 2d ser. 8 (1819): 120–53.

Mather, Cotton. *Decennium Luctuosum: An History of Remarkable Occurrences, in the Long War, which New-England Hath Had with the Indian Salvages, from the Year 1688. to the Year 1698; Faithfully Composed and Improved.* Boston: Printed by B. Green for Samuel Phillips, 1699.

> Reprinted in Cotton Mather, *Magnalia Christi Americana.* Also reprinted in Lincoln, *Narratives of the Indian Wars.*

———. *Frontiers Well-Defended: An Essay, to Direct the Frontiers of a Countrey Exposed unto the Incursions of a Barbarous Enemy, How to Behave Themselves in Their Uneasy Station? Containing Admonitions of Piety, Propos'd by the Compassion of Some Friends unto Their Welfare, to be Lodg'd in the Families of Our Frontier Plantations.* Boston: T. Green, 1706.

———. *Humiliations follow'd with Deliverances: A Brief Discourse on the Matter and Method, of that Humiliation which Would be an Hopeful Symptom of Our Deliverance from Calamity; Accompanied and Accomodated with a Narrative, of a Notable Deliverance Lately Received by Some English Captives, from the Hands of Cruel Indians; and Some Improvement of that Narrative.* Boston: B. Green and J. Allen, 1697.

———. *Magnalia Christi Americana: Or, The Ecclesiastical History of New-England, from its First Planting in the Year 1620, unto the Year of Our Lord, 1698.* 2 vols. Hartford: Silas Andrus, 1820.

————. *The Short History of New-England: A Recapitulation of Wonderful Passages which Have Occurr'd, First in the Protections, and then in the Afflictions, of New-England; with a Representation of Certain Matters Calling for the Singular Attention of the Country; Made at Boston-lecture, in the Audience of the Great and General Assembly of the Province of the Massachusetts-Bay, June 7, 1694.* Boston: Printed by B. Green for Samuel Phillips, 1694.

————. *The Wonders of the Invisible World: Observations as well Historical as Theological, upon the Nature, the Number, and the Operations of the Devils; Accompany'd with I. Some Accounts of the Grievous Molestations, by Daemons and Witchcrafts, which Have Lately Annoy'd the Countrey; and the Trials of some Eminent Malefactors Executed upon Occasion Thereof; with Several Remarkable Curiosities Therein Occurring; II. Some Counsils, Directing a Due Improvement of the Terrible Things, Lately Done, by the Unusual and Amazing Range of Evil Spirits, in Our Neighbourhood; and the Methods to Prevent the Wrongs which Those Evil Angels May Intend Against All Sorts of People Among Us; Especially in Accusations of the Innocent; III. Some Conjectures upon the Great Events, Likely to Befall the World in General, and New-England in Particular; as also upon the Advances of the Time, When We Shall See Better Dayes; IV. A Short Narrative of a Late Outrage Committed by a Knot of Witches in Swedeland, very much Resembling, and so far Explaining, that Under which Our Parts of America Have Laboured! V. The Devil Discovered; in a Brief Discourse upon Those Temptations, which are the More Ordinary Devices of the Wicked One.* Boston: Printed by Benjamin Harris for Samuel Phillips, 1693.

Mather, Increase. *A Brief History of the Warr with the Indians in New-England, (From June 24, 1675. when the First Englishman Was Murdered by the Indians, to August 12, 1676. when Philip, alias Metacomet, the Principal Author and Beginner of the Warr, Was Slain): Wherein the Grounds, Beginning, and Progress of the Warr, Is Summarily Expressed; Together with a Serious Exhortation to the Inhabitants of the Land.* Boston: John Foster, 1676.

    Includes *An Earnest Exhortation,* listed below.

————. *Early History of New England: Being a Relation of Hostile Passages Between the Indians and European Voyagers and First Settlers; and a Full Narrative of Hostilities, to the Close of the War with the Pequots, in the Year 1637; also a Detailed Account of the Origin of the War with King Philip.* Edited by Samuel G. Drake. Albany: J. Munsell, 1864.

    Reprint, with a new title, of *A Relation of the Troubles* (Boston, 1677).

————. *An Earnest Exhortation to the Inhabitants of New-England: To Hearken to the Voice of God in His Late and Present Dispensations, as Ever They Desire to Scape another Judgement, Seven Times Greater Then Any Thing Which Yet Hath Been.* Boston: John Foster, 1676.

————. *A Relation of the Troubles Which Have Hapned in New-England, by Reason of the Indians There, from the Year 1614 to the Year 1675: Wherein the Frequent Conspiracyes of the Indians to Cutt Off the English, and the Wonderfull Providence of God, in Disappointing Their Devices, Is Declared; Together with an Historical Discourse Concerning the Prevalency of Prayer; Shewing that New-Englands Late Deliverance from the Rage of the Heathen Is an Eminent Answer to Prayer.* Boston: John Foster, 1677.

————. *Remarkable Providences: Illustrative of the Earlier Days of American Colonisation*. Edited by George Offor. London: Reeves and Turner, 1890.
Partially reprinted in Burr, *Narratives of the Witchcraft Cases*.

Matthiessen, F. O. *American Renaissance: Art and Expression in the Age of Emerson and Whitman*. New York: Oxford University Press, 1941.

Maxson, Charles Hartshorn. *The Great Awakening in the Middle Colonies*. Gloucester, Mass.: Peter Smith, 1958.

Maylem, John. *The Conquest of Louisbourg: A Poem*. [Boston: Benjamin Mecom?, 1758.]

————. *Gallic Perfidy: A Poem*. Boston: Benjamin Mecom, 1758.

Melville, Herman. *The Confidence-Man: His Masquerade*. New York: Grove Press, 1949.

————. *Moby-Dick: Or, The White Whale*. New York: Modern Library, 1950.

————. *Selected Tales and Poems*. Edited by Richard Chase. New York: Holt, Rinehart and Winston, Rinehart Editions, 1965.

Metcalf[e], Samuel Lytler. "A Collection of Some of the Most Interesting Narratives of Indian Warfare in the West: Containing an Account of the Adventures of Col. Daniel Boone. . . ." Reprinted from the Lexington, Ky., 1821, edition. *Magazine of History with Notes and Queries* 26, extra no. 26 (1913).
Contains a reprint of Filson's Boone narrative from the original text of the Wilmington, 1784, edition of *Kentucke*.

Meyers, Marvin. *The Jacksonian Persuasion: Politics and Belief*. Stanford: Stanford University Press, 1957.

Miller, Perry. *Errand into the Wilderness*. New York: Harper and Row, Harper Torchbooks, 1964.

————. *Jonathan Edwards*. New York: Meridian Books, 1964.

————. *The New England Mind: From Colony to Province*. Cambridge: Harvard University Press, 1953.

————. *The New England Mind: The Seventeenth Century*. Cambridge: Harvard University Press, 1954.

————. *Roger Williams: His Contribution to the American Tradition*. New York: Atheneum, 1962.

Miller, Perry, and Johnson, Thomas H., eds. *The Puritans*. Rev. ed., edited by George McCandlish. 2 vols. New York: Harper and Row, Harper Torchbooks, 1963.

Miller, William. *Evidence from Scripture and History of the Second Coming of Christ, about the Year 1843: Exhibited in a Course of Lectures*. Boston: B. B. Mussey, 1840.

Miner, William H. *Daniel Boone: Contributions Towards a Bibliography of Works Concerning Daniel Boone*. New York: Dibdin Club, 1901.

Monk, Maria. *Awful Disclosures of Maria Monk: As Exhibited in a Narrative of Her Sufferings During a Residence of Five Years as a Novice, and Two Years as a Black Nun, in the Hotel Dieu Nunnery at Montreal; Revised, with an Appendix. . . .* New York: Maria Monk, 1836.

Moore, Arthur Keister. *The Frontier Mind: A Cultural Analysis of the Kentucky Frontiersman*. Lexington: University of Kentucky Press, 1957.

Morgan, Edmund S. *The Puritan Dilemma: The Story of John Winthrop*. Boston: Little, Brown, 1958.

Morison, Samuel Eliot. *The Puritan Pronaos.* New York: New York University Press, 1936.

Morton, Thomas. "New English Canaan or New Canaan: Containing an Abstract of New England Composed in Three Bookes; the First Setting forth the Originall of the Natives, Their Manners and Customs; Together with Their Tractable Nature and Love Towards the English; II. The Natural Indowments of the Countrie, and what Staple Commodities it Yeeldeth; III. What People are Planted There, Their Prosperity, What Remarkable Accidents Have Happened Since Their First Planting of it; together with Their Tenets and Practice of Their Church." Edited by Peter Force. [Force's] *Tracts and Other Papers Relating Principally to the Origin, Settlement, and Progress of the Colonies in North America, from the Discovery of the Country to the Year 1776* 2, no. 5 (1838).

> Apparently reprinted from the Amsterdam, 1637, edition; the title-page facsimile of a "London, 1632" edition printed by Charles Green is possibly a ghost and almost certainly a misreading of the date (see Vail, *Voice of the Old Frontier*, p. 122).

Moses, Montrose J., ed. *Representative Plays by American Dramatists.* Vol. 1. New York: Benjamin Blom, 1964.

Mott, Frank Luther. *Golden Multitudes: The Story of Best-Sellers in the United States.* New York: Macmillan, 1947.

———. *A History of American Magazines.* Vol. 1. New York: D. Appleton, 1930. Vols. 2–5. Cambridge: Harvard University Press, 1938–40.

"The Mournful Elegy on Mr. Jonathan Frye, 1725." *Magazine of History with Notes and Queries* 2, extra no. 5, part 1 (1909).

> See Kidder, "Expeditions of Captain John Lovewell."

[Mourt (or Morton), George, ed.]. *A Relation or Iournall of the Beginning and Proceedings of the English Plantation Setled at Plimoth in New England. . . .* London: Iohn Bellamie, 1622.

New and Further Narrative of the State of New-England: Being, a Continued Account of the Bloudy Indian-War, from March till August, 1676; Giving a Perfect Relation of the Several Devastations, Engagements and Transactions There; as also the Great Successes Lately Obtained Against the Barbarous Indians, the Reducing of King Philip, and the Killing of One of the Queens, &c; Together with a Catalogue of the Losses in the Whole, Sustained on Either Side, Since the Said War Began, as Near as Can Be Collected, A. London: Printed by J. B. for Dorman Newman, 1676.

Nowell, Samuel. *Abraham in Arms: Or, The First Religious General with His Army Engaging in a War for which He Had Wisely Prepared, and by which, Not Only an Eminent Victory was Obtained, but a Blessing Gained also; Delivered in an Artillery-Election-Sermon, June 3, 1678.* Boston: John Foster, 1678.

O'Dea, Thomas F. *The Mormons.* Chicago: University of Chicago Press, 1957.

Osborn, Chase Salmon, and Osborn, Stellanova. *Schoolcraft, Longfellow, Hiawatha.* Lancaster, Pa.: Jacques Cattell Press, 1942.

Owen, Roger C.; Deetz, James J. F.; and Fisher, Anthony D., eds. *The North American Indians: A Sourcebook.* New York: Macmillan, 1967.

Parkman, Francis. *Count Frontenac and New France under Louis XIV.* Boston: Beacon Press, 1966.

————. *A Half-Century of Conflict.* New York: Macmillan, Collier Books, 1962.

————. *The Old Regime in Canada.* Boston: Little, Brown, 1898.

Parrington, Vernon Louis. *Main Currents in American Thought.* 3 vols. New York: Harcourt, Brace, and World, 1930.

————, ed. *The Connecticut Wits.* New York: Harcourt, Brace, 1926.

Pearce, Roy Harvey. *Historicism Once More: Problems and Occasions for the American Scholar.* Princeton: Princeton University Press, 1969.

————. *The Savages of America: A Study of the Indian and the Idea of Civilization.* Baltimore: Johns Hopkins Press, 1953.

————. "The Significances of the Captivity Narrative." *American Literature* 19, no. 1 (March 1949): 1–20.

————, ed. *Colonial American Writing.* New York: Holt, Rinehart, and Winston, Rinehart Editions, 1964.

Peck, John M. "The Life of Daniel Boon." *The Library of American Biography.* Vol. 13. Edited by Jared Sparks. Boston: Charles C. Little and James Brown, 1847.

Penhallow, Samuel. *The History of the Wars of New-England, with the Eastern Indians: Or, A Narrative of Their Continued Perfidy and Cruelty, from the 10th of August, 1703. to the Peace Renewed 13th of July, 1713. . . .* Boston: Printed by T. Fleet for S. Gerrish, 1726.

Peterson, Merrill D. *The Jefferson Image in the American Mind.* New York: Oxford University Press, 1960.

Pierson, Roscoe M. *Preliminary Check List of Lexington Kentucky Imprints: 1821–1850.* Charlottesville: Bibliographical Society of the University of Virginia, 1953.

Porte, Joel Miles. *The Romance in America: Studies in Cooper, Poe, Hawthorne, Melville, and James.* Middletown, Conn.: Wesleyan University Press, 1969.

Porter, William Trotter. *Big Bear's Adventures and Travels: Containing the Whole of the Big Bear of Arkansaw and Stray Subjects, Illustrative of Characters and Incidents in the South and South-west, in a Series of Sixty-eight Southern and Southwestern Sketches. . . .* Philadelphia: T. B. Peterson and Brothers, 1858.

Potter, Israel Ralph. *The Life and Remarkable Adventures of Israel Ralph Potter.* Edited by Leonard Kriegel. Facsimile of the original Providence, 1824, edition. American Experience Series. New York: Corinth Books, 1962.

Pritts, Joseph. *Incidents of Border Life, Illustrative of the Times and Conditions of the First Settlements in Parts of the Middle and Western States: Comprising Narratives of Strange and Thrilling Adventure. . . .* Chambersburg, Pa.: Joseph Pritts, 1839.

Providence Typographical Union, Committee of the. *Printers and Printing in Providence: 1762–1907.* [Providence: Providence Typographical Union, 1908.]

Randall, Randolph C. *James Hall: Spokesman of the New West.* Columbus: Ohio University Press, 1964.

Raskin, Marcus G., and Fall, Bernard B., eds. *The Viet-Nam Reader: Articles and Documents on American Foreign Policy and the Viet-Nam Crisis.* Rev. ed. New York: Vintage Books, 1967.

Raynal, [Guillaume-Thomas François] Abbé. *A Philosophical and Political History of the Settlements and Trade of the Europeans in the East and West Indies.*

Vols. 5–8. Translated by J. O. Justamond. London: W. S. Trahan and T. Cadell, 1788.

————. *The Revolution of America.* London: Printed for Lockyer Davis, Holborn, 1781.

Rexroth, Kenneth. "Classics Revisited LXI: Parkman's History." *Saturday Review of Literature,* 24 February 1968, p. 35.

Rice, Howard C. *Le Cultivateur américain: Etude sur l'oeuvre de St.-Jean de Crèvecoeur.* Paris: Librairie Ancienne Honoré Champion, 1933.

Rickels, Milton. *Thomas Bangs Thorpe: Humorist of the Old Southwest.* Baton Rouge: Louisiana State University Press, 1962.

Ridgely, J. V. *William Gilmore Simms.* New York: Twayne, 1962.

Rogers, Robert. *A Concise Account of North America: Containing a Description of the Several British Colonies on that Continent, Including the Islands of Newfoundland, Cape Breton, &c; As to Their Situation, Extent, Climate, Soil, Produce, Rise, Government, Religion, Present Boundaries, and the Number of Inhabitants Supposed to be in Each; Also of the Interior, or Westerly Parts of the Country, Upon the Rivers St. Laurence, the Mississippi, Christino, and the Great Lakes; To which is subjoined an Account of the Several Nations and Tribes of Indians Residing in Those Parts, as to Their Customs, Manners, Government, Numbers, &c; Containing Many Useful and Entertaining Facts, Never Before Treated Of.* London: Printed for the Author, 1765.

————. *Journals of Major Robert Rogers: Reprinted from the Original Edition of 1765.* Edited by Howard H. Peckham. American Experience Series. New York: Corinth Books, 1961.

[————.] *Ponteach: Or The Savages of America; a Tragedy.* London: Printed for the Author by J. Millam, 1766.

————. *Reminiscences of the French War: Containing Rogers' Expeditions with the New-England Rangers Under His Command. as Published in London in 1765; with Notes and Illustrations; to which is added an Account of the Life and Military Services of Maj. Gen. John Stark; with Notices and Anecdotes of Other Officers Distinguished in the French and Revolutionary Wars.* [Edited by Luther Roby.] Concord, N.H.: Luther Roby, 1831.

Rogin, Michael Paul. "Liberal Society and the Indian Question." *Politics and Society* 1, no. 3 (May 1971): 269–312.

Rougemont, Denis de. *Love in the Western World.* Translated by Montgomery Belgion. New York: Fawcett, 1966.

Rourke, Constance Mayfield. *American Humor: A Study of the National Character.* Garden City, N.Y.: Doubleday, Anchor Books, 1955.

Rousseau, Jean Jacques. *Emile.* Translated by Barbara Foxley. Introduction by André Boutet de Monvel. New York: Dutton, Everyman's Library, [1957].

————. *Social Contract. Discourses.* Translated and edited by G. D. H. Cole. London: Dent, Everyman's Library, 1961.

Rowlandson, Mary. *The Soveraignty and Goodness of God, Together with the Faithfulness of His Promises Displayed: Being a Narrative of the Captivity and Restauration of Mrs. Mary Rowlandson; Commended by Her, to All that Desires to Know the Lords Doings to, and Dealings with Her; Especially to Her Dear Children and Relations . . . Written by Her Own Hand for Her Private*

Use, and Now Made Publick at the Earnest Desire of Some Friends, and for the Benefit of the Afflicted. 2d ed., corrected and amended. Cambridge, Mass.: Samuel Green, 1682.

No copy of the first edition exists. This is the first issue of the second edition, with the misspelling "Addition" on the title page. Charles Lincoln reprints this title page in *Narratives of the Indian Wars*, but the text of the reprint is derived from this edition and from the London, 1682, edition described below, since the extant copies of this edition are damaged and incomplete.

————. *A True History of the Captivity & Restoration of Mrs. Mary Rowlandson, a Minister's Wife in New-England; Wherein is Set Forth, the Cruel and Inhumane Usage She Underwent Amongst the Heathens, for Eleven Weeks Time; and Her Deliverance from Them; Written by Her Own Hand, for Her Private Use; and Now Made Publick at the Earnest Desire of Some Friends, for the Benefit of the Afflicted; Whereunto is Annexed, a Sermon of the Possibility of God's Forsaking a People that Have Been Near and Dear to Him; Preached by Mr. Joseph Rowlandson, Husband to the Said Mrs. Rowlandson; it Being His Last Sermon.* Printed first at New-England, and re-printed at London: Joseph Poole, 1682.

The first English edition. The sermon was also printed in the two American editions and also issued separately. For reprint, see note on preceding entry.

Rusk, Ralph Leslie. "The Adventures of Gilbert Imlay." *Indiana University Studies* 10, no. 57 (March 1923): 6–23.

————. *The Literature of the Middle Western Frontier.* 2 vols. New York: Columbia University Press, 1925.

Sabin, Joseph; Eames, Wilberforce; and Vail, R. W. G. *Bibliotheca Americana: A Dictionary of Books Relating to America, from Its Discovery to the Present Time.* 29 vols. New York: [Bibliographical Society of America], 1868–1936.

S[altonstall], N[athaniel]. *A Continuation of the State of New-England: Being a Farther Account of the Indian Warr, and of the Engagement betwixt the Joynt Forces of the United English Collonies and the Indians, on the 19th. of December 1675: With the True Number of the Slain and Wounded, and the Transactions of the English Army Since the Said Fight; With All Other Passages that Have There Hapned from the 10th. of November, 1675. to the 8th. of February 167⁶/₇: Together with an Account of the Intended Rebellion of the Negroes in the Barbadoes.* London: Printed by T. M. for Dorman Newman, 1676.

————. *A New and Further Narrative of the State of New-England: Being, a Continued Account of the Bloudy Indian-War, from March till August, 1676. . . .* London: Printed by J. B. for Dorman Newman, 1676.

————. *The Present State of New-England, with Respect to the Indian War: Wherein is an Account of the True Reason Thereof, (as Far as Can Be Judged by Men); Together with Most of the Remarkable Passages that Have Happened from the 20th of June, till the 10th of November, 1675.* London: Printed for Dorman Newman, 1675.

These three works by Nathaniel Saltonstall are reprinted in Lincoln, *Narratives of the Indian Wars.*

Schoolcraft, Henry Rowe. *Algic Researches: Comprising Inquiries Respecting the Mental Characteristics of the North American Indians; First Series; Indian Tales and Legends.* 2 vols. New York: Harper and Brothers, 1839.

———. *The Myth of Hiawatha: And Other Legends, Mythologic and Allegoric, of the North American Indians.* Philadelphia: J. B. Lippincott, 1856.

Scott, Walter, Sir. *Rob Roy. The Waverly Novels.* Vol. 5. New York: Harper and Brothers, n.d.

Seaver, James E. *A Narrative of the Life of Mrs. Mary Jemison: Who Was Taken by the Indians, in the Year 1755, When Only About Twelve Years of Age, and Has Continued to Reside Amongst Them to the Present Time. . . .* Edited by Allen W. Trelease. Facsimile of the original Canandaigua, N.Y., 1824, edition. American Experience Series. New York: Corinth Books, 1961.

Sebeok, Thomas, ed. *Myth: A Symposium.* Bloomington: University of Indiana Press, 1965.

Sedgwick, Catherine Maria. *Hope Leslie: Or, Early Times in the Massachusetts.* 1827. 2 vols. New York: Harper and Brothers, 1842.

Shaw, Ralph R., and Shoemaker, Richard. *American Bibliography: A Preliminary Check List, 1801–1820.* 20 vols. New York: Scarecrow Press, 1958.

[Shepard, Thomas.] "The Day-Breaking, If Not the Sun-Rising of the Gospell with the Indians in New-England." Reprinted from the London, 1647, edition. *Collections of the Massachusetts Historical Society,* 3d ser. 4 (1834): 1–23.

Sherwood, James Manning, ed. *Memoirs of the Rev. David Brainerd, Missionary to the Indians of North America: Based on the Life of Brainerd Prepared by Jonathan Edwards and Afterwards Revised and Enlarged by Sereno E. Dwight. . . . Also an Essay on God's Hand in Missions, by Arthur T. Pierson.* New York: Funk and Wagnalls, 1884.

Shipton, Clifford K., and Mooney, James E. *National Index of American Imprints Through 1800: The Short-Title Evans.* 2 vols. N.p.: American Antiquarian Society and Barre Publishers, 1969.

Silver, Rollo G. *The Boston Book Trade: 1800–1825.* New York: New York Public Library, 1949.

Silverman, Kenneth, ed. *Colonial American Poetry.* New York: Hafner, 1968.

Simms, William Gilmore. *Guy Rivers: A Tale of Georgia. The Works of William Gilmore Simms.* Vol. 3. New York: A. C. Armstrong and Son, 1882.

———. *The Kinsmen: Or, The Black Riders of the Congaree; a Tale.* Philadelphia: Lea and Blanchard, 1841.

———. *Views and Reviews in American Literature, History and Fiction.* Edited by C. Hugh Holman. Cambridge: Harvard University Press, Belknap Press, 1962.

———. *The Yemassee.* Edited by C. Hugh Holman. Boston: Houghton Mifflin, Riverside Editions, 1961.

Slotkin, Richard S. "Dreams and Genocide: The American Myth of Regeneration through Violence." *Journal of Popular Culture* 5, no. 1 (Summer 1971): 38–59.

———. *Emergence of a Myth: John Filson's "Boon Narrative" and the Literature of the Indian Wars, 1638–1848.* Ann Arbor, Mich.: University Microfilms, 1966.

Smith, Elbert H. *Ma-Ka-Tai-Me-She-Kia-Kiak: or, Black Hawk, and Scenes in the West; a National Poem in Six Cantos . . .* New York: Edward Kearny, 1848.

Smith, Ethan. *Views of the Hebrews: Exhibiting the Destruction of Jerusalem; the*

Certain Restoration of Judah and Israel; the Present State of Judah and Israel; and an Address of the Prophet Isaiah Relative to Their Restoration. Poultney, Vt.: Smith and Shute, 1823.

Smith, Henry Nash. *Virgin Land: The American West as Symbol and Myth.* New York: Vintage Books, 1950.

Smith, Horatio. *Festivals, Games, and Amusements: Ancient and Modern. . . . With additions by Samuel Woodworth.* New York: J. and J. Harper, 1836.

Smith, James. *An Account of the Remarkable Occurrences in the Life and Travels of Col. James Smith, During His Captivity with the Indians, in the Years 1755, '56, '57, '58, and '59: With an Appendix of Illustrative Notes.* Edited by William M. Darlington. Biographical and bibliographical account by Robert Clarke. Ohio Valley Historical Series, no. 5. Cincinnati: Robert Clarke and Company, 1870.

    Reprint of Smith's *Account* (1799), together with his *Treatise* (1812). See following entries.

————. *An Account of the Remarkable Occurrences in the Life and Travels of Col. James Smith, (Now a Citizen of Bourbon County, Kentucky,) During His Captivity with the Indians, in the Years 1755, '56, '57, '58, & '59, in which the Customs, Manners, Traditions, Theological Sentiments, Mode of Warfare, Military Tactics, Discipline and Encampments, Treatment of Prisoners, &c. Are Better Explained, and More Minutely Related, Than Has Been Heretofore Done, by Any Author on that Subject: To which is added, a Brief Account of Some Very Uncommon Occurrences, which Transpired After His Return from Captivity; as well as of the Different Campaigns Carried On Against the Indians to the Westward of Fort Pitt, since the Year 1755, to the Present Date.* Lexington, Ky.: John Bradford, 1799.

————. *A Treatise, On the Mode and Manner of Indian War: Their Tactics, Discipline and Encampments, the Various Methods They Practise, in Order to Obtain the Advantage, by Ambush, Surprise, Surrounding, &c.; Ways and Means Proposed to Prevent the Indians from Obtaining the Advantage. . . .* Paris, Ky.: Joel R. Lyle, 1812.

Smith, John, Captain. *A Description of New England: Or, The Observations, and Discoueries, of Captain Iohn Smith (Admirall of that Country) in the North of America, in the Year of Our Lord 1614. . . .* London: Humfrey Lownes, 1616.

————. *The Generall History of Virginia, New-England, and the Summer Isles: With the Names of the Adventurers, Planters, and Governours from Their First Beginning, Ano: 1584. to this Present 1624. . . .* London: Printed by I. D. and I. H. for Michael Sparkes, 1624.

Smith, John, Captain, and Symonds, William. *A Map of Virginia: With a Description of the Countrey, the Commodities, People, Government and Religion. . . .* Oxford: Joseph Barnes, 1612.

[Smith, Joseph, Jr., and Pratt, Orson.] *The Book of Mormon: An Account Written by the Hand of Mormon, Upon Plates Taken from the Plates of Nephi. Translated by Joseph Smith, Jun.* Salt Lake City: Deseret News Company, 1888.

[Smith, William.] *Historical Account of Bouquet's Expedition Against the Ohio Indians, in 1764.* Edited by Francis Parkman. Ohio Valley Historical Series, no. 1. Cincinnati: Robert Clarke and Company, 1868.

Reprint, with additions, of *An Historical Account* (1765). See following entry.

———. *An Historical Account of the Expedition Against the Ohio Indians, in the Year 1764, Under the Command of Henry Bouquet, Esq., Colonel of Foot, and Now Brigadier General in America: Including His Transactions with the Indians, Relative to the Delivery of Their Prisoners, and the Preliminaries of Peace; With an Introductory Account of the Preceeding Campaign, and Battle at Bushy-Run; To which are Annexed Military Papers, Containing Reflections on the War with the Savages. . . .* Philadelphia: William Bradford, 1765.

"Song of Lovewell's Fight." *Magazine of History with Notes and Queries* 2, extra no. 5, part 1 (1909).

See Kidder, "Expeditions of Captain John Lovewell."

Southey, Robert. *The Poetical Works of Robert Southey: With a Memoir of the Author.* Edited by Henry T. Tuckerman. 10 vols. Boston: Little, Brown, 1860.

Speck, Frank Goldsmith. *Penobscot Man: The Life History of a Forest Tribe in Maine.* Philadelphia: University of Pennsylvania Press, 1940.

———. *A Study of the Delaware Indian Big House Ceremony: In Native Text Dictated by Witapanóxwe.* Harrisburg, Pa.: Pennsylvania Historical Commission, 1931.

Spence, Lewis. *Myth and Ritual in Dance, Game, and Rhyme.* London: Watts, 1947.

Spencer, Benjamin Townley. *The Quest for Nationality: An American Literary Campaign.* Syracuse, N.Y.: Syracuse University Press, 1957.

Starkey, Marion L. *The Devil in Massachusetts: A Modern Enquiry into the Salem Witch Trials.* Garden City, N.Y.: Doubleday, Dolphin Books, 1961.

Stearns, Raymond P. "Underhill, John." *Dictionary of American Biography* 19: 110–11. New York: Charles Scribner's Sons, 1936.

Stone, John Augustus. "Metamora: Or The Last of the Wampanoags." *Favorite American Plays of the Nineteenth Century.* Edited by Barrett H. Clark. Princeton: Princeton University Press, 1934.

Stowe, Harriet Beecher. *Uncle Tom's Cabin: Or, Life among the Lowly.* New York: Harper and Row, Perennial Classics, 1965.

Strange News from Virginia: Being a Full and True Account of the Life and Death of Nathaniel Bacon Esquire, Who was the Only Cause and Original of All the Late Troubles in that Country; With a Full Relation of All the Accidents which Have Happened in the Late War There Between the Christians and the Indians. London: William Harris, 1677.

Strutt, Joseph. *The Sports and Pastimes of the People of England: Including the Rural and Domestic Recreations, May Games, Mummeries, Shows, Processions, Pageants, and Pompous Spectacles, from the Earliest Period to the Present Time.* London: William Tegg, 1867.

Stubbes, Phillip. "Anatomy of the Abuses in England in Shakespeare's Youth, A.D. 1583. . . ." Edited by Frederick J. Furnivall. *New Shakespeare Society Publications,* 6th ser., nos. 4, 6, 12 (1877–79).

Sutton, Walter. *The Western Book Trade: Cincinnati as a Nineteenth-Century Publishing and Book-Trade Center; Containing a Directory of Cincinnati Publishers, Booksellers, and Members of Allied Trades, 1796–1880.* Columbus: Ohio University Press for the Ohio Historical Society, 1961.

Symmes, Thomas. *Historical Memoirs of the Late Fight at Piggwacket: With a Sermon Occasion'd by the Fall of the Brave Capt John Lovewell and Several of His Valiant Company, in the Late Heroic Action There; Pronounc'd at Bradford, May, 16. 1725.* 2d ed., corrected. Boston: Printed by B. Green, Jr., for S. Gerrish, 1725.

      For first edition, see following entry. For reprint, see Kidder, "Expeditions of Captain John Lovewell."

————. *Lovewell Lamented: Or, A Sermon Occasion'd by the Fall of the Brave Capt. John Lovewell and Several of His Valiant Company, in the Late Heroic Action at Piggwacket; Pronounc'd at Bradford, May 16, 1725.* Boston: Printed by B. Green, Jr., for S. Gerrish, 1725.

      For reprint, see Kidder, "Expeditions of Captain John Lovewell."

Tawney, Richard H. *Religion and the Rise of Capitalism: A Historical Study.* New York: Harcourt, Brace, and World, 1926.

Taylor, William R. *Cavalier and Yankee: The Old South and American National Character.* New York: George Braziller, 1961.

Tebbel, John, and Jennison, Keith. *The American Indian Wars.* New York: Bonanza Books, 1960.

Thatcher, B[enjamin] B[ussey]. *Indian Biography: Or, An Historical Account of Those Individuals Who Have Been Distinguished Among the North American Natives as Orators, Warriors, Statesmen, and Other Remarkable Characters.* 2 vols. New York: J. and J. Harper, 1834.

————. *Tales of the Indians: Being Prominent Passages of the History of the North American Natives; Taken from Authentic Sources.* Boston: Waitt and Dow, 1831.

Thoreau, Henry David. *Walden and Civil Disobedience: Authoritative Texts, Background, Reviews and Essays in Criticism.* Edited by Owen Thomas. New York: W. W. Norton, Norton Critical Editions, 1966.

————. *A Week on the Concord and Merrimack Rivers.* Edited by Denham Sutcliffe. New York: New American Library, 1961.

————. *The Works of Henry David Thoreau.* Selected and edited by Henry Seidel Canby. Boston: Houghton Mifflin, 1937.

[Thorpe, Thomas Bangs.] *The Big Bear of Arkansas, and Other Sketches, Illustrative of Characters and Incidents in the South and Southwest.* Philadelphia: Carey and Hart, 1845.

Thwaites, Reuben Gold, ed. *The Jesuit Relations and Allied Documents: Travels and Explorations of the Jesuit Missionaries in New France, 1619–1791; the Original French, Latin, and Italian Texts, with English Translations and Notes.* . . . 73 vols. Cleveland: Burrows Brothers, 1900.

Timberlake, Henry. *Lieutenant Henry Timberlake's Memoirs: 1756–1765.* Edited by Samuel Cole Williams. Reprinted from the London, 1765, edition. Johnson City, Tenn.: Watauga Press, 1927.

[Tompson, Benjamin.] *New Englands Crisis: Or A Brief Narrative, of New-Englands Lamentable Estate at Present, Compar'd with Her Former (but Few) Years of Prosperity; Occasioned by Many Unheard-of Crueltyes Practised Upon the Persons and Estates of its United Colonyes, Without Respect of Sex, Age or Quality of Persons, by the Barbarous Heathen Thereof; Poetically Described.* Boston: John Foster, 1676.

————. *New-Englands Tears for Her Present Miseries: Or, A Late and True Relation of the Calamities of New-England Since April Last Past, with an Account of the Battel between the English and Indians Upon Seaconck Plain and of the Indians Burning and Destroying of Marlbury, Rehoboth, Chelmsford, Sudbury, and Providence; with the Death of Antononies the Grand Indian Sachem; and a Relation of the Fortification Made by Women Upon Boston Neck; Together with an Elegy on the Death of John Winthrop Esq.; Late Governour of Connecticut, and Fellow of the Royal Society.* Boston: John Foster, 1676.

True Account of the Most Considerable Occurrences that Have Hapned in the Warre between the English and the Indians in New-England. . . . The Most Exact Account yet Printed, A. London: Benjamin Billingsley, 1676.

[Trumbull, Henry.] *History of the Discovery of America: of the Landing of Our Forefathers, at Plymouth, and of Their Most Remarkable Engagements with the Indians, in New-England, from Their First Landing in 1620, until the Final Subjugation of the Natives in 1669* [sic, but actually 1679]: *To which is Annexed, the Defeat of Generals Braddock, Harmer & St. Clair, by the Indians at the Westward, &c.* Brooklyn: Printed by Grant and Wells for J. W. Carew, 1810.

————. *History of the Discovery of America. . . .* Norwich, Conn.: For the Author, at his office, 1810. Also: 2d ed., corrected. Norwich: Published for the Author, 1810. Also: Norwich: Published for the Author, 1811.

————. *History of the Discovery of America. . . .* Norwich: Published for the Author, 1812.

————. *History of the Discovery of America. . . . Also, the Official Account of the Late Defeat of the Indians on the Wabash, by Gov. Harrison.* Trenton: Republished by D. Fenton, 1812.

The following editions were also published, all at Boston: Printed by S. Sewell, for the Author, 1819. — Published by George Clark, proprietor of the copy-right. Printed by Jonathan Howe, 1822. — J. P. Peaselee, 1828. — George Clark, 1830. Also 1831. — Published by George Clark. J. Page, printer, 1832. — Published by George Clark. E. G. House, printer, 1833. — [No publisher], 1834 — George Clark, 1835. Also 1836, 1840.

————. *History of the Indian Wars. . . .* Boston: N. C. Barton, 1846.

Reprint of *History of the Discovery of America* under a new title. Text is substantially the same as that of the second edition.

————. *Western Emigration: Journal of Doctor Jeremiah Smipleton's* [sic for Simpleton's] *Tour to Ohio; Containing an Account of the Numerous Difficulties, Hair-breadth Escapes, Mortifications, and Privations, which the Doctor and His Family Experienced on Their Journey from Maine, to the "Land of Promise," and During a Residence of Three Years in that Highly Extolled Country.* Boston: S. Sewell, [1819].

Turner, Frederick Jackson. *The Significance of the Frontier in American History.* New York: Holt, Rinehart, and Winston, Rinehart Editions, 1962.

Turner, George. *Traits of Indian Character: As Generally Applicable to the Aborigines of North America; Drawn from Various Sources; — Partly from Personal Observation of the Writer.* 2 vols. Philadelphia: Key and Biddle, 1836.

Tyler, Lyon Gardiner, ed. *Narratives of Early Virginia: 1606–1625.* Original Narratives of Early American History Series. New York: Charles Scribner's Sons, 1907.

Tyler, Moses Coit. *A History of American Literature During the Colonial Period: 1607–1765.* New York: G. P. Putnam's Sons, Knickerbocker Press, 1909.

Underhill, John. "Newes from America: Or, A New and Experimentall Discoverie of New England; Containing, a True Relation of Their War-like Proceedings These Two Years Last Past, with a Figure of the Indian Fort, or Palizado; Also a Discovery of These Places, that as Yet Have Very Few or No Inhabitants which Would Yeeld Speciall Accomodation to Such as Will Plant There. . . ." Reprinted from the London, 1638, edition. *Collections of the Massachusetts Historical Society,* 3d ser. 6 (1837): 1–28.

Vail, Robert William Glenroie. *The Voice of the Old Frontier.* Philadelphia: University of Pennsylvania Press, 1949.

Van Nostrand, Albert D. *Everyman His Own Poet: Romantic Gospels in American Literature.* New York: McGraw-Hill, 1968.

Vinal, William. *A Sermon on the Accursed Thing that Hinders Success and Victory in War: Occasioned by the Defeat of the Hon. Edward Braddock, Esq., General of the English Forces in North-America, Who Was Mortally Wounded in an Engagement with the French and Indians, Near Fort DuQuesne; and Died of his Wounds the Third Day After the Battle, which Was Fought July 5, 1755.* . . . Newport, R.I.: James Franklin, 1755.

Vincent, P[hilip]. "A True Relation of the Late Battell Fought in New-England, between the English and the Pequet Salvages: In which were Slaine and Taken Prisoners about 700 of the Salvages, and Those which Escaped, Had Their Heads Cut Off by the Mohocks; with the Present State of Things There." Reprinted from the London, 1638, edition. *Collections of the Massachusetts Historical Society,* 3d ser. 6 (1837): 29–44.

Volney, Constantin François Chasseboeuf. *A View of the Soil and Climate of the United States of America: with Supplementary Remarks upon Florida; on the French Colonies on the Mississippi and Ohio, and in Canada; and on the Aboriginal Tribes of America.* Translated and annotated by C[harles] B[rockden] Brown. Philadelphia: Published by J. Conrad and Company. Printed by T. and G. Palmer, 1804.

Voltaire, François-Marie Arouet de. "Alzire: ou, les Américains." *Oeuvres complètes.* Nouvelle edition. Vol. 3. Paris: Garnier Frères, 1879.

————. *Lettres philosophiques (1734). Oeuvres complètes.* Nouvelle edition. Vol. 22. Paris: Garnier Frères, 1879.

Waggoner, Hyatt Howe. *Hawthorne: A Critical Study.* Rev. ed. Cambridge: Harvard University Press, Belknap Press, 1963.

Walker, Thomas Capell. *Chateaubriand's Natural Scenery: A Study of His Descriptive Art.* Baltimore: Johns Hopkins Press, 1946.

Walker, Warren S., ed. *Leatherstocking and the Critics.* Chicago: Scott, Foresman, 1965.

Walker, Willard, et al. "The Indians of Maine." Unpublished ms., Wesleyan University, 1968.

Walton, John. *John Filson of Kentucke.* Lexington: University of Kentucky Press, 1956.

Ward, Edward. *A Trip to New-England: With a Character of the Country and People, both English and Indians.* London: [no publisher], 1699.

Ward, John William. *Andrew Jackson: Symbol for an Age.* New York: Oxford University Press, 1955.

Wardle, Ralph M. *Mary Wollestonecraft: A Critical Biography.* Lawrence: University of Kansas Press, 1951.

Washburn, Wilcomb F., ed. *The Indian and the White Man.* Garden City, N.Y.: Doubleday, Anchor Books, 1964.

Watts, Alan. *Myth and Ritual in Christianity.* London: Thames and Hudson, 1953.

Weber, Max. *The Protestant Ethic and the Spirit of Capitalism.* Translated by Talcott Parsons. Foreword by R. H. Tawney. New York: Charles Scribner's Sons, 1948.

Weems, M[ason] L[ocke]. *The Life of George Washington: with Curious Anecdotes, Equally Honourable to Himself, and Exemplary to His Young Countrymen.* Philadelphia: J. B. Lippincott, 1856.

[Wharton, Edward.] *New-England's Present Sufferings, Under Their Cruel Neighbouring Indians: Represented in Two Letters, Lately Written from Boston to London.* London: [B. Clark], 1675.

Wheeler, Thomas. *A Thankfull Remembrance of Gods Mercy to Several Persons at Quabaug or Brookfield: Partly in a Collection of Providences about Them, and Gracious Appearances for Them; and Partly in a Sermon Preached by Mr. Edward Bulkley, Pastor of the Church of Christ at Concord, upon a Day of Thanksgiving, Kept by Divers for Their Wonderfull Deliverance There.* Cambridge, Mass.: Samuel Green, 1676.

White, John. *The Planters Plea: Or the Grounds of Plantations Examined, and Usual Objections Answered; Together with a Manifestation of the Causes Mooving Such as Have Lately Undertaken a Plantation in New-England; for the Satisfaction of Those that Question the Lawfulnesse of the Action.* London: William Iones, 1630.

White, T. H., ed. and trans. *The Book of Beasts: Being a Translation from a Latin Bestiary of the Twelfth Century.* New York: G. P. Putnam's Sons, 1954.

Whitfield, Henry. "The Light Appearing More and More To-wards the Perfect Day: Or, A Farther Discovery of the Present State of the Indians in New-England, Concerning the Progress of the Gospel Amongst Them; Manifested by Letters from Such as Preacht to Them There." Reprinted from the London, 1651, edition. *Collections of the Massachusetts Historical Society,* 3d ser. 4 (1834): 101–47.

Whitman, Walt. *Leaves of Grass and Selected Prose.* Edited by James E. Miller. Boston: Houghton Mifflin, Riverside Editions, 1959.

Whittier, John Greenleaf. *The Poems of John G. Whittier.* New York: F. A. Stolles, 1893.

Wilbur, Richard. *The Poems of Richard Wilbur.* New York: Harcourt, Brace, and World, 1963.

Williams, John. *The Redeemed Captive Returning to Zion: Or, A Faithful History of Remarkable Occurrences in the Captivity and Deliverance of Mr. John Williams, Minister of the Gospel in Deerfield, Who in the Desolation which Befel the Plantation by an Incursion of the French and Indians, Was by Them Car-*

ried Away, with His Family and His Neighbourhood, into Canada, Drawn Up by Himself; to which is added, a Biographical Memoir of the Reverend Author, with an Appendix and Notes, by Stephen Williams. . . . 6th ed. Northampton, Mass.: Hopkins, Bridgman, 1853.
    First printed in 1706; numerous later editions and printings.

Williams, Oscar, ed. *A Little Treasury of American Poetry.* New York: Charles Scribner's Sons, 1952.

Williams, Roger. *A Key into the Language of America: Or, An Help to the Language of the Natives in That Part of America, Called New-England; Together, with Briefe Observations of the Customes, Manners and Worships, &c of the Aforesaid Natives, in Peace and Warre, in Life and Death.* . . . London: Gregory Dexter, 1643.

Williams, Solomon. *The Power and Efficacy of the Prayers of the People of God When Rightly Offered to Him; and the Obligation and Encouragement thence Arising to be Much in Prayer: A Sermon Preached at Mansfield, Aug. 4, 1741; at a Time Set Apart for Prayer for the Revival of Religion; and on Behalf of Mrs. Eunice, the Daughter of the Reverend Mr. John Williams (formerly Pastor of Deerfield) Who was Then on a Visit There, from Canada; Where She has been in a Long Captivity.* . . . Boston: S. Kneeland and T. Green, 1742.

Williams, William Carlos. *In the American Grain.* New York: New Directions, 1953.

Wilson, Edmund. *Apologies to the Iroquois: With a Study of the Mohawks in High Steel by Joseph Mitchell.* New York: Farrar, Straus, and Cudahy, 1960.

Winkfield, Unca Eliza. *The Female American: Or, The Extraordinary Adventures of Unca Eliza Winkfield, Compiled by Herself.* London, 1767. 2 vols. Newburyport, Mass.: Angier March, 1800.

Withers, Alexander Scott. *Chronicles of Border Warfare: Or, A History of the Settlement by the Whites, of North-Western Virginia; and of the Indian Wars and Massacres, in that Section of the State; with Reflections, Anecdotes, &c.* Clarksburg, Va.: Joseph Israel, 1831.

Wolcott, Roger. *The Poems of Roger Wolcott.* Boston: Club of Odd Volumes, 1898.

Woolman, John. *John Woolman's Journal.* Edited by Frederick B. Tolles. Facsimile of the original Philadelphia, 1774, edition of *The Works of John Woolman.* New York: Corinth Books, 1961.

Worsley, Israel. *A View of the American Indians: Their General Character, Customs, Languages, Public Festivals, Religious Rites, and Traditions; Shewing Them to be the Descendants of the Ten Tribes of Israel.* . . . London: Printed for the Author and sold by R. Hunter, 1828.

Wright, Louis B. *The Cultural Life of the American Colonies.* New York: Harper and Row, Harper Torchbooks, 1957.

Wright, Lyle Henry. *American Fiction: 1774–1850.* San Marino, Cal.: Huntington Library, 1948.

Index

A

Abendsland, America as, 28
Abnaki Indians, 26, 132
abolition, -ism, -ists, 211, 217, 441–4 (*see also* slavery)
aborigines, *see* Indians
Abraham in Arms, see Nowell, Samuel
Absalom, Absalom!, see Faulkner, William
acculturation, *myth-theme,* 5–6, 18–22, 39–40, 63, 66, 76, 83, 86, 102, 121, 126,
    142–3, 147–9, 153–4, 157–8, 161, 166, 180–1, 183, 188–9, 191, 194–5, 212,
    235–6, 259–63, 267, 273–4, 310, 364, 406–7, 420, 473, 537, 553, 558–9; fear of,
    15, 18, 22, 37, 40–2, 64–5, 76, 98–9, 121, 125, 146–8, 153–4, 191–2, 195, 291,
    249, 563 (*see also* adoption, anxiety, cannibalism, Indianization, initiation,
    marriage)
Actaeon, 307, 490, 544
Adair, James, 247, 361–2
————, *History of the American Indians,* 255, 360
Adam, *myth-figure,* 46, 148, 184, 199, 286, 309, 382, 409, 436, 505, 522–3, 533–4
    (*see also* Eve; garden)
adoption by Indians, *myth-theme,* 123, 127, 241, 244, 247, 252–5, 263–7, 287–8,
    328–30, 333, 353, 421–23, 429–30, 445–6, 448, 455 (*see also* captives; initia-
    tion; Indianization)
Adventures of Col. Daniel Boone, see Filson, John
Aeneas, 28, 208, 555
Aeneid, see Virgil
Africans, 194, 443, 541 (*see also* Negroes, slavery)
Age of Discovery, 27–9
Age of Reason, *see* rationalism
Ahab, Capt., *see* Melville, Herman, *Moby-Dick*
Alamo, the, 446, 557
Alden (Aldin), John, 128, 141
Algonkian Indians, 26, 55, 530 (*see also* Schoolcraft, Henry R.)
Allen, Ethan, 251–2, 262, 267, 323, 447
Amadis de Gaul, 33
Amalek, -ites (*see* Indians, myth figure, in religion)
America, *myth-images* of (New World), 3, 5, 22, 26–39, 44, 56, 59–61, 71, 79, 85,
    90, 95, 99, 102, 104, 116–8, 126, 144, 147, 157, 166, 178–9, 190, 203, 214, 240,
    243, 261, 263, 277, 311, 314, 319–20, 333–4, 337, 340–2, 347, 348, 352, 357,
    375, 380, 396, 432–3, 447, 471–3, 494, 505, 516, 521, 533, 535 (*see also*
    Abendsland; arcadia; Abel; Cain; Caliban; chivalric romances; garden; land-
    scape; pre-Columbian myths of West; Promised Land; underworld; utopia;
    wilderness)

J

K

M